There are about 300 species of prickly pear cacti.

The prickly pear cactus grows in areas with as little as 150 millimeters of rain a year.

One cactus survived 6 years after it was taken out of the ground. It used 24 pounds of stored water to live.

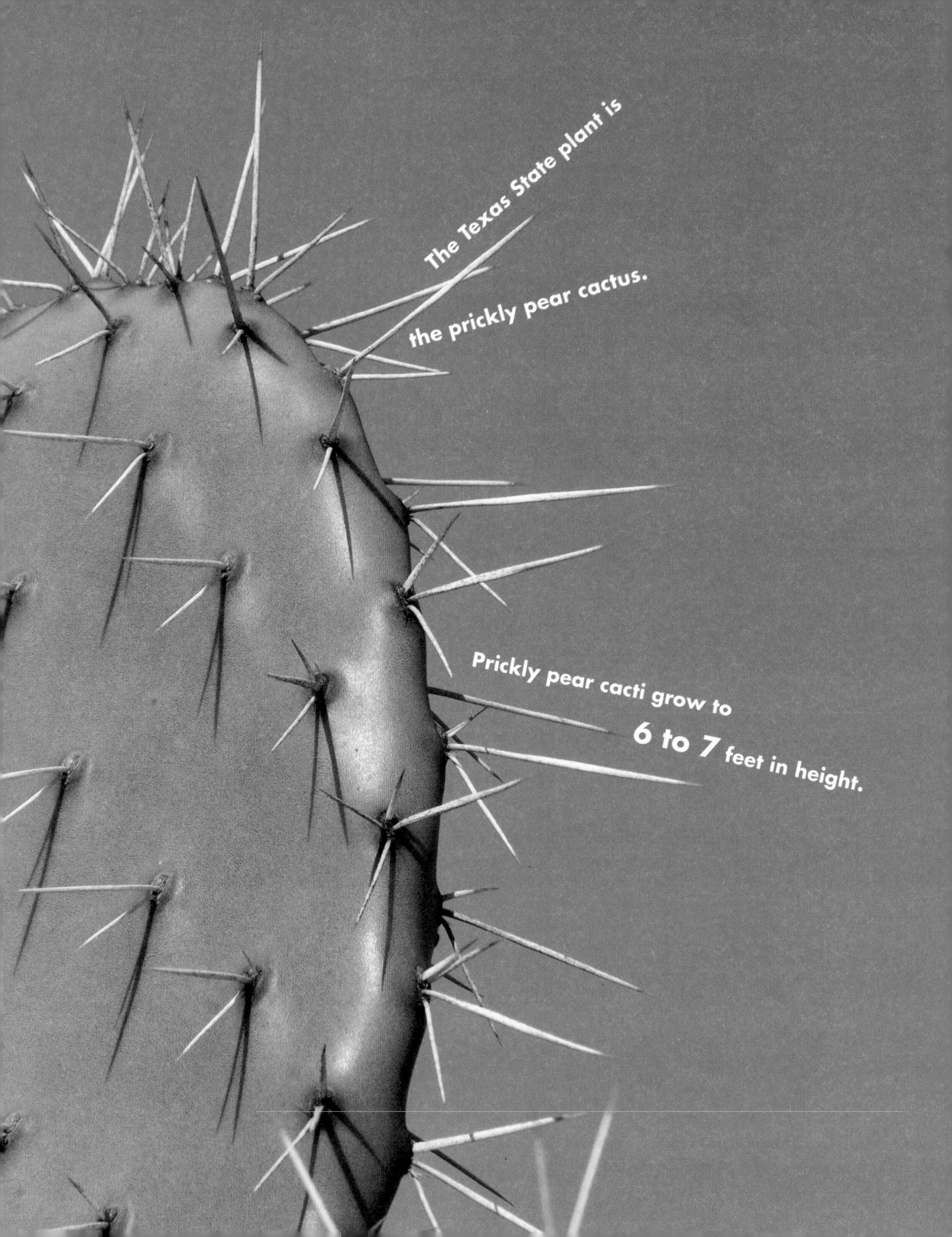

The Texas State plant is

the prickly pear cactus.

Prickly pear cacti grow to

6 to 7 feet in height.

TEXAS
HSP Math

Visit *The Learning Site!*
www.harcourtschool.com

Printed in the United States of America

ISBN 13: 978-0-15-354176-6
ISBN 10: 0-15-354176-8

2 3 4 5 6 7 8 9 10 032 16 15 14 13 12 11 10 09 08

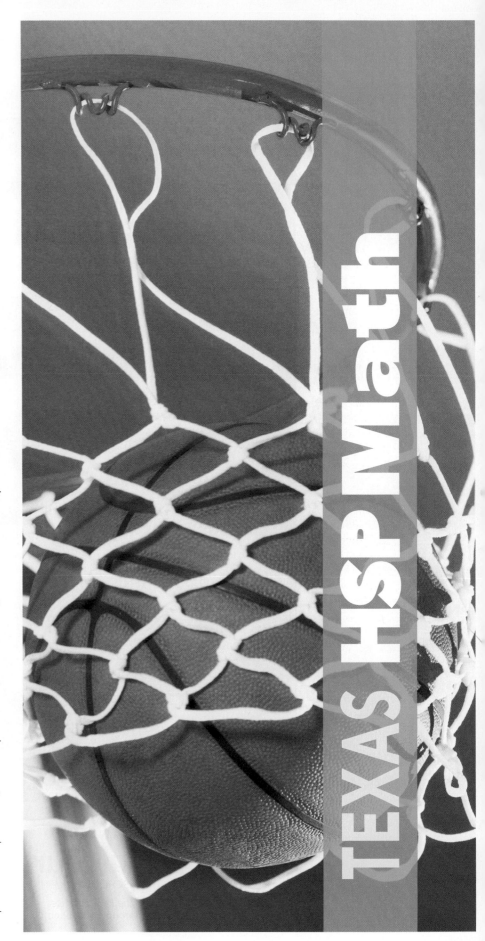

TEXAS HSP Math

Mathematics Advisor

James Epperson
Associate Professor, Department of Mathematics
The University of Texas at Arlington
Arlington, Texas

Senior Authors

Evan M. Maletsky
Professor Emeritus
Montclair State University
Upper Montclair, New Jersey

Joyce McLeod
Visiting Professor, Retired
Rollins College
Winter Park, Florida

Authors

Angela G. Andrews
Assistant Professor, Math Education
National-Louis University
Lisle, Illinois

Minerva Cordero-Epperson
Associate Professor of Mathematics and Associate Dean of the Honors College
The University of Texas at Arlington
Arlington, Texas

James Epperson
Associate Professor
Department of Mathematics
The University of Texas at Arlington
Arlington, Texas

Barbara Montalto
Mathematics Consultant
Assistant Director of Mathematics, Retired
Texas Education Agency
Austin, Texas

Karen S. Norwood
Associate Professor of Mathematics Education
North Carolina State University
Raleigh, North Carolina

Janet K. Scheer
Executive Director
Create-A-Vision
Foster City, California

Jennie M. Bennett
Mathematics Teacher
Houston Independent School District
Houston, Texas

Juli Dixon
Associate Professor of Mathematics Education
University of Central Florida
Orlando, Florida

Lynda Luckie
Director, K–12 Mathematics
Gwinnett County Public Schools
Suwanee, Georgia

David D. Molina
Program Director, Retired
The Charles A. Dana Center
The University of Texas at Austin

Vicki Newman
Classroom Teacher
McGaugh Elementary School
Los Alamitos Unified School District
Seal Beach, California

Tom Roby
Associate Professor of Mathematics
Director, Quantitative Learning Center
University of Connecticut
Storrs, Connecticut

David G. Wright
Professor
Department of Mathematics
Brigham Young University
Provo, Utah

Program Consultants and Specialists

Russell Gersten
Director, Instructional Research Group
Long Beach, California
Professor Emeritus of Special Education
University of Oregon
Eugene, Oregon

Valerie Johse
Elementary Math Specialist
Office of Curriculum & Instruction
Pearland I.S.D.
Pearland, Texas

Robin C. Scarcella
Professor and Director, Program of Academic English and ESL
University of California, Irvine
Irvine, California

Michael DiSpezio
Writer and On-Air Host, JASON Project
North Falmouth, Massachusetts

Tyrone Howard
Assistant Professor, UCLA Graduate School of Education—Information Studies
University of California at Los Angeles
Los Angeles, California

Concepcion Molina
Southwest Educational Development Lab
Austin, Texas

Place Value

1 Understand Place Value 2

2 Compare, Order, and Round Numbers 28

MATH ON LOCATION

GO ONLINE Technology

Harcourt Mega Math: Chapter 1, p. 14; Chapter 2, p. 32; Extra Practice, pp. 22, 44
The Harcourt Learning Site: www.harcourtschool.com
Multimedia Math Glossary www.harcourtschool.com/hspmath

The World Almanac for Kids

Addition, Subtraction, and Money

3 Addition 54

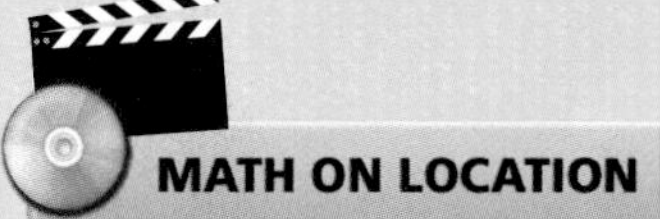

MATH ON LOCATION

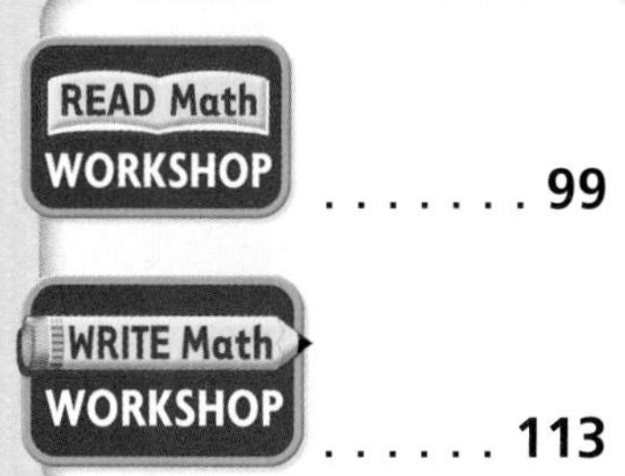

GO ONLINE Technology

Harcourt Mega Math: Chapter 3, p. 65; Chapter 4, p. 91; Chapter 5, p. 112; Extra Practice, pp. 76, 102, 122
The Harcourt Learning Site: www.harcourtschool.com
Multimedia Math Glossary www.harcourtschool.com/hspmath

Time, Data, and Patterns

MATH ON LOCATION

Technology

Harcourt Mega Math: Chapter 6, p. 137; Chapter 7, p. 164; Chapter 8, p. 179; Extra Practice, pp. 144, 170, 190
The Harcourt Learning Site: www.harcourtschool.com
Multimedia Math Glossary www.harcourtschool.com/hspmath

The World Almanac for Kids

Multiplication Concepts and Facts

9 Understand Multiplication 200

10 Multiplication Facts 226

11 Facts and Strategies 248

12 Algebra: Facts and Properties 270

MATH ON LOCATION

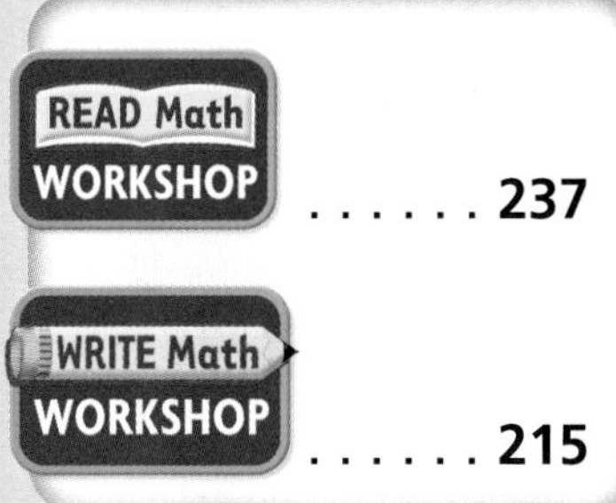

Technology

Division Concepts and Facts

13 Understand Division 294

14 Division Facts 318

15 Facts through 12 338

MATH ON LOCATION

DVD from The Futures Channel with Texas Chapter Projects and VOCABULARY POWER 293

READ Math WORKSHOP 329

WRITE Math WORKSHOP 307

GO ONLINE Technology

Harcourt Mega Math: Chapter 13, p. 303; Chapter 14, p. 328; Chapter 15, p. 354; Extra Practice, pp. 312, 332, 356
The Harcourt Learning Site: www.harcourtschool.com
Multimedia Math Glossary www.harcourtschool.com/hspmath

The World Almanac for Kids

The Wheel Is a Big Deal 362

Geometry

16 2-Dimensional Figures 366

17 Congruence and Symmetry 394

MATH ON LOCATION

GO ONLINE Technology

The Harcourt Learning Site: www.harcourtschool.com

Multimedia Math Glossary www.harcourtschool.com/hspmath

The World Almanac for Kids

Measurement

19 Customary Measurement 436

20 Metric (SI) Measurement 464

21 Perimeter, Area, and Volume 484

MATH ON LOCATION

GO ONLINE Technology

Harcourt Mega Math: Chapter 19, p. 444; Chapter 20, p. 473; Chapter 21, p. 490; Extra Practice, pp. 458, 478, 502
The Harcourt Learning Site: www.harcourtschool.com
Multimedia Math Glossary www.harcourtschool.com/hspmath

The World Almanac for Kids

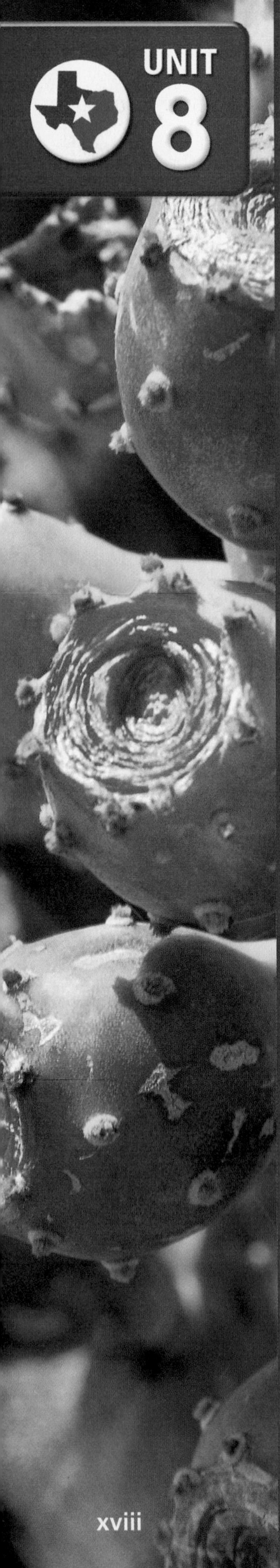

Fractions, Multiplication, and Probability

24 Probability 564

Student Handbook

MATH ON LOCATION

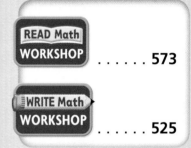

GO ONLINE Technology

Harcourt Mega Math: Chapter 22, p. 516; Chapter 23, p. 551; Chapter 24, p. 572; Extra Practice, pp. 536, 558, 580
The Harcourt Learning Site: www.harcourtschool.com
Multimedia Math Glossary www.harcourtschool.com/hspmath

The World Almanac for Kids

TALK, READ, and WRITE About Math

Mathematics is a language of numbers, words, and symbols.

This year, you will learn ways to communicate about math as you **talk**, **read**, and **write** about what you are learning.

The tally table and the bar graph show the number of long-legged wading birds seen along the bay shore of South Padre Island. Marta and her family counted the birds they saw.

Long-Legged Wading Birds	
Name	Tallies
Glossy Ibis	卌
Great Blue Heron	卌 I
Roseate Spoonbill	卌 IIII
Snowy Egret	IIII

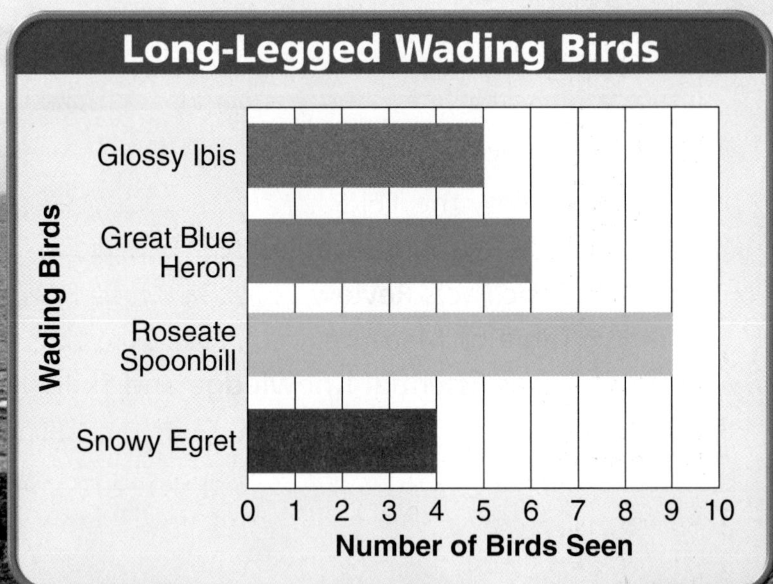

TALK Math

Talk about the tally table and the bar graph.

1. Why are the titles of the tally table and the bar graph the same?
2. How is the information on the tally table and the bar graph alike? How is it different?
3. How do you use the numbers along the bottom of the bar graph?

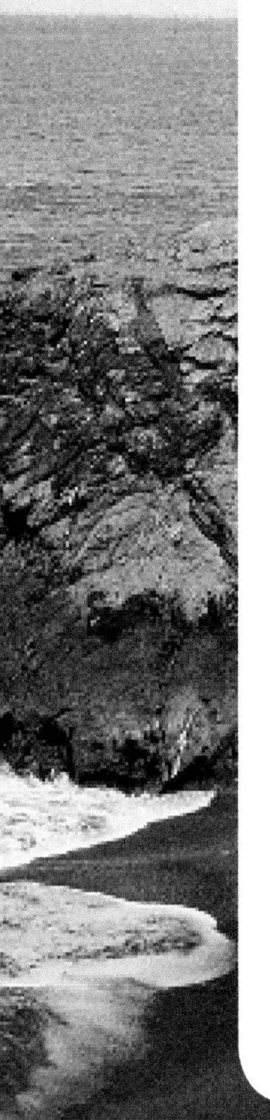

READ Math

Read the data on the bar graph.

4. How many Snowy Egrets were seen?
5. Were more Glossy Ibises or Snowy Egrets seen?
6. How many more Roseate Spoonbills than Great Blue Herons were seen?
7. How many birds were counted in all?

WRITE Math

Write a problem about the graph.

This year, you will write many problems. When you see **Pose a Problem**, you look at a problem on the page and use it to write your own problem.

In your problem, you can
- change the numbers or some of the information.
- exchange the known and unknown information.
- write an open-ended problem that can have more than one correct answer.

These problems are examples of ways you can pose your own problem. Solve each problem.

Problem How many more Roseate Spoonbills than Snowy Egrets were seen?

- **Change the Numbers or Information.**
  Marta saw 2 more Great Blue Herons, but she forgot to put tally marks on the tally table. How many more Great Blue Herons than Snowy Egrets did she see?
- **Exchange the Known and Unknown Information.**
  Marta tallied a total of 13 Roseate Spoonbills and Snowy Egrets. If she tallied 4 Snowy Egrets, how many Roseate Spoonbills did she tally?
- **Open-Ended**
  Marta visited the seashore again and counted the same birds. She counted a total of 14 birds. She saw 3 Snowy Egrets. How many Glossy Ibises, Great Blue Herons, and Roseate Spoonbills might she have seen?

Pose a Problem Choose one of the three ways to write a new problem. Use the information on the tally table and the bar graph.

UNIT

1 Place Value

1. The biologists visit thousands of acres of refuges by airboat to keep track of birds and other animals.

2. The biologist counts and records the number of egrets to tell if the number is increasing or decreasing.

3. Great numbers of birds and ducks arrive daily, so totals are estimated.

VOCABULARY POWER

TALK Math

What math do you see in the **Math on Location** photographs?

READ Math

REVIEW VOCABULARY You learned the words below when you learned about place value last year. How do these words relate to **Math on Location**?

compare to describe whether numbers are equal to, less than, or greater than each other

estimate to find about how many or how much

place value the value of each digit in a number, based on the location of the digit

WRITE Math

Copy and complete a Word Association Tree Diagram like the one below. Use what you know about place value to fill in the blanks.

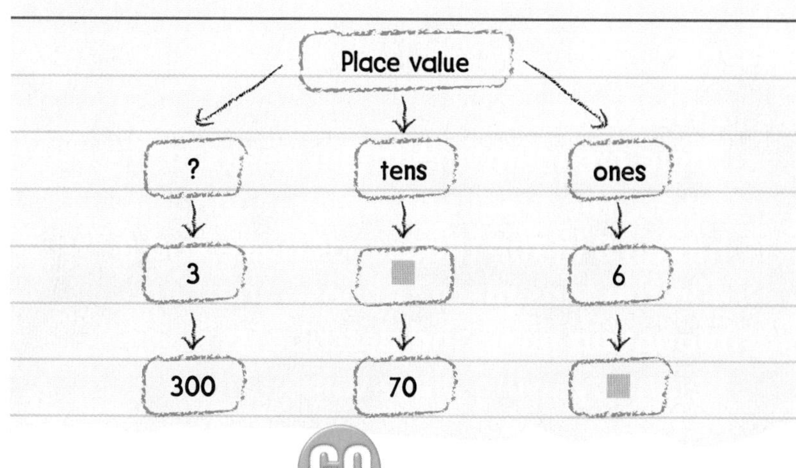

GO ONLINE Technology
Multimedia Math Glossary link at
www.harcourtschool.com/hspmath

1 Understand Place Value

The Big Idea The position of a digit determines its value.

The Chisos Mountains are in Big Bend National Park. The highest peak of this mountain range is Emory Peak. It is 7,825 feet high.

Investigate

There are many mountain peaks in Texas. The height of which mountain has an 8 in the thousands place and a 4 in the tens place? Choose another mountain peak and describe its height by using place value.

Mountain Peaks in Texas

Name	Height in Feet
Baldy Peak	8,378
Eagle Peak	7,484
Emory Peak	7,825
Guadalupe Peak	8,749

GO ONLINE **Technology**
Student pages are available in the Student eBook.

Show What You Know

Check your understanding of important skills needed for success in Chapter 1.

▶ Place Value: Tens and Ones to 100

Write the value of the blue digit.

1. 37 **2.** 81 **3.** 53 **4.** 29 **5.** 14

▶ Understand Place Value

Write the number shown.

6. 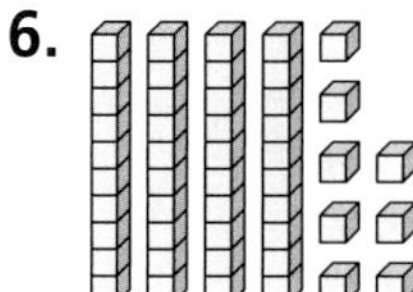

7.

8. 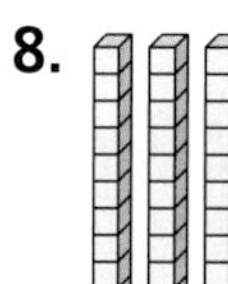

9.

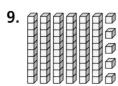

10.

11. 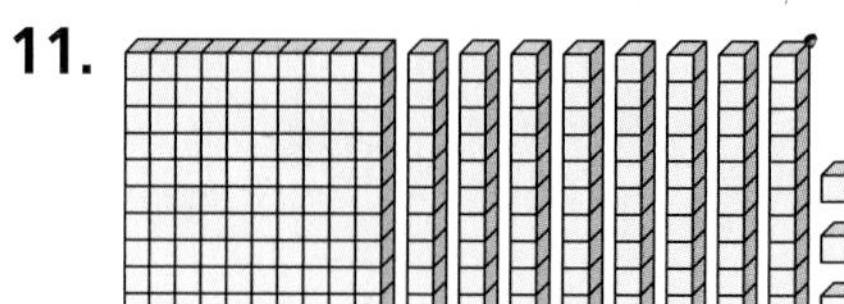

▶ Tens and Ones

Write each number.

12. $90 + 3$

13. $20 + 6$

14. seventeen

15. thirty-one

VOCABULARY POWER

CHAPTER VOCABULARY

digits
even
expanded form
odd
standard form
word form

WARM-UP WORDS

even A whole number that has a 0, 2, 4, 6, or 8 in the ones place

odd A whole number that has a 1, 3, 5, 7, or 9 in the ones place

digits The symbols 0, 1, 2, 3, 4, 5, 6, 7, 8, and 9

Ways to Use Numbers

OBJECTIVE: Use numbers to count, to measure, to label, and to describe position or order.

Quick Review

Write the next number.

1. 4, 5, 6, ■
2. 31, 32, 33, 34, ■
3. 46, 47, 48, 49, ■
4. 297, 298, 299, ■
5. 509, 510, 511, ■

Learn

Numbers are used in many ways.

A Count or tell how many.

Mark has 2 boxes of crayons.

There are 10 crayons in each box.

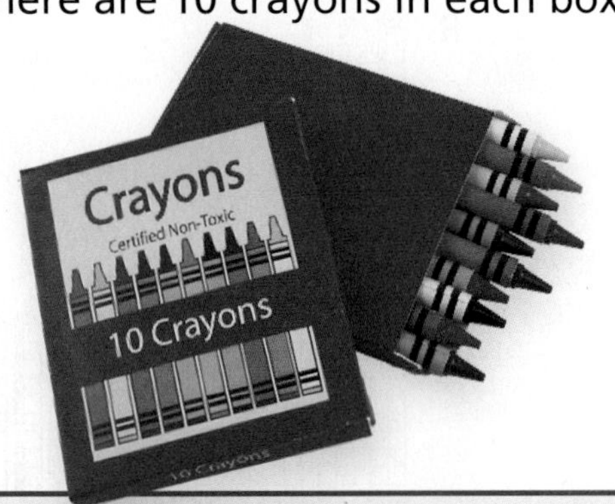

B Measure.

Sarah's book is 8 inches wide.

The book weighs 5 pounds.

C Tell order or position.

Anita is third in line.

Anita won first prize in the spelling contest.

D Name or label.

Mr. Sanchez teaches in Room 27.

The school's address is 400 Main Street.

Tom's phone number is 555-2610.

- Look at example C. How many students are in front of Anita in line?

Guided Practice

1. Kathy's sweater has 5 buttons. Is the number 5 here used to count or to label?

TEKS 3.14A Identify the mathematics in everyday situations. *also* **3.14A, 3.15A, 3.15B**

Tell how each number is used. Write *count, measure, label,* or *position*.

2. 

3. 

4. 

5. TALK Math **Explain** three ways that you use numbers to count, measure, label, or tell position.

Independent Practice and Problem Solving

Tell how each number is used. Write *count, measure, label,* or *position*.

6. 

7. 

8. 

9. Eddie is in the third grade.

10. There are 25 students in a class.

USE DATA For 11–12, use the Texas Facts.

11. Which Texas fact uses numbers to measure?

12. Which Texas fact uses a number to show position or order?

13. WRITE Math Write a list of things you did to get ready for school this morning. In your list, use numbers that tell order or position.

TEXAS FACTS

A Texas became a state in 1845.

B Texas was the twenty-eighth state to join the United States.

C Texas is 773 miles wide and 801 miles long.

D Texas has 254 counties.

Mixed Review and TAKS Prep

14. Which figure has more sides, a square or a triangle? (Grade 2, TEKS 2.7A)

15. Tim has $1 in pennies. How many pennies does he have? (Grade 2, TEKS 2.3D)

16. **TAKS Prep** Which represents a number used to count? (Obj. 6)

A fifth grade

B 27 Elm Street

C 52 cards

D 36 inches

Extra Practice on page 22, Set A

LESSON 2 HANDS ON

ALGEBRA

Patterns on a Hundred Chart

OBJECTIVE: Find number patterns on a hundred chart.

Quick Review

Find the sum.

1. 5 + 5
2. 10 + 5
3. 15 + 5
4. 20 + 5
5. 25 + 5

Vocabulary

even odd

Investigate

Materials ■ hundred chart

You can use a hundred chart to find number patterns.

A Choose a number from 2 through 5.

B Shade that box on the hundred chart.

C Skip-count by your number and shade each box you land on.

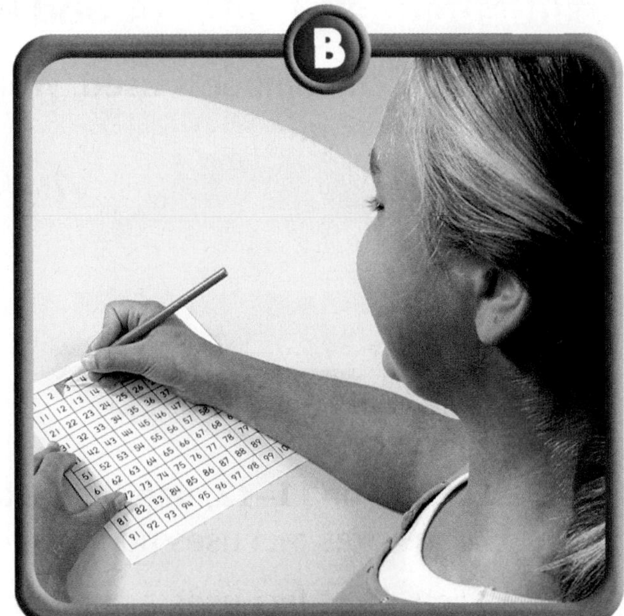

1	2	3	4	5	6	7	8	9	[illegible]
[illegible]	12	13	14	15	16	17	18	19	[illegible]
[illegible]	22	23	24	25	26	27	28	29	30
[illegible]	32	33	34	35	36	37	38	39	40
41	42	43	44	45	46	47	48	49	50
51	52	53	54	55	56	57	58	59	60
61	62	63	64	65	66	67	68	69	70
71	72	73	74	75	76	77	78	79	80
81	82	83	84	85	86	87	88	89	90
91	92	93	94	95	96	97	98	99	100

Draw Conclusions

1. Describe the pattern you see on your hundred chart.
2. Compare your hundred chart with those of other classmates. What do you notice about the patterns?
   How are they alike?
   How are they different?
3. **Analysis** Look at a hundred chart. What pattern will you get if you start at 10 and skip-count by tens?

TEKS 3.6A Identify and extend whole-number and geometric patterns to make predictions and solve problems.
also **3.14A, 3.14C, 3.14D, 3.15A, 3.15B, 3.16A**

Connect

You can use a hundred chart to identify even and odd numbers.

Step 1

Start at 2. Shade the box on the hundred chart.

1	2	3	4	5	6	7	8	9	10
11	12	13	14	15	16	17	18	19	20
21	22	23	24	25	26	27	28	29	30
31	32	33	34	35	36	37	38	39	40
41	42	43	44	45	46	47	48	49	50
51	52	53	54	55	56	57	58	59	60
61	62	63	64	65	66	67	68	69	70
71	72	73	74	75	76	77	78	79	80
81	82	83	84	85	86	87	88	89	90
91	92	93	94	95	96	97	98	99	100

Step 2

Skip-count by twos. Shade each box you land on. What pattern do you see?

1	2	3	4	5	6	7	8	9	10
11	12	13	14	15	16	17	18	19	20
21	22	23	24	25	26	27	28	29	30
31	32	33	34	35	36	37	38	39	40
41	42	43	44	45	46	47	48	49	50
51	52	53	54	55	56	57	58	59	60
61	62	63	64	65	66	67	68	69	70
71	72	73	74	75	76	77	78	79	80
81	82	83	84	85	86	87	88	89	90
91	92	93	94	95	96	97	98	99	100

The numbers that are shaded are **even** numbers. Even numbers end in 2, 4, 6, 8, or 0.

The numbers that are not shaded are **odd** numbers. Odd numbers end in 1, 3, 5, 7, or 9.

- How does a hundred chart help you identify even and odd numbers?

TALK Math

How can you tell whether a number is odd or even?

Practice

Use the hundred chart. Find the next number in the pattern.

1. 10, 20, 30, 40, ■
2. 5, 10, 15, 20, ■
3. 77, 75, 73, 71, ■
4. 3, 6, 9, 12, ■

Use the hundred chart. Tell whether each number is *odd* or *even*.

5. 16
6. 25
7. 34
8. 23
9. 81
10. 92
11. 47
12. 78

13. **WRITE Math** If you start at 3 and skip-count by twos, will the pattern include even numbers, odd numbers, or both? **Explain.**

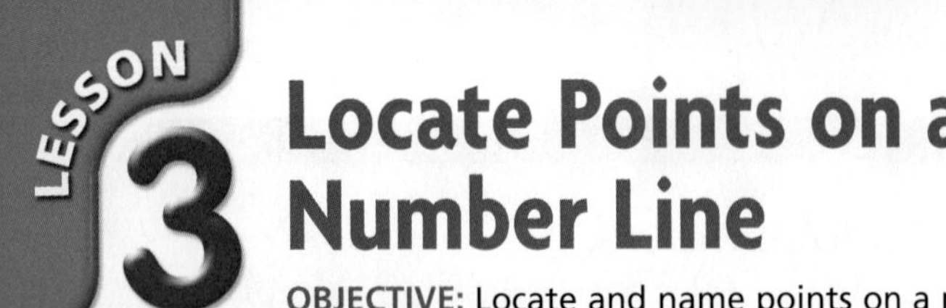

Locate Points on a Number Line

OBJECTIVE: Locate and name points on a number line.

Quick Review

Write the next number in the pattern.

1. 2, 4, 6, 8, ■

2. 5, 10, 15, 20, ■

3. 1, 3, 5, 7, ■

4. 10, 20, 30, 40, ■

5. 4, 8, 12, 16, ■

Learn

PROBLEM Ryan is playing a game that uses a number line. His game piece is on the point labeled *X*. What number does point *X* represent?

A number line is a way to show numbers in order from least to greatest.

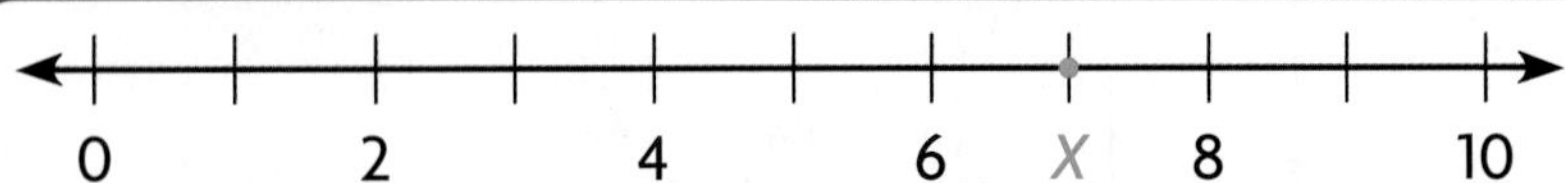

This number line shows marks for numbers from 0 to 10. The numbers shown count by twos from left to right. Point *X* is between 6 and 8.

So, point *X* represents 7.

Examples **Find the number represented by the letter.**

A

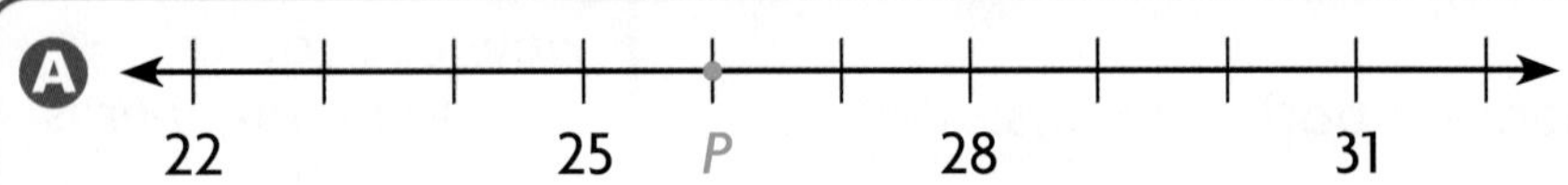

Point *P* is between 25 and 28.

Think: There are two marks between 25 and 28. Those marks represent 26 and 27. Point *P* is the first mark.

So, point *P* represents 26.

B

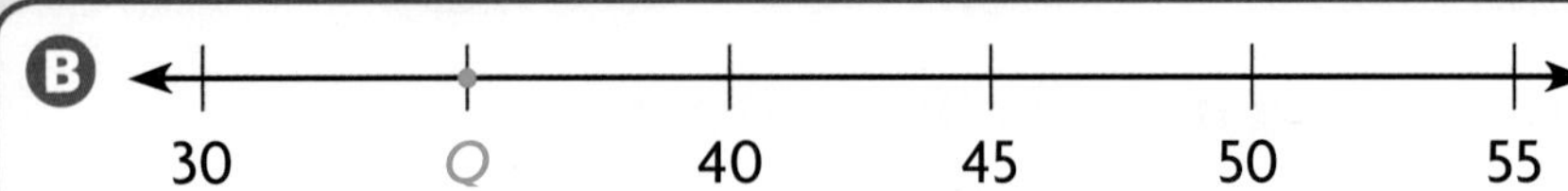

Point *Q* is between 30 and 40.

Think: The number line shows counting by fives. Count on 5 to find the number that *Q* represents.

So, point *Q* represents 35.

Guided Practice

1. Skip-count by threes to find the number that point *Z* represents on the number line.

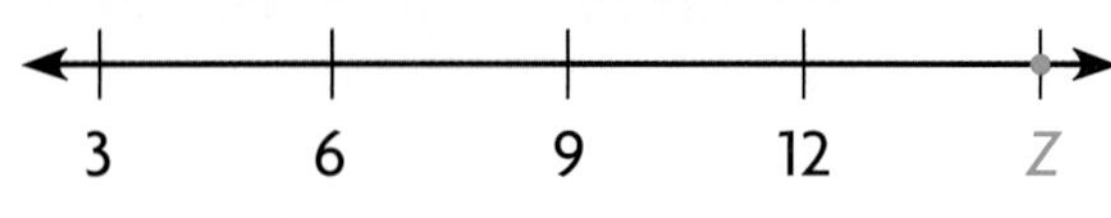

TEKS 3.10 The student is expected to locate and name points on a number line using whole numbers and fractions, including halves and fourths. *also* **3.14A, 3.15A, 3.15B, 3.16B**

Find the number that point *X* represents on the number line.

4. **TALK Math** **Explain** how you can use the marks and numbers that are on a number line to find the missing numbers.

Independent Practice and Problem Solving

Find the number that point *X* represents on the number line.

5. 17 20 X 23 26 29

6.

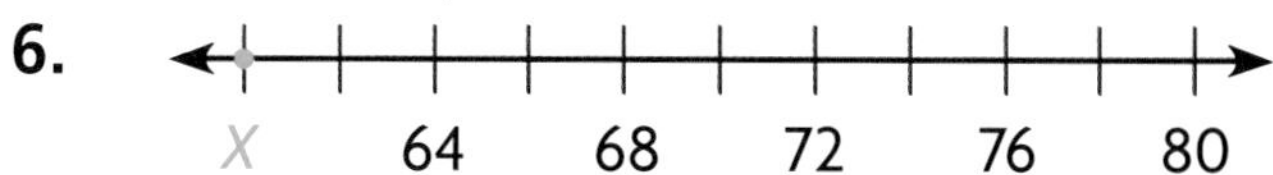

For 7–8, use the number line.

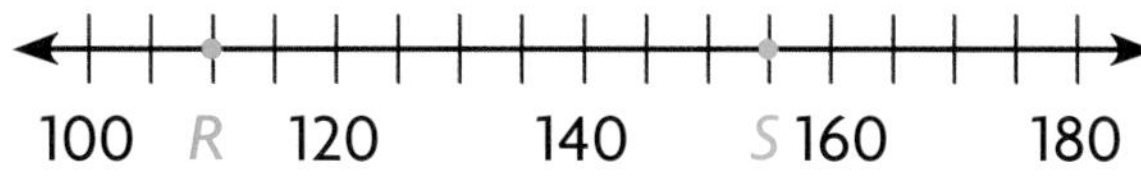

7. Robin's score is shown by point *R* on the number line above. What is her score?

8. Steve's score is shown by point *S*. What will Steve's next score be if he gets 10 more points? 5 fewer points?

9. **What's the Error?** On the number line below, Laura says that point *X* represents 35. What error did Laura make?

10. **WRITE Math** **Sense or Nonsense** Brian says every other whole number on a number line is an even number. Does Brian's statement make sense?

Mixed Review and TAKS Prep

11. Darius rides bus 29 to school. Is that number used to count, label, or measure? (TEKS 3.14A, p. 4)

12. Each pen costs $4. What is the total cost of 5 pens? (Grade 2, TEKS 2.4A)

13. **TAKS Prep** What number does point *X* represent? (Obj. 3)

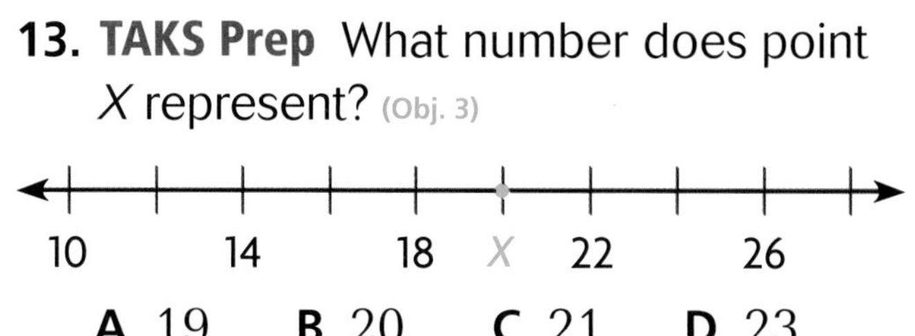

A 19 **B** 20 **C** 21 **D** 23

Extra Practice on page 22, Set B

Place Value: 3 Digits

OBJECTIVE: Use place value to read, write, and represent 3-digit numbers.

Quick Review

Write the value of the underlined digit.

1. $1\underline{8}$ **2.** $\underline{2}5$
3. $\underline{1}0$ **4.** $\underline{6}1$
5. $4\underline{2}$

Vocabulary

digits, expanded form, standard form, word form

Learn

The symbols 0, 1, 2, 3, 4, 5, 6, 7, 8, and 9 are **digits**. Numbers are made up of digits.

PROBLEM The Otto family visited the world's longest cave at Mammoth Cave National Park. The cave is 367 miles long. What is the value of the digit 6 in 367?

You can show the number 367 with base-ten blocks and a place-value chart.

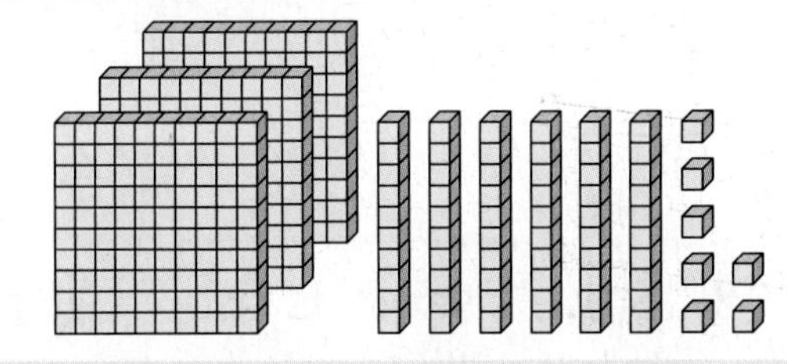

HUNDREDS	TENS	ONES
3	6	7

3 hundreds — 6 tens — 7 ones
300 — 60 — 7

So, the value of the digit 6 in 367 is 6 tens, or 60.

▲ Mammoth Cave National Park is located in Kentucky.

You can write a number in different ways.
Standard form: 367
Expanded form: 300 + 60 + 7
Word form: three hundred sixty-seven

READ Math

When you read whole numbers, do not say "and." The number 367 is read "three hundred sixty-seven."

Guided Practice

1. Write the value of each digit in the chart.

HUNDREDS	TENS	ONES
4	9	5

Write the value of the underlined digit.

2. $9\underline{2}1$ **3.** $53\underline{7}$ ✓**4.** $\underline{6}24$ ✓**5.** $75\underline{0}$

6. **TALK Math** The Headquarters Campground has 109 campsites. **Explain** what the zero in 109 means.

TEKS 3.1A Use place value to read, write (in symbols and words), and describe the value of whole numbers through 999,999. *also* **3.14A, 3.14D, 3.15A, 3.15B**

Independent Practice and Problem Solving

Write the value of the underlined digit.

7. 581   8. 672   9. 120   10. 208

11. 914   12. 845   13. 713   14. 693

Write each number in standard form.

15. $700 + 80 + 1$
16. $200 + 10 + 9$
17. $600 + 40 + 3$
18. three hundred eighty-five
19. 5 hundreds 4 ones
20. eight hundred nine

Write each number in expanded form.

21. 842
22. 329
23. four hundred fifty-four

USE DATA For 24–25, use the table.

24. What is the length of Fisher Ridge Cave written in expanded form?

25. Which cave's length has a 1 in the tens place?

United States Caves

Cave	Length (in miles)
Jewel Cave	129
Wind Cave	116
Fisher Ridge Cave	107

26. **FAST FACT** Jewel Cave in South Dakota has a depth of 632 feet. What is the value of the digit 3 in 632?

27. **WRITE Math** **What's the Error?** Tanya wrote four hundred seven as 470. Explain her error. Write the number in standard form.

28. **Reasoning** Write as many 3-digit numbers as you can with the digits 1, 2, and 3 in each number. Write the greatest number in expanded form.

Mixed Review and TAKS Prep

29. Cory read 43 pages. Blake read 28 pages. How many more pages did Cory read than Blake? (Grade 2, TEKS 2.3C)

30. Jordan has three $1 dollar bills and one quarter. How much money does he have? (Grade 2, TEKS 2.3D)

31. **TAKS Prep** Which shows 806 written in expanded form? (Obj. 1)

A $800 + 60$

B $800 + 6$

C $80 + 60$

D $80 + 6$

Extra Practice on page 22, Set C

LESSON 5

Place Value: 4 Digits

OBJECTIVE: Use place value to read, write, and represent 4-digit numbers

Quick Review

Write the value of the underlined digit.

1. $8\underline{2}5$ **2.** $\underline{4}17$
3. $\underline{2}51$ **4.** $19\underline{8}$
5. $6\underline{3}4$

Learn

PROBLEM Most peanuts grown in the United States are used to make peanut butter. It takes about 1,000 peanuts to make a jar of peanut butter! What does 1,000 of an object look like?

▲ Did you know that the peanut is not a nut? The peanut is actually a vegetable.

Activity

Materials ■ paper clips

Model 1,000 using paper clips.

Step 1

Make a chain of 10 linked paper clips. Then make 9 more chains of 10 paper clips.

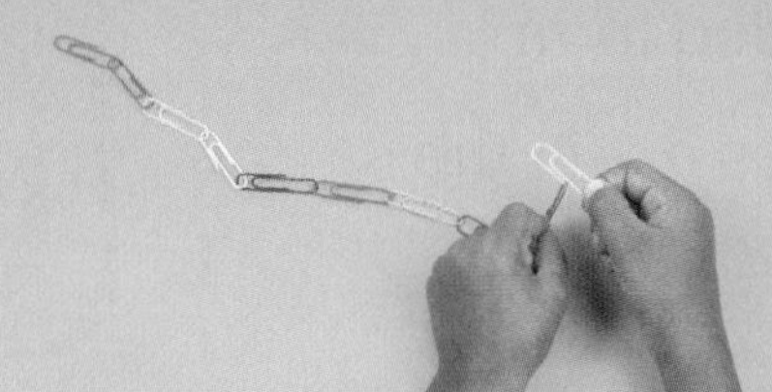

Step 2

Skip-count by tens.
How many paper clips have you used?

Step 3

Now link your 10 chains to make one long chain of 100 paper clips.

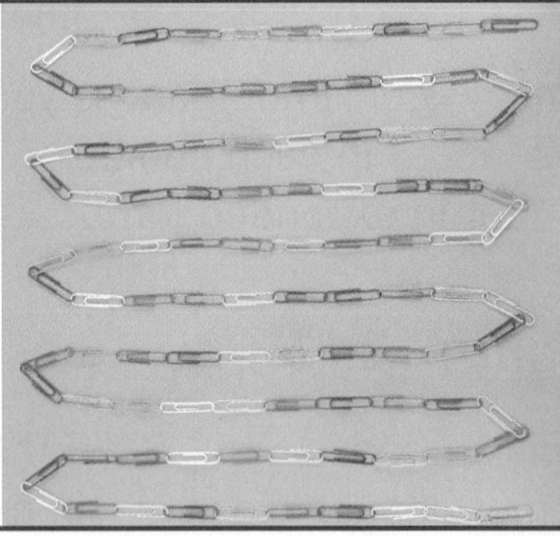

Step 4

Combine your chain of 100 paper clips with the chains from 9 other groups.

- How many chains of 100 paper clips did it take to make 1,000?

So, now you know what 1,000 looks like.

TEKS 3.1A Use place value to read, write (in symbols and words), and describe the value of whole numbers through 999,999. *also* **3.14A, 3.14D, 3.15A, 3.15B, 3.16A, 3.16B**

Understand Thousands

Base-ten blocks can help you understand thousands.

There are 10 ones in 10.

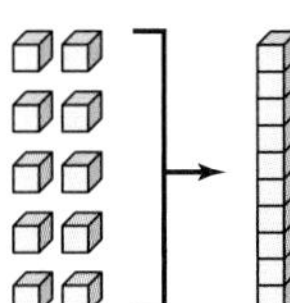

There are 10 tens in 100.

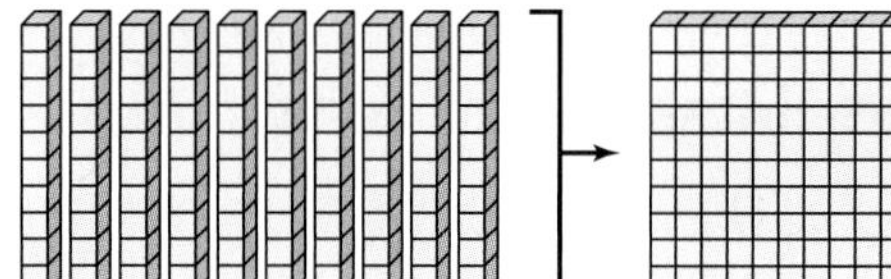

There are 10 hundreds in 1,000.

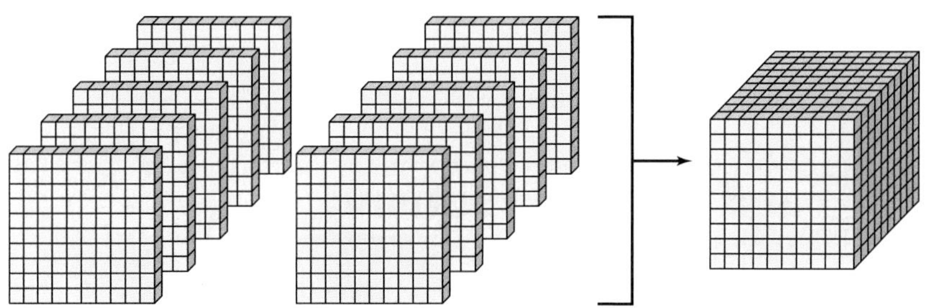

- How many hundreds are in 3,000?

Mr. Jackson sold 2,186 jars of homemade peanut butter. What is the value of the digit 2 in 2,186?

Model the number with base-ten blocks.

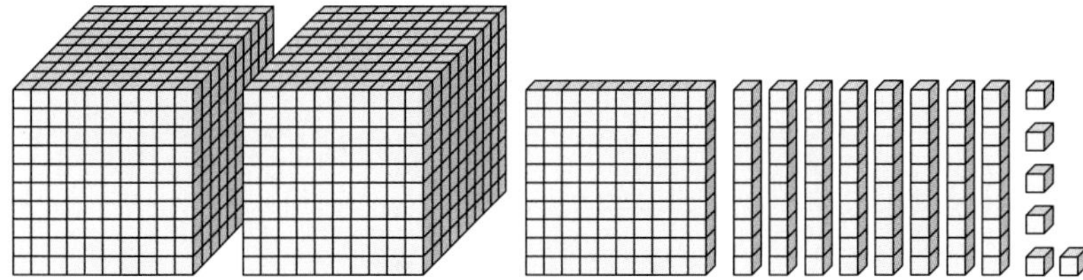

Write the number in a place-value chart.

THOUSANDS	HUNDREDS	TENS	ONES
2,	1	8	6

2 thousands	1 hundred	8 tens	6 ones
2,000	100	80	6

Math Idea
A comma is used to separate the thousands and the hundreds.

So, the value of the digit 2 in 2,186 is 2 thousands, or 2,000.

Here are three ways to write this number.

Standard form: 2,186
Expanded form: 2,000 + 100 + 80 + 6
Word form: two thousand, one hundred eighty-six

Guided Practice

1. Write this number in standard form and in expanded form.

THOUSANDS	HUNDREDS	TENS	ONES
1,	3	4	7

Write each number in standard form.

2. 8,000 + 200 + 50 + 8
3. three thousand, one hundred fourteen
4. 1,000 + 300 + 8
5. two thousand, thirty-four
6. TALK Math **Explain** how to find the value of each digit in the number 9,248.

Independent Practice and Problem Solving

Write each number in standard form.

7. 9,000 + 700 + 30 + 1
8. 1,000 + 20 + 4
9. eight thousand, five hundred two
10. seven thousand, three hundred ninety-one

Write each number in expanded form.

11. 2,389
12. 7,241
13. 6,170
14. 4,502
15. one thousand, eighteen
16. six thousand, four

Write the value of the underlined digit.

17. $\underline{6}$,452
18. 3,$\underline{8}$01
19. $\underline{5}$,018
20. 7,3$\underline{1}$4

Algebra Find the missing number.

21. 1,000 + ■ + 40 + 8 = 1,748
22. 3,000 + 200 + ■ + 6 = 3,296
23. 4,000 + 600 + ■ = 4,620
24. ■ + 50 + 4 = 8,054
25. Write a 4-digit number that has a 7 in the hundreds place.
26. Write a number that is 1,000 more than 6,243.
27. How many hundreds are in 6,000? How many tens?
28. WRITE Math **Sense or Nonsense** Brett says that the greatest possible 4-digit number is 9,000. Does Brett's statement make sense? **Explain**.

CD ROM **Technology**
Use Harcourt Mega Math, The Number Games, *Tiny's Think Tank*, Level A; Country Countdown, *Block Busters*, Level T

Extra Practice on page 22, Set D

USE DATA **For 29–30, use the graph.**

29. Use both standard form and expanded form to write the number of jars of peanut butter sold in 2005.

30. **What's the Question?** The answer is 3,500. What is the question?

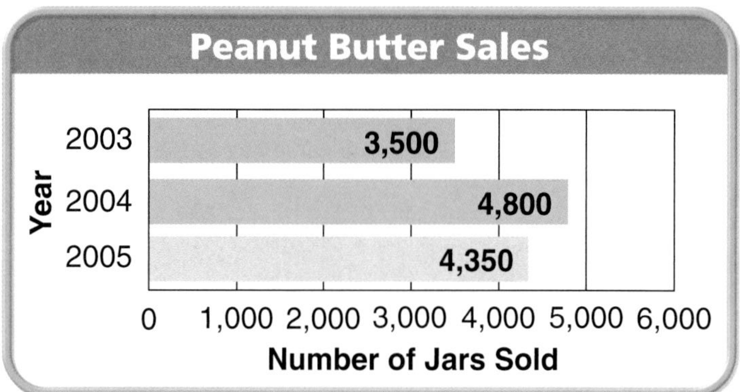

Mixed Review and TAKS Prep

31. Paul drew a figure that has 3 sides and 3 vertices. What shape could he have drawn? (Grade 2 TEKS 2.7A)

32. In a class survey of favorite pets, 6 students chose dogs, 7 students chose cats, and 3 students chose fish. How many students in all voted? (Grade 2 TEKS 2.3A)

33. **TAKS Prep** Which number shows eight thousand ninety? (Obj. 1)

A 890 **B** 8,009 **C** 8,090 **D** 8,900

34. **TAKS Prep** What is the value of the underlined digit in 6,4<u>7</u>2? (Obj. 1)

F 7 **G** 70 **H** 700 **J** 7,000

Problem Solving and Reasoning

NUMBER SENSE You can use base-ten blocks to show a number in many different ways. The model at the right is one way to show the number 128.

1 hundred 2 tens 8 ones

Here are two other ways to show the number 128.

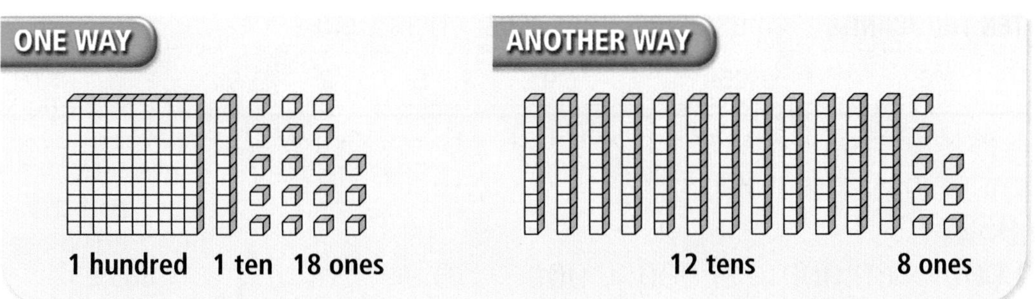

Draw base-ten blocks to show each number in two different ways. Label your drawings.

1. 75 **2.** 94 **3.** 37 **4.** 322 **5.** 243

LESSON 6

Place Value: 5 and 6 Digits

OBJECTIVE: Use place value to read and write 5- and 6-digit numbers.

Quick Review

Write each number in expanded form.

1. 672 **2.** 1,056
3. 980 **4.** 2,362
5. 9,005

Learn

PROBLEM The highest peak in California is Mount Whitney. It has a height of 14,494 feet. What is the value of the digit 1 in 14,494?

▲ Mount Whitney is part of the mountain range called the Sierra Nevada.

Use a place-value chart. The place to the left of the thousands place is the ten-thousands place.

TEN THOUSANDS	THOUSANDS	HUNDREDS	TENS	ONES
1	4,	4	9	4

So, the value of the digit 1 in 14,494 is 1 ten thousand, or 10,000.

You can write this number in different ways.
Standard form: 14,494
Expanded form: 10,000 + 4,000 + 400 + 90 + 4
Word form: fourteen thousand, four hundred ninety-four

Mount Whitney is in Sequoia National Park, which is next to Kings Canyon National Park. These parks have a total area of 865,952 acres.

Look at this number in a place-value chart. The place to the left of the ten-thousands place is the hundred-thousands place.

HUNDRED THOUSANDS	TEN THOUSANDS	THOUSANDS	HUNDREDS	TENS	ONES
8	6	5,	9	5	2

Remember
Put a comma between the thousands place and the hundreds place.
865,952
↑
comma

You can write this number in different ways.
Standard form: 865,952
Expanded form: 800,000 + 60,000 + 5,000 + 900 + 50 + 2
Word form: eight hundred sixty-five thousand, nine hundred fifty-two

Guided Practice

1. Complete the expanded form for 17,598. 10,000 + ■ + 500 + 90 + ■

TEKS 3.1A use place value to read, write (in symbols and words), and describe the value of whole numbers through 999,999. *also* **3.14A, 3.15A, 3.15B**

Write the value of the underlined digit.

2. 1<u>4</u>0,278
3. 5<u>2</u>,167
4. <u>2</u>3,890
5. <u>5</u>74,302

6. TALK Math **Explain** how to show the value of each digit in the number 623,714.

Independent Practice and Problem Solving

Write the value of the underlined digit.

7. 7<u>2</u>,180
8. <u>8</u>26,351
9. 2<u>6</u>5,817
10. 19,<u>3</u>42

Write each number in standard form.

11. 200,000 + 500 + 90 + 4
12. 60,000 + 8,000 + 700 + 40 + 3
13. nine hundred twelve thousand, two hundred six

USE DATA For 14–15, use the graph.

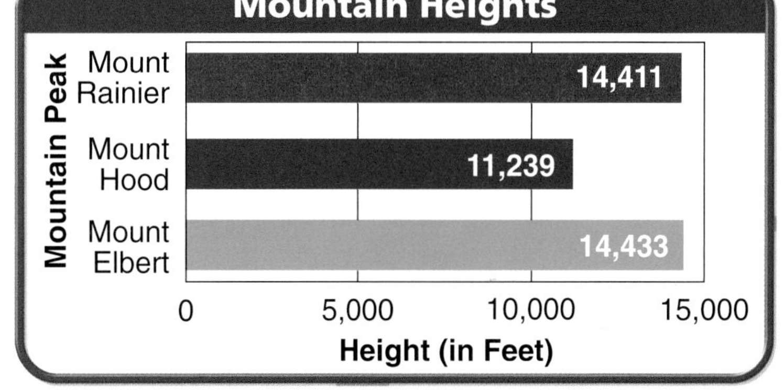

14. Write the height of Mount Rainier in expanded form.
15. Find the height of Mount Hood. What is the value of the digit in the hundreds place?
16. **Reasoning** Tammy baked 21 cookies. She ate 2 cookies and put the rest in bags with 3 cookies in each bag. How many cookies are not in a bag?
17. WRITE Math Write a 6-digit number that has a zero in the thousands place. **Explain** how to write your number in expanded form.

Mixed Review and TAKS Prep

18. Which part of this square is shaded? (Grade 2, TEKS 2.2A)

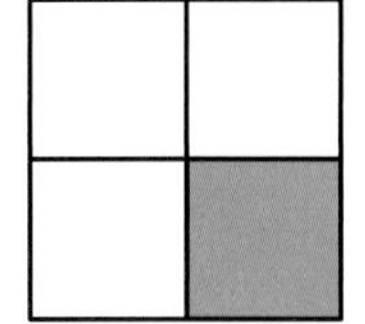

19. Beth's dog weighs 18 pounds more than her cat. Her cat weighs 9 pounds. How much does Beth's dog weigh? (Grade 2, TEKS 2.3C)

20. **TAKS Prep** How is 43,867 written in expanded form? (Obj. 1)

A 4,000 + 800 + 60 + 7

B 40,000 + 800 + 60 + 7

C 40,000 + 3,000 + 60 + 7

D 40,000 + 3,000 + 800 + 60 + 7

Extra Practice on page 22, Set E

Problem Solving Workshop
Strategy: Use Logical Reasoning

OBJECTIVE: Solve problems by using the strategy *use logical reasoning*.

Learn the Strategy

Logical reasoning can help you solve problems. When you use logical reasoning, you compare facts and think about clues.

Sometimes the facts or clues can be organized in a list.

Vince plays soccer. The players on his team have the numbers 1 to 11 on their uniforms.

Vince's uniform has an odd number.

His number is greater than 6.

You can skip-count by threes to find his number.

What is Vince's number?

~~1~~ ~~2~~ ~~3~~ ~~4~~ ~~5~~ ~~6~~ 7 ~~8~~ (9) ~~10~~ 11

Sometimes the facts or clues can be put in a table or chart.

Sue, Rick, and Heather were in a race.

Sue finished first.

Rick did not finish second.

In what position did Heather finish?

	1st	2nd	3rd
Sue	yes	no	no
Rick	no	no	yes
Heather	no	yes	no

TALK Math

Explain why there is a *yes* for Heather in the second column.

TEKS 3.16B Justify why an answer is reasonable and explain the solution process. *also* 3.14A, 3.14B, 3.14C, 3.15A

Use the Strategy

PROBLEM Anna used a riddle for the invitations to her birthday party. Her friends had to use the clues at the right to find her address on Pine Street.

My address is a 2-digit number. The number is greater than 80. The sum of the digits is 15. The ones digit is 1 less than the tens digit.

What is my address?

You're Invited!

Read to Understand
Plan
Solve
Check

Read to Understand

- Use a graphic aid to understand the clues.
- What information is given?

Plan

- What strategy can you use to solve the problem?

You can use logical reasoning.

Solve

- How can you use the strategy to solve the problem?

Look at one clue at a time. Use a hundred chart.

The number has two digits, so cross out 1 through 9 and 100. The number is greater than 80, so cross out 80 and all the numbers less than 80.

1	2	3	4	5	6	7	8	9	10
11	12	13	14	15	16	17	18	19	20
21	22	23	24	25	26	27	28	29	30
31	32	33	34	35	36	37	38	39	40
41	42	43	44	45	46	47	48	49	50
51	52	53	54	55	56	57	58	59	60
61	62	63	64	65	66	67	68	69	70
71	72	73	74	75	76	77	78	79	80
81	82	83	84	85	86	87	88	89	90
91	92	93	94	95	96	97	98	99	100

Add the digits of each number that is not crossed out. Circle the numbers with digits whose sum is 15.

81	82	83	84	85	86	87	88	89	90
91	92	93	94	95	96	97	98	99	100

Find the circled number with a ones digit that is 1 less than its tens digit.

$96 \rightarrow 9 - 6 = 3$ ✗
$87 \rightarrow 8 - 7 = 1$ ✓

So, Anna's address is 87 Pine Street.

Check

- How do you know your answer is correct?

Guided Problem Solving

Read to Understand
Plan
Solve
Check

1. Anna wants to mail an invitation to Steve. He gave her his address on Oak Road in the riddle below.

   - My address is a 2-digit number between 46 and 64.
   - The sum of the digits is 12.
   - The ones digit is 2 more than the tens digit.

   What is Steve's address?

   First, use a hundred chart and read the first clue. Cross out numbers less than 46 and greater than 64.

   Then, add the digits of each number not crossed out. Circle the numbers whose sum is 12.

   Finally, use the last clue to find Steve's address.

1	2	3	4	5	6	7	8	9	10
11	12	13	14	15	16	17	18	19	20
21	22	23	24	25	26	27	28	29	30
31	32	33	34	35	36	37	38	39	40
41	42	43	44	45	46	47	48	49	50
51	52	53	54	55	56	57	58	59	60
61	62	63	64	65	66	67	68	69	70
71	72	73	74	75	76	77	78	79	80
81	82	83	84	85	86	87	88	89	90
91	92	93	94	95	96	97	98	99	100

2. **What if** the sum of the digits is 10? What is Steve's address?

3. Julie is thinking of an even number between 12 and 29. The sum of the digits is the same as the digit in the tens place. What is Julie's number?

Problem Solving Strategy Practice

Use logical reasoning to solve.

4. Use the hundred chart and the clues. Cary is thinking of an odd number between 32 and 48. The sum of the digits is 5. What is Cary's number?

5. Copy the chart and use the clues. Andy, Beth, Mary, and Rod brought Anna gifts.

   Rod's gift had to be put together.
   Beth's gift was not the teddy bear or the soccer ball.
   Andy's gift was not the skates.
   Mary's gift was the soccer ball.

   What was Andy's gift?

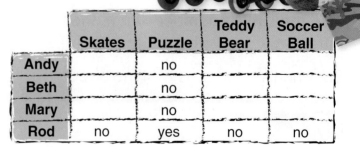

	Skates	Puzzle	Teddy Bear	Soccer Ball
Andy		no		
Beth		no		
Mary		no		
Rod	no	yes	no	no

Mixed Strategy Practice

USE DATA For 6–11, use the calendars.

6. Jami's birthday is on a Saturday in July. It is not July 7. It is not an even number. What date is Jami's birthday?

7. Carl's birthday invitations have a riddle theme. He wants his friends to find the date of his party. He gave them the following clues.

   My party is on a Friday in July.
   The date of my party is a two-digit even number.

   What date is Carl's party?

8. Michelle's birthday is June 22. Kim's birthday is 9 days before Michelle's birthday. What date is Kim's birthday?

9. Jon's birthday is June 30. Rachel's birthday is 12 days after Jon's. What date is Rachel's birthday?

10. **Open-Ended** Shawn's birthday is June 16. Mark's birthday is two weeks later. Tell two ways you could find the date of Mark's birthday.

11. **Pose a Problem** Look back at Problem 9. Write a similar problem by changing the date of Rachel's birthday.

Choose a STRATEGY

- Draw a Diagram or Picture
- Make a Model or Act It Out
- Make an Organized List
- Look for a Pattern
- Make a Table or Graph
- Guess and Check
- Work Backward
- Solve a Simpler Problem
- Write a Number Sentence
- Use Logical Reasoning

June

Sun	Mon	Tue	Wed	Thu	Fri	Sat
					1	2
3	4	5	6	7	8	9
10	11	12	13	14	15	16
17	18	19	20	21	22	23
24	25	26	27	28	29	30

July

Sun	Mon	Tue	Wed	Thu	Fri	Sat
1	2	3	4	5	6	7
8	9	10	11	12	13	14
15	16	17	18	19	20	21
22	23	24	25	26	27	28
29	30	31				

CHALLENGE YOURSELF

Thirteen children in Kim's class have a birthday in either June, July, or August.

12. Two more children have a birthday in July than in June. There is the same number of birthdays in July and August. How many children have a birthday in August?

13. Michael's birthday falls on a Thursday in August. The sum of the digits of his birthday is 5. **Explain** how you know when Michael's birthday is.

Extra Practice

Set A Tell how each number is used. Write *count, measure, label,* or *position*. (pp. 4–5)

1. Tim lives at 37 Park Avenue.
2. Joe has 89 baseball cards.

Set B Find the number that point *X* represents on the number line. (pp. 8–9)

1. 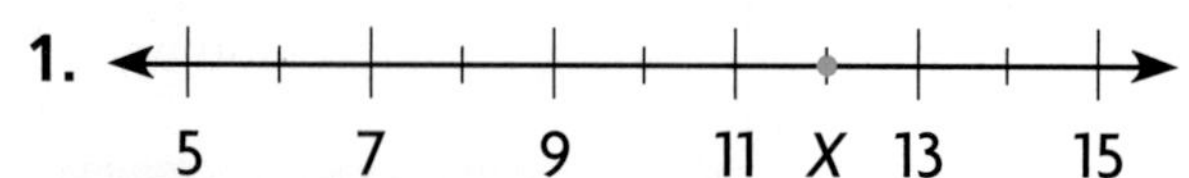

2. 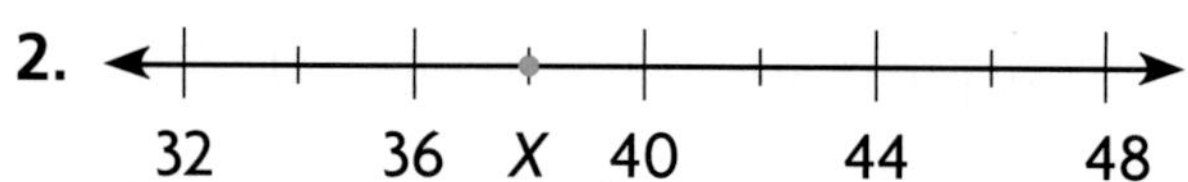

Set C Write the value of the underlined digit. (pp. 10–11)

1. $67\underline{2}$
2. $\underline{1}58$
3. $8\underline{9}0$
4. $\underline{4}35$
5. There are 253 students in Talia's school. How do you write the number in expanded form?
6. There are 922 seats in the theater. What is the value of the digit 9 in 922?

Set D Write each number in standard form. (pp. 12–15)

1. 4,000 + 800 + 10 + 3
2. 9,000 + 600 + 50 + 2
3. 7,000 + 20 + 2
4. Mr. Price drove 2,947 miles in one week. What is the value of the digit 2 in 2,947?
5. The library has 7,163 children's books. How do you write 7,163 in expanded form?

Set E Write the value of the underlined digit. (pp. 16–17)

1. $1\underline{3},781$
2. $8\underline{4}0,526$
3. $\underline{5}71,903$
4. $7\underline{1}4,200$

Write each number in standard form.

5. eighty thousand, seven hundred ninety-six
6. two hundred fifteen thousand, thirty

CD ROM **Technology**
Use Harcourt Mega Math, Country Countdown, *Block Busters*, Levels S, T.

TECHNOLOGY CONNECTION

iTools: Base-Ten Blocks (TEKS 3.1A, 3.1B, 3.14D, 3.15A)

Use Base-Ten Blocks to Show Numbers.

Bob has 6 hundreds, 8 tens, and 16 ones.
What number does this show?

Step 1	Click on *Base-Ten Blocks*. Then click on the third tab at the bottom. Click on *Hide*.
Step 2	Click on the hundreds block at the left. Click 6 times in the hundreds column. Do the same thing with 8 tens and 16 ones. If you make a mistake, click on the eraser.
Step 3	Click on *Line Up* at the bottom. Then click on the *Regroup* arrow in the **ones** column. Ten **ones** blocks will group together and move to the tens column.
Step 4	Count the hundreds, tens, and ones blocks. Write the 3-digit number. Click on *Show* to check your answer.

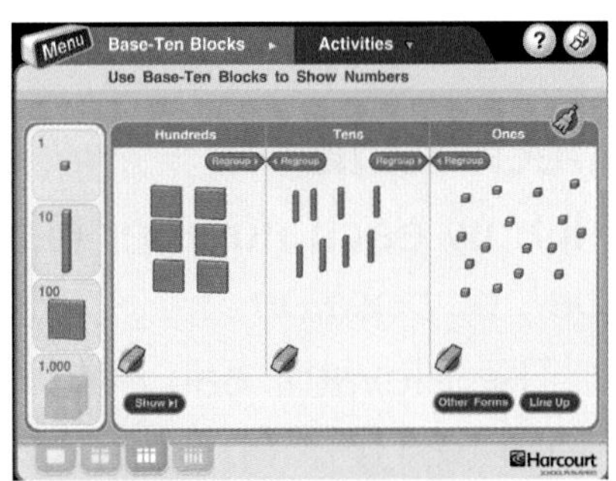

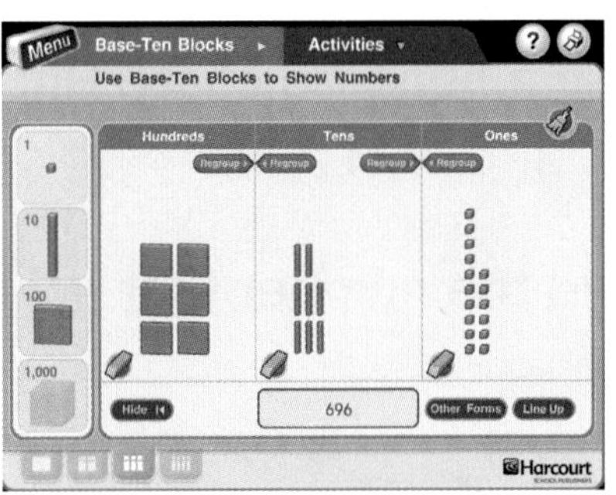

So, Bob's number is 696.
Click on the broom to clear the workspace.

Try It

Follow the steps above to make each 3-digit number.

1. 7 hundreds, 12 tens, 6 ones
2. 3 hundreds, 5 tens, 14 ones

Use Base-Ten Blocks to show each number.

3. 825
4. 917
5. 256
6. 379
7. 568

8. **Explore More** Karen has 4 hundreds, 9 tens, and 11 ones. Benson has 3 hundreds, 19 tens, and 12 ones. Use Base-Ten Blocks to show the numbers. Who has the greater number? **Explain.**

Chapter 1 Review/Test

Check Vocabulary and Concepts

Choose the best term from the box.

VOCABULARY
digits even odd
standard form
expanded form

1. Numbers ending with 2, 4, 6, 8, or 0 are _?_ numbers. (TEKS 3.6A, p. 6)
2. There are six _?_ in the number 457,390. (TEKS 3.1A, p. 10)
3. _?_ is a way to write numbers by showing the value of each digit. (TEKS 3.1A, p. 10)

Check Skills

Tell how each number is used. Write *count, measure, label,* or *position*. (TEKS 3.14A, pp. 4–5)

4. The elevator can hold up to 10 people.
5. Tyler got to third base after he hit the ball.
6. Lauren is 52 inches tall.

Use a hundred chart. Find the next number in the pattern. (TEKS 3.6A, pp. 6–7)

7. 3, 6, 9, 12, ■
8. 65, 70, 75, 80, ■

Find the number that point *X* represents on each number line. (TEKS 3.10, pp. 8–9)

9. Number line: 11, 13, *x*, 15, 17, 19

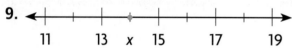

10. 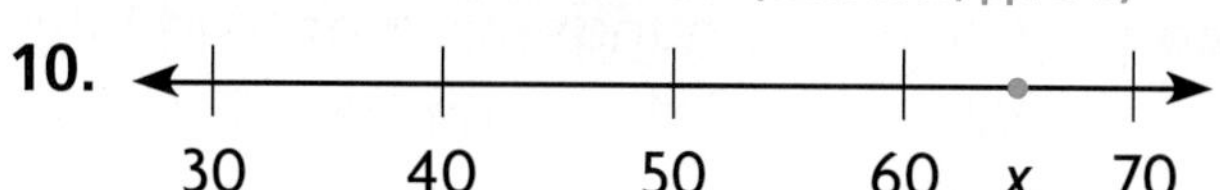

Write the value of the underlined digit. (TEKS 3.1A, pp. 10–11, 12–15, 16–17)

11. 4<u>7</u>6,521
12. 1,<u>9</u>64
13. <u>8</u>30,795
14. 63,4<u>2</u>8

Write each number in standard form. (TEKS 3.1A, pp. 10–11, 12–15)

15. five hundred thirty-two
16. seven thousand, three hundred five
17. 5,000 + 100 + 40 + 8
18. 60,000 + 2,000 + 10 + 7

Check Problem Solving

For 19, use the table. Solve. (TEKS 3.16B, pp. 18–21)

19. Jack's score is a 4-digit number. The hundreds digit is an even number. The tens digit is odd. What is his score?

20. WRITE Math Beth, Sasha, Jake, and Tyrone ran in a race. Tyrone finished first. Sasha did not finish second. Beth finished last. **Explain** how you can tell in which place Jake finished.

Game Scores

Players	Scores
Player A	4,602
Player B	897
Player C	3,415

GO ONLINE **Technology** Use *Online Assessment.*

Enrich • More Patterns
Design by Numbers

You have found **column patterns** and **diagonal patterns** on a hundred chart.

You can also use other kinds of number charts to find patterns.

1	2	3
4	5	6
7	8	9

column ▲ pattern

1	2	3	4	5
6	7	8	9	10
11	12	13	14	15

▲ diagonal pattern

Materials ■ Charts A, B, and C

Look at Chart A. It has 5 numbers in each row. Skip-count by threes. Shade each box you land on.

- What boxes did you shade?
- Is your pattern a diagonal pattern or a column pattern?

A

1	2	3	4	5
6	7	8	9	10
11	12	13	14	15
16	17	18	19	20
21	22	23	24	25

Choose another number from 2 to 5. Use it to skip-count on Chart A.

- What pattern do you see?
- Is it the same kind of pattern you made when you skip-counted by threes?

Now look at Chart B. It has 4 numbers in each row. Skip-count by threes. Shade each box you land on.

- Is your pattern a diagonal pattern or a column pattern?
- How is this pattern like the pattern you made skip-counting by threes on Chart A? How is it different?

B

1	2	3	4
5	6	7	8
9	10	11	12
13	14	15	16
17	18	19	20
21	22	23	24

Try It

Use Chart B to solve.

1. Skip-count by twos. What kind of pattern did you make?
2. What other number could you skip-count by that will make a diagonal pattern?

Wrap Up

WRITE Math Use Chart C. What numbers can you skip-count by to make a diagonal pattern? **Explain.**

C

1	2	3	4	5	6
7	8	9	10	11	12
13	14	15	16	17	18
19	20	21	22	23	24

Getting Ready for the TAKS
Chapter 1

Number, Operation, and Quantitative Reasoning (Obj. 1)

1. Lily put 43 marbles in a jar. Joe put 28 marbles in the jar. How many marbles did they put in the jar in all?

A 15

B 25

C 61

D 71

Choose the answer.

See item 2. If your answer doesn't match one of the choices, check your computation.

2. $53 - 26 =$

F 23 **H** 33

G 27 **J** 77

3. Which fraction names the shaded part?

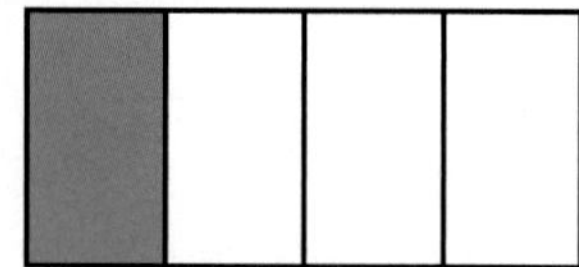

A $\frac{1}{4}$ **C** $\frac{1}{2}$

B $\frac{1}{3}$ **D** $\frac{3}{4}$

4. WRITE Math **Explain** how you can find the value of the digit 6 in the number 16,782.

Patterns, Relationships, and Algebraic Thinking (Obj. 2)

5. Which addition fact helps you find the difference $17 - 8 = ■$?

F $10 + 10 = 20$

G $8 + 9 = 17$

H $4 + 4 = 8$

J $1 + 7 = 8$

6. What is the next number in the pattern?

20, 24, 28, 32, ■

A 30 **C** 36

B 34 **D** 37

7. How many wheels do 6 bicycles have?

Bicycles	2	3	4	5	6
Wheels	4	6	8	■	■

F 10 **H** 12

G 11 **J** 13

8. WRITE Math Find the difference. **Explain** how you can check your answer by using addition.

70¢ − 24¢

Measurement (Obj. 4)

9. Lexi drew this figure. What is the area of Lexi's figure?

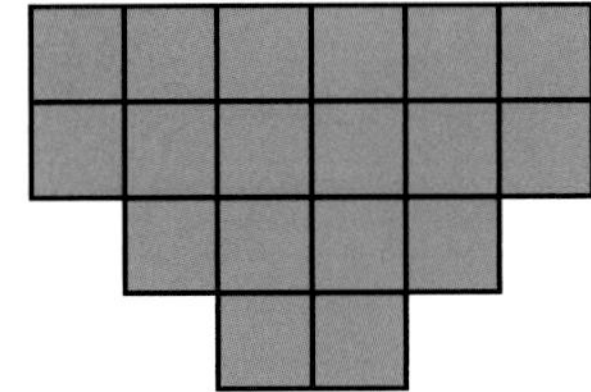

A 9 units

B 12 units

C 18 units

D 20 units

10. What time is shown on the clock?

F 3:15

G 3:25

H 5:15

J 5:25

11. WRITE Math About how long does it take to wash your hands, 2 minutes or 2 hours? **Explain**.

Probability and Statistics (Obj. 5)

12. How many boxes of cookies were sold during Week 3?

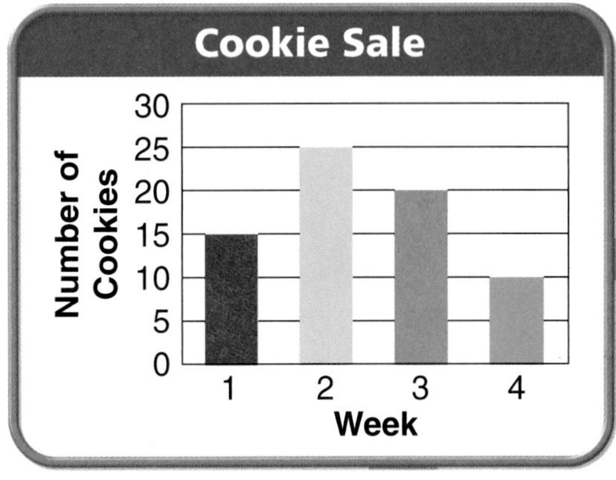

A 10

B 15

C 20

D 25

13. How many students in all voted for their favorite fruit?

Favorite Fruit	
Banana	
Orange	
Apple	
Key: Each fruit = 1 vote.	

F 13

G 15

H 21

J 23

14. WRITE Math From which bag would you be more likely to pull a red cube than a blue cube? **Explain**.

Bag A

Bag B

2 Compare, Order, and Round Numbers

The Big Idea Place value is used to compare, order, and round numbers.

TEXAS FAST FACT

The JPMorgan Chase Tower in Houston is the tallest building in Texas and the tallest five-sided building in the world. It is 1,002 feet high and has 75 floors.

Investigate

There are many tall buildings in Houston. Round the heights of three of the buildings to the nearest hundred, and then order those building heights from least to greatest. Explain how ordering rounded numbers can be misleading.

Buildings in Houston, Texas

Building	Height in Feet
Bank of America Center	780
First City Tower	662
Fullbright Tower	725
Wells Fargo Plaza	992
Williams Tower	901

Technology
Student pages are available in the Student eBook.

Show What You Know

Check your understanding of important skills needed for success in Chapter 2.

▶ Order on a Number Line to 100

Write the numbers in order from least to greatest.

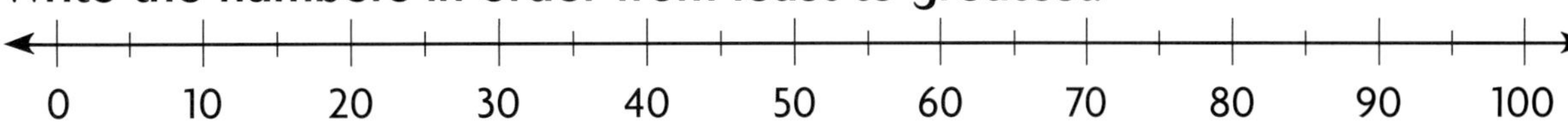

1. 27, 34, 22

2. 41, 38, 50

3. 80, 90, 60

4. 83, 86, 72

5. 20, 14, 19

6. 61, 52, 68

▶ Compare 2-Digit Numbers Using Place Value

Write <, >, or = for each ●.

7. 15 ● 23

8. 77 ● 58

9. 31 ● 34

10. 82 ● 82

11. 91 ● 19

12. 46 ● 61

13. 27 ● 28

14. 45 ● 40

15. 53 ● 63

VOCABULARY POWER

CHAPTER VOCABULARY

compare
equal to =
greater than >
less than <
order
round

WARM-UP WORDS

compare To describe whether numbers are equal to, less than, or greater than each other

greater than > A symbol used to compare two numbers, with the greater number given first

less than < A symbol used to compare two numbers, with the lesser number given first

Compare Numbers

OBJECTIVE: Use models, place value, and number lines to compare 2- and 3-digit numbers.

Quick Review

Write the greater number.

1. 9 or 12 **2.** 8 or 3
3. 13 or 4 **4.** 5 or 17
5. 6 or 14

Vocabulary

compare
equal to =
less than <
greater than >

Learn

PROBLEM Cedar Point in Ohio has 68 rides. Hersheypark in Pennsylvania has 59 rides. Which amusement park has more rides?

You can **compare** numbers in different ways to find which number is greater.

greater than > **less than <** **equal to =**

ONE WAY **Use base-ten blocks.**

Compare from left to right.

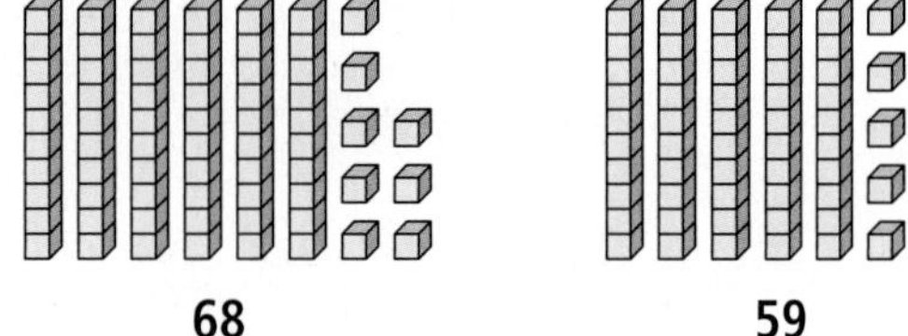

6 tens is greater than 5 tens. $68 > 59$

So, Cedar Point has more rides than Hersheypark.

OTHER WAYS

A **Use a number line.**
Compare 37 and 45.

The numbers are in order from least to greatest.

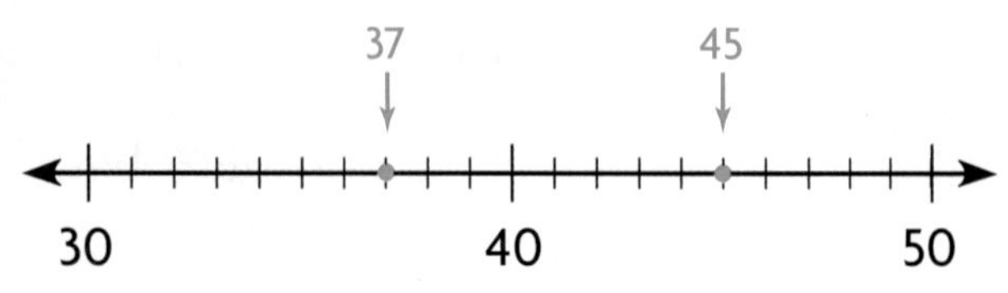

37 is to the left of 45.

So, $37 < 45$.

B **Use a place-value chart.**
Compare 85 and 77.

Compare digits in the same place-value position from left to right.

TENS	ONES
8	5
7	7

↑

8 tens is greater than 7 tens.

So, $85 > 77$.

• In Example B, why don't you have to compare the ones?

TEKS 3.1B use place value to compare and order whole numbers through 9,999. *also* **3.10, 3.14A, 3.14D, 3.15A, 3.15B, 3.16B**

Compare 3-Digit Numbers

Example

Compare 329 and 341.

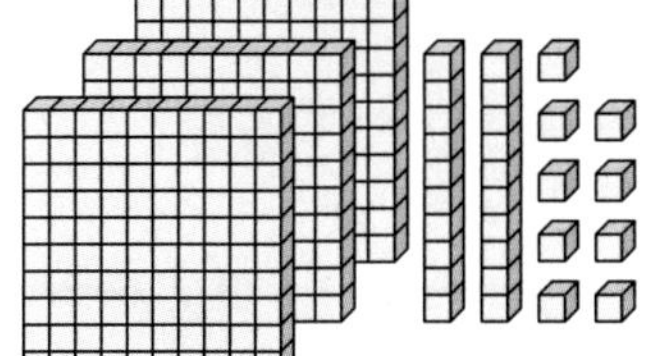

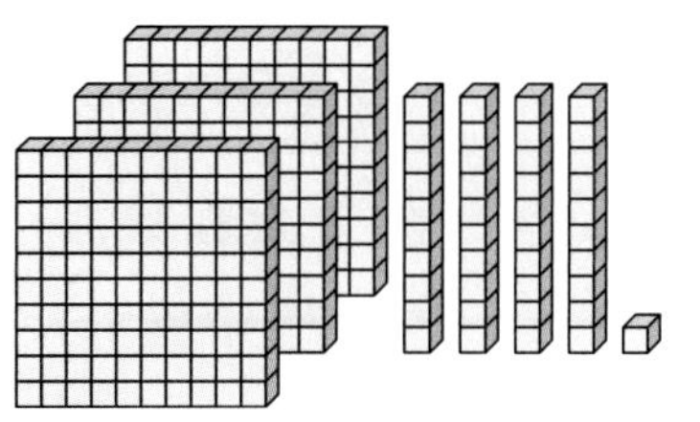

The hundreds are the same, so compare the tens. 2 tens is less than 4 tens. So, 329 < 341.

More Examples

A Compare 185 and 256.

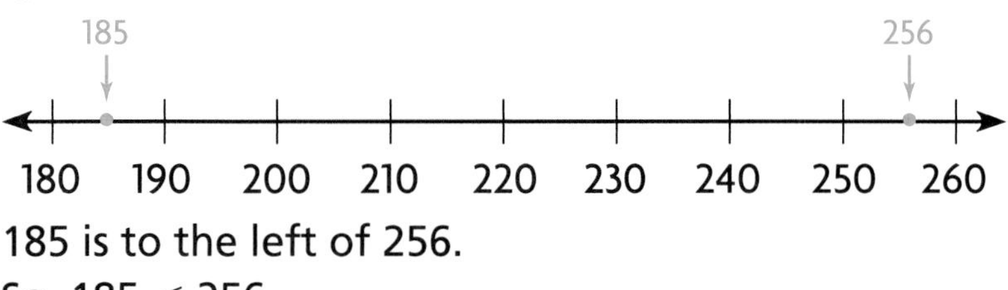

185 is to the left of 256.
So, 185 < 256.

B Compare 658 and 653.

HUNDREDS	TENS	ONES
6	5	8
6	5	3

↑ Hundreds are the same. ↑ Tens are the same. ↑ 8 > 3

So, 658 > 653.

C Compare 75 and 117.

HUNDREDS	TENS	ONES
	7	5
1	1	7

75 has no hundreds.
So, 75 < 117.

Guided Practice

1. Which number has more tens? Which number is greater?

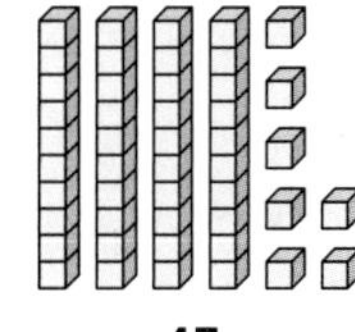
47

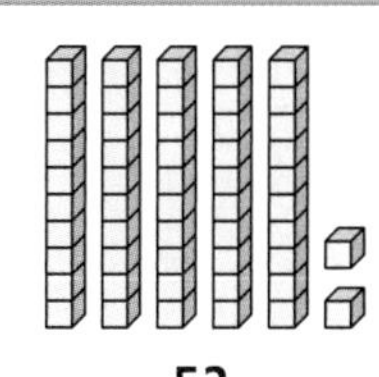
52

Compare the numbers. Write <, >, or = for each ●.

2. 53 ● 39
3. 78 ● 91
✓ 4. 221 ● 316
✓ 5. 414 ● 85

6. TALK Math **Explain** two ways to compare 435 and 460.

Independent Practice and Problem Solving

Compare the numbers. Write <, >, or = for each ●.

7. 63 ● 36
8. 87 ● 92
9. 756 ● 756
10. 344 ● 427
11. 504 ● 98
12. 617 ● 671
13. 832 ● 823
14. 458 ● 467
15. 200 ● 300
16. 65 ● 69
17. 190 ● 190
18. 573 ● 537

USE DATA For 19–21, use the table.

Fastest Steel Roller Coasters

State	Roller Coaster	Speed in miles per hour
Texas	Titan	85
New Jersey	Kingda Ka	128
California	Superman: The Escape	100
Ohio	Millennium Force	93

19. Compare the speeds of the fastest steel roller coasters in Texas and New Jersey.

20. The speed of Kingda Ka is how many miles per hour faster than Superman: The Escape?

21. WRITE Math **What's the Error?** Dana compared the speeds of Kingda Ka and Millennium Force. She said Millennium Force is faster because 9 is greater than 1. What's her error?

22. ***FAST FACT*** The tallest roller coaster in the United States is Kingda Ka. It is 456 feet tall. The tallest roller coaster in Japan is Steel Dragon 2000. It is 318 feet tall. Which roller coaster is taller?

Mixed Review and TAKS Prep

23. Karen read a book that had 1,028 pages. Is 1,028 an even number or an odd number? What is the value of the 2 in 1,028? (TEKS 3.1A, pp. 6, 12)

24. Sam said that it is 278 days until his birthday. What is 278 written in expanded form? (TEKS 3.1A, p. 10)

25. **TAKS Prep** Which number is greater than 822? (Obj. 1)

A 637 **B** 743 **C** 798 **D** 826

26. **TAKS Prep** Which number is less than 648? (Obj. 1)

F 647 **G** 670 **H** 704 **J** 722

Technology
Use Harcourt Mega Math, Country Countdown, *Harrison's Comparisons,* Levels L and M; Fraction Action, *Number Line Mine,* Level B

 Extra Practice on page 44, Set A

Write to Explain

Justin is using data from the table to compare the heights of the Trump Building and the Key Tower. He wants to find out which building is taller.

This is how Justin explained how he compared the heights of the buildings.

Tall Buildings in the United States

Building	City	Height (in feet)
Chase Tower	Indianapolis	811
Bloomberg Tower	New York	806
Key Tower	Cleveland	947
Trump Building	New York	927
Woolworth Building	New York	792

First, I looked at the table to find the heights of the Trump Building and Key Tower.

Next, I recorded the heights of the buildings.

Trump Building	*927 feet*
Key Tower	*947 feet*

Then, I compared the heights. Since both numbers have a 9 in the hundreds place, I compared the tens digits. The Trump Building has a 2 and the Key Tower has a 4 in the tens place. Since $4 > 2$, I know that the Key Tower is taller than the Trump Building.

Tips

To write an explanation:

- Write the steps you took to solve the problem.
- Use words such as first, next, and then.
- State your answer in the last sentence of your explanation.

Problem Solving Use the data in the table. Explain how to solve each problem.

1. Is the Woolworth Building or the Chase Tower taller?
2. Is the Chase Tower or the Bloomberg Tower taller?

LESSON 2

Order Numbers

OBJECTIVE: Use a number line and place value to order 2- and 3-digit numbers.

Quick Review

Compare. Write <, >, or = for each ●.

1. 45 ● 57 **2.** 458 ● 487
3. 34 ● 29 **4.** 613 ● 613
5. 798 ● 789

Vocabulary

order

Learn

When you **order** numbers, you write them from least to greatest or from greatest to least.

PROBLEM The table lists the heights of three tall buildings in Houston, Texas. Which building in the table is the tallest?

Tall Buildings in Houston, Texas

Building	Height
Bank of America Center	780 feet
Wells Fargo Plaza	970 feet
Williams Tower	901 feet

ONE WAY **Use a number line.**

From least to greatest, the numbers are 780, 901, 970.

So, Wells Fargo Plaza is the tallest building.

OTHER WAYS

A **Use base-ten blocks. Order 24, 38, and 32 from least to greatest.**

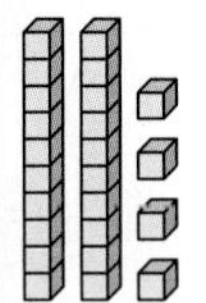
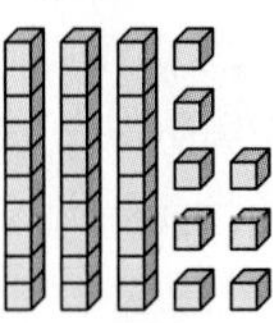
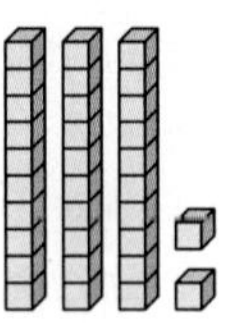

Compare the tens.
2 < 3, so 24 is the least number.
Compare the ones.
8 > 2, so 38 is the greatest number.

So, the order is 24, 32, 38.

B **Use a place-value chart. Order 220, 226, and 238 from greatest to least.**

HUNDREDS	TENS	ONES
2	2	0
2	2	6
2	3	8
↑ Hundreds are the same.	↑ 3 > 2, so 238 is the greatest number.	↑ 6 > 0, so 220 is the least number.

So, the order is 238, 226, 220.

- In Example B, which place-value positions helped you order the numbers?

TEKS **3.1B** use place value to compare and order whole numbers through 9,999. *also* **3.10, 3.14A, 3.14D, 3.15A, 3.15B, 3.16B**

Guided Practice

1. Use the number line. Order 45, 38, and 53 from least to greatest.

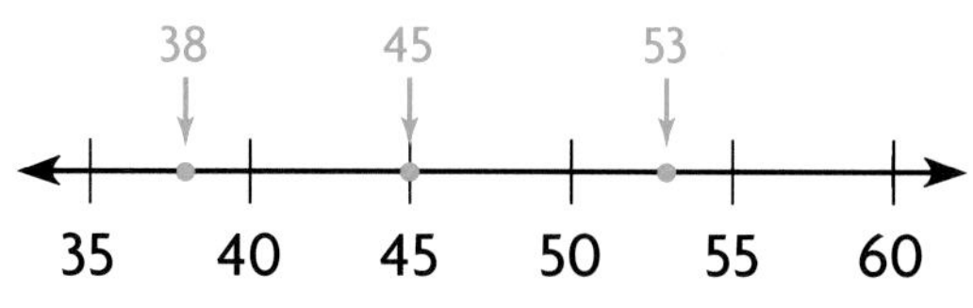

Write the numbers in order from least to greatest.

2. 72, 58, 67
3. 312, 331, 324
4. 708, 684, 699

5. TALK Math **Explain** how you know 176, 202, and 234 are in order from least to greatest.

Independent Practice and Problem Solving

Write the numbers in order from least to greatest.

6. 540, 527, 536
7. 784, 699, 808
8. 914, 896, 910

Write the numbers in order from greatest to least.

9. 395, 483, 475
10. 671, 740, 613
11. 594, 612, 601

USE DATA For 12–13, use the table.

12. List the Dallas building heights in order from greatest to least.

13. WRITE Math **What's the Error?** Alex wanted to order the three heights from least to greatest. He wrote 886 feet, 787 feet, 927 feet. What is Alex's error? Write the numbers in the correct order.

Tallest Buildings in Dallas, Texas

Building	Height in Feet
Bank One Center	787
Bank of America Plaza	927
Renaissance Tower	886

Mixed Review and TAKS Prep

14. Casey, Ben, and Ted ran a race. Casey did not finish last. Ted finished before Casey. Who finished first? (TEKS 3.14C, p. 18)

15. Texas Stadium in Irving seats sixty-five thousand, six hundred seventy-five people. Write this number in standard form. (TEKS 3.1A, p. 16)

16. **TAKS Prep** Which number is less than 408 but greater than 390? (Obj. 1)

A 400

B 408

C 410

D 480

Extra Practice on page 44, Set B

Compare and Order Greater Numbers

OBJECTIVE: Use place-value concepts to compare and order 4-digit numbers.

Quick Review

Order from least to greatest.

1. 23, 41, 37
2. 86, 79, 90
3. 404, 365, 391
4. 700, 698, 743
5. 141, 95, 114

Learn

PROBLEM The table shows some major league baseball players who have made 3,000 or more base hits in a career. Which player has the greatest number of base hits?

3,000 Hit Club	
Player	**Number of Base Hits**
Willie Mays	3,283
Stan Musial	3,630
Cap Anson	3,418

ONE WAY Use a number line.

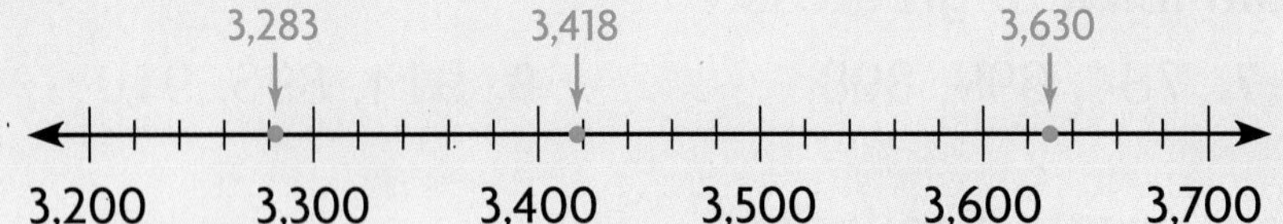

Since 3,630 is to the right of the other numbers, it is the greatest number. So, Stan Musial has the greatest number of base hits.

ANOTHER WAY Use place value.

Order 1,628; 976; and 1,645 from greatest to least.

Step 1	Step 2	Step 3
1,628 976 1,645 Compare thousands. 976 has no thousands. It is the least number.	1,628 1,645 Compare hundreds. $6 = 6$	1,628 1,645 Compare tens. $4 > 2$, so 1,645 is the greatest number.

So, the order is 1,645; 1,628; 976.

- Look at Step 3. **What if** the tens were the same? What would you do next?

Guided Practice

1. Which number is least? How can you tell?

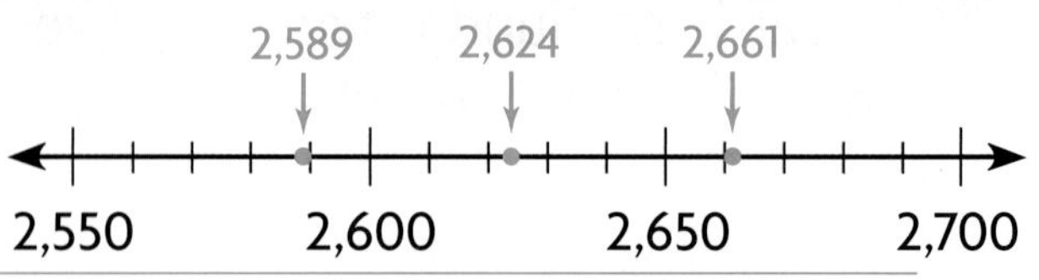

TEKS 3.1B use place value to compare and order whole numbers through 9,999. *also* **3.10, 3.14A, 3.14D, 3.15A, 3.15B, 3.16B**

Write the numbers in order from least to greatest.

2. 2,400; 2,397; 2,415

3. 3,088; 2,986; 3,165

4. 7,214; 742; 7,412

5. TALK Math **Explain** how you know 1,479; 1,523; and 1,601 are in order from least to greatest.

Independent Practice and Problem Solving

Write the numbers in order from least to greatest.

6. 1,250; 1,137; 1,314

7. 425; 4,015; 4,351

8. 2,519; 3,443; 2,567

9. 6,548; 6,456; 6,871

10. 5,091; 5,136; 5,109

11. 6,019; 6,090; 6,010

Write the numbers in order from greatest to least.

12. 898; 3,786; 3,981

13. 8,119; 8,284; 8,595

14. 559; 5,871; 5,071

15. 4,695; 4,297; 4,477

16. 9,223; 9,280; 9,275

17. 7,321; 7,318; 7,276

USE DATA For 18–20, use the table.

18. Which major league baseball pitcher in the table has the greatest number of strikeouts?

19. Write the number of strikeouts in order from greatest to least.

20. WRITE Math **Sense or Nonsense?** Karen says Don Sutton has more strikeouts than Tom Seaver because $7 > 4$. Does her answer make sense? **Explain.**

Major League Baseball Career Strikeouts

Player	Number of Strikeouts
Gaylord Perry	3,534
Tom Seaver	3,640
Don Sutton	3,574

Mixed Review and TAKS Prep

21. Dean had 2 dimes, 3 nickels, and 4 pennies. He lost 2 nickels. How much money does he have now?
(Grade 2, TEKS 2.3D)

22. Write forty thousand, five hundred thirty-one in standard form.
(TEKS 3.1A, p. 16)

23. **TAKS Prep** Which number is greater than 4,387 but less than 5,081? (Obj. 1)

A 4,198

B 4,275

C 4,981

D 5,248

Extra Practice on page 44, Set C

Round to the Nearest Ten

OBJECTIVE: Use the number line and place value to round numbers to the nearest ten.

Quick Review

1. Is 17 closer to 10 or 20?
2. Is 42 closer to 40 or 50?
3. Is 76 closer to 70 or 80?
4. Is 33 closer to 30 or 40?
5. Is 88 closer to 80 or 90?

Vocabulary

round

Learn

When you **round** a number, you find a number that tells you *about* how much or *about* how many.

PROBLEM Pet stores sell many kinds of freshwater fish. One store sold 253 guppies and 268 silver dollars. To the nearest ten, about how many of each kind of fish did the pet store sell?

Round to the nearest ten by finding the ten that is closer.

ONE WAY **Use a number line.**

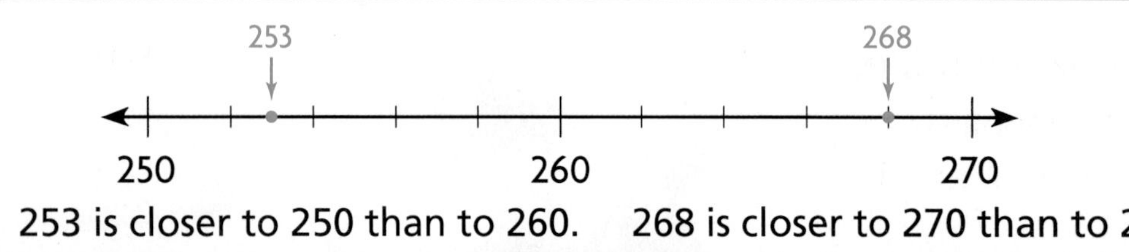

253 is closer to 250 than to 260. 268 is closer to 270 than to 260.

So, the pet store sold about 250 guppies and about 270 silver dollars.

ANOTHER WAY

Use place value.

- Find the place to which you want to round.
- Look at the digit to the right.
- If the digit is less than 5, the digit in the rounding place stays the same.
- If the digit is 5 or more, the digit in the rounding place increases by 1.
- Write a zero for the digit to the right.

Examples

Round 253 to the nearest ten.

Look at the ones digit.

253
↑

Since the ones digit is less than 5, the tens digit stays the same. Write a zero for the digit to the right.
So, 253 rounds to 250.

Round 268 to the nearest ten.

Look at the ones digit.

268
↑

Since the ones digit is greater than 5, the tens digit increases by 1. Write a zero for the digit to the right.
So, 268 rounds to 270.

TEKS 3.5A round whole numbers to the nearest ten or hundred to approximate reasonable results in problem situations. *also* **3.10, 3.14A, 3.15A, 3.15B**

Guided Practice

1. Write the two tens the number 318 is between. Then tell which ten is closer.

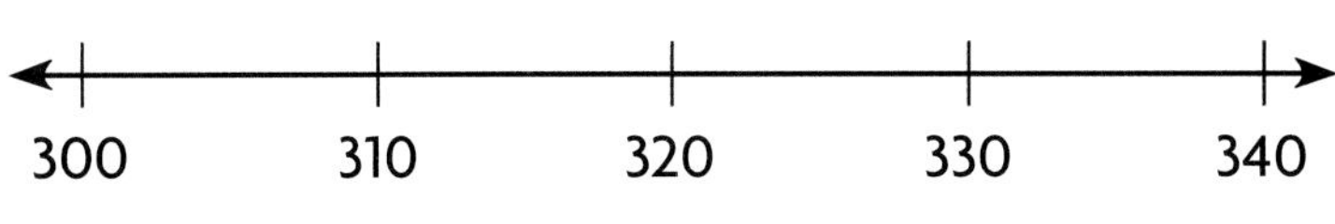

Round the number to the nearest ten.

2. 364 **3.** 283 **4.** 467 **5.** 981 **6.** 736

7. TALK Math **Explain** how to round 546 to the nearest ten.

Independent Practice and Problem Solving

Round the number to the nearest ten.

8. 152 **9.** 576 **10.** 298 **11.** 392 **12.** 178

13. 516 **14.** 843 **15.** 609 **16.** 290 **17.** 844

USE DATA **For 18–20, use the table.**

18. To the nearest ten pounds, about how much did the striped marlin weigh?

19. Which fish's record weight rounds to 220 pounds?

20. WRITE Math **Explain** how you would round the weight of the Pacific tuna to the nearest ten pounds.

Record Weights of Saltwater Fish

Fish	Weight in Pounds
Striped marlin	494
Pacific sailfish	221
Pacific tuna	435

21. **Reasoning** When numbers are rounded to the nearest ten, what is the least number that rounds to 100? What is the greatest number?

Mixed Review and TAKS Prep

22. I am an odd 3-digit number. The sum of my digits is 17. My hundreds digit is 2 more than my tens digit. My tens digit is 4. What number am I?
(TEKS 3.1A, p. 18)

23. Write 43,708 in expanded form.
(TEKS 3.1A, p. 16)

24. **TAKS Prep** Rounded to the nearest ten, Stella has 520 seashells. How many seashells could Stella have?
(Obj. 1)

A 552 **C** 527

B 531 **D** 522

Extra Practice on page 44, Set D

Round to the Nearest Hundred

OBJECTIVE: Use the number line and place value to round numbers to the nearest hundred.

Quick Review

Round to the nearest ten.

1. 28 **2.** 35
3. 104 **4.** 532
5. 697

Learn

PROBLEM Texas has 367 miles of coastline. To the nearest hundred, how many miles of coastline does Texas have?

▼ **Coastline is the edge of a body of water.**

Example **Use a number line.**

Round 367 to the nearest hundred.

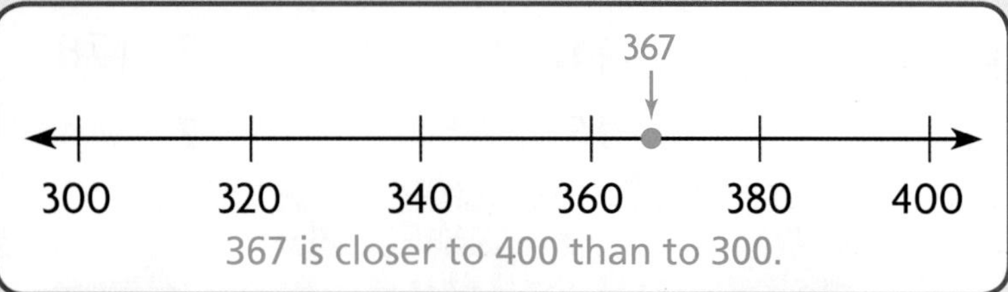

So, Texas has about 400 miles of coastline.

Sometimes you need to decide whether to round to the nearest hundred or to the nearest ten.
Louisiana has 397 miles of coastline. To what place value would you round in order to compare the number of miles of coastline for Texas and Louisiana?

Round to the nearest hundred.

397
$9 > 5$, so 397 rounds to 400.

367
$6 > 5$, so 367 rounds to 400.

Round to the nearest ten.

397
$7 > 5$, so 397 rounds to 400.

367
$7 > 5$, so 367 rounds to 370.

Both 397 and 367 round to 400 when rounded to the nearest hundred. So, in order to compare the rounded numbers, you need to round to the nearest ten.

- **What if** the number being rounded to the nearest hundred is 1,356? Explain how to round 1,356 by using place value.

TEKS 3.5A round whole numbers to the nearest ten or hundred to approximate reasonable results in problem situations. *also* **3.10, 3.14A, 3.15A, 3.15B, 3.16A**

Guided Practice

1. Between which two hundreds is 643? To which hundred is it closer?

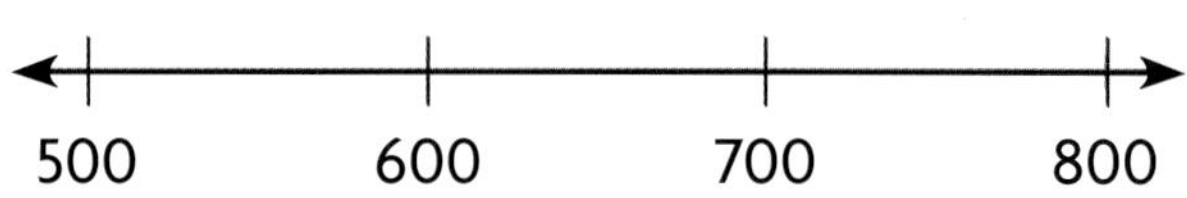

Round the number to the nearest hundred.

2. 218 ✓3. 764 4. 4,555 5. 3,366 ✓6. 8,205

7. TALK Math **Explain** how to round 396 to the nearest hundred.

Independent Practice and Problem Solving

Round the number to the nearest hundred.

8. 473 9. 894 10. 2,637 11. 7,849 12. 518

13. 332 14. 6,652 15. 721 16. 5,361 17. 956

USE DATA For 18–19 and 23, use the table.

18. Rounded to the nearest hundred, how many miles of shoreline does Oregon have?

19. WRITE Math Explain how to round the miles of California shoreline to the nearest hundred.

Miles of Shoreline

State	Number
Oregon	1,410
Washington	3,026
California	3,427

20. **Reasoning** What is the greatest 3-digit number you can write that rounds to 600 if three of the digits 4, 5, 6, and 8 can be used?

21. **Reasoning** A 4-digit number rounded to the nearest ten is 2,470. Rounded to the nearest hundred, it is 2,500. What is the number?

Mixed Review and TAKS Prep

22. What is the value of the 7 in 23,764? (TEKS 3.1A, p. 16)

23. Write the miles of shoreline in order from greatest to least. (TEKS 3.1B, p. 34)

24. **TAKS Prep** Which number does NOT round to 300 when rounded to the nearest hundred? (Obj. 1)

A 350 **C** 325

B 300 **D** 284

Extra Practice on page 44, Set E

Problem Solving Workshop
Skill: Use a Number Line

OBJECTIVE: Solve problems by using the skill *use a number line.*

Read to Understand
Plan
Solve
Check

Use the Skill

PROBLEM Jason and his family are visiting the zoo. They see a black leopard that weighs 168 pounds, a jaguar that weighs 274 pounds, and a zebra that weighs 412 pounds. What is the weight of each animal, rounded to the nearest hundred pounds?

Find the weight of each animal on the number line. To which hundred is each number closer?

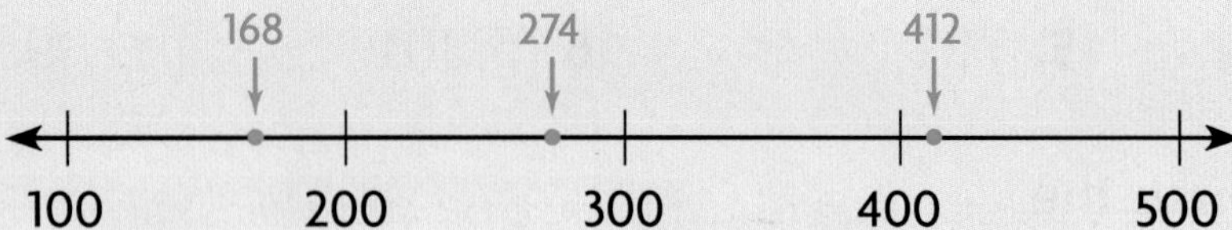

168 is closer to 200, 274 is closer to 300, and 412 is closer to 400.

So, the black leopard weighs about 200 pounds. The jaguar weighs about 300 pounds, and the zebra weighs about 400 pounds.

Think and Discuss

a. The petting zoo had 587 visitors on the weekend. Rounded to the nearest ten, how many people visited the petting zoo on the weekend?

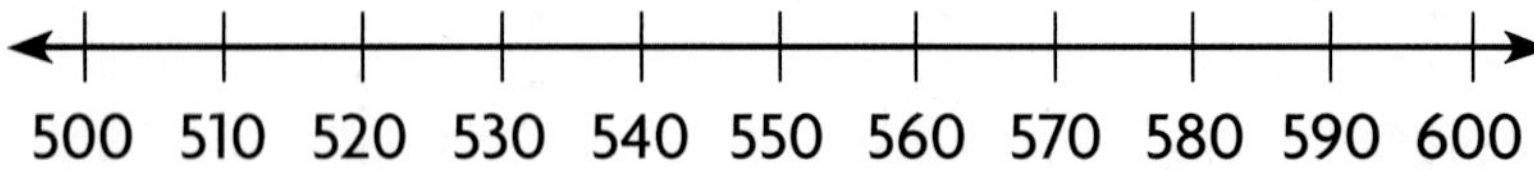

b. One of the giant pandas in the zoo ate 288 pounds of bamboo in one week. Rounded to the nearest hundred, how many pounds of bamboo did the panda eat?

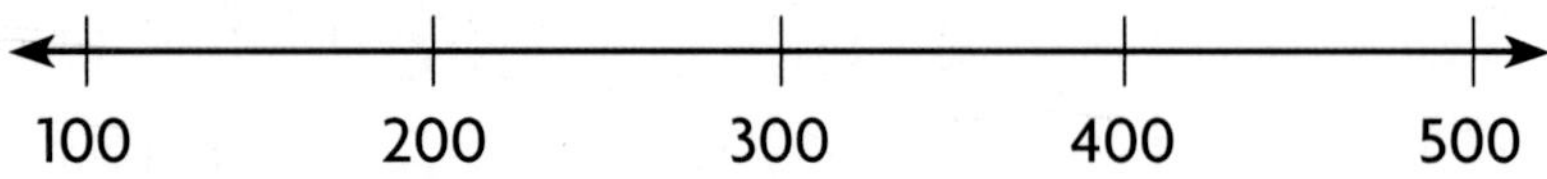

TEKS 3.5A round whole numbers to the nearest ten or hundred to approximate reasonable results in problem situations. *also* **3.10, 3.14A, 3.14C, 3.14D, 3.15A, 3.15B, 3.16B**

Guided Problem Solving

Use the number line to solve the problem.

1. The zoo has 725 kinds of mammals. To the nearest hundred, how many kinds of mammals does the zoo have?

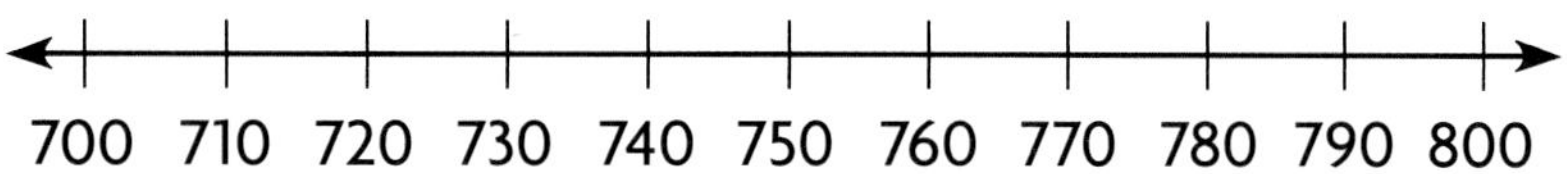

Use the number line.

Is 725 closer to 700 or to 800?

To the nearest hundred, how many kinds of mammals does the zoo have?

2. **What if** the kinds of mammals increased by 150? To the nearest ten, how many kinds of mammals would the zoo have?

3. The zoo has 268 kinds of birds. To the nearest hundred, how many kinds of birds does the zoo have?

Mixed Applications

USE DATA For 4–5, use the table.

4. Write the names of the animals in order from least to greatest number of minutes of sleep each day.

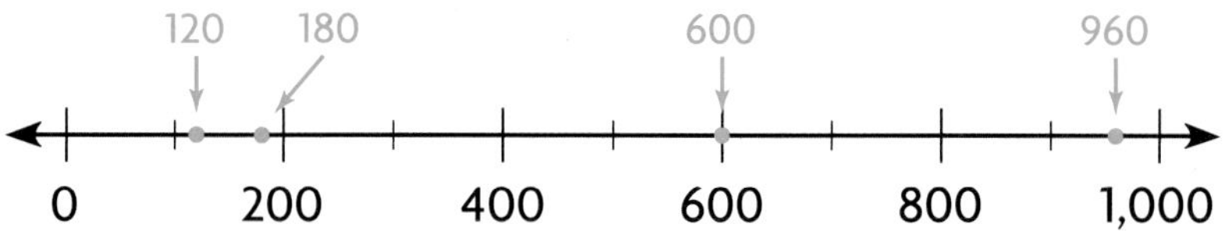

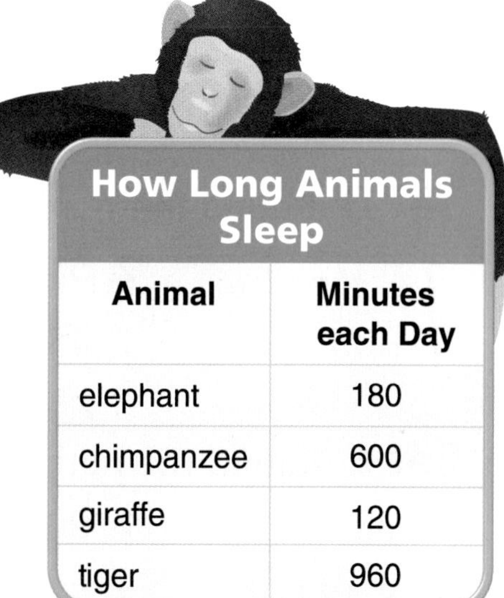

How Long Animals Sleep

Animal	Minutes each Day
elephant	180
chimpanzee	600
giraffe	120
tiger	960

5. How many more minutes each day does a tiger sleep than a chimpanzee?

6. Kelly bought 2 pencils for 25¢ each and an eraser for 50¢ in the zoo gift shop. How much did Kelly spend in all?

7. Hector's family lives 46 miles from the zoo. They have driven 28 miles. How many more miles do they have to drive to reach the zoo?

Extra Practice

Set A **Compare the numbers. Write $<$, $>$, or $=$ for each ●.** (pp. 30–33)

1. 87 ● 94
2. 100 ● 94
3. 381 ● 381
4. 426 ● 439
5. 317 ● 771
6. 733 ● 732
7. 218 ● 218
8. 69 ● 112

Set B **Write the numbers in order from least to greatest.** (pp. 34–35)

1. 49, 31, 36
2. 362, 609, 572
3. 753, 738, 797
4. 623, 641, 625
5. 811, 118, 181
6. 453, 65, 781
7. Sabrina's first throw in the softball-toss competition was 57 feet. Her second throw was 54 feet, and her third throw was 60 feet. Which throw was her longest?
8. There are a total of 254 counties in the state of Texas. There are 102 counties in Illinois, and 159 counties in Georgia. Which of these states has the second-greatest number of counties?

Set C **Write the numbers in order from least to greatest.** (pp. 36–37)

1. 5,260; 5,899; 5,624
2. 1,728; 1,717; 1,731
3. 8,015; 9,317; 6,273
4. 3,956; 1,516; 3,870
5. 2,719; 3,818; 1,011
6. 8,102; 5,973; 7,318
7. A farm produced 1,099 pounds of cherries in June. It produced 998 pounds of cherries in July, and another 901 pounds in August. During which month did the farm produce the most cherries?
8. Ryan's class collected 3,598 pennies for the playground fundraiser. Allen's class collected 3,618 pennies, and Marla's class collected 3,600 pennies. Order the numbers from least to greatest.

Set D **Round the number to the nearest ten.** (pp. 38–39)

1. 657
2. 518
3. 642
4. 109
5. 756
6. 235
7. 456
8. 313
9. 711
10. 544

Set E **Round the number to the nearest hundred.** (pp. 40–41)

1. 875
2. 907
3. 189
4. 1,296
5. 7,557
6. 8,432
7. 562
8. 4,209
9. 6,750
10. 9,917

CD ROM **Technology**
Use Harcourt Mega Math, Fraction Action, *Number Line Mine*, Levels C, D.

PRACTICE GAME Building Numbers

Prepare!
3 players

Plan!
- Number cube numbered 1–6
- 1 gameboard for each player

A

THOUSANDS HUNDREDS TENS ONES

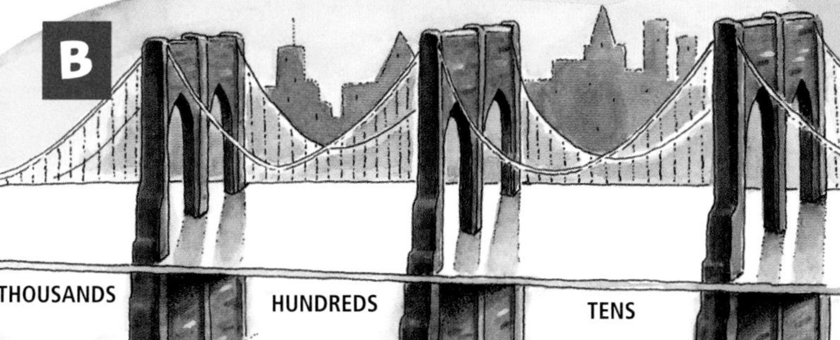

Build!

- Players take turns rolling the number cube.
- Player 1 writes the rolled number in the ones, tens, hundreds, or thousands place in one of the place-value charts.
- Once a number is placed in a chart, it cannot be moved to another place-value position.
- Play continues until each player has built a 4-digit number.
- Players compare their 4-digit numbers. The player with the greater number earns 1 point.
- The game continues until each player has built a 4-digit number in each place-value chart.
- The player with more points wins.

Chapter 2 Review/Test

Check Vocabulary and Concepts

VOCABULARY
- compare
- order
- round

Choose the best term from the box.

1. One way to __?__ numbers is to use $<$, $>$, or $=$. (TEKS 3.1B, p. 30)
2. You __?__ a number to find *about* how much or how many. (TEKS 3.5A, p. 38)

Check Skills

Compare the numbers. Write $<$, $>$, or $=$ for each ●. (TEKS 3.1B, pp. 30–33)

3. 78 ● 84 **4.** 600 ● 500 **5.** 42 ● 42 **6.** 268 ● 218

7. 980 ● 890 **8.** 65 ● 76 **9.** 98 ● 89 **10.** 585 ● 585

Write the numbers in order from greatest to least. (TEKS 3.1B, pp. 34–37)

11. 498, 569, 389 **12.** 1,267; 1,098; 1,330 **13.** 240, 221, 320

14. 8,780; 8,870; 8,078 **15.** 843, 627, 762 **16.** 6,636; 6,950; 5,910

Round each number to the nearest hundred and to the nearest ten. (TEKS 3.5A, pp. 38–41)

17. 687 **18.** 341 **19.** 924 **20.** 4,567 **21.** 1,212

22. 6,478 **23.** 3,633 **24.** 5,295 **25.** 9,526 **26.** 2,877

Check Problem Solving

Solve. Use a number line. (TEKS 3.5A, 3.15A, 3.15B, pp. 42–43)

27. The zoo sold 378 tickets to its new panda exhibit. Rounded to the nearest hundred, how many tickets did the zoo sell?

28. The concession stand at the zoo sold 723 sandwiches. Rounded to the nearest ten, how many sandwiches did the concession stand sell?

29. WRITE Math Jenny has 261 stamps in her collection. **Explain** how you can find the number of stamps Jenny has, rounded to the nearest hundred.

GO ONLINE **Technology** Use *Online Assessment.*

Enrich • Number Sense

Use the clues to solve the riddle.

1. • I am an odd number.
• When rounded to the nearest ten, I round to 60.
• I am greater than 61.

What number am I?

2. • I am an odd 4-digit number.
• Two of my digits are zero.
• I am less than 5,000.
• The difference between my ones digit and thousands digits is 7.

What number am I?

3. • I am an even number.
• I am greater than 5,685 and less than 5,691.
• My ones digit is less than my hundreds digit.

What number am I?

4. • I am a 3-digit number.
• My ones digit is twice my hundreds digit.
• When rounded to the nearest hundred, I round to 500.
• My tens digit is less than 6.

What number am I?

5. • I am an odd number.
• My hundreds digit is 4.
• My ten thousands digit is 2 more than my hundreds digit.
• My thousands digit is 3 less than my hundreds digit.
• My tens digit is twice my hundreds digit.
• The sum of my digits is 22.

What number am I?

6. • I am a 4-digit number.
• All of my digits are even numbers.
• The sum of my ones and tens digits is 8.
• My hundreds and ones digits are both 4.
• The sum of my digits is 18.

What number am I?

WRITE Math Write a number riddle. Exchange riddles with a classmate. **Explain** how you solved your classmate's riddle.

Unit Review/Test
Chapters 1–2

Multiple Choice

1. Which is twenty thousand, five hundred four written in standard form? (TAKS Obj. 1)

   A 25,004

   B 20,540

   C 20,504

   D 20,054

2. Use the number line below to order these numbers from greatest to least: 3,350; 3,240; 3,150; 3,260

   (TAKS Obj. 1)

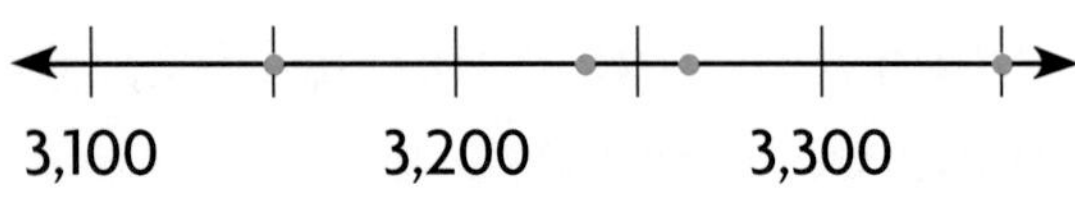

   F 3,150; 3,240; 3,260; 3,350

   G 3,350; 3,240; 3,260; 3,150

   H 3,350; 3,260; 3,240; 3,150

   J 3,260; 3,240; 3,350; 3,150

3. Martin has 287 rocks in his collection. What is 287 rounded to the nearest hundred? (TAKS Obj. 1)

   A 200

   B 280

   C 290

   D 300

4. Which shows 603,410 in word form? (TAKS Obj. 1)

   F Six hundred thirty thousand, four hundred ten

   G Sixty three thousand, forty-one

   H Six hundred three thousand, four hundred one

   J Not here

5. The table shows the video game scores of four players.

Video Game Scores	
Anne	459
Brian	462
Paula	426
Richard	460

   Who had the greatest score?

   (TAKS Obj. 1)

   A Anne　　**C** Paula

   B Brian　　**D** Richard

6. What is the value of the underlined digit in the number $4\underline{1}3{,}783$?

   (TAKS Obj. 1)

   F 100,000　　**H** 1,000

   G 10,000　　**J** 100

GO ONLINE Technology Use *Online Assessment.*

7. Use the hundred chart.

1	2	3	4	5	6	7	8	9	10
11	12	13	14	15	16	17	18	19	20
21	22	23	24	25	26	27	28	29	30
31	32	33	34	35	36	37	38	39	40
41	42	43	44	45	46	47	48	49	50
51	52	53	54	55	56	57	58	59	60
61	62	63	64	65	66	67	68	69	70
71	72	73	74	75	76	77	78	79	80
81	82	83	84	85	86	87	88	89	90
91	92	93	94	95	96	97	98	99	100

What is the next number in the pattern? (TAKS Obj. 2)

45, 55, 65, 75, ■

A 80 **C** 90

B 85 **D** 95

8. What number does point *P* best represent on this number line? (TAKS Obj. 3)

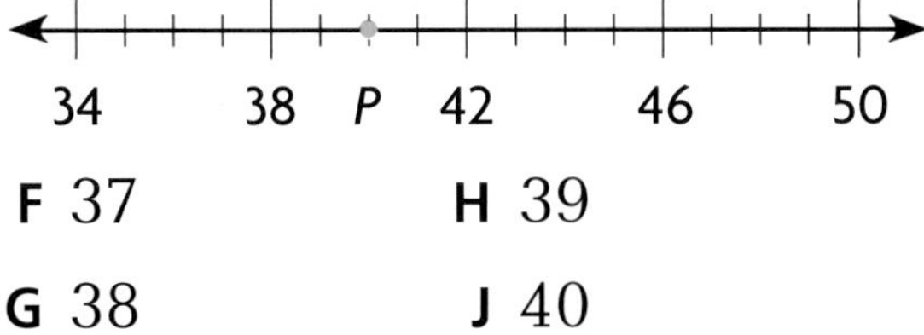

F 37 **H** 39

G 38 **J** 40

9. Mr. Miller wrote a number on the board that has a 7 in the thousands place. Which number could Mr. Miller have written? (TAKS Obj. 1)

A 57,893 **C** 83,795

B 78,359 **D** 95,873

Short Response

10. Alicia ran the race in 47 seconds. Tanya's time was 44 seconds, and Bev's time was 49 seconds. Who won the race? (TAKS Obj. 1)

11. When rounded to the nearest ten, what is the least number that rounds to 500? (TAKS Obj. 1)

12. What is the greatest 4-digit number you can write with digits that are all different even numbers? (TAKS Obj. 1)

Extended Response WRITE Math

13. Andy scored 4,730 points on a computer game. Carlos scored 4,703 points on the same game. Who got the higher score? **Explain** your answer. (TAKS Obj. 1)

14. There were 347 students at the science center. Is it more reasonable to round the number of students to the nearest ten or to the nearest hundred? **Explain.** (TAKS Obj. 1)

Texas Problem Solving

Rivers of the World

Winding Water

There are rivers on every continent. Rivers can be used for transportation, to generate electricity, to water crops, for water to drink, and for fun. Over many thousands of years, rivers can even cut through rock. In the United States, the Colorado River carved out the Grand Canyon, which is about one mile deep.

The Nile River flows north through Africa from Lake Victoria to the Mediterranean Sea.

Mediterranean Sea
AFRICA
Nile River
Lake Victoria
N
S
E
W

FACT ACTIVITY

Use the data in the table to answer the questions.

Longest Rivers on Six Continents

Continent	River	Length
Africa	Nile	4,160 miles
Asia	Chang (Yangtze)	3,964 miles
Australia	Murray-Darling	2,310 miles
Europe	Volga	2,290 miles
North America	Mississippi	2,340 miles
South America	Amazon	4,000 miles

1. How many rivers are longer than the Mississippi River?
2. Which river is longer than the Mississippi River but shorter than the Amazon River?
3. Write the lengths of the rivers in order from the longest to the shortest.
4. Two different rivers have a 4 in the thousands place. Which two rivers are they?

ALMANAC Fact

The Rio Grande River is the longest river in Texas, with a length of 1,896 miles! In Spanish, Rio Grande means "Great River."

The Rio Grande River

Texas River Riddles

A river has a mouth. At its mouth, a river flows into another body of water. A river begins at its source. A source may be an underground spring or a place high in the mountains where rain or melting snow collects to form a small stream.

Some Texas Rivers

Name of River	Mouth	Length
Colorado	Gulf of Mexico	894 miles
Lampasas	Leon River	110 miles
Mission	Copano Bay	25 miles
Pease	Red River	75 miles
Rio Grande	Gulf of Mexico	1,896 miles
San Jacinto	Galveston Bay	130 miles
White	Brazos River	100 miles
Wichita	Red River	250 miles

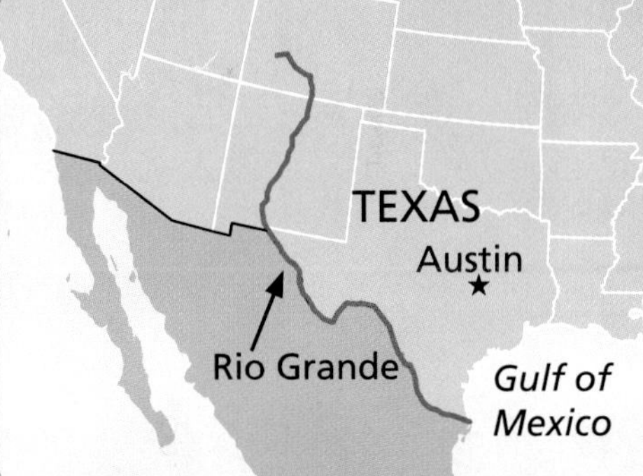

FACT·ACTIVITY

Use the data in the table to answer the questions.

1. When rounded to the nearest hundred, my length is 100 miles. My name has two words. Which river am I?
2. I am the second longest river shown in the table. Which river am I? Compare my length to the length of shortest river in the table.
3. **Pose a Problem** Write three riddles using the river lengths. Have a classmate solve your riddles.

UNIT

2 Addition, Subtraction, and Money

Math on Location

with
Chapter Projects

1

As old computers are taken apart, the number of cases, circuit boards, and keyboards increase.

2

An equal number of CRT's (cathode ray tubes) are placed on wood pallets for safe handling.

3

Three men can recycle 600 computers a day. That is 75 computers an hour in an 8-hour day.

VOCABULARY POWER

TALK Math

What math do you see in the **Math on Location** photographs? If 3 men recycle 75 computers an hour, how many can they recycle in 4 hours?

READ Math

REVIEW VOCABULARY You learned the words below when you learned about addition, subtraction, and money. How do these words relate to **Math on Location**?

sum the answer in an addition problem

difference the answer in a subtraction problem

estimate to find about how many or how much

WRITE Math

Copy and complete the table using the word pairs shown below. Use what you know about numbers and operations.

addition, subtraction — addition, sum — odd, even — subtraction, count backward — regroup, compare — digit, place value — fact family, number sentence — subtraction, difference — sum, difference — compare, order — greater than, less than — sum, total

Same	Opposite	Go Together	Not Related
	addition, subtraction		

Technology
Multimedia Math Glossary link at www.harcourtschool.com/hspmath

CHAPTER

3 Addition

The Big Idea Addition of multi-digit numbers is based on single-digit addition facts and base-ten and place-value concepts.

TEXAS FAST FACT

Corpus Christi, Texas, is the largest city on the coast of Texas and the sixth-largest port in the United States. The Municipal Marina has over 500 spots for boats to park.

Investigate

A marina has several boat docks. The pictograph shows the number of boats at each dock. Choose three of the docks, and tell how many boats are at those three docks altogether.

Boats at Marina

Dock A	🚤 🚤 🚤 🚤 🚤 🚤
Dock B	🚤 🚤 🚤 🚤
Dock C	🚤 🚤 🚤 🚤 🚤
Dock D	🚤 🚤 🚤
Dock E	🚤 🚤 🚤 🚤 🚤 🚤 🚤

Key: Each 🚤 = 4 boats.

GO ONLINE **Technology** Student pages are available in the Student eBook.

Show What You Know

Check your understanding of important skills needed for success in Chapter 3.

▶ Add 1-Digit Numbers

Add.

1. $5 + 2$ **2.** $3 + 7$ **3.** $8 + 6$ **4.** $9 + 4$ **5.** $1 + 8$

▶ Model 2-Digit Addition

Use the models. Find the sum.

6. $15 + 18 = ■$

7. $27 + 31 = ■$

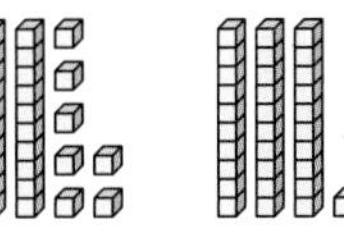

8. $45 + 19 = ■$

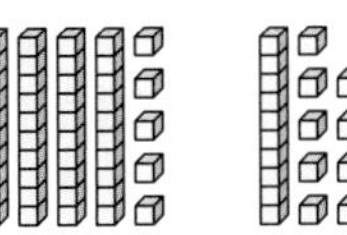

9. $50 + 24 = ■$

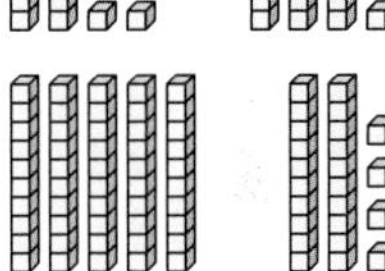

▶ 2-Digit Addition Without Regrouping

Add.

10. $14 + 11$ **11.** $32 + 24$ **12.** $27 + 62$ **13.** $48 + 30$ **14.** $34 + 15$

VOCABULARY POWER

CHAPTER VOCABULARY

Associative Property of Addition
Commutative Property of Addition
compatible numbers
estimate
Identity Property of Addition
missing addend
number sentence

WARM-UP WORDS

Commutative Property of Addition The property that states that you can add two or more numbers in any order and get the same sum

Identity Property of Addition The property that states that when you add zero to a number, the result is that number

Associative Property of Addition The property that states that you can group addends in different ways and still get the same sum

ALGEBRA

Addition Properties

OBJECTIVE: Use properties of addition to solve problems.

Quick Review

1. 5 + 8 **2.** 6 + 6
3. 7 + 3 **4.** 8 + 7
5. 9 + 6

Vocabulary

Commutative Property of Addition
Identity Property of Addition
Associative Property of Addition

Learn

PROBLEM Ana saw 9 seagulls on Monday and 5 seagulls on Tuesday. How many seagulls did she see in all?

Commutative Property of Addition

You can add numbers in any order and get the same sum.

9 + 5 = 14
addend + addend = sum

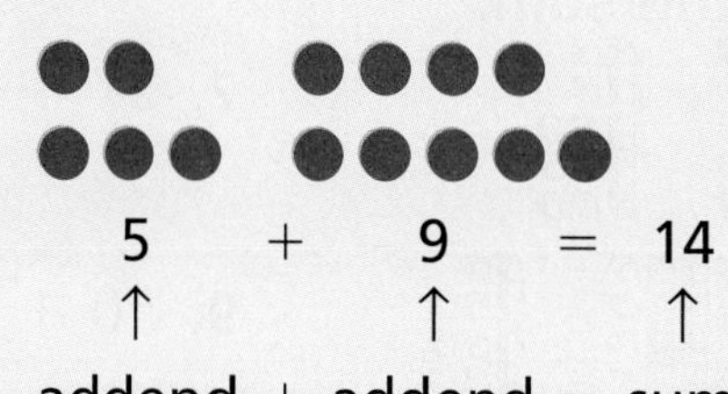

5 + 9 = 14
addend + addend = sum

So, 9 + 5 = 5 + 9. Ana saw 14 birds.

Identity Property of Addition

Ana saw 8 fish. Beth did not see any. How many fish did the girls see in all?

If you add zero to any number, the sum is that number.

8 + 0 = 8

So, the girls saw 8 fish in all.

Associative Property of Addition

Ana collected 7 brown shells, 4 white shells, and 6 gray shells. How many shells did she collect in all?

You can group addends in different ways, and the sum will be the same.

(7 + 4) + 6 = 7 + (4 + 6)
11 + 6 = 7 + 10
17 = 17

Math Idea
Parentheses ( ) show which numbers to add first.

So, Ana collected 17 shells in all.

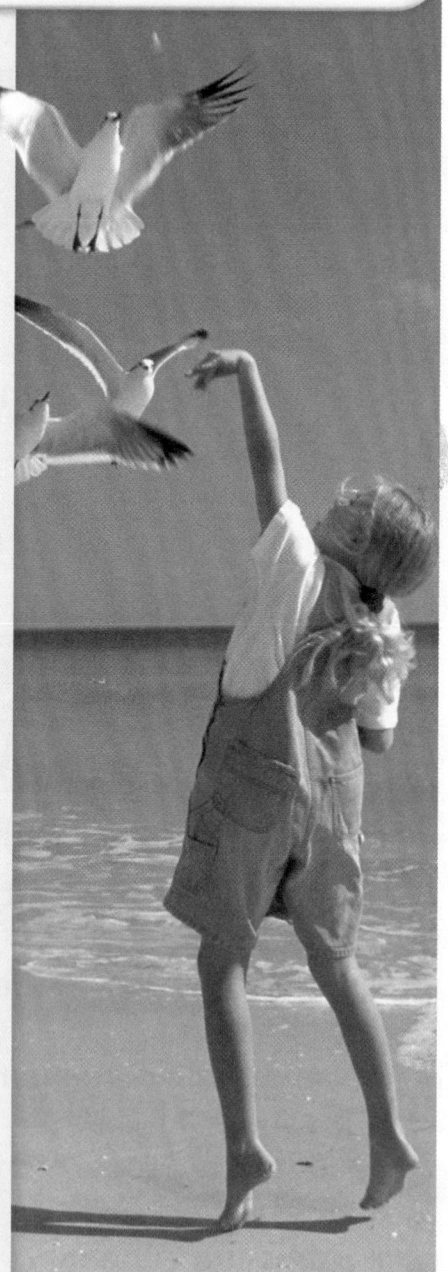

TEKS 3.3A model addition and subtraction using pictures, words, and numbers. *also* **3.3B, 3.14A, 3.15A, 3.15B**

Guided Practice

1. What is the sum when you add 0 to 6?
   6 turtles + 0 turtles = ■ turtles

Find each sum. Name the property used.

2. $8 + 4 =$ ■
   $4 + 8 =$ ■
3. $0 + 23 =$ ■
   $23 + 0 =$ ■
4. ✓ $6 + 3 =$ ■
   $3 + 6 =$ ■
5. ✓ $(2 + 7) + 1 =$ ■
   $2 + (7 + 1) =$ ■
6. TALK Math **Explain** how you can use the Associative Property of Addition to find $15 + 7 + 3$.

Independent Practice and Problem Solving

Find each sum. Name the property used.

7. $10 + 2 =$ ■
   $2 + 10 =$ ■
8. $1 + (16 + 4) =$ ■
   $(1 + 16) + 4 =$ ■
9. $6 + 0 =$ ■
   $0 + 6 =$ ■
10. $3 + (5 + 9) =$ ■
    $(3 + 5) + 9 =$ ■

Find each sum two different ways. Use parentheses to show which numbers you added first.

11. $8 + 9 + 1 =$ ■
12. $25 + 25 + 15 =$ ■
13. $30 + 70 + 15 =$ ■
14. A saltwater fishtank has 2 starfish, 3 sea horses, and 5 clown fish. How many animals are in the tank in all? Draw a picture and write a number sentence.
15. **What if** 4 of each animal are added to the tank? How many animals are there in all now?
16. WRITE Math Do you think there is a Commutative Property of Subtraction? **Explain** why or why not.

Mixed Review and TAKS Prep

17. What is 759 rounded to the nearest hundred? (TEKS 3.5A, p. 40)
18. **TAKS Prep** Which is the sum? (Obj. 1)

    $(6 + 6) + 7 =$ ■

    A 12 **B** 13 **C** 19 **D** 20
19. There are 2 red marbles and 5 green marbles in a bag. Which color marble are you more likely to choose? (Grade 2 TEKS 2.11C)

Extra Practice on page 76, Set A

LESSON 2

ALGEBRA

Missing Addends

OBJECTIVE: Identify missing addends in addition sentences.

Quick Review

1. 4 + 7
2. 5 + 9
3. 8 + 4
4. 9 + 3
5. 7 + 6

Learn

PROBLEM Nick's family spent the day at an amusement park. They rode roller coasters a total of 12 times. They rode roller coasters 7 times before lunch. How many times did they ride roller coasters after lunch?

ONE WAY **Use an addition fact.**

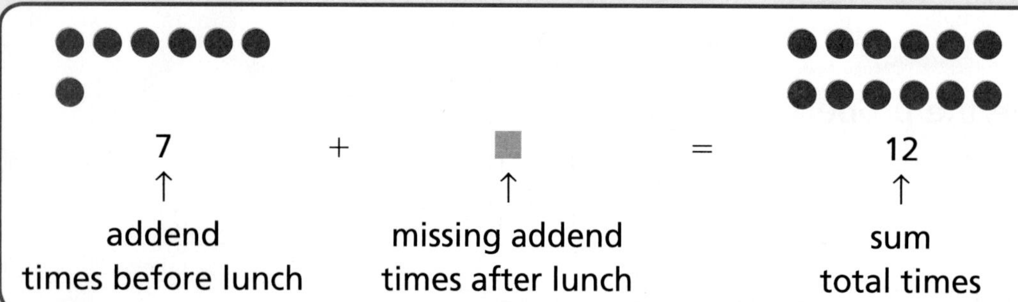

7 + 5 = 12

ANOTHER WAY **Use a related subtraction fact.**

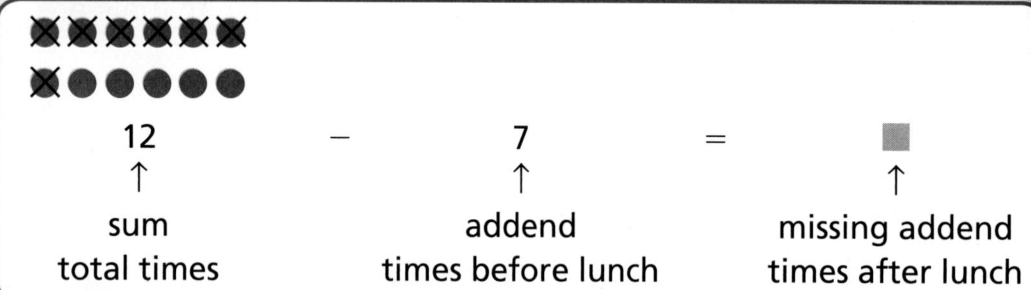

12 − 7 = 5

So, Nick's family rode roller coasters 5 times after lunch.

- **What if** Nick's family rode roller coasters 3 times before lunch? How many times would they have ridden roller coasters after lunch?

Guided Practice

1. What addition fact can help you find 3 + ■ = 10? What related subtraction fact can help you?

TEKS 3.3A model addition and subtraction using pictures, words, and numbers. *also* 3.3B, 3.14A, 3.14D, 3.15A, 3.15B

Find the missing addend. You may want to use counters.

2. $4 + ■ = 12$ **3.** $■ + 6 = 6$ ✓**4.** $8 + ■ = 10$ ✓**5.** $■ + 5 = 11$

6. TALK Math **Explain** how to use a related subtraction fact to find $8 + ■ = 13$.

Independent Practice and Problem Solving

Find the missing addend. You may want to use counters.

7. $6 + ■ = 16$ **8.** $■ + 5 = 12$ **9.** $■ + 17 = 17 + 6$ **10.** $■ + 9 = 9$

11. $6 + ■ = 20$ **12.** $19 + 12 = 12 + ■$ **13.** $5 + ■ = 13$ **14.** $■ + 3 = 18$

Find the missing number.

15. $7 + 8 = ■$ **16.** $9 + ■ = 18$ **17.** $■ + 8 = 14$ **18.** $10 + 0 = ■$

USE DATA For 19–21, use the table.

19. The table shows the amount of food sold at an amusement park on Friday. How many more hot dogs and nachos were sold than hamburgers?

Food Sold

Food	Number Sold
Hamburgers	41
Hot dogs	29
Nachos	35

20. **Pose a Problem** Look back at Problem 19. Write a similar problem by changing the number of items sold to numbers less than 20 and by changing the question.

21. WRITE Math If Sue's family bought 8 hot dogs, how many hot dogs were bought by other people? **Explain** how you know.

Mixed Review and TAKS Prep

22. Leah wrote eight thousand, three hundred four. What is Leah's number in standard form? (TEKS 3.1A, p.12)

23. Dan caught 12 baseballs. Jim didn't catch any. Which addition property is shown by this example? $12 + 0 = 12$ (TEKS 3.3B, p.56)

24. **TAKS Prep** Which is the missing addend for $12 + ■ = 17$? (Obj. 1)

A 3

B 4

C 5

D 6

LESSON 3

Estimate Sums

OBJECTIVE: Estimate sums of 2- and 3-digit numbers by using rounding and compatible numbers.

Quick Review

Round each number to the nearest ten.

1. 83
2. 96
3. 55
4. 19
5. 74

Vocabulary

estimate

compatible numbers

Learn

PROBLEM There are many types of birds at Lake Whitney, in Texas. One day Jacob counted 128 birds. Paul counted 73 birds. About how many birds did Jacob and Paul count in all?

To find *about* how many, you can **estimate**.

Example Estimate. 128 + 73

ONE WAY **Use rounding.**

Round each number to the nearest ten. Then add.

$$\begin{array}{r} 128 \\ +\ 73 \end{array} \rightarrow \begin{array}{r} 130 \\ +\ 70 \\ \hline 200 \end{array}$$

ANOTHER WAY **Use compatible numbers.**

Compatible numbers are close numbers that are easy to compute mentally.

$$\begin{array}{r} 128 \\ +\ 73 \end{array} \rightarrow \begin{array}{r} 125 \\ +\ 75 \\ \hline 200 \end{array}$$

So, 200 is a reasonable estimate of how many birds were counted.

- What other compatible numbers could be used to estimate the sum?

More Examples

A **Use rounding.**

$$\begin{array}{r} 19 \\ +66 \end{array} \rightarrow \begin{array}{r} 20 \\ +70 \\ \hline 90 \end{array}$$

B **Use rounding.**

$$\begin{array}{r} 492 \\ +219 \end{array} \rightarrow \begin{array}{r} 500 \\ +200 \\ \hline 700 \end{array}$$

C **Use compatible numbers.**

$$\begin{array}{r} 306 \\ +286 \end{array} \rightarrow \begin{array}{r} 300 \\ +285 \\ \hline 585 \end{array}$$

Guided Practice

1. Copy the problem at the right. Round both 324 and 48 to the nearest ten. Then estimate their sum.

$$\begin{array}{r} 324 \\ +\ 48 \\ \hline \end{array}$$

TEKS 3.5B use strategies including rounding and compatible numbers to estimate solutions to addition and subtraction problems. *also* **3.3B, 3.14A, 3.15A, 3.15B**

Use rounding or compatible numbers to estimate each sum.

2. $37 + 51$

3. $307 + 181$

4. $476 + 239$

5. $29 + 44$

6. $148 + 151$

7. TALK Math Use rounding and then use compatible numbers to estimate 128 + 381. Which way do you think gives an answer closer to the exact sum for this problem? **Explain.**

Independent Practice and Problem Solving

Use rounding to estimate each sum.

8. $42 + 35$

9. $61 + 95$

10. $319 + 54$

11. $289 + 407$

12. $526 + 361$

Use compatible numbers to estimate each sum.

13. $42 + 37$

14. $51 + 48$

15. $172 + 27$

16. $326 + 176$

17. $248 + 121$

USE DATA For 18–20, use the table.

18. Reasoning If you went along the shoreline of Lake Conroe two times, would that distance be about the same as going one time along Lake Fork? **Explain** using compatible numbers.

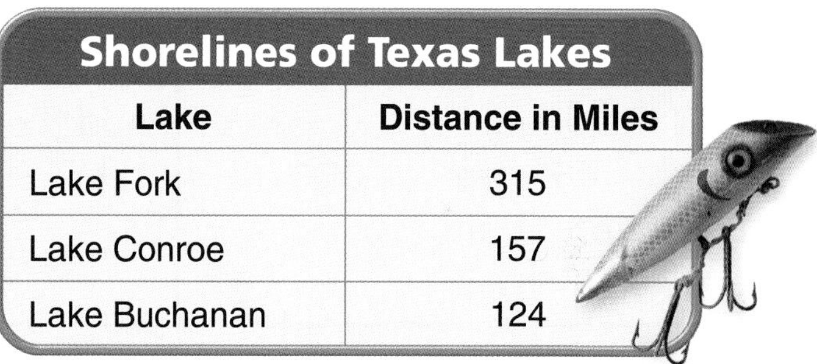

Shorelines of Texas Lakes

Lake	Distance in Miles
Lake Fork	315
Lake Conroe	157
Lake Buchanan	124

19. WRITE Math Some lakes in Texas have shorelines along which people hike and fish. **Explain** how you would estimate the sum of Lake Fork's and Lake Conroe's shorelines.

20. ***FAST FACT*** Lake Livingston is the second-largest lake in Texas. It has 450 miles of shoreline. Estimate the sum of Lake Livingston's and Lake Buchanan's shorelines.

Mixed Review and TAKS Prep

21. Write the numbers in order from least to greatest. (TEKS 3.1B, p. 36)

2,219; 2,178; 2,198

22. What is the missing addend?
9 + ■ = 18 (TEKS 3.3B, p. 58)

23. TAKS Prep A plane flew 732 miles and then flew 476 miles. About how many miles did the plane fly in all? (Obj. 1)

A 200 **B** 1,000 **C** 1,200 **D** 2,000

Extra Practice on page 76, Set C

Add 2-Digit Numbers

OBJECTIVE: Add 2-digit numbers with and without regrouping.

Quick Review

1. 6 + 8
2. 8 + 9
3. 7 + 7
4. 8 + 4
5. 6 + 4 + 5

Learn

PROBLEM Shannon picked 29 red apples at the orchard. Katrina picked 57 green apples. How many apples did Shannon and Katrina pick in all?

Example 1 **Add.** 29 + 57 **Estimate.** 30 + 60 = 90

ONE WAY **Use mental math.**

	Add the tens.	Add the ones.	Add the sums.
29 + 57	20 + 50 70	9 + 7 16	70 + 16 86

ANOTHER WAY **Use place value.**

Step 1

Add the ones.
9 + 7 = 16 ones
Regroup 16 ones as 1 ten 6 ones.

$$\begin{array}{r} ^{1} \\ 29 \\ +\,57 \\ \hline 6 \end{array}$$

Step 2

Add the tens.
1 + 2 + 5 = 8 tens

$$\begin{array}{r} ^{1} \\ 29 \\ +\,57 \\ \hline 86 \end{array}$$

So, Shannon and Katrina picked 86 apples in all. Since 86 is close to the estimate of 90, the answer is reasonable.

Sometimes when you add 3 addends, you can make a ten.

Example 2 **Add.** 35 + 26 + 54

Step 1

Add the ones.
5 + (6 + 4) = 15 ones
Regroup 15 ones as 1 ten 5 ones.

$$\begin{array}{r} ^{1} \\ 35 \\ 26 \\ +\,54 \\ \hline 5 \end{array}$$

Make a ten.

Step 2

Add the tens.
1 + 3 + 2 + 5 = 11 tens
Regroup 11 tens as 1 hundred 1 ten.

$$\begin{array}{r} ^{1} \\ 35 \\ 26 \\ +\,54 \\ \hline 115 \end{array}$$

- How can you use mental math to find 43 + 22 + 18?

ERROR ALERT

Remember to add the regrouped ten.

TEKS 3.3B select addition or subtraction and use the operation to solve problems involving whole numbers through 999. *also* **3.5A, 3.5B, 3.14A, 3.15A, 3.15B, 3.16B**

Guided Practice

1. Find 45 + 68 using mental math. Complete the number sentences.

$$\begin{array}{r} 45 \\ +\,68 \\ \hline \end{array}$$

40 + 60 = ■
5 + ■ = 13

Estimate. Then find each sum using place value or mental math.

2. $\begin{array}{r} 17 \\ +\,54 \\ \hline \end{array}$

3. $\begin{array}{r} 22 \\ 48 \\ +\,13 \\ \hline \end{array}$

4. $\begin{array}{r} 84 \\ +\,35 \\ \hline \end{array}$

✓5. $\begin{array}{r} 24 \\ +\,39 \\ \hline \end{array}$

✓6. $\begin{array}{r} 47 \\ 23 \\ +\,28 \\ \hline \end{array}$

7. **TALK Math** **Explain** how you would use place value to find 56 + 19 + 31.

Independent Practice and Problem Solving

Estimate. Then find each sum using place value or mental math.

8. $\begin{array}{r} 98 \\ +\,36 \\ \hline \end{array}$

9. $\begin{array}{r} 19 \\ +\,42 \\ \hline \end{array}$

10. $\begin{array}{r} 53 \\ +\,29 \\ \hline \end{array}$

11. $\begin{array}{r} 16 \\ 12 \\ +\,28 \\ \hline \end{array}$

12. $\begin{array}{r} 33 \\ 10 \\ +\,85 \\ \hline \end{array}$

13. 66 + 35 = ■
14. 21 + 46 = ■
15. 18 + 18 = ■
16. 21 + 37 + 19 = ■

For 17–19, use the picture.

17. For the class party, Carlos brought 2 gallons of apple juice. How many cups can he pour?

18. Kate brought 2 dozen apples for the class party. Only 22 apples were eaten. How many apples were left?

19. **WRITE Math** Sarah bought 3 dozen apples to make applesauce. How many apples did Sarah buy? **Explain** how you know.

Apple juice
16 cups = 1 gallon
Apples
12 apples = 1 dozen

Mixed Review and TAKS Prep

20. What is 576 rounded to the nearest hundred? (TEKS 3.5A, p. 40)

21. Kyle cut apart a square. What figures did he make? (Grade 2 TEKS 2.7C)

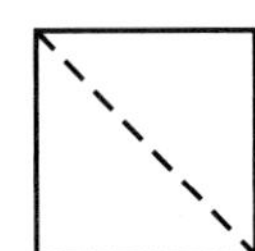

22. **TAKS Prep** Which is the sum? (Obj. 1)

56 + 41 + 73 = ■

A 160 **C** 170
B 161 **D** 171

Extra Practice on page 76, Set D

LESSON HANDS ON

5 Model 3-Digit Addition

OBJECTIVE: Explore adding 3-digit numbers with and without regrouping.

Quick Review

Regroup.

1. 10 ones = ■ ten 0 ones
2. 17 ones = 1 ten ■ ones
3. ■ ones = 1 ten 4 ones
4. 12 tens = ■ hundred 2 tens
5. 19 tens = 1 hundred ■ tens

Investigate

Materials ■ base-ten blocks

You can use base-ten blocks to help add numbers.

A Model the numbers 246 and 175.

Use your model to find the sum of 246 and 175.
Add the ones, tens, and hundreds.
Regroup the blocks when needed.

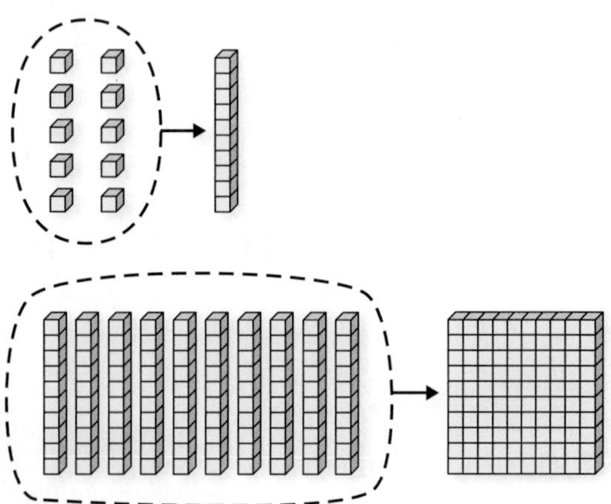

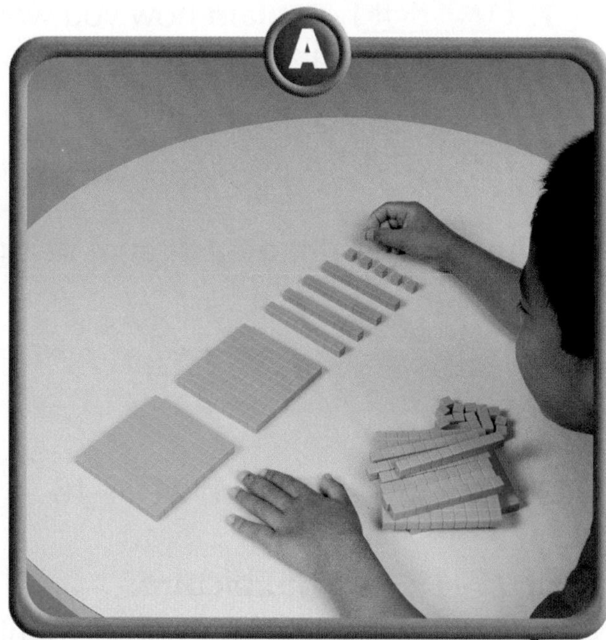

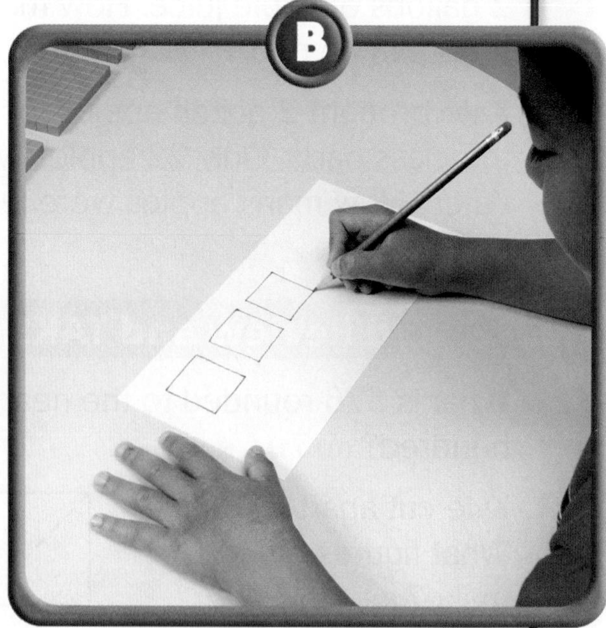

B Draw a picture to show the sum.
Record your answer.

Draw Conclusions

1. Explain how your model helped you find the sum.
2. When do you need to regroup?
3. **Analysis** Can the sum of two 3-digit numbers equal a 4-digit number? Explain. Give an example.

TEKS 3.3A model addition and subtraction using pictures, words, and numbers. *also* **3.14A, 3.14D, 3.15A, 3.15B**

Connect

Here is a way to record addition.

To add 138 and 267, first line up the hundreds, tens, and ones.

H	T	O
1	3	8
+2	6	7

Step 1

Add the ones.
8 + 7 = 15 ones
Regroup.
15 ones = 1 ten 5 ones

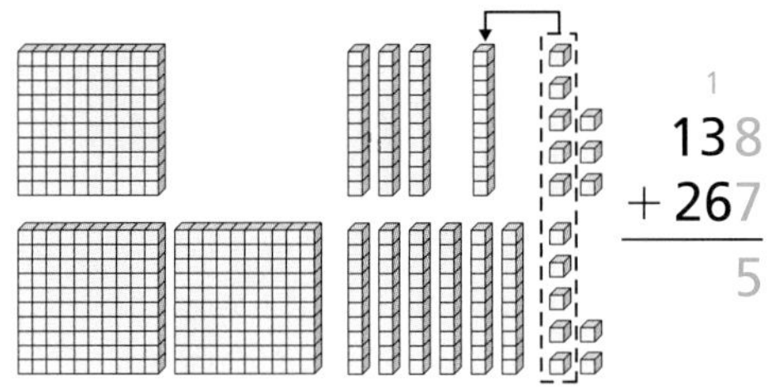

Step 2

Add the tens.
1 + 3 + 6 = 10 tens
Regroup.
10 tens = 1 hundred 0 tens

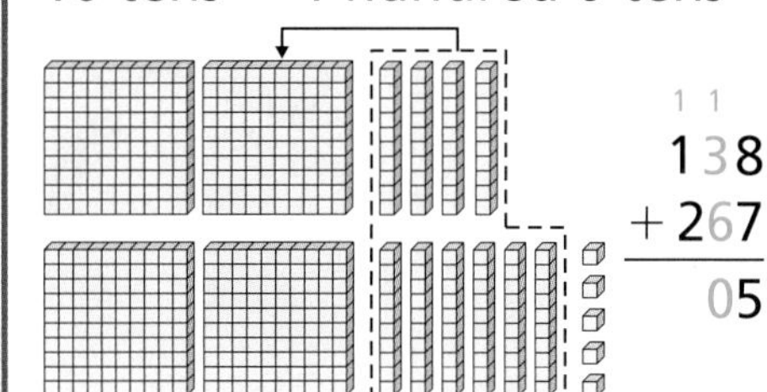

Step 3

Add the hundreds.
1 + 1 + 2 =
4 hundreds

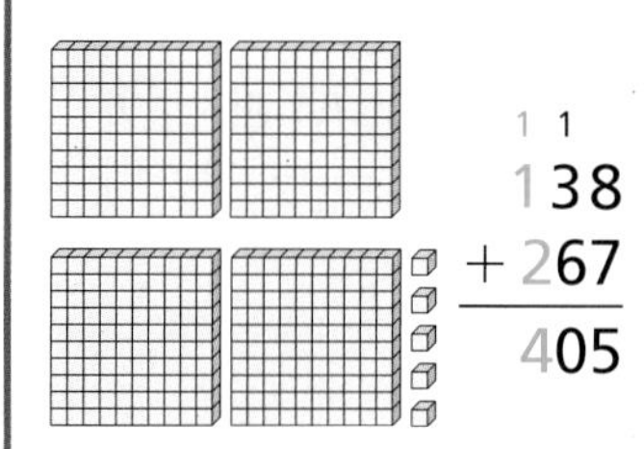

So, 138 + 267 = 405.

TALK Math

Explain how to find the sum of 485 and 429. Tell if you need to regroup.

Practice

Use base-ten blocks to find each sum.

1. 511 + 253 = ■
2. 183 + 214 = ■
3. 455 + 346 = ■
4. 268 + 258 = ■
5. 123 + 155 = ■
6. 352 + 191 = ■

Find each sum.

7. $\begin{array}{r} 434 \\ +517 \\ \hline \end{array}$
8. $\begin{array}{r} 185 \\ +309 \\ \hline \end{array}$
9. $\begin{array}{r} 594 \\ +156 \\ \hline \end{array}$
10. $\begin{array}{r} 233 \\ +128 \\ \hline \end{array}$
11. $\begin{array}{r} 457 \\ +465 \\ \hline \end{array}$
12. $\begin{array}{r} 193 \\ +796 \\ \hline \end{array}$
13. $\begin{array}{r} 216 \\ +261 \\ \hline \end{array}$
14. $\begin{array}{r} 377 \\ +140 \\ \hline \end{array}$
15. $\begin{array}{r} 615 \\ +284 \\ \hline \end{array}$
16. $\begin{array}{r} 545 \\ +389 \\ \hline \end{array}$

17. **Reasoning** Will the sum of 625 and 718 be greater than or less than 1,000? How do you know?

18. **WRITE Math** **Explain** how to use base-ten blocks to model 182 + 376. What is the sum?

Technology
Use Harcourt Mega Math, Country Countdown, *Block Busters,* Levels U, V.

LESSON 6

Add 3-Digit Numbers

OBJECTIVE: Add 3-digit numbers with and without regrouping.

Quick Review

1. 12 + 14
2. 13 + 18
3. 20 + 35
4. 36 + 17
5. 68 + 29

Learn

PROBLEM Mia is planning a trip to Texas. Her airplane leaves from Chicago, Illinois, and stops in Tulsa, Oklahoma. Then it flies from Tulsa to Dallas, Texas. What is the total distance of Mia's trip?

Example **Add.** 585 + 236 **Estimate.** 600 + 200 = 800

Step 1	Step 2	Step 3
Add the ones. Regroup. 11 ones = 1 ten 1 one	Add the tens. Regroup. 12 tens = 1 hundred 2 tens	Add the hundreds.
$\begin{array}{r} {\scriptstyle 1} \\ 585 \\ +236 \\ \hline 1 \end{array}$	$\begin{array}{r} {\scriptstyle 1\,1} \\ 585 \\ +236 \\ \hline 21 \end{array}$	$\begin{array}{r} {\scriptstyle 1\,1} \\ 585 \\ +236 \\ \hline 821 \end{array}$

So, the total distance of Mia's trip is 821 miles. Since 821 is close to the estimate of 800, the answer is reasonable.

More Examples

Ⓐ Regrouping	Ⓑ No regrouping	Ⓒ Regrouping
$\begin{array}{r} {\scriptstyle 1} \\ 436 \\ +182 \\ \hline 618 \end{array}$	$\begin{array}{r} 242 \\ +354 \\ \hline 596 \end{array}$	$\begin{array}{r} {\scriptstyle 1\,1} \\ 974 \\ 337 \\ +521 \\ \hline 1{,}832 \end{array}$

- How could you use compatible numbers to check the reasonableness of the sum in Example B?

TEKS 3.3B select addition or subtraction and use the operation to solve problems involving whole numbers through 999. *also* **3.5A, 3.5B, 3.14A, 3.15A, 3.15B, 3.16B**

Guided Practice

1. Copy the problem at the right. Do you have to regroup? Find the sum.

$$\begin{array}{r} 146 \\ +218 \\ \hline \end{array}$$

Estimate. Then find each sum.

2. $\begin{array}{r} 533 \\ +314 \\ \hline \end{array}$

3. $\begin{array}{r} 625 \\ +127 \\ \hline \end{array}$

4. $\begin{array}{r} 781 \\ +256 \\ \hline \end{array}$

✓5. $\begin{array}{r} 453 \\ +168 \\ \hline \end{array}$

✓6. $\begin{array}{r} 813 \\ 415 \\ +144 \\ \hline \end{array}$

7. TALK Math **Explain** how to add 219 and 326.

Independent Practice and Problem Solving

Estimate. Then find each sum.

8. $\begin{array}{r} 414 \\ +352 \\ \hline \end{array}$

9. $\begin{array}{r} 206 \\ +325 \\ \hline \end{array}$

10. $\begin{array}{r} 538 \\ +268 \\ \hline \end{array}$

11. $\begin{array}{r} 321 \\ 584 \\ +906 \\ \hline \end{array}$

12. $\begin{array}{r} 124 \\ 289 \\ +576 \\ \hline \end{array}$

13. $793 + 643 = \blacksquare$

14. $437 + 365 = \blacksquare$

15. $591 + 708 = \blacksquare$

USE DATA For 16–17, use the table.

16. Scott flies from Boston to Washington, D.C., and then from Washington, D.C., to Atlanta. He flies the same distance to return home. What is the total distance he flies?

17. WRITE Math **What's the Error?** An airplane flies from San Antonio to St. Louis and then to New York City. Keith says the total flight distance is 1,662 miles. Describe his error. Find the correct distance.

Flight Distances Between Cities

Cities	Distance in Miles
Boston to Washington, D.C.	394
Washington, D.C. to Atlanta	541
San Antonio to St. Louis	787
St. Louis to New York City	885

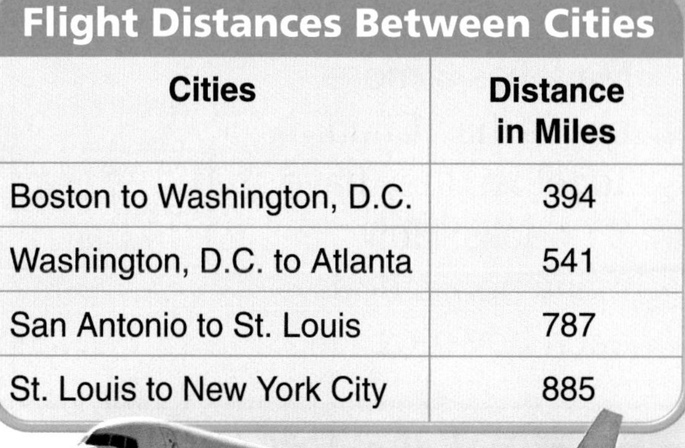

Mixed Review and TAKS Prep

18. Write $<$, $>$, or $=$ to compare. (TEKS 3.1B, p. 30)

    218 ■ 281

19. What is $60{,}000 + 400 + 30 + 5$ written in standard form? (TEKS 3.1A, p. 16)

20. **TAKS Prep** What is the sum of 579 and 123? (Obj. 1)

    A 456 **C** 692

    B 602 **D** 702

Extra Practice on page 76, Set E

Problem Solving Workshop
Strategy: Guess and Check

OBJECTIVE: Solve problems by using the strategy *guess and check*.

Learn the Strategy

Sometimes, the best way to solve a problem is to guess and check. After reading the problem, you guess, or predict, what the answer might be. Then you use information in the problem to check, or test, if your answer is too low, too high, or just right.

Guess and check to find numbers whose sum is 39.

Three numbers in a row have a sum of 39. What are the numbers?

Guess	Check	Notes
9, 10, 11	9 + 10 + 11 = 30	too low
13, 14, 15	13 + 14 + 15 = 42	too high
12, 13, 14	12 + 13 + 14 = 39	just right

Guess and check to find the number of books each boy has.

Mark has 3 more books than Chad. Together, they have 25 books. How many books does each boy have?

Guess: 12 and 9 Check: 12 + 9 = 21 too low	Guess: 16 and 13 Check: 16 + 13 = 29 too high	Guess: 14 and 11 Check: 14 + 11 = 25 just right

Guess and check to find the amount of time spent on each activity.

Melanie spends 60 minutes reading and exercising. She exercises 10 minutes more than she reads. How much time does Melanie spend doing each activity?

Guess		Check	
Read	Exercise	Total	Notes
30	30 + 10 = 40	30 + 40 = 70	too high
20	20 + 10 = 30	20 + 30 = 50	too low
25	25 + 10 = 35	25 + 35 = 60	just right

TALK Math

Explain how you can use the results from one guess to make another guess.

TEKS 3.14C select or develop an appropriate problem-solving plan or strategy, including drawing a picture, looking for a pattern, systematic guessing and checking, acting it out, making a table, working a simpler problem, or working backwards to solve a problem. *also* **3.3B, 3.14A, 3.14B, 3.15A, 3.15B, 3.16B**

Use the Strategy

PROBLEM Jacob and Gabe play on different football teams. Jacob's team scored 7 more points than Gabe's team. There were 35 points total scored in the game. How many points did each team score?

Read to Understand
Plan
Solve
Check

Read to Understand

- **Use graphic aids to organize your guesses and check the results.**
- **What information is given?**
- **Is there information you will not use? If so, what?**

Plan

- **What strategy can you use to solve the problem?**
  You can guess and check to help you solve the problem.

Solve

- **How can you use the strategy to solve the problem?**
  Make a table to organize your guesses and check the results.

  Guess the number of points scored by Gabe's team. Add 7 to that number to find the points scored by Jacob's team. Then check to see if the sum of the numbers is 35.

  So, Gabe's team scored 14 points, and Jacob's team scored 21 points.

Guess		Check	
Gabe's Team	Jacob's Team	Total	Notes
11	11 + 7 = 18	11 + 18 = 29	too low
16	16 + 7 = 23	16 + 23 = 39	too high
14	14 + 7 = 21	14 + 21 = 35	just right

Check

- **How do you know your answer is correct?**

Guided Problem Solving

Read to Understand
Plan
Solve
Check

1. Fifty children signed up for the youth basketball league. There were 20 more boys than girls. How many girls and how many boys signed up for the basketball league?

First, guess the number of girls.

Then, add 20 to that number to find the number of boys.

Finally, check to see if the sum is 50. If the sum is not 50, try other numbers.

Guess		Check	
Girls	Boys	Total	Notes
20	20 + 20 = 40	20 + 40 = 60	too high
10	10 + 20 =		

2. **What if** 72 children signed up for the league and there were still 20 more boys than girls? How many girls and how many boys would have signed up?

3. In a survey, 100 students were asked to choose swimming or soccer as their favorite sport. Of those, 14 more chose soccer than swimming. How many students chose soccer?

Problem Solving Strategy Practice

Guess and check to solve.

4. For a volleyball game, 200 tickets were sold. There were 70 more student tickets sold than adult tickets. How many of each type of ticket were sold?

5. The snack bar at the football field has 500 cups. There are 80 more small cups than large cups. How many small cups are there?

6. The youth softball league ordered 48 T-shirts in two colors. There were 10 fewer red shirts ordered than blue shirts. How many of each color were ordered?

7. WRITE Math During basketball practice, Jacob attempted 40 free-throw shots. He made 6 more than he missed. How many free-throw shots did Jacob make? **Explain** how you know.

Mixed Strategy Practice

USE DATA For 8–10, use the graph.

8. For Game 1, the number of fans for the home team was 200 more than the number of fans for the visiting team. How many visiting fans were at Game 1?

9. The coach said that the number of fans at Game 2 was 235 fewer than he expected. How many fans did the coach expect at Game 2?

10. **Pose a Problem** Look back at Problem 9. Write a similar problem by changing the number of fans the coach expected to a number greater than 300.

11. **Open-Ended** At Game 3, each fan was given a 3-digit number for a prize drawing. Justin's number had three even digits. The digit in the tens place was greater than the digit in the ones place. The digit in the hundreds place was greater than the digit in the tens place. What could Justin's number have been?

CHALLENGE YOURSELF

In the first three games of the season, Sam scored 23, 18, and 26 points.

12. In Game 4, Sam scored 5 more points than he did in one of the first three games. He scored fewer than 94 points in all for the first four games. How many points did he score in Game 4?

13. Sam scored more than 100 points over the first 5 games. He scored the same number of points in Games 4 and 5. What is the least number of points he could have scored in Game 5?

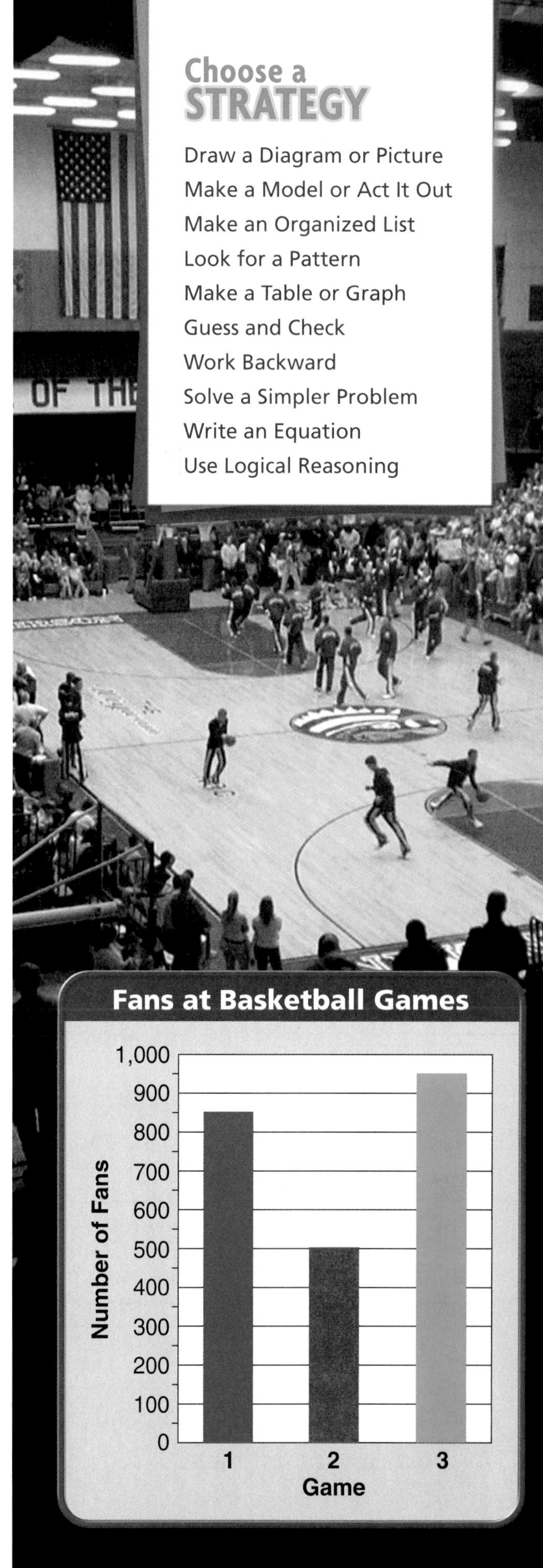

LESSON 8

Choose a Method

OBJECTIVE: Choose paper and pencil, a calculator, or mental math to add 3-digit numbers.

Quick Review

There are 130 students at Prairie School. There are 275 students at Lincoln School. What is the total number of students at both schools?

Learn

PROBLEM Lisa is helping her cousins plant vegetable seeds at their farm. The table shows the number of seeds planted. How many lettuce and bean seeds did they plant?

Seeds Planted

Seed	Number Planted
Cucumber	331
Carrot	877
Bean	175
Lettuce	246

Example 1 Use paper and pencil.

Add. 246 + 175 = ■ **Estimate.** 200 + 200 = 400

The problem involves regrouping and adding two numbers. So, using paper and pencil is a good choice.

Step 1	Step 2	Step 3
Add the ones. Regroup. 11 ones = 1 ten 1 one	Add the tens. Regroup. 12 tens = 1 hundred 2 tens	Add the hundreds.
$\begin{array}{r} {}^{1} \\ 246 \\ +175 \\ \hline 1 \end{array}$	$\begin{array}{r} {}^{1\,1} \\ 246 \\ +175 \\ \hline 21 \end{array}$	$\begin{array}{r} {}^{1\,1} \\ 246 \\ +175 \\ \hline 421 \end{array}$

So, 421 lettuce and bean seeds were planted. Since 421 is close to the estimate of 400, the answer is reasonable.

Example 2 Use a calculator.

How many cucumber, carrot, and bean seeds were planted in all?

331 + 877 + 175 = ■

The problem involves regrouping and adding three numbers. So, using a calculator is a good choice.

So, 1,383 cucumber, carrot, and bean seeds were planted.

- How can you estimate to see if your answer is reasonable?

Math Idea

Since you may enter a wrong number when using a calculator, it is important to check your answer.

TEKS 3.14D use tools such as real objects, manipulatives, and technology to solve problems. *also* 3.3B, 3.14A, 3.15A, 3.15B

Example 3 Use mental math.

Pete and Michael bought vegetable plants for their farm. They bought 120 radish plants and 438 broccoli plants. How many plants did they buy?

$$120 + 438 = \blacksquare$$

No regrouping is needed. So, using mental math is a good choice.

Think: Add the hundreds. $100 + 400 = 500$
Add the tens. $20 + 30 = 50$
Add the ones. $0 + 8 = 8$
Find the sum. $500 + 50 + 8 = 558$

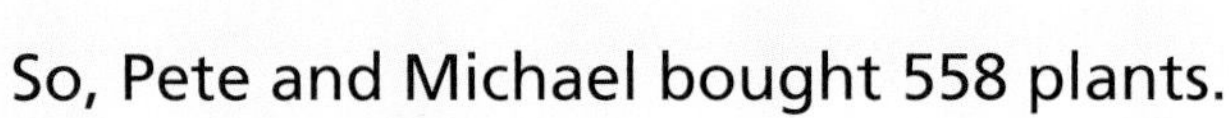

So, Pete and Michael bought 558 plants.

More Examples

A Use paper and pencil.

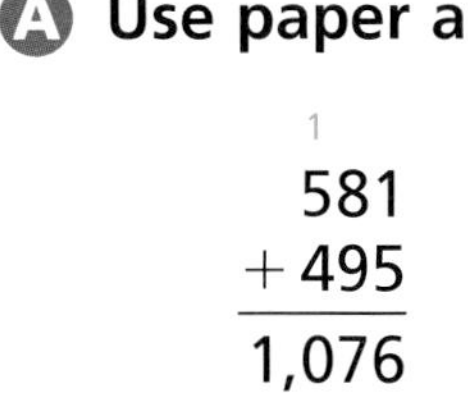

$$\begin{array}{r} {}^{1} \\ 581 \\ +\,495 \\ \hline 1{,}076 \end{array}$$

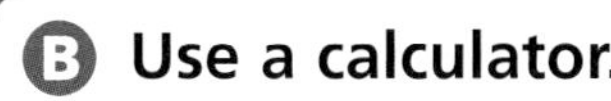

B Use a calculator.

$$\begin{array}{r} 895 \\ 462 \\ +\,784 \\ \hline 2{,}141 \end{array}$$

C Use mental math.

$$\begin{array}{r} 503 \\ +\,324 \\ \hline 827 \end{array}$$

- What is another method you could use to find the sum in Example B?

Guided Practice

1. Find 247 + 230 using mental math. Use the number sentences to help you.

$$\begin{array}{r} 247 \\ +\,230 \\ \hline \end{array}$$

$200 + 200 = \blacksquare$
$40 + 30 = \blacksquare$
$7 + 0 = \blacksquare$

Find the sum. Tell which method you used.

2. $\begin{array}{r} 656 \\ +\,103 \\ \hline \end{array}$

3. $\begin{array}{r} 862 \\ +\,839 \\ \hline \end{array}$

4. $\begin{array}{r} 784 \\ 257 \\ +\,836 \\ \hline \end{array}$

5. $\begin{array}{r} 611 \\ +\,350 \\ \hline \end{array}$

✓6. $\begin{array}{r} 465 \\ +\,528 \\ \hline \end{array}$

7. $611 + 156 = \blacksquare$

8. $754 + 426 = \blacksquare$

✓9. $782 + 518 + 359 = \blacksquare$

10. TALK Math **Explain** which strategy would be a good choice to add 457 and 963. Then find the sum.

Independent Practice and Problem Solving

Find the sum. Tell which method you used.

11. $\begin{array}{r} 612 \\ +273 \\ \hline \end{array}$ **12.** $\begin{array}{r} 195 \\ +142 \\ \hline \end{array}$ **13.** $\begin{array}{r} 456 \\ +372 \\ \hline \end{array}$ **14.** $\begin{array}{r} 211 \\ 384 \\ +970 \\ \hline \end{array}$ **15.** $\begin{array}{r} 865 \\ 559 \\ +273 \\ \hline \end{array}$

16. $\begin{array}{r} 570 \\ +695 \\ \hline \end{array}$ **17.** $\begin{array}{r} 786 \\ +274 \\ \hline \end{array}$ **18.** $\begin{array}{r} 154 \\ +622 \\ \hline \end{array}$ **19.** $\begin{array}{r} 110 \\ +373 \\ \hline \end{array}$ **20.** $\begin{array}{r} 588 \\ +567 \\ \hline \end{array}$

21. $\begin{array}{r} 904 \\ 675 \\ +418 \\ \hline \end{array}$ **22.** $\begin{array}{r} 805 \\ +191 \\ \hline \end{array}$ **23.** $\begin{array}{r} 324 \\ 510 \\ +103 \\ \hline \end{array}$ **24.** $\begin{array}{r} 398 \\ +271 \\ \hline \end{array}$ **25.** $\begin{array}{r} 432 \\ +686 \\ \hline \end{array}$

26. $942 + 578 + 896 = ■$ **27.** $264 + 305 = ■$ **28.** $615 + 789 = ■$

29. $424 + 253 = ■$ **30.** $558 + 762 = ■$ **31.** $341 + 129 + 473 = ■$

USE DATA For 32–35, use the table.

32. Sarah's family owns a farm that is 950 acres. How many acres planted with corn, broccoli, and lettuce does the family have?

33. Eric's family plants 778 more acres of lettuce than Sarah's family does. How many acres of lettuce does Eric's family plant?

34. Reasoning Is the total number of acres planted with corn and peas greater than or less than the number of acres planted with broccoli? **Explain** your answer.

35. WRITE Math **What's the Question?** Jessica used the data in the table. The answer is 507.

36. On Friday, Dan and his father picked some tomatoes. On Saturday, they picked 36 more tomatoes. Now they have 89 tomatoes. How many tomatoes did they pick on Friday?

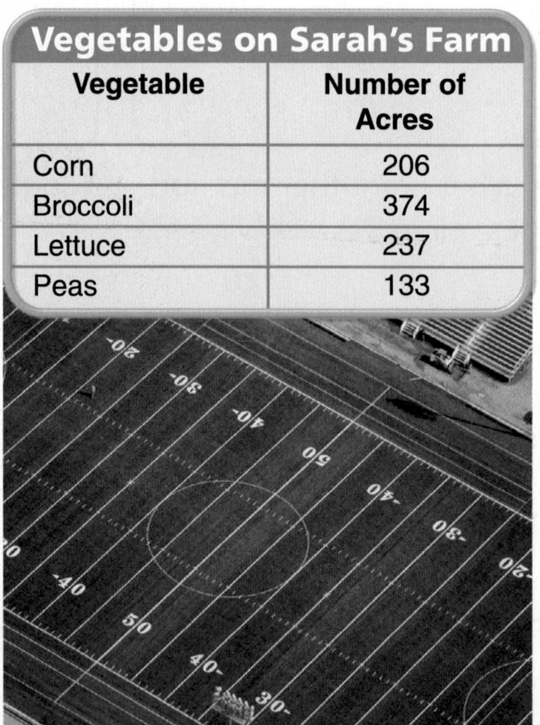

Vegetables on Sarah's Farm

Vegetable	Number of Acres
Corn	206
Broccoli	374
Lettuce	237
Peas	133

▲ An acre of land is about the size of a football field.

 Extra Practice on page 76, Set F

Mixed Review and TAKS Prep

37. Write the numbers in order from least to greatest. (TEKS 3.1B, p. 34)

45, 78, 36

38. **TAKS Prep** Drew's family drove 512 miles to his uncle's farm. Then they drove 173 miles to Drew's grandmother's house. How many miles did Drew's family drive in all? (Obj. 6)

A 339 miles **C** 572 miles

B 456 miles **D** 685 miles

39. What is the greatest whole number you can make by using the digits 4, 7, 3, and 5? Use each digit exactly once. (TEKS 3.1A, p. 12)

40. **TAKS Prep** Junie's father runs a shipping business. He shipped 870 boxes on Tuesday. He shipped 765 boxes on Wednesday. How many boxes did he ship on both days? **Explain** what method you used. (Obj. 6)

Problem Solving and Reasoning

PUZZLE Use mental math to find each sum.

S 216 + 153	B 352 + 617	O 750 + 248	A 332 + 504	I 425 + 250
E 793 + 206	T 526 + 361	R 319 + 320	G 182 + 607	C 453 + 116
H 853 + 134	N 630 + 230	K 445 + 424	y 223 + 513	

To answer the riddle, match the letters from the sums above to the numbers below.

What food likes to listen to music? Why?

___ ___ ___ ___. ___ ___ ___ ___ ___ ___ ___ ___ ___!

569 998 639 860 675 887 987 836 369 999 836 639 369

Extra Practice

Set A Find each sum. Name the property used. (pp. 56–57)

1. $8 + 3 = \blacksquare$
   $3 + 8 = \blacksquare$
2. $0 + 14 = \blacksquare$
   $14 + 0 = \blacksquare$
3. $13 + 5 = \blacksquare$
   $5 + 13 = \blacksquare$
4. $(4 + 2) + 3 = \blacksquare$
   $4 + (2 + 3) = \blacksquare$

Set B Find the missing addend. You may want to use counters. (pp. 58–59)

1. $\blacksquare + 2 = 8$
2. $9 + \blacksquare = 10$
3. $\blacksquare + 5 = 22$
4. $15 + \blacksquare = 2 + 15$
5. $13 + \blacksquare = 20$
6. $\blacksquare + 9 = 17$
7. $6 + \blacksquare = 13$
8. $\blacksquare + 8 = 8 + 11$

Set C Use rounding to estimate each sum. (pp. 60–61)

1. $51 + 47$
2. $89 + 56$
3. $22 + 72$
4. $678 + 113$
5. $487 + 391$

Use compatible numbers to estimate each sum.

6. $49 + 52$
7. $63 + 21$
8. $354 + 126$
9. $477 + 226$
10. $761 + 131$

Set D Estimate. Then find each sum using place value or mental math. (pp. 62–63)

1. $43 + 31 + 22$
2. $38 + 93$
3. $86 + 64 + 54$
4. $27 + 18$
5. $53 + 67$

Set E Estimate. Then find each sum. (pp. 66–67)

1. $367 + 243$
2. $142 + 461$
3. $890 + 539$
4. $502 + 319$
5. $284 + 678$

6. Andy's family drove 214 miles on Friday and 329 miles on Saturday. How many miles did they drive in all?

Set F Find the sum. Tell which method you used. (pp. 72–75)

1. $329 + 693$
2. $965 + 711 + 179$
3. $404 + 294$
4. $433 + 376$
5. $258 + 640$

Technology
Use Harcourt Mega Math, Country Countdown, *Block Busters*, Levels M, U, V.

PRACTICE GAME

Auto Addition

Get in the Car!
2 players

Start Your Engines!
- 2 two-color counters

Drive to the Picnic!

- Each player selects a different color counter and places it on the matching START color.
- Players follow the highway color that matches the color of their counter.
- Players complete the addition problem to get to the first Stop Sign. Use paper and pencil to solve. Players will check each other's answers.
- If the player's answer to a problem is wrong, the player does not move forward. The player must wait until his or her next turn to try to solve the problem again.
- Each player continues to solve addition problems in order to move to the next Stop Sign.
- The first player to reach the picnic wins the game.

Chapter 3 Review/Test

Check Vocabulary and Concepts

Choose the best term from the box.

VOCABULARY
Associative Property of Addition
Commutative Property of Addition
Identity Property of Addition

1. The __?__ says that if you add zero to any number, the sum is that number. (TEKS 3.3B, p. 56)
2. The __?__ says you can add numbers in any order and get the same sum. (TEKS 3.3B, p. 56)

Check Skills

Find each sum. Name the property used. (TEKS 3.3B, pp. 56–57)

03. $4 + 0 = ■$
    $0 + 4 = ■$

4. $8 + (2 + 4) = ■$
   $(8 + 2) + 4 = ■$

5. $7 + 6 = ■$
   $6 + 7 = ■$

Find the missing addend. (TEKS 3.3B, pp. 58–59)

6. $■ + 8 = 13$
7. $5 + ■ = 9 + 5$
8. $6 + ■ = 12$
9. $■ + 3 = 12$

Use rounding or compatible numbers to estimate each sum. (TEKS 3.5B, pp. 60–61)

10. $57 + 24$
11. $782 + 131$
12. $34 + 59$
13. $542 + 279$

Estimate. Then find each sum. (TEKS 3.3B, pp. 62–63, 66–67)

14. $49 + 23$
15. $394 + 278$
16. $145 + 266$
17. $213 + 732$

Check Problem Solving

Solve. (TEKS 3.3B, 3.14C, pp. 68–71)

18. There were 150 fans at a soccer game. There were 30 more students than parents. How many students were at the game?

19. Caleb and Mary scored a total of 14 points at the basketball game. Mary scored 6 more points than Caleb. How many points did each player score?

20. WRITE Math **Sense or Nonsense** Three numbers in a row have a sum of 45. Kathy says the numbers are 15, 16, and 17. Does her statement make sense? **Explain.**

GO ONLINE **Technology** Use *Online Assessment.*

Enrich • Finding Sums

Magic SQUARES

Magic Squares are a fun way to practice finding the sum of three numbers. In a Magic Square, the sums of each column, row, and diagonal are the same.

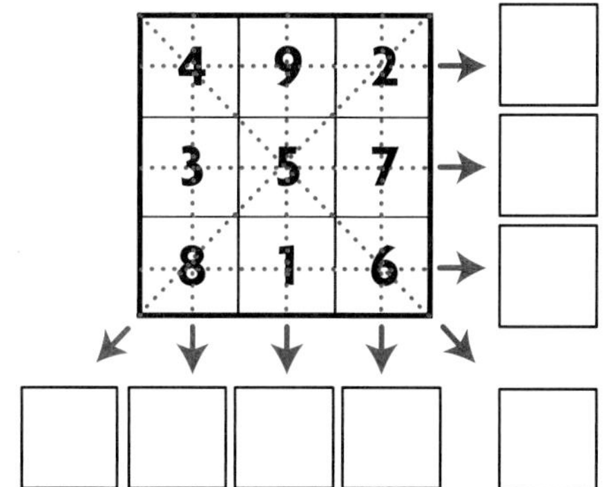

How To

The Magic Square to the right is called the *Lo Shu* Magic Square. To find the answer to this Magic Square, follow these steps.

Step 1 Find the sums of the horizontal rows.
4 + 9 + 2 = ■, 3 + 5 + 7 = ■, 8 + 1 + 6 = ■

Step 2 Find the sums of the vertical columns.
4 + 3 + 8 = ■, 9 + 5 + 1 = ■, 2 + 7 + 6 = ■

Step 3 Find the sums of the diagonals.
4 + 5 + 6 = ■, 8 + 5 + 2 = ■

So, the answer to the Magic Square is 15.

Make Your Own

Copy and complete the Magic Square by using the numbers below. The answer is 15.

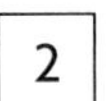

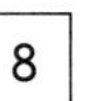
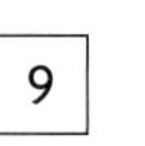

■	■	6
3	■	7
■	■	■

Figure It Out

WRITE Math ▸ Work with a partner to find the sum of one row in Benjamin Franklin's Magic Square. **Explain** how you found your answer.

Benjamin Franklin's Magic Square

14	3	62	51	46	35	30	19
52	61	4	13	20	29	36	45
11	6	59	54	43	38	27	22
53	60	5	12	21	28	37	44
55	58	7	10	23	26	39	42
9	8	57	56	41	40	25	24
50	63	2	15	18	31	34	47
16	1	64	49	48	33	32	17

Getting Ready for the TAKS
Chapters 1–3

Number, Operation, and Quantitative Reasoning (TAKS Obj. 1)

1. Which numeral means the same as $500 + 30 + 7$?

A 537

B 573

C 5,037

D 5,307

Test Tip **Eliminate choices.**

See item 2. First, estimate the sum. Then, find the answer choices that are close to your estimate. Finally, add to find the correct answer choice.

2. The school library has 289 science books and 332 animal books. How many science and animal books does the library have altogether?

F 511

G 521

H 611

J Not here

3. WRITE Math On Sunday there were 643 visitors at the amusement park. Rounded to the nearest hundred, about how many people were at the park? **Explain** how to find the answer using the tens digit.

Patterns, Relationships, and Algebraic Thinking (TAKS Obj. 2)

4. Cars have 4 wheels. Greg wants to find out how many wheels are on 5 cars. Use the table below to find the answer.

number of cars	1	2	3	4	5
number of wheels	4	8	12	16	■

A 24 **C** 20

B 22 **D** 18

5. Which are the next two figures in the pattern below?

□ △ ○ □ △ ○ □ △ ○ ? ?

F □ △

G □ ○

H ○ □

J △ ○

6. WRITE Math Brad had 4 toy cars and got 3 more. Pete had 3 toy cars and got 4 more. Who has more toy cars now? **Explain** which addition property helps you to solve the problem.

Measurement (TAKS Obj. 4)

7. Which time is shown on the clock?

A 3:30

B 6:15

C 6:30

D 7:15

8. Which temperature does the thermometer show?

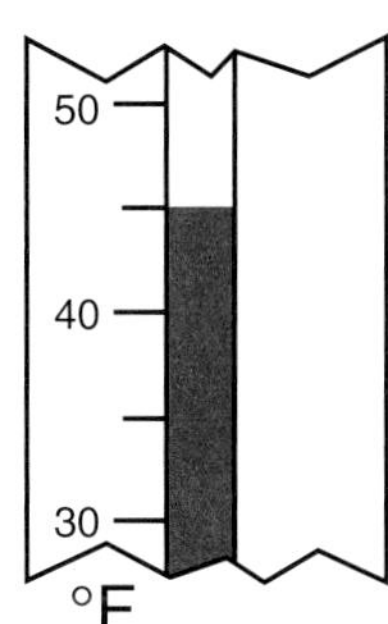

F 50°F

G 45°F

H 40°F

J 35°F

9. **WRITE Math** Keith ate a snack at three forty. **Explain** where the hands of the clock point at three forty.

Probability and Statistics (TAKS Obj. 5)

10. Betty has 10 crayons in a bag. There are 2 blue, 1 green, 1 yellow, and 6 red crayons. Which color crayon is Betty most likely to choose?

A Blue

B Red

C Yellow

D Green

11. Mrs. Totten's class made a tally table to show the number of books they read in each subject. How many science and social studies books did they read altogether?

Books Read	
Subject	**Number of Books**
Social Studies	||||
Science	~~||||~~ |||
Music	||

F 4

G 6

H 11

J 12

12. **WRITE Math** If Mrs. Totten's class wanted to make a picture graph using the data shown in Problem 11, how many pictures would they use? **Explain**.

4 Subtraction

The Big Idea Subtraction of multi-digit numbers is based on single-digit subtraction facts and base-ten and place-value concepts.

TEXAS FAST FACT

The Texas longhorn is one of the state mammals of Texas. Each horn of this breed of cattle can grow to be up to 36 inches long!

Investigate

Look at the horn lengths in the table. Pick two animals, and compare their lengths to the maximum length of the Texas longhorn. Write about the differences in horn length.

Horned Animals

Animal	Horn Length
Grant's Gazelle	32 inches
Greater Kudu Antelope	70 inches
Sable Antelope	65 inches
Waterbuck	40 inches
Oryx	30 inches

GO ONLINE **Technology**
Student pages are available in the Student eBook.

Show What You Know

Check your understanding of important skills needed for success in Chapter 4.

▶ Subtract 1-Digit from 2-Digit Numbers

Subtract.

1. $\begin{array}{r} 12 \\ -\ 8 \\ \hline \end{array}$ **2.** $\begin{array}{r} 17 \\ -\ 7 \\ \hline \end{array}$ **3.** $\begin{array}{r} 15 \\ -\ 6 \\ \hline \end{array}$ **4.** $\begin{array}{r} 11 \\ -\ 0 \\ \hline \end{array}$ **5.** $\begin{array}{r} 18 \\ -9 \\ \hline \end{array}$

▶ Model 2-Digit Subtraction

Use the models. Find the difference.

6. $35 - 12 = ■$

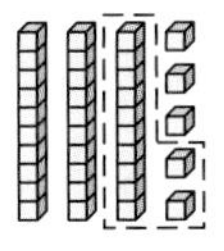

7. $48 - 26 = ■$

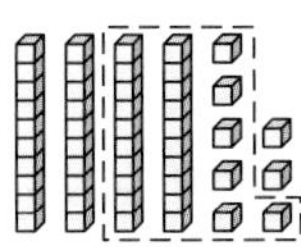

8. $53 - 43 = ■$

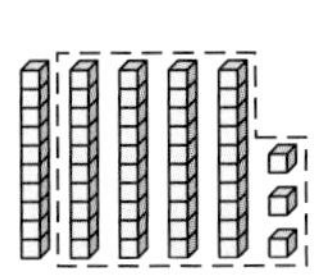

9. $69 - 23 = ■$

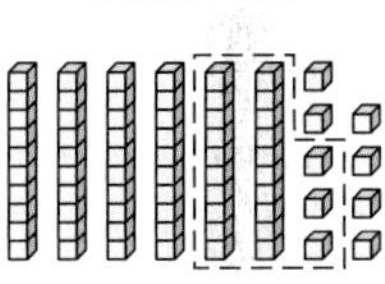

▶ 2-Digit Subtraction Without Regrouping

Subtract.

10. $\begin{array}{r} 76 \\ -32 \\ \hline \end{array}$ **11.** $\begin{array}{r} 29 \\ -13 \\ \hline \end{array}$ **12.** $\begin{array}{r} 65 \\ -54 \\ \hline \end{array}$ **13.** $\begin{array}{r} 92 \\ -50 \\ \hline \end{array}$ **14.** $\begin{array}{r} 38 \\ -18 \\ \hline \end{array}$

VOCABULARY POWER

CHAPTER VOCABULARY

fact family
inverse operations

WARM-UP WORDS

fact family A set of related addition and subtraction, or multiplication and division, number sentences

inverse operations Opposite operations, or operations that undo each other, such as addition and subtraction or multiplication and division

LESSON 1

ALGEBRA

Fact Families

OBJECTIVE: Identify and write addition and subtraction fact families.

Quick Review

1. 4 + 5
2. 12 − 4
3. 3 + 8
4. 5 + 6
5. 13 − 7

Vocabulary

fact family

inverse operations

Learn

PROBLEM Rory is baking a cake. She has 12 eggs. She uses 3 eggs to make the cake. How many eggs does Rory have left?

You can write a number sentence to solve the problem.

$12 - 3 = 9$ So, Rory has 9 eggs left.

The numbers 3, 9, and 12 can be used to make a fact family. A **fact family** is a group of related number sentences that use the same numbers.

Addition and subtraction are opposite, or **inverse operations**. Fact families are examples of inverse operations.

Fact Family for 3, 9, and 12

$3 + 9 = 12$ $9 + 3 = 12$

$12 - 9 = 3$ $12 - 3 = 9$

If both addends are the same, there are only two facts in a fact family.

Fact Family for 4, 4, and 8

$4 + 4 = 8$ $8 - 4 = 4$

Guided Practice

1. Copy and complete the fact family.

$8 + 5 = 13$ $5 + 8 = ■$ $13 - 5 = 8$ $13 - 8 = ■$

Complete.

2. $12 - 6 = 6$, so $6 + 6 = ■$.

✓3. $4 + 3 = 7$, so $■ - 3 = 4$.

TEKS 3.3A model addition and subtraction using pictures, words, and numbers. *also* **3.3B, 3.14A, 3.15A, 3.15B**

Write the fact family for each set of numbers.

4. 4, 5, 9
5. 5, 9, 14
6. 1, 6, 7
7. 5, 7, 12

8. TALK Math **Explain** why some fact families have four facts and others only have two facts.

Independent Practice and Problem Solving

Complete.

9. $11 - 2 = 9$, so $2 + ■ = 11$.
10. $4 + 8 = 12$, so $■ - 8 = 4$.
11. $6 + 9 = 15$, so $15 - 6 = ■$.
12. $10 - 5 = 5$, so $5 + ■ = 10$.
13. $16 - 5 = 11$, so $■ + ■ = 16$.
14. $7 + 6 = 13$, so $■ - 7 = ■$.

Write the fact family for each set of numbers.

15. 2, 8, 10
16. 4, 7, 11
17. 3, 6, 9
18. 7, 7, 14

For 19–21, use the picture.

19. Write a number sentence that shows the total number of muffins sold. Then write the fact family for the number sentence.
20. On Tuesday, 3 blueberry muffins and 4 apple muffins were sold. How many more muffins were sold on Monday than on Tuesday?
21. **Pose a Problem** Look back at Problem 20. Write a similar problem by changing the day and the numbers of muffins sold.
22. WRITE Math Draw and label four pictures to show the fact family for 2, 4, and 6. **Explain** how you used inverse operations to find the facts.

Mixed Review and TAKS Prep

23. The school store has 325 black pens and 115 blue pens. How many pens are there altogether? (TEKS 3.3B, p. 66)
24. What is the name of a figure with 6 sides? (Grade 2 TEKS 2.7A)
25. **TAKS Prep** Which number sentence is in the same fact family as $3 + 4 = 7$? (Obj. 1)

    A $3 + 5 = 8$

    B $7 + 3 = 10$

    C $4 + 7 = 11$

    D $4 + 3 = 7$

Extra Practice on page 102, Set A

LESSON 2

Estimate Differences

OBJECTIVE: Estimate differences of 2- and 3-digit numbers by using rounding and compatible numbers.

Quick Review

Round each number to the greatest place value.

1. 24
2. 65
3. 391
4. 847
5. 588

Learn

PROBLEM The largest Mekong giant catfish caught by fishers weighed 646 pounds. The largest blue catfish caught weighed 124 pounds. About how much more did the Mekong giant catfish weigh than the blue catfish?

▲ The Mekong giant catfish is the largest known freshwater fish and is an endangered species.

To find *about* how much more, you can estimate.

Example **Estimate.** 646 − 124

ONE WAY **Use rounding.**

Round each number to the nearest hundred. Then subtract.

$$\begin{array}{rcr} 646 & \rightarrow & 600 \\ -\,124 & \rightarrow & -\,100 \\ \hline & & 500 \end{array}$$

ANOTHER WAY **Use compatible numbers.**

$$\begin{array}{rcr} 646 & \rightarrow & 650 \\ -\,124 & \rightarrow & -\,125 \\ \hline & & 525 \end{array}$$

So, both 500 and 525 are reasonable estimates of how much more the Mekong giant catfish weighed.

- Why are 650 and 125 compatible numbers?

Remember

Compatible numbers are numbers that are easy to compute mentally.

More Examples

A **Use compatible numbers.**

$$\begin{array}{rcr} 73 & \rightarrow & 75 \\ -\,22 & \rightarrow & -\,25 \\ \hline & & 50 \end{array}$$

B **Use compatible numbers.**

$$\begin{array}{rcr} 476 & \rightarrow & 475 \\ -\,248 & \rightarrow & -\,250 \\ \hline & & 225 \end{array}$$

C **Use rounding.**

$$\begin{array}{rcr} 87 & \rightarrow & 90 \\ -\,19 & \rightarrow & -\,20 \\ \hline & & 70 \end{array}$$

Guided Practice

1. Copy the problem at the right. Round both 319 and 133 to the nearest hundred. Then estimate their difference.

$$\begin{array}{r} 319 \\ -\,133 \\ \hline \end{array}$$

TEKS 3.5B use strategies including rounding and compatible numbers to estimate solutions to addition and subtraction problems. *also* **3.14A, 3.15A, 3.15B**

Use rounding or compatible numbers to estimate each difference.

2. $52 - 24$ **3.** $94 - 56$ **4.** $691 - 137$ ✓**5.** $736 - 327$ ✓**6.** $487 - 248$

7. TALK Math **Explain** ways you could estimate $567 - 209$.

Independent Practice and Problem Solving

Use rounding or compatible numbers to estimate each difference.

8. $88 - 41$ **9.** $65 - 19$ **10.** $98 - 67$ **11.** $378 - 312$ **12.** $42 - 19$

13. $774 - 349$ **14.** $936 - 421$ **15.** $415 - 187$ **16.** $587 - 208$ **17.** $86 - 24$

18. $694 - 593$ **19.** $94 - 42$ **20.** $798 - 726$ **21.** $561 - 349$ **22.** $63 - 37$

Algebra Estimate to compare. Write <, >, or = for each ●.

23. $456 - 162$ ● 200 **24.** $798 - 726$ ● 10 **25.** $542 - 331$ ● 300

USE DATA For 26–27, use the table.

26. About how much more is the total weight of the Pacific halibut and conger than the weight of the yellowfin tuna?

27. WRITE Math About how much more did the yellowfin tuna weigh than the conger? **Explain** how you know.

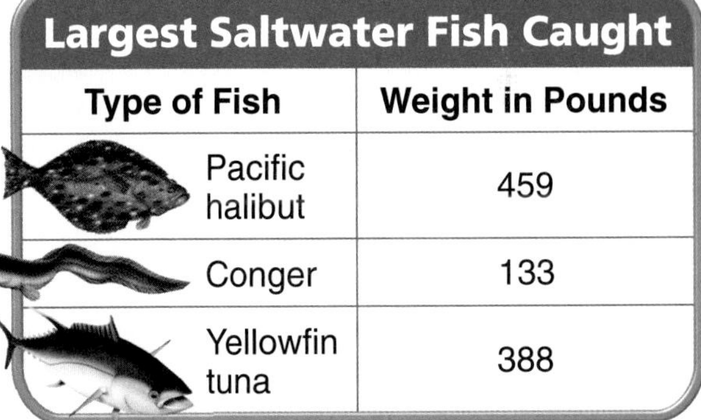

Largest Saltwater Fish Caught

Type of Fish	Weight in Pounds
Pacific halibut	459
Conger	133
Yellowfin tuna	388

Mixed Review and TAKS Prep

28. Use the Associative Property to complete the number sentence. (TEKS 3.3A, p. 56)

$$3 + (2 + 5) = (\blacksquare + \blacksquare) + 5$$

29. Which color marble is more likely to be pulled from the bag? (Grade 2 TEKS 2.11C)

30. **TAKS Prep** Fred estimated $591 - 128$. He rounded each number to the nearest hundred. Then he subtracted. What was Fred's estimate? (Obj. 1)

A 400 **C** 600

B 500 **D** 700

LESSON 3

Subtract 2-Digit Numbers

OBJECTIVE: Subtract 2-digit numbers with and without regrouping.

Quick Review

1. 9 − 4
2. 12 − 5
3. 18 − 9
4. 7 − 3
5. 15 − 7

Learn

PROBLEM Ken saw a grizzly bear that was 39 inches tall. He saw a polar bear that was 62 inches tall. How much taller was the polar bear than the grizzly bear?

▲ When standing on all four legs, a polar bear can be up to 64 inches tall.

Example 1 Subtract. 62 − 39 Estimate. 60 − 40 = 20

ONE WAY Use mental math.

Step 1

Add to the lesser number to make a ten.

$$\begin{array}{r} 62 \\ -39 \\ \hline \end{array} \rightarrow 40$$

Think: 39 + 1 = 40

Step 2

Add the same number to the greater number.

$$\begin{array}{rcl} 62 & \rightarrow & 63 \\ -39 & \rightarrow & 40 \end{array}$$

Think: 62 + 1 = 63

Step 3

Subtract your answers.

$$\begin{array}{r} 62 \\ -39 \\ \hline \end{array} \rightarrow \begin{array}{r} 63 \\ -40 \\ \hline 23 \end{array}$$

Math Idea
Adding the same amount to both numbers does not change the difference.

ANOTHER WAY Use place value.

Step 1

Since 9 > 2, regroup 62 as 5 tens 12 ones.

$$\begin{array}{r} \scriptstyle 5\,12 \\ \not{6}\not{2} \\ -39 \\ \hline \end{array}$$

Step 2

Subtract the ones.
Subtract the tens.

$$\begin{array}{r} \scriptstyle 5\,12 \\ \not{6}\not{2} \\ -39 \\ \hline 23 \end{array} \qquad \begin{array}{r} 23 \\ +39 \\ \hline 62 \end{array}$$

Add to check.

So, the polar bear was 23 inches taller than the grizzly bear.

Since 23 is close to the estimate of 20, the answer is reasonable.

Example 2 Subtract. 43 − 16

Use mental math.

Think: 16 + 4 = 20
43 + 4 = 47

$$\begin{array}{r} 43 \\ -16 \\ \hline \end{array} \rightarrow \begin{array}{r} 47 \\ -20 \\ \hline 27 \end{array}$$

Use place value.

Regroup 43 as 3 tens 13 ones.
Subtract the ones.
Subtract the tens.

$$\begin{array}{r} \scriptstyle 3\,13 \\ \not{4}\not{3} \\ -16 \\ \hline 27 \end{array}$$

TEKS 3.3B select addition or subtraction and use the operation to solve problems involving whole numbers through 999. *also* **3.5A, 3.5B, 3.14A, 3.15A, 3.15B, 3.16B**

Guided Practice

1. To find 31 − 17 by using mental math, what number should you add to both 17 and 31?

Estimate. Then find each difference.

2. $\begin{array}{r} 94 \\ -15 \\ \hline \end{array}$
3. $\begin{array}{r} 58 \\ -29 \\ \hline \end{array}$
4. $\begin{array}{r} 87 \\ -54 \\ \hline \end{array}$
5. $\begin{array}{r} 72 \\ -24 \\ \hline \end{array}$
6. $\begin{array}{r} 79 \\ -36 \\ \hline \end{array}$

7. **TALK Math** **Explain** how to use place value to find 93 − 68.

Independent Practice and Problem Solving

Estimate. Then find each difference.

8. $\begin{array}{r} 61 \\ -48 \\ \hline \end{array}$
9. $\begin{array}{r} 46 \\ -23 \\ \hline \end{array}$
10. $\begin{array}{r} 77 \\ -19 \\ \hline \end{array}$
11. $\begin{array}{r} 51 \\ -34 \\ \hline \end{array}$
12. $\begin{array}{r} 45 \\ -27 \\ \hline \end{array}$

Find each difference. Use addition to check.

13. 55 − 31 = ■
14. 86 − 28 = ■
15. 68 − 14 = ■
16. 93 − 76 = ■

USE DATA For 17–18, use the graph.

17. A brown bear grew 6 inches more than the average height. An American black bear grew 3 inches more than the average height. What is the difference between their heights?

18. **WRITE Math** **Explain** how you can use mental math to find how much taller the polar bear is than the brown bear.

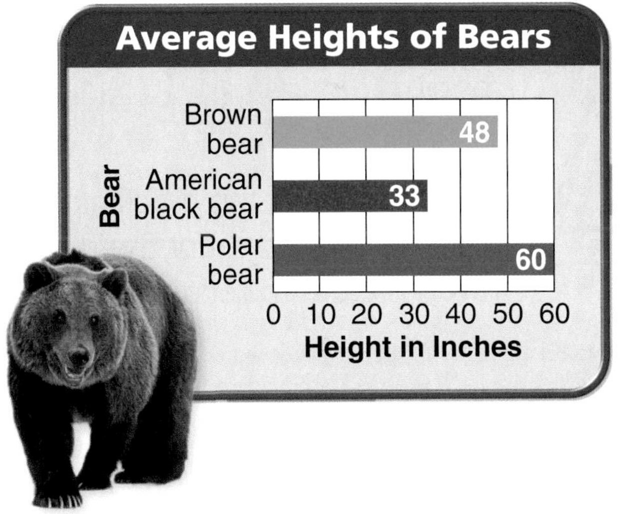

 Mixed Review and TAKS Prep

19. What is 539 rounded to the nearest hundred? (TEKS 3.5A, p. 40)

20. There are 324 girls and 271 boys at school. About how many students are at school? (TEKS 3.5B, p. 60)

21. **TAKS Prep** Craig sold 54 shirts to raise money for the swim team. He has delivered 17 of them. How many shirts does he have left to deliver? (Obj. 1)

A 17 **B** 37 **C** 47 **D** 71

Extra Practice on page 102, Set C

LESSON 4 HANDS ON

Model 3-Digit Subtraction

OBJECTIVE: Explore subtracting 3-digit numbers with and without regrouping.

Quick Review

Write the numbers in expanded form.

1. 656
2. 703
3. 182
4. 599
5. 250

Investigate

Materials ■ base-ten blocks

You can use base-ten blocks to subtract numbers.

A Model the number 345.

B Use your model to find 345 − 158. Subtract the ones, tens, and hundreds. Regroup the blocks when needed.

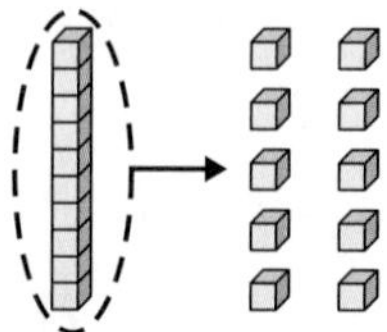

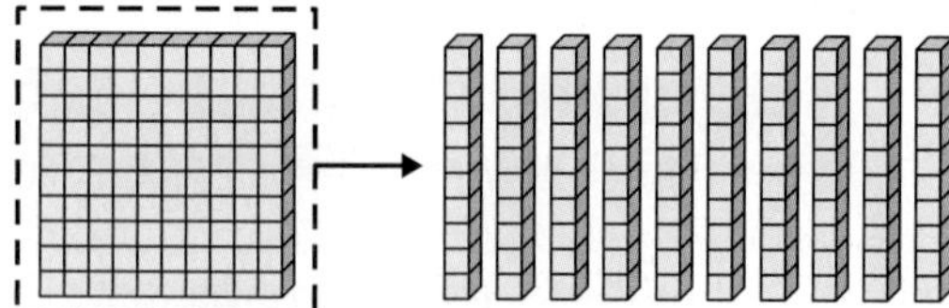

C Look at the base-ten blocks that are left. These blocks represent the difference. Draw a picture to record your answer.

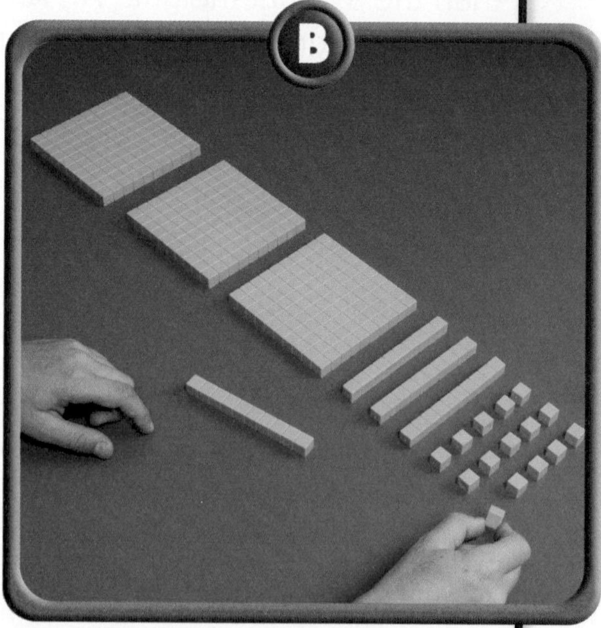

Draw Conclusions

1. **Explain** why there are 3 hundreds, 3 tens, and 15 ones in Picture B.
2. How did you know you had to regroup one of the hundreds?
3. **Synthesis** How could you use base-ten blocks and addition to check your answer?

TEKS 3.3A model addition and subtraction using pictures, words, and numbers. *also* 3.14A, 3.14D, 3.15A, 3.15B

Connect

You can record your steps with paper and pencil.

Example **Subtract.** 221 − 146

Step 1

Subtract the ones.
Since 6 > 1, regroup.
2 tens 1 one =
1 ten 11 ones

$$\begin{array}{r} \overset{1\ 11}{2\,2\,\not{1}} \\ -\,1\,4\,6 \\ \hline 5 \end{array}$$

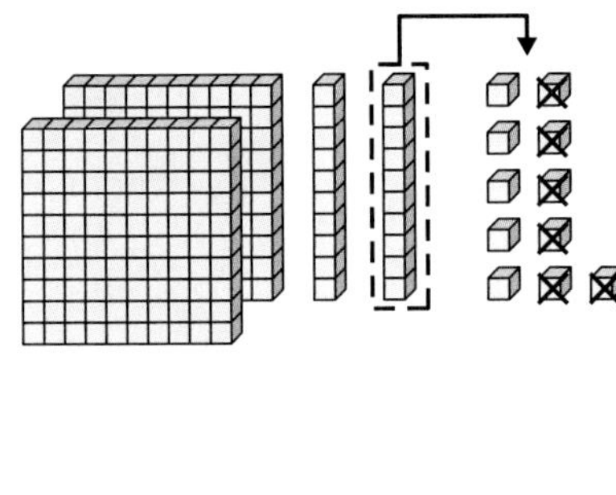

Step 2

Subtract the tens.
Since 4 > 1, regroup.
2 hundreds 1 ten =
1 hundred 11 tens

$$\begin{array}{r} \overset{11}{\overset{1\ \not{1}\ 11}{2\,\not{2}\,\not{1}}} \\ -\,1\,4\,6 \\ \hline 7\,5 \end{array}$$

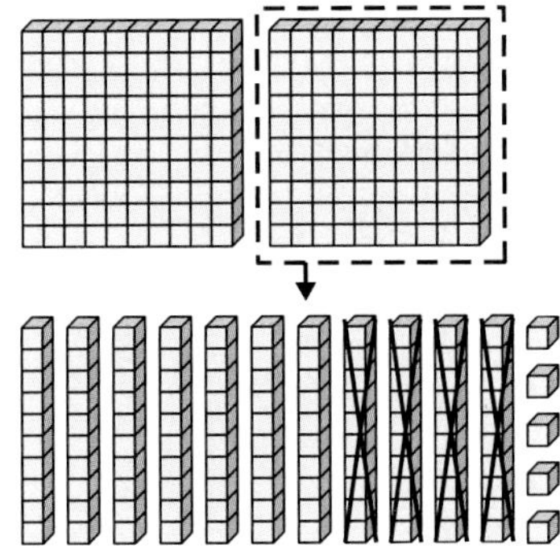

Step 3

Subtract the hundreds.

$$\begin{array}{r} \overset{11}{\overset{1\ \not{1}\ 11}{\not{2}\,\not{2}\,\not{1}}} \\ -\,1\,4\,6 \\ \hline 7\,5 \end{array}$$

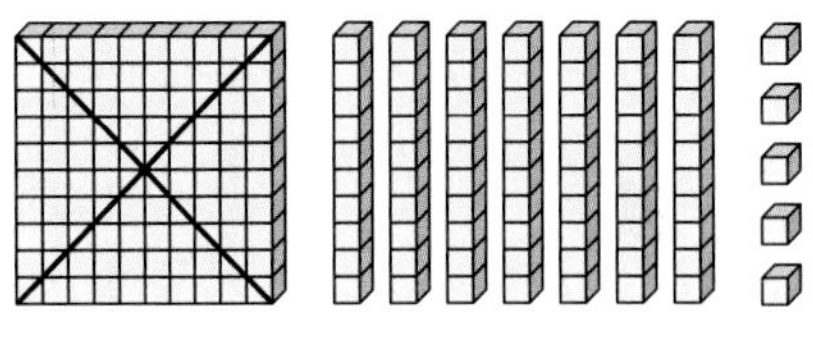

TALK Math

Explain how to find 462 − 299.

So, 221 − 146 = 75.

Practice

Use base-ten blocks to find each difference.

1. 299 − 186 = ■
2. 309 − 281 = ■
3. 443 − 267 = ■

Find each difference.

4. 435 − 319
5. 585 − 124
6. 458 − 283
7. 796 − 435
8. 851 − 615
9. 909 − 350
10. 374 − 126
11. 614 − 327
12. 451 − 286
13. 640 − 337

14. **WRITE Math** **Explain** how modeling with base-ten blocks helps you see when you need to regroup for subtraction.

Technology
CD ROM Use Harcourt Mega Math, Country Countdown, *Block Busters*, Levels X, Y.

Subtract 3-Digit Numbers

OBJECTIVE: Subtract 3-digit numbers with and without regrouping.

Quick Review

1. 25 − 12 **2.** 68 − 34
3. 37 − 16 **4.** 52 − 25
5. 83 − 59

Learn

PROBLEM Kingda Ka is a roller coaster in Jackson, New Jersey. It is 456 feet tall. The Superman Krypton Coaster, in San Antonio, Texas, is 168 feet tall. How much taller is Kingda Ka than the Superman Krypton Coaster?

▲ The Kingda Ka is the tallest and fastest roller coaster in the world.

Example **Subtract.** 456 − 168 **Estimate.** 500 − 200 = 300

Step 1	Step 2	Step 3
Subtract the ones. Regroup. 5 tens 6 ones = 4 tens 16 ones	Subtract the tens. Regroup. 4 hundreds 4 tens = 3 hundreds 14 tens	Subtract the hundreds.
4 16 45̸6̸ −168 8	14 3 4̸ 16 4̸5̸6̸ −168 88	14 3 4̸ 16 4̸5̸6̸ −168 288

So, Kingda Ka is 288 feet taller than the Superman Krypton Coaster. Since 288 is close to the estimate of 300, the answer is reasonable.

More Examples

A Regrouping	**B** No Regrouping	**C** Regrouping
4 14 5̸4̸8 −383 165	896 −524 372	12 8 2̸ 15 9̸3̸5̸ −277 658

- How could you use compatible numbers to check the reasonableness of the answer in Example B?

Guided Practice

1. Copy the problem at the right. Do you have to regroup? Find the difference.

853
−486

TEKS 3.3B select addition or subtraction and use the operation to solve problems involving whole numbers through 999. *also* 3.5A, 3.5B, 3.14A, 3.15A, 3.15B, 3.16B

Estimate. Then find each difference.

2. $\begin{array}{r} 654 \\ -547 \\ \hline \end{array}$ 3. $\begin{array}{r} 887 \\ -457 \\ \hline \end{array}$ 4. $\begin{array}{r} 744 \\ -458 \\ \hline \end{array}$ ✓5. $\begin{array}{r} 460 \\ -186 \\ \hline \end{array}$ ✓6. $\begin{array}{r} 314 \\ -281 \\ \hline \end{array}$

7. **TALK Math** **Explain** why you need to regroup a ten to subtract the ones in 292 − 173. Solve.

Independent Practice and Problem Solving

Estimate. Then find each difference.

8. $\begin{array}{r} 518 \\ -305 \\ \hline \end{array}$ 9. $\begin{array}{r} 644 \\ -329 \\ \hline \end{array}$ 10. $\begin{array}{r} 871 \\ -488 \\ \hline \end{array}$ 11. $\begin{array}{r} 968 \\ -679 \\ \hline \end{array}$ 12. $\begin{array}{r} 235 \\ -154 \\ \hline \end{array}$

Algebra Copy and complete each table.

	Subtract 236.	
13.	498	■
14.	562	■
15.	715	■

	Subtract 651.	
16.	718	■
17.	943	■
18.	859	■

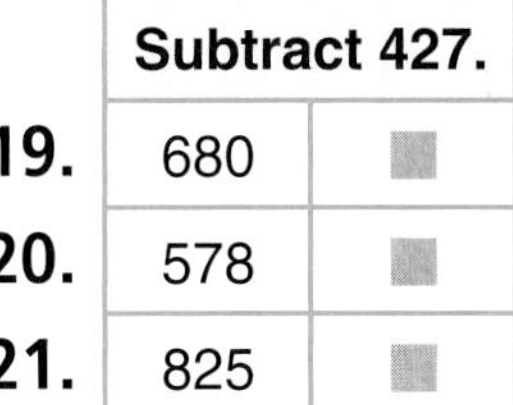

	Subtract 427.	
19.	680	■
20.	578	■
21.	825	■

USE DATA For 22–24, use the table.

22. How much taller is Millennium Force than the Texas Giant?

23. How much taller is the roller coaster in New Jersey than the two roller coasters in Texas put together?

24. **Reasoning** Which roller coaster is 146 feet shorter than Kingda Ka? **Explain** how you know.

Roller Coaster Heights

Roller Coaster	Location	Height
Texas Giant	Texas	143 feet
Kingda Ka	New Jersey	456 feet
Millennium Force	Ohio	310 feet
Titan	Texas	245 feet

25. **WRITE Math** Find 526 − 239. **Explain** how an estimate can show that your answer is reasonable.

Mixed Review and TAKS Prep

26. Amy's bookmobile has 327 books. She ordered 156 more books. How many books will there be in all? (TEKS 3.3B, p. 66)

27. Find the missing addend.
23 + ■ = 41 (TEKS 3.3B, p. 58)

28. **TAKS Prep** What is the difference between 973 and 481? (Obj. 1)

A 482 **C** 512
B 492 **D** 592

LESSON 6

Subtract Across Zeros

OBJECTIVE: Subtract 3-digit numbers across zeros.

Quick Review

1. 700 − 200
2. 516 − 300
3. 324 − 102
4. 479 − 281
5. 815 − 347

Learn

PROBLEM Colin is playing arcade games to win tickets. He wants to collect 300 tickets to exchange for a coloring book. He already has 184 tickets. How many more tickets does Colin need?

300 Tickets

COLORING BOOK LETS GO FISHING

Example **Subtract.** 300 − 184 **Estimate.** 300 − 200 = 100

Step 1

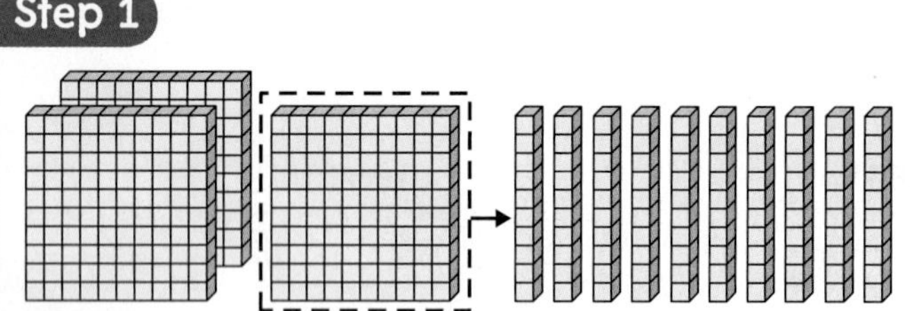

4 > 0. Since there are 0 tens, regroup hundreds.
3 hundreds 0 tens = 2 hundreds 10 tens

```
  2 10
  3̸ 0̸ 0
− 1 8 4
```

Step 2

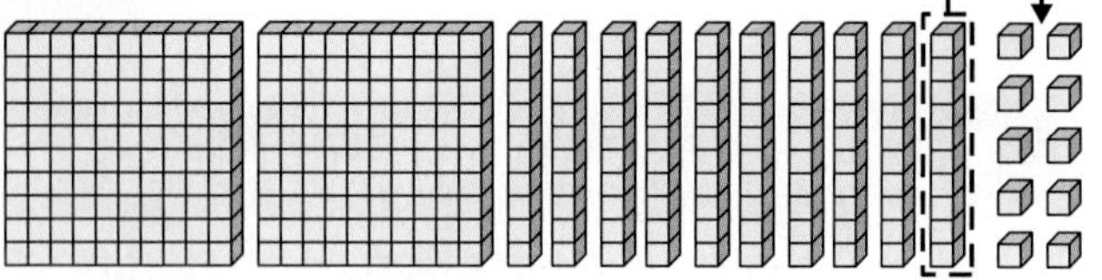

Now you can regroup tens.
10 tens 0 ones = 9 tens 10 ones

```
     9
  2 10̸ 10
  3̸ 0̸ 0̸
− 1 8 4
```

Step 3

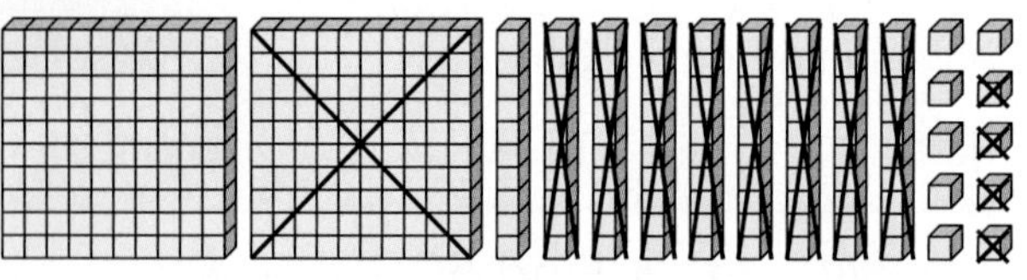

Subtract the ones.
Subtract the tens.
Subtract the hundreds.

```
     9
  2 10̸ 10
  3̸ 0̸ 0̸
− 1 8 4
  1 1 6
```

So, Colin needs to collect 116 more tickets. Since 116 is close to the estimate of 100, the answer is reasonable.

ERROR ALERT

Don't forget to regroup the tens after regrouping the hundreds.

More Examples

A

```
     9
  5 10̸ 15
  6̸ 0̸ 5̸
− 3 1 7
  2 8 8
```

B

```
     9
  7 10̸ 10
  8̸ 0̸ 0̸
− 4 8 1
  3 1 9
```

C

```
     9
  4 10̸ 12
  5̸ 0̸ 2̸        473
−   2 9      +  29
  4 7 3         502
```

Add to check.

TEKS 3.3B select addition or subtraction and use the operation to solve problems involving whole numbers through 999. *also* **3.5A, 3.5B, 3.14A, 3.14D, 3.15A, 3.15B, 3.16B**

Guided Practice

1. Look at the model for 203. What do you need to do to find 203 − 174?

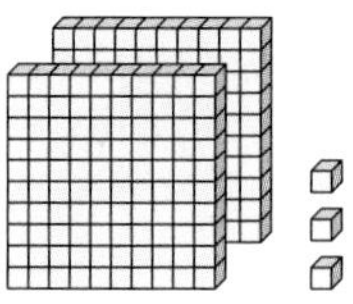

Estimate. Then find each difference.

2.	3.	4.	✓5.	✓6.
306 − 157	700 − 374	547 − 238	901 − 486	400 − 161

7. TALK Math Explain how to find 300 − 226.

Independent Practice and Problem Solving

Estimate. Then find each difference.

8.	9.	10.	11.	12.
202 − 65	500 − 326	989 − 472	504 − 137	600 − 263

Find each difference. Use addition to check.

13. 705 − 346 = ■ 14. 200 − 114 = ■ 15. 800 − 259 = ■

USE DATA For 16–18, use the picture.

16. How many more tickets are needed for a football than for a hat? Draw a picture of base-ten blocks to show how to find the answer.

17. Sheila has 100 tickets. Tim gives her 54 tickets. How many more tickets does Sheila need to get a calendar?

18. WRITE Math What's the Question? Sheila looked at the prize wall. The answer is 460.

Mixed Review and TAKS Prep

19. How many edges does a cube have? (Grade 2 TEKS 2.7A)

20. What is the value of the 7 in 59,734? (TEKS 3.1A, p. 16)

21. **TAKS Prep** Which number will make the number sentence true? (Obj. 1)

700 − 386 = ■

A 424 **B** 324 **C** 314 **D** 304

Extra Practice on page 102, Set E

Choose a Method

OBJECTIVE: Choose paper and pencil, a calculator, or mental math to subtract 3-digit numbers.

Quick Review

1. 120 − 110
2. 365 − 50
3. 400 − 20
4. 436 − 257
5. 405 − 116

Learn

PROBLEM For her science project, Ella compared the weights of different animals that she saw at the zoo. How much more does the zebra weigh than the ostrich?

Example 1 Use paper and pencil.

Subtract. 625 − 245 = ■ **Estimate.** 600 − 200 = 400

The problem involves one regrouping. So, using paper and pencil is a good choice.

Step 1	Step 2	Step 3
Subtract the ones. 5 − 5 = 0	Subtract the tens. Since 4 > 2, regroup. 12 − 4 = 8	Subtract the hundreds. 5 − 2 = 3
625 − 245 0	5 12 625 − 245 80	5 12 625 − 245 380

So, the zebra weighs 380 pounds more than the ostrich. Since 380 is close to the estimate of 400, the answer is reasonable.

Example 2 Use a calculator.

How much more does the grizzly bear weigh than the gazelle?

800 − 165 = ■

The problem involves subtracting across zeros. So, using a calculator is a good choice.

So, the grizzly bear weighs 635 pounds more than the gazelle.

- How can you use addition to check your answer?

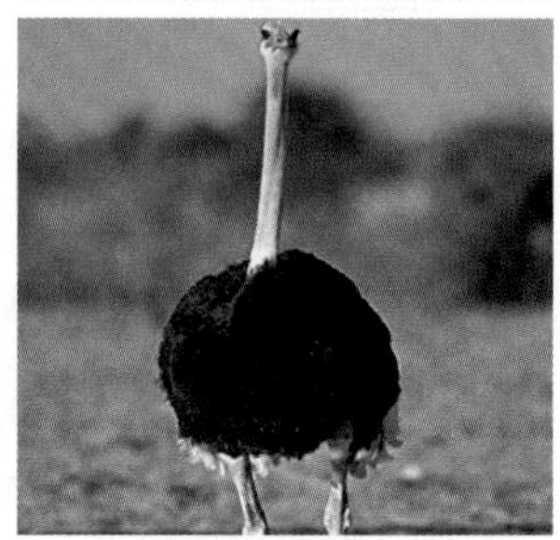

Ostrich
weight: 245 pounds

Gazelle
weight: 165 pounds

Grevy's zebra
weight: 625 pounds

Grizzly bear
weight: 800 pounds

TEKS 3.14D use tools such as real objects, manipulatives, and technology to solve problems. *also* 3.3B, 3.14A, 3.15A, 3.15B

Example 3 Use mental math.

A giraffe can be 218 inches tall.
An ostrich can be 108 inches tall.
How much taller is the giraffe than the ostrich?

$$218 - 108 = \blacksquare$$

There is no regrouping. So, using mental math is a good choice.

Think: Subtract the hundreds. $200 - 100 = 100$
Subtract the tens. $10 - 0 = 10$
Subtract the ones. $8 - 8 = 0$
110

So, the giraffe is 110 inches taller than the ostrich.

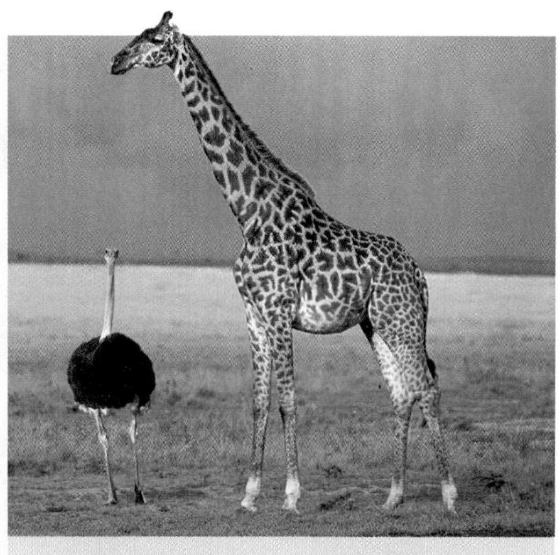

▲ The tallest bird is the ostrich.

▲ The tallest mammal is the giraffe.

More Examples

A Use paper and pencil.

$$\begin{array}{r} \overset{7}{\not 8}\overset{12}{\not 2} \\ 7\;\;\;\;\;\; \\ -457 \\ \hline 325 \end{array}$$

B Use mental math.

$$\begin{array}{r} 677 \\ -430 \\ \hline 247 \end{array}$$

C Use a calculator.

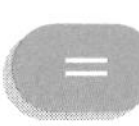

5 0 1 − 1 5 9 = 342.

Guided Practice

1. Find $561 - 120$ using mental math. Use the number sentences to help you.

$$\begin{array}{r} 561 \\ -120 \\ \hline \end{array}$$

$500 - 100 = \blacksquare$
$60 - 20 = \blacksquare$
$1 - 0 = \blacksquare$

Find the difference. Tell which method you used.

2. $\begin{array}{r} 746 \\ -232 \\ \hline \end{array}$

3. $\begin{array}{r} 816 \\ -482 \\ \hline \end{array}$

4. $\begin{array}{r} 912 \\ -357 \\ \hline \end{array}$

5. $\begin{array}{r} 495 \\ -305 \\ \hline \end{array}$

✓6. $\begin{array}{r} 700 \\ -218 \\ \hline \end{array}$

7. $307 - 189 = \blacksquare$

8. $540 - 336 = \blacksquare$

✓9. $895 - 722 = \blacksquare$

10. TALK Math **Explain** what method you would use to subtract 131 from 526. Then find the difference.

Independent Practice and Problem Solving

Find the difference. Tell which method you used.

11. $600 - 278$ **12.** $895 - 784$ **13.** $719 - 372$ **14.** $310 - 100$ **15.** $737 - 259$

16. $570 - 269$ **17.** $411 - 286$ **18.** $954 - 622$ **19.** $850 - 376$ **20.** $520 - 419$

21. 907 − 506 = ■ **22.** 244 − 105 = ■ **23.** 823 − 789 = ■

Algebra **Find the missing number.**

24. 683 − ■ = 331 **25.** ■ − 165 = 164 **26.** 397 − ■ = 255

USE DATA **For 27–29, use the table.**

27. How many more kinds of animals does the San Antonio Zoo have than the El Paso Zoo and the Fort Worth Zoo put together?

28. **Reasoning** There are 47 kinds of endangered animals at the Gladys Porter Zoo. How many animals are not endangered?

29. WRITE Math **What's the Error?** Aaron said that the Gladys Porter Zoo has 150 more kinds of animals than the Fort Worth Zoo. **Explain** his error. Find the correct answer.

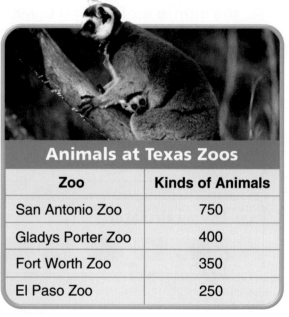

Animals at Texas Zoos

Zoo	Kinds of Animals
San Antonio Zoo	750
Gladys Porter Zoo	400
Fort Worth Zoo	350
El Paso Zoo	250

30. ***FAST FACT*** The heaviest African lion in the wild weighed 690 pounds. The heaviest African lion at a zoo weighed 826 pounds. What is the difference between their weights?

Mixed Review and TAKS Prep

31. On Friday, 784 children and 522 adults visited the zoo. How many people visited the zoo in all? (TEKS 3.3B, p. 66)

32. How is 5,920 written in expanded form? (TEKS 3.1A, p. 12)

33. **TAKS Prep** A zebra weighs 625 pounds, and a grizzly bear weighs 703 pounds. How much more does the grizzly bear weigh? (Obj. 6)

A 78 pounds **C** 178 pounds
B 122 pounds **D** 188 pounds

 Extra Practice on page 102, Set F

▲ Emus sometimes eat things like nails, keys, and bottle tops.

◀ The size of 1 ostrich egg equals up to 24 chicken eggs!

Emus live in Australia and weigh about 120 pounds. They can grow to be about 6 feet tall and can run as fast as 40 miles per hour.

Ostriches live in Africa and weigh about 300 pounds. They can grow to be about 9 feet tall and can run as fast as 40 miles per hour.

When you compare things, you decide how they are alike. When you contrast things, you decide how they are different. Use the table to compare and contrast the birds. How are they different?

	Emus	Ostriches
Where do they live?	Australia	Africa
How much do they weigh?	120 pounds	300 pounds
How tall are they?	6 feet tall	9 feet tall
How fast can they run?	40 miles per hour	40 miles per hour

Problem Solving **Compare and contrast to solve.**

1. Solve the problem above using the table to tell how the birds are different.
2. Ostriches have 2 toes on each foot. They protect themselves by kicking with their toes. Emus have 3 toes on each foot. They use them for protection. How are the birds alike?

Problem Solving Workshop
Skill: Choose the Operation

OBJECTIVE: Solve problems by using the skill *choose the operation.*

Use the Skill

PROBLEM Ms. Wells counted books in the school library. She counted 123 animal books in one section. She counted 305 sports books in another section. How many more sports books did Ms. Wells count than animal books?

This chart will help you decide which operation you can use to solve the problem.

Add	Join groups to find how many in all, or the total.
Subtract	Take away, or compare, to find how many more, how many fewer, or how many are left.

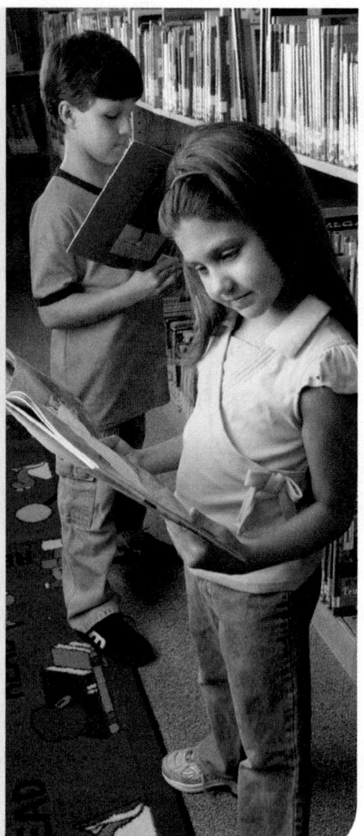

Since the question asks you to find how many more sports books Ms. Wells counted than animal books, you can subtract.

number of sports books		number of animal books		how many more sports books than animal books
↓		↓		↓
305	−	123	=	182

$$\begin{array}{r} \overset{2}{\cancel{3}}\overset{10}{\cancel{0}}5 \\ -\,123 \\ \hline 182 \end{array}$$

So, Ms. Wells counted 182 more sports books than animal books.

Think and Discuss

Tell which operation you would use. Then solve the problem.

a. Gina's family has 165 books on shelves. They also have 277 books in the attic. How many books does Gina's family have in all?

b. Carlos likes word puzzles. He bought a puzzle book that has 275 word puzzles. He has 132 puzzles left to complete. How many puzzles has Carlos already completed?

TEKS 3.3B select addition or subtraction and use the operation to solve problems involving whole numbers through 999. *also* **3.14A, 3.14C, 3.15A, 3.15B, 3.16B**

Guided Problem Solving

1. Zack has 65 photos of his vacation and 48 photos of his family in his photo album. He has room for 137 more photos. How many photos can Zack's album hold in all?

   Copy and complete the table.

Clues	Meaning
has ■ photos of vacation and ■ photos of family	has a total of ■ photos
has room for ■ more photos	■ more photos can go in the album
How many photos can Zack's album hold in all?	What is the total number of __?__ the album holds?

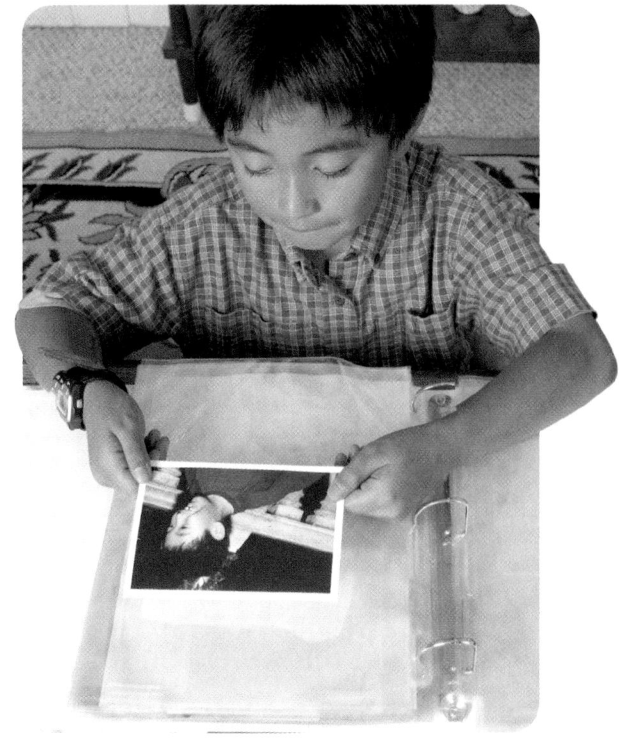

   Which operation can you use to find how many in all? Write a number sentence that shows the answer.

2. **What if** Zack had room for 175 more photos? How many photos would Zack's album hold in all?

3. Brad has room for 100 baseball cards in his binder. He has 64 cards already. How many more cards does he need to fill his binder?

Mixed Applications

4. Erin collects stamps. She has 279 stamps in an album. She gives away 47 stamps to her friends. How many stamps does Erin have left?

5. Kyle and Josh have a total of 64 CDs. Kyle has 12 more CDs than Josh. How many CDs does each boy have?

6. Joseph has 2 coins in his pocket. Their total is 30¢. What are the two coins?

7. Mrs. Gregory has 189 books in her office. Mrs. Moore has 168 books in her office. Who has more books? How many more?

8. **WRITE Math** Kim is reading a book that has 382 pages. She reads 28 pages each night. How many more pages will she have left to read after 3 nights? **Explain** how you know.

9. **Reasoning** Brad's album can hold 225 photos. He has 144 photos in the album. He wants to put 79 more photos in the album. **Explain** how to tell if he has enough space left for the photos.

Extra Practice

Set A **Write the fact family for each set of numbers.** (pp. 84–85)

1. 4, 9, 13
2. 2, 5, 7
3. 6, 8, 14
4. 3, 8, 11
5. 6, 6, 12
6. 1, 7, 8
7. 4, 6, 10
8. 7, 9, 16

Set B **Use rounding or compatible numbers to estimate each difference.** (pp. 86–87)

1. $76 - 24$
2. $89 - 12$
3. $506 - 354$
4. $795 - 133$
5. $448 - 227$
6. Maggie read 87 pages of her book. Alan read 51 pages of his book. About how many more pages did Maggie read?

Set C **Estimate. Then find each difference.** (pp. 88–89)

1. $93 - 59$
2. $78 - 37$
3. $56 - 11$
4. $85 - 26$
5. $62 - 44$

Set D **Estimate. Then find each difference.** (pp. 92–93)

1. $386 - 107$
2. $519 - 185$
3. $865 - 378$
4. $786 - 432$
5. $429 - 236$
6. Sue is saving money to buy a bike for $220. So far she has saved $136. How much more money does Sue need to save?

Set E **Estimate. Then find each difference.** (pp. 94–95)

1. $600 - 328$
2. $402 - 238$
3. $330 - 119$
4. $800 - 183$
5. $906 - 557$

Set F **Find the difference. Tell which method you used.** (pp. 96–99)

1. $580 - 461$
2. $792 - 521$
3. $843 - 376$
4. $900 - 263$
5. $478 - 105$

CD ROM **Technology**
Use Harcourt Mega Math, Country Countdown, *Block Busters*, Levels R, X, Y.

PRACTICE GAME

Time to Subtract

On Your Mark!
2 players

Get Set!
- Timer

18 33 46 61 80 98

24 38 50 65 76 92

Play!

- Each player chooses a type of animal. Each player uses the 6 numbers on his or her animals to write and solve problems.
- Using their 6 numbers, players write and solve as many subtraction problems as they can in 2 minutes.
- When both players are ready, set the timer for 2 minutes and begin.
- After the 2 minutes are up, players trade papers and check each other's answers.
- The player with more correct answers receives a point.
- Each player chooses a different animal and continues to play.
- The first player to reach 3 points wins.

Chapter 4 Review/Test

Check Vocabulary and Concepts

Choose the best term from the box.

VOCABULARY
fact family
inverse operations
regrouping

1. Addition and subtraction are opposite, or ? . (TEKS 3.3B, p. 84)
2. A group of related number sentences that use the same numbers is a ? . (TEKS 3.3B, p. 84)

Check Skills

Write the fact family for each set of numbers. (TEKS 3.3B, pp. 84–85)

3. 2, 8, 10
4. 6, 6, 12
5. 3, 4, 7
6. 7, 8, 15

Use rounding or compatible numbers to estimate each difference. (TEKS 3.5B, pp. 86–87)

7. $56 - 19$
8. $64 - 23$
9. $661 - 185$
10. $942 - 316$

Estimate. Then find each difference. (TEKS 3.3B, pp. 88–89, 92–93, 94–95)

11. $48 - 17$
12. $77 - 49$
13. $80 - 35$
14. $374 - 253$
15. $507 - 230$
16. $583 - 179$
17. $97 - 58$
18. $800 - 567$
19. $605 - 386$
20. $700 - 411$
21. $864 - 775$
22. $624 - 248$

Check Problem Solving

Solve. (TEKS 3.3B, 3.14A, pp. 100–101)

23. Mr. Patrick read 216 pages of his book. Mrs. Wu read 197 pages of her book. How many pages have they read in all?
24. A car show had 329 visitors. Of the visitors, 47 were children and the rest were adults. How many of the visitors were adults?
25. WRITE Math What operation did you use to solve Problem 24? **Explain** how you knew which operation to use.

GO ONLINE **Technology** Use *Online Assessment.*

Enrich • Sums and Differences

Odd or EVEN?

Every number is either **odd** or **even**.

Odd numbers end in 1, 3, 5, 7, or 9.

41, 197, and 1,433 are odd.

Even numbers end in 0, 2, 4, 6, or 8.

28, 374, and 4,562 are even.

▲ Mancala is one of the oldest board games in the world. The game has 6 small holes on each side. Is the total number of small holes an odd or even number?

You can look for patterns to predict if the sum or difference of two numbers will be odd or even.

Examples

Addition Complete the table to find each answer.

NUMBERS	EXAMPLE	SUM	ODD OR EVEN?
even + even	2 + 6	8	even
odd + odd	73 + 7	■	■
odd + even	45 + 30	■	■
even + odd	2,116 + 517	■	■

Subtration Complete the table to find each answer.

NUMBERS	EXAMPLE	DIFFERENCE	ODD OR EVEN?
even − even	8 − 4	4	even
odd − odd	87 − 49	■	■
odd − even	835 − 22	■	■
even − odd	474 − 367	■	■

Remember
The ones digit helps you see if a number is even or odd.

Try It

Find the sum or difference. Write *odd* or *even*.

1. 7 + 3 **2.** 1 + 12 **3.** 84 + 18 **4.** 734 + 15 **5.** 565 + 259

6. 10 − 5 **7.** 33 − 12 **8.** 196 − 80 **9.** 775 − 401 **10.** 9,827 − 6,378

WRITE Math Choose two numbers to add. Is the sum of your numbers an odd or even number? **Explain** how you know.

Getting Ready for the TAKS
Chapters 1–4

Number, Operation, and Quantitative Reasoning (TAKS Obj. 1)

1. Building A is 890 feet tall. Building B is 564 feet tall. About how much taller is Building A than Building B?

   A about 200 feet

   B about 300 feet

   C about 400 feet

   D about 500 feet

Test Tip **Check your work.**

See item 2. Make sure you regroup correctly when subtracting across zeros. You can add to check your work.

2. Gavin has a score of 300 on a computer game. Ben needs 188 more points to tie Gavin's score. What is Ben's score?

   F 112

   G 122

   H 212

   J Not here

3. **WRITE Math** On Tuesday, 435 people visited the history museum. What is 435 rounded to the nearest hundred? **Explain** how to find the answer using the tens digit.

Patterns, Relationships, and Algebraic Thinking (TAKS Obj. 2)

4. Which number completes the fact family?

   $8 + \blacksquare = 13$ $\quad 13 - 8 = \blacksquare$

   $\blacksquare + 8 = 13$ $\quad 13 - \blacksquare = 8$

   A 7

   B 6

   C 5

   D 4

5. Which number is missing in the pattern below?

   19, 23, 27, 31, 35, ___

   F 37

   G 38

   H 39

   J 40

6. **WRITE Math** Which number is missing from the table below? **Explain** how you know.

number of nickels	2	3	4	5	6
number of pennies	10	15	20	25	■

Geometry and Spatial Reasoning (TAKS Obj. 3)

7. How many faces does a rectangular prism have?

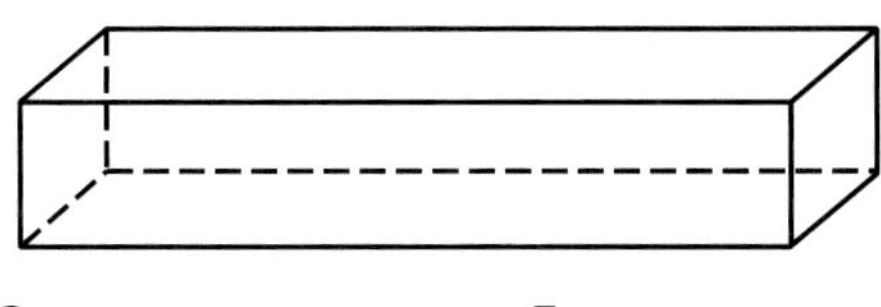

A 3 **C** 5

B 4 **D** 6

8. Which shape has more than 5 vertices?

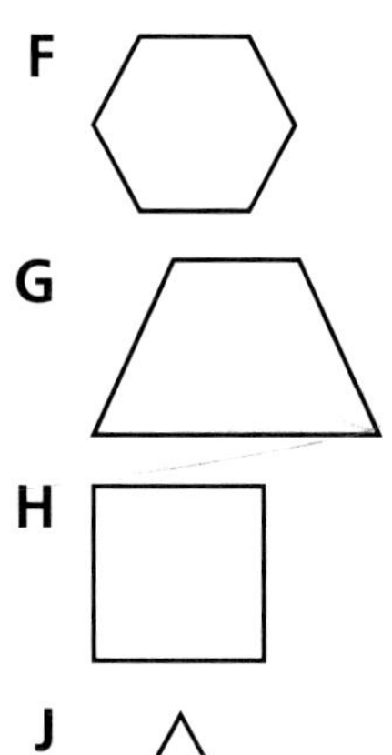

F

G

H

J

9. WRITE Math Jackie put two trapezoid pattern blocks together to make a hexagon. **Explain** how to make a hexagon using different pattern blocks.

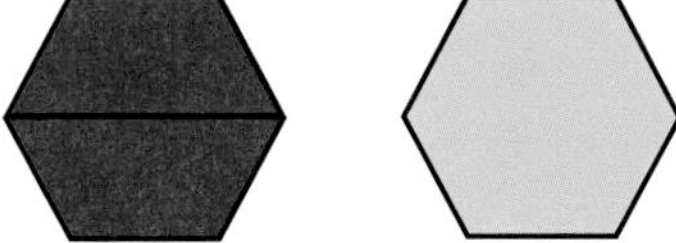

Probability and Statistics (TAKS Obj. 5)

10. Miss Handy's class researched countries for a project. How many students did research?

Countries Researched

Country	Number of Students
Spain	𝍸 ||||
Canada	||||
Japan	||||
Norway	𝍸

A 20

B 21

C 22

D 23

11. Julia has 8 blue shirts in a drawer. She also has 3 red shirts, 3 white shirts, and 1 purple shirt in the same drawer. What color shirt is she more likely to choose?

F Blue

G Red

H White

J Purple

12. WRITE Math Henry has 4 green marbles and 10 blue marbles in a bag. Without looking, which color marble is he less likely to choose? **Explain** how you know.

5 Money

The Big Idea Money amounts can be added, subtracted, and compared just like whole numbers.

Investigate

A quarter has a value of 25 cents. Choose two items from the chart. Tell how many quarters you would need to buy the two items.

Texas Collectibles

Item	Cost
Small Texas flag	$0.79
Texas pencil	$0.45
Texas license plate	$3.50
Texas coffee mug	$2.30
Texas keychain	$2.80

TEXAS FAST FACT

The United States Mint made a quarter for each state. The 28th state quarter was the one for Texas. Texas became the 28th state of the United States on December 29, 1845.

GO ONLINE Technology
Student pages are available in the Student eBook.

Show What You Know

Check your understanding of important skills needed for success in Chapter 5.

▶ Count Coins

Count and write the amount.

1.

2.

3.

4.

▶ Quarters

Count and write the amount.

5.

6.

7.

8.

9.

10.

VOCABULARY POWER

CHAPTER VOCABULARY

change
decimal point
dollar
equivalent

WARM-UP WORDS

equivalent Two or more sets that name the same amount

decimal point A symbol used to separate dollars from cents in money

change The money you get back if you have paid for an item with coins or bills that have a value greater than the cost of the item

1 Count Bills and Coins

OBJECTIVE: Count, read, and write money amounts with groups of coins and bills.

Quick Review

Find the next number in the pattern.

1. 5, 10, 15, ■
2. 10, 20, 30, ■
3. 25, 30, 35, ■
4. 15, 25, 35, ■
5. 25, 50, 75, ■

Vocabulary

equivalent **dollar**
decimal point

Learn

PROBLEM Brian has some coins in his piggy bank. How much money does he have?

Brian's Money

half dollar	quarter	dime	nickel	penny
50¢	25¢	10¢	5¢	1¢

50¢ →	75¢ →	85¢ →	90¢ →	91¢

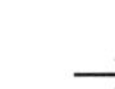

Start with the coin of greatest value. Count on to find the total.

So, Brian has 91¢ in his bank.

Remember
Every coin has a "heads" side and a "tails" side.

heads

tails

Example

A

25¢ → 50¢ → 60¢ → 70¢ → 80¢ → 85¢ → 86¢

Activity

Materials ■ play money coins

- Choose a handful of play money coins.
- Count the value of the coins. Start with the coins of greatest value.
- Record your count. Then count the value of the coins in a different order.
- Is the value of the set of coins different when you count in a different order? Explain.

TEKS 3.1C determine the value of a collection of bills and coins. *also* **3.14A, 3.14D, 3.15A, 3.15B**

Equivalent Amounts

Sets of money that have the same value are **equivalent**.

Example 1 Show $1.06 two different ways.

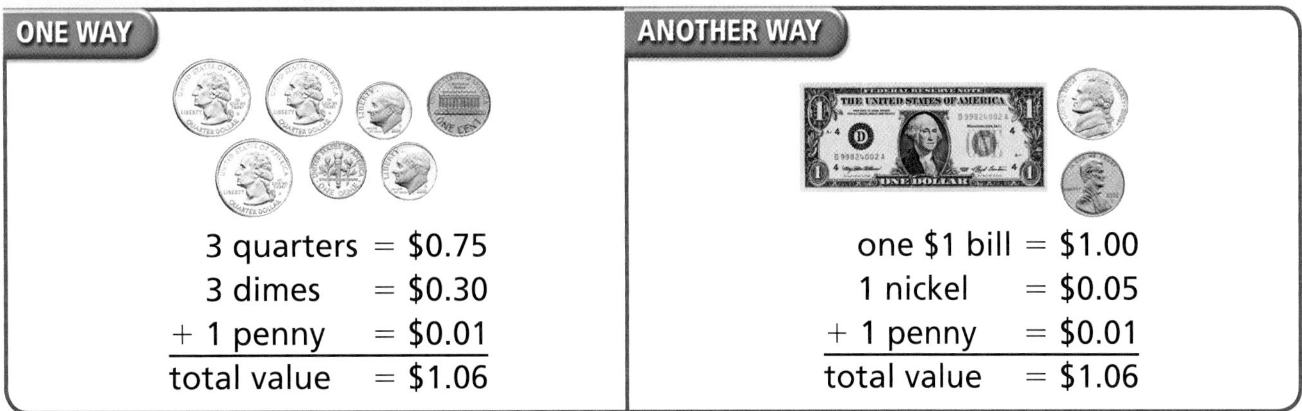

ONE WAY

3 quarters	=	$0.75
3 dimes	=	$0.30
+ 1 penny	=	$0.01
total value	=	$1.06

ANOTHER WAY

one $1 bill	=	$1.00
1 nickel	=	$0.05
+ 1 penny	=	$0.01
total value	=	$1.06

Each set has a value of $1.06. The sets are equivalent.

Write	Read
dollar sign → $1.06 ↑ **decimal point**	one **dollar** and six cents

• What does the 0 in $1.06 mean?

Example 2 Juanita and Tony have the money shown below.

Juanita's money

one $5 bill	→ $5.00
two $1 bills	→ $2.00
2 quarters	→ $0.50
3 pennies	→ $0.03
	$7.53

Tony's money

seven $1 bills	→ $7.00
1 half-dollar	→ $0.50
3 pennies	→ $0.03
	$7.53

So, Juanita and Tony each have $7.53. The amounts are equivalent.

Guided Practice

1. What is the value of 5 nickels?     

Write the amount.

2. 

3.  

4. TALK Math **Explain** two ways to show $1.25.

Independent Practice and Problem Solving

Write the amount.

5. 

6. 

Find two equivalent sets for each. List the coins and bills.

7. 70¢ 8. 38¢ 9. $1.20 10. $6.74

Algebra Write the missing number.

11. 2 quarters + ■ dimes = 80¢

12. 2 nickels + ■ pennies = 23¢

USE DATA For 13–14, use the pictures.

13. Tom wants to buy a smoothie. List the fewest bills and coins he can use.

14. **Reasoning** Kayla wants to buy a fruit chiller. List two ways Kayla can pay for it. **Explain** your choices.

15. How can you make 87¢ by using the fewest coins? the most coins?

16. WRITE Math Alex has $1.48. **Explain** how you know he has at least six coins.

Mixed Review and TAKS Prep

17. Josh wants to collect 200 cards. He has 159 cards. How many more cards does he need? (TEKS 3.3B, p. 94)

18. What number goes in the ■ to make the number sentence true?

63 + ■ = 89 (TEKS 3.3B, p. 58)

19. **TAKS Prep** Jared has two $1 bills, 1 quarter, and 3 nickels. How much money does Jared have in all? (Obj. 1)

A $1.40 **C** $2.35

B $1.90 **D** $2.40

Technology
Use Harcourt Mega Math, The Number Games, *Buggy Bargains*, Levels A and B.

 Extra Practice on page 122, Set A

Write a Conclusion

Writing a conclusion helps you use the information you are given and what you find out to make a decision.

Jessica and Alex are comparing the bills and coins they have. Do they have equivalent amounts of money?

Jessica's Money

Alex's Money

Jessica wrote this paragraph to explain her answer.

First, I counted my money. I have \$3.00 + \$1.00 + \$0.20 + \$0.05. I have \$4.25.

Next, I counted Alex's money. He has \$2.00 + \$2.00 + \$0.10 + \$0.15. He has \$4.25.

Then, I compared the two amounts of money. Alex and I have equivalent amounts.

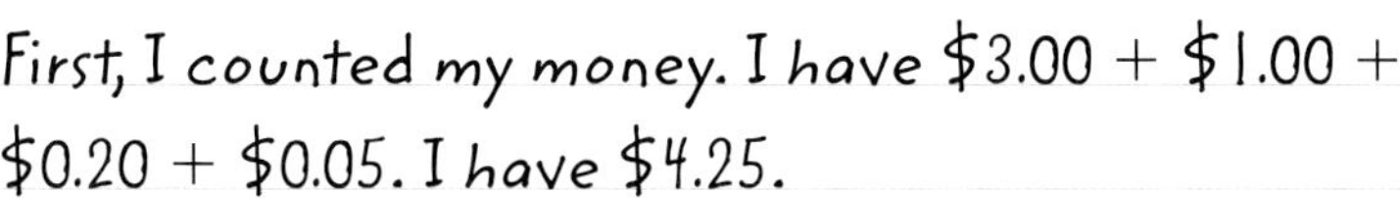

Tips

- To write a conclusion, first, study the information you are given.
- Then, write the steps you took to help you make a decision.
- Use words such as first and next.
- Then state your conclusion in the last sentence.

Problem Solving Write a conclusion for each problem.

1. Tina has 2 quarters, 2 dimes, and 2 pennies. Jacob has 5 dimes, 5 nickels, and 2 pennies. Do they have equivalent amounts of money?

2. Ron has two \$1 bills, 3 dimes, and 4 nickels. Lois has one \$1 bill, 4 quarters, and 5 dimes. Do they have equivalent amounts of money?

LESSON 2

Compare Money Amounts

OBJECTIVE: Compare money amounts with bills and coins.

Quick Review

Compare. Use <, >, or = for each.

1. 6 ● 8
2. 11 ● 13
3. 15 ● 12
4. 134 ● 145
5. 229 ● 226

Learn

PROBLEM Sarah and Zoey each bought a pair of sunglasses. They paid the amounts shown below. Who spent more money?

Example 1 Count and compare the money amounts.

Sarah

Sarah spent $5.27.

Zoey

Zoey spent $5.30.

$5.27 < $5.30, or $5.30 > $5.27

So, Zoey spent more money.

- If you have a greater number of bills and coins than someone else, do you always have the greater amount of money? Explain.

Remember

< means is less than.

> means is greater than.

Example 2 Use place value to compare $3.56 and $3.54.

DOLLARS	.	DIMES	PENNIES
$3	.	5	6
$3	.	5	4

The number of dollars and dimes are equal.
Compare the number of pennies.
6 > 4, so $3.56 > $3.54.

Guided Practice

1. Which is the greater money amount, 2 quarters or 6 dimes?

TEKS 3.1C determine the value of a collection of coins and bills. *also* 3.14A, 3.15A, 3.15B

Use <, >, or = to compare the amounts of money.

2.  

3.  

4. **TALK Math** **Explain** how to compare $5.28 and $5.41 by using place value.

Independent Practice and Problem Solving

Use <, >, or = to compare the amounts of money.

5.  

Which amount is greater?

6. $6.82 or $6.90
7. $1.10 or 5 quarters
8. $1.90 or 7 quarters
9. $3.26 or $2.63
10. 4 dimes or 4 quarters
11. 3 dimes 3 nickels, or 5 dimes

USE DATA For 12–13, use the table.

12. Write the prices in order from greatest to least. What is the difference between the greatest and the least amount?
13. **WRITE Math** Hayley has $5.00. Which item can she buy at the Beach Shop? **Explain** how you know.

Beach Shop

Item	Price
Towel	$5.82
Water Bottle	$2.87
Sunscreen	$5.12

Mixed Review and TAKS Prep

14. Marcus poured milk into his glass. What tool should he use to measure how much milk he poured? (TEKS 2.9 Grade 2)
15. Bianca estimated 688 − 432 by rounding each number to the nearest hundred. What was her estimate? (TEKS 3.5B, p. 86)
16. **TAKS Prep** Amber has only quarters. She has more than 75¢. Which amount could Amber have? (Obj. 1)

    A $0.85 **C** $1.50

    B $1.05 **D** $1.70

Extra Practice on page 122, Set B

Problem Solving Workshop
Strategy: Make a Table

OBJECTIVE: Solve problems by using the strategy *make a table.*

Learn the Strategy

Using a table can help you understand the information in some problems.

A table can help you see how items in a problem are related. This table shows a number pattern.

Matt and his dad build wagons. Each wagon has 4 wheels.

Wagons	1	2	3
Wheels	4	8	12

A table can help you record choices. This table shows how students voted.

Mika asked his classmates to vote for their favorite meal.

Favorite Meal	
Meal	Votes
Breakfast	HHT II
Lunch	HHT IIII
Dinner	HHT HHT

A table can help you find possible answers. This table shows equivalent sets of money.

Opal has a $1 bill, some dimes, and some nickels. She uses it all to buy a fruit drink for $1.50.

$1 bills	Dimes	Nickels	Total Value
1	2	6	$1.50
1	3	4	$1.50
1	4	2	$1.50

TALK Math

What questions can be answered by using each of the tables above?

TEKS 3.1C determine the value of a collection of coins and bills. *also* 3.14A, 3.14B, 3.14C, 3.14D, 3.15A, 3.15B, 3.16B

Use the Strategy

PROBLEM Damon has the bills and coins pictured below. He wants to rent ice skates for $3.25. How many different ways can Damon make $3.25?

Read to Understand

- **What information is given in the graphic aid?**
- **Is any information not needed?**

Plan

- **What strategy can you use to solve the problem?**
  You can make a table to help you solve the problem.

Solve

- **How can you use the strategy to solve the problem?**
  Make a table to show all the equivalent sets of bills and coins Damon can make to equal $3.25.

$1 bills	Quarters	Dimes	Nickels	Pennies	Total Value
3	1	0	0	0	$3.25
3	0	2	1	0	$3.25
3	0	2	0	5	$3.25
2	4	2	1	0	$3.25
2	4	2	0	5	$3.25

So, there are 5 equivalent sets Damon can make to equal $3.25.

Check

- **How can you make sure each set of bills and coins equals $3.25?**
- **What other way could you solve the problem?**

Guided Problem Solving

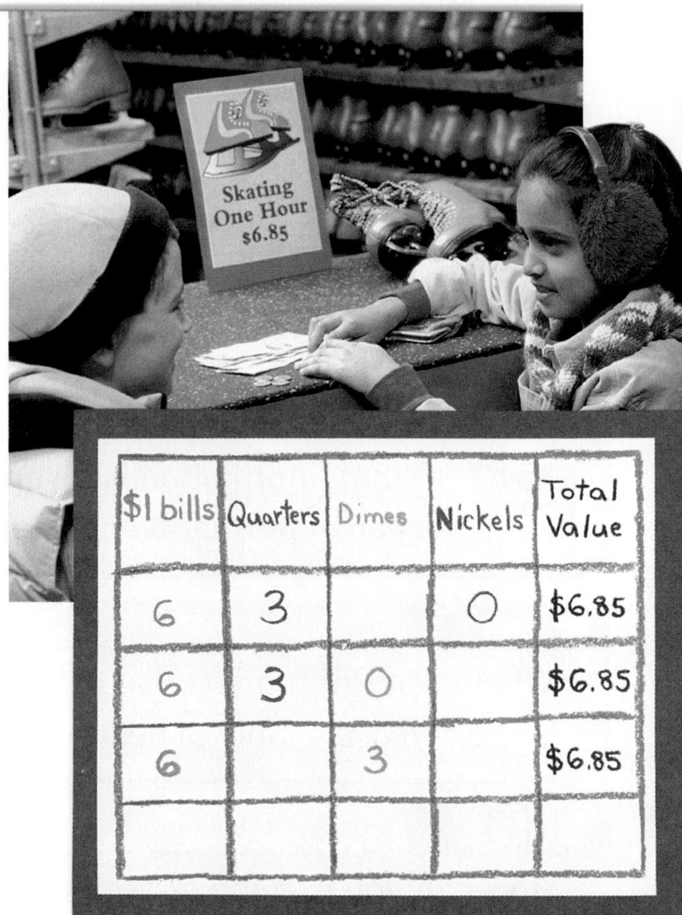

$1 bills	Quarters	Dimes	Nickels	Total Value
6	3		0	$6.85
6	3	0		$6.85
6		3		$6.85

1. Amy has six $1 bills, 4 quarters, 3 dimes, and 4 nickels. She needs to pay $6.85 to ice skate for an hour. How many different ways can Amy make $6.85?

Copy and complete the table. Find all the equivalent sets that equal $6.85. Make sure Amy has enough bills and coins for each set.

2. **What if** Amy had one $5 bill, two $1 bills, 3 quarters, 3 dimes, and 3 nickels? Name two ways Amy could make $6.85.

3. Tyler has 7 quarters, 4 dimes, and 6 nickels. He wants to buy a hot dog for $1.45. How many different ways can Tyler make $1.45?

Problem Solving Strategy Practice

USE DATA For 4–6, use the list. Make a table to solve.

List your favorite juice.
grape apple apple berry
grape berry apple grape
berry grape grape berry
apple apple berry grape
berry berry apple
grape berry berry
apple grape grape grape

4. Kim had a class skating party for her birthday. Each student chose one juice flavor. How many students were at Kim's party? How many students chose each flavor?

5. How many more students chose grape juice than chose apple juice?

6. Kim's mother bought 2 juice boxes for each student at the party. How many juice boxes did she buy in all?

7. Eric has five $1 bills, 3 quarters, 5 dimes, 1 nickel, and 5 pennies. How many different equivalent sets of bills and coins can he use to pay for earmuffs that cost $5.75?

Mixed Strategy Practice

USE DATA For 8–10, use the table below.

8. Jen and Tina sold lemonade and cookies to raise money for an ice-skating class. On Friday, they counted 11 coins. List the coins they could have on Friday.

9. On Saturday, Taylor bought 4 cookies. He gave Jen and Tina 5 dimes and 8 pennies. How much more than that did the girls earn on Saturday?

10. After selling the lemonade and cookies on Sunday, the girls had 2 bills and 6 coins. What bills and coins did the girls have?

Friday	$2.75
Saturday	$5.58
Sunday	$6.30
Monday	$3.65

Choose a STRATEGY

- Draw a Diagram or Picture
- Make a Model or Act It Out
- Make an Organized List
- Look for a Pattern
- Make a Table or Graph
- Guess and Check
- Work Backward
- Solve a Simpler Problem
- Write an Equation
- Use Logical Reasoning

11. WRITE Math Duane scored 2 goals during ice hockey practice. Robbie scored 2 more goals than Duane. Jack scored 1 less goal than Robbie. **Explain** how you can find the number of goals each boy scored.

12. Casey bought ice hockey supplies. She spent $5 and bought 3 items. Which items did she buy?

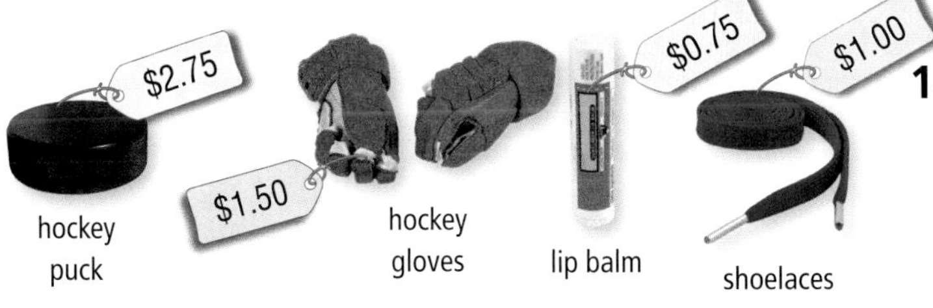

13. Pose a Problem Look back at Problem 9. Write a similar problem by changing the amount of money the girls had on Saturday.

14. Open-Ended Becca dropped her coins on the ice. The coins were four different sizes. There were more of the smallest coin than of any other coin. What coins could Becca have dropped? How much money would that be?

CHALLENGE YOURSELF

The Snow Cats are playing against the Polar Bears in ice hockey. Tickets for the game are $8.00 for adults and $5.00 for children.

15. Mr. Meyers buys 1 adult ticket. He pays with 3 bills and 6 coins. What bills and coins does he use?

16. Mr. Hall pays $31 for tickets. Explain how you can find the number of adult tickets and the number of children's tickets that he buys.

LESSON 4

Model Making Change

OBJECTIVE: Make change by counting on.

Quick Review

Jody has a $1 bill, 3 pennies, and 1 quarter. How much money does Jody have in all?

Vocabulary

change

Learn

PROBLEM Marla buys a toy kitten for $3.68. She pays with a $5 bill. How much change should she get?

Change is the money you get back if you have paid for an item with coins or bills that have a value greater than the cost of the item.

Activity 1 Make change from $5.00.

Materials ■ play money

Start with the cost of the item.
Count up with coins and bills to the amount Marla paid.

cost of item     

$3.68 → $3.69 → $3.70 → $3.75 → $4.00 → $5.00 ← amount paid

Then count the value of the bills and coins she received.

So, Marla should get $1.32 in change.

Activity 2 Make change from $10.00.

Alex buys a leash for his dog for $7.70. He pays with a $10 bill. What change should Alex get?

cost of item    

$7.70 → $7.80 → $7.90 → $8.00 → $9.00 → $10.00 ← amount paid

So, Alex should get $2.30 in change.

TEKS 3.1C determine the value of a collection of coins and bills. *also* 3.14A, 3.14D, 3.15A, 3.15B

Guided Practice

1. Count up from $5.18 to $6.00. Name the coins that are missing.

Find the amount of change. Use play money to help.

2. Brenda buys a comic book for $3.42. She pays with a $5 bill.
3. Ivy buys a sandwich for $5.25. She pays with a $10 bill.
4. TALK Math **Explain** how to count up from $2.09 to $5.00.

Independent Practice and Problem Solving

Find the amount of change. Use play money to help.

5. Pete buys a new dictionary for $4.59. He pays with a $5 bill.
6. Rose buys a carton of yogurt for $0.68. She pays with a $5 bill.
7. Omar buys a dog collar for $7.22. He pays with a $10 bill.
8. Morgan buys a stuffed animal for $3.85. She pays with a $10 bill.

USE DATA For 9–10, use the picture.

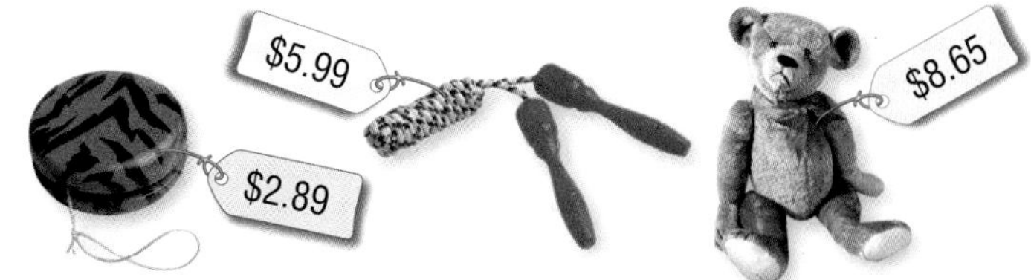

9. Ed buys a yo-yo. He pays with a $5 bill. How much change should he receive?
10. WRITE Math Mena buys a stuffed bear. She pays with a $10 bill. How much is Mena's change? What bills and coins does she get? **Explain** how you know.
11. **Reasoning** Jane bought a book. She paid with $3.00. She got 2 quarters, 2 dimes, and 3 pennies in change. What did her book cost?

Mixed Review and TAKS Prep

12. A year usually has 365 days. What is the value of the digit 3 in 365? (TEKS 3.1A, p. 10)
13. There are 328 boys and 182 girls at camp. Estimate the total number of campers. (TEKS 3.5B, p. 60)
14. **TAKS Prep** Kim buys lunch for $4.17. She pays with a $5 bill. How much change does she get? (Obj. 1)

    A $0.75 **C** $0.81
    B $0.78 **D** $0.83

Extra Practice on page 122, Set C

Extra Practice

Set A Write the amount. (pp. 110–113)

1.

2.

Find two equivalent sets for each. List the coins and bills.

3. 68¢
4. 80¢
5. $2.57
6. $1.14

Set B Use <, >, or = to compare the amounts of money. (pp. 114–115)

1.   

2.   

Which amount is greater?

3. $8.61 or $8.60
4. $2.25 or 8 quarters
5. $4.32 or $4.23
6. Marcus wants to buy a souvenir pin that costs $1.29. He has 6 quarters in his pocket. Does he have enough money to buy the pin?
7. Janelle and Fay emptied the coins in their banks. Janelle found $7.67 in change in hers. Fay counted $7.18 in her bank. Who had more money?

Set C Find the amount of change. Use play money to help. (pp. 120–121)

1. Sofia buys a sandwich for $3.42. She pays with a $5 bill.
2. Kim buys a fruit salad for $4.74. She pays with a $5 bill.
3. Grace buys a calculator for $8.37. She pays with a $10 bill.
4. Brett buys a puzzle book for $7.99. He pays with a $10 bill.
5. Tony buys a model car for $6.70. He pays with a $10 bill.
6. Matt buys a dog toy for $5.59. He pays with a $10 bill.

Technology
Use Harcourt Mega Math, The Number Games, *Buggy Bargains*, Levels A, B.

PRACTICE GAME

Money Mania

Make a Money Team!

2 players

Money Materials!

- 1 set of money cards for each team
- play money coins and bills
- 1 Comparing Chart for each player

place card here

place card here

Master the Game!

- Shuffle the cards and place them facedown in two equal piles.
- Players each pick up the top card from their pile. Do not show the card.
- Both players turn their cards over at the same time.
- The first player reads the money amount on his or her card aloud. Both players record that amount on their chart.
- Repeat for the second player's card.
- Write <, >, or = between the two amounts on your chart. You may use play money to help.
- The player whose card showed the greater amount keeps both cards in a separate pile. If the two amounts are equal, each player keeps his or her own card.
- The player with more cards at the end wins the game.

Chapter 5 Review/Test

Check Vocabulary and Concepts

Choose the best term from the box.

VOCABULARY
change
decimal point
dollar
equivalent

1. __?__ is the money you get back if you have paid for an item with a money amount greater than the cost of the item. (TEKS 3.1, p. 120)
2. A __?__ separates dollars and cents when you write money amounts. (TEKS 3.1C, p. 110)
3. Sets of money that have the same value are __?__. (TEKS 3.1C, p. 110)

Check Skills

Find two equivalent sets for each. List the coins and bills. (TEKS 3.1C, pp. 110–113)

4. 72¢
5. 43¢
6. $3.35

Use <, >, or = to compare the amounts of money. (TEKS 3.1C, pp. 114–115)

7. 
8. 

Which amount is greater? (TEKS 3.1C, pp. 114–115)

9. $7.18 or $8.14
10. $10.15 or ten $1 bills, 2 nickels

Find the amount of change. Use play money to help. (TEKS 3.1C, pp. 120–121)

11. 

Pay with a $5 bill

12. 

Pay with a $10 bill

Check Problem Solving

Solve. (TEKS 3.1C, pp. 116–119)

13. Ryan wants to buy a snow globe for $2.17. What are two ways to use coins and bills to show $2.17?
14. Ava has 4 $1 bills, 5 quarters, 6 dimes, and 2 nickels. She buys a book for $3.95. What are two ways Ava can make $3.95?
15. **WRITE Math** Yolanda bought a map for $1.50, sun block for $4.75, and a bottle of water for $2.25. Write two ways Yolanda can pay for all three items. **Explain** how you found your answers.

GO ONLINE **Technology** Use *Online Assessment.*

Enrich • Comparing Amounts

What's Your Name Worth?

There are 26 letters in the English alphabet. These 26 letters can be arranged to make many different words and names.

PUZZLES			
A	1¢	N	14¢
B	2¢	O	15¢
C	3¢	P	16¢
D	4¢	Q	17¢
E	5¢	R	18¢
F	6¢	S	19¢
G	7¢	T	20¢
H	8¢	U	21¢
I	9¢	V	22¢
J	10¢	W	23¢
K	11¢	X	24¢
L	12¢	Y	25¢
M	13¢	Z	26¢

From A to Z

The chart to the right lists each letter of the alphabet. The letter A is the first letter, so it has been assigned a value of 1¢. The letter Z is the last letter, so it has been assigned a value of 26¢.

What is the value of the name **MARK**?

Step 1	Find the letter **M**. Write down the value.
Step 2	Find the letter **A**. Write down the value.
Step 3	Find the letter **R**. Write down the value.
Step 4	Find the letter **K**. Write down the value.
Step 5	Add to find the total amount.

So, the value for **MARK** is 43¢.

M = 13 ¢
A = 1 ¢
R = 18 ¢
K = 11 ¢
TOTAL: = 43 ¢

Alphabet Adding

Use the chart to find the value of these names.

1. BARRY
2. NICK
3. ZOE
4. TEVA
5. SAM
6. DOUG
7. ABBIE
8. MICHAEL
9. JESSICA

Lots of Letters

WRITE Math ▸ What is the total value of your first and last names? **Explain** how you found your answer.

Unit Review/Test
Chapters 3–5

Multiple Choice

1. Kyle has 6 quarters, 5 dimes, and 2 nickels. Kyle bought a juice drink for $1.75. How much money does Kyle have left? (TAKS Obj. 1)

   A $0.20

   B $0.25

   C $0.30

   D $0.35

2. Meg has a collection of 89 marbles. Her parents gave her 15 more marbles. How many marbles does Meg have now? (TAKS Obj. 1)

   F 104

   G 94

   H 93

   J 74

3. On Monday, 447 people were at a basketball game. On Tuesday, 821 people were at a basketball game. About how many more people were at the basketball game on Tuesday than on Monday? (TAKS Obj. 1)

   A 200

   B 300

   C 400

   D 500

4. Which number sentence is in the same fact family as $3 + 2 = 5$? (TAKS Obj. 2)

   F $5 - 3 = 2$

   G $3 - 2 = 1$

   H $2 + 5 = 7$

   J $5 + 3 = 8$

5. What is the missing addend? (TAKS Obj. 1)

   $$17 + ■ = 35$$

   A 17

   B 18

   C 19

   D 20

6. Juan wants to read 300 books this year. So far, he has read 163 books. How many more books does Juan need to read? (TAKS Obj. 1)

   F 463

   G 263

   H 247

   J 137

GO ONLINE **Technology** Use *Online Assessment.*

7. Renee has the amount of money shown below. How much money does Renee have? (TAKS Obj. 1)

A $2.46 C $2.56

B $2.51 D $2.71

8. A new play opened at the theater last weekend. On the first night, 579 people saw the play. On the second night, 393 people saw the play. How many more people saw the play on the first night than on the second night? (TAKS Obj. 1)

F 286 H 186

G 226 J 126

9. Scott's family drove 195 miles from San Antonio to Houston to visit relatives. Then, they drove 240 miles from Houston to Dallas. How many miles did Scott's family drive in all? (TAKS Obj. 1)

A 335 miles

B 435 miles

C 535 miles

D Not here

Short Response

10. What is the sum of 189 and 28? (TAKS Obj. 1)

11. Shannon has 2 one-dollar bills, 5 quarters, 4 dimes, and 3 nickels. She needs $2.75 to buy a bag of pretzels. List two different ways Shannon can pay for the pretzels. (TAKS Obj. 1)

12. A scout troop collected 200 cans of green beans and 121 cans of corn. How many more cans of green beans did the troop collect than cans of corn? (TAKS Obj. 1)

Extended Response WRITE Math

13. Jaime and Kathy bought games at a sale. Jaime's game cost $8.05. Kathy's game cost $7.95. Who spent more money? **Explain** how you know. (TAKS Obj. 1)

14. Marcus had 3 apples and bought 4 more. Bryan had 4 apples and bought 3 more. Who has more apples? **Explain** how you know using a property of addition. (TAKS Obj. 1)

Texas

Problem Solving

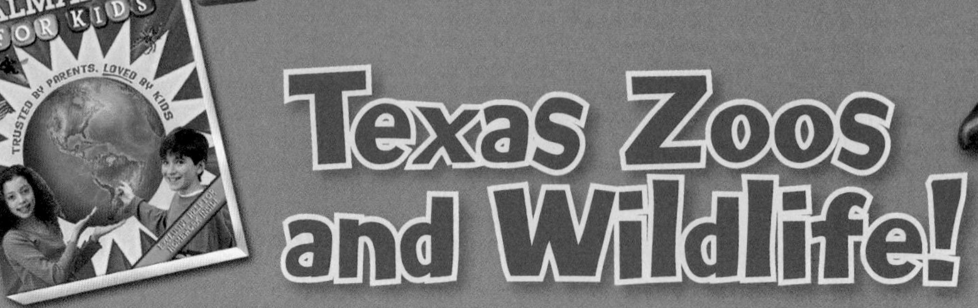

Texas Zoos and Wildlife!

Zoos in Texas

Do you enjoy going to the zoo? The Dallas Zoo has about 8,000 different animals. You can see and learn about Texas animals and animals from far away. Would you like to get closer to animals or go on a safari? You can do that at the Exotic Resort Zoo in Johnson City, Texas, and the Fossil Rim Wildlife Center in Glen Rose, Texas. These two centers allow animals to live in their natural habitats. Visitors can view the animals by driving through the preserve or by taking a guided tour.

FACT · ACTIVITY

Answer the questions.

1. The Dallas Zoo monorail takes people on a tour through six habitats. In the morning, 87 people rode the monorail, and in the afternoon 62 people rode the monorail. Estimate how many people rode the monorail all day.
2. There are 145 bird species and 70 mammal species at the Dallas Zoo. How many bird and mammal species does the zoo have in all?
3. The Exotic Resort Zoo has 137 acres of wildlife. The Dallas Zoo has 95 acres. How many more acres does the Exotic Resort Zoo have than the Dallas Zoo?
4. **WRITE Math** In the wild, ostriches can form groups of up to 50 members. Meerkats in the wild can be found in groups of up to 40. **Explain** a way to find how many more ostriches can be in a group than meerkats.

ALMANAC **Fact**

The Dallas Zoo opened in 1888 and was the first zoo in Texas. Today, it continues to be one of the largest zoos in Texas.

Children's Programs

The Dallas Zoo has a number of programs for children. To learn about the animals, the programs offer different activities.

Twilight Safaris are offered in the fall for children ages 8 to 13. At the Twilight Safari, children can enjoy the zoo at night.

If you like creepy, crawly bugs, then the Bug Club is for you. Six times a year, the Bug Club meets and learns about different insects. Most meetings include crafts, working at a science table, nature play, and a snack.

FACT·ACTIVITY

Answer the questions.

1. On Friday night, 28 children came to the Twilight Safari. On Saturday, 39 children came. How many children attended the Twilight Safari in all?
2. At the Bug Club, there are 11 children at the science table and 44 at nature play. How many more children are at nature play than at the science table?

For questions 3–4, use the table.

Souvenirs at the Dallas Zoo

Souvenir	Cost
Talking Turtle	$1.70
Elephant Ears	$0.85
Giraffe Game	$2.50
Penguin Patch	$0.32

3. Name four coins you could use to buy elephant ears.
4. You have 1 dollar bill and 3 quarters. Do you have enough money to buy a talking turtle? **Explain.**

UNIT

3 Time, Data, and Patterns

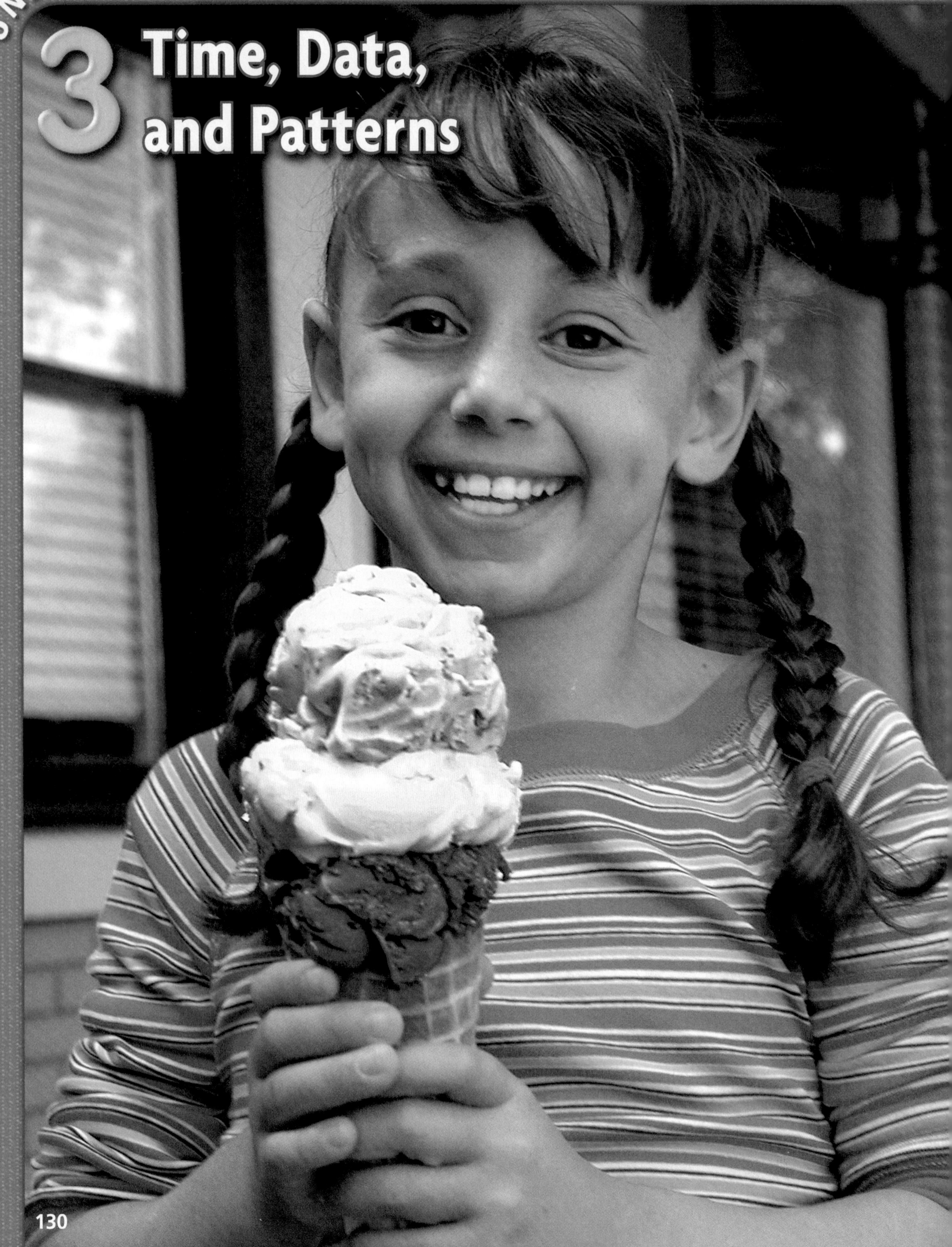

Math on Location

with **Texas Chapter Projects**

1

Maria checks that there will be enough gallons of each flavor to meet the needs for that day.

2

The time is recorded from cleaning the machine to filling the containers with the ice cream.

3

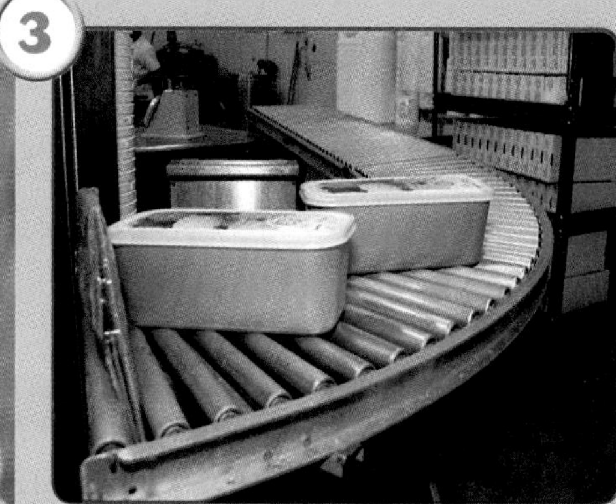

The cost of the ice cream is affected by the cost of the ingredients.

Vocabulary Power

TALK Math

What information is collected and talked about in the **Math on Location** photographs?

READ Math

REVIEW VOCABULARY You learned the words below when you learned about time and data. How do these words relate to **Math on Location**?

graph a picture that represents a mathematical relationship

hour a unit used to measure time; in one hour, the hour hand on a clock moves from one number to the next

WRITE Math

Copy and complete a Freyer Model like the one below. Use what you know about data to add more words.

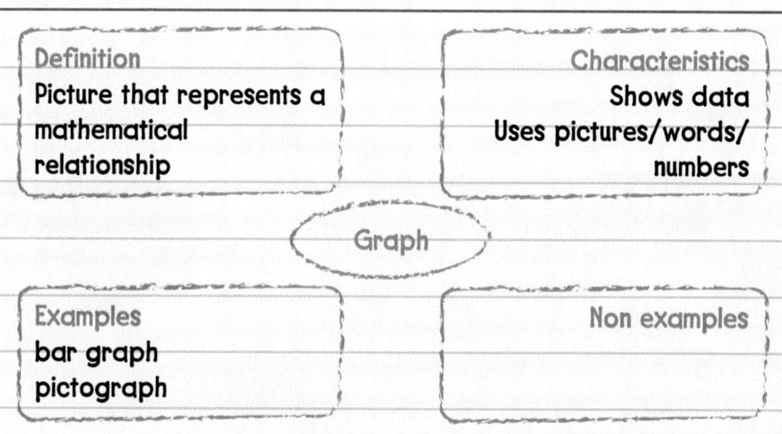

Definition
Picture that represents a mathematical relationship
Characteristics
Shows data
Uses pictures/words/numbers
Graph
Examples
bar graph
pictograph
Non examples

Chapter 6 Time

The Big Idea

Time is the duration of an event.

TEXAS FAST FACT

All space shuttle flights are controlled from NASA's Mission Control Center in Houston, Texas. During a mission, the control center is operated by about 20 flight controllers.

Investigate

Clocks come in many different shapes and sizes. Look at the four clocks. Write the time shown on each. Then tell what you might be doing at that time on a school day.

GO ONLINE Technology
Student pages are available in the Student eBook.

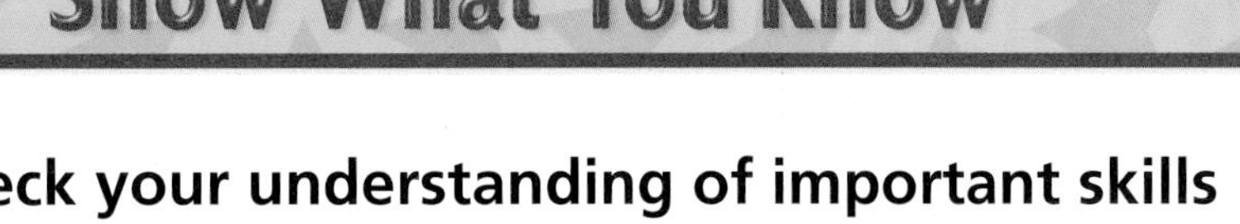

Show What You Know

Check your understanding of important skills needed for success in Chapter 6.

▶ Time to Hour

Write the time shown.

1. 

2. 

3. 

▶ Time to Half Hour

Write the time shown.

4. 

5. 

6. 

▶ Time to Quarter Hour

Write the time shown.

7. 

8. 

9. 

VOCABULARY POWER

CHAPTER VOCABULARY

A.M.
digital clock
hour
minute
P.M.
second
analog clock
half hour
midnight
noon
quarter hour
second hand

WARM-UP WORDS

quarter hour 15 minutes

half hour 30 minutes

noon 12:00 in the day

Understand Time

OBJECTIVE: Read, write, and tell time to the nearest half hour, quarter hour, and five minutes.

Quick Review

Roberto skip-counted to 60 by fives. What numbers did he count?

Vocabulary

hour **minute**
quarter hour **half hour**
analog clock **digital clock**

Learn

In one **hour**, the hour hand on a clock moves from one number to the next. In one **minute**, the minute hand on a clock moves from one mark to the next.

PROBLEM Carrie is visiting the Texas Seaport Museum in the port at Galveston, Texas. The movie about *Elissa*, a tall sailing ship, begins at 12:30. Where are the hour and minute hands when the clock shows 12:30?

An hour can be divided into 2 equal parts, or half hours. A **half hour** has 30 minutes.
Write: 12:30
Read: • twelve thirty
• thirty minutes after twelve
• half past twelve

So, at 12:30, the hour hand is between 12 and 1 and the minute hand is on the 6.

An hour can be divided into 4 equal parts, or quarter hours. A **quarter hour** has 15 minutes.
Write: 8:15
Read: • eight fifteen
• fifteen minutes after eight
• quarter past eight

An hour has 60 minutes.
It can be divided into 12 equal parts. Each part has 5 minutes.
Write: 10:05
Read: • five minutes after ten

• How does the hour hand move when the time changes from 8:00 to 9:00?

READ Math

An **analog clock** has a minute hand and an hour hand. Some clocks have second hands.

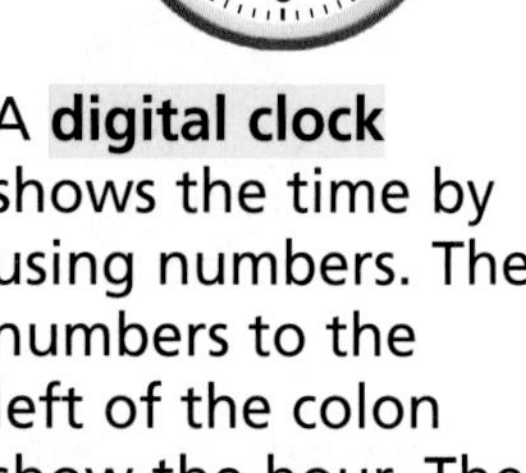

A **digital clock** shows the time by using numbers. The numbers to the left of the colon show the hour. The numbers to the right show the minutes after the hour.

  TEKS **3.12B** tell and write time shown on analog and digital clocks. *also* **3.14A, 3.15A, 3.15B**

Guided Practice

1. How would you count by fives to 35 minutes after an hour?

Write the time. Write two ways you can read the time.

2. 

3. 

4. 

5. 

6. **TALK Math** **Explain** how the minute hand moves when the time changes from 2:00 to 3:00.

Independent Practice and Problem Solving

Write the time. Write two ways you can read the time.

7. 

8. 

9. 

10. 

USE DATA For 11–12, use the museum information.

11. Mark saw the movie, *Elissa*. He arrived 5 minutes before it started. At what time did Mark arrive?

12. **WRITE Math** **What's the Error?** Colleen says the movie ends at 11:27. Explain Colleen's error.

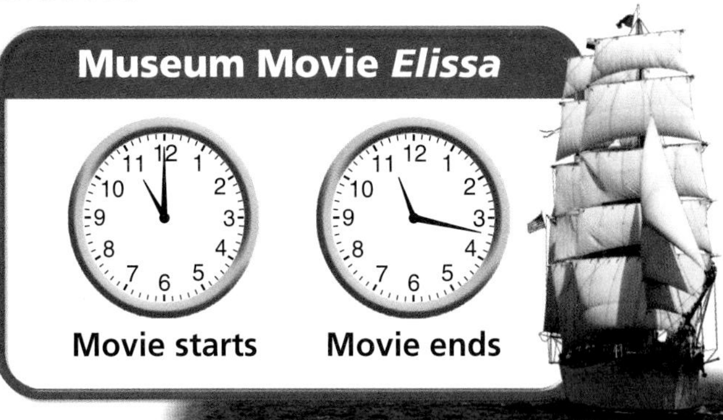

Mixed Review and TAKS Prep

13. Bryan has 3 quarters and 4 dimes. Tim has 4 quarters and 2 dimes. Who has more money? How much more? (TEKS 3.1C, p.114)

14. Tim has three hundred six marbles. Write this number in standard form. (TEKS 3.1A, p.10)

15. **TAKS Prep** Laura ate lunch at quarter to one. Which is one way to write the time? (Obj. 4)

A 12:15 **C** 1:15
B 12:45 **D** 1:45

Extra Practice on page 144, Set A

LESSON 2

Time to the Minute

OBJECTIVE: Read, write, and tell time to the nearest minute.

Quick Review

Dan got home from school at the time shown on the clock. At what time did Dan get home?

Learn

PROBLEM Groundhog Day is February 2. People say that if a groundhog named Punxsutawney Phil can see his shadow on that morning, winter will last another 6 weeks. At what time did the groundhog see his shadow?

ONE WAY

Count forward by fives and ones.

Write: 7:31

Read: • thirty-one minutes after seven
• seven thirty-one

ANOTHER WAY

Count back by fives and ones.

Write: 7:31

Read: • twenty-nine minutes before eight
• seven thirty-one

So, the groundhog saw his shadow at 7:31.

More Examples

A Minutes after the hour

Write: 3:26

Read: • three twenty-six
• twenty-six minutes after three

B Minutes before the hour

Write: 8:47

Read: • eight forty-seven
• thirteen minutes before nine

TEKS 3.12B tell and write time shown on analog and digital clocks. *also* 3.14A, 3.15A, 3.15B

Guided Practice

1. How would you count to find the time shown on the clock?

Write the time. Write one way you can read the time.

2. 

3. 

4. 

5. 

6. **TALK Math** **Explain** how you know when to stop counting by fives and start counting by ones when counting minutes after an hour.

Independent Practice and Problem Solving

Write the time. Write one way you can read the time.

7. 

8. 

9. 

10. 

USE DATA For 11–12, use the clocks.

11. **What if** Phil saw his shadow 5 minutes later in 2007 than in 2003? What time would this be?

12. How many minutes later did Phil see his shadow in 2003 than in 2002?

13. **WRITE Math** **Explain** where the hands on the clock are pointing at four forty-five.

Punxsutawney Phil Saw His Shadow

2002 2003

Mixed Review and TAKS Prep

14. Ann has 2 quarters and 1 nickel. Tania has 5 dimes and 3 nickels. How much does each have? (TEKS 3.1.C, p. 112)

15. Tom had a piece of string 36 inches long. He used 18 inches of it. How many inches of string are left? (TEKS 3.3.B, p. 88)

16. **TAKS Prep** What time is shown on this clock? (Obj. 4)

A 4:20

B 4:45

C 9:20

D 9:23

CD ROM **Technology**
Use Harcourt Mega Math, Country Countdown, *Clock-a-Doodle-Doo*, Level J.

Extra Practice on page 144, Set B

Minutes and Seconds

OBJECTIVE: Read, write, and tell time on analog and digital clocks to the nearest minute and second.

Quick Review

Ellen's soccer game ended at ten minutes before five. Write that time in numbers.

Vocabulary

second

Learn

PROBLEM Marathon race times are measured in hours, minutes, and seconds. Paul Tergat set a world record for a marathon in 2003. If he finished the race at 55 seconds after 10:04 A.M., how would that time be shown on a clock?

▲ Paul Tergat set the world record by running a marathon in 2 hours, 4 minutes, 55 seconds.

Example Time on an analog clock

A **second** is a very short time. It takes about one second to take a step. Some clocks have second hands. To write a time including seconds, write hours: minutes: seconds.

Seconds: 55 Minutes: 4 Hours: 10

Write: 10:04:55
Read: 10:04 and 55 seconds

So, the time shown on the clock is 10:04:55.

More Examples Time on a digital clock

A 

4:11 and 6 seconds

B 8:15:02

8:15 and 2 seconds

- Where will the second hand be when an analog clock shows 2:15:00?

Math Idea
60 seconds = 1 minute
60 minutes = 1 hour

Guided Practice

1. How many seconds after 11:15 does this clock show?

TEKS 3.12B tell and write time shown on analog and digital clocks. *also* **3.14A, 3.15A, 3.15B**

Write the time. Then write how you would read the time.

✓ 2. 

3. 

✓ 4. 

5. 

6. **TALK Math** **Explain** how to tell where the second hand is on an analog clock for 2:30:25.

Independent Practice and Problem Solving

For 7–8, write the time. Then write how you would read the time.

7. 

8. 

For 9–10, write the letter of the clock that shows the time.

9. 6:20:45

10. 6:15:20

a. 

b. 

11. James ran a relay race. The race began at 10:00 A.M. He finished the race at the time shown on the clock. At what time did he finish the race?

12. Lilly played her favorite song on the piano. It took 2 minutes and 30 seconds to play. How many seconds did it take her to play the song?

13. **WRITE Math** Where will the hands of a clock be when the time is 4:35:55? **Explain.**

Mixed Review and TAKS Prep

14. What digit is in the thousands place of 374,916? (TEKS 3.1.A, p. 16)

15. Jim counted 26 marbles. Then he found more. He counted 47 in all. How many marbles did Jim find? (TEKS 3.3.B, p. 58)

16. **TAKS Prep** Which shows one thirty and 5 seconds? (Obj. 4)

A 1:05:30 **C** 1:30:50

B 1:30:05 **D** 1:50:30

Extra Practice on page 144, Set C

A.M. and P.M.

OBJECTIVE: Read, write, and tell time in the A.M. and P.M.

Quick Review

Tom sees this time on his clock. What time is it?

Vocabulary

midnight **A.M.**
noon **P.M.**

Learn

PROBLEM Kendra's family is going hiking tomorrow at 8:00. They are going in the morning, not in the evening. How should Kendra write the time?

12:00 A.M. Midnight | 6:00 A.M. | 12:00 P.M. Noon | 6:00 P.M. | 12:00 A.M. Midnight

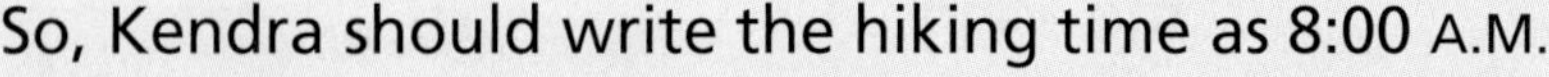

A time line can help you understand the hours in a day.

Midnight is 12:00 at night.	**Noon** is 12:00 during the day.
For times from midnight to noon, write **A.M.** Midnight is 12:00 A.M.	For times from noon to midnight, write **P.M.** Noon is 12:00 P.M.
You wake up, eat breakfast, and get ready for school in the a.m. hours.	You come home from school, eat dinner, and go to bed in the p.m. hours.

So, Kendra should write the hiking time as 8:00 A.M.

- How do you write the time when it is one minute after noon?

Guided Practice

1. Name something you do in the A.M. hours. Name something you do in the P.M. hours.

Write the time for each activity. Use A.M. or P.M.

✓ 2. play soccer

3. go shopping

✓ 4. look up at the stars

5. put on pajamas

6. TALK Math **Explain** how you decide whether to use A.M. or P.M. when you write the time.

TEKS 3.12B tell and write time shown on analog and digital clocks. *also* 3.14A, 3.15A, 3.15B

Independent Practice and Problem Solving

Write the time for each activity. Use A.M. or P.M.

7. eat breakfast

8. have math class

9. play outside

10. watch a sunset

Write the time by using numbers. Use A.M. or P.M.

11. quarter after 8 in the morning

12. 5 minutes before 9 at night

13. half past midnight

14. 20 minutes before noon

15. ***FAST FACT*** Daylight Saving Time begins on the second Sunday in March at 2:00 in the morning. Write the time, and use A.M. or P.M.

USE DATA For 16–18, use the table.

16. Ken wants to go to the tile art class. Write the time for the class, using A.M. or P.M.

17. Brad took the earliest classes in the morning and afternoon. Which classes did he take?

18. **WRITE Math** Mary eats lunch at noon. What classes are before Mary's lunch? **Explain** how you know.

Morning and Afternoon Craft Classes	
Scrapbooking	8:50
Tile Art	10:30
Stamp a Card	1:00
Make Soap	2:45

Mixed Review and TAKS Prep

19. Use $<$, $>$, or $=$ to make this number sentence true.

$14 - 2 \bigcirc 10 + 2$ (TEKS 3.1B, p. 30)

20. Carlos had 17 markers. He found 4 more. Then he gave Louis 9 markers. How many does Carlos have now? (TEKS 3.3B, p. 100)

21. **TAKS Prep** At which of the times shown are most third graders asleep? (Obj. 4)

A 8 A.M.
B 12:00 P.M.
C 7:00 P.M.
D 12:00 A.M.

Problem Solving Workshop
Skill: Too Much/Too Little Information

OBJECTIVE: Solve problems by using the skill *too much/too little information.*

Read to Understand
Plan
Solve
Check

PROBLEM Neil Armstrong is a famous astronaut. On July 20, 1969, at 10:56 P.M., he became the first man to walk on the moon. He walked on the moon for 2 hours and 32 minutes. Where should the clock hands be to show the time Neil Armstrong walked on the moon?

To solve a problem, first decide what information is needed. Sometimes too much information is given. Sometimes too little information is given.

Information	Is it needed?
Neil Armstrong is a famous astronaut.	no
On July 20, 1969, at 10:56 P.M. he became the first man to walk on the moon.	yes
He walked on the surface of the moon for 2 hours and 32 minutes.	no

Use the needed information to solve the problem.

Since the time was 10:56, the hour hand should be between 10 and 11, but closer to 11.

56 minutes after an hour is the same as 4 minutes before the next hour.

So, Neil Armstrong returned to the lunar module at 1:28 A.M.

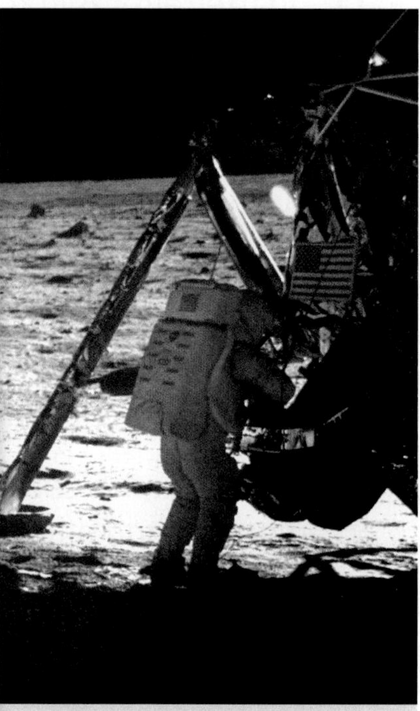

▲ **The astronauts set the United States flag on the moon.**

Think and Discuss

Tell whether there is too much or too little information. Solve if there is enough information.

a. Ella began working on her science project about the moon at 9:00 A.M. She has lunch 2 hours later. Did Ella work on her project in the morning or evening?

b. Matt watched a movie about the moon. It began at 3:45 P.M. How long was the movie?

TEKS 3.12B tell and write time shown on analog and digital clocks. *also* **3.14A, 3.14C, 3.15A, 3.15B**

Guided Problem Solving

Tell whether there is too much or too little information. Solve if there is enough information.

1. The lunar module landed on the moon at 4:18 P.M. The landing site was called Tranquility Base. At what time did the astronauts begin their space flight to the moon?
   a. What is the question?
   b. What information do you need to answer the question?
   c. Is there too much information? If so, what?
   d. Is there too little information? If so, what more is needed?
   e. Can you solve the problem? If so, then solve it.

2. **What if** the Apollo 11 spacecraft began its orbit around the moon at 1:26 P.M. on July 19? Did it begin orbiting the moon in the morning or in the afternoon?

3. The first manned space flight to the moon began at 9:32 A.M. on July 16, 1969. How many years before July 16, 2008 was that?

Mixed Applications

For 4–5, tell whether there is too much or too little information. Solve if there is enough information.

4. Donna has 6 coins in her pocket. She got the coins from her piggy bank. Does Donna have enough money to buy a popsicle that costs 25¢?

5. Justin wants to buy a book. He arrives at the bookstore at 8:45 A.M. How much did Justin pay for his book?

6. WRITE Math Tina has a box of 43 crayons. After working on her art project, 6 crayons were broken. How many crayons were not broken? **Explain** how you know.

7. Nora has a $5 bill, two $1 bills, 5 quarters, and 6 dimes. She wants to buy a puzzle book that costs $6.95. How much money will Nora have left after she buys the book?

Extra Practice

Set A **Write the time. Write two ways you can read the time.** (pp. 134–135)

1. 

2. 
3. 
4. 

Set B **Write the time. Write one way you can read the time.** (pp. 136–137)

1. 

2. 
3. 
4. 

Set C **Write the time. Then write how you would read the time.** (pp. 138–139)

1. 

2. 
3. 

For 4–6, write the letter of the clock that shows the time.

4. 3:40:15
5. 3:20:10
6. 8:21:15

A. 
B. 
C. 

Set D **Write the time for each activity. Use A.M. or P.M.** (pp. 140–141)

1. 

science class
2. 
baseball game
3. 
eat breakfast
4. 
get ready for bed

CD ROM
Technology
Use Harcourt Mega Math, Country Countdown, *Clock-a-Doodle-Doo*, Level J.

PRACTICE GAME Matching Time

On Your Mark!
2 players

Get Set!
- 1 set of time cards for each player

MATCHING TIME	MATCHING TIME	MATCHING TIME	MATCHING TIME	MATCHING TIME
MATCHING TIME	MATCHING TIME	MATCHING TIME	MATCHING TIME	MATCHING TIME
MATCHING TIME	MATCHING TIME	MATCHING TIME	MATCHING TIME	MATCHING TIME
MATCHING TIME	MATCHING TIME	MATCHING TIME	MATCHING TIME	MATCHING TIME

Match!

- Players shuffle the time cards and place them face down on the gameboard, covering each square.
- Players take turns choosing a card and turning it face up on the gameboard, and reading the time aloud.
- The player chooses a second card, turns it face up, and reads the time aloud.
- If the times match on the cards, the player removes the 2 cards and places them in a collection pile.
- If the times do not match, the cards are turned back over and play passes to the next player.
- Play continues until all cards have been collected. The player with more cards in his or her collection pile at the end of the game wins.

Chapter 6 Review/Test

Check Vocabulary and Concepts

Choose the best term from the box.

VOCABULARY
analog clock
digital clock
half hour
second

1. The amount of time it takes to clap your hands once is a __?__. (TEKS 3.12B, p. 138)
2. A __?__ is the same as thirty minutes. (TEKS 3.12B, p. 134)
3. The clock that has a minute hand and hour hand is an __?__. (TEKS 3.12B, p. 134)

Check Skills

Write the time. Write one way you can read the time. (TEKS 3.12B, pp. 134–135, 136–137)

4. 

5. 

6. 

7. 

Write the time another way. (TEKS 3.12B, pp. 136–137)

8. 25 minutes after two
9. 40 minutes after 9
10. half past five

For 11–13, write the letter of the clock that shows the time. (TEKS 3.12B, pp. 138–139)

11. 3:15:35
12. 3:25:50
13. 8:40:06

a. 

b.

c. 

Write the time by using numbers. Use A.M. or P.M. (TEKS 3.12B, pp. 140–141)

14. quarter after 7 in the morning
15. 10 minutes before 9 at night
16. half past noon
17. half past midnight

Check Problem Solving

Solve if there is enough information. (TEKS 3.12B, 3.14B, pp. 142–143)

18. Melanie's soccer game starts at 9:30 A.M. She played in the game for 10 minutes and scored one goal. What was her team's score?
19. Mr. Travis ordered pizza at 6:15 P.M. His pizza will be delivered in 30 minutes. At what time will Mr. Travis receive his pizza?
20. WRITE Math Ava's favorite book is 28 pages long. She has read 12 pages. How many pages are left for Ava to read? **Explain** how you know.

GO ONLINE **Technology** Use *Online Assessment.*

Enrich • Time Zones

Telephone Time

There are four time zones in the continental United States. There is a difference of one hour between each time zone.

Dial the Phone

Beth lives in San Francisco and her sister Shannon lives in Denver. If Beth calls Shannon when it is 9 A.M. in San Francisco, what time will it be in Denver?

Step 1	Find San Francisco on the map. San Francisco is in the Pacific time zone.
Step 2	Find Denver on the map. Denver is in the Mountain time zone.
Step 3	Find the difference in hours between the Pacific and Mountain time zones. It is one hour later in the Mountain time zone than in the Pacific time zone.

So, when it is 9 A.M. in San Francisco, it will be 10 A.M. in Denver.

It's Ringing!

Use the map to solve.

1. Beth's cousin Randy lives in Dallas. If Beth calls him when it is 3:00 P.M. in San Francisco, what time will it be in Dallas?
2. Beth calls her grandmother at 8:00 A.M. each Sunday. Beth's grandmother lives in Miami. What time is it in Miami when Beth calls?
3. Beth calls her brother Mike when it is 4:00 P.M. in Chicago. What time is it in San Francisco when Beth calls her brother?
4. Beth's parents live in Seattle. If they call Beth at 7:00 P.M. once a week, what time is it in San Francisco?

Hang Up

WRITE Math ▸ Beth's brother Lewis lives in Boston. If Lewis calls Beth at 9:00 P.M. Eastern time, what time will it be in San Francisco? **Explain** how you know.

Getting Ready for the TAKS

Chapters 1–6

Number, Operation, and Quantitative Reasoning (TAKS Obj. 1)

1. The deepest part of the Gulf of Mexico is Sigsbee Deep. It is 12,714 feet deep. What is the value of the digit 2 in 12,714?

   A 20 **C** 2,000

   B 200 **D** 20,000

2. Lucy's book has 39 pages. Angela's book has 48 pages. How many more pages are in Angela's book?

   F 6 **H** 8

   G 7 **J** Not here

Understand the problem.

See item 3. What is the question? What information do you need to answer the question? Write down all of the numbers in the problem and solve.

3. **WRITE Math** Joe ran 3 miles on Monday and 4 miles on Friday. Ed ran 6 miles on Monday and 2 miles on Friday. Write a number sentence to show who ran the greater number of miles. **Explain.**

Patterns, Relationships, and Algebraic Thinking (TAKS Obj. 2)

4. Which number completes the fact family?

   $6 + \blacksquare = 13$ $\blacksquare + 6 = 13$

   $13 - 6 = \blacksquare$ $13 - \blacksquare = 6$

   A 6

   B 7

   C 13

   D 19

5. How many wheels are on 6 bicycles?

Bicycles	1	2	3	4	5	6
Wheels	2	4	6	8	10	■

   F 11

   G 12

   H 14

   J 18

6. **WRITE Math** Describe the pattern unit and draw the next two shapes. **Explain** how to continue the pattern.

Measurement (TAKS Obj. 4)

7. What is the correct temperature?

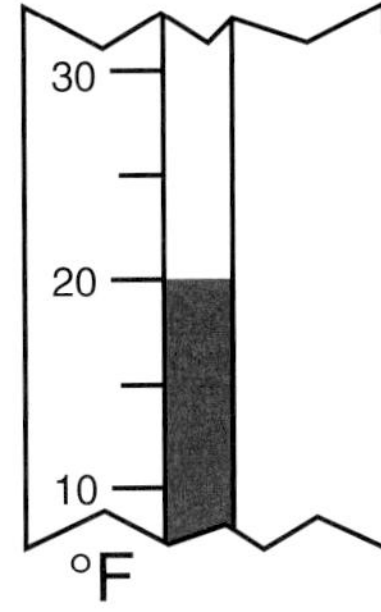

A 20°F C 30°F

B 25°F D 35°F

8. The clock shows the time Michael eats dinner. At what time does he eat?

F 5:00

G 5:30

H 6:25

J 6:30

9. WRITE Math **Explain** where the hands on the clock will be when the time is 9:25:15.

Probability and Statistics (TAKS Obj. 5)

10. How many more students chose orange juice than apple juice?

Juices We Like	
Apple	🍎 🍎 🍎
Orange	🍎 🍎 🍎 🍎 🍎
Grape	🍎 🍎
Key: Each 🍎 = 1 student.	

A 1

B 2

C 3

D 4

11. Which pizza topping did the most students choose?

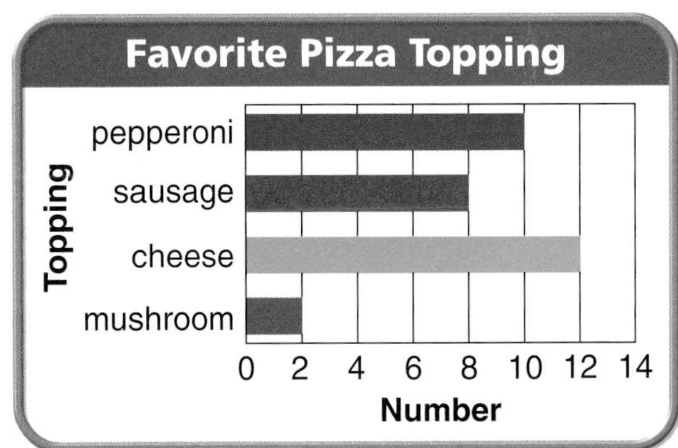

F Pepperoni H Cheese

G Sausage J Mushroom

12. WRITE Math A bag has 4 green tiles, 3 yellow tiles, and 7 red tiles. Which color are you most likely to pull? **Explain** how you know.

CHAPTER

7 Data and Graphs

The Big Idea Data can be collected, analyzed, and displayed in various graphical forms.

TEXAS FAST FACT

El Paso, Texas, usually gets only about 5 inches of snow each year. But in December 1987, a snowstorm dropped over 22 inches of snow on El Paso in a single day!

Investigate

The pictograph shows the most snowfall in each month for Wichita Falls, Texas. Show another way you can display the data.

Greatest Snowfalls in Wichita Falls, Texas	
November	❄ ❄ ❄ ½❄
December	❄ ❄ ❄ ❄
January	❄ ❄ ❄ ❄ ❄ ❄
February	❄ ❄ ❄ ❄ ❄ ❄
March	❄ ❄ ❄ ❄ ❄ ½❄
Key: Each ❄ = 2 inches.	

Technology
Student pages are available in the Student eBook.

Show What You Know

Check your understanding of important skills needed for success in Chapter 7.

▶ Read a Tally Table

For 1–3, use the tally table.

Which pet do you have?	
Dog	𝍸 𝍸 IIII
Cat	𝍸 𝍸 II
Bird	IIII
Fish	𝍸 III

1. How many students have a dog?
2. How many students have fish?
3. How many students answered the question?

▶ Column Addition

Find the sum.

4. $\begin{array}{r} 3 \\ 2 \\ 5 \\ +7 \\ \hline \end{array}$ **5.** $\begin{array}{r} 9 \\ 3 \\ 1 \\ +4 \\ \hline \end{array}$ **6.** $\begin{array}{r} 6 \\ 2 \\ 8 \\ +3 \\ \hline \end{array}$ **7.** $\begin{array}{r} 8 \\ 1 \\ 4 \\ +6 \\ \hline \end{array}$ **8.** $\begin{array}{r} 7 \\ 9 \\ 2 \\ +7 \\ \hline \end{array}$

▶ Read a Chart

For 9–11, use the bar graph.

9. How many students ate a sandwich?
10. Which food did most students eat?
11. How many students ate lunch?

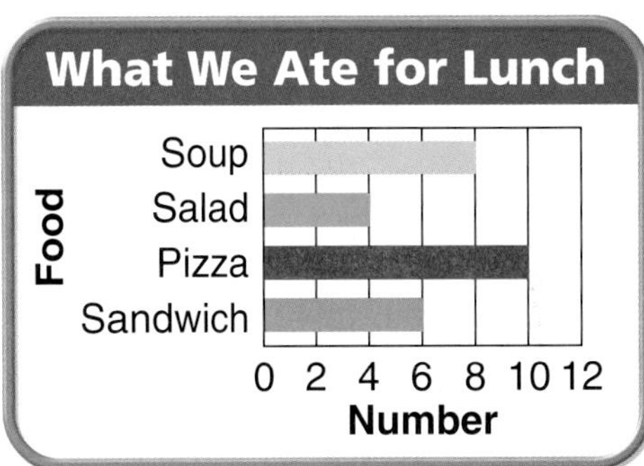

VOCABULARY POWER

CHAPTER VOCABULARY

bar graph
classify
data
frequency table
horizontal bar graph
key
pictograph
results
scale
survey
tally table
vertical bar graph

WARM-UP WORDS

data Information that is collected about people or things

tally table A table that uses tally marks to record data

frequency table A table that uses numbers to record data

Collect Data

OBJECTIVE: Collect, organize, and record data in tally tables and frequency tables.

Quick Review

Write numbers for the tally marks.

1. 卌 | **2.** |||
3. |||| **4.** 卌
5. 卌 |||

Vocabulary

data **tally table**
frequency table

Learn

Data is information that is collected about people or things.

PROBLEM The students in Moira's class voted for their favorite ice cream flavors. Moira showed the results two ways. Which flavor got the greatest number of votes? Which flavor got the least number of votes?

You can record data in a **tally table** by making tally marks as you gather data.

Favorite Ice Cream	
Flavor	**Tally**
Rocky Road	卌 |
Vanilla	卌 ||
Chocolate	卌 |||
Strawberry	||||

You can show the number of tally marks in a **frequency table** to make the data easier to read.

Favorite Ice Cream	
Flavor	**Number**
Rocky Road	6
Vanilla	7
Chocolate	8
Strawberry	4

The number of votes from greatest to least is 8, 7, 6, and 4.

So, chocolate got the greatest number of votes.
Strawberry got the least number of votes.

Activity **Materials** ■ tally table

Collect data about your classmates' favorite ice cream flavors. Organize the data in a tally table. Then make a frequency table.

Favorite Ice Cream
Flavor | Tally

Favorite Ice Cream
Flavor | Number

Step 1

Make a tally table. Write the title and headings. List the possible flavors. Make a tally mark for each vote.

Step 2

Count the number of tally marks. Record the numbers in a frequency table.

TEKS 3.13A collect, organize, record, and display data in pictographs and bar graphs where each picture or cell might represent more than one piece of data. *also* **3.14A, 3.14D, 3.15A, 3.15B**

Guided Practice

1. What number would you write in a frequency table to show 𝍸 𝍸 |||?

For 2–3, use the Favorite Sport table.

2. How many students in all voted for soccer and baseball?
3. How many students voted in all?
4. **TALK Math** **Explain** why a frequency table can be a good way to show data.

Favorite Sport	
Sport	**Tally**
Basketball	𝍸 ||
Soccer	𝍸 ||||
Baseball	𝍸 |

Independent Practice and Problem Solving

For 5–6, use the Shirt Color list.

5. Kelly made this list of the shirt colors the students in her class were wearing. Make a tally table and a frequency table to organize her data.
6. How many more students are wearing white or blue shirts than red or green shirts?

Shirt Color

Jen	white	Kim	blue
Patty	red	Lee	red
Matt	blue	Pam	white
Jared	white	Brad	red
Carl	green	Jake	blue

For 7–8, use the Favorite Juice table.

7. How many students voted for their favorite juice in this survey?
8. **What if** 13 more students voted for orange juice? How would the table change?
9. **WRITE Math** How are a tally table and a frequency table alike? How are they different?

Favorite Juice	
Flavor	**Number**
Grape	16
Orange	4
Berry	5
Apple	6

Mixed Review and TAKS Prep

10. Julie had a 45-inch piece of ribbon. She cut 9 inches off each end. How many inches of ribbon are left? (TEKS 3.3B, p. 88)
11. What fraction of this figure is shaded? (Grade 2 TEKS 2.2A)

12. **TAKS Prep** Jen made a tally table to record her friends' votes for their favorite pet. Her chart shows 𝍸 𝍸 || next to dog. How many voted for dogs? (Obj. 5)

A 7 **B** 10 **C** 12 **D** 15

Extra Practice on page 170, Set A

LESSON 2

Read a Pictograph

OBJECTIVE: Read and interpret data in a pictograph.

Quick Review

Use the tally table.

Favorite Pet	
Pet	**Tally**
Dog	卌 卌 |
Cat	卌 ||||
Bird	||||

How many people voted for cat?

Vocabulary

pictograph **key**

Learn

A **pictograph** uses pictures to show information.

PROBLEM Areas that are part of the national park system are good places to vacation and to learn about plants and animals. The pictograph shows the number of those areas in some states. How many are there in Pennsylvania?

Number of National Parks	
Massachusetts	🌲🌲🌲🌲🌲
Michigan	🌲 (half 🌲)
New Jersey	🌲🌲 (half 🌲)
New York	🌲🌲🌲🌲🌲🌲🌲
Pennsylvania	🌲🌲🌲🌲🌲🌲
Key: Each 🌲 = 4 national parks.	

Math Idea
In this graph, 🌲 = 4 parks, so (half 🌲) = 2 parks.

The title tells that the pictograph is about national parks.

Each row has a label that tells the name of a state.

The **key** tells that each picture stands for 4 national parks.

To find the number of national parks in Pennsylvania, count the number of 🌲 by fours.

$4 + 4 + 4 + 4 + 4 + 4 = 24$

So, there are 24 national parks in Pennsylvania.

- Which state in the pictograph has the most national parks? How many parks does it have?
- Explain how many national parks are in New Jersey.

▲ Yellowstone National Park, in Wyoming, was the first named national park in the United States.

Guided Practice

1. How many national parks are in Massachusetts?

$4 + 4 + 4 + 4 + 4 = ■$

For 2–3, use the National Parks pictograph on page 154.

2. Which state in the pictograph has the fewest national parks?

3. How many more national parks are there in Pennsylvania than in Massachusetts?

4. TALK Math Explain why you need a key to read a pictograph.

Independent Practice and Problem Solving

For 5–7, use the National Parks pictograph at the right.

5. Kyle has visited every national park in Arizona. How many parks has he visited?

6. Which two states combined have the same number of national parks as Arizona?

7. Pose a Problem Look back at problem 5. Write a similar problem by changing the name of the state.

Number of National Parks	
Arizona	🌲🌲🌲🌲🌲
Colorado	🌲🌲🌲
Kansas	🌲🌲
Oregon	🌲🌲
Key: Each 🌲 = 5 National Parks.	

For 8–10, use the Favorite Park Activity pictograph.

8. How many people in all voted?

9. How many more people voted for hiking and fishing than for biking?

10. WRITE Math What if 25 people had voted for swimming? How would you show this in the pictograph?

Favorite Park Activity	
Biking	☼ ☼ ☼ ◐
Hiking	☼ ☼ ☼ ☼
Boating	☼ ☼ ☼
Fishing	☼ ◐
Key: Each ☼ = 10 Votes.	

Mixed Review and TAKS Prep

11. Find the missing addend.
$19 + \blacksquare = 32$ (TEKS 3.3B, p. 58)

12. Wendy bought a book for $7.59. She paid with a $10 bill. How much change did she receive? (TEKS 3.3B, p. 120)

13. TAKS Prep Lester made a pictograph to show how many books he owns. This is his key.
Each 📕 = 10 books.
How many books does 📕 📕 📕 ▯ stand for? (Obj. 5)

A 7 **B** 8 **C** 35 **D** 40

Extra Practice on page 170, Set B

Problem Solving Workshop
Strategy: Make a Graph

OBJECTIVE: Solve problems by using the strategy *make a graph*.

Learn the Strategy

There are many ways to show data. Some ways are lists, tables, and graphs.

You can show the data in this table in a pictograph.

Students' Pets	
Type of Pet	**Number**
Cat	9
Dog	12
Fish	4
Hamster	3

Step 1

Write the title at the top of the graph. Write a label for each row.

Students' Pets	
Cat	
Dog	
Fish	
Hamster	

Step 2

Look at the numbers. Choose a key that tells how many each picture represents.

Write the key at the bottom of the graph.

Students' Pets	
Cat	
Dog	
Fish	
Hamster	
Key: Each = 2 students.	

Step 3

Draw the correct number of pictures for each type of pet.

Students' Pets	
Cat	
Dog	
Fish	
Hamster	
Key: Each = 2 students.	

TALK Math

What do the pictures in the row for Dog in the pictograph tell you?

Remember

A half picture has half the value of a whole picture.
= 2 students
= 1 student

TEKS 3.13A collect, organize, record, and display data in pictographs and bar graphs where each picture or cell might represent more than one piece of data. *also* **3.13B, 3.14A, 3.14B, 3.14C, 3.15A, 3.15B, 3.16B**

Read to Understand
Plan
Solve
Check

Use the Strategy

PROBLEM Mrs. Keller asked all the third grade students where they would like to go for a field trip. Eight students voted for the art museum, 26 students voted for the science center, 28 students voted for the aquarium, and 14 students voted for the zoo. What is one way the votes could be shown in a graph?

Read to Understand

- **Is there any information you will not use? If so, what?**

Plan

- **What graphic aid could help you solve the problem?**
- **What strategy can you use?**
  You can make a pictograph.

Solve

- **How can you use the strategy to solve the problem?**
  Make a pictograph.

  Choose a title.
  Write a label for each row.
  Choose a key to tell how many votes each picture stands for.
  Decide how many pictures should be placed next to each field trip choice.
  Show the correct number of pictures beside each field trip choice.

Field Trip Choices

Art museum	☺☺
Science center	☺☺☺☺☺☺ half ☺
Aquarium	☺☺☺☺☺☺☺
Zoo	☺☺☺ half ☺

Key: Each ☺ = 4 votes.

Check

- **How do you know whether each row has the correct number of pictures? Give an example.**
- **Could you have used another number for the key? Explain.**

Guided Problem Solving

Read to Understand
Plan
Solve
Check

1. The science center gift shop sold 20 stuffed animals, 30 books, 15 stickers, and 10 T-shirts. How can you display the data?

   Copy the pictograph. Complete it by using the data. In your key, let each 🛍 stand for 10 items.

2. **What if** the gift shop sold 25 posters? Explain how you would display that on the pictograph.

3. Which item at the gift shop was bought the most? The least?

Science Center Gift Shop	
Stuffed Animals	🛍 🛍

Key: Each 🛍 = 10 items.

Problem Solving Strategy Practice

Make a pictograph to solve.

4. Some students voted for their favorite science center exhibit. The results are in the table at the right. Make a pictograph for the data. Let each picture stand for 3 students.

5. **Reasoning** If the key is changed so that each picture stands for 6 students, how many pictures should be used for the number of students who voted for the nature exhibit?

6. WRITE Math **Explain** how you knew how many pictures to draw for the light and sound exhibit.

Favorite Exhibit	
Nature	𝍸 ||||
Solar system	𝍸 |
Light and sound	𝍸 𝍸 𝍸
Human body	𝍸 𝍸 ||

Mixed Strategy Practice

For 7–10, use the information about the constellations.

7. Make a pictograph to show the number of stars in each constellation. Which constellation has the fewest stars?

8. How many more stars are in Orion than in Ursa Minor? Write a number sentence that shows your answer.

9. **Pose a Problem** Look back at problem 8. Write a similar problem about Ursa Major and Ursa Minor.

10. WRITE Math **What's the Error?** Gina says that Ursa Minor has 2 fewer stars than Cassiopeia. What error did Gina make? **Explain.**

11. **Open-Ended** After the constellation show, Rick bought a poster for $1.45. He gave the clerk $2.00. What are three combinations of coins Rick could have received as change?

Choose a STRATEGY

- Draw a Diagram or Picture
- Make a Model or Act It Out
- Make an Organized List
- Look for a Pattern
- Make a Table or Graph
- Guess and Check
- Work Backward
- Solve a Simpler Problem
- Write a Number Sentence
- Use Logical Reasoning

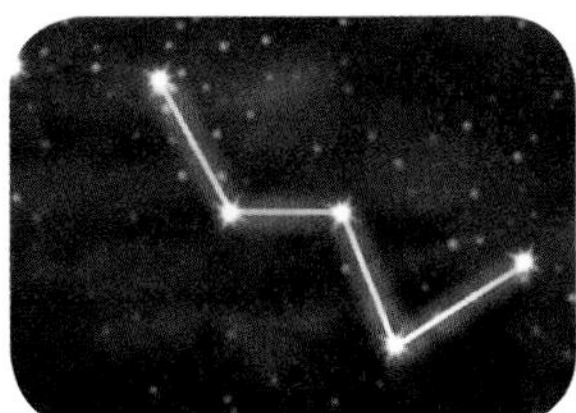

▲ Cassiopeia: 5 stars

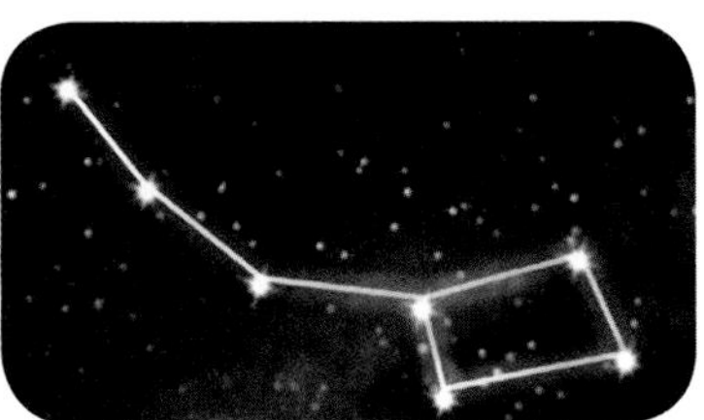

▲ Ursa Minor: 7 stars

▲ Ursa Major: 18 stars

▲ Orion: 20 stars

CHALLENGE YOURSELF

The seats in the Science Center's planetarium are divided into 3 sections. Each section has 48 seats. The table shows the numbers of third-grade students from Cypress Park School who are visiting the planetarium.

Third Grade Students from Cypress Park School

Class Teacher	Number of Students
Mrs. Parker	31
Mr. Daniel	28
Ms. McCarthy	26

12. Mrs. Parker's students took their seats first, followed by Mr. Daniel's students. After the first section was filled, how many of Mr. Daniel's students sat in the second section of seats?

13. Ms. McCarthy's class was seated last. Explain how you can find the number of empty seats in the planetarium after everyone, including the teachers, took a seat.

LESSON 4

Read a Bar Graph

OBJECTIVE: Read and interpret data in a bar graph.

Quick Review

Write the numbers that are between:

1. 8 and 10
2. 14 and 18
3. 28 and 32
4. 54 and 60
5. 36 and 40

Vocabulary

bar graph scale
horizontal bar graph
vertical bar graph

Learn

PROBLEM Erin's family is planning to visit an amusement park. They want to ride as many roller coasters as possible. Which amusement park has the greatest number of roller coasters?

A **bar graph** uses bars to show data. A **scale** of numbers helps you read the number each bar shows. On the bar graphs below, the scale shows the numbers 0, 4, 8, 12, and 16. Each space between the numbers represents 4 roller coasters.

These bar graphs show the same data.

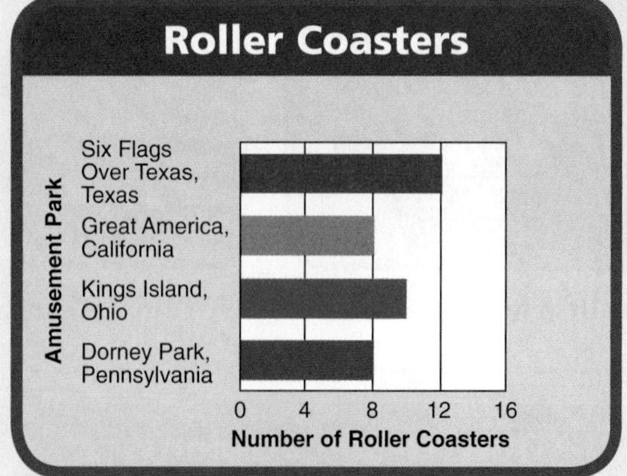

In a **horizontal bar graph**, the bars go across from left to right.

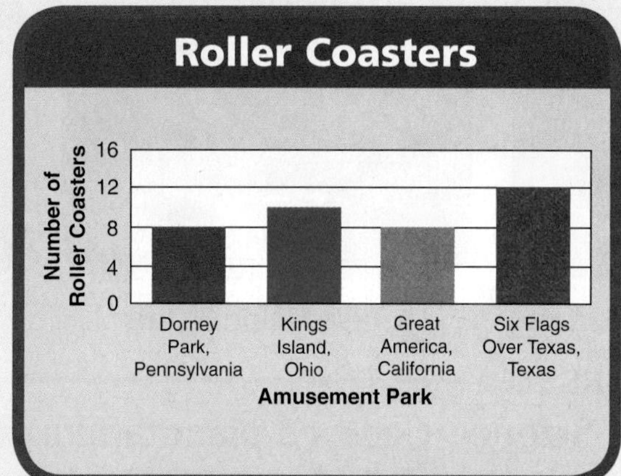

In a **vertical bar graph**, the bars go up from the bottom.

The longest bar ends at 12. It is for Six Flags Over Texas.

So, Six Flags Over Texas has the greatest number of roller coasters.

▲ The Texas Giant is a wooden roller coaster. It has 81,370 bolts holding it together!

Guided Practice

For 1–4, use the Roller Coasters graphs above.

1. Which amusement parks have the same number of roller coasters? Think: Which bars have the same length?

TEKS 3.13B interpret information from pictographs and bar graphs. *also* 3.13A, 3.14A, 3.15A, 3.15B

2. How many roller coasters does Dorney Park have?

3. How many more roller coasters does Six Flags Over Texas have than Great America?

4. **TALK Math** **Explain** how you would use the bar graph to tell how many roller coasters Kings Island has.

Independent Practice and Problem Solving

For 5–7, use the Favorite Ride graph.

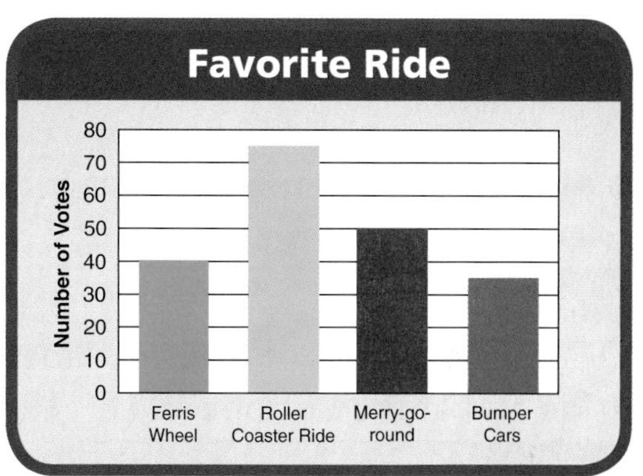

5. How many students voted for roller coaster?

6. Did more students vote for ferris wheel and merry-go-round or for roller coaster and bumper cars? **Explain** your answer.

7. How many students voted in all?

For 8–10, use the Roller Coaster Speed graph.

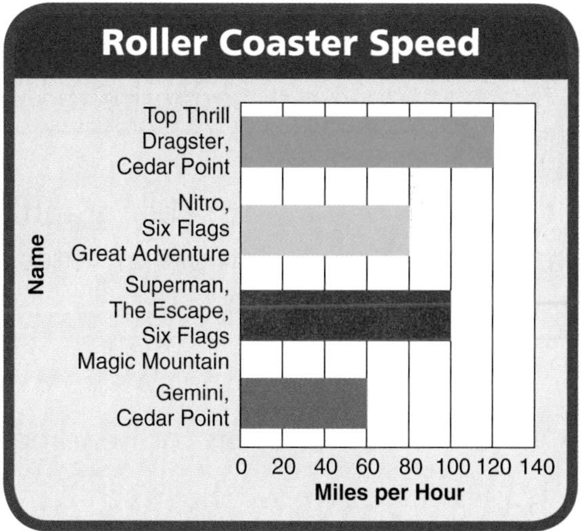

8. How much faster is Superman, The Escape than Nitro?

9. Which roller coaster is twice as fast Gemini?

10. **WRITE Math** **Sense or Nonsense?** Jane says that Gemini is faster than Nitro. Does her statement make sense? **Explain.**

Mixed Review and TAKS Prep

11. What time does this clock show? (TEKS 3.12B, p. 136)

12. Arthur placed two squares together side by side. What shape did he make? (Grade 2, TEKS 2.7C)

13. **TAKS Prep** Melinda makes a bar graph to show how many pets her friends have. Which of these will have the shortest bar? (Obj. 5)

A 8 dogs
B 6 cats
C 4 hamsters
D 3 birds

Extra Practice on page 170, Set C

Make a Bar Graph

OBJECTIVE: Make a bar graph to show data.

Quick Review

Write the numbers that are between.

1. 10 and 12
2. 16 and 20
3. 18 and 24
4. 24 and 32
5. 30 and 40

Learn

PROBLEM Julian's classmates voted for their favorite school subjects. He showed the data in a pictograph. How can he display the data in a bar graph?

Activity

Materials ■ inch or cm grid paper or bar graph pattern, colored pencils or crayons

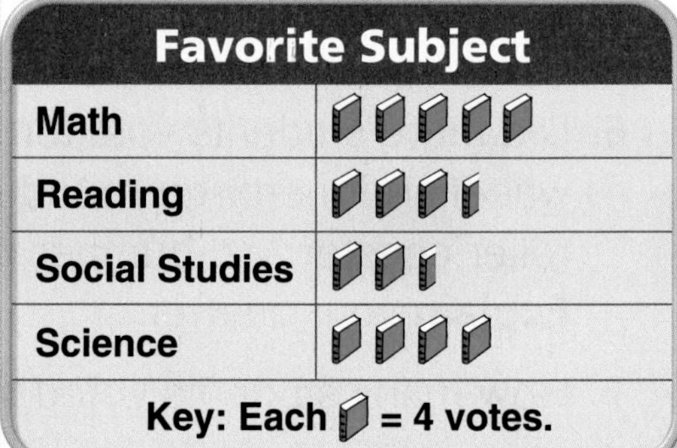

Step 1

Write the title at the top and labels on the side and at the bottom.

Step 2

Choose a scale to show the number of votes. You can use a scale of 0 to 24, counting by fours. Start with 0, and write the numbers.

Step 3

Copy and complete the bar graph. Draw a bar to match the number of votes for each subject.

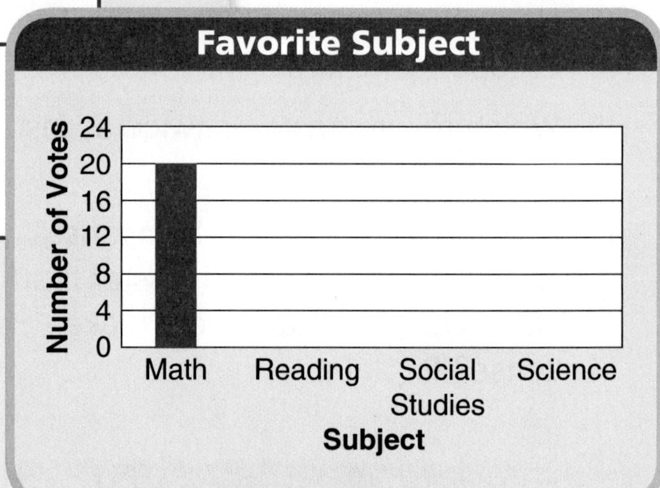

So, Julian can display the data in a bar graph.

- Where should the bar for Reading end?
- How will you know that each bar in your graph is the correct height?
- How do you know what scale to use when you make a bar graph?

TEKS 3.13A collect, organize, record, and display data in pictographs and bar graphs where each picture or cell might represent more than one piece of data. *also* **3.13B, 3.14A, 3.15A, 3.15B**

Use Data in a Frequency Table

You can make a bar graph from data in a frequency table.

Favorite Season	
Season	**Number of Votes**
Spring	6
Summer	11
Fall	8
Winter	3

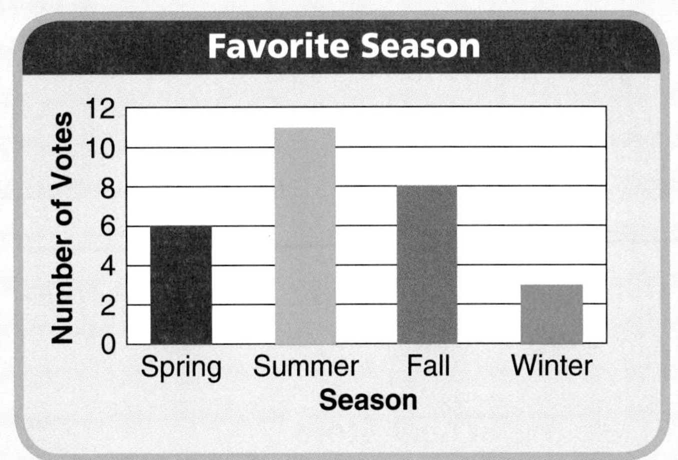

• Where does the bar for summer end?

Guided Practice

For 1–5, use the Favorite Drink pictograph.

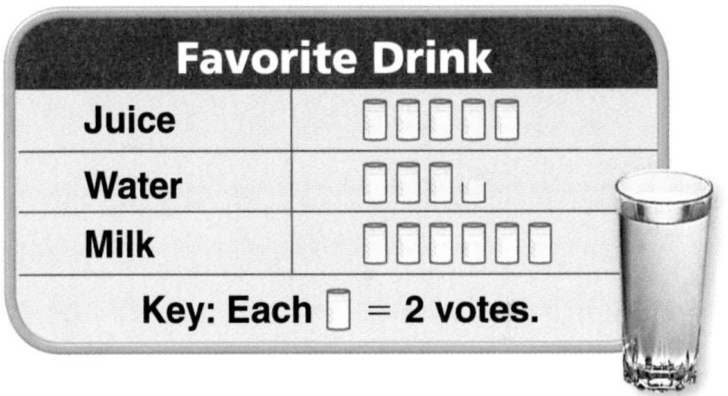

Favorite Drink
Juice
Water
Milk
Key: Each = 2 votes.

1. Which of these scales would be best for a bar graph of the data?

0, 5, 10, 15, 20, 25
0, 4, 8, 12, 16, 20
0, 2, 4, 6, 8, 10, 12

2. Use the data in the pictograph to make a bar graph.

3. How many more votes did juice receive than water?

4. Which drink received the most votes?

5. TALK Math How are your bar graph and the pictograph alike? How are they different?

Independent Practice and Problem Solving

For 6–8, use the Favorite Breakfast Food pictograph.

6. Use the data in the pictograph to make a bar graph.

7. Did more people vote for cereal and waffles or for eggs and toast? **Explain.**

8. Mike voted for the breakfast food that got the least number of votes. What did Mike vote for?

Favorite Breakfast Food	
Cereal	
Waffles	
Eggs and Toast	
Key: Each = 4 votes.	

Extra Practice on page 170, Set D

For 9–12, use the Lunch Choices table.

Lunch Choices

Lunch	Number Bought
Taco	8
Chicken	10
Hamburger	6
Pizza	12

9. Use the data in the table to make a bar graph. What scale did you choose?

10. Which lunch choice did the most students buy?

11. Did more students buy tacos and hamburgers or pizza? **Explain**.

12. What if 4 more students had bought chicken for lunch? **Explain** what the bar graph would look like.

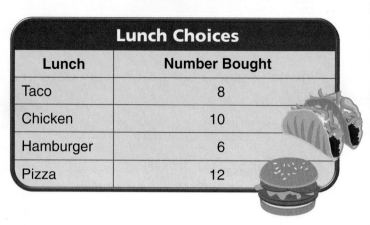

For 13–15, use the School Store Items graph.

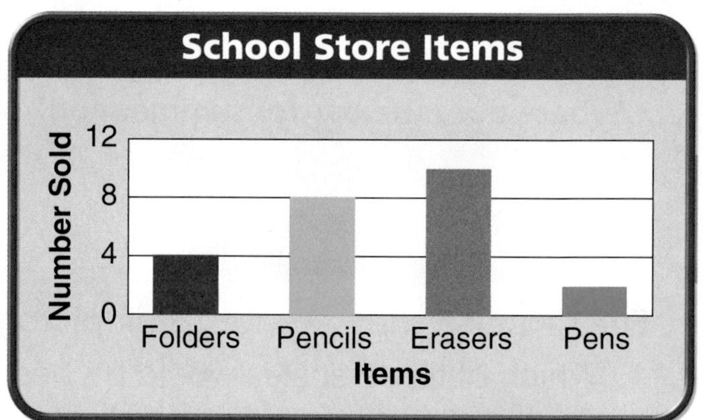

13. How many more pencils were sold than pens? **Explain** how you used the graph to solve the problem.

14. Four more of an item were sold than folders. Two fewer of this item were sold than erasers. What is this item?

15. WRITE Math **What's the Error?** Jamal says that there were 22 items sold at the school store. What is his error?

16. ***FAST FACT*** The pencil was invented in 1564. How many years ago was that?

Mixed Review and TAKS Prep

17. Write the fact family for 4, 6, and 10. (TEKS 3.3A, p. 84)

18. What time is shown on this clock? (TEKS 3.12B, p. 136)

19. TAKS Prep Which vegetable did exactly 4 students choose? (Obj. 5)

A potato

B broccoli

C corn

D beans

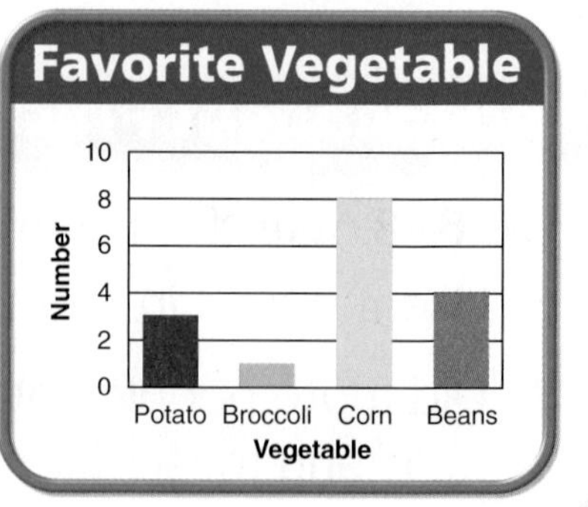

Technology
Use Harcourt Mega Math, Country Countdown, *White Water Graphing*, Level F, and The Number Games, *ArachnaGraph*, Level C.

Science Fair

Summarize

Ms. Jansen's third grade class is getting ready for the science fair. The students are voting for their favorite science topics. Eight students choose space. Five students choose energy because they like to perform experiments. Plants are chosen by six students, and animals are chosen by nine students.

When you summarize, you restate the most important information in a shorter way to help you understand what you have read.

Rewrite the paragraph above in a shorter form.

Ms. Jansen's class voted for their favorite science topics. 8 students voted for space, 5 voted for energy, 6 voted for plants, and 9 voted for animals.

Problem Solving Summarize to understand what you read.

1. Which is the favorite science topic of students in Ms. Jansen's class?
2. Mr. Miller's class recorded the types of art they will display at the art show. Four students chose painting. Nine students chose clay sculptures. Six students chose chalk. Which type of art was chosen by the greatest number of students? Summarize the important information. Then solve the problem.

Hands On: Take a Survey

OBJECTIVE: Take a survey, and record the results in a tally table, pictograph, and bar graph.

Quick Review

Write numbers for the tally marks.

1. 𝍸 ||
2. 𝍸 𝍸
3. 𝍸 𝍸 ||||
4. 𝍸 𝍸 𝍸 |
5. 𝍸 𝍸 𝍸 𝍸 |||

Vocabulary

survey **results**

Investigate

Materials ■ tally table

A **survey** is a way of collecting information or data. The answers collected are the **results** of the survey.

Take a survey in your classroom. Record the results in a tally table.

A Think of a survey question that has several answer choices. For example, you could ask, *What is your favorite breakfast food?*

B Make a tally table. Write a title and labels. List the answer choices.

C Ask your classmates the survey question. Record the results by making tally marks in the *Tally* column.

Favorite Breakfast Food	
Food	**Tally**
Cereal	
Toast	
Waffles	
Pancakes	

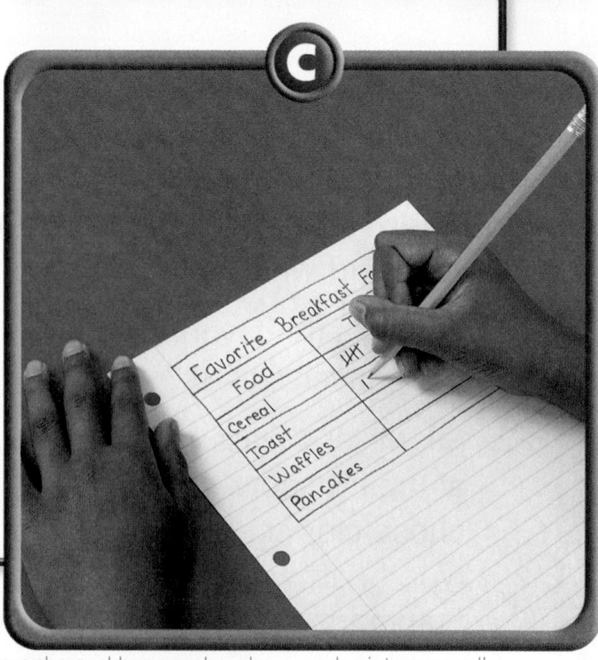

D Count the tally marks for each answer. Share the results with the class.

Draw Conclusions

1. What answer choices did you use for your survey?
2. Which answer choice for your survey has the most tally marks? Which has the fewest?
3. **Analysis** Do you think each classmate collected the same results in his or her survey? Explain.

TEKS 3.13A collect, organize, record, and display data in pictographs and bar graphs where each picture or cell might represent more than one piece of data. *also* **3.13B, 3.14A, 3.14D, 3.15A. 3.15B**

Connect

You can show the data you collected by making a pictograph and a bar graph.

ONE WAY **Make a pictograph.**

Write a title and a label for each row.
Choose a key to tell how many each picture stands for.
Write the key at the bottom.
Copy and complete your pictograph.

Favorite Breakfast Food	
Cereal	
Toast	
Waffles	
Pancakes	
Key: Each ▪ = ▪ students.	

ANOTHER WAY **Make a bar graph.**

Write a title and labels.
Write the answer choices.
Choose a scale to show the number of answers.
Copy and complete your bar graph.

TALK Math

How do your graphs show the choice with the least number of tally marks? the greatest number?

Favorite Breakfast Food

Practice

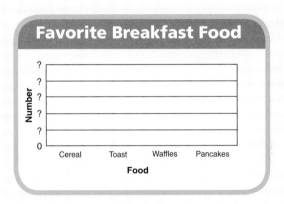

For 1–2, use your tally table and graph.

1. What is the title of your tally table and your graph?
2. How many classmates in all answered your survey?
3. Think of another survey question. Write several possible answer choices. Ask your classmates your survey question. Show the results in a pictograph and in a bar graph.
4. **WRITE Math** How is the data in your pictograph and bar graph alike? How is it different?

LESSON 7

Classify Data

OBJECTIVE: Use a table to organize data.

Quick Review

Find the sum.

1. 2 + 3 + 4
2. 4 + 6 + 3
3. 2 + 7 + 5
4. 3 + 5 + 8
5. 7 + 6 + 5

Vocabulary

classify

Learn

To **classify** means to group pieces of data according to how they are the same. You can classify by shape, color, or size.

PROBLEM Cathy and Tom are playing a game. Their game pieces are shown below. What are some ways Cathy and Tom can classify the game pieces?

Data can be organized into a table. A table can show two ways at a time to classify the data.

ONE WAY **By shape and color**

Game Pieces

	triangle	circle	square
red	3	2	3
yellow	4	2	2
blue	2	2	4

ANOTHER WAY **By shape and size**

Game Pieces

	triangle	circle	square
small	2	2	4
medium	3	2	3
large	4	2	2

So, Cathy and Tom can classify the game pieces by shape and color and by shape and size.

- What other way can Cathy and Tom classify the game pieces?

TEKS 3.13 The student solves problems by collecting, organizing, displaying, and interpreting sets of data. *also* **3.14A, 3.15A, 3.15B**

Guided Practice

For 1–5, use the Juice Boxes table.

Juice Boxes	orange	apple	grape
small	4	5	6
medium	5	4	4
large	5	5	4

1. How are the juice boxes classified?
2. How many large apple juice boxes are there?
3. How many grape juice boxes are there?
4. How many more small juice boxes than large juice boxes are there?
5. TALK Math **Explain** how to find the total number of juice boxes.

Independent Practice and Problem Solving

For 6–8, use the Class Shoe Color table.

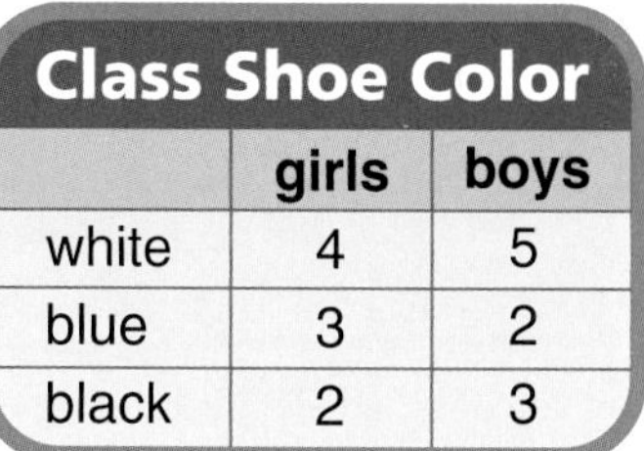

Class Shoe Color	girls	boys
white	4	5
blue	3	2
black	2	3

6. How many girls are wearing black shoes?
7. How many students are wearing blue shoes?
8. How many students were surveyed in all?
9. Look at the stickers at the right. Make a table to classify them two ways. **Explain** how you classified them.

10. WRITE Math **Explain** 3 ways you can classify the students in your class.

Mixed Review and TAKS Prep

11. What is the value of the digit 9 in 93,462? (TEKS 3.1A, p. 16)
12. If = 10 books, how many books are represented by ? (TEKS 3.13B, p. 154)
13. **TAKS Prep** Which shows two ways to classify a group of hats? (Obj. 5)

   A happy or sad
   B quiet or loud
   C size and color
   D sweet or salty

Extra Practice on page 170, Set E

Extra Practice

Set A For 1–3, use the Favorite Animal table. (pp. 152–153)

1. How many more students voted for cat than fish?
2. Which animals received the greatest number of votes, cat and fish, or dog?
3. How many students voted in this survey?

Favorite Animal

Animal	Number
Cat	8
Dog	10
Fish	5

Sets B and D For 1–3, use the Goals Scored pictograph. (pp. 154–155, 162–165)

1. How many more goals did Tony score than Clara?
2. What is the difference between the greatest number of goals and the least number of goals scored?
3. Use the data in the pictograph to make a bar graph.

Goals Scored

Tony	⚽ ⚽ ⚽ ⚽
Clara	⚽ ⚽ ⚽
Darrell	⚽ ⚽ ◖
Monica	⚽ ⚽ ⚽ ⚽ ⚽

Key: Each ⚽ = 2 goals.

Set C For 1–2, use the Favorite Instrument graph. (pp. 160–161)

1. How many students voted for their favorite instrument in this survey?
2. There was one more vote for piano than for what other instrument?

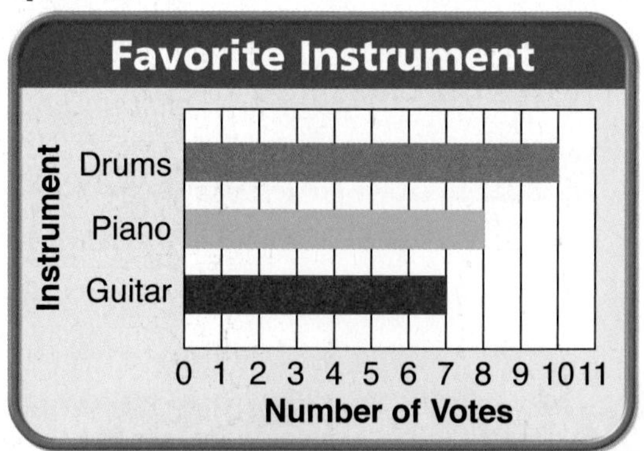

Set E For 1–2, use the Books Read table. (pp. 168–169)

1. How many mystery books have Jamie and Maddie read?
2. Who has read the greatest number of books?

Books Read

	Jamie	Maddie
biography	4	1
mystery	6	3
fiction	6	9

Technology
Use Harcourt Mega Math, The Number Games, *ArachnaGraph*, Levels A, B.

TECHNOLOGY ★ CONNECTION

Computer: Spreadsheet (TEKS 3.14A, 3.14D)

Use a Spreadsheet to Show Data

Carol studied 3 humpback whales during June, July, and August. She recorded how many times she saw each whale each month. Carol's findings are shown below.

BANDIT	
June	𝍸
July	||
August	|

MIDNIGHT	
June	|||
July	𝍸 |
August	||||

OWEN	
June	𝍸
July	𝍸 |||
August	𝍸 |||

Record Carol's data on a spreadsheet.

Step 1	Type labels in Row 1. Tab across the row, or use the mouse or arrow keys to move. Type *Name* in Column A, *June* in Column B, *July* in Column C, and *August* in Column D.
Step 2	Use the mouse or arrow keys to move to Row 2. Type *Bandit* in Column A. Then type the data for Bandit in Columns B, C, and D.
Step 3	Fill in the data for the other whales in Rows 3 and 4.

	A	B	C	D
1	Name	June	July	August
2				
3				

	A	B	C	D
1	Name	June	July	August
2	Bandit	5	2	1
3				
4				

Try It

1. Ed kept track of how many food pellets his fish ate on 4 days. Fin ate 1, 0, 2, and 3 pellets. Flip ate 2, 1, 0, and 3. Stripe ate 0, 2, 2, and 2. Make a spreadsheet to show the amount of food eaten by each fish on the 4 days.

2. **Explore More** Record how many pages of homework you had on each day of one week. Ask four friends to do the same. Enter all the data on a spreadsheet. **Explain** what labels you need on the spreadsheet.

Chapter 7 Review/Test

Check Vocabulary and Concepts

Choose the best term from the box.

VOCABULARY
frequency table
pictograph
tally table

1. A way to record the number of tally marks is in a __?__. (TEKS 3.13A, p. 152)
2. A __?__ uses pictures to show information. (TEKS 3.13A, p. 154)

Check Skills

For 3–4, use the Miles Max Biked pictograph. (TEKS 3.13B, pp. 154–155)

3. How many miles did Max bike on Friday and Saturday?
4. How many more miles did Max bike on Saturday than on Sunday?

Miles Max Biked

Friday	🚲 🚲 🚲 🚲 🚲
Saturday	🚲 🚲 🚲 🚲 🚲 🚲
Sunday	🚲 🚲 🚲 🚲 half 🚲

Key Each 🚲 = 10 miles.

Favorite Pet

Pet: Cat, Dog, Hamster

0 4 8 12 16

Number of Votes

For 5–6, use the Favorite Pet bar graph. (TEKS 3.13B, pp. 160–161)

5. How many more students voted for dog than for cat?
6. What if birds got 4 fewer votes than hamsters? Where would the bar end?

Check Problem Solving

Solve. (TEKS 3.13A, pp. 156–159)

7. The third grade voted on locations for their field trip. The results are shown in the table. Make a pictograph for the data. Let each picture stand for 4 votes.
8. WRITE Math **Explain** how you knew how many pictures to draw for Amusement Park.

Field Trip Locations

Location	Number of Votes
Zoo	16
Amusement park	20
History museum	8
Science center	24

GO ONLINE **Technology** Use *Online Assessment.*

Enrich • Circle Graphs

Mr. Spear's class asked 100 third grade students where they went for summer vacation. Some students went to the beach, some went to a theme park, and some went camping. The class showed the data in a circle graph. A **circle graph** shows data as parts of a whole circle.

Are We There Yet?

- The whole circle represents all 100 students in the survey.
- The section for beach is half of the circle. Since $50 + 50 = 100$, 50 students went to the beach.
- The sections for camping and theme park are the same size. Since $25 + 25 = 50$, 25 students went camping, and 25 students went to a theme park.

Have Fun!

For 1–2, use the Third-Grade Vacations graph.

1. What if the 25 students who went camping went to the beach instead? How would the graph change?
2. What if 25 of the students who went to the beach went to a family reunion instead? How would the graph change?
3. Make your own circle graph using these data: Robbie surveyed 60 students about their favorite fruit. Half chose apples, 10 chose oranges, and 20 chose grapes.

Coming Home

WRITE Math ▸ The fourth grade classes did their own vacation survey. Half of the students went camping. If 120 students were surveyed, how many went camping? **Explain**.

Getting Ready for the TAKS
Chapters 1–7

Number, Operation, and Quantitative Reasoning (TAKS Obj. 1)

Check the answer.

See Item 1. Subtract to find the answer. If the difference does not match one of the answer choices, check your subtraction.

1. On Tuesday, the cafeteria at Ramon's school served 300 lunches. On Wednesday, the cafeteria served 257 lunches. How many more lunches were served on Tuesday?

   A 42 **C** 52

   B 43 **D** 53

2. Meredith and her friend James live 182 miles apart. What is the value of the digit 8 in 182?

   F 8,000 **H** 80

   G 800 **J** 8

3. **WRITE Math** Cheryl has a collection of 413 stamps. Patty has a collection of 329 stamps. How many stamps do they have altogether? Which method did you use to solve the problem? **Explain**.

Patterns, Relationships, and Algebraic Thinking (TAKS Obj. 2)

4. Look at the pattern. What are the next two shapes?

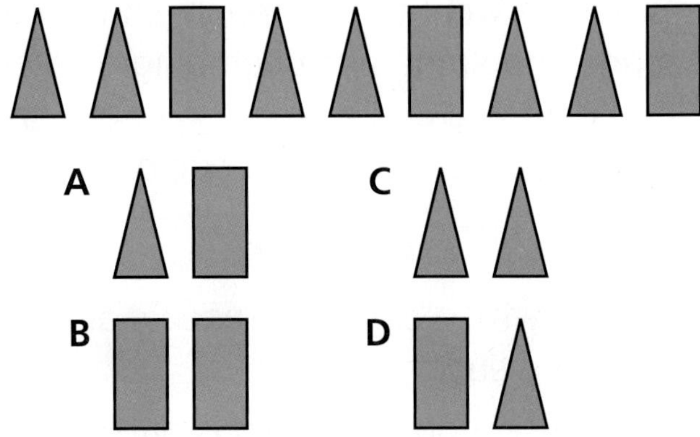

5. Look at the pattern. What comes next?

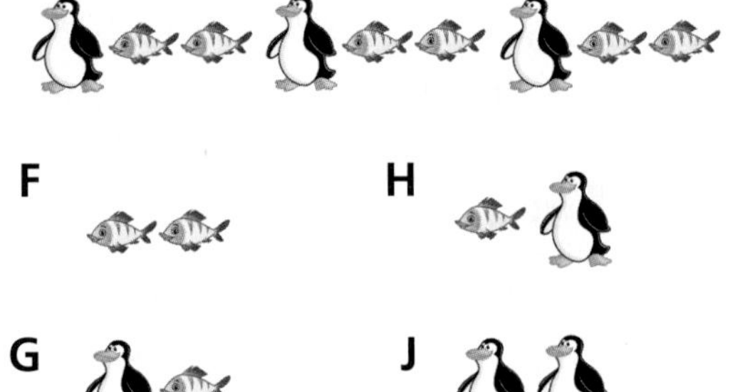

6. **WRITE Math** Sarah had 4 puzzle books. She got 9 more. Her sister Emily had 9 puzzle books. She got 4 more. Who has more puzzle books? **Explain**.

Geometry and Spatial Reasoning (TAKS Obj. 3)

7. What is the name of the shape?

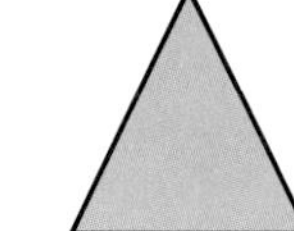

A Square

B Hexagon

C Rectangle

D Not here

8. Look at the solid figure. Which plane figure is one face of the solid figure?

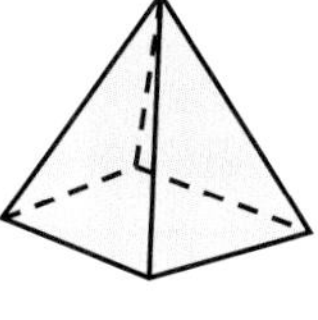

F 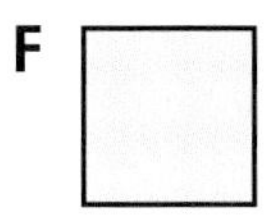

G 

H 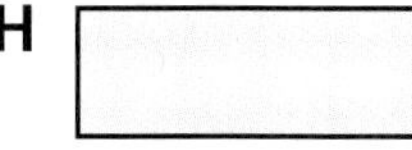

J

9. WRITE Math **Explain** how this cube and rectangular prism are alike.

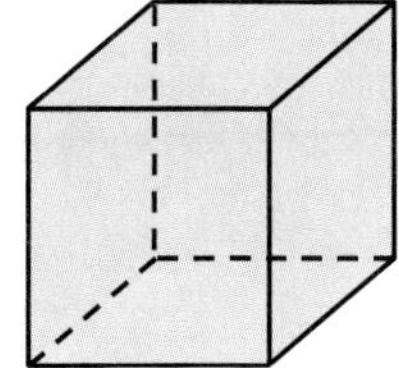

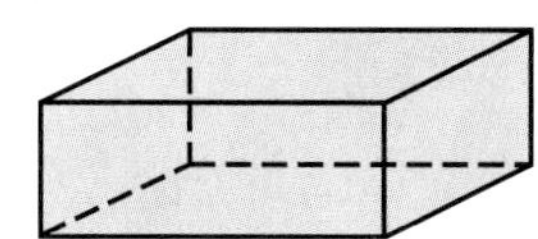

Probability and Statistics (TAKS Obj. 4)

10. Students voted for their favorite ice cream topping. How many students in all voted?

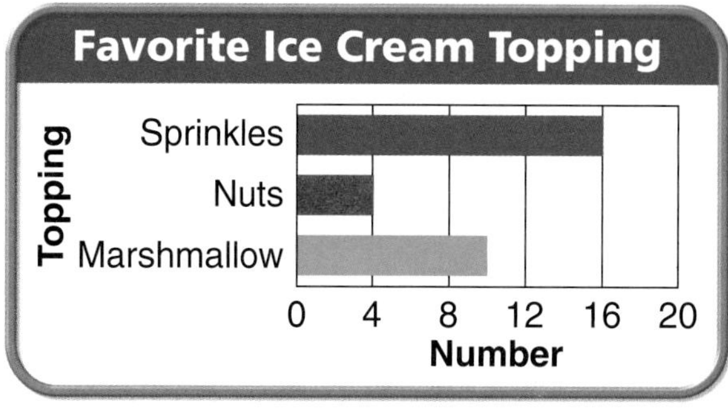

A 16 C 26

B 20 D 30

11. Which color marble is least likely to be pulled?

F Yellow

G Blue

H Green

J Red

12. WRITE Math Sherri is making a pictograph to show the number of books the students in her class have read. The key is Each [book] = 5 books. There are 3 books next to Eric's name. How many books did he read? **Explain**.

CHAPTER

8 Algebra: Patterns

The Big Idea Growing and repeating patterns can be identified, described, extended, and generalized with words and symbols.

TEXAS FAST FACT

At the Dallas Farmers Market, farmers sell fresh fruits and vegetables. Fruits and vegetables have lots of vitamins and minerals. Eat 5 to 9 servings a day to stay healthy.

Investigate

Fruits and vegetables come in many different colors. Bell peppers, for example, are fruits that are most often green, red, orange, or yellow. Create a pattern using the colors of bell peppers. Describe or draw your pattern.

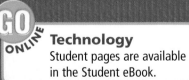

GO ONLINE **Technology**
Student pages are available in the Student eBook.

Show What You Know

Check your understanding of important skills needed for success in Chapter 8.

▶ Find a Number Pattern

Write a rule. Then copy and complete the table.

1.

Boxes	1	2	3	4	5
Pencils	4	8	12	16	■

2.

Bicycles	1	2	3	4	5
Wheels	2	4	6	■	■

3.

T-shirt	1	2	3	4	5
Cost	\$5	\$10	■	\$20	■

4.

Shelf	1	2	3	4	5
Books	10	■	30	40	■

▶ Plane Shape Patterns

Describe the pattern. Then draw the next two shapes.

5. ■ ● ■ ● ■ ● ■

6. 

7. ▬ ▲ ▬ ▲ ▬ ▲ ▬

8. 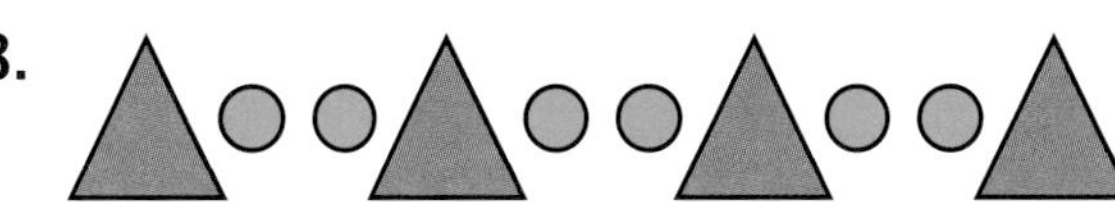

VOCABULARY POWER

CHAPTER VOCABULARY

growing pattern
pattern unit
repeating pattern

WARM-UP WORDS

pattern unit The part of a pattern that repeats

repeating pattern A pattern that uses the same pattern unit over and over again

growing pattern A pattern in which the number or number of figures increases by the same amount each time

Patterns

OBJECTIVE: Identify and extend number and geometric patterns to solve problems.

Quick Review

Name each shape.

1. △
2. □
3. ○
4. ▭
5. ☆

Vocabulary

pattern unit

Learn

A pattern is an ordered set of numbers or objects. A **pattern unit** is the part of a pattern that repeats.

PROBLEM Karen enjoys sewing and making pillows. The chart shows the number of pillows she made each week. If the pattern continues, how many pillows will she make in Week 10?

Week	one	two	three	four	five	six	seven	eight	nine	ten
Number of pillows	3	2	4	3	2	4	3	2	4	■

Example

Look at the number pattern. Find the pattern unit.

The number pattern is 3, 2, 4, 3, 2, 4, 3, 2, 4,

The pattern unit is *3, 2, 4.*

To continue the pattern, repeat the pattern unit.
3, 2, 4, 3, 2, 4, 3, 2, 4, 3, 2, 4

So, Karen will make 3 pillows in Week 10.

Math Idea
Both numbers and shapes can form patterns.

Another Example

Karen sewed shapes around the edge of a pillow. Look at the pattern she used. What is the missing shape?

   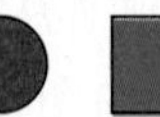   ? 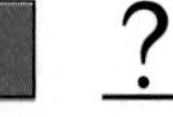  

The pattern unit is *red circle, blue square.*

So, the missing shape is a red circle.

- Predict what the next two shapes in her pattern will be.
- **What if** the pattern unit was *red circle, blue square, green circle?* What would the pattern look like?

TEKS 3.6.A identify and extend whole-number and geometric patterns to make predictions and solve problems.
also **3.14A, 3.15A, 3.15B, 3.16A**

Guided Practice

1. What are the next two shapes in this pattern? 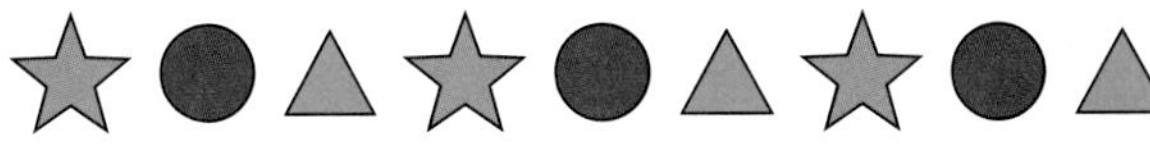

Name a pattern unit. Find the missing number or shape.

2. 6, 6, 5, 6, 6, 5, 6, 6, 5, 6, ■, 5

3. ▲ ▮ ▫ ▲ ▮ ▫ ▲ ▮ ▫ ? ▮

4. TALK Math **Explain** how to find a pattern unit.

Independent Practice and Problem Solving

Name a pattern unit. Find the missing number or shape.

5. 8, 4, 2, 8, 4, 2, 8, 4, 2, 8, ■, 2

6. 2, 0, 0, 1, 2, 0, 0, 1, 2, 0, 0, 1, 2, 0, ■

7. ☆ ▬ ▭ ☆ ▬ ▭ ☆ ▬ ▭ ☆ ▬ ▭ ? ▬ ▭

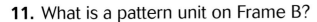

Predict the next two numbers or shapes in each pattern.

8. 5, 1, 1, 5, 5, 1, 1, 5, 5, 1, 1, 5, ■, ■

9. ▽▽△▽▽△▽▽△ ? ?

USE DATA For 10–11, use the photo frames.

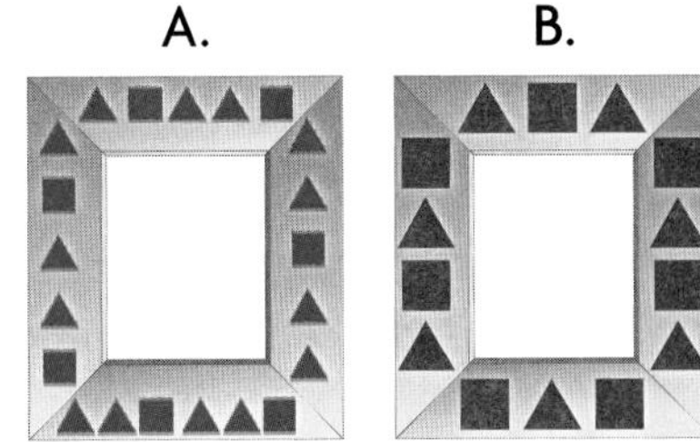

10. Greg put a photo of his dog in one of the frames. A pattern unit on the frame is *triangle, square, triangle*. Which frame did Greg use?

11. What is a pattern unit on Frame B?

12. WRITE Math **Sense or Nonsense** Helena lost a bead from her pattern bracelet. She says the missing bead is a green square. Does that make sense?

Mixed Review and TAKS Prep

13. The bottom view and top view of a solid figure is a circle. Name the solid figure. (Grade 2 TEKS 2.7A)

14. I am a polygon with four sides the same length. I have four vertices. What am I? (Grade 2 TEKS 2.7A)

15. **TAKS Prep** What are the next two numbers in this pattern? (Obj. 2)

1, 6, 1, 1, 6, 1, 1, 6, 1, 1, 6, ■, ■

A 6, 1 **C** 6, 6

B 1, 6 **D** 1, 1

Extra Practice on page 190, Set A

CD ROM **Technology**
Use Harcourt Mega Math, The Number Games, *Tiny's Think Tank*, Levels J and K.

LESSON 2

Geometric Patterns

OBJECTIVE: Identify and extend geometric patterns to solve problems.

Quick Review

Kylie drew this pattern.

What is the pattern unit?

Vocabulary

repeating pattern

growing pattern

Learn

PROBLEM Vicky and Will use rubber stamps to make patterns. What are the next two shapes in each pattern?

Vicky's pattern is a **repeating pattern** because it uses the same pattern unit over and over again.

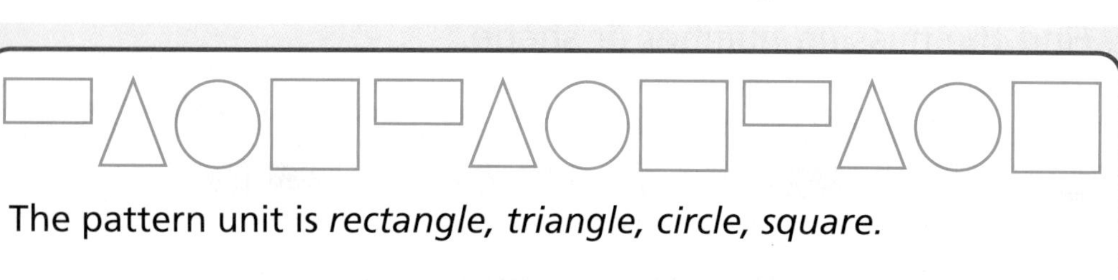

The pattern unit is *rectangle, triangle, circle, square.*

To continue a repeating pattern, use the pattern unit.

So, the next two shapes in Vicky's pattern are: *rectangle, triangle.*

Will's pattern is called a **growing pattern** because the number of rectangles increases by the same amount from one figure to the next.

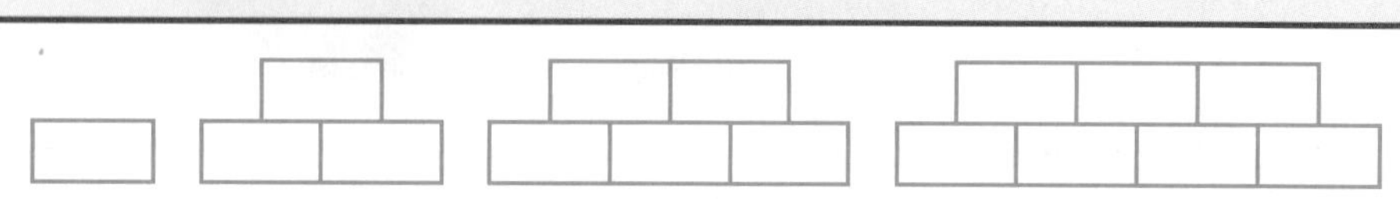

The rule is *add 2 rectangles.*

To continue a growing pattern, use a rule.

So, the next two figures in Will's pattern will have 9 rectangles and 11 rectangles.

- This is Lee's pattern. Is it a repeating or a growing pattern?

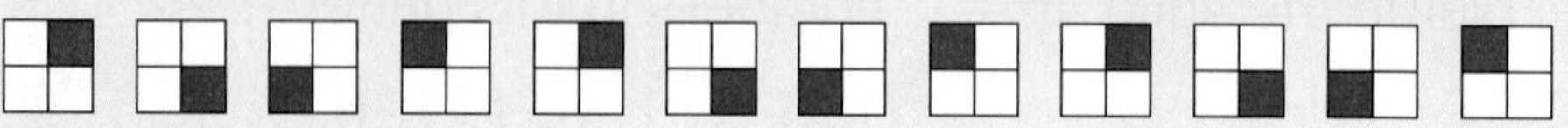

Guided Practice

1. Draw the pattern unit Lee used to make the pattern shown above.

TEKS 3.6.A identify and extend whole number and geometric patterns to make predictions and solve problems. *also* **3.14A, 3.14C, 3.15A, 3.15B, 3.16A**

Find the pattern unit or rule. Then name the next figure.

✓2. 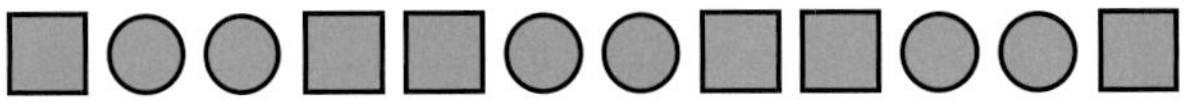 ■●●■■●●■■●●■ ✓3.  [2 squares] [3 squares] [4 squares] [5 squares]

4. **TALK Math** **Explain** the difference between a repeating pattern and a growing pattern. Draw an example of each.

Independent Practice and Problem Solving

Find the pattern unit or rule. Then name the next figure.

5. 

6.  ☆ △ ☆ △ ☆ △

Find the pattern unit or rule. Draw the missing figure.

7. 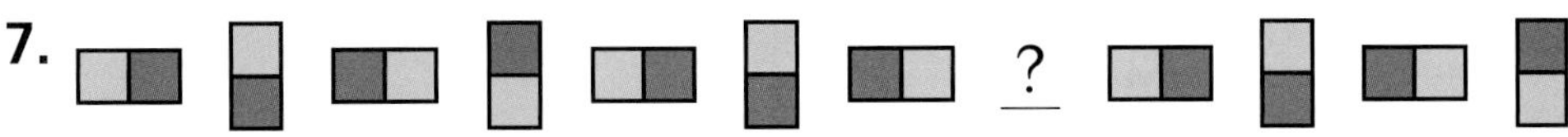

8. 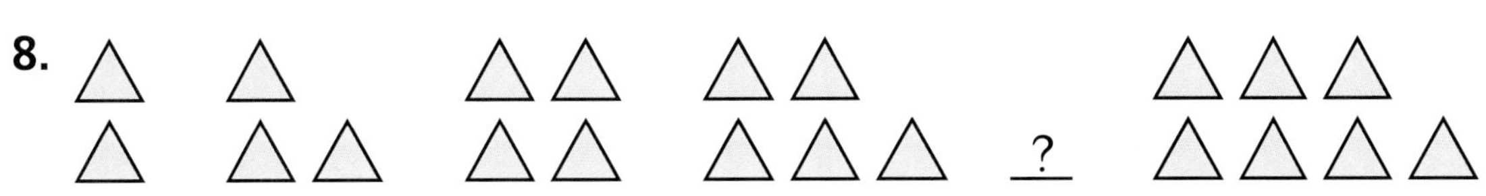

9. **FAST FACT** The non-venomous king snake looks much like the venomous coral snake. Look at the photos. Describe the color pattern unit for each.

king snake

coral snake

10. Draw a pattern. Tell whether your pattern is repeating or growing.

11. **WRITE Math** **What's the Question?** The answer is 9 tiles.

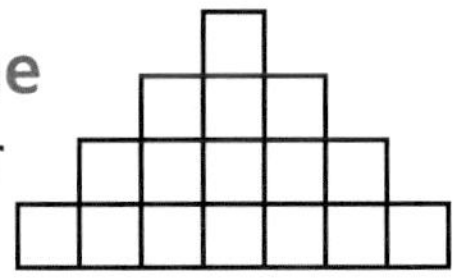

Mixed Review and TAKS Prep

12. The zoo sold 785 adult tickets and 418 child tickets. To the nearest hundred, how many were sold?
(TEKS 3.5B, p. 60)

13. What mailbox number is missing?
(TEKS 3.6A, p. 178)

14. **TAKS Prep** Which is the missing figure? (Obj. 2)

▲ ▼ ▼ ▲ ▼ ▼ ▲ ▼ ? ▲

A ▲

B ◀

C 

D ▼

LESSON 3

Number Patterns

OBJECTIVE: Identify and extend whole-number patterns to find rules and solve problems.

Quick Review

Skip-count to complete.

1. 3, 6, 9, 12, 15, ■
2. 5, 10, 15, 20, ■
3. 2, 4, 6, 8, 10, ■
4. 10, 20, 30, 40, 50, ■
5. 1, 3, 5, 7, 9, 11, ■

Learn

A rule can be used to describe a pattern.

PROBLEM Mr. Rome wrote a number pattern. What rule did he use for the pattern? What will the next number be?

2, 5, 8, 11, 14

Example

Look at the number pattern. Find the rule.

Think: What do I do to 2 to get 5? What do I do to 5 to get 8?

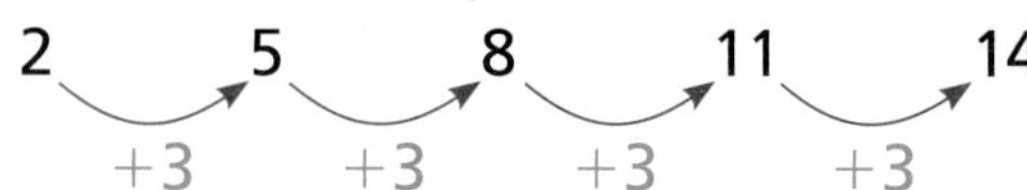

The numbers increase by 3. So, Mr. Rome used the rule *add* 3.

Use the rule to extend the pattern.

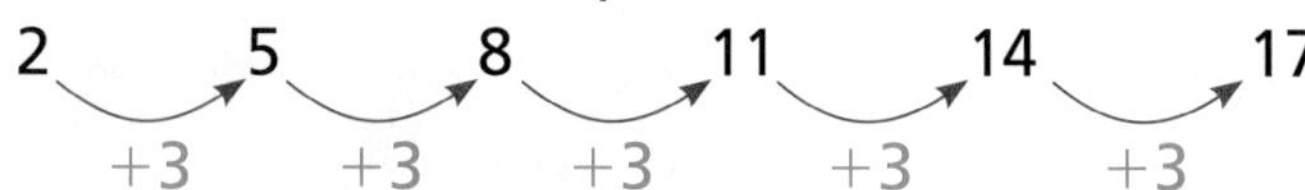

Math Idea
A rule must be true for all the numbers in the pattern.

So, the next number in the pattern is 17.

More Examples

A 27, 23, 19, 15, __, 7

Think: What do I do to 27 to get 23?
What do I do to 23 to get 19?

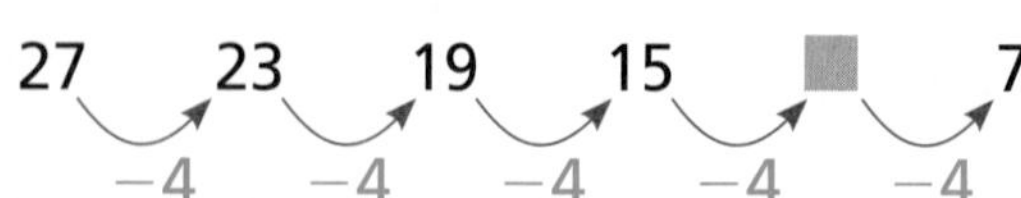

So, the rule is *subtract* 4.

To find the missing number, subtract 4.

$15 - 4 = 11$

So, the missing number is 11.

B 1, 2, 4, 7, 11, 16, __

Think: What do I do to 1 to get 2?
to 2 to get 4? to 4 to get 7?

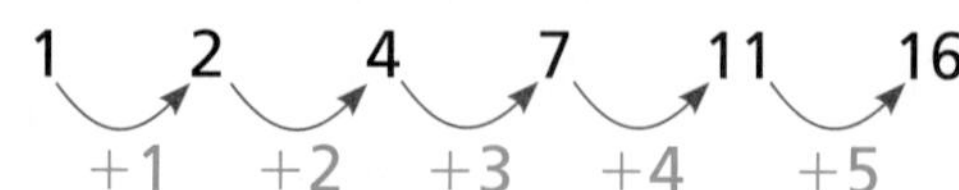

So, the rule is add 1, then add 2, then add 3 and so on.

To find the next number, add 6.

$16 + 6 = 22$

So, the next number is 22.

TEKS 3.6.A identify and extend whole-number and geometric patterns to make predictions and solve problems.
also **3.14A, 3.15A, 3.15B, 3.16A**

Guided Practice

1. What is a rule for this number pattern? 1, 5, 9, 13, 17

Write a rule for each pattern. Then find the next number.

2. 28, 33, 38, 43, 48
3. 52, 45, 38, 31, 24
4. 4, 12, 20, 28, 36
5. TALK Math **Explain** how you can find a rule for a pattern.

Independent Practice and Problem Solving

Write a rule for each pattern. Then find the next number.

6. 7, 16, 25, 34, 43, 52
7. 81, 75, 69, 63, 57, 51
8. 211, 198, 185, 172, 159
9. 3, 5, 8, 10, 13, 15, 18, 20, 23
10. 12, 18, 17, 23, 22, 28, 27, ■

Find the missing numbers.

11. 109, 119, 129, ■, 149, 159, 169
12. 96, 93, 90, 87, ■, ■, 78, 75
13. 5, 15, 13, 23, ■, 31, 29, ■, 37, ■
14. 324, 316, 308, ■, 292, ■, ■, 268, ■

USE DATA For 15–17, use the chart.

15. How much money does Erik save each week?
16. How much money is in Erik's account in Week 5?
17. **Reasoning** Erik wants a bike that costs $76. If he continues the savings pattern, will he have enough saved by Week 10? Explain.
18. WRITE Math **What's the Error?** Tim wrote this pattern: 5, 12, 15, 22, 25, 32, 35. Louie said the rule is *add* 7. Describe his error. Write a correct rule.

Erik's Savings

Week	Amount
1	$25
2	$31
3	$37
4	$43
5	■
6	$55

Mixed Review and TAKS Prep

19. Morgan has 2 quarters, 3 dimes, and 6 nickels. How much money does she have in all? (TEKS 3.1C, p. 110)
20. Zoey ate breakfast at the time shown on the clock. At what time did she eat? (TEKS 3.12B, p. 134)

21. **TAKS Prep** Valerie wrote the following pattern: (Obj. 2)

    262, 259, 256, 253, ■, 247, ■

    What numbers are missing?

    A 250, 245 **C** 250, 244

    B 249, 243 **D** 256, 250

Extra Practice on page 190, Set C

LESSON

4 Extend Patterns

OBJECTIVE: Extend number and geometric patterns to solve problems.

Quick Review

Identify each rule or pattern unit.

1. 6, 10, 14, 18, 22

2. 97, 91, 85, 79, 73

3. 2, 3, 6, 7, 10, 11, 14

4. ○ ▯ ▯ ○ ▯ ▯ ○ ▯ ▯

5. ★ ★ ▲ ▲ ★ ★ ▲ ▲ ★ ★ ▲ ▲

Learn

PROBLEM Yoshi is drawing a border around the title page of his report about Texas. He has 3 more shapes to draw. If he extends the pattern, or continues it, what are the next three shapes he will draw?

Example

Look at Yoshi's border pattern.

It is a repeating pattern.

The pattern unit is *blue rectangle, white star, red rectangle, white rectangle.*

What are the next three shapes?

So, the next three shapes Yoshi will draw are *white star, red rectangle, white rectangle.*

More Examples **Extend the pattern.**

A Find the next three figures in this growing pattern.

  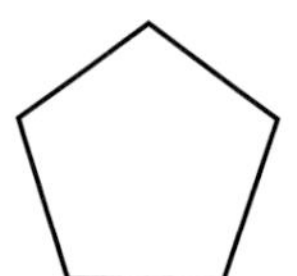 

The number of sides increases by 1 from one figure to the next. The rule is *add 1 side*.

So, the next three figures will have 7 sides, 8 sides, and 9 sides.

B Find the next three numbers in this repeating pattern.

175, 164, 153, 142, 131

The rule is *subtract 11*.

So, the next three numbers will be 120, 109, and 98.

- What is the 10th number for the pattern in Example B?

Remember

A repeating pattern uses a pattern unit. A growing pattern uses a pattern rule.

TEKS 3.6.A identify and extend whole-number and geometric patterns to make predictions and solve problems. *also* **3.14A, 3.15A, 3.15B, 3.16A**

Guided Practice

1. Kurt started with the number 5 and used the rule *add 3* to make a pattern. Write the first five numbers of his pattern.

Name the rule or pattern unit. Find the next three numbers or shapes.

✓2. 7, 11, 15, 19, 23, 27

✓3. 

4. TALK Math **Explain** how to find the next three figures in this pattern.

Independent Practice and Problem Solving

Name the rule or pattern unit. Find the next three numbers or shapes.

5. 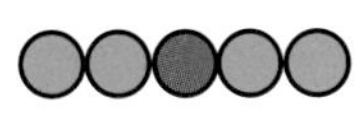 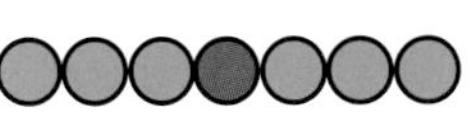 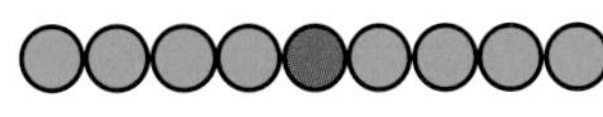

6. 5, 10, 8, 13, 11, 16, 14, 19, 17

Draw the next three shapes in each pattern.

7. 8. 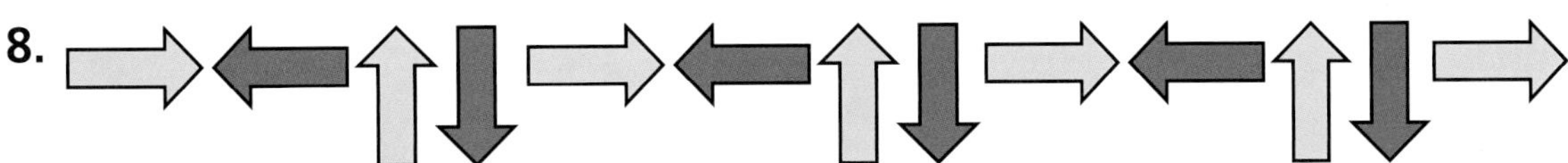

9. **Reasoning** Brooke is making a repeating pattern with 2 squares and 3 triangles. She will draw 25 shapes. How many squares will she draw? How many triangles?

10. WRITE Math Rob made this number pattern. Write the rule. **Explain** how to find the next two numbers in his pattern.

6, 8, 7, 9, 8, 10, 9, 11

Mixed Review and TAKS Prep

11. What is the missing shape? (TEKS 3.6A, p. 180)

12. Jessie has these coins in her purse. How much money does she have? (TEKS 3.1C, p. 110)

13. **TAKS Prep** Cindy drew a shape pattern. The pattern unit is *star, circle, square, triangle*. What will the 10th and 11th shapes be? (Obj. 2)

A star, circle

B square, triangle

C circle, square

D triangle, star

Extra Practice on page 190, Set D

LESSON 5 Problem Solving Workshop
Strategy: Look for a Pattern

OBJECTIVE: Solve problems by using the strategy *look for a pattern*.

Learn the Strategy

Finding patterns can help you solve problems. To find a pattern, see whether the numbers in the problem increase or decrease or if the colors or shapes repeat.

Number Patterns

Hannah is saving money to buy a new bike. She saved $3 the first week, $6 the second week, $9 the third week, and $12 the fourth week.

Week	1	2	3	4
Savings	$3	$6	$9	$12

Color Patterns

Josie made this bracelet in art class. She used red and blue beads to make a pattern.

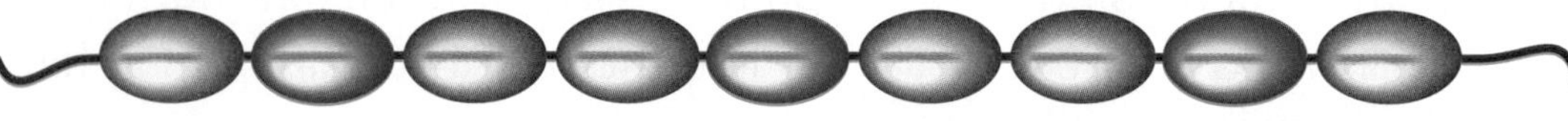

Geometric Patterns

Dan made this pattern with pattern blocks.

TALK Math

Look at each pattern above. Is the pattern repeating or growing? What number, color, or shape comes next in each pattern?

TEKS 3.14C select or develop an appropriate problem-solving plan or strategy, including drawing a picture, looking for a pattern, systematic guessing and checking, acting it out, making a table, working a simpler problem, or working backwards to solve a problem. *also* **3.6A, 3.14A, 3.14B, 3.14C, 3.15A, 3.15B, 3.16A, 3.16B**

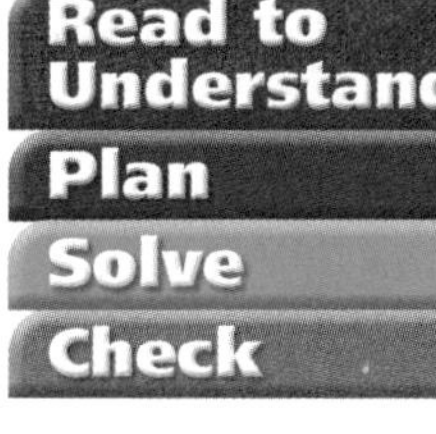

Use the Strategy

PROBLEM Sean is using square tiles to make patterns. He used 20 tiles to make the 4 rows in the pattern at the right.

How many tiles will he need for the fifth row?

1st row
2nd row
3rd row
4th row

Read to Understand

- **Summarize what you are asked to find.**
- **What information is given?**

Plan

- **What strategy can you use to solve the problem?**
  You can look for a pattern.

Solve

- **How can you use the picture of tiles and the strategy to solve the problem?**
  Look at the tile pattern. Is the pattern repeating or growing? How are the rows related?

  The number of tiles increases by 2 from one row to the next. *Add 2 tiles* is a rule that describes the pattern.

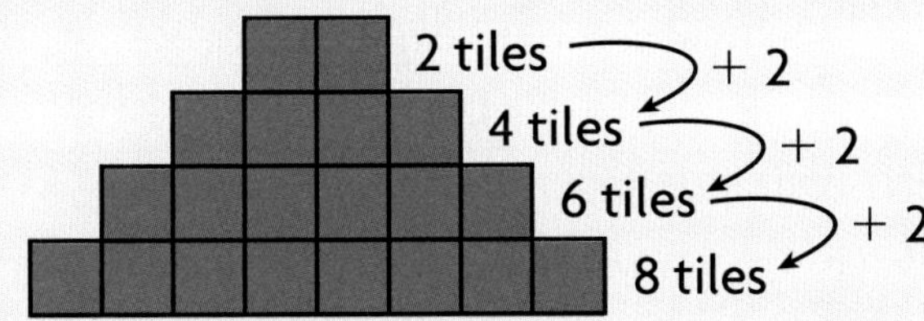

To make the fifth row, add 2 tiles to the number of tiles in the fourth row.

$$8 + 2 = 10$$

So, Sean will need 10 tiles for the fifth row.

Check

- **How can you check your answer?**
- **In what other ways could you solve the problem?**

Guided Problem Solving

Read to Understand
Plan
Solve
Check

1. Dylan and his dad are putting a Native American border on his bedroom wall. The pattern shows two bears facing each other with a paw print between them. How many figures are in the pattern unit?

   First, look at all of the figures in the border.

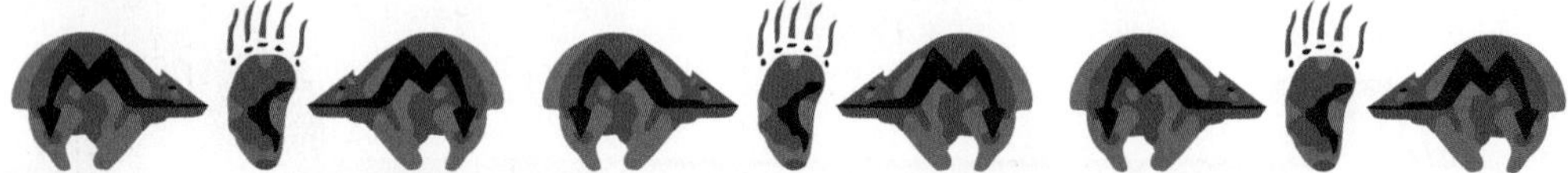

   Next, find the pattern unit where the pattern repeats.

   Then, count the number of figures in the pattern unit.

2. **What if** the border pattern included a right paw print between every other pair of facing bears? How many figures would be in this pattern unit?

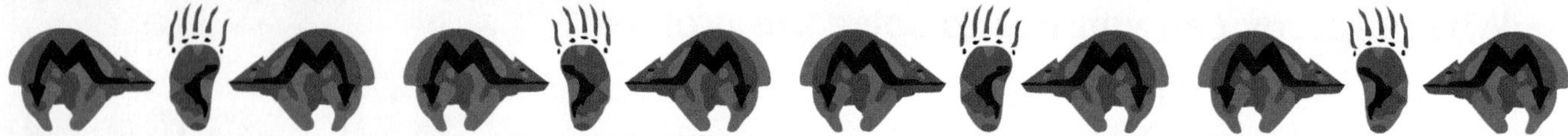

3. Steven painted a border around a picture frame. His pattern unit was *3 circles, 1 triangle.* He painted a total of 24 figures. What shape was the 12th figure?

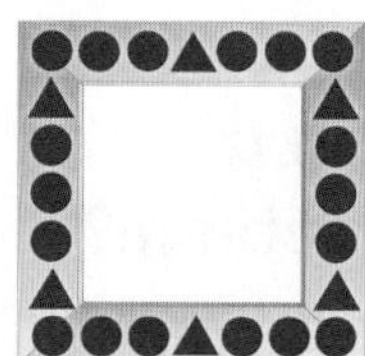

Problem Solving Strategy Practice

Find a pattern to solve.

4. A spider has 8 legs. How many legs do 7 spiders have?

Spiders	2	3	4	5	6	7
Legs	16	24	32	40	■	■

5. Mr. Tanner wrote this number pattern. What is the rule and the next two numbers?
   385, 381, 377, 373, 369, 365, ■, ■

6. Elise arranged shape cards to make a pattern. Then she turned 2 of the cards face down. What shapes are on those 2 cards?

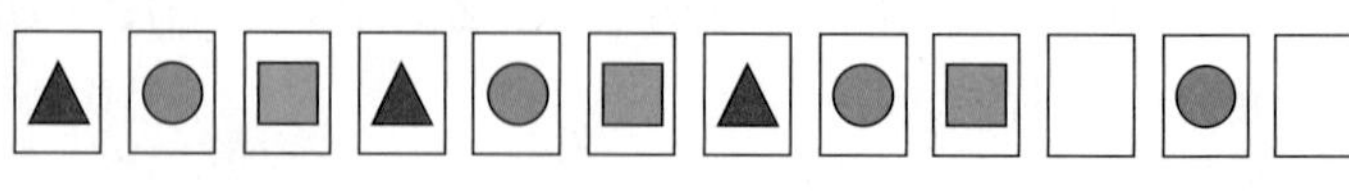

7. WRITE Math Curt is using 35 tiles to make a pattern. The bottom 3 rows are shown at the right. How many rows will Curt make? How many tiles will be in each row? Explain how you found the answer.

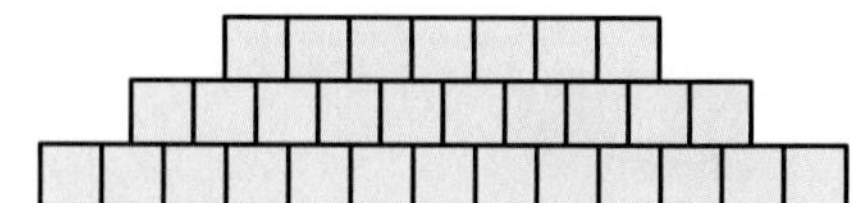

Mixed Strategy Practice

8. Some of the seat numbers in the stadium have worn off. Here is a row of seats. What seat numbers are missing?

9. Abe made a spinner that has 4 colors. The pointer is most likely to land on blue and equally likely to land on red, yellow, and green. What could Abe's spinner look like?

Choose a STRATEGY

- Look for a Pattern
- Draw a Diagram or Picture
- Make a Model or Act It Out
- Make an Organized List
- Make a Table or Graph
- Guess and Check
- Work Backward
- Solve a Simpler Problem
- Write an Equation
- Use Logical Reasoning

USE DATA For 10–12, use the jersey information.

10. Some students in Mr. Jenson's class play soccer. They wore their soccer jerseys to school. Write the numbers in order from least to greatest.

11. Lisa's jersey number is a two-digit number. The ones digit is greater than the tens digit. The sum of the digits is less than 6. What is Lisa's jersey number?

12. **Open-ended** Use all of the numbers on the soccer jerseys to write a pattern. Find a rule for your pattern. Then tell what the next two numbers would be if you continued your pattern.

CHALLENGE YOURSELF

Five teams played in a soccer tournament.
Each team played each other only 1 time.

13. How many games in all were played in the tournament?

14. During the season, Team 1 won 2 fewer games than Team 5. Team 2 won 2 fewer games than Team 1. Team 1 won twice as many games as Team 3. Team 4 won 3 more games than Team 3. Team 5 won 10 games. How many games did Team 4 win?

Extra Practice

Set A Name a pattern unit. Find the missing number or shape. (pp. 178–179)

1. 7, 6, 3, 7, 6, 3, ■, 6, 3, 7, 6, 3
2. 9, 1, 7, 9, 1, 7, 9, 1, 7, 9, 1, ■
3. ?

Predict the next two numbers in each pattern.

4. 3, 0, 8, 8, 3, 0, 8, 8, 3, 0, 8, ■, ■
5. 4, 5, 6, 5, 4, 5, 6, 5, 4, 5, 6, 5, ■, ■
6. Madison ran the following number of miles during training so far this month: 3, 3, 2, 3, 3, 2, 3, 3. If he continues the same pattern of miles, what are the next two distances he will run?

Set B Find the pattern unit or rule. Then name the next figure. (pp. 180–181)

1.
2.

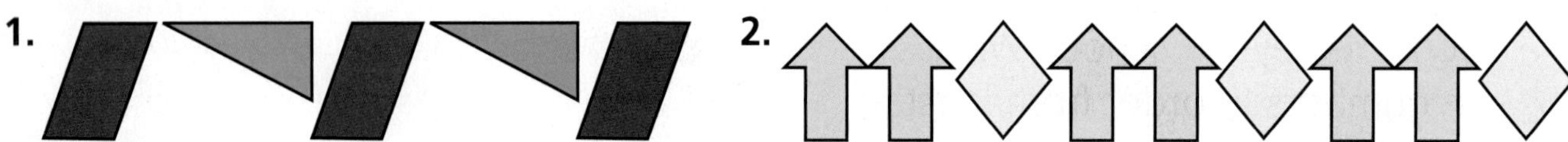

Find the pattern unit or rule. Draw the missing figures.

3. ? ?

Set C Write a rule for each pattern. Then find the next number. (pp. 182–183)

1. 25, 37, 49, 61, 73, 85
2. 65, 58, 51, 44, 37, 30
3. 4, 8, 13, 17, 22, 26, 31, 35
4. The balances in Vivian's bank account for the last six months were $112, $127, $142, $157, $172, and $187. How much did Vivian save each month?

Set D Name the rule or pattern unit. Find the next three numbers or shapes in the pattern. (pp. 184–185)

1.
2. 26, 34, 33, 41, 40, 48, 47, 55, 54
3.

CD ROM **Technology**
Use Harcourt Mega Math, The Number Games, *Tiny's Think Tank*, Levels J, K.

TECHNOLOGY CONNECTION

Calculator: Number Patterns (TEKS 3.6A)

Use a calculator to find number patterns.

Elizabeth is taking a bead-making class. In her first lesson, she makes 8 beads. In each of the next lessons, she makes 3 more beads than in the lesson before. How many beads does she make in her fifth lesson?

Identify the first number and a rule for the pattern.

First lesson: 8 beads **Pattern rule:** add 3

Add 3 to find out how many beads Elizabeth made in the second lesson.

So, Elizabeth made 11 beads in the second lesson.

To continue the pattern, press the = key for the next three lessons. You do not have to press + 3 again.

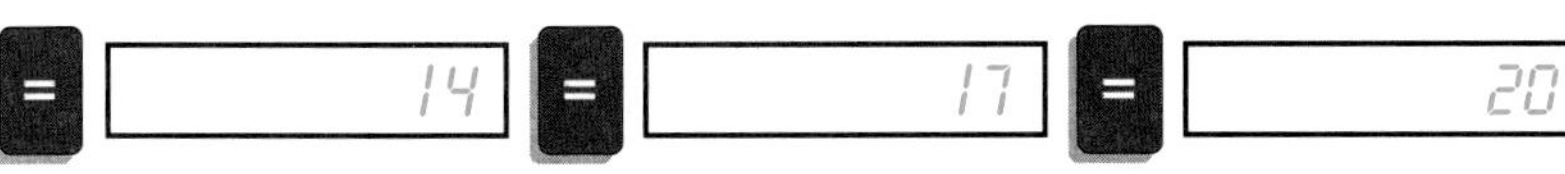

third lesson **fourth lesson** **fifth lesson**

So, Elizabeth made 20 beads in the fifth lesson.

Try It

Use a calculator to find the first five numbers in each number pattern.

1. First number: 5
   Pattern rule: add 9
2. First number: 74
   Pattern rule: subtract 8
3. First number: 15
   Pattern rule: add 12

Use a calculator to find a rule for each pattern. Fill in the missing numbers.

4. 56, 50, ■, 38, 32
5. 26, 39, 52, ■, 78
6. 140, 122, 104, 86, ■
7. **Explore More** Ethan made this table to show how long he read on each day of one week. How many minutes did he read on Friday? **Explain** your answer.

	Monday	Tuesday	Wednesday	Thursday	Friday
minutes	18	31	44	57	■

Chapter 8 Review/Test

Check Vocabulary and Concepts

Choose the best term from the box.

VOCABULARY
repeating pattern
pattern unit
growing pattern
geometric pattern

1. A _?_ is a pattern that adds to each pattern unit. (TEKS 3.6A, p. 180)
2. The part of the pattern that repeats is the _?_. (TEKS 3.6A, p. 178)
3. A pattern that uses the same pattern unit over and over is a _?_. (TEKS 3.6A, p. 180)

Check Skills

Find the pattern unit or rule. Then draw the missing figure. (TEKS 3.6A, pp. 180–181)

4.  _?_

5. 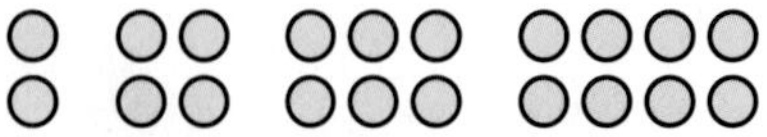 _?_

6. 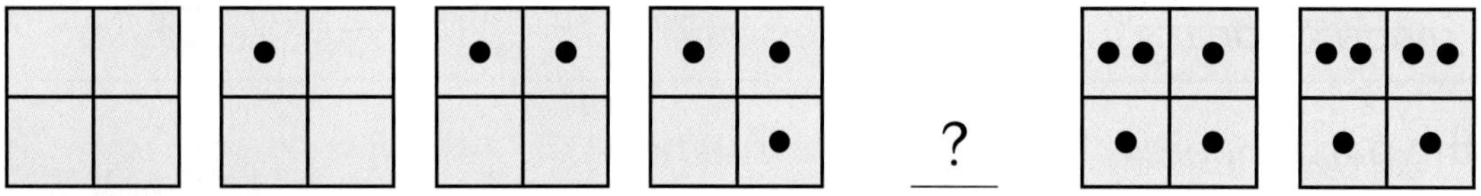

Write a rule for each pattern. Then find the next number. (TEKS 3.6A, pp. 182–183)

7. 27, 34, 41, 48, 55, 62, ■
8. 8, 14, 19, 25, 30, 36, ■
9. 7, 9, 13, 19, 27, 37, ■
10. 93, 87, 85, 79, 77, 71, ■
11. 19, 28, 36, 43, 49, 54 ■
12. 1, 2, 4, 7, 11, 16, 22, 29, 37, ■

Check Problem Solving

Solve. (TEKS 3.14C, pp. 186–189)

13. Malik has a border on his bedroom wall that follows a pattern unit of two trees, a deer, and a leaf. What is the 14th figure in the pattern?

14. Melissa's rug has this pattern:

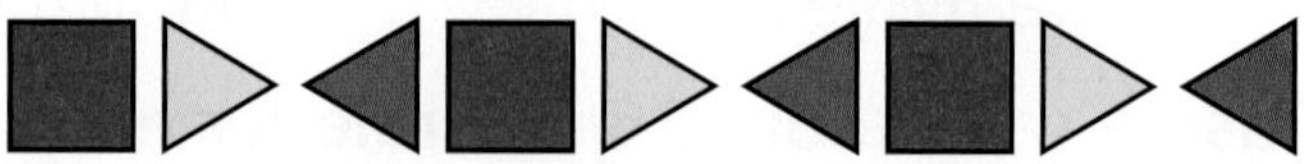

What is the pattern unit for the rug? What is the next shape?

15. WRITE Math Keisha is making a necklace with 9 red beads, 6 blue beads, and 3 yellow beads. What pattern can Keisha use so that she includes all the beads in the necklace? **Explain.**

GO ONLINE **Technology** Use *Online Assessment.*

Enrich • Calculator Patterns

Nifty Numbers

You can use a calculator to find number patterns with large numbers.

One

Start with 0. Add 99 five times. What patterns do you see?

Step 1	Enter the starting number, 99.    Press the plus key and then the equal key.
Step 2	Record each sum. 99 198 297 396 495 594
Step 3	Look for patterns. • What did you notice about the ones digits? the tens digits? the hundreds digits?
Step 4	Predict the next four numbers in the pattern. Check your predictions on your calculator.

So, you can predict the results of adding 99, using patterns.

Two

Find a pattern. Write the next 3 numbers in each pattern.

1. Multiply 2 x 6. Record the product. Press the equal key 10 times. Record the products. What pattern do you notice in the ones digits?

2. Start with 7. Add 6 ten times. What patterns do you notice in the ones digits of the sums?

Three

WRITE Math ▸ Choose a number from 1 through 9. Then choose a second number from 1 through 9 to add at least 10 times. Record each sum. Describe the patterns you find in the ones digits.

Unit Review/Test
Chapters 6–8

Multiple Choice

1. Michelle made a tally table to record her friends' votes for their favorite activity. Her chart shows 卌 卌 |||| next to reading. How many friends voted for reading? (TAKS Obj. 5)

   A 6

   B 12

   C 14

   D Not here

2. Which time shows 20 minutes before midnight? (TAKS Obj. 4)

   F 12:20 P.M.

   G 11:40 P.M.

   H 12:20 A.M.

   J 11:40 A.M.

3. Ken made the bar graph to show the number of books he read each month. How many books did Ken read in June? (TAKS Obj. 5)

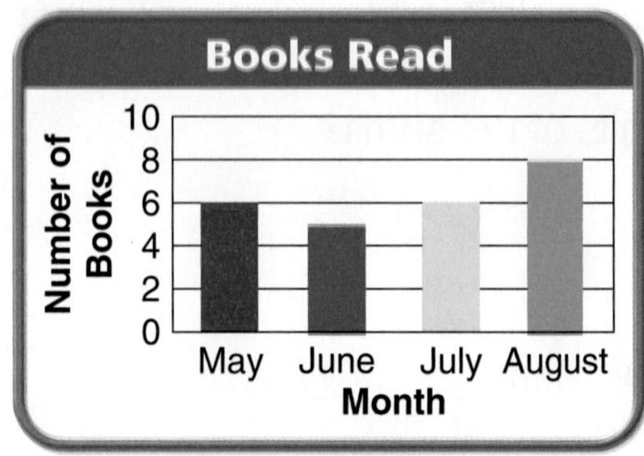

   A 8 C 6

   B 7 D 5

4. What is the pattern unit in this number pattern? (TAKS Obj. 2)

   3, 2, 1, 3, 2, 1, 3, 2, 1

   F 3, 2, 1

   G 2, 3, 1

   H 2, 3, 4

   J 1, 2, 3

5. Which is NOT a way to write the time shown on this clock? (TAKS Obj. 4)

   A Fifteen minutes after five

   B 5:15

   C Quarter to five

   D Five fifteen

6. Linda made a pictograph to show how many games she has. She used the key: Each □ = 3 games. How many games does □□□□□ stand for? (TAKS Obj. 5)

   F 5 H 15

   G 10 J 20

GO ONLINE Technology Use *Online Assessment.*

7. Rosanna made a number pattern. The rule for the pattern was add 3, subtract 1. Which could be her number pattern? (TAKS Obj. 2)

   A 5, 8, 11, 14, 17, 21

   B 5, 8, 7, 10, 9, 12

   C 5, 4, 7, 6, 9, 8

   D 5, 8, 9, 12, 13, 16

8. Sarah surveyed her classmates about their favorite food. She displayed her data in a bar graph. Which could be the title of her graph? (TAKS Obj. 5)

   F Favorite Foods

   G Number of Students

   H Favorite Color

   J Sarah's Lunch

9. Which is the missing shape in this pattern? (TAKS Obj. 2)

   △ □ ○ △ □ ○ △ □ ○ ? □

   A ○ **C** □

   B △ **D** ▯

10. At what time would a third grader eat breakfast? (TAKS Obj. 4)

   F 3:00 A.M. **H** 8:00 P.M.

   G midnight **J** 8:00 A.M.

Short Response

11. What time is shown on the clock? (TAKS Obj. 4)

12. What is the missing number? (TAKS Obj. 2)

1	2	3	4	5	6
17	23	29	35	41	■

13. Stephen made the pictograph to show how many models he has in his collection. How many cars does Stephen have? (TAKS Obj. 5)

Models in Collection	
Airplanes	◻◻◧
Cars	◻◻◻◻◻◻◧
Trucks	◻◻◻◻
Boats	◻◻
Key: Each ◻ = 4 models.	

Extended Response WRITE Math

14. Barry made towers with blocks. The towers form a pattern. How many blocks would be needed to make the 5th tower in the pattern? **Explain.** (TAKS Obj. 2)

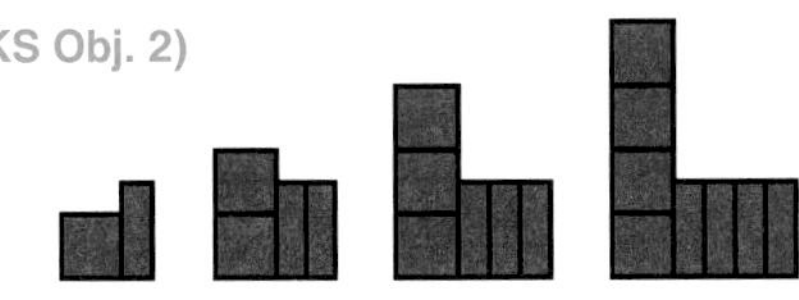

Texas Problem Solving

Butterflies

A butterfly watcher at the Butterfly Festival

Texas Butterfly Festival

The Texas Butterfly Festival is held every October in Mission, Texas. People come from all over to see hundreds of butterfly species that live in Texas. At the three-day festival, children can learn about butterflies at different exhibits, feed butterflies by hand, and march in a nature-themed costume parade.

FACT·ACTIVITY

Read the time to answer the questions.

1. The festival begins at 7:30 A.M. Which clock shows this time?

A 

B 

C 

2. The costume parade begins at 2:15 P.M. Which clock shows this time?

A 

B 

C 

3. The clock on the right shows when the butterfly exhibit opens each morning. Write the time in two different ways.

4. 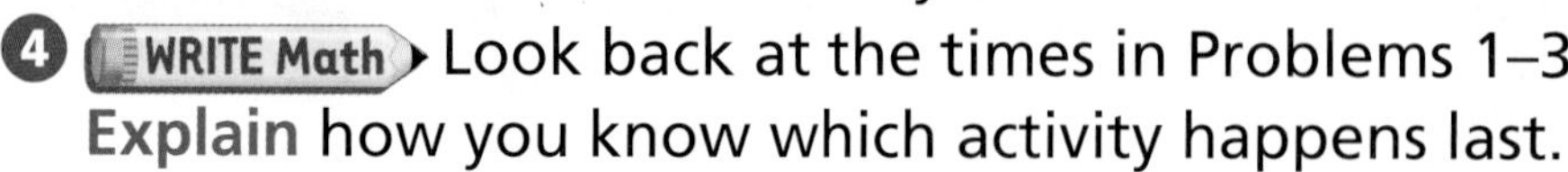 WRITE Math Look back at the times in Problems 1–3. **Explain** how you know which activity happens last.

Texas Butterflies

You can see hundreds of butterflies during the festival or any other time at the International Butterfly Park in Mission, Texas. Butterflies are everywhere—on flowers, in chrysalises, or just flying by.

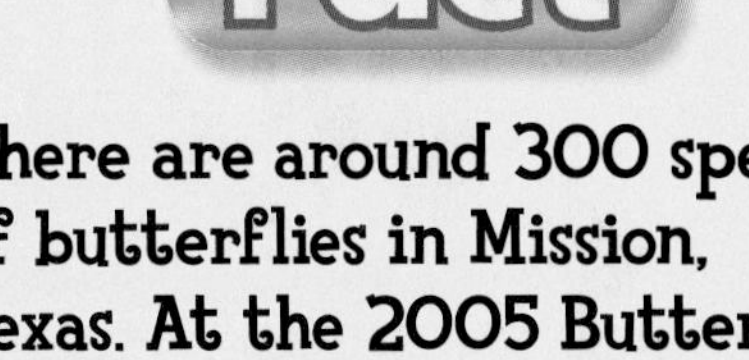

There are around 300 species of butterflies in Mission, Texas. At the 2005 Butterfly Festival, 106 species were seen.

Texas even has a state butterfly! The monarch butterfly became the state butterfly of Texas in 1995.

Monarch

Blue-eyed sailor

Two-barred flasher

FACT ACTIVITY

The Rivera family counted the number of times they saw different butterflies at the park. Some of their results are in the table.

Butterflies Seen by the Riveras

Butterfly	Number
Monarch	25
Blue-eyed sailor	10
Two-barred flasher	5

1. Make a bar graph using the data shown on the table.
   - Is 2 a good scale to use? Is 5 a good scale? Decide on a scale.
   - Write a title for the graph. Color a bar for each butterfly.
   - Label the bars.
2. Write an addition and a subtraction problem that can be answered by the data in your graph.

UNIT

4 Multiplication Concepts and Facts

Math on Location

with **Texas Chapter Projects**

1

A new toy is invented by starting with an idea, making a drawing, and combining pieces for a kit.

2

The unassembled kit shows multiple numbers of different pieces.

3

The designers use imagination and creativity when designing small toys or large, movable toys.

VOCABULARY POWER

TALK Math

What math is shown in the **Math on Location** photographs? How can you use multiplication to tell how many pieces there are?

READ Math

REVIEW VOCABULARY You learned the words below when you learned about multiplication last year. How do these words relate to **Math on Location**?

factor a number that is multiplied by another number to find a product

multiply to combine equal groups to find how many in all

product the answer in a multiplication problem

WRITE Math

Copy and complete a Word Definition Map like the one below. Use what you know about multiplication.

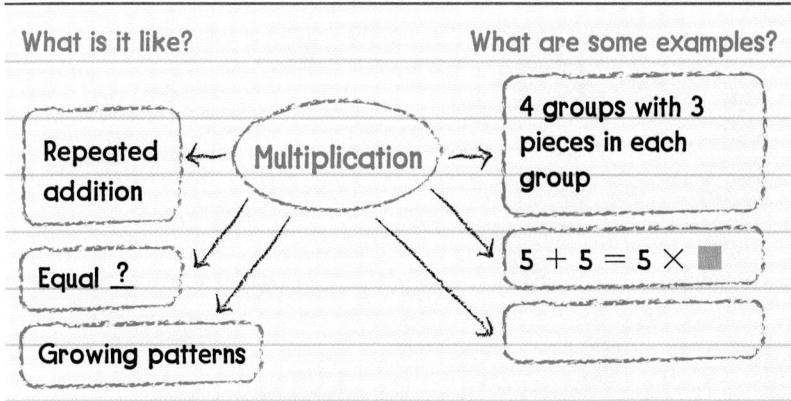

Technology
Multimedia Math Glossary link at
www.harcourtschool.com/hspmath

9 Understand Multiplication

The Big Idea Multiplication is related to repeated addition and tells how many in equal groups.

TEXAS FAST FACT

The state folk dance of Texas is the square dance. Square dancing is done in groups of 8. The 4 pairs of dancers form a square. A caller tells the dancers what steps to do.

Investigate

The table shows the types and numbers of classes offered at a dance studio each week. Choose a dance style. Tell how many classes of that style are offered in 4 weeks and in 8 weeks.

Dance Class Schedule

Dance Style	Classes per Week
Square Dancing	2
Line Dancing	1
Ballet	4
Tap	3
Jazz/Hip Hop	5
Ballroom	4

Technology
Student pages are available in the Student eBook.

Show What You Know

Check your understanding of important skills needed for success in Chapter 9.

▶ Skip-Count

Skip-count to find the missing numbers.

1. 2, 4, 6, 8, ■, ■, ■

2. 3, 6, 9, ■, ■, ■

3. 5, 10, 15, ■, 25, ■, ■

4. 10, 20, ■, ■, 50, ■, ■

▶ Equal Groups

Write how many there are in all.

5.

4 groups of 3 = ■

6.

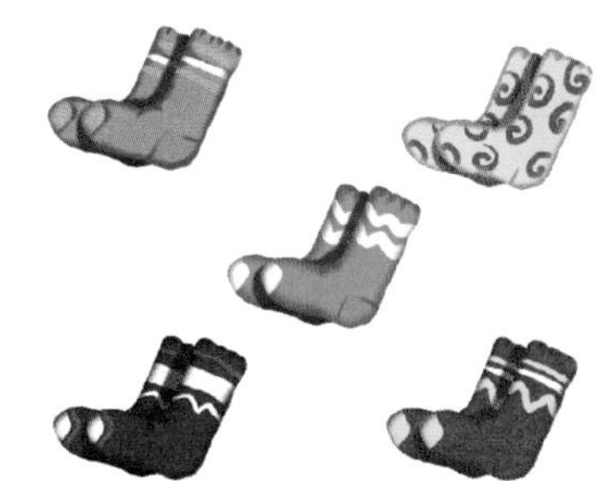

5 groups of 2 = ■

7.

2 groups of 4 = ■

Find how many in all. You may wish to draw a picture.

8. 3 groups of 6

9. 2 groups of 2

10. 4 groups of 5

11. 2 groups of 4

12. 4 groups of 3

13. 5 groups of 6

VOCABULARY POWER

CHAPTER VOCABULARY

array
Commutative Property of Multiplication
factor
Identity Property of Multiplication
multiplication
multiply
product
square number
Zero Property of Multiplication

WARM-UP WORDS

array An arrangement of objects in rows and columns

factor A number that is multiplied by another number to find a product

product The answer in a multiplication problem

ALGEBRA

Relate Addition to Multiplication

OBJECTIVE: Relate addition and multiplication.

Quick Review

Add.

1. 4 + 4 + 4
2. 5 + 5 + 5 + 5
3. 7 + 7 + 7
4. 2 + 2 + 2
5. 3 + 3 + 3

Vocabulary

multiplication multiply

Learn

PROBLEM Jasmine needs 3 bananas to make 1 loaf of banana bread. The same number of bananas are in each loaf. How many bananas does Jasmine need to make 4 loaves?

ONE WAY **Use addition.**

Use counters to show the bananas.
Show 3 counters for each loaf of bread.
Make 4 groups to show the 4 loaves.

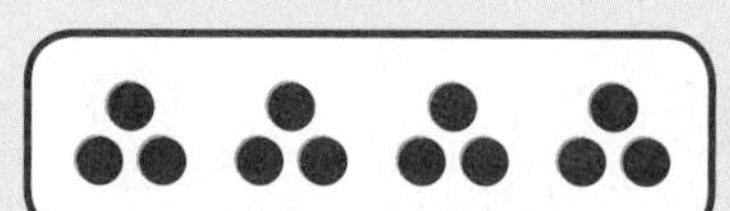

3 + 3 + 3 + 3 = 12

Find the total number of counters.
Write the addition sentence.

So, Jasmine needs 12 bananas to make 4 loaves of bread.

▲ There are about 200 bananas in some bunches.

ANOTHER WAY **Use multiplication.**

When groups are equal, you can use **multiplication** to find the total. When you **multiply**, you combine equal groups to find how many in all.

Think: 4 groups of 3

Write: $4 \times 3 = 12$ **Read:** 4 times 3 equals 12.

A table can show the addition and multiplication.

Equal Groups	Think:	Addition Sentence	Multiplication Sentence
●●● ●●● ●●● ●●●	4 groups of 3	3 + 3 + 3 + 3 = 12	$4 \times 3 = 12$

- **What if** Jasmine makes 5 loaves of bread? How many bananas will she need? Use multiplication to show your answer.

TEKS 3.4A learn and apply multiplication facts through 12 by 12 using concrete models and objects. *also* 3.4B, 3.14A, 3.14D, 3.15A, 3.15B

Guided Practice

1. Write a multiplication sentence that shows $2 + 2 + 2 + 2 + 2 = 10$.

Use counters to model. Then write an addition sentence and a multiplication sentence for each.

2. 2 groups of 4
3. 3 groups of 2
4. 5 groups of 4
5. 3 groups of 3

6. TALK Math **Explain** how you know that both $3 + 3$ and 2×3 equal 6.

Independent Practice and Problem Solving

Use counters to model. Then write an addition sentence and a multiplication sentence for each.

7. 3 groups of 4
8. 2 groups of 5
9. 4 groups of 6
10. 3 groups of 7

Write a multiplication sentence for each.

11.
12.
13.
14.

15. $2 + 2 + 2 + 2 = 8$
16. $4 + 4 + 4 + 4 = 16$
17. $9 + 9 + 9 = 27$

USE DATA For 18–19, use the table.

18. John bought 3 oranges. How much do the oranges weigh in all?

19. Which weighs more, 3 apples or 4 bananas? How much more?

Weight of Fruit

Fruit	Weight in ounces
Apple	6
Orange	5
Banana	4

20. WRITE Math **Sense or Nonsense** Jared says that he can write a multiplication sentence and an addition sentence for $5 + 4 + 4$. Does Jared's statement make sense? **Explain.**

Mixed Review and TAKS Prep

21. Find the missing number in the pattern.
15, 30, 45, ■, 75, 90 (TEKS 3.6A, p.182)

22. Is it more or less likely that Drew will pull a red marble from this bag? (Grade 2, TEKS 2.11C)

23. **TAKS Prep** Which is another way to show $2 + 2 + 2 + 2$?

A 2×2 **B** 6×2 **C** 4×2 **D** 2×8 (Obj. 1)

Extra Practice on page 220, Set A

ALGEBRA

Model with Arrays

OBJECTIVE: Use arrays to understand multiplication and the Commutative Property of Multiplication.

Quick Review

Find how many in all.

1. 3 groups of 2
2. 2 groups of 6
3. 4 groups of 3
4. 3 groups of 5
5. 5 groups of 2

Vocabulary

array factor product
Commutative Property of Multiplication
Square number

Learn

PROBLEM Mark has a garden. He planted 2 rows of tomato plants with 3 plants in each row. How many tomato plants did Mark put in his garden?

An **array** is a group of objects in rows and columns.

Activity

Materials ■ square tiles

Make an array with 2 rows and 3 columns to show Mark's tomato plants.

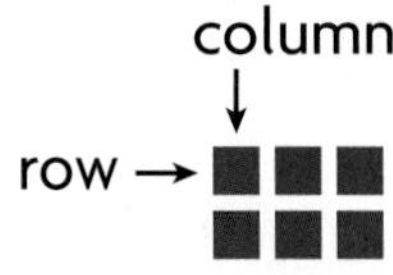

2 rows of 3 = ■

Now find the total number of tiles.

Add. $3 + 3 = 6$

Multiply. $2 \times 3 = 6$

So, Mark put 6 tomato plants in his garden.

You can turn your array to show 3 rows of 2.

3 rows of 2 = ■

Find the total number of tiles.

Add. $2 + 2 + 2 = 6$

Multiply. $3 \times 2 = 6$

- What happened to the number of tiles in the array when you turned it?

▲ Tomatoes are a good source of vitamins.

TEKS 3.4A learn and apply multiplication facts through 12 by 12 using concrete models and objects. *also* 3.6B, 3.14A, 3.14D, 3.15A, 3.15B

Commutative Property of Multiplication

In multiplication, the numbers you multiply together are called **factors**. The answer is called the **product**.

2	$\times$	3	$=$	6
↑		↑		↑
factor		factor		product

The **Commutative Property of Multiplication**, or Order Property of Multiplication, states that factors can be multiplied in any order and their product is the same.

You can use a table to see the Commutative Property.

Model	Draw	Write a Multiplication Sentence
2 rows of 3		$2 \times 3 = 6$
3 rows of 2		$3 \times 2 = 6$
2 rows of 5		$2 \times 5 = 10$
5 rows of 2		$5 \times 2 = 10$
3 rows of 4		$3 \times 4 = 12$
4 rows of 3		$4 \times 3 = 12$

Guided Practice

1. Write the multiplication sentences these arrays show.

Write a multiplication sentence for each array.

2. 

3. 

4. 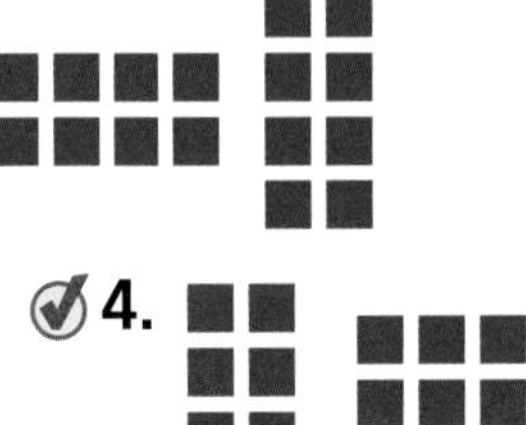

5. TALK Math **Explain** why the Commutative Property is also called the Order Property.

Independent Practice and Problem Solving

Write a multiplication sentence for each array.

6. 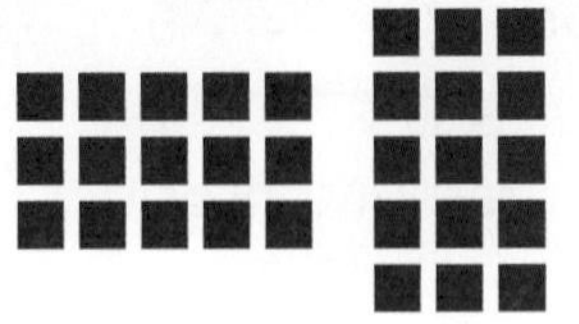

7. 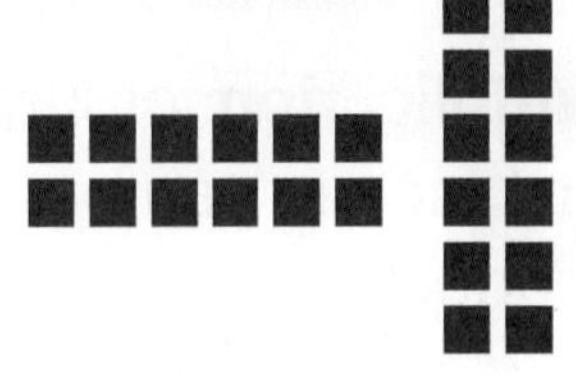

8. 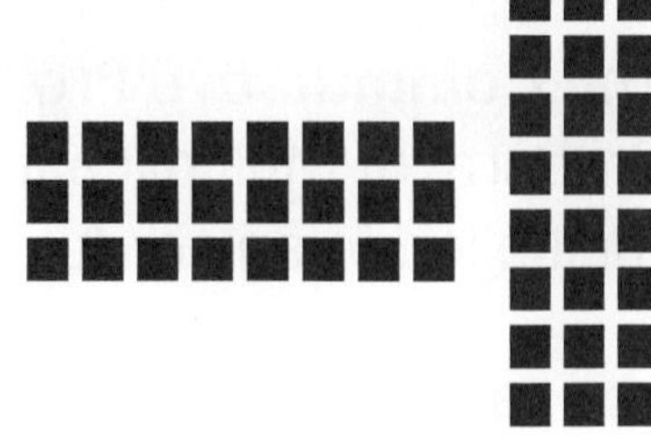

9. 

10. 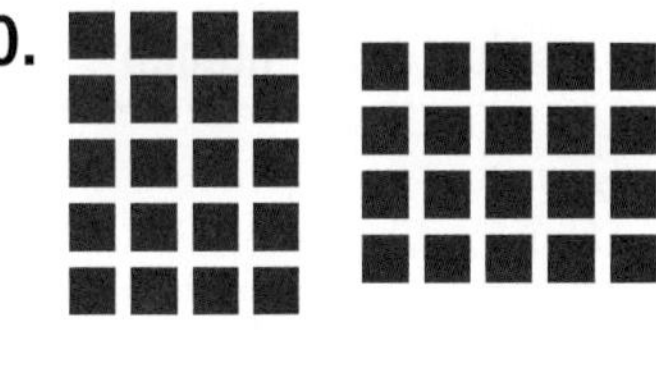

11. 

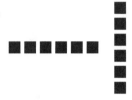

Write the multiplication sentence for each array.
Then draw the array that shows the Commutative Property.

12. 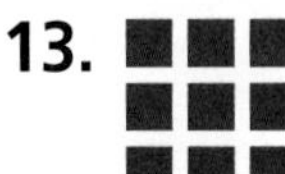

13.

14. 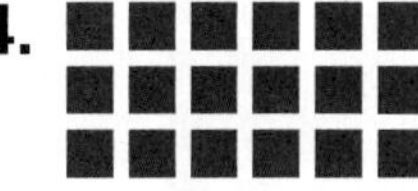

15. Mary placed 24 cans of tomato sauce in 6 rows. How many cans were in each row?

6 rows of ■ = 24

16. Mark picked 5 peppers from each of the 2 rows in his garden. He used 3 peppers to make a salad. How many peppers does he have left?

17. **Reasoning** Jenna and her mother baked apple pies. They picked 18 apples and put the same number of apples in each of 3 pies. Draw an array to show how many apples they put in each pie.

18. John planted 4 rows of strawberries. There are 8 plants in each row. How many strawberry plants did John grow? Draw an array to show your answer.

19. **WRITE Math** Eddie and Jackie both used 12 square tiles to make an array. Eddie's array had 4 rows. Jackie's array had 3 rows. Is this possible? **Explain.**

CD ROM Technology
Use Harcourt Mega Math, Country Countdown, Counting Critters, Level W.

 Extra Practice on page 220, Set B

Mixed Review and TAKS Prep

20. **FAST FACT** The world's largest ketchup bottle is one hundred seventy feet tall. Write this number in standard form. (TEKS 3.1A, p. 10)

21. A notebook has 2 pockets for loose paper. Write an addition sentence and a multiplication sentence to show how many pockets 4 notebooks would have.
(TEKS 3.4A, p. 202)

22. **TAKS Prep** Which is an example of the Commutative Property of Multiplication? (Obj. 1)

A $6 + 4 = 2 + 4$ C $4 \times 6 = 6 \times 4$

B $4 \times 6 = 4 + 6$ D $4 \times 6 = 3 \times 8$

23. **TAKS Prep** The art students hung up their paintings. There are 5 rows with 6 paintings in each row. How many paintings are there in all? (Obj. 1)

F 11 G 30 H 35 J 56

Problem Solving and Reasoning

NUMBER SENSE If both factors are the same, the product is called a **square number**. A square array has the same number of rows and columns.

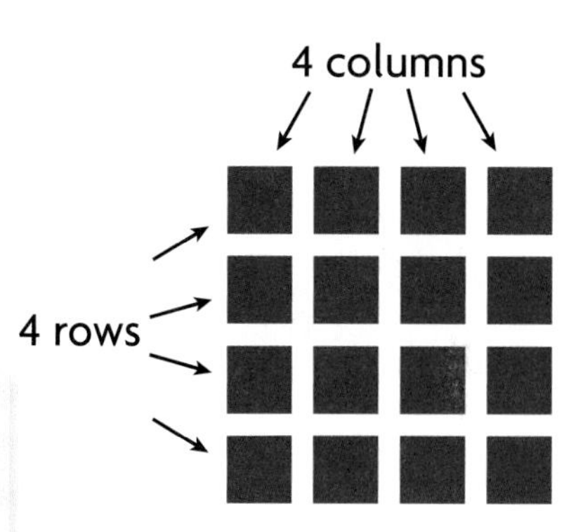

$4 \times 4 = 16$
16 is a square number.

Work with a partner to draw arrays that show square numbers.

Use tiles to make a square array with 3 rows and 3 columns.

Draw the array and write the multiplication sentence.

$3 \times 3 = 9$

So, 9 is a square number.

Draw each array. Write the multiplication sentence. Then circle the square number in each sentence.

1. 5×5
2. 7×7
3. 8×8
4. 6×6
5. 9×9
6. **Reasoning** Is 10 a square number? How do you know?

LESSON 3 Multiply with 2

OBJECTIVE: Multiply with the factor 2.

Quick Review

1. 3 + 3
2. 4 + 4
3. 8 + 8
4. 6 + 6
5. 9 + 9

Learn

PROBLEM Four students are putting on a play for their class. Each of the 4 students has 2 costumes. How many costumes do the students have in all?

Find $4 \times 2 = \blacksquare$.

HANDS ON Activity

Materials ■ counters

Use counters.

MODEL	THINK	RECORD
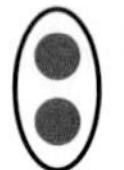  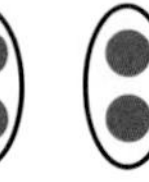 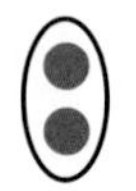	4 groups of 2 2 + 2 + 2 + 2	$4 \times 2 = 8$ $\begin{array}{r} 2 \\ \times 4 \\ \hline 8 \end{array}$

Draw a picture.

DRAW	THINK	RECORD
	4 groups of 2 2 + 2 + 2 + 2	$4 \times 2 = 8$ $\begin{array}{r} 2 \\ \times 4 \\ \hline 8 \end{array}$

So, the students have 8 costumes in all.

Example

You can also multiply by 2 by doubling the other factor.

$3 \times 2 = 2 \times 3 = 3 + 3 = 6$

$4 \times 2 = 2 \times 4 = 4 + 4 = 8$

$5 \times 2 = 2 \times 5 = 5 + 5 = 10$

Guided Practice

1. Write the multiplication sentence the drawing shows.

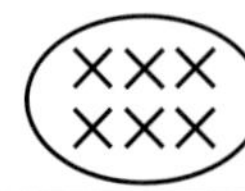 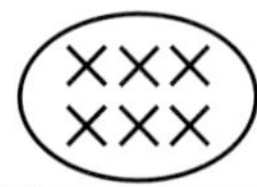

TEKS 3.4A learn and apply multiplication facts through 12 by 12 using concrete models and objects. *also* **3.6B, 3.14A, 3.15A, 3.15B**

Write the multiplication sentence for each.

2. 

3.

4. 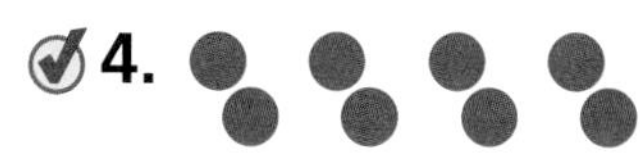

5. TALK Math **Explain** how 6×2 can help you find the product for 2×6.

Independent Practice and Problem Solving

Write a multiplication sentence for each.

6.

7. 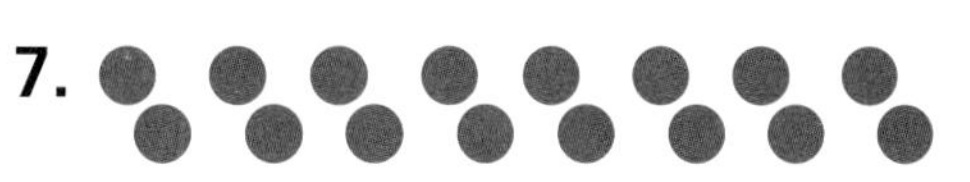

8. 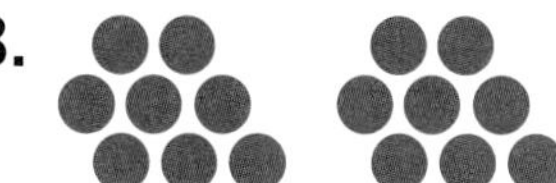

Find the product.

9. $\begin{array}{r} 1 \\ \times 2 \\ \hline \end{array}$

10. $\begin{array}{r} 2 \\ \times 2 \\ \hline \end{array}$

11. $\begin{array}{r} 4 \\ \times 2 \\ \hline \end{array}$

12. $\begin{array}{r} 2 \\ \times 9 \\ \hline \end{array}$

13. $\begin{array}{r} 6 \\ \times 2 \\ \hline \end{array}$

14. $\begin{array}{r} 2 \\ \times 7 \\ \hline \end{array}$

Copy and complete.

15.

×	1	2	3	4	5	6	7	8	9
2	■	■	■	■	■	■	■	■	■

USE DATA For 16–18, use the graph.

16. How many tickets did Tyrone and Julia sell in all?

17. WRITE Math **Explain** how you find out how many tickets Lee sold for the school play.

18. How many more tickets did Lee sell than Julia? (p. 96)

Play Tickets

Name	Tickets Sold
Tyrone	
Julia	
Lee	
Key: Each = 2 tickets.	

Mixed Review and TAKS Prep

19. James had 498 cards. Marta has 346 cards. How many cards do they have in all? (TEKS 3.3B, p. 66)

20. $600 - 357 = ■$ (TEKS 3.3B, p. 94)

21. **TAKS Prep** Jenna and Matt each wear 5 costumes. Which shows their total number of costumes? (obj. 1)

A $2 + 5 = 7$

B $5 + 2 = 7$

C $2 \times 2 = 4$

D $2 \times 5 = 10$

Extra Practice on page 220, Set C

LESSON 4

Multiply with 4

OBJECTIVE: Multiply with the factor 4.

Quick Review

1. 2 × 3
2. 2 × 5
3. 8 × 2
4. 2 × 6
5. 10 × 2

Learn

PROBLEM Matchbox® cars were invented by Jack Odell in 1952. Caleb has 3 Matchbox cars. Each car has 4 wheels. What is the total number of wheels on Caleb's cars?

Find 3 × 4 = ■.

HANDS ON **Activity** **Materials** ■ counters, number line

ONE WAY **Use counters.**

MODEL	THINK	RECORD
	3 groups of 4 4 + 4 + 4	3 × 4 = 12 $\begin{array}{r} 4 \\ \times 3 \\ \hline 12 \end{array}$

So, Caleb's cars have a total of 12 wheels.

OTHER WAYS **Use a number line.**

MODEL	THINK	RECORD
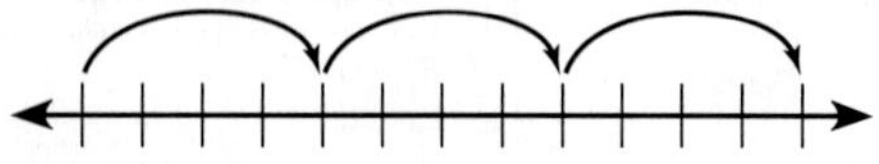	Skip count by 4. 4, 8, 12	3 × 4 = 12 $\begin{array}{r} 4 \\ \times 3 \\ \hline 12 \end{array}$

Use doubles.

Multiplying with 4 is the same as multiplying by 2 and doubling the product.

	Multiply by 2.	Double the product.
3 × 4 = ■ Think: 2 + 2	3 × 2 = 6	6 + 6 = 12, so, 3 × 4 = 12
5 × 4 = ■ Think: 2 + 2	5 × 2 = 10	10 + 10 = 20, so, 5 × 4 = 20

- How can you double a 2's fact to find 6 × 4?

TEKS 3.4A learn and apply multiplication facts through 12 by 12 using concrete models and objects. *also* **3.6B, 3.14A, 3.15A, 3.15B**

Guided Practice

1. How can you use this number line to find 4×4?

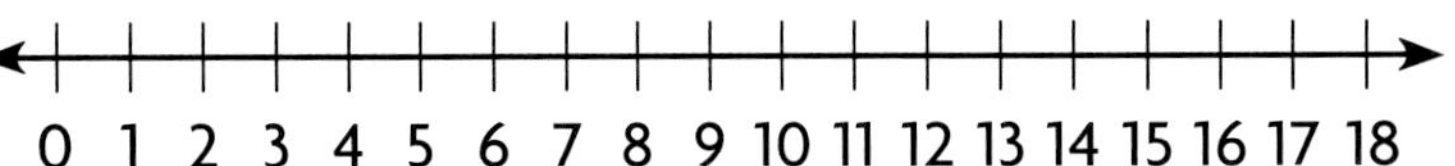

Find the product.

2. $6 \times 4 = ■$
3. $3 \times 4 = ■$
4. $5 \times 4 = ■$
5. $8 \times 4 = ■$

6. **TALK Math** **Explain** how knowing the product of 2×8 helps you find the product of 4×8.

Independent Practice and Problem Solving

Find the product.

7. $4 \times 4 = ■$
8. $7 \times 4 = ■$
9. $6 \times 4 = ■$
10. $4 \times 5 = ■$

Copy and complete.

	×	1	2	3	4	5	6	7	8	9	10
11.	2	■	■	■	■	■	■	■	■	■	■
12.	4	■	■	■	■	■	■	■	■	■	■

Algebra Write the missing factor.

13. $8 + 8 + 8 + 8 = ■ \times 8$
14. $4 + 4 + 4 = ■ \times 4$
15. $6 \times 4 = 4 \times ■$

USE DATA For 16–17, use the graph.

16. Tina, Charlie, and Amber have Matchbox cars. How many wheels do their cars have altogether?

17. **WRITE Math** **What's the Error?** Charlie says that since $5 \times 2 = 10$, his cars have a total of 10 wheels. What is Charlie's error?

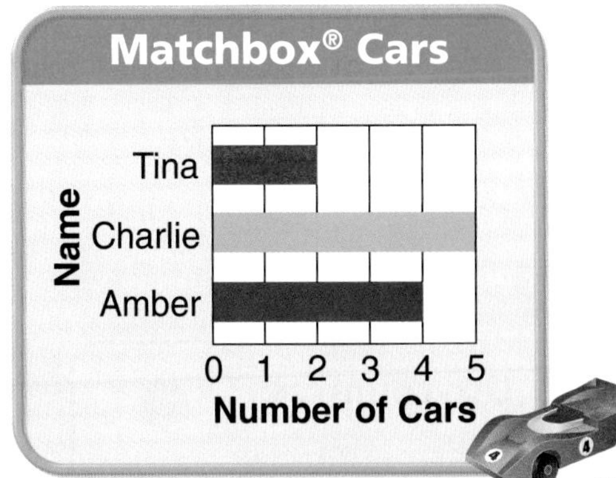

Mixed Review and TAKS Prep

18. In a pictograph, how would you show 9 votes using the key ☺ = 3 votes? (TEKS 3.13B, p. 152)

19. What shape has 4 equal sides and 4 square corners? (Grade 2, TEKS 2.7A)

20. **TAKS Prep** There are 5 rows of 4 cars on the toy shelf. How many cars are there in all? (Obj. 1)

A $5 + 4 = 9$ **C** $5 \times 4 = 20$
B $4 \times 4 = 16$ **D** $5 \times 5 = 25$

Extra Practice on page 221, Set D

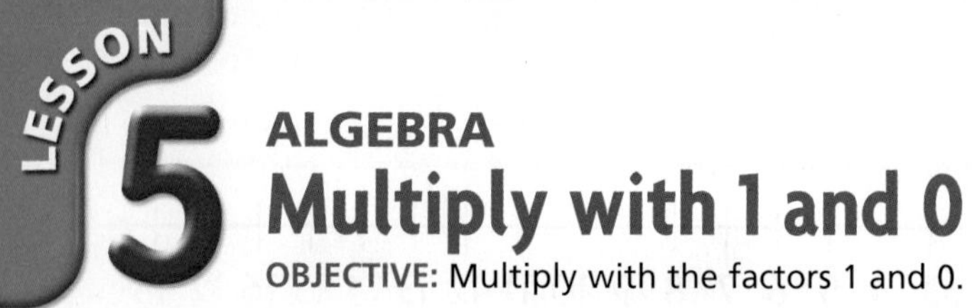

LESSON 5

ALGEBRA

Multiply with 1 and 0

OBJECTIVE: Multiply with the factors 1 and 0.

Quick Review

1. 6 + 1
2. 5 + 0
3. 1 + 4
4. 7 + 0
5. 9 + 1

Vocabulary

Identity Property of Multiplication

Zero Property of Multiplication

Learn

PROBLEM Luke saw 4 doghouses. Each doghouse had 1 dog in it. How many dogs were there in all?

ONE WAY **Draw a picture.**

Step 1

Step 2

Write the multiplication sentence.

4	×	1	=	4
↑		↑		↑
number of groups		number in each group		number in all

So, there were 4 dogs in all.

The **Identity Property of Multiplication** states that the product of any number and 1 is that number.

$7 \times 1 = 7$ $\quad$ $6 \times 1 = 6$

$1 \times 7 = 7$ $\quad$ $1 \times 6 = 6$

OTHER WAYS

A **Use counters.**

4 groups

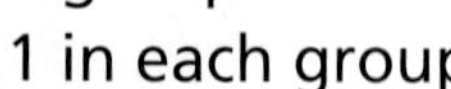

1 in each group

4 in all

$4 \times 1 = 4$

B **Use a number line.**

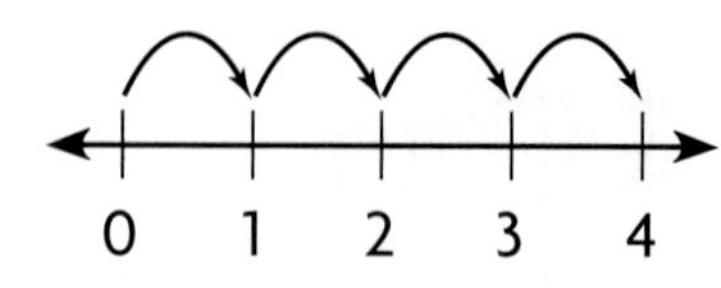

4 jumps of 1

4 in all

$4 \times 1 = 4$

ERROR ALERT

Be sure to look carefully at the operation signs.

$4 + 1 = 5$

$4 \times 1 = 4$

$1 + 5 = 6$

$1 \times 5 = 5$

TEKS 3.4A learn and apply multiplication facts through 12 by 12 using concrete models and objects. *also* **3.6B, 3.14A, 3.15A, 3.15B**

Multiply with Zero

Lilly saw 4 doghouses. There were 0 dogs in each doghouse. How many dogs were there in all?

ONE WAY **Draw a picture.**

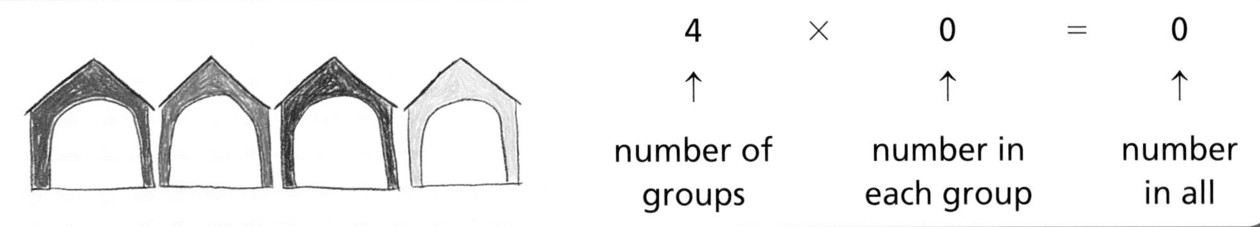

So, there were 0 dogs in all.

The **Zero Property of Multiplication** states that the product of zero and any number is zero.

$0 \times 10 = 0 \qquad 5 \times 0 = 0$

ANOTHER WAY **Use a multiplication table.**

Look at the row and column for 0.

- What do you notice about the products that have 0 as a factor?

Look at the row and column for 1.

- What do you notice about the products that have 1 as a factor?

×	0	1	2	3	4	5	6	7	8	9	10
0	0	0	0	0	0	0	0	0	0	0	0
1	0	1	2	3	4	5	6	7	8	9	10
2	0	2									
3	0	3									
4	0	4									
5	0	5									
6	0	6									
7	0	7									
8	0	8									
9	0	9									
10	0	10									

Guided Practice

1. What multiplication sentence is shown in this picture? Find the product.

2. $3 \times 1 = ■$ 3. $0 \times 2 = ■$ ✓4. $4 \times 0 = ■$ ✓5. $1 \times 6 = ■$

6. **TALK Math** **Explain** how 3×1 and $3 + 1$ are different. Draw a picture to show your answer.

Independent Practice and Problem Solving

Find the product.

7. $5 \times 1 = \blacksquare$ **8.** $8 \times 0 = \blacksquare$ **9.** $1 \times 9 = \blacksquare$ **10.** $0 \times 7 = \blacksquare$ **11.** $1 \times 1 = \blacksquare$

12. $\begin{array}{r} 1 \\ \times 0 \\ \hline \end{array}$ **13.** $\begin{array}{r} 1 \\ \times 7 \\ \hline \end{array}$ **14.** $\begin{array}{r} 0 \\ \times 6 \\ \hline \end{array}$ **15.** $\begin{array}{r} 2 \\ \times 1 \\ \hline \end{array}$ **16.** $\begin{array}{r} 8 \\ \times 1 \\ \hline \end{array}$ **17.** $\begin{array}{r} 0 \\ \times 5 \\ \hline \end{array}$

Write a multiplication sentence shown on each number line.

18. 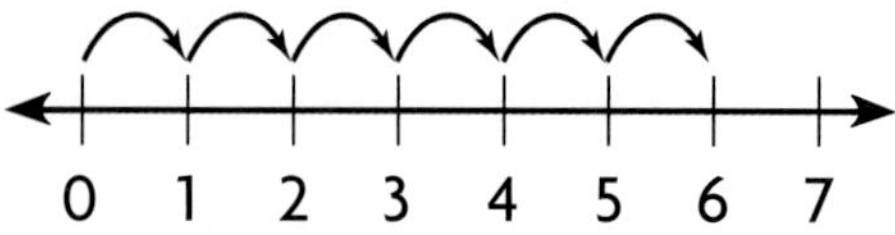

19. 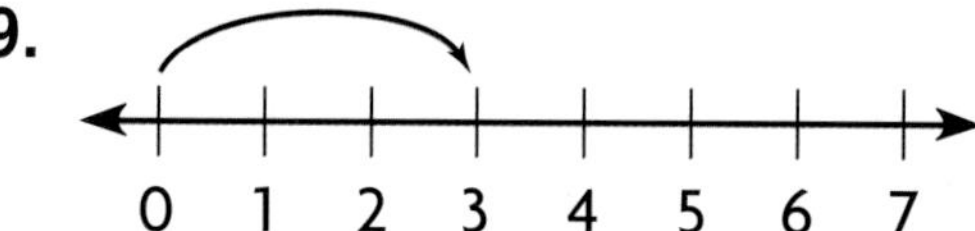

Find the missing number.

20. $3 \times \blacksquare = 0$ **21.** $5 \times 1 = \blacksquare \times 5$ **22.** $\blacksquare \times 28 = 28$ **23.** $0 \times 46 = \blacksquare$

USE DATA For 24–26, use the table.

Vehicle	Number of Wheels
Car	4
Tricycle	3
Bicycle	2
Unicycle	1

24. At the circus Jon saw 5 unicycles. How many wheels are on the unicycles in all? Draw a picture and write a multiplication sentence.

25. Brian's family has 3 bicycles and 1 tricycle. How many wheels are there in all?

26. WRITE Math **What's the Question?** Josh used multiplication by 1 and the information in the table. The answer is 6.

Mixed Review and TAKS Prep

27. Write a 4-digit number with an 8 in the tens place. (TEKS 3.1A, p. 14)

28. **TAKS Prep** Eric has 6 boxes. He has 1 pencil in each box. Which shows how many pencils Eric has? (Obj. 1)

A $6 + 1 = 7$ **C** $0 \times 6 = 0$

B $6 - 1 = 5$ **D** $6 \times 1 = 6$

29. Which shape is missing from this pattern? (TEKS 3.6A, p. 180)

30. **TAKS Prep** Which number sentence is correct? (Obj. 1)

F $3 \times 1 = 0$ **H** $1 \times 3 = 0$

G $0 \times 3 = 0$ **J** $0 \times 1 = 3$

Extra Practice on page 221, Set E

Pose a Problem

Writing a problem helps you become a better problem solver. Sarah is learning how to multiply with 1 and 0. Her teacher asked her to write a problem about multiplying with 1 and another problem about multiplying with 0. Sarah wrote the problems below.

Marcos bought 1 box of crayons. There are 8 crayons in the box. How many crayons does Marcos have?

Each box of crayons has 8 crayons in it. James did not get a box. How many crayons does James have now?

Tips

To pose a problem, think about these things:

- the information you will give
- the question you will ask
- the math idea your problem will be about
- the numbers you will use in your problem
- how to solve the problem

Problem Solving Write problems to show that you understand how to multiply with 1 and 0.

1. Multiply with 1.

2. Multiply with 0.

Problem Solving Workshop
Strategy: Draw a Picture

OBJECTIVE: Solve problems by using the *draw a picture* strategy.

Learn the Strategy

Drawing a picture can help you understand a problem and see how to solve it. You can draw pictures to solve different types of problems.

A picture can show how many in all.

There are 4 flower pots on the Langs' front porch. Mrs. Lang wants to plant 3 flowers in each pot. How many flowers will she plant in all?

A picture can show how to divide a whole.

Lucy bought a sub sandwich. She wants to share it with 3 friends for lunch. Into how many pieces should Lucy cut the sandwich? How many cuts will she need to make?

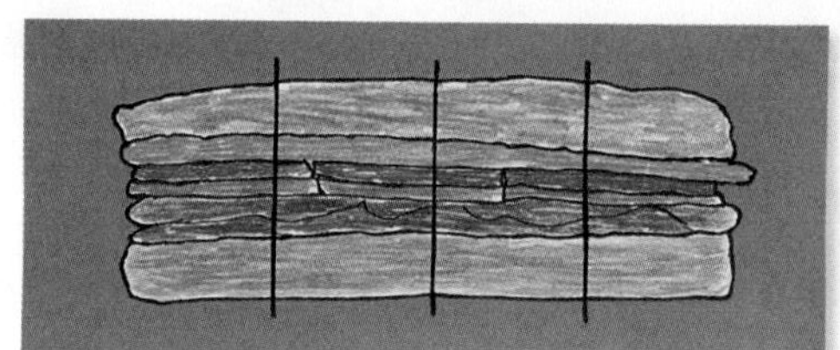

A picture can show order.

Morgan built a snowman. She put 5 buttons on it. The blue button was below the red button. The green button was above the red one. The black button was between the red and blue buttons. The yellow button was just above the green button. Which button was at the top?

To draw a picture, carefully read the information in the problem. Keep your drawing simple.

TALK Math

Choose one of the problems. Tell how the picture helps you solve it.

TEKS 3.14C select or develop an appropriate problem-solving strategy including drawing a picture, looking for a pattern, systematic guessing and checking, acting it out, making a table, working a simpler problem, or working backwards to solve a problem. *also* **3.4A, 3.6B, 3.14A, 3.14B, 3.15A**

Use the Strategy

PROBLEM There are 2 rows of drummers in the drum section of a marching band. There are 7 drummers in each row. How many drummers are there in all?

Read to Understand
Plan
Solve
Check

Read to Understand

- **Summarize what you are asked to find.**
- **What information will you use?**

Plan

- **What strategy can you use to solve the problem?**
  You can draw a picture to help you solve the problem.

Solve

- **How can you use the strategy to solve the problem?**
  Draw a picture with stick people to show the drummers.

  Draw 2 rows.
  Show 7 stick people in each row.

  Add or multiply to find the total number of drummers in all.

  $7 + 7 = 14$
  $2 \times 7 = 14$

  So, there are 14 drummers in all in the drum section.

Check

- **How can you check your answer?**
- **What other ways could you solve the problem?**

Guided Problem Solving

Read to Understand
Plan
Solve
Check

1. The marching band has 6 groups of 4 people who play the trumpet. How many people play the trumpet?

   First, draw a picture of the problem.
   Show 6 circles with 4 dots in each circle.

   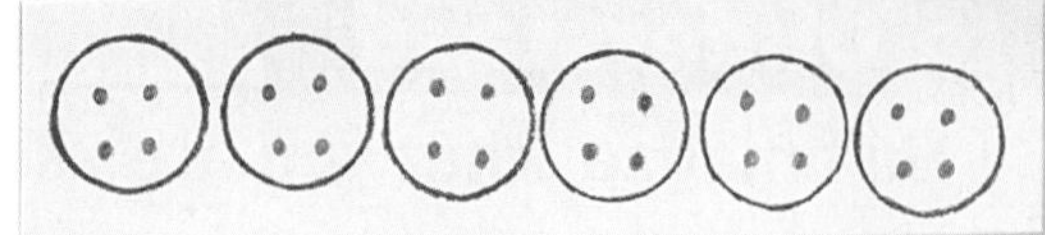

   Next, find the total number of dots.

   $6 \times 4 = \blacksquare$

2. **What if** there are 5 groups instead of 6 in Problem 1? How many people would play the trumpet?

3. There are 7 rows of flute players in the marching band. There are 5 people in each row. How many flute players are in the marching band?

Problem Solving Strategy Practice

For 4–6, draw a picture to solve.

4. Each drummer needs 2 drum sticks. How many drum sticks do 6 drummers need?

5. During band practice, 7 students each twirled 1 flag. How many total flags did the students twirl?

6. Twelve students in Mrs. Taylor's class want to start a band. Seven of the students made drums. The rest made 2 maracas each. How many maracas in all were made?

USE DATA For 7–8, use the table.

Materials Needed for Making Instruments

Drum	Maracas
1 coffee can	2 plastic water bottles
1 large rubber band	1 roll of tape
1 trash bag	Dried beans

7. How many rubber bands will seven students need to make their drums?

8. WRITE Math Three students want to use maracas in the class band. How many water bottles do they need in all to make their maracas? Explain how you can draw a picture to find the answer.

9. **Reasoning** The class band has 12 students. Show two different ways the band members can stand in equal rows to march.

Mixed Strategy Practice

USE DATA For 10–12, use the Favorite Instrument Survey.

10. The table shows how students in Jillian's class voted. How many students voted for the guitar? Draw a picture to show your answer.

11. On the day of Jillian's survey, two students in the class were absent. The table shows the votes of all other students in the class, including Jillian. How many students in all are in Jillian's class?

12. **Reasoning** Jillian added the number of votes for two instruments and got a total of 12 students. Which two instruments did she add?

13. ***FAST FACT*** The electric guitar was invented in 1931. How many years ago was that?

14. **Open-Ended** Tony and Mike surveyed 50 students about their favorite instrument: flute, trumpet, drum, or guitar. Choose a key and show a possible survey result in a table like the one at the right.

Choose a STRATEGY

- Draw a Diagram or Picture
- Make a Model or Act It Out
- Make an Organized List
- Look for a Pattern
- Make a Table or Graph
- Guess and Check
- Work Backward
- Solve a Simpler Problem
- Write an Equation
- Use Logical Reasoning

Favorite Instrument Survey

Instrument	Number of Children
Flute	☺ ☺
Trumpet	☺ ☺ ☺
Drums	☺ ☺ ☺ ☺
Guitar	☺ ☺ ☺ ☺ ☺

Key: Each ☺ = 2 children.

CHALLENGE YOURSELF

Ari, Beth, Corey, and Dan each play a different instrument. One plays the flute, one plays the trumpet, one plays the drum, and one plays the guitar. Read the clues to find out who plays which instrument.

Clues

a. Ari's instrument does not have strings.

b. Beth uses her mouth to play her instrument.

c. Corey does not use sticks with his instrument.

d. Dan's instrument is shaped like a cylinder.

e. Ari's instrument is wider at one end than at the other.

15. Who plays the guitar? Who plays the trumpet?

16. Explain how you know which instrument Ari plays.

Extra Practice

Set A Use counters to model. Then write an addition sentence and a multiplication sentence for each. (pp. 202–203)

1. 3 groups of 4
2. 2 groups of 2
3. 2 groups of 3
4. 5 groups of 2
5. 6 groups of 1
6. 4 groups of 5
7. 3 groups of 6
8. 7 groups of 3

Write a multiplication sentence for each.

9. $3 + 3 + 3 = 9$
10. $2 + 2 + 2 + 2 = 8$
11. $4 + 4 = 8$
12. $7 + 7 + 7 + 7 = 28$
13. $1 + 1 + 1 = 3$
14. $6 + 6 + 6 + 6 = 24$
15. $5 + 5 + 5 = 15$
16. $3 + 3 = 6$
17. $8 + 8 + 8 = 24$

Set B Write a multiplication sentence for each array. (pp. 204–207)

1. ■■■ ■■ / ■■■ ■■ / ■■

2. 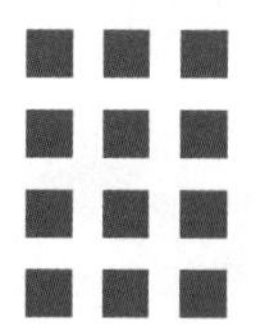

3.  

4. Jamal put 20 model cars in 5 rows. How many cars were in each row?
   5 rows of ■ cars = 20 cars

5. Mary picked 6 tomatoes from each of the 3 rows in her garden. She used 4 tomatoes to make salsa. How many tomatoes does she have left?

Set C Find the product. (pp. 208–209)

1. $2 \times 4 = ■$
2. $9 \times 2 = ■$
3. $2 \times 2 = ■$
4. $2 \times 1 = ■$
5. $2 \times 3 = ■$
6. $5 \times 2 = ■$
7. $2 \times 7 = ■$
8. $8 \times 2 = ■$
9. $3 \times 2 = ■$
10. $2 \times 6 = ■$
11. $2 \times 9 = ■$
12. $4 \times 2 = ■$

13. 2×7
14. 5×2
15. 2×2
16. 6×2
17. 2×4
18. 3×2
19. 8×2
20. 2×1
21. 9×2
22. 2×8
23. 4×2
24. 7×2

Technology
Use Harcourt Mega Math, Country Countdown, *Counting Critters*, Levels V, Z.

Set D Find the product. (pp. 210–211)

1. $2 \times 4 = ■$ 2. $9 \times 4 = ■$ 3. $4 \times 4 = ■$ 4. $4 \times 1 = ■$

5. $4 \times 3 = ■$ 6. $5 \times 4 = ■$ 7. $4 \times 7 = ■$ 8. $8 \times 4 = ■$

9. $1 \times 4 = ■$ 10. $4 \times 6 = ■$ 11. $4 \times 9 = ■$ 12. $4 \times 2 = ■$

13. 4×4 14. 5×4 15. 4×2 16. 2×4 17. 4×6 18. 3×4

19. 9×4 20. 2×4 21. 7×4 22. 8×4 23. 1×4 24. 6×4

25. Marla has 4 bins. Each bin has 2 jump ropes in it. How many jump ropes does Marla have?

26. Arwin has 3 pencil boxes. He has 4 pencils in each box. How many pencils does Arwin have in all?

Copy and complete.

	×	1	2	3	4	5	6	7	8	9
27.	2									
28.	4									

Set E Find the product. (pp. 212–215)

1. $6 \times 0 = ■$ 2. $4 \times 1 = ■$ 3. $3 \times 0 = ■$ 4. $0 \times 1 = ■$

5. $1 \times 5 = ■$ 6. $0 \times 9 = ■$ 7. $1 \times 1 = ■$ 8. $4 \times 0 = ■$

9. 2×0 10. 7×1 11. 8×0 12. 6×1 13. 0×3 14. 9×1

15. 1×2 16. 0×0 17. 0×5 18. 5×1 19. 4×0 20. 0×7

Find the missing number.

21. $5 \times ■ = 0$ 22. $3 \times 1 = ■ \times 3$ 23. $■ \times 14 = 14$ 24. $0 \times 89 = ■$

25. $■ \times 8 = 8$ 26. $24 \times 0 = ■$ 27. $11 \times ■ = 11$ 28. $1 \times 7 = ■ \times 1$

Solve.

29. Tom had 4 boxes. He put 1 car in each box. How many cars does he have in all?

30. Lucy has 2 fish bowls. There are no fish in the bowls. How many fish does she have in all?

Chapter 9 Review/Test

Check Vocabulary and Concepts

Choose the best term from the box.

VOCABULARY
array
Identity Property of Multiplication
multiply
Zero Property of Multiplication

1. When you __?__, you combine equal groups to find how many in all. (TEKS 3.4A, p. 202)

2. The __?__ states that the product of any number and 1 is that number. (TEKS 3.4A, p. 212)

Check Skills

Use counters to model. Then write an addition sentence and a multiplication sentence for each. (TEKS 3.4A, pp. 202–203)

3. 7 groups of 3 **4.** 3 groups of 6 **5.** 4 groups of 5 **6.** 2 groups of 8

Write a multiplication sentence for each array. (TEKS 3.4A, pp. 204–207)

7. **8.**

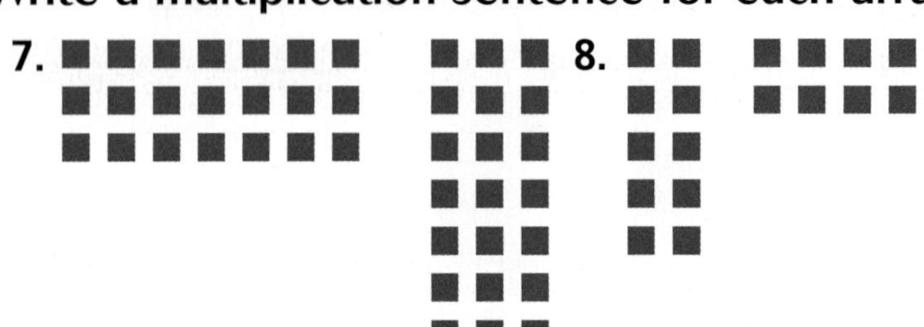

9.

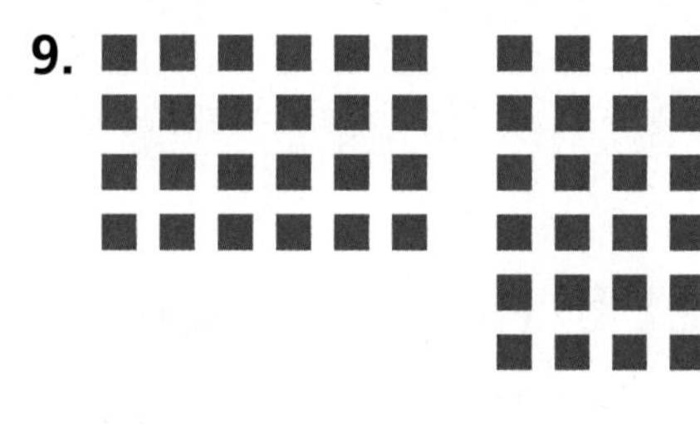

Find the product. (TEKS 3.4A, pp. 208–209, 210–211, 212–215)

10. $5 \times 2 =$ ■ **11.** $4 \times 1 =$ ■ **12.** $0 \times 7 =$ ■ **13.** $4 \times 4 =$ ■

14. $2 \times 8 =$ ■ **15.** $9 \times 0 =$ ■ **16.** $1 \times 1 =$ ■ **17.** $9 \times 4 =$ ■

18. $\begin{array}{r} 2 \\ \times 2 \\ \hline \end{array}$ **19.** $\begin{array}{r} 0 \\ \times 6 \\ \hline \end{array}$ **20.** $\begin{array}{r} 7 \\ \times 1 \\ \hline \end{array}$ **21.** $\begin{array}{r} 6 \\ \times 2 \\ \hline \end{array}$ **22.** $\begin{array}{r} 4 \\ \times 3 \\ \hline \end{array}$ **23.** $\begin{array}{r} 8 \\ \times 4 \\ \hline \end{array}$

Check Problem Solving

Solve. (TEKS 3.4A, pp. 216–219)

24. Ten students are in the school play. Three students will play instuments and one student will sing a song. The rest of the students will make 2 props each. How many props will the students make in all?

25. WRITE Math Three students sold tickets for the play. They sold 10 tickets each. How many tickets did they sell in all? **Explain** how you know.

GO ONLINE **Technology** Use *Online Assessment.*

Enrich • Value of Shapes

Problems with Shapes

Using shapes instead of numbers can help you practice addition, subtraction, and multiplication facts.

Shape Solvers

Find the value of the ♥ and ✿ by answering the questions.

♥ − ✿ = 3

✿ × ✿ = 16

Step 1	**Step 2**
The ✿ is in both problems, so find the value of the ✿ first. Think: What number multiplied by itself equals 16? 4 × 4 = 16, so ✿ = 4.	Now you can find the value of the . Using the value of the ✿, you know that ♥ − 4 = 3. Find the value of ♥ by adding. 4 + 3 = 7. 7 − 4 = 3, so ♥ = 7.

So, ✿ = 4 and ♥ = 7.

Try It

Find the value for each shape in the puzzles below.

1. ▲ + ⬢ = 8
⬢ × ▲ = 12

▲ = ■
⬢ = ■

2. ⬟ + ⬟ = 6
⬟ × ⬟ = 9

⬟ = ■

3. 🍁 − 🌳 = 5
🍁 × 🌳 = 24

🍁 = ■
🌳 = ■

WRITE Math How can knowing ★ = 3 help you to solve the puzzle below? **Explain.**

★ + ⏢ = 12
★ × ★ = ⏢

Getting Ready for the TAKS
Chapters 1–9

Number, Operation, and Quantitative Reasoning (TAKS Obj. 1)

1. How many miles did Larry and Mike walk altogether?

School Walk-a-Thon	
Sue	👟 👟 👟 👟 👟
Mike	👟 👟 👟
Jenny	👟
Larry	👟 👟 👟 👟
Key: Each 👟 = 2 miles.	

A 18 miles

B 16 miles

C 14 miles

D 12 miles

2. Johanna's family drove 618 miles during their vacation. What is 618 rounded to the nearest ten?

F 600

G 610

H 620

J Not here

3. WRITE Math **Explain** how knowing the product 2×9 can help you to find the product 4×9.

Patterns, Relationships, and Algebraic Thinking (TAKS Obj. 2)

4. Which array shows the product 6×3?

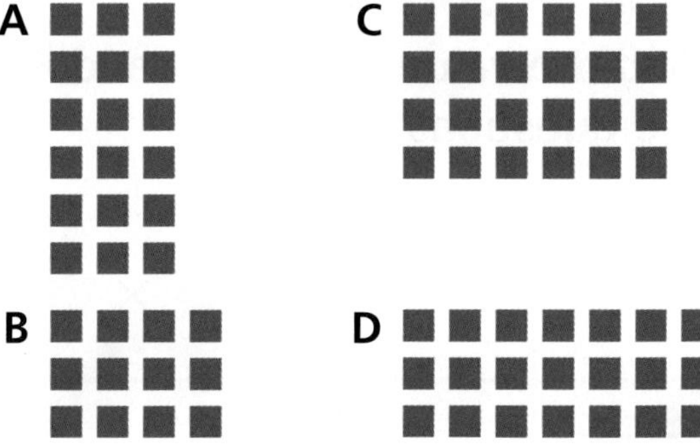

5. Which multiplication sentence is shown by the counters?

F $6 \times 3 = 18$

G $4 \times 3 = 12$

H $2 \times 6 = 12$

J $4 \times 2 = 8$

6. WRITE Math Write the addition sentence $5 + 5 + 5 + 5 = 20$ as a multiplication sentence. **Explain** how you know.

Measurement (TAKS Obj. 4)

Test Tip **Eliminate choices.**

See item 7. First find the time that names the correct hour shown on the clock. Then find the time that names the correct minutes.

7. Walter's swim practice ends at the time shown on the clock. What time does Walter's swim practice end?

A 5:15

B 4:45

C 4:15

D 3:45

8. Jim is playing outside in the snow. Which temperature does the thermometer show?

F 5° F

G 15° F

H 25° F

J 35° F

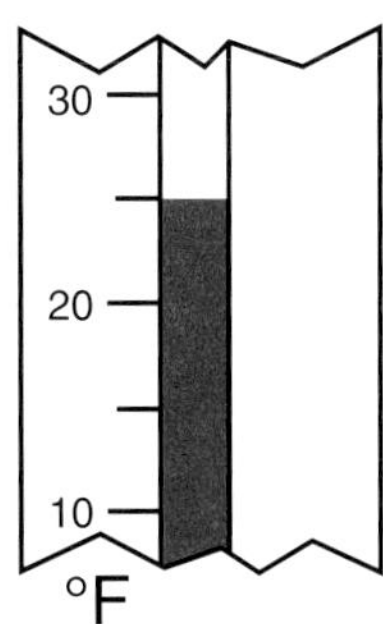

9. WRITE Math Would you use inches, feet, or yards to measure the length of the school palyground? **Explain**.

Probability and Statistics (TAKS Obj. 5)

10. Randy recorded the results of a probability experiment. How many marbles did Randy pull in all?

A 12

B 13

C 14

D 15

Marbles Pulled

Color	Number of Times Pulled
orange	|||
red	||
green	~~||||~~ |||
blue	||

11. How many more red shirts than blue shirts does Matt have?

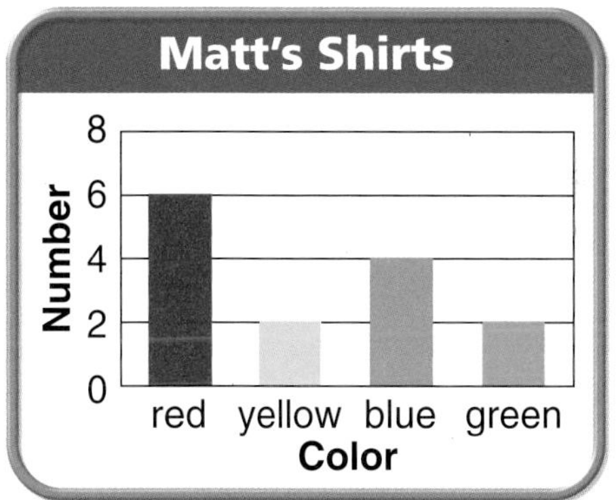

F 4

G 3

H 2

J 1

12. WRITE Math List the possible outcomes of spinning the pointer 1 time. **Explain** how you know.

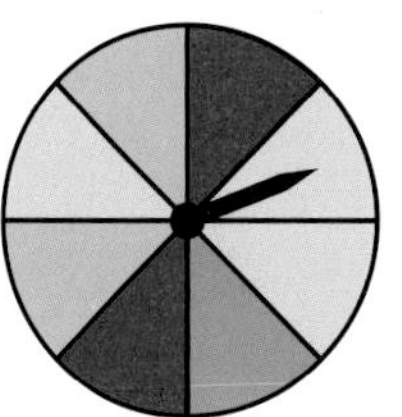

10 Multiplication Facts

The Big Idea Basic facts strategies for multiplication are based on properties, patterns, and number relationships.

TEXAS FAST FACT

A wind farm is a group of wind turbines that are placed together. The wind is used to make electricity. A wind turbine has 3 blades that are 30 to 70 meters across.

Investigate

A windmill looks similar to a wind turbine. A windmill uses wind energy to turn a machine or pump water. Draw a picture of a windmill with 9 blades. Suppose you want to make more than one windmill. How can you find how many blades you would need?

GO ONLINE **Technology** Student pages are available in the Student eBook.

Show What You Know

Check your understanding of important skills needed for success in Chapter 10.

▶ Equal Groups

Write how many there are in all.

1. 

2 groups of 7 = ■

2.   

3 groups of 4 = ■

3.  

6 groups of 2 = ■

▶ Arrays

Find the product.

4. 

$3 \times 5 =$ ■

5. ■ ■ ■ ■ ■ ■ ■

$2 \times 7 =$ ■

6. 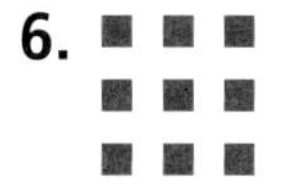

$3 \times 3 =$ ■

7. 

$4 \times 6 =$ ■

▶ Multiply with 2 and 4

Multiply.

8. $4 \times 4 =$ ■ **9.** $3 \times 2 =$ ■ **10.** $5 \times 4 =$ ■ **11.** $2 \times 9 =$ ■

VOCABULARY POWER

CHAPTER VOCABULARY

array
factor
multiple
multiplication
multiply
product
square number

WARM-UP WORDS

multiple A number that is the product of a given number and a counting number

multiply When you combine equal groups, you can multiply to find how many in all.

LESSON 1

Multiply with 5 and 10

OBJECTIVE: Multiply with the factors 5 and 10.

Quick Review

1. 5 + 5
2. 10 + 10
3. 5 + 5 + 5 + 5
4. 10 + 10 + 10 + 10
5. 5 + 5 + 5 + 5 + 5

Learn

PROBLEM Mandi is singing in the school chorus. For the first song, there are 3 rows with 5 students in each row. How many students sing the first song?

Multiply. $3 \times 5 = \blacksquare$

ONE WAY **Make an array.**

Use tiles to make an array with 3 rows of 5.

Count the tiles. $3 \times 5 = 15$

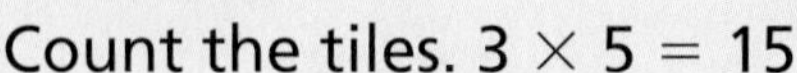

So, 15 students sing the first song.

ANOTHER WAY **Use a number line.**

Start at 0. Make 3 jumps of 5 spaces each.

$3 \times 5 = 15$ $\quad \begin{array}{r} 5 \\ \times 3 \\ \hline 15 \end{array}$

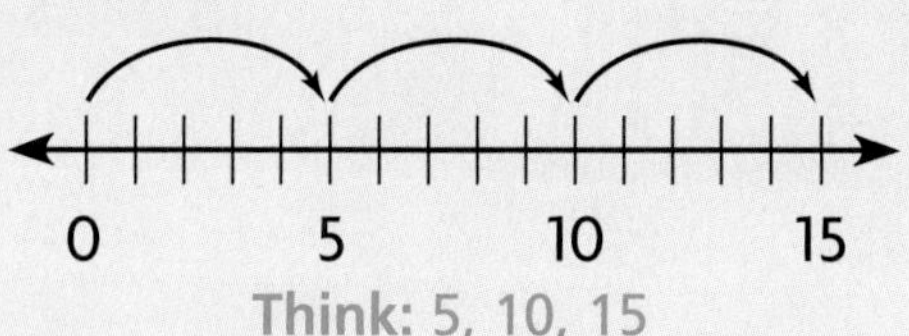

Think: 5, 10, 15

For the last song, there are 3 rows with 10 students in each row. How many students sing the last song?

Multiply. $3 \times 10 = \blacksquare$

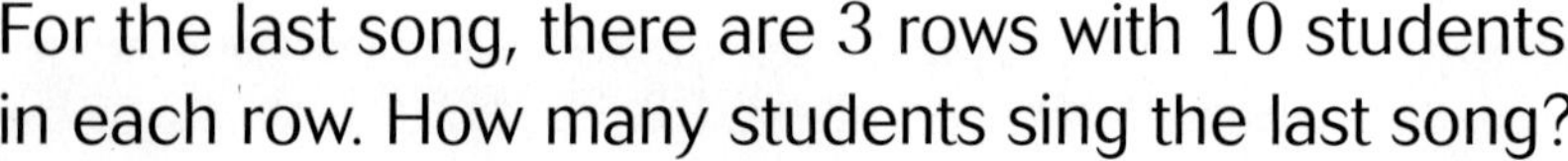

ONE WAY **Use zeros.**

To find a 10s product, write a zero after the 1s product.	$1 \times 1 = 1$	$1 \times 10 = 10$
	$2 \times 1 = 2$	$2 \times 10 = 20$
	$3 \times 1 = 3$	$3 \times 10 = 30$

So, 30 students sing the last song.

ANOTHER WAY **Use doubles.**

Find the 5s product. $3 \times 5 = 15$

Double that product. $15 + 15 = 30$

So, $3 \times 10 = 30$.

Math Idea

The product of 10 and any factor always looks like the other factor followed by a zero.

TEKS 3.4A learn and apply multiplication facts through 12 by 12 using concrete models and objects. *also* **3.6B, 3.14A, 3.15A, 3.15B**

Guided Practice

1. How can you use this number line to find 4×10?

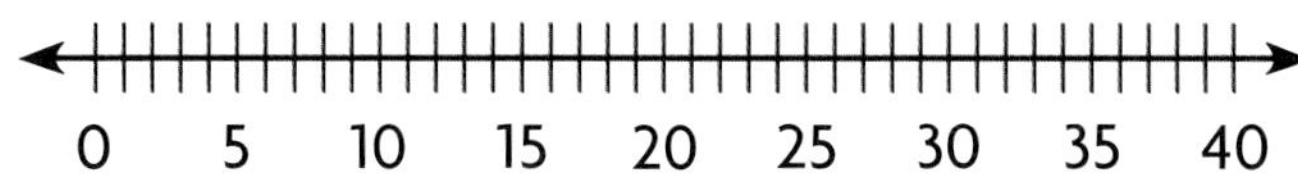

Find the product.

2. $2 \times 5 = \blacksquare$
3. $\blacksquare = 6 \times 10$
4. $\blacksquare = 5 \times 5$
5. $10 \times 7 = \blacksquare$
6. TALK Math **Explain** how 4×5 can help you find 4×10.

Independent Practice and Problem Solving

Find the product.

7. $10 \times 2 = \blacksquare$
8. $\blacksquare = 5 \times 3$
9. $\blacksquare = 10 \times 10$
10. $6 \times 5 = \blacksquare$
11. $10 \times 5 = \blacksquare$
12. $9 \times 5 = \blacksquare$
13. $\blacksquare = 2 \times 10$
14. $\blacksquare = 5 \times 9$
15. 10×0
16. 7×5
17. 5×8
18. 10×9
19. 5×6
20. 10×8

USE DATA For 21–22, use the table.

21. Draw a picture to show how many strings are on 4 banjos. Then write a multiplication sentence.
22. Mr. Case has 2 guitars, 4 banjos, and 1 mandolin. What is the total number of strings on Mr. Case's instruments?

Stringed Instruments

Instrument	Number of Strings
Guitar	6
Banjo	5
Mandolin	8
Violin	4

Mandolin

23. WRITE Math What do you notice about the products for 5 and 10? **Explain.**

Mixed Review and TAKS Prep

24. A music store sold 586 guitar books and 297 piano books. How many more guitar books were sold? (TEKS 3.3B, p. 92)
25. Which symbol makes this number sentence true?

    $7 \bullet 4 = 28$ (TEKS 3.4A, p. 210)

26. **TAKS Prep** A music store has guitars displayed on 5 shelves. There are 5 guitars on each shelf. How many guitars are there in all? (Obj. 1)

    A 10 **C** 20

    B 15 **D** 25

Extra Practice on page 242, Set A

LESSON 2

Multiply with 3

OBJECTIVE: Multiply with the factor 3.

Quick Review

1. $3 + 3 + 3 = \blacksquare$
2. $3 + 3 + 3 + 3 = \blacksquare$
3. $5 \times 3 = \blacksquare \times 5$
4. $1 \times 7 = \blacksquare \times 1$
5. $\blacksquare \times 2 = 2 \times 6$

Learn

PROBLEM Paula is making a design with 4 triangles. How many sides do 4 triangles have?

$$4 \times 3 = \blacksquare$$

A triangle has 3 sides. To find the number of sides in 4 triangles, find 4×3.

equilateral triangle

3 inches 3 inches 3 inches

ONE WAY **Draw a picture.**

Step 1 **Draw 4 triangles.**

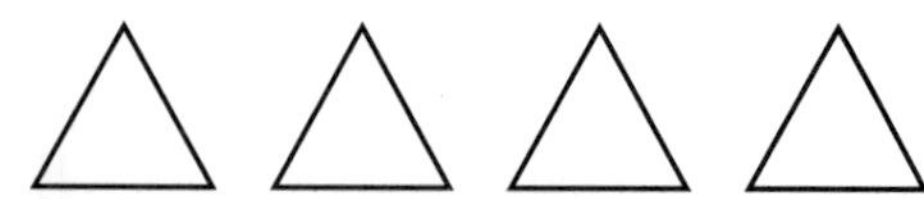

Step 2 **Count the sides.**

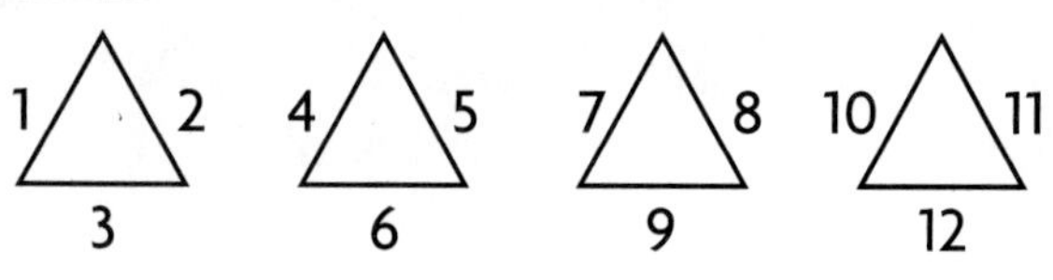

$$4 \times 3 = 12$$

So, 4 triangles have 12 sides.

OTHER WAYS

A **Use counters.**
Make 4 groups of 3.

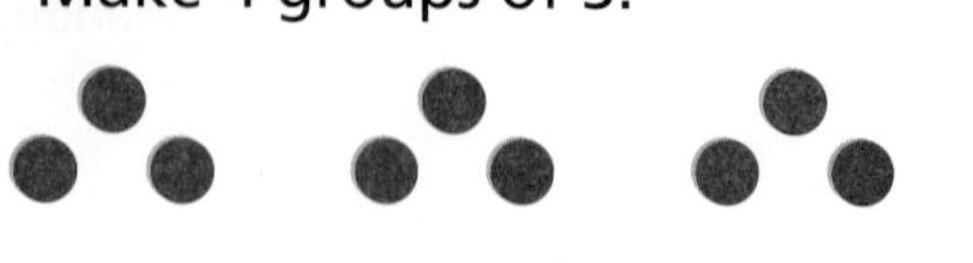

$$4 \times 3 = 12$$

B **Look for a pattern.**

Triangles	Sides	Total
1	3	3
2	3	6
3	3	9
4	3	12

$$4 \times 3 = 12$$

Guided Practice

1. Use the picture and tell how to find the number of sides in 6 triangles.

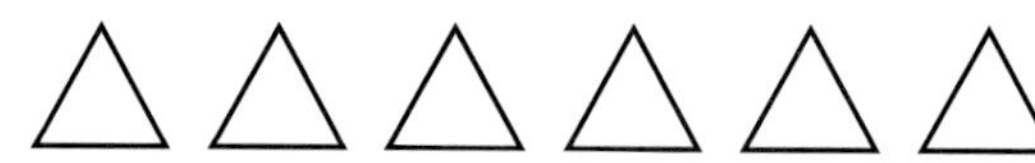

TEKS 3.4A learn and apply multiplication facts through 12 by 12 using concrete models and objects. *also* **3.6B, 3.14A, 3.14C, 3.14D, 3.15A, 3.15B**

Find the product.

2. $3 \times 5 = ■$ 3. $■ = 3 \times 6$ ✓4. $■ = 7 \times 3$ ✓5. $9 \times 3 = ■$

6. **TALK Math** **Explain** how you can use counters to find 5×3.

Independent Practice and Problem Solving

Find the product.

7. $6 \times 3 = ■$ 8. $■ = 8 \times 3$ 9. $■ = 3 \times 0$ 10. $3 \times 3 = ■$

11. $2 \times 3 = ■$ 12. $■ = 9 \times 3$ 13. $■ = 3 \times 1$ 14. $3 \times 7 = ■$

15. 3×6 16. 8×3 17. 5×3 18. 3×2 19. 7×3 20. 3×9

Algebra **Complete.**

21. $2 \times 3 = ■ \times 2$ 22. $8 \times 1 = ■ \times 8$ 23. $5 \times 2 = ■ \times 5$

24. $2 \times 3 = ■ + 1$ 25. $8 \times 1 = ■ + 1$ 26. $5 \times 2 = ■ + 1$

27. A square has 4 sides. Which have more sides, 5 squares or 6 triangles? Show your work.

28. **Reasoning** Use the factors 3 and 4 to show the Commutative Property of Multiplication. Draw a picture.

USE DATA **For 29–30, use the table.**

29. How many squares are there in 3 pieces of the quilt pattern? Draw a picture to show your answer.

30. **WRITE Math** **Explain** how to find the total number of sides of all the shapes in the quilt pattern. Some sides will be counted more than once.

Quilt Pattern

Shape	Number in 1 pattern piece
Square	6
Triangle	4
Rectangle	4

Amish pattern used in making quilts.

Mixed Review and TAKS Prep

31. Jon has 2 quarters, 2 dimes, and 3 nickels. Tom has 1 quarter, 5 nickels, and 27 pennies. Who has more money? How much more? (TEKS 3.1C, p. 114)

32. Name the fraction for the part that is shaded. (Grade 2, TEKS 2.2A)

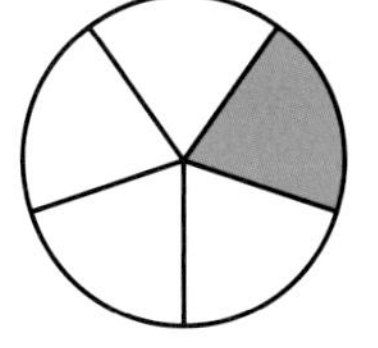

33. **TAKS Prep** There are 9 color pencils in each of 3 packages. How many color pencils are there in all? (Obj. 1)

A 6 **B** 12 **C** 24 **D** 27

Extra Practice on page 242, Set B

LESSON 3

Multiply with 6

OBJECTIVE: Multiply with the factor 6.

Quick Review

1. 3×2 **2.** 9×3

3. 5×3 **4.** 3×4

5. 6×3

Vocabulary

multiple

Learn

PROBLEM A lightning bug has 6 legs. How many legs do 5 lightning bugs have?

$$5 \times 6 = \blacksquare$$

ONE WAY **Use an array.**

Make 5 rows with 6 tiles in each row.

Count the tiles.

$5 \times 6 = 30$ $\begin{array}{r} 6 \\ \times 5 \\ \hline 30 \end{array}$

So, 5 lightning bugs have 30 legs.

▲ Lightning bugs are also called fireflies.

OTHER WAYS

A Use a number line.

Make 5 jumps of 6 spaces each.

$5 \times 6 = 30$

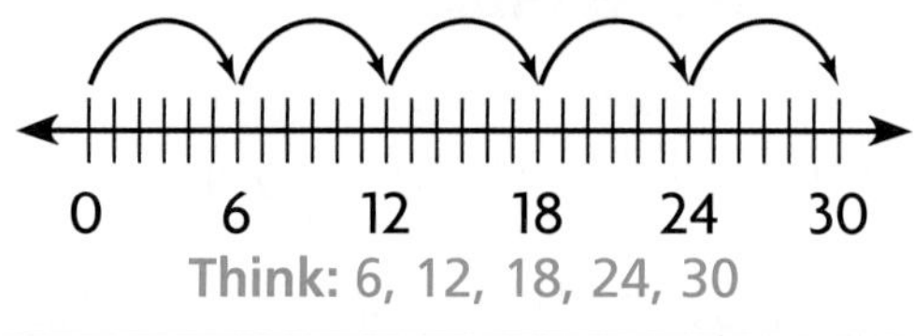

Think: 6, 12, 18, 24, 30

A **multiple** of 6 is any product that has a 6 as one of its factors. Some multiples of 6 are 6, 12, 18, 24, and 30.

B Use a multiplication table.

Find the product for 5×6 where row 5 and column 6 meet. $5 \times 6 = 30$

column ↓ (6); row → (5)

×	0	1	2	3	4	5	6	7	8	9
0	0	0	0	0	0	0	0	0	0	0
1	0	1	2	3	4	5	6	7	8	9
2	0	2	4	6	8	10	12	14	16	18
3	0	3	6	9	12	15	18	21	24	27
4	0	4	8	12	16	20	24	28	32	36
5	0	5	10	15	20	25	30	35	40	45
6	0	6	12	18	24	30	36	42	48	54
7	0	7	14	21	28	35	42	49	56	63
8	0	8	16	24	32	40	48	56	64	72
9	0	9	18	27	36	45	54	63	72	81

C Use doubles.

First, find the 3s product. $5 \times 3 = 15$

Then double that product. $15 + 15 = 30$

So, $5 \times 6 = 30$.

- Look at the columns for 3 and 6 in the table. What do you notice about their products?

TEKS 3.4A learn and apply multiplication facts through 12 by 12 using concrete models and objects. *also* 3.6B, 3.14A, 3.14D, 3.15A, 3.15B

Guided Practice

1. Use the array to find 3×6.

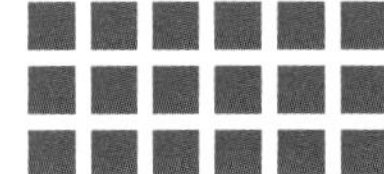

Find the product.

2. $6 \times 1 =$ ■
3. ■ $= 3 \times 6$
4. ✓ ■ $= 6 \times 4$
5. ✓ $6 \times 8 =$ ■
6. TALK Math Name a product that is a multiple of 3 and 6. **Explain** how you know.

Independent Practice and Problem Solving

Find the product.

7. $6 \times 5 =$ ■
8. ■ $= 8 \times 6$
9. ■ $= 6 \times 6$
10. $0 \times 6 =$ ■
11. $10 \times 6 =$ ■
12. $4 \times 5 =$ ■
13. ■ $= 1 \times 6$
14. ■ $= 5 \times 5$
15. $\begin{array}{r} 6 \\ \times 5 \\ \hline \end{array}$
16. $\begin{array}{r} 3 \\ \times 5 \\ \hline \end{array}$
17. $\begin{array}{r} 9 \\ \times 6 \\ \hline \end{array}$
18. $\begin{array}{r} 6 \\ \times 7 \\ \hline \end{array}$
19. $\begin{array}{r} 6 \\ \times 6 \\ \hline \end{array}$
20. $\begin{array}{r} 6 \\ \times 3 \\ \hline \end{array}$

USE DATA For 21–23, use the table.

21. How many wings do 6 honeybees have?
22. How many more wings do 6 beetles have than 6 flies?
23. WRITE Math Write a number sentence that shows how many wings 3 flies have. **Explain** how this fact can help you find the number of wings 6 flies have.

Winged Insects

Insect	Number of Wings
Fly	2
Beetle	4
Honeybee	4

Mixed Review and TAKS Prep

24. Sharon saw 10 butterflies. Each one had 4 wings. How many wings did the butterflies have in all? (TEKS 3.4B, p. 210)
25. Jeff made this figure with square tiles. What is the area of the figure? (Gr. 2, TEKS 2.9B)

26. **TAKS Prep** Sean saw 8 ladybugs while he was camping. Each one had 6 legs. How many legs did the 8 ladybugs have in all? (Obj. 1)

A 12 **B** 16 **C** 48 **D** 54

Extra Practice on page 242, Set C

ALGEBRA

Practice the Facts

OBJECTIVE: Practice multiplication facts with factors 0, 1, 2, 3, 4, 5, 6, and 10.

Quick Review

1. 6×5
2. 4×4
3. 3×7
4. 9×2
5. 4×8

Learn

PROBLEM Stephen's family lives on a dairy farm. One of the cows on the farm produces 3 gallons of milk each day. How many gallons of milk does the cow produce in 6 days?

$6 \times 3 = ■$

◀ One dairy cow can produce 200,000 glasses of milk in a year!

ONE WAY **Use a multiplication table.**

Find where the row for the 6 and the column for the 3 meet.
$6 \times 3 = 18$

So, the cow produces 18 gallons of milk in 6 days.

The gray shaded part of the table shows the products for multiplication facts you have already learned.

×	0	1	2	3	4	5	6	7	8	9	10
0	0	0	0	0	0	0	0	0	0	0	0
1	0	1	2	3	4	5	6	7	8	9	10
2	0	2	4	6	8	10	12	14	16	18	20
3	0	3	6	9	12	15	18	21	24	27	30
4	0	4	8	12	16	20	24	28	32	36	40
5	0	5	10	15	20	25	30	35	40	45	50
6	0	6	12	18	24	30	36	42	48	54	60
7	0	7	14	21	28	35	42	49	56	63	70
8	0	8	16	24	32	40	48	56	64	72	80
9	0	9	18	27	36	45	54	63	72	81	90
10	0	10	20	30	40	50	60	70	80	90	100

ERROR ALERT

When finding where a row and column meet in a multiplication table, be careful to follow the numbers in a straight line.

OTHER WAYS

Ⓐ Use a number line.

Skip-count by 3s. $6 \times 3 = 18$

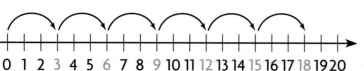

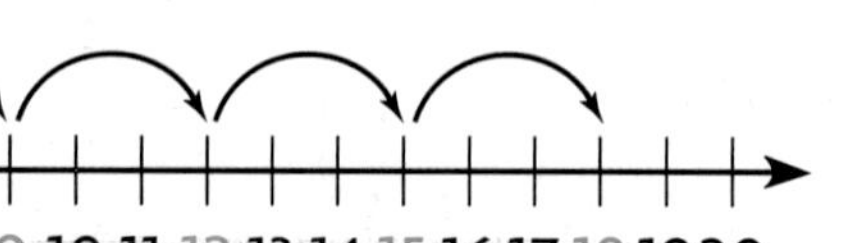

Think: 3, 6, 9, 12, 15, 18

Ⓑ Use counters.

Make 6 groups of 3.

$6 \times 3 = 18$

TEKS 3.4A learn and apply multiplication facts through 12 by 12 using concrete models and objects. *also* 3.6B, 3.14A, 3.14D, 3.15A, 3.15B

C Make an array.

Make 6 rows of 3 tiles.

$6 \times 3 = 18$

D Draw a picture.

Draw 6 groups of 3.

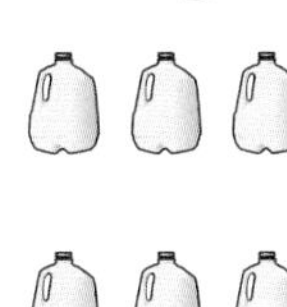

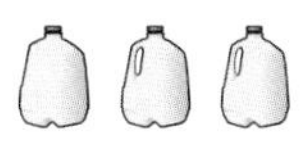

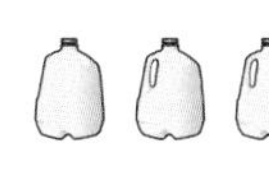

$$\begin{array}{r} 3 \\ \times 6 \\ \hline 18 \end{array}$$

$6 \times 3 = 18$

E Use Doubles.

Find the 3s product. $3 \times 3 = 9$

Double that product. $9 + 9 = 18$

So, $6 \times 3 = 18$.

F Use the Commutative Property.

Change the order of the factors.

$3 \times 6 = 18$, so $6 \times 3 = 18$.

- How would you find 3×6 by using a number line?

Guided Practice

1. Write the multiplication sentence shown by these counters.

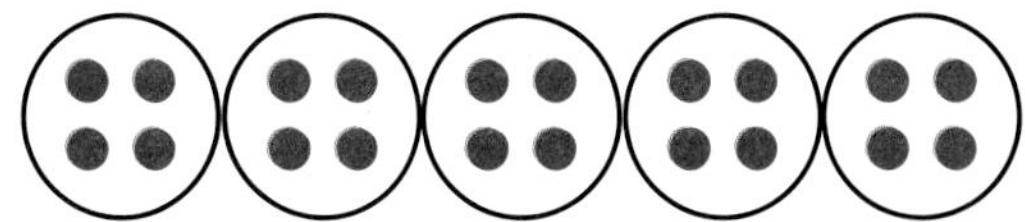

Find the product.

2. $4 \times 8 = \blacksquare$ **3.** $\blacksquare = 7 \times 3$ **✓4.** $\blacksquare = 9 \times 4$ **✓5.** $6 \times 6 = \blacksquare$

6. TALK Math **Explain** two ways to find 7×5.

Independent Practice and Problem Solving

Find the product.

7. $6 \times 8 = \blacksquare$ **8.** $\blacksquare = 5 \times 6$ **9.** $\blacksquare = 4 \times 2$ **10.** $0 \times 9 = \blacksquare$

11. $4 \times 7 = \blacksquare$ **12.** $2 \times 6 = \blacksquare$ **13.** $\blacksquare = 5 \times 5$ **14.** $\blacksquare = 6 \times 7$

15. $\blacksquare = 10 \times 1$ **16.** $7 \times 2 = \blacksquare$ **17.** $8 \times 3 = \blacksquare$ **18.** $6 \times 9 = \blacksquare$

19. $\begin{array}{r} 5 \\ \times 6 \\ \hline \end{array}$ **20.** $\begin{array}{r} 10 \\ \times 8 \\ \hline \end{array}$ **21.** $\begin{array}{r} 1 \\ \times 9 \\ \hline \end{array}$ **22.** $\begin{array}{r} 7 \\ \times 5 \\ \hline \end{array}$ **23.** $\begin{array}{r} 6 \\ \times 6 \\ \hline \end{array}$ **24.** $\begin{array}{r} 7 \\ \times 4 \\ \hline \end{array}$

25. $\begin{array}{r} 8 \\ \times 2 \\ \hline \end{array}$ **26.** $\begin{array}{r} 4 \\ \times 4 \\ \hline \end{array}$ **27.** $\begin{array}{r} 3 \\ \times 6 \\ \hline \end{array}$ **28.** $\begin{array}{r} 4 \\ \times 2 \\ \hline \end{array}$ **29.** $\begin{array}{r} 3 \\ \times 3 \\ \hline \end{array}$ **30.** $\begin{array}{r} 4 \\ \times 8 \\ \hline \end{array}$

Extra Practice on page 242, Set D

CD ROM **Technology**
Use Harcourt Mega Math, The Number Games, *Up, Up, and Array,* Levels A and B.

Show two different ways to find each product.

31. $3 \times 2 =$ ■ **32.** $1 \times 7 =$ ■ **33.** $9 \times 6 =$ ■

34. $4 \times 9 =$ ■ **35.** $10 \times 6 =$ ■ **36.** $8 \times 2 =$ ■

37. $3 \times 6 =$ ■ **38.** $7 \times 5 =$ ■ **39.** $5 \times 9 =$ ■

USE DATA For 40–42 and 44, use the recipe.

Macaroni and Cheese

3 cups uncooked macaroni
$\frac{1}{2}$ cup butter
6 tablespoons flour
3 teaspoons dried mustard
6 cups milk
4 cups American cheese (cubed)
2 cups shredded cheddar cheese
salt and pepper to taste

serves 12 people

40. Molly made macaroni and cheese 3 times last month. How many cups of macaroni did she use? Write a multiplication sentence to show your answer.

41. Sasha doubled the macaroni-and-cheese recipe for a picnic. How many cups of cheese in all did she use?

42. Reasoning Paul multiplied the macaroni-and-cheese recipe. He used 12 tablespoons of flour in all. How many people will Paul be able to serve?

43. Choose a multiplication fact. Show three different ways to find the product.

44. **WRITE Math** **What's the Error?** Sasha says she will use 24 cups of milk to double this recipe. Describe her error.

Mixed Review and TAKS Prep

45. Corey goes to soccer practice at the time shown on the clock. At what time does Corey go to soccer practice? (TEKS 3.12B, p. 134)

46. There are 9 red marbles and 1 blue marble in a bag. Sam pulls a marble without looking. Is it more likely or less likely that Sam will pull a red marble from the bag? (Grade 2 TEKS 2.11C)

47. TAKS Prep Which multiplication fact does the picture show? (Obj. 1)

A $3 \times 4 = 12$ **C** $4 \times 6 = 24$

B $3 \times 6 = 18$ **D** $4 \times 8 = 32$

48. TAKS Prep Sharon has 4 necklaces. There are 6 beads on each one. **Explain** how you would find the total number of beads on all of the necklaces. (Obj. 1)

Healthy Foods for Good Health

Use Graphic Aids

The food pyramid shows amounts of different food groups people need for good health. The person climbing up the stairs reminds us that it is important to exercise as well as eat healthy foods.

To help you stay healthy, you should eat a balanced diet and exercise every day. The table shows the recommended daily servings for third graders. For good health, you should eat the right amounts of each food group. To stay healthy, you also need to limit the amount of foods you eat that have a lot of fat and sugar in them.

Recommended Daily Servings

Food Group	Servings
Whole grains (bread, cereal)	6 ounces
Vegetables (beans, corn)	2 cups
Fruits (apples, oranges)	1 cup
Dairy products (milk, cheese)	3 cups
Meat, beans, fish, eggs, nuts	5 ounces
8 ounces = 1 cup	

Problem Solving **Look at the graphic aids. Use the information to solve the problems.**

1. A slice of wheat bread weighs about 1 ounce. How many ounces of whole grains, such as bread and cereal, should a third grader eat in 1 week? Think: 1 week = 7 days

2. How many cups of vegetables and fruits should a third grader eat in 1 day? In 1 week?

3. How many cups of dairy products, such as milk and cheese, should a third grader have in 1 day? In 10 days?

4. WRITE Math **What's the Question?** Kendra ate the recommended number of vegetable servings each day for 7 days. The answer is 14 cups.

Problem Solving Workshop
Strategy: Act It Out

OBJECTIVE: Solve problems by using the *act it out* strategy.

Learn the Strategy

Acting out a problem can help you understand the problem and find the solution.

Act out a problem with cups and counters.

Stacy has 3 vases. She puts 5 flowers in each vase. How many flowers does Stacy have in all?

Act out a problem with classmates.

Four friends are in a line for lunch. Abby is ahead of Max. Nicky is behind Max. Abby is behind Kim. Who is first in line?

Act out a problem with coins.

Emily has 2 quarters, 2 dimes, and 1 nickel. Tom has an equal amount of money in dimes and nickels. Tom has 9 coins. How many of each coin does Tom have?

TALK Math

In what other ways could you act out each of the problems above?

3.14C select or develop an appropriate problem-solving strategy including drawing a picture, looking for a pattern, systematic guessing and checking, acting it out, making a table, working a simpler problem, or working backwards to solve a problem. *also* **3.4A, 3.6B, 3.14A, 3.15A, 3.15B**

Read to Understand
Plan
Solve
Check

Use the Strategy

PROBLEM Jamie is planning a party. She wants to have 4 cookies for each person. How many cookies should she bake if there will be 5 people at her party?

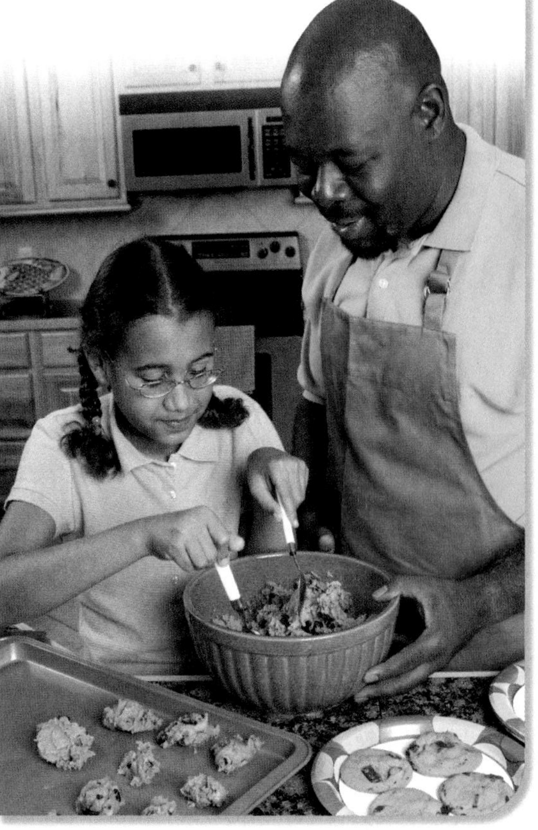

Read to Understand

- **Identify the details in the problem.**
- **What information is given?**

Plan

- **What strategy can you use to solve the problem?**

  You can act out the problem to find the solution.

Solve

- **How can you use the strategy to solve the problem?**

  You can use paper plates and counters to act out the problem.

  Put 5 paper plates on your desk to represent 1 plate for each person at the party.

  Place 4 counters on each plate to represent 4 cookies for each person.
  Write the multiplication sentence.

$$5 \times 4 = 20$$

  So, Jamie should bake 20 cookies.

Check

- **How can you check your answer?**

Guided Problem Solving

Read to Understand
Plan
Solve
Check

1. Kim is having a party. Everyone at Kim's party will get 3 party favors. There will be 6 people at Kim's party. Act out the problem to find how many party favors she needs.

   First, decide how to act out the problem. You can use counters as the party favors. Act out the problem using the counters.

   Then, find the total number of counters.

   $$6 \times 3 = \blacksquare$$

6 people with 3 party favors each.

2. **What if** there will be 7 people at Kim's party? How many party favors will she need?

3. At Kim's party, the children line up to play a game. Lisa is in front of Tim. Matt is behind Avery but ahead of Lisa. Kim is in front of Brett. Brett is in front of Avery. In what order are the children lined up?

Problem Solving Strategy Practice

Act out the problem to solve.

4. Ed made 10 sandwiches for a party. He used 2 slices of bread for each sandwich. How many slices of bread did Ed use in all?

5. Ed set up 3 tables for the party. He tied 4 balloons to each table. How many balloons did Ed tie on the tables?

USE DATA For 6–8 use the table.

6. Carol bought 4 packages of plates. How many plates did Carol buy?

7. Jason needs 17 gift bags. He buys 2 packages of gift bags. How many gift bags will Jason have left over?

8. Which has more items, 2 packages of napkins or 3 packages of cups?

9. WRITE Math Sierra played 8 games at her party. Each game took about 6 minutes to play. About how long did it take to play all the games? **Explain** your answer.

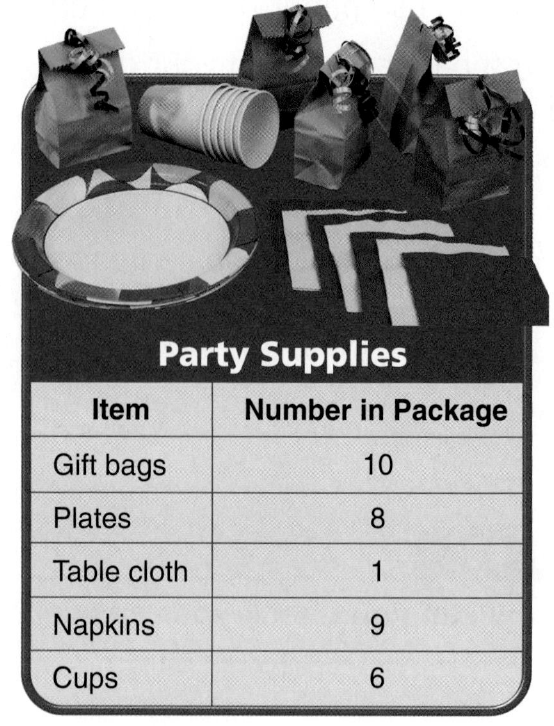

Party Supplies

Item	Number in Package
Gift bags	10
Plates	8
Table cloth	1
Napkins	9
Cups	6

Mixed Strategy Practice

USE DATA For 10–12, use the recipe information.

10. Miriam only has a cup for measuring ingredients for the recipe. How many cups of grape juice does she need to make the fruit punch? **Think**: 2 cups = 1 pint; 2 pints = 1 quart.

11. **Reasoning** Miriam mixed all of the ingredients in a large punch bowl. How many cups can she fill with punch?

12. **Reasoning** For the school open house, Tommy's mother doubled the fruit punch recipe 3 times. How much grape juice did she use in all?

13. Mary, John, Peter, and David are standing in line. Mary is behind John. John is not first. Peter is last. In what order are the children standing?

14. **Pose a Problem** Look back at problem 13. Write and solve a similar problem by changing the number of children.

15. **Open Ended** There are 12 cookies on a plate. How many different numbers of students could share them equally without breaking any of the cookies? Draw a picture to show your work.

Choose a STRATEGY

- Make a Model or Act It Out
- Draw a Diagram or Picture
- Make an Organized List
- Look for a Pattern
- Make a Table or Graph
- Guess and Check
- Work Backward
- Solve a Simpler Problem
- Write an Equation
- Use Logical Reasoning

Fruit Punch Recipe

1 cup lemonade
1 cup orange juice
1 quart ginger ale
1 quart club soda
2 quarts grape juice

Arcade Games

Game	Tokens Needed
Arctic Racer	3
Space Quest	4
Adventurer	2

CHALLENGE YOURSELF

Collin is having his party at an arcade. The table shows the number of tokens required to play each of his favorite games.

16. How many more tokens would he need to play 8 games of Space Quest than to play 6 games of Arctic Racer and 2 games of Adventurer?

17. Collin started with 28 tokens. He played one game 6 times, and another game 4 times. He still has tokens left over. Which 2 games could he have played? **Explain** how you know.

Extra Practice

Set A Find the product. (pp. 228–229)

1. $4 \times 5 = ■$
2. $■ = 3 \times 10$
3. $■ = 5 \times 2$
4. $■ = 6 \times 10$
5. $10 \times 7 = ■$
6. $■ = 2 \times 5$
7. $■ = 5 \times 10$
8. $5 \times 5 = ■$
9. $\begin{array}{r} 9 \\ \times 5 \\ \hline \end{array}$
10. $\begin{array}{r} 10 \\ \times 0 \\ \hline \end{array}$
11. $\begin{array}{r} 8 \\ \times 5 \\ \hline \end{array}$
12. $\begin{array}{r} 10 \\ \times 2 \\ \hline \end{array}$
13. $\begin{array}{r} 5 \\ \times 6 \\ \hline \end{array}$
14. $\begin{array}{r} 3 \\ \times 10 \\ \hline \end{array}$
15. A music store has CDs in 10 boxes. There are 8 CDs in each box. How many CDs are there in all?
16. A grocery store has boxes of cereal on 5 shelves. There are 6 boxes on each shelf. How many boxes of cereal in all are there?

Set B Find the product. (pp. 230–231)

1. $3 \times 5 = ■$
2. $■ = 4 \times 3$
3. $■ = 3 \times 10$
4. $7 \times 3 = ■$
5. $3 \times 9 = ■$
6. $■ = 3 \times 2$
7. $■ = 4 \times 6$
8. $3 \times 3 = ■$
9. $\begin{array}{r} 5 \\ \times 3 \\ \hline \end{array}$
10. $\begin{array}{r} 3 \\ \times 4 \\ \hline \end{array}$
11. $\begin{array}{r} 9 \\ \times 3 \\ \hline \end{array}$
12. $\begin{array}{r} 3 \\ \times 1 \\ \hline \end{array}$
13. $\begin{array}{r} 0 \\ \times 3 \\ \hline \end{array}$
14. $\begin{array}{r} 6 \\ \times 3 \\ \hline \end{array}$

Set C Find the product. (pp. 232–233)

1. $7 \times 6 = ■$
2. $■ = 3 \times 6$
3. $■ = 5 \times 6$
4. $6 \times 2 = ■$
5. $4 \times 6 = ■$
6. $1 \times 7 = ■$
7. $■ = 2 \times 5$
8. $■ = 1 \times 6$
9. $\begin{array}{r} 6 \\ \times 6 \\ \hline \end{array}$
10. $\begin{array}{r} 5 \\ \times 6 \\ \hline \end{array}$
11. $\begin{array}{r} 6 \\ \times 8 \\ \hline \end{array}$
12. $\begin{array}{r} 6 \\ \times 4 \\ \hline \end{array}$
13. $\begin{array}{r} 1 \\ \times 6 \\ \hline \end{array}$
14. $\begin{array}{r} 10 \\ \times 6 \\ \hline \end{array}$

Set D Find the product. (pp. 234–237)

1. $7 \times 6 = ■$
2. $■ = 3 \times 1$
3. $■ = 2 \times 8$
4. $0 \times 8 = ■$
5. $6 \times 9 = ■$
6. $4 \times 9 = ■$
7. $■ = 8 \times 9$
8. $■ = 5 \times 5$
9. $\begin{array}{r} 5 \\ \times 9 \\ \hline \end{array}$
10. $\begin{array}{r} 10 \\ \times 9 \\ \hline \end{array}$
11. $\begin{array}{r} 1 \\ \times 4 \\ \hline \end{array}$
12. $\begin{array}{r} 3 \\ \times 7 \\ \hline \end{array}$
13. $\begin{array}{r} 4 \\ \times 4 \\ \hline \end{array}$
14. $\begin{array}{r} 8 \\ \times 3 \\ \hline \end{array}$
15. Maria has 6 bracelets. There are 7 beads on each bracelet. How many beads are there in all?
16. Neil has 3 bookcases. There are 8 books on each bookcase. How many books does Neil have?

Technology
Use Harcourt Mega Math, The Number Games, *Up, Up, and Array*, Level C.

PRACTICE GAME

Super Spinners

Get Ready!

2 players

Get Set!

- 1 blue spinner and 1 red spinner

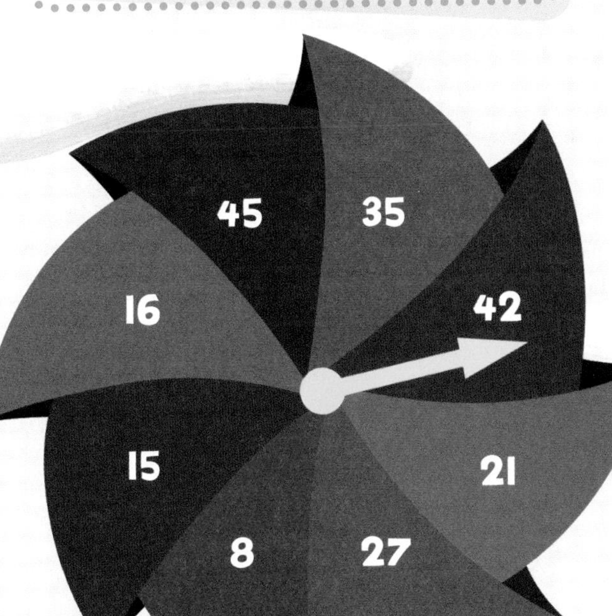

7 3 9 4 8 5 2 6

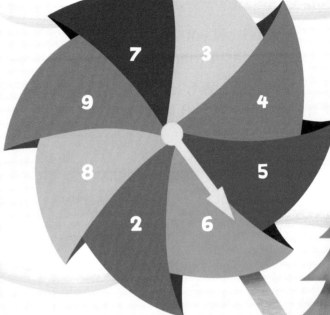

Yes! 6 × 7 = 42

Does 6 × ☐ = 42?

6 × 7 = 42

7 × 6 = 42

SPIN!

- Players take turns spinning both spinners.
- The first player decides if the blue number can be multiplied by a number to equal the red number.
- The first player then writes both of the multiplication sentences that can be made with the numbers shown on both spinners.
- If the blue number cannot be multiplied by a number to equal the red number, play passes to the next player.
- The player with more number sentences after 5 rounds wins!

Chapter 10 Review/Test

Check Concepts

1. **Explain** how knowing 3×5 can help you find 3×10. (TEKS 3.4A, pp. 228–229)

2. **Explain** how you can use the picture to find how many sides 4 triangles have. (TEKS 3.4A, pp. 230–231)

3. A ladybug has 6 legs. Draw an array to show how many legs 3 ladybugs have. (TEKS 3.4A, pp. 232–233)

Check Skills

Find the product. (TEKS 3.4A, pp. 228–229, 230–231, 232–233, 234–237)

4. $4 \times 6 = ■$
5. $2 \times 10 = ■$
6. $6 \times 3 = ■$
7. $5 \times 3 = ■$
8. $6 \times 2 = ■$
9. $6 \times 5 = ■$
10. $10 \times 8 = ■$
11. $3 \times 1 = ■$
12. $9 \times 10 = ■$
13. $■ = 3 \times 4$
14. $6 \times 6 = ■$
15. $■ = 3 \times 7$
16. $■ = 9 \times 6$
17. $5 \times 10 = ■$
18. $■ = 3 \times 3$
19. $8 \times 6 = ■$
20. 7×3
21. 10×10
22. 6×4
23. 8×3
24. 6×9
25. 10×1
26. 7×4
27. 2×5
28. 8×8
29. 0×3
30. 4×10
31. 7×5

Check Problem Solving

Solve. (TEKS 3.14C, pp. 238–241)

32. Matt, Joe, Bryan, and Rick are standing in line. Bryan is in front of Joe. Matt is behind Rick, but ahead of Bryan. In what order are the children standing?

33. WRITE Math Irene has 4 flowers in a pot. Each flower has 6 petals. How many petals are on 4 flowers? **Explain** how you know.

GO ONLINE **Technology** Use *Online Assessment.*

Enrich • Multiplication Facts
Multiplication Circles

A multiplication circle has a product in the center square. Multiplication facts are written in the sections around the circle. Their product is the center number. Multiplication circles can have many solutions.

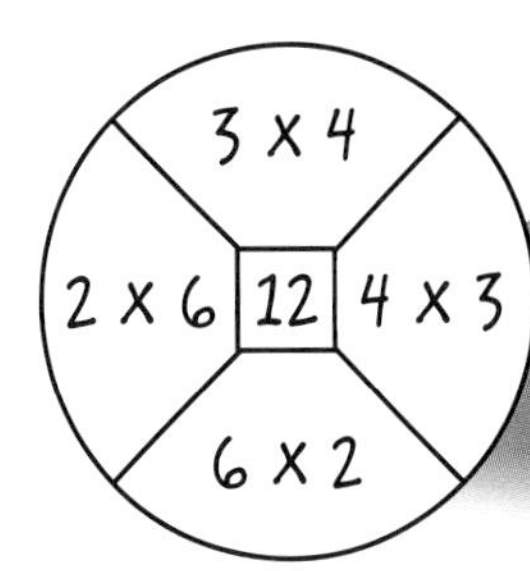

Going in Circles

The center square shows the prduct, 10.

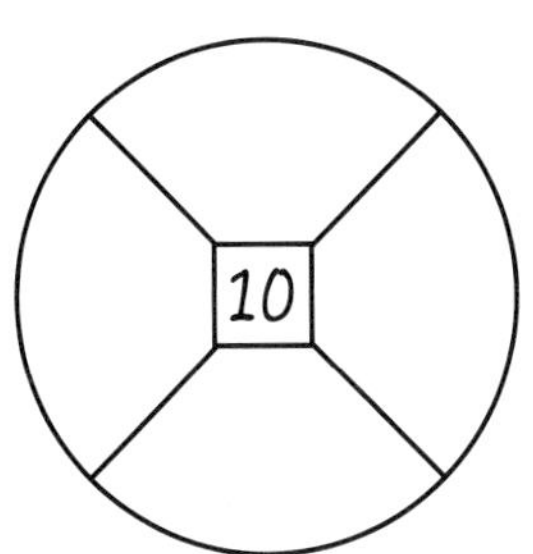

Think of a fact whose product is 10. Then use the Commutative Property to find the "turn-around" fact.

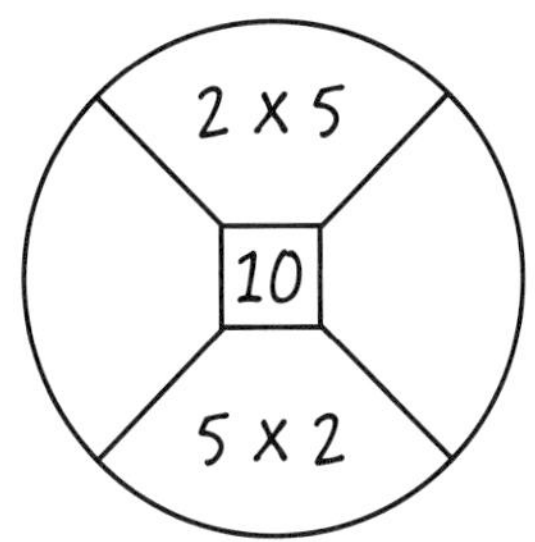

Think of another fact and complete the circle.

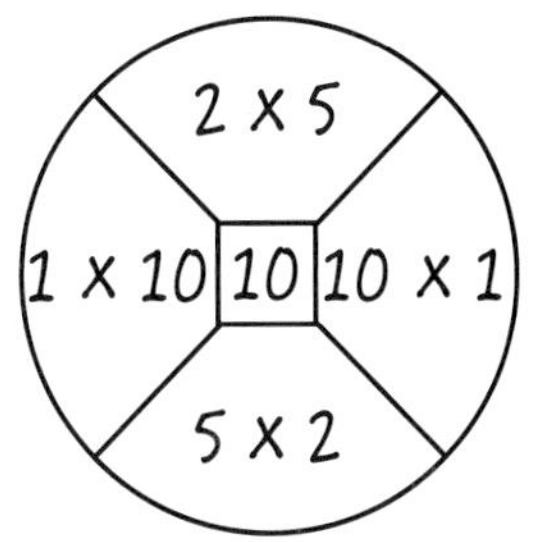

A Roundabout Way

Copy and complete each multiplication circle.

1.

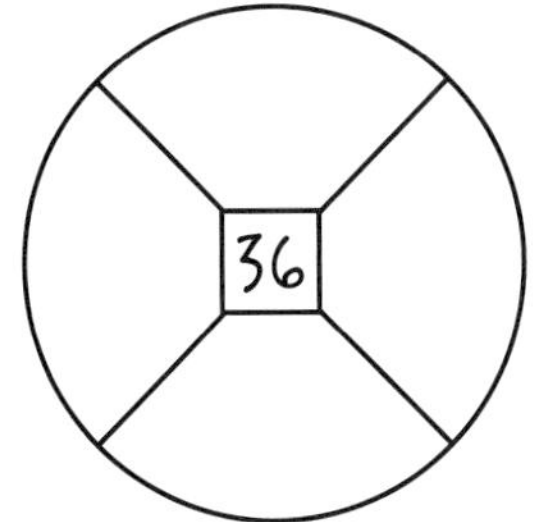

2.

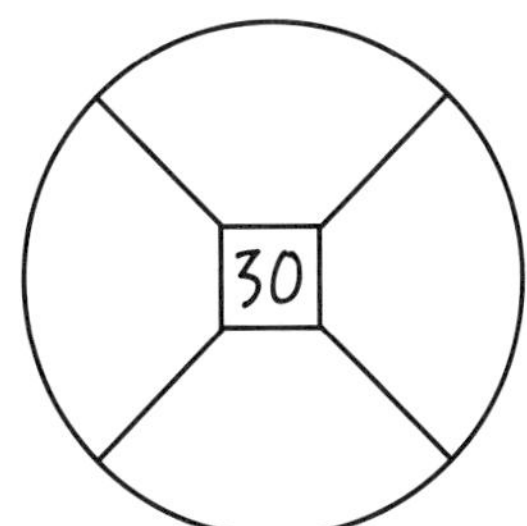

3.

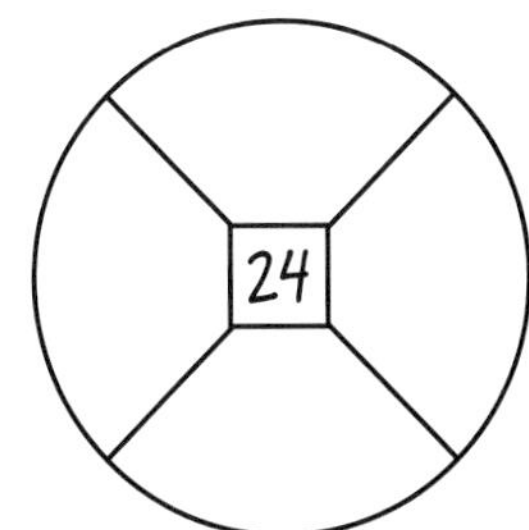

Cool Down

WRITE Math Copy this circle. Think of a product to write in the center square. What facts can you use to complete your circle? **Explain** how you know.

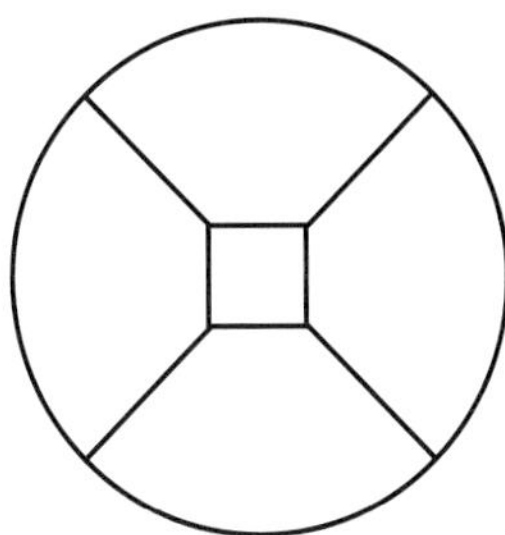

Getting Ready for the TAKS
Chapters 1–10

Number, Operation, and Quantitative Reasoning (TAKS Obj. 1)

1. Jody's school is having a craft fair. There are 7 rows of tables with 5 tables in each row. How many tables are set up for the craft fair?

A 25

B 30

C 35

D 40

Understand the problem.

See item 2. What is the question asking you to find? Read the problem again to find the information you need to answer the question.

2. There was a talent show at Wanda's school on Friday and Saturday. On Friday, 495 people saw the talent show. In all, 867 people saw the talent show. How many people saw the talent show on Saturday?

F 262 **H** 362

G 272 **J** 372

3. WRITE Math How can this picture help you find 5×6? **Explain.**

Patterns, Relationships, and Algebraic Thinking (TAKS Obj. 2)

4. What is a rule for the number pattern below?

84, 87, 90, 93, 96

A Add 4.

B Add 3.

C Subtract 4.

D Not here

5. What are the next 2 figures in Nate's pattern?

F ◁ ▽ **H** ▽ ◁

G △ ▽ **J** △ ◁

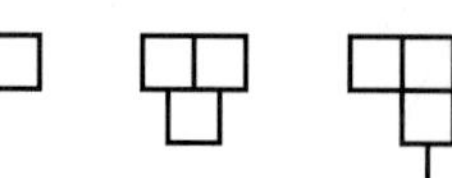

6. WRITE Math **Explain** how you can draw a picture to find the number of tiles in the fifth figure.

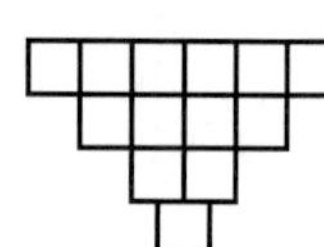

Geometry and Spatial Reasoning (TAKS Obj. 3)

7. These faces can be put together to make which solid figure?

A Rectangular prism

B Cylinder

C Cube

D Square pyramid

8. Which solid figure has exactly 5 faces?

F 

H 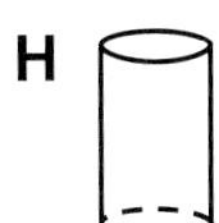

G 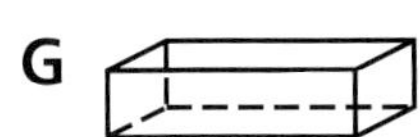

J 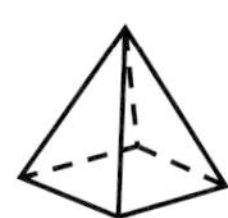

9. **WRITE Math** **Explain** how this square and this rectangle are alike.

Probability and Statistics (TAKS Obj. 5)

10. How many more students chose blue than green as their favorite color?

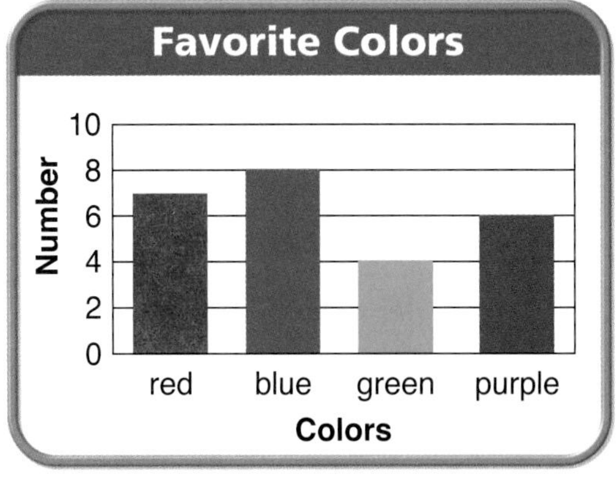

A 1

B 2

C 3

D 4

11. Which color block is Brian least likely to pull?

F Blue

G Green

H Red

J Yellow

12. **WRITE Math** What if Brian's bag had 10 yellow blocks and 2 green blocks. Which color would he be more likely to pull? **Explain** your answer.

Chapter 11 Facts and Strategies

The Big Idea Basic facts strategies for multiplication are based on properties, patterns, and number relationships.

Investigate

The boat used in sport rowing is called a shell. There also are other boats that use oars or paddles. Select a boat from the graph. Explain how you can use multiplication to find how many boats you would need to rent for your whole class.

Boat Sizes

Type of Boat	Number of People
Kayak	2
Canoe	4
Raft	8
Row-boat	3

TEXAS FAST FACT

Rowing is the oldest college sport in the United States. The University of Texas has a women's and a men's rowing team. The teams practice on Town Lake in Austin.

GO ONLINE **Technology** Student pages are available in the Student eBook.

Show What You Know

Check your understanding of important skills needed for success in Chapter 11.

▶ Multiply with 2 and 5

Find the product.

1. $1 \times 5 = \blacksquare$ **2.** $3 \times 2 = \blacksquare$ **3.** $4 \times 5 = \blacksquare$ **4.** $9 \times 2 = \blacksquare$

5. 5×5 **6.** 8×5 **7.** 5×2 **8.** 2×2

▶ Multiply with 4

Find the product.

9. $4 \times 3 = \blacksquare$ **10.** $7 \times 4 = \blacksquare$ **11.** $4 \times 5 = \blacksquare$ **12.** $9 \times 4 = \blacksquare$

13. 6×4 **14.** 2×4 **15.** 8×4 **16.** 4×4

▶ Multiply with 6

Find the product.

17. $2 \times 6 = \blacksquare$ **18.** $5 \times 6 = \blacksquare$ **19.** $3 \times 6 = \blacksquare$ **20.** $8 \times 6 = \blacksquare$

21. 9×6 **22.** 7×6 **23.** 6×6 **24.** 1×6

VOCABULARY POWER

CHAPTER VOCABULARY

array
Commutative Property of Multiplication
multiple
square number

WARM-UP WORDS

Commutative Property of Multiplication The property that states that you can multiply two factors in any order and get the same product

square number The product of two factors that are the same

LESSON 1

Multiply with 8

OBJECTIVE: Multiply with the factor 8.

Quick Review

1. 2×4 **2.** 8×4
3. 3×4 **4.** 5×4
5. 7×4

Learn

PROBLEM A scorpion has 8 legs. How many legs do 4 scorpions have?

$4 \times 8 = ■$

◀ **Scorpions are found in hot dry places, such as Arizona, Texas, and central Oklahoma.**

ONE WAY **Make an array.**

Use tiles to make an array with 4 rows of 8.
Count the tiles. $4 \times 8 = 32$

So, 4 scorpions have 32 legs.

OTHER WAYS

A **Use the Commutative Property.**

Use facts you know to find 4×8.

$8 \times 4 = 32$, so $4 \times 8 = 32$.

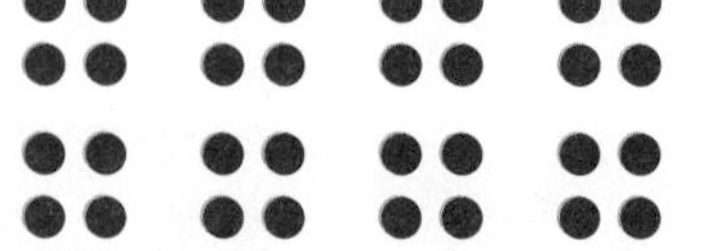

8 groups of 4

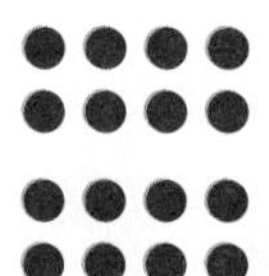

4 groups of 8

B **Use doubles.**

$4 \times 4 = 16$

$16 + 16 = 32$

So, $4 \times 8 = 32$.

Guided Practice

1. **Explain** how you would use this array to find 7×8.

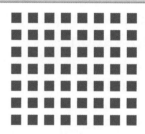

Find the product.

2. $6 \times 8 = ■$ **3.** $■ = 3 \times 8$ ✓**4.** $■ = 8 \times 8$ ✓**5.** $9 \times 8 = ■$

6. TALK Math **Explain** how you can use 5×4 to help you find 5×8.

TEKS 3.4A learn and apply multiplication facts through 12 by 12 using concrete models and objects. *also* **3.6B, 3.14A, 3.14D, 3.15A, 3.15B**

Independent Practice and Problem Solving

Find the product.

7. $10 \times 8 = \blacksquare$ **8.** $2 \times 8 = \blacksquare$ **9.** $\blacksquare = 3 \times 8$ **10.** $\blacksquare = 8 \times 7$

11. $8 \times 4 = \blacksquare$ **12.** $\blacksquare = 6 \times 8$ **13.** $\blacksquare = 0 \times 8$ **14.** $5 \times 8 = \blacksquare$

15. 8×8 **16.** 10×3 **17.** 9×8 **18.** 1×8 **19.** 8×2 **20.** 5×7

21. 6×4 **22.** 7×3 **23.** 5×5 **24.** 3×8 **25.** 6×5 **26.** 7×8

Algebra Copy and complete each table.

	Multiply by 4.	
27.	9	■
28.	3	■
29.	5	■

	Multiply by 8.	
30.	4	■
31.	■	56
32.	■	24

33.	Multiply by ■.	
	3	18
	6	36
34.	9	■

USE DATA For 35–37 use the table.

Average Yearly Rainfall in North American Deserts

Desert	Inches
Chihuahuan	8
Great Basin	9
Mojave	4
Sonoran	9

35. About how much rain falls in the Chihuahuan Desert in 4 years? **Explain** how you can use doubles to find the answer.

36. In 2 years, how many more inches of rainfall are there in the Sonoran Desert than in the Mojave Desert?

37. WRITE Math **Explain** how you can find about how many inches of rain fall in the Chihuahuan Desert in 5 years.

Mixed Review and TAKS Prep

38. About 460 inches of rain falls on Mt. Waialeale, Hawaii each year. What is the value of the 4 in 460? (TEKS 3.1A, p. 10)

39. Carrie has 3 bags of oranges. Each bag has 4 oranges. How many oranges is that? (TEKS 3.4B, p. 210)

40. **TAKS Prep** A black widow spider has 8 legs. How many legs do 7 black widow spiders have? (Obj. 1)

A 1 **C** 48

B 15 **D** 56

on page 264, Set A

LESSON 2

ALGEBRA

Patterns with 9

OBJECTIVE: Multiply with the factor 9.

Quick Review

1. 9×4
2. 7×10
3. 6×10
4. 9×2
5. 9×3

Learn

PROBLEM Melissa's class is studying the solar system. Students are making models of 9 planets that orbit, or revolve around, the sun. How many planets are in 5 solar system models?

$5 \times 9 = ■$

▲ Planets orbit the sun.

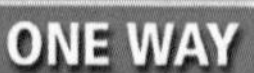

Use patterns of 9.

Look at the products in the table of 9s facts.

The tens digit is 1 less than the factor that is multiplied by 9.

$5 \times 9 = 4■$

↓ ↑

$5 - 1 = 4$

The sum of the digits in the product equals 9.

$4 + 5 = 9$

So, $5 \times 9 = 45$

So, there are 45 planets in 5 solar system models.

- How can you use patterns of 9 to complete the table?

Table of 9's	
Factors	**Product**
$1 \times 9 =$	9
$2 \times 9 =$	18
$3 \times 9 =$	27
$4 \times 9 =$	36
$5 \times 9 =$	■
$6 \times 9 =$	54
$7 \times 9 =$	63
$8 \times 9 =$	■
$9 \times 9 =$	■
$10 \times 9 =$	■

ANOTHER WAY **Use a related 10s fact.**

To multiply by 9, first multiply by 10.

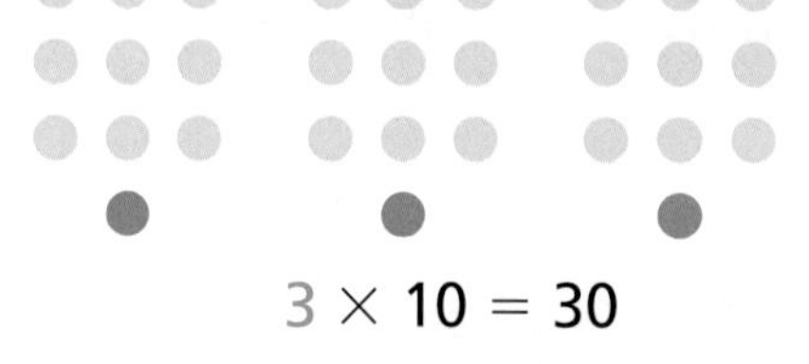

$3 \times 10 = 30$

Then subtract the first factor.

$30 - 3 = 27$

So, $3 \times 9 = 27$

Guided Practice

1. How can you use a related 10s fact to find 4×9?

TEKS 3.4A learn and apply multiplication facts through 12 by 12 using concrete models and objects. *also* 3.6B, 3.14A, 3.15A, 3.15B

Find each product.

2. $9 \times 8 = ■$ **3.** $■ = 2 \times 9$ ✓**4.** $■ = 9 \times 6$ ✓**5.** $9 \times 1 = ■$

6. TALK Math **Explain** how to use the 9s pattern to find 7×9.

Independent Practice and Problem Solving

Find each product.

7. $■ = 9 \times 0$ **8.** $5 \times 9 = ■$ **9.** $■ = 6 \times 9$ **10.** $■ = 1 \times 9$

11. $9 \times 2 = ■$ **12.** $■ = 9 \times 9$ **13.** $9 \times 4 = ■$ **14.** $3 \times 9 = ■$

15. 9×8 **16.** 9×7 **17.** 10×5 **18.** 4×6 **19.** 8×4 **20.** 9×5

Algebra Compare. Write <, >, or = for each ●.

21. 2×9 ● 3×6 **22.** 5×9 ● 6×7 **23.** 1×9 ● 3×3

24. 9×4 ● 7×5 **25.** 9×0 ● 2×3 **26.** 5×8 ● 3×9

USE DATA For 27–29, use the table.

27. The number of moons of one of the planets can be found by multiplying 7×9. Which planet is it?

28. **Reasoning** This planet has 9 times as many moons as Mars and Earth together have. Which planet is it? **Explain** your answer.

29. WRITE Math Nine groups of students made models of Mars and its moons. How many moons were made in all? **Explain** how to find the answer.

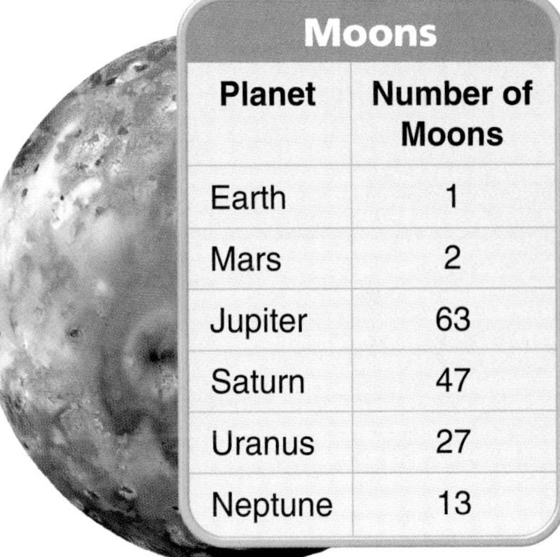

Moons

Planet	Number of Moons
Earth	1
Mars	2
Jupiter	63
Saturn	47
Uranus	27
Neptune	13

Mixed Review and TAKS Prep

30. The school library has 87 books about space. John checked out 9 of them. How many books about space does the library have left? (TEKS 3.3B, p. 88)

31. Ten students each returned 3 books to the library. How many books did the students return? (TEKS 3.4B, p. 230)

32. **TAKS Prep** Mary has 5 sheets of star stickers. Each sheet has 9 stars on it. How many stickers are there in all? (Obj. 1)

A 50 **B** 45 **C** 36 **D** 14

CD ROM **Technology**
Use Harcourt Mega Math, The Number Games, *Up, Up, and Array,* Level B and C.

Extra Practice on page 264, Set B

LESSON 3

Multiply with 7

OBJECTIVE: Multiply with the factor 7.

Quick Review

1. 7×1
2. 7×4
3. 7×3
4. 7×2
5. 7×5

Learn

PROBLEM Jason's family has a new puppy. Jason walks the puppy once a day. How many times will Jason walk the puppy in 4 weeks?

$$4 \times 7 = \blacksquare$$

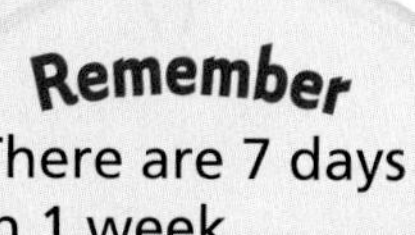

ONE WAY **Make an array.**

Make 4 rows of 7 tiles.

$$\begin{array}{r} 7 \\ \times 4 \\ \hline 28 \end{array}$$

So, Jason will walk the puppy 28 times.

OTHER WAYS

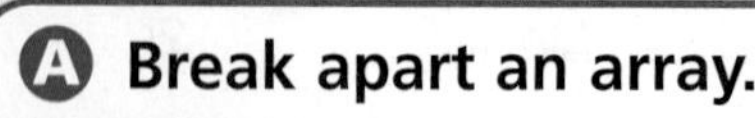

A Break apart an array.

Step 1

Make an array that shows 4 rows of 7.

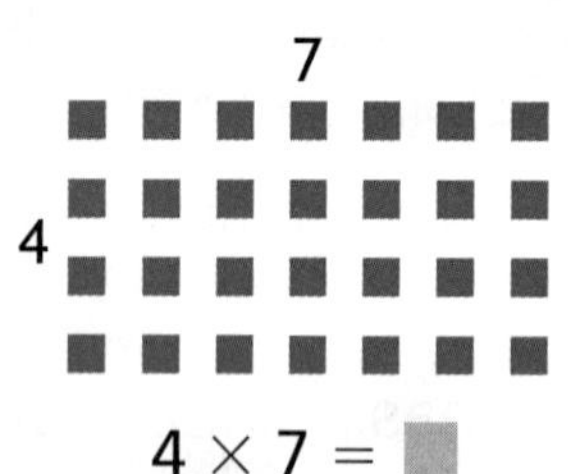

$4 \times 7 = \blacksquare$

Step 2

Break the array into two smaller arrays.

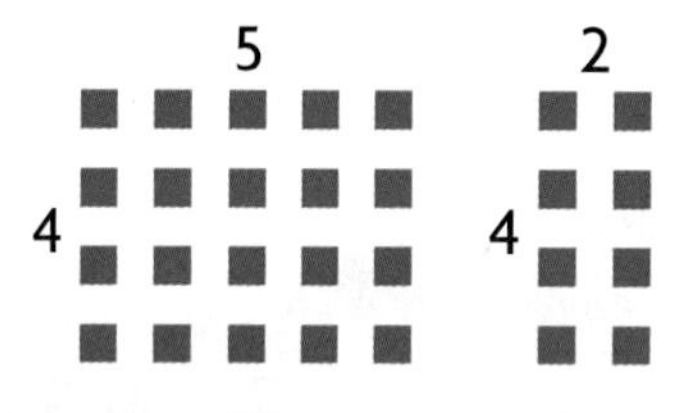

$4 \times 5 = 20$ $4 \times 2 = 8$

Step 3

Add the products of the two arrays.

$$\begin{array}{r} 20 \\ +\ 8 \\ \hline 28 \end{array}$$

So, $4 \times 7 = 28$.

- What is another way to break apart the 4×7 array?

B Use the Commutative Property.

If you know 7×4, use that fact to find 4×7.

$7 \times 4 = 28$, so $4 \times 7 = 28$.

TEKS 3.4A learn and apply multiplication facts through 12 by 12 using concrete models and objects. *also* **3.6B, 3.14A, 3.14C, 3.15A, 3.15B**

Guided Practice

1. **Explain** how you could break apart 8×7 into two arrays to help you find the product. Use tiles to help.

Find the product.

2. $9 \times 7 =$ ■ 3. ■ $= 6 \times 7$ 4. ■ $= 3 \times 7$ 5. $7 \times 1 =$ ■

6. TALK Math How could you use the Commutative Property to find 6×7?

Independent Practice and Problem Solving

Find the product.

7. ■ $= 7 \times 7$ 8. $5 \times 7 =$ ■ 9. ■ $= 1 \times 8$ 10. ■ $= 7 \times 2$

11. 7×3 12. 10×6 13. 9×7 14. 5×7 15. 6×8 16. 7×6

17. 8×9 18. 0×7 19. 8×8 20. 7×4 21. 3×6 22. 8×7

USE DATA For 23 and 25, use the table.

Midnight's Care	
Food	3 cups a day
Water	4 cups a day
Bath	2 times a month

23. Lori has a dog named Midnight. How many baths will Midnight have in 7 months?

24. **FAST FACT** A dog's heartbeat depends on its size. Some dogs' hearts beat 70 times a minute. What 7s fact equals 70?

25. WRITE Math Jose's dog, Sunny, eats 4 cups of food a day. In 7 days, does Sunny eat more or less than Midnight eats? **Explain**.

Mixed Review and TAKS Prep

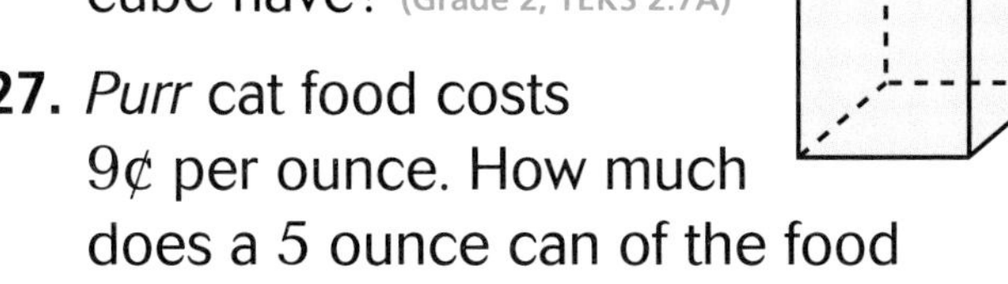

26. How many faces does a cube have? (Grade 2, TEKS 2.7A)

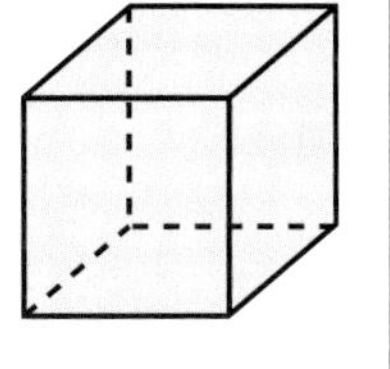

27. *Purr* cat food costs 9¢ per ounce. How much does a 5 ounce can of the food cost? (TEKS 3.4B, p. 252)

28. **TAKS Prep** Sam walks 3 miles a day. How many miles does he walk in one week? (Obj. 1)

A 3 **B** 10 **C** 21 **D** 28

Extra Practice on page 264, Set C

ALGEBRA

Practice the Facts

OBJECTIVE: Practice multiplication facts with factors 0 through 10.

Quick Review

1. 5×8 **2.** 7×6
3. 2×4 **4.** 1×8
5. 6×6

Learn

PROBLEM A volleyball team has 6 players. How many players do 8 teams have?

$8 \times 6 = \blacksquare$

ONE WAY **Draw a picture.**

Draw 8 groups of 6.

$8 \times 6 = 48$

$$\begin{array}{r} 6 \\ \times 8 \\ \hline 48 \end{array}$$

So, 8 teams have 48 players.

OTHER WAYS

A **Use a number line.**

Skip-count by 6s.

$8 \times 6 = 48$

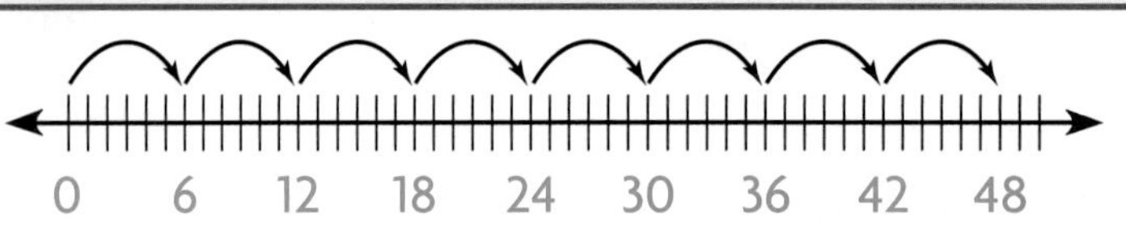

B **Use counters.**

Make 8 groups of 6.

$8 \times 6 = 48$

C **Make an array.**

Make 8 rows of 6 tiles.

$$\begin{array}{r} 6 \\ \times 8 \\ \hline 48 \end{array}$$

$8 \times 6 = 48$

• How could you break apart the 8×6 array into two arrays to find the product?

Math Idea
There are many ways to solve multiplication problems.

TEKS 3.4A learn and apply multiplication facts through 12 by 12 using concrete models and objects. *also* **3.6B, 3.14A, 3.15A, 3.15B**

D Use doubles.

Find the 3s product. $8 \times 3 = 24$

Double that product. $24 + 24 = 48$

So, $8 \times 6 = 48$

E Use the Commutative Property.

If you know 6×8, use it to find 8×6.

$6 \times 8 = 48$, so $8 \times 6 = 48$.

F Use a multiplication table.

Find where the row for 8 and the column for 6 meet.

$8 \times 6 = 48$

- How would you use the multiplication table to find 6×8?

×	0	1	2	3	4	5	6	7	8	9	10	11	12
0	0	0	0	0	0	0	0	0	0	0	0	0	0
1	0	1	2	3	4	5	6	7	8	9	10	11	12
2	0	2	4	6	8	10	12	14	16	18	20	22	24
3	0	3	6	9	12	15	18	21	24	27	30	33	36
4	0	4	8	12	16	20	24	28	32	36	40	44	48
5	0	5	10	15	20	25	30	35	40	45	50	55	60
6	0	6	12	18	24	30	36	42	48	54	60	66	72
7	0	7	14	21	28	35	42	49	56	63	70	77	84
8	0	8	16	24	32	40	48	56	64	72	80	88	96
9	0	9	18	27	36	45	54	63	72	81	90	99	108
10	0	10	20	30	40	50	60	70	80	90	100	110	120
11	0	11	22	33	44	55	66	77	88	99	110	121	132
12	0	12	24	36	48	60	72	84	96	108	120	132	144

Guided Practice

1. How could you draw a picture to find 9×3?

Find the product.

2. ■ $= 10 \times 8$ **3.** $3 \times 7 =$ ■ ✓**4.** ■ $= 9 \times 5$ ✓**5.** $7 \times 7 =$ ■

6. TALK Math **Explain** two different ways to find 7×6.

Independent Practice and Problem Solving

Find the product.

7. ■ $= 2 \times 6$ **8.** $8 \times 7 =$ ■ **9.** ■ $= 4 \times 9$ **10.** $5 \times 1 =$ ■

11. $10 \times 7 =$ ■ **12.** ■ $= 8 \times 3$ **13.** $9 \times 5 =$ ■ **14.** $4 \times 6 =$ ■

15. $0 \times 10 =$ ■ **16.** $7 \times 9 =$ ■ **17.** ■ $= 6 \times 8$ **18.** ■ $= 9 \times 6$

19. 8×8 **20.** 6×3 **21.** 2×4 **22.** 5×5 **23.** 10×3 **24.** 7×6

25. 9×8 **26.** 3×7 **27.** 6×5 **28.** 10×6 **29.** 1×4 **30.** 2×9

Extra Practice on page 264, Set D

Find the missing number.

31. $5 \times 2 = \blacksquare$
32. $\blacksquare = 3 \times 4$
33. $9 \times \blacksquare = 9$
34. $\blacksquare \times 6 = 0$
35. $5 \times \blacksquare = 35$
36. $4 \times \blacksquare = 20$
37. $7 \times \blacksquare = 28$
38. $3 \times \blacksquare = 30$
39. $\blacksquare \times 4 = 24$

Explain two different ways to find the product.

40. $9 \times 9 = \blacksquare$
41. $4 \times 8 = \blacksquare$
42. $2 \times 5 = \blacksquare$
43. $5 \times 10 = \blacksquare$
44. $10 \times 10 = \blacksquare$
45. $3 \times 9 = \blacksquare$

Compare. Write <, >, or = for each ●.

46. 2×3 ● 1×6
47. 5×6 ● 3×9
48. 6×8 ● 7×7
49. 4×9 ● 5×8
50. 10×3 ● 6×6
51. 4×7 ● 8×3
52. 8×9 ● 9×8
53. 6×5 ● 4×8
54. 3×9 ● 5×4

55. How does knowing that $5 \times 8 = 40$ help you find 6×8?

56. **Reasoning** Is the product of 6×5 greater or less than the product of 7×4? How do you know?

USE DATA For 57–59 and 61–62, use the table.

57. Marianne's town has 10 baseball teams. How many baseball players is that?

58. Carl's town has 6 baseball teams and 8 basketball teams. Are there more basketball players or baseball players? **Explain** your answer.

59. Steve plays one of the sports listed in the table. The number of players on his team is a multiple of both 2 and 3. Which sport does Steve play? **Explain** your answer.

Sports Teams

Sport	Number of Players
Ice hockey	6
Baseball	9
Basketball	5
Soccer	11

60. ***FAST FACT*** A hockey puck is 1 inch thick and weighs about 6 ounces. About how many ounces do 4 pucks weigh?

61. **Pose a Problem** Look back at Problem 57. Write a similar problem using a different number of baseball teams.

62. WRITE Math **What's the Question?** There are 10 basketball teams at Sandi's school. The answer is 50. What is the question?

Mixed Review and TAKS Prep

63. Paul put 2 basketballs in each of 4 bins. Write a number sentence that shows the number of basketballs in all. (TEKS 3.4B, p. 208)

64. **TAKS Prep** Jim played in 5 baseball games. Each was 9 innings long. For how many innings did Jim play baseball? (Obj. 1)

    A 25   **C** 45

    B 35   **D** 59

65. Zoey plays tennis. What solid figure has the same shape as the tennis ball she uses? (Grade 2, TEKS 2.7A)

66. **TAKS Prep** Which multiplication fact does this array show? (Obj. 1)

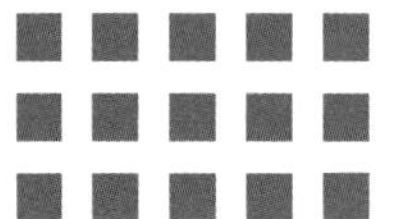

F $3 \times 5 = 15$ **H** $5 \times 5 = 25$

G $3 \times 6 = 18$ **J** $3 \times 3 = 9$

Problem Solving and Reasoning

VISUAL THINKING When two factors are the same, the product is called a square number. A multiplication table can help you find square numbers. Look at the table. Since $2 \times 2 = 4$, then 4 is a square number.

Use the multiplication table to find other square numbers.

A Find where the row and column with the same number meet.

B Write the multiplication sentence. The product is a square number.

C Find other square numbers. Be sure both factors are the same.

×	0	1	2	3	4	5	6	7	8	9	10
0	0	0	0	0	0	0	0	0	0	0	0
1	0	1	2	3	4	5	6	7	8	9	10
2	0	2	4	6	8	10	12	14	16	18	20
3	0	3	6	9	12	15	18	21	24	27	30
4	0	4	8	12	16	20	24	28	32	36	40
5	0	5	10	15	20	25	30	35	40	45	50
6	0	6	12	18	24	30	36	42	48	54	60
7	0	7	14	21	28	35	42	49	56	63	70
8	0	8	16	24	32	40	48	56	64	72	80
9	0	9	18	27	36	45	54	63	72	81	90
10	0	10	20	30	40	50	60	70	80	90	100

1. What is the square number that has 5 and 5 as factors?
2. Find the rest of the products on the multiplication table where 2 of the same factors meet. What do you notice?
3. **WRITE Math** **What's the Error?** Gerri said that 100 is not a square number. What is her error? **Explain.**

LESSON 5

Multiply with 11 and 12

OBJECTIVE: Multiply with the factors 11 and 12.

Quick Review

1. $11 + 11$
2. $12 + 12$
3. 1×10
4. 2×10
5. $11 + 11 + 11$

Learn

PROBLEM It takes Bobby 11 minutes to walk to school each morning. How many minutes will Bobby spend walking to school in 5 days?

$5 \times 11 = ■$

ONE WAY **Break apart an array.**

Make 5 rows of 11.

Use the 10s facts and the 1s facts to multiply by 11.

$5 \times 10 = 50$ $5 \times 1 = 5$

$5 \times 11 = 50 + 5 = 55$

5×10 5×1

So, Bobby will spend 55 minutes walking to school.

ANOTHER WAY

Look at the table of 11s facts.

To find 5×11, write the first factor twice.

$5 \times 11 = 55$

- What pattern do you see in the 11s facts through 9?

11s Facts
$1 \times 11 = 11$
$2 \times 11 = 22$
$3 \times 11 = 33$
$4 \times 11 = 44$
$5 \times 11 = ■$
$6 \times 11 = 66$
$7 \times 11 = 77$
$8 \times 11 = 88$
$9 \times 11 = 99$
$10 \times 11 = 110$

It takes Joan 12 minutes to ride her bike to school. How many minutes will Joan spend riding to school in 5 days?

$5 \times 12 = ■$

ONE WAY **Break apart an array.**

Make 5 rows of 12.

Use the 10s facts and the 2s facts to multiply by 12.

5×10 5×2

$5 \times 10 = 50$ $5 \times 2 = 10$

$5 \times 12 = 50 + 10 = 60$

So, Joan will spend 60 minutes riding to school.

ANOTHER WAY **Double a 6s fact.**

Find the 6s product. Double that product.

$5 \times 6 = 30$

$30 + 30 = 60$

So, $5 \times 12 = 60$.

12s Facts
$0 \times 12 = 0$
$1 \times 12 = 12$
$2 \times 12 = 24$
$3 \times 12 = 36$
$4 \times 12 = 48$
$5 \times 12 = 60$
$6 \times 12 = 72$
$7 \times 12 = 84$
$8 \times 12 = 96$
$9 \times 12 = 108$
$10 \times 12 = 120$
$11 \times 12 = 132$
$12 \times 12 = 144$

TEKS 3.4A learn and apply multiplication facts through 12 by 12 using concrete models and objects. *also* **3.6B, 3.14A, 3.15A, 3.15B**

Guided Practice

1. How can you use the 10s facts and the 2s facts to find 4×12?

Find the product.

2. $9 \times 11 = \blacksquare$
3. $\blacksquare = 12 \times 7$
4. $\blacksquare = 4 \times 11$
5. $12 \times 3 = \blacksquare$
6. **TALK Math** How does knowing $11 \times 6 = 66$ help you find 11×12?

Independent Practice and Problem Solving

Find the product.

7. $\blacksquare = 11 \times 11$
8. $6 \times 12 = \blacksquare$
9. $\blacksquare = 10 \times 9$
10. $\blacksquare = 0 \times 12$
11. $10 \times 11 = \blacksquare$
12. $\blacksquare = 11 \times 8$
13. $11 \times 3 = \blacksquare$
14. $2 \times 12 = \blacksquare$
15. $\begin{array}{r} 11 \\ \times\ 4 \\ \hline \end{array}$
16. $\begin{array}{r} 12 \\ \times\ 9 \\ \hline \end{array}$
17. $\begin{array}{r} 12 \\ \times\ 0 \\ \hline \end{array}$
18. $\begin{array}{r} 11 \\ \times\ 9 \\ \hline \end{array}$
19. $\begin{array}{r} 12 \\ \times\ 7 \\ \hline \end{array}$
20. $\begin{array}{r} 12 \\ \times\ 6 \\ \hline \end{array}$

USE DATA For 21–22, use the graph.

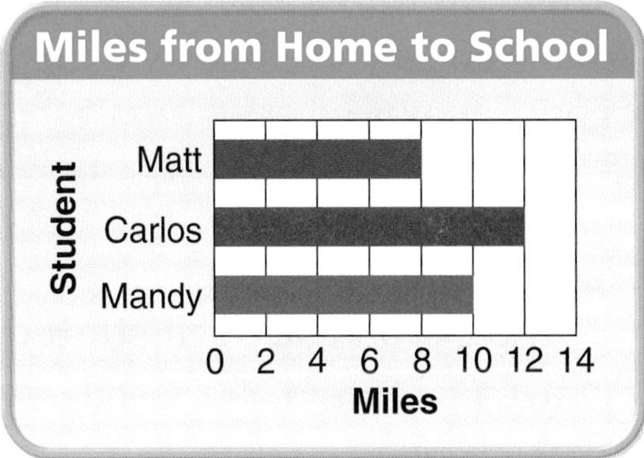

21. The graph shows the number of miles some students travel to school. How many miles will Carlos travel to school in 10 days?
22. Mandy takes 11 trips to school. Matt takes 12 trips to school. Who travels more miles? **Explain** your answer.
23. **WRITE Math** Mr. Lane is putting 6 cartons of eggs on the shelf. There are 12 eggs in each carton. How many eggs in all are there? **Explain** two ways to find the answer.

Mixed Review and TAKS Prep

24. A school has 199 third graders and 208 fourth graders. How many students in all are there? (TEKS 3.3B, p. 66)
25. What is the missing number in $5 \times 9 = \blacksquare$? (TEKS 3.4B, p. 252)
26. **TAKS Prep** There are 12 desks in each of 3 rows. How many desks in all are there? (Obj. 1)

A 8 **C** 36

B 16 **D** 48

Extra Practice on page 264, Set E

Problem Solving Workshop
Strategy: Compare Strategies

OBJECTIVE: Compare different strategies to solve problems.

PROBLEM The nine-banded armadillo usually has 9 bands across its back. How many bands would 4 armadillos have?

▲ The armadillo is the state small animal of Texas.

Read to Understand

- **Summarize what you are asked to find.**
- **What information is given?**

Plan

- **What strategy can you use to solve the problem?**
  Many times you can use more than one strategy to solve a problem. For example, you can *draw a picture* or *make a table* to solve this problem.

Solve

- **How can you use each strategy to solve the problem?**

Draw a picture of 4 armadillos with 9 bands on each one.

$4 \times 9 = 36$

So, 4 armadillos will have 36 bands.

Make a table to show the number of bands on four armadillos.

Armadillo Bands				
Number of armadillos	1	2	3	4
Number of bands	9	18	27	36

Check

- **How do you know your answer is correct?**

TALK Math

Which strategy would you use to solve the problem? Explain.

TEKS **3.14C** select or develop an appropriate problem-solving strategy including drawing a picture, looking for a pattern, systematic guessing and checking, acting it out, making a table, working a simpler problem, or working backwards to solve a problem. *also* **3.4A, 3.6B, 3.14A, 3.15A, 3.15B**

Guided Problem Solving

1. The mockingbird is the state bird of Texas. Julie saw 6 mockingbirds each time she went bird-watching. How many mockingbirds did Julie see in 5 days?

Draw a picture.

First, draw a picture of 6 birds.

Next, draw 4 more groups of 6 birds so there are 5 groups in all.

Last, count to find the total number of birds.

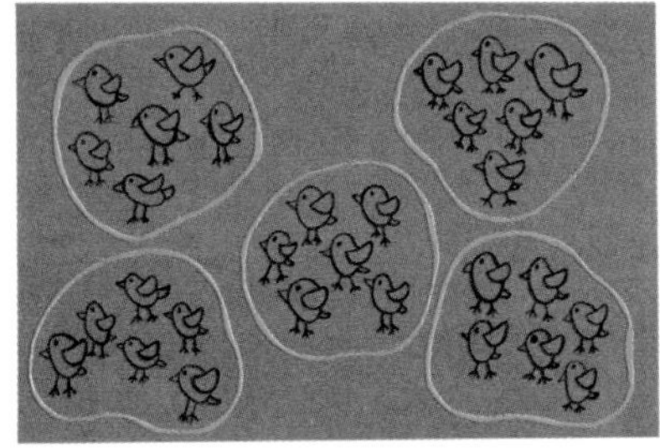

$5 \times 6 = \blacksquare$

Make a table.

First, decide what information should be in each row.

Next, write the information from the problem in the table.

Last, fill in the table through 5 days.

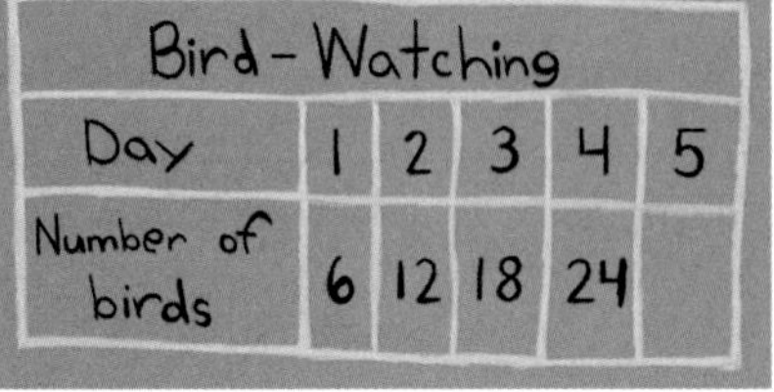

Bird-Watching					
Day	1	2	3	4	5
Number of birds	6	12	18	24	

Choose a STRATEGY

- Make a Model or Act It Out
- Draw a Diagram or Picture
- Make an Organized List
- Look for a Pattern
- Make a Table or Graph
- Guess and Check
- Work Backward
- Solve a Simpler Problem
- Write an Equation
- Use Logical Reasoning

2. **What if** Julie saw 6 mockingbirds every day for 6 days? How many in all would she have seen?

3. Mark hiked a trail every day for 5 days. Each day he saw 9 cactus plants. How many cactus plants did he see in all?

Mixed Strategy Practice

USE DATA For 4–6, use the recipe.

Cactus Fruit Jelly

- 3 Pounds of ripe cactus fruit
- 3 cups juice from cooked fruit
- 1 cup water
- 1 bottle liquid pectin
- Juice of 2 lemons
- 8 cups sugar

4. Jane doubles the cactus jelly recipe. How many lemons does she need?

5. Joan, Michelle, Samantha, and Gerri each use the recipe to make cactus fruit jelly. How many cups of sugar do they use in all?

6. **Reasoning** Joel has 7 pounds of ripe cactus fruit. How many pounds will he have left if he makes 2 batches of jelly? **Explain** your answer.

7. Lilly took a 4-mile walk every day for 9 days. How many miles in all did Lilly walk?

8. **WRITE Math** Louis planted a cactus garden. He bought 48 cactus. He planted 8 cactus each day. How many days did it take Louis to plant all of the cactus? Explain how you know.

Extra Practice

Set A Find the product. (pp. 250–251)

1. $3 \times 8 = ■$ 2. $1 \times 8 = ■$ 3. $5 \times 8 = ■$ 4. $8 \times 0 = ■$

5. 6×6 6. 0×8 7. 7×8 8. 2×7 9. 4×8 10. 8×9

11. Elena has 3 small loaves of bread. Each loaf has 8 pieces of bread. How many pieces of bread in all does Elena have?

12. Cole has 4 bags of 10 action figures. Owen has 6 bags of 8 action figures. Who has more action figures, Cole or Owen? How many more?

Set B Find each product. (pp. 252–253)

1. $3 \times 9 = ■$ 2. $9 \times 5 = ■$ 3. $0 \times 9 = ■$ 4. $9 \times 7 = ■$

Compare. Write <, >, or = for each ●.

5. 9×3 ● 7×4 6. 4×3 ● 2×6 7. 9×2 ● 6×3

Set C Find the product. (pp. 254–255)

1. $7 \times 10 = ■$ 2. $3 \times 7 = ■$ 3. $5 \times 7 = ■$ 4. $7 \times 4 = ■$

5. A photo album has 7 pictures on 8 pages. How many photos are there in all?

6. Malik rides his bike 7 miles every day. How many miles does he ride in one week?

Set D Find the product. (pp. 256–259)

1. $■ = 8 \times 3$ 2. $4 \times 7 = ■$ 3. $5 \times 5 = ■$ 4. $■ = 2 \times 9$

5. 6×6 6. 7×5 7. 9×2 8. 8×5 9. 10×7 10. 5×6

Set E Find the product. (pp. 260–261)

1. $11 \times 9 = ■$ 2. $11 \times 3 = ■$ 3. $12 \times 2 = ■$ 4. $11 \times 8 = ■$

5. $7 \times 11 = ■$ 6. $3 \times 12 = ■$ 7. $6 \times 12 = ■$ 8. $8 \times 12 = ■$

Technology
Use Harcourt Mega Math, The Number Games, *Up, Up, and Array*, Levels B, D.

TECHNOLOGY CONNECTION

Calculator: Multiplication Facts (TEKS 3.4A, 3.4B)

Use a Calculator for Multiplication

Eleanor is making a food mix for her hamsters. She wants equal numbers of sunflower seeds, corn kernels, peanuts, round pellets, and flat pellets. If she uses 12 of each item, how many items will be in the mix?

Write a number sentence for the word problem.

$5 \times 12 = \blacksquare$

Use a calculator to solve.

So, Eleanor will use 60 items in the food mix.

Try It

Use a calculator to multiply.

1. $11 \times 7 = \blacksquare$
2. $8 \times 4 = \blacksquare$
3. $12 \times 6 = \blacksquare$
4. $7 \times 4 = \blacksquare$
5. $8 \times 5 = \blacksquare$
6. $12 \times 8 = \blacksquare$
7. $10 \times 11 = \blacksquare$
8. $9 \times 4 = \blacksquare$
9. $3 \times 12 = \blacksquare$
10. $7 \times 3 = \blacksquare$
11. $6 \times 9 = \blacksquare$
12. $2 \times 11 = \blacksquare$
13. Ferris went bird watching 7 times in May. On each trip, he wrote about 9 new bird sightings in his journal. How many new birds did he see in May?
14. Carter collects old coins. He has 6 dimes, 6 quarters, and 6 half dollars. How many coins does he have in all? Write a number sentence, and then use a calculator to multiply.
15. Maria has 12 pennies, 12 nickels, 12 dimes, and 12 silver dollars in her wallet. How many coins does she have in all? Write a number sentence, and then use a calculator to multiply.
16. **Explore More** Yvette has invited 8 friends to her party. She plans to give each friend 4 party favors. She has 35 favors in all. How many will she have left over? **Explain.**

Chapter 11 Review/Test

Check Concepts

Make an array to solve. (TEKS 3.4A, pp. 250–251, 254–255)

1. Maria puts 8 ice cubes into each of 3 glasses for her friends. How many ice cubes has she used in all?

2. There are 7 days in a week. How many days are there in 4 weeks?

Check Skills

Find the product. (TEKS 3.4A, pp. 250–251, 252–253, 254–255, 256–259, 260–261)

3. $2 \times 12 = ■$
4. $8 \times 4 = ■$
5. $3 \times 11 = ■$
6. $7 \times 5 = ■$
7. $5 \times 8 = ■$
8. $11 \times 7 = ■$
9. $9 \times 8 = ■$
10. $12 \times 4 = ■$
11. 5×4
12. 3×8
13. 5×5
14. 11×9
15. 12×3
16. 8×4

Compare. Write <, >, or = for each ●. (TEKS 3.4A, pp. 252–253)

17. 4×3 ● 5×2
18. 6×5 ● 7×4
19. 4×5 ● 10×2
20. 8×2 ● 5×3
21. 8×3 ● 12×2
22. 7×5 ● 9×3

Check Problem Solving

Solve. (TEKS 3.14, pp. 262–263)

23. Linda can paint 4 pictures in one day. How many pictures can she paint in 5 days?

Number of days	1	2	3	4	5
Pictures painted	4	8	■	■	■

24. Jerod buys 4 packages of markers and 5 packages of paper. Each package of markers costs \$5, and each package of paper costs \$3. How much does Jerod spend in all?

25. WRITE Math What if each package of paper costs \$6? How much does Jerod spend in all for paper and markers then? **Explain** how you found your answer.

GO ONLINE **Technology** Use *Online Assessment.*

Enrich • Facts and Strategies

MYSTERY NUMBER RIDDLES

Everybody loves a good mystery! Use addition, subtraction, and multiplication to solve the riddle below.

Math Mystery

Follow the steps to begin solving the riddle.

		A
Start with 5.	5	
Add 4.	$5 + 4 = 9$	
Multiply by 2.	$2 \times 9 = 18$	
Subtract 3.	$18 - 3 = 15$	
END NUMBER: ■	15	
	So, A = 15.	

Funny Facts

Copy the riddle. Find the value of each letter. Then write the letters in the correct spaces.

Q	C	K
Start with 9. Subtract 3. Multiply by 4. Subtract 4. END NUMBER: ■	Start with 4. Add 2. Subtract 3. Multiply by 6. END NUMBER: ■	Start with 8. Multiply by 3. Subtract 10. Add 5. END NUMBER: ■

U	E	R
Start with 7. Subtract 3. Multiply by 9. Add 4. END NUMBER: ■	Start with 10. Multiply by 5. Subtract 6 Add 11. END NUMBER: ■	Start with 6. Multiply by 8. Add 9. Subtract 22. END NUMBER: ■

- **What is a duck's favorite food?**

A	?	?	?	?	?	?	?!
15	20	40	15	18	19	55	35

Writing a Riddle

WRITE Math ▸ Write a riddle with at least 4 steps. **Explain** your riddle.

Getting Ready for the TAKS

Chapters 1–11

Number, Operation, and Quantitative Reasoning (TAKS Obj. 1)

1. Randy looked up the population of Williamstown and found census data from 1932. He learned that in 1932 Williamstown's population was 7,610. What is the value of the 7 in 7,610?

   A 70

   B 700

   C 7,000

   D 70,000

2. I am a number less than 1,000. My hundreds digit is 3 times my tens digit. My tens digit is 1 greater than my ones digit. My ones digit is 1. What number am I?

   F 931

   G 642

   H 621

   J 31

3. **WRITE Math** Order the numbers from least to greatest. **Explain** the steps you used.

421	411	412

Patterns, Relationships, and Algebraic Thinking (TAKS Obj. 2)

4. Look at the function table. How many legs are on 4 spiders?

Number of spiders	Number of Legs
1	8
2	16
3	24
4	■

   A 26

   B 28

   C 32

   D Not here

Test Tip **Eliminate choices.**

See item 5. Read each answer choice. Cross off the answers that do not make sense.

5. Which number sentence is in the same fact family as $3 + 4 = 7$?

   F $4 + 2 = 6$

   G $3 + 7 = 10$

   H $7 - 1 = 6$

   J $7 - 3 = 4$

6. **WRITE Math** How can you use the product of 8×3 to find 8×6? **Explain**.

Measurement (TAKS Obj. 4)

7. What time does the clock show?

A 5:15

B 5:45

C 6:15

D 6:45

8. Measure the length of the ribbon in inches.

F 1 inch

G 2 inches

H 3 inches

J 4 inches

9. **WRITE Math** Would you use inches, centimeters, or feet to measure the length of a fence around a playground? **Explain** your choice.

Probability and Statistics (TAKS Obj. 5)

10. The graph shows the number of students who voted for each color. How many students voted for blue as their favorite color?

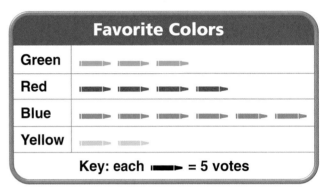

Favorite Colors	
Green	
Red	
Blue	
Yellow	
Key: each = 5 votes	

A 10

B 15

C 20

D 30

11. Which color is the pointer on this spinner most likely to stop on?

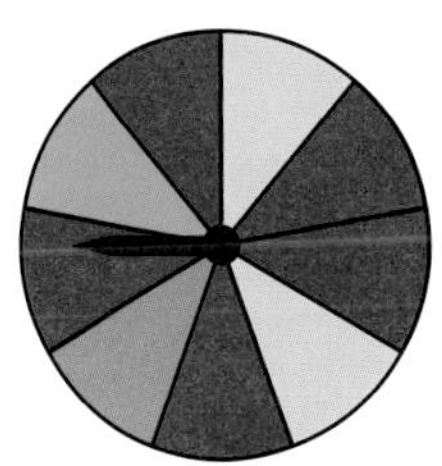

F Red

G Blue

H Green

J Yellow

12. **WRITE Math** Molly's class took a survey of their favorite pets. The results were: dog, 13; cat, 12; and hamster, 4. **Explain** how you would display these data in a bar graph.

CHAPTER

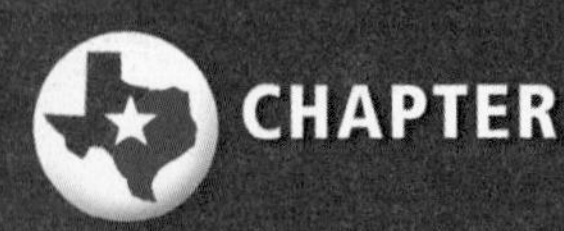

12 Algebra: Facts and Properties

The Big Idea Basic facts strategies for multiplication are based on properties, patterns, and number relationships.

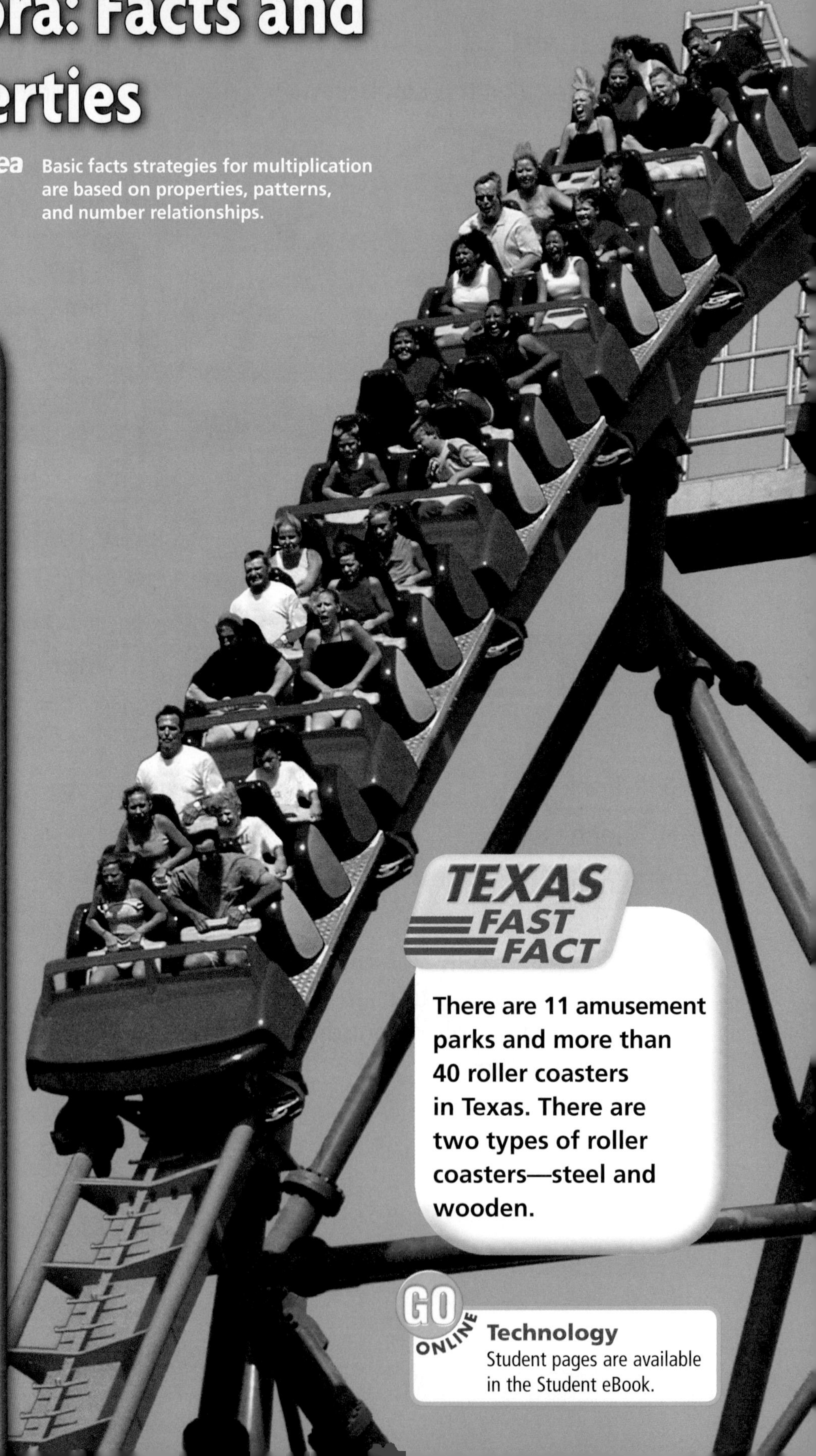

Investigate

Each train in the Titan at Six Flags Over Texas has 5 cars that hold 6 riders each, for a total of 30 riders. Choose a roller coaster from the graph. How many cars and riders per car could each train have? Make a list of possible combinations.

Texas Roller Coasters

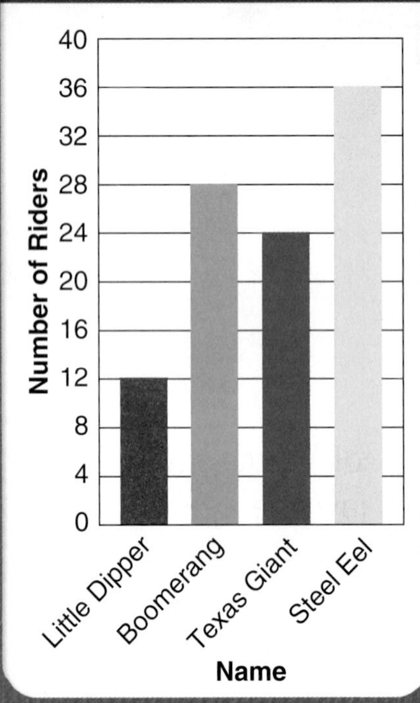

TEXAS FAST FACT

There are 11 amusement parks and more than 40 roller coasters in Texas. There are two types of roller coasters—steel and wooden.

GO ONLINE **Technology** Student pages are available in the Student eBook.

Show What You Know

Check your understanding of important skills needed for success in Chapter 12.

▶ Arrays

Complete.

1.

2 rows of ■ = 16

$2 \times 8 =$ ■

2.

4 rows of ■ = 20

$4 \times 5 =$ ■

3.

3 rows of ■ = 21

$3 \times 7 =$ ■

4. 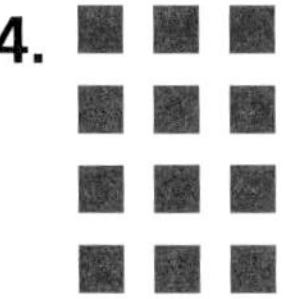

4 rows of ■ = 12

$4 \times 3 =$ ■

5. 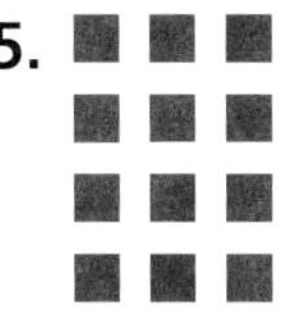

5 rows of ■ =15

$5 \times 3 =$ ■

6. 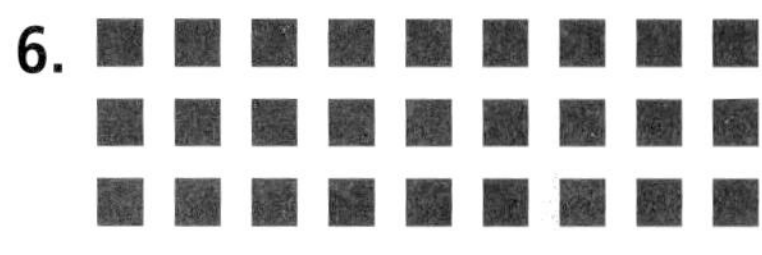

3 rows of ■ = 27

$3 \times 9 =$ ■

▶ Multiplication Facts Through 10

Find the product.

7. $4 \times 4 =$ ■ **8.** $3 \times 6 =$ ■ **9.** $7 \times 9 =$ ■ **10.** $5 \times 10 =$ ■

VOCABULARY POWER

CHAPTER VOCABULARY

Associative Property of Multiplication
Commutative Property of Multiplication
Identity Property of Multiplication
variable
Zero Property of Multiplication

WARM-UP WORDS

variable A symbol or a letter that stands for an unknown number

Associative Property of Multiplication The property that states that when the grouping of factors is changed, the product remains the same

Zero Property of Multiplication The property that states that the product of zero and any number is 0

LESSON 1 Find a Rule

OBJECTIVE: Find a rule for a numerical pattern shown on a function table.

Quick Review

1. $6 \times 7 = \blacksquare$
2. $8 \times 4 = \blacksquare$
3. $1 \times 8 = \blacksquare$
4. $6 \times 9 = \blacksquare$
5. $8 \times 7 = \blacksquare$

Learn

PROBLEM The camping club is planning a trip. Each camper will need a flashlight. One flashlight uses 3 batteries. How many batteries are needed for 7 flashlights?

▲ The flashlight was invented in 1896.

Example Look for a pattern. Write a rule.

Flashlights	1	2	3	4	5	6	7
Batteries	3	6	9	12	15	18	■

Pattern: The number of batteries equals the number of flashlights times 3 batteries per flashlight.

Rule: Multiply the number of flashlights by 3.

To find how many batteries are needed for 7 flashlights, multiply 7 times 3.

$$7 \times 3 = 21$$

So, 21 batteries are needed for 7 flashlights.

More Examples Describe the pattern. Write a rule.

Packs of batteries	1	2	3	4	5
Number of batteries	4	8	■	16	■

Pattern: The number of batteries equals the number of packs times 4 batteries per pack.

Rule: Multiply the number of packs of batteries by 4.

- How many batteries are in 3 packs? 5 packs?

Packs of batteries	1	2	3	4
Cost	$5	$10	$15	■

Pattern: The cost equals the number of packs times $5 per pack.

Rule: Multiply the number of packs of batteries by $5.

- How much do 4 packs cost? 7 packs?

- How does knowing the pattern rule help you find the next number in the pattern?

TEKS 3.7A generate a table of paired numbers based on a real-life situation such as insects and legs. *also* **3.6B, 3.7B, 3.14A, 3.15A, 3.15B**

Guided Practice

1. **Explain** how to use a rule to find how many batteries are needed for 9 flashlights.

Flashlights	1	2	3
Batteries	3	6	9

Write a rule for each table. Then copy and complete the table.

2.

Tents	2	3	4	5	6	7
Campers	4	6	8	10	■	■

3.

Campers	1	2	3	4	5
Flashlights	1	2	3	■	■

4. TALK Math **Explain** how you can make a table to find how many plates are on 6 tables. Pattern: The number of plates equals the number of tables times 4.

Independent Practice and Problem Solving

Write a rule for each table. Then copy and complete the table.

5.

Hours	1	2	3	4	5
Miles Hiked	2	4	■	■	■

6.

Cabins	3	4	5	6	7
Campers	27	36	■	■	■

USE DATA For 7–9, use the table.

7. Write a rule for the table at the right. What pattern do you see?

8. The camping club rents 4 rafts. How many people can 4 rafts hold?

9. WRITE Math **What's the Question?** The answer is 30 people. What is the question?

Rafts	1	2	3	4
People	6	12	18	■

10. The cost to rent a raft is $10 per person. There is a $2 launch fee per raft. What is the cost for a group of 6 people?

Mixed Review and TAKS Prep

11. Are you more likely or less likely to spin blue on this spinner? (Grade 2 TEKS 2.11C)

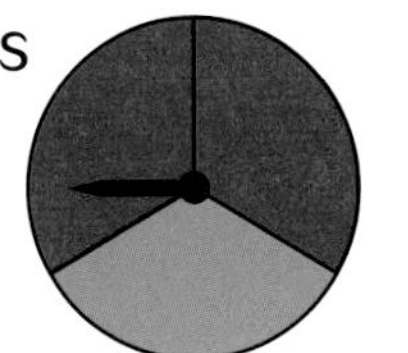

12. Tim bought 4 boxes of granola bars. There are 6 bars in each box. How many bars did Tim buy? (TEKS 3.4B, p. 232)

13. **TAKS Prep** Two notebooks cost $4 and 3 notebooks cost $6. Jenny bought 6 notebooks. How much did she spend? (Obj. 1)

A $6 **B** $10 **C** $12 **D** $24

Extra Practice on page 284, Set A

LESSON 2

Missing Factors

OBJECTIVE: Use an array and a multiplication table to find missing factors.

Quick Review

1. $7 \times 3 = \blacksquare$
2. $9 \times 6 = \blacksquare$
3. $8 \times 5 = \blacksquare$
4. $5 \times 7 = \blacksquare$
5. $2 \times 0 = \blacksquare$

Vocabulary

variable

Learn

PROBLEM Brandy plans to invite 24 people to a picnic. The invitations come in packs of 8. How many packs of invitations does Brandy need to buy?

$$\blacksquare \times 8 = 24$$

A **variable** is a letter or symbol that stands for an unknown number.

8 invitations

ONE WAY **Make an array.**

Activity

Materials ■ square tiles

Make an array with 24 tiles.
Use 8 tiles in each row.

Count the rows of 8 tiles.

column

row →

■	×	8	=	24
↑		↑		↑
factor		factor		product
rows		columns		total number of tiles

There are 3 rows of 8 tiles. The missing factor is 3.

$$3 \times 8 = 24$$

So, Brandy needs 3 packs of invitations.

ANOTHER WAY **Use a multiplication table.**

Start at the column for 8.
Look down to the product, 24.
Look left across the row from 24.
The missing factor is 3.

$a \times 8 = 24$

$3 \times 8 = 24$

×	0	1	2	3	4	5	6	7	8	9
0	0	0	0	0	0	0	0	0	0	0
1	0	1	2	3	4	5	6	7	8	9
2	0	2	4	6	8	10	12	14	16	18
3	0	3	6	9	12	15	18	21	24	27
4	0	4	8	12	16	20	24	28	32	36
5	0	5	10	15	20	25	30	35	40	45
6	0	6	12	18	24	30	36	42	48	54
7	0	7	14	21	28	35	42	49	56	63
8	0	8	16	24	32	40	48	56	64	72
9	0	9	18	27	36	45	54	63	72	81

TEKS 3.4A learn and apply multiplication facts through 12 by 12 using concrete models and objects. *also* **3.6B, 3.14A, 3.15A, 3.15B**

Guided Practice

1. What is the missing factor shown by this array?

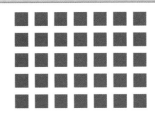

$$5 \times ■ = 35$$

Find the missing factor.

2. $■ \times 3 = 27$
3. $6 \times b = 30$
✓4. $c \times 5 = 20$
✓5. $■ \times 2 = 14$

6. TALK Math **Explain** how to use the multiplication table on page 274 to find the missing factor in $■ \times 6 = 42$.

Independent Practice and Problem Solving

Find the missing factor.

7. $■ \times 2 = 18$
8. $4 \times ■ = 28$
9. $■ \times 3 = 9$
10. $■ \times 7 = 63$
11. $5 \times ■ = 40$
12. $8 \times ■ = 56$
13. $■ \times 6 = 36$
14. $9 \times ■ = 72$
15. $a \times 4 = 24$
16. $7 \times y = 7$
17. $m \times 3 = 15$
18. $b \times 8 = 48$
19. $3 \times 6 = n \times 9$
20. $9 \times d = 70 + 2$
21. $5 \times g = 35 - 5$

USE DATA For 22–24, use the table.

Picnic Supplies

Item	Number per pack	Cost
Bowls	6	$4
Cups	8	$3
Tablecloth	1	$2
Napkins	36	$6
Forks	50	$3

22. Brandy needs 48 bowls for the picnic. How many packs of bowls should she buy?
23. What is the total cost for 3 tablecloths and 2 packs of napkins?
24. WRITE Math **What's the Error?** Brandy needs 5 packs of cups. She gives the cashier $8. What is Brandy's error?

Mixed Review and TAKS Prep

25. Eric bounced the ball 170 times. What is 170 in expanded notation? (TEKS 3.1A, p. 10)
26. The gym teacher divides the class into 4 teams. There are 9 students on each team. How many students are in the class? (TEKS 3.4B, p. 252)
27. **TAKS Prep** What is the missing factor? (Obj. 1)

$$■ \times 6 = 12$$

A 18 **C** 3
B 6 **D** 2

CD ROM **Technology**
Use Harcourt Mega Math, Ice Station Exploration, *Arctic Algebra*, Level C.

Extra Practice on page 284, Set B

LESSON 3

Multiply 3 Factors

OBJECTIVE: Multiply with three factors using the Associative (Grouping) Property of Multiplication.

Quick Review

1. $6 + 3 + 5$
2. $8 + 4 + 8$
3. $5 + 2 + 7$
4. $2 + 6 + 9$
5. $4 + 8 + 1$

Vocabulary

Associative Property of Multiplication

Learn

PROBLEM The Mr. Freeze Roller Coaster in Texas has 5 cars. Each car has 2 rows of seats. Each row has 2 seats. How many seats in all are on the ride?

ONE WAY Multiply $5 \times (2 \times 2) = ■$.

Make an array to show 5 groups of 2 times 2.

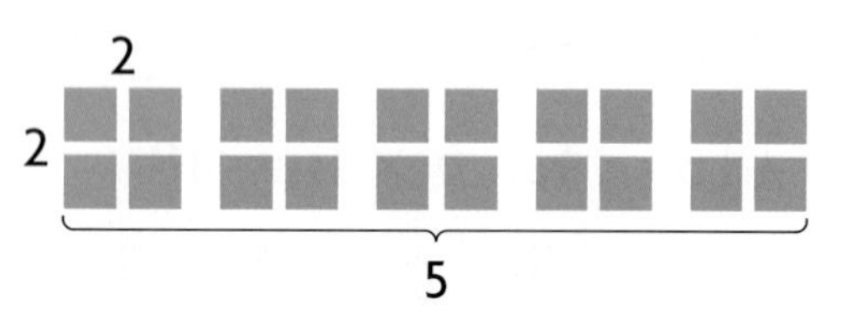

$5 \times (2 \times 2) = ■$

↓

$5 \times 4 = 20$

Multiply the numbers in parentheses first.

ANOTHER WAY Multiply $(5 \times 2) \times 2 = ■$.

Make an array to show 2 groups of 5 times 2.

$(5 \times 2) \times 2 = ■$

↓

$10 \times 2 = 20$

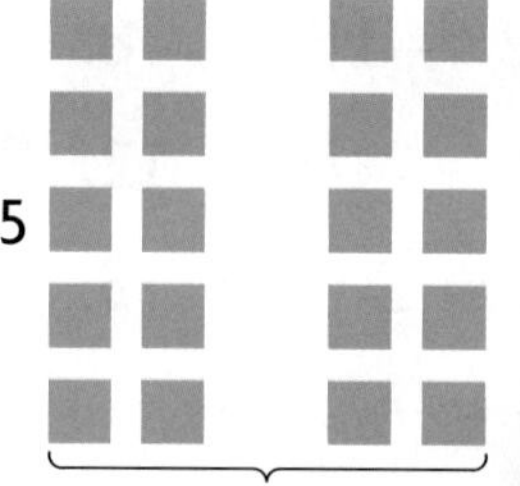

So, there are 20 seats in all on the roller coaster.

The **Associative Property of Multiplication**, or Grouping Property, states that when the grouping of factors is changed, the product remains the same.

- What if you change the order of the factors and multiply $(2 \times 5) \times 2$? What will the product be?

▲ Mr. Freeze Roller Coaster in Arlington, Texas, can go from 0 to 70 miles per hour in 4 seconds!

Guided Practice

1. What number sentence does this array represent? Use tiles. Write another way to group the factors.

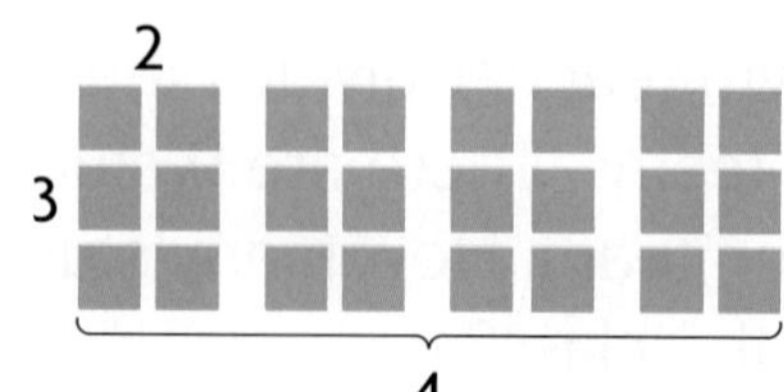

TEKS 3.4A learn and apply multiplication facts through 12 by 12 using concrete models and objects. *also* **3.6B, 3.14A, 3.15A, 3.15B**

Find the product. Write another way to group the factors.

2. $(2 \times 1) \times 7$ **3.** $3 \times (5 \times 2)$ ✓**4.** $4 \times (3 \times 3)$ ✓**5.** $(3 \times 2) \times 6$

6. TALK Math Heidi multiplies $(3 \times 2) \times 5$, and Jesse multiplies $3 \times (2 \times 5)$. Will they get the same product? **Explain**.

Independent Practice and Problem Solving

Find the product. Write another way to group the factors.

7. $(5 \times 2) \times 2$ **8.** $8 \times (3 \times 2)$ **9.** $(1 \times 3) \times 2$ **10.** $(3 \times 2) \times 7$

11. $(6 \times 1) \times 4$ **12.** $(2 \times 2) \times 7$ **13.** $9 \times (3 \times 3)$ **14.** $5 \times (2 \times 4)$

Use parentheses. Find the product.

15. $3 \times 1 \times 9$ **16.** $1 \times 3 \times 5$ **17.** $4 \times 2 \times 6$ **18.** $2 \times 3 \times 6$

Find the missing factor.

19. $(2 \times \blacksquare) \times 7 = 28$ **20.** $6 \times (5 \times \blacksquare) = 30$ **21.** $\blacksquare \times (3 \times 2) = 54$

USE DATA For 22–23, use the graph.

22. Each car on Steel Force has 3 rows with 2 seats in each row. How many seats are on a train?

23. **Reasoning** A Kingda Ka train has 4 seats per car but the last car has only 2 seats. How many people can ride in one Kingda Ka train?

24. WRITE Math **Sense or Nonsense** Ken works 2 days for 4 hours each day and earns \$5 an hour. Len works 5 days for 2 hours each day and earns \$4 an hour. Ken says they both earn the same. Does his statement make sense? **Explain**.

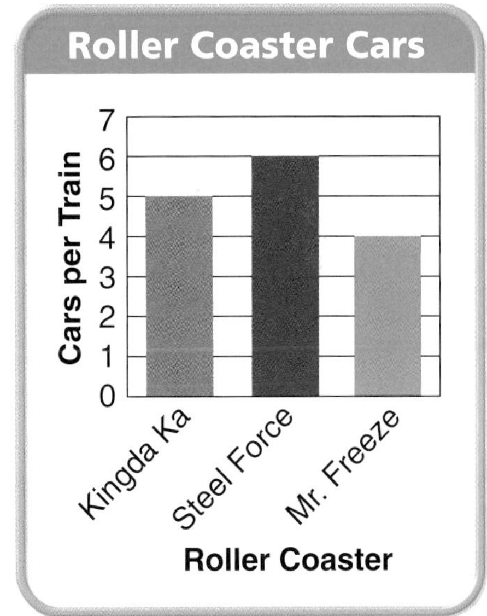

Mixed Review and TAKS Prep

25. Renee is 3 times as old as Jim. Jim is 5 years old. Write a number sentence to show Renee's age. (TEKS 3.4B, p. 228)

26. The product of two factors is 24. One factor is 4. What is the other factor? (TEKS 3.4B, p. 210)

27. **TAKS Prep** Multiply. $3 \times 2 \times 5 = \blacksquare$ (Obj. 1)

A 11 **B** 13 **C** 16 **D** 30

Extra Practice on page 284, Set C

Multiplication Properties

OBJECTIVE: Use the Identity, Zero, Commutative, and Associative Properties of Multiplication to find products.

Quick Review

1. 9×1
2. 0×5
3. 4×2
4. 2×4
5. $(2 \times 3) \times 5$

Vocabulary

Identity Property
Zero Property
Commutative Property
Associative Property

Learn

PROBLEM Mandy knit 3 scarves. She used 1 ball of yarn for each scarf. How many balls of yarn did she use in all?

You can use multiplication properties to help you find products.

Example Multiply 3 × 1.

The **Identity Property** states that the product of 1 and any number equals that number.

$3 \times 1 = 3$

So, Mandy used 3 balls of yarn.

Math Idea
Using multiplication properties makes finding products easier.

More Examples

Zero Property The product of zero and any number equals 0.

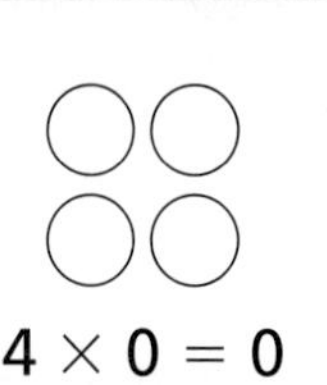

$4 \times 0 = 0$

Commutative Property When you multiply two factors in any order the product is the same.

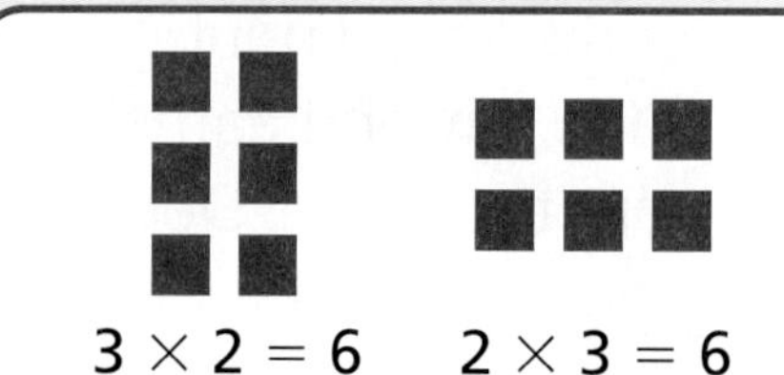

$3 \times 2 = 6$ $2 \times 3 = 6$

Associative Property
When you group factors in different ways the product is the same.

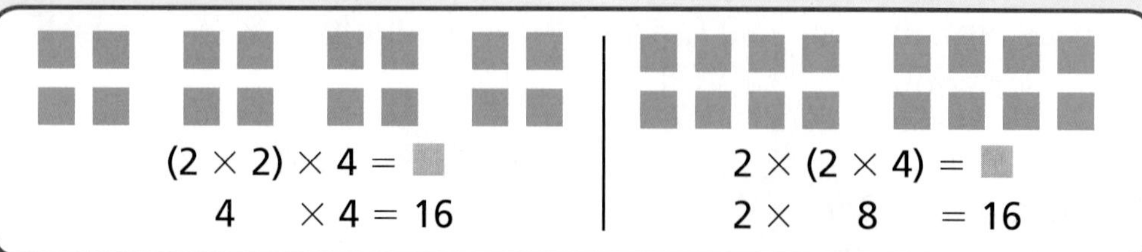

$(2 \times 2) \times 4 = \square$
$4 \times 4 = 16$

$2 \times (2 \times 4) = \square$
$2 \times 8 = 16$

• Which multiplication property can you use to find 85×0?

TEKS 3.4A learn and apply multiplication facts through 12 by 12 using concrete models and objects. *also* **3.6B, 3.14A, 3.15A, 3.15B**

Guided Practice

1. Which property is shown in this array?

Find the product. Tell which property you could use.

2. 5×1
3. 8×4
4. 0×9
5. $3 \times (3 \times 7)$

6. TALK Math Which costs more—5 balls of yarn for \$3 each or 3 balls of yarn for \$5 each? **Explain** your answer.

Independent Practice and Problem Solving

Find the product. Tell which property you could use.

7. 0×7
8. 8×1
9. 9×2
10. 7×2
11. $(5 \times 2) \times 7$
12. 9×3
13. 6×0
14. $(3 \times 3) \times 8$

Algebra Find the missing factor.

15. $5 \times \blacksquare = 6 \times 5$
16. $3 \times (2 \times 4) = (\blacksquare \times 2) \times 4$
17. $\blacksquare \times 3 = 3 \times 9$

USE DATA For 18–19 and 21, use the pictograph.

Knitting Supplies	
Needles	💵 💵 💵
Book	💵 💵 💵 💵 💵
Yarn	💵 💵

Key: Each 💵 = \$1.

18. Amy bought 3 balls of yarn. How much did she spend?

19. Katie bought one pack of needles, a knitting book, and 2 balls of yarn. What was the total cost?

20. **Reasoning** What is the missing number? **Explain** your answer.

$$\blacksquare \times 0 = 0$$

21. WRITE Math Sandy bought 8 balls of yarn. **Explain** how you can use the Commutative Property to find the cost.

Mixed Review and TAKS Prep

22. Kevin has 3 packs of baseball cards. Each pack has 9 cards. How many baseball cards does he have? (TEKS 3.4B, p. 252)

23. A school's auditorium has 950 seats. There were 843 students who attended an assembly. How many seats were empty? (TEKS 3.3B, p. 92)

24. **TAKS Prep** Which is an example of the Identity Property? (Obj. 1)

A $5 \times 3 = 3 \times 5$

B $0 \times 6 = 0$

C $7 \times 1 = 7$

D $(8 \times 1) \times 4 = 8 \times (1 \times 4)$

Extra Practice on page 284, Set D

Problem Solving Workshop
Skill: Multistep Problems

OBJECTIVE: Solve problems by using the skill multistep problems.

Use the Skill

PROBLEM The circus is in town! Tickets cost $7 for adults and $5 for children. Mr. Kimble buys 5 tickets for his family. He buys 2 adult tickets and 3 child tickets. How much does it cost for the Kimble family to go to the circus?

Use the tickets to help you solve the problem.

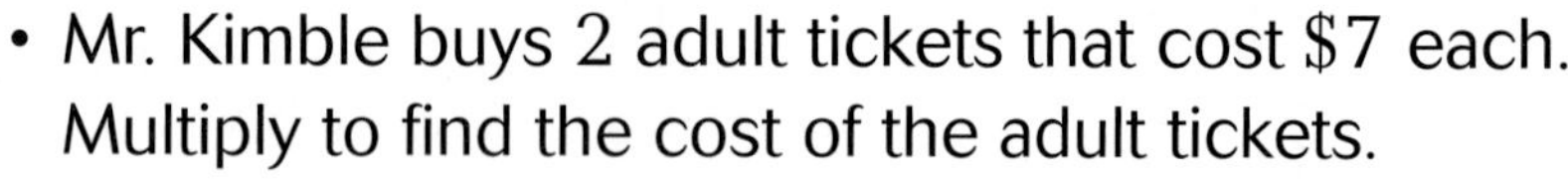

- Mr. Kimble buys 2 adult tickets that cost $7 each. Multiply to find the cost of the adult tickets.

$$2 \times \$7 = \$14$$

- He buys 3 child tickets that cost $5 each. Multiply to find the cost of the child tickets.

$$3 \times \$5 = \$15$$

- Add to find the total cost.

$14	+	$15	=	$29
↑		↑		↑
Cost of adult tickets		Cost of child tickets		Total cost

So, it costs $29 for the Kimble family to go to the circus.

TALK Math

Why did you multiply in this problem?

Think and Discuss

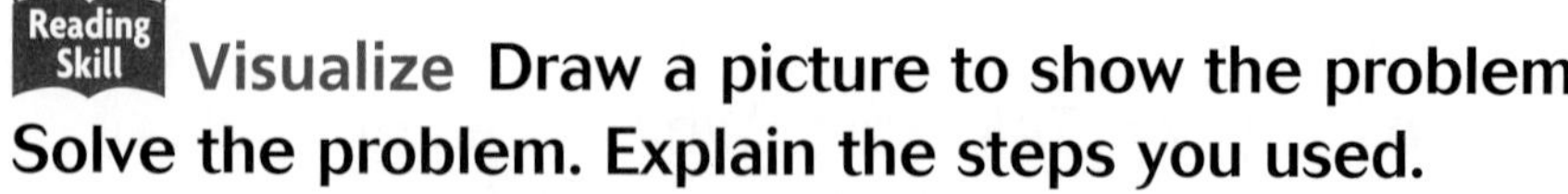

Reading Skill **Visualize** **Draw a picture to show the problem. Solve the problem. Explain the steps you used.**

a. There are 5 clowns with balloons. Four of the clowns have 8 balloons each. One clown has only 6 balloons. How many balloons in all do the clowns have?

b. Sam has a $20 bill. He buys 4 sheets of circus stickers. Each sheet costs $3. How much money does Sam have left?

TEKS 3.14A identify the mathematics in everyday situations. *also* **3.3B, 3.4A, 3.15A, 3.15B**

Guided Problem Solving

1. Maddie and Sasha buy 2 bags of popcorn and 4 balloons. The popcorn costs $5 a bag. Each balloon costs $2. How much do Maddie and Sasha spend in all?

   Visualize the problem.

   Which operation combines equal amounts?

   Which operation can you use to find the total cost?

   Solve the problem.

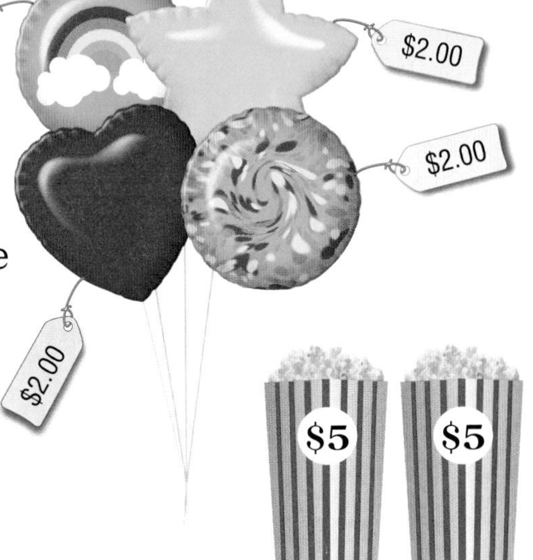

2. **What if** each balloon costs $3? How much do Maddie and Sasha spend in all for balloons and popcorn?

3. The animal trainers give 6 horses apples as rewards. The trainers reward each with 3 apples. If the trainers started with 30 apples, how many apples are left?

$5 $5

Mixed Applications

4. Mr. Brown's four children all have pets. Three of his children have 2 hamsters each. One child has 3 goldfish. How many pets in all do Mr. Brown's children have?

5. Jodi is saving money to buy a new bike. The bike costs $127. She has saved $75. How much more does Jodi need to buy the bike?

USE DATA For 6–8 use the menu.

6. Mr. Werner ordered turkey on rye, a salad, and juice. He paid with a $20 bill. How much change did he get back?

7. The baseball team went to David's Deli after the game. Each player ordered a hamburger and milk. There are 9 players on the team. What was the total cost of the team's order?

8. WRITE Math Mrs. Quigley bought twice as many apples as bananas. She bought 4 bananas. How much did Mrs. Quigley spend on fruit? **Explain** how you got your answer.

David's Deli

Item	Price
Hot Roast Beef Sandwich	$8
Turkey on Rye	$6
Hamburger	$4
Macaroni and Cheese	$5
Salad	$2
Fruit per piece (banana, apple, orange)	$1
Juice	$3
Milk	$2

LESSON HANDS ON

6 Multiples on a Hundred Chart

OBJECTIVE: Use a hundred chart to find multiples.

You can use a hundred chart to find multiples. A **multiple** is the product of a given whole number and another whole number. Some multiples of 3 are 3, 6, 9, and 12.

$1 \times 3 = 3$ $2 \times 3 = 6$ $3 \times 3 = 9$ $4 \times 3 = 12$

Quick Review

1. 2, 4, 6, 8, ■
2. 3, 6, ■, 12, 15
3. 4, 8, 12, ■, 20
4. ■, 10, 15, 20, 25
5. 10, 20, 30, 40, ■

Vocabulary

multiple

Investigate

Materials ■ hundred chart, crayons

Ⓐ Choose a number from 2 to 10. Shade that number on the chart. Then, skip count and shade all the multiples of that number.

Ⓑ Choose another number from 2 to 10. On a different hundred chart and with a different color, shade all the multiples of that number.

Ⓒ Display your charts in the classroom.

A

1	2	3	4	5	6	7	8	9	10
11	12	13	14	15	16	17	18	19	20
21	22	23	24	25	26	27	28	29	30
31	32	33	34	35	36	37	38	39	40
41	42	43	44	45	46	47	48	49	50
51	52	53	54	55	56	57	58	59	60
61	62	63	64	65	66	67	68	69	70
71	72	73	74	75	76	77	78	79	80
81	82	83	84	85	86	87	88	89	90
91	92	93	94	95	96	97	98	99	100

B

1	2	3	4	5	6	7	8	9	10
11	12	13	14	15	16	17	18	19	20
21	22	23	24	25	26	27	28	29	30
31	32	33	34	35	36	37	38	39	40
41	42	43	44	45	46	47	48	49	50
51	52	53	54	55	56	57	58	59	60
61	62	63	64	65	66	67	68	69	70
71	72	73	74	75	76	77	78	79	80
81	82	83	84	85	86	87	88	89	90
91	92	93	94	95	96	97	98	99	100

Draw Conclusions

1. Compare your hundred charts with those of your classmates. How are all the 3s and 6s charts alike? How are they different?
2. Which other charts are alike? Which charts are different?
3. **ANALYSIS** Why are some of the same numbers shaded on more than one of the charts? Give an example.

TEKS 3.6B identify patterns in multiplication facts using concrete objects, pictorial models, or technology. *also* **3.6A, 3.4A, 3.14A, 3.15A, 3.15B**

Connect

Compare the 2s chart and the 4s chart.

2s chart

1	2	3	4	5	6	7	8	9	10
11	12	13	14	15	16	17	18	19	20
21	22	23	24	25	26	27	28	29	30
31	32	33	34	35	36	37	38	39	40
41	42	43	44	45	46	47	48	49	50
51	52	53	54	55	56	57	58	59	60
61	62	63	64	65	66	67	68	69	70
71	72	73	74	75	76	77	78	79	80
81	82	83	84	85	86	87	88	89	90
91	92	93	94	95	96	97	98	99	100

The numbers shaded pink are multiples of 2.

4s chart

1	2	3	4	5	6	7	8	9	10
11	12	13	14	15	16	17	18	19	20
21	22	23	24	25	26	27	28	29	30
31	32	33	34	35	36	37	38	39	40
41	42	43	44	45	46	47	48	49	50
51	52	53	54	55	56	57	58	59	60
61	62	63	64	65	66	67	68	69	70
71	72	73	74	75	76	77	78	79	80
81	82	83	84	85	86	87	88	89	90
91	92	93	94	95	96	97	98	99	100

The numbers shaded blue are multiples of 4.

The numbers shaded *both* pink and blue are multiples of 2 *and* 4.

- How are the 2s chart and the 4s chart alike? How are they different?
- What are some numbers that are not shaded on either chart? Why aren't they shaded?
- Look at your classmates' charts for all of the multiples. Are there any numbers that are shaded on every chart? Are there any numbers not shaded on any of the charts? Explain.

TALK Math

How does a hundred chart help you find the multiples of two different numbers?

Practice

Find and write the missing multiples.

1. Multiples of 5

1	2	3	4	5	6	7	8	9	10
11	12	13	14	15	16	17	18	19	20
21	22	23	24	25	26	27	28	29	30
31	32	33	34	35	36	37	38	39	40
41	42	43	44	45	46	47	48	49	50

2. Multiples of 7

11	12	13	14	15	16	17	18	19	20
21	22	23	24	25	26	27	28	29	30
31	32	33	34	35	36	37	38	39	40
41	42	43	44	45	46	47	48	49	50
51	52	53	54	55	56	57	58	59	60
61	62	63	64	65	66	67	68	69	70

3. Multiples of 8

31	32	33	34	35	36	37	38	39	40
41	42	43	44	45	46	47	48	49	50
51	52	53	54	55	56	57	58	59	60
61	62	63	64	65	66	67	68	69	70
71	72	73	74	75	76	77	78	79	80
81	82	83	84	85	86	87	88	89	90

4. In the 4s chart, what would be the next shaded number after 100?

5. In the 8s chart, what would be the next shaded number after 88?

6. Look at the 4s chart and a 5s chart. What numbers are multiples of both 4 and 5?

7. **Reasoning** Are all multiples of 9 also multiples of 3? How do you know?

8. WRITE Math **Explain** what the word *multiple* means. Give an example.

Extra Practice

Set A **Write a rule for each table. Then copy and complete the table.** (pp. 272–273)

1.

Cars	1	2	3	4	5
Wheels	4	8	■	■	■

2.

Weeks	3	4	5	6	7
Days	21	28	■	■	■

Set B **Find the missing factor.** (pp. 274–275)

1. $3 \times ■ = 21$
2. $b \times 5 = 35$
3. $a \times 3 = 30$
4. $5 \times ■ = 25$
5. There are 18 scoops of ice cream. If there are 6 bowls, how many scoops will go in each bowl?
6. There are 32 children and 8 slides on the playground. If the students are divided evenly into groups, how many can play on each slide?

Set C **Find the product. Write another way to group the factors.** (pp. 276–277)

1. $(2 \times 2) \times 4 = ■$
2. $(1 \times 3) \times 3 = ■$
3. $(5 \times 2) \times 3 = ■$
4. $8 \times (1 \times 2) = ■$

Use parentheses. Find the product.

5. $3 \times 3 \times 1 = ■$
6. $2 \times 4 \times 5 = ■$
7. $1 \times 7 \times 4 = ■$
8. $2 \times 2 \times 2 = ■$
9. For Arbor Day, Nora wants to plant 3 groups of 3 trees in 4 different parks. How many trees in all will she plant?
10. Nora's friend Dion plants 2 groups of 4 trees in 7 different parks. How many trees will he plant?

Find the missing factor.

11. $(1 \times ■) \times 2 = 8$
12. $4 \times (2 \times ■) = 16$
13. $■ \times (5 \times 2) = 80$

Set D **Find the product. Tell which property you used.** (pp. 278–279)

1. $(2 \times 1) \times 5$
2. $(3 \times 3) \times 5$
3. 8×3
4. 6×1

Find the missing factor.

5. $2 \times ■ = 10 \times 1$
6. $(2 \times 2) \times ■ = 6 \times 2$
7. $0 \times 7 = 7 \times ■$
8. $7 \times ■ = 5 \times 7$
9. $(4 \times ■) \times 3 = 4 \times 6$
10. $■ \times 9 = 9$

CD ROM **Technology**
Use Harcourt Mega Math, Ice Station Exploration, *Arctic Algebra*, Level C.

PRACTICE GAME

Guess My Numbers

Ready!
2 players

Set!
- 2 pieces of paper
- 2 pencils

Think!

- Each player thinks of a multiplication problem with one-digit factors.
- Players draw 3 blank lines on their papers. Draw a multiplication sign between the first two lines and an equal sign before the third line.
- Player 1 guesses a number. If that number is in Player 2's problem, Player 2 writes the number in the blank.
- Then Player 2 tries to guess a number in Player 1's problem. If the guess is correct, Player 1 writes the number in the blank.
- The players take turns guessing numbers.
- The first player to guess all the numbers in the other player's multiplication problem is the winner.

Chapter 12 Review/Test

Check Vocabulary and Concepts

Choose the best term from the box.

VOCABULARY
Associative Property of Multiplication
multiple
Identity Property
variable

1. A ___?___ is a letter or symbol that stands for an unknown number. (TEKS 3.4A, p. 274)
2. The product of a number and another whole number is a ___?___. (TEKS 3.6B, p. 282)
3. The ___?___ states that when the grouping of factors is changed, the product remains the same. (TEKS 3.4A, p. 278)

Check Skills

Find the missing factor. (TEKS 3.4A, pp. 274–275)

4. $7 \times a = 28$
5. ■ $\times 5 = 45$
6. $6 \times$ ■ $= 30$
7. $d \times 3 = 9$
8. $8 \times$ ■ $= 64$
9. ■ $\times 4 = 20$
10. $g \times 10 = 40$
11. $9 \times b = 27$

Find the product. (TEKS 3.4A, pp. 276–277)

12. $3 \times (5 \times 2) =$ ■
13. $(2 \times 4) \times 8 =$ ■
14. $(1 \times 9) \times 5 =$ ■
15. $6 \times (3 \times 3) =$ ■
16. $7 \times (2 \times 2) =$ ■
17. $(4 \times 2) \times 3 =$ ■

Find the missing factor. (TEKS 3.4A, pp. 278–279)

18. $3 \times (3 \times$ ■$) = 27$
19. ■ $\times (4 \times 2) = 40$
20. $5 \times ($■ $\times 10) = 50$
21. $3 \times 4 =$ ■ $\times 2$
22. ■ $\times 5 = 3 \times 10$
23. $6 \times$ ■ $= 9 \times 2$

Check Problem Solving

Solve. (TEKS 3.14A, pp. 280–281)

24. Michelle bought 2 necklaces for \$3 each and 3 rings for \$4 each. How much money did Michelle spend in all?

25. WRITE Math Rick put 5 baseball cards on each of 2 pages, and 8 cards on each of 4 pages. How many baseball cards did he put in the book altogether? **Explain** how you solved the problem.

GO ONLINE **Technology** Use *Online Assessment.*

Enrich • Multiplication Table Parts

Little Pieces

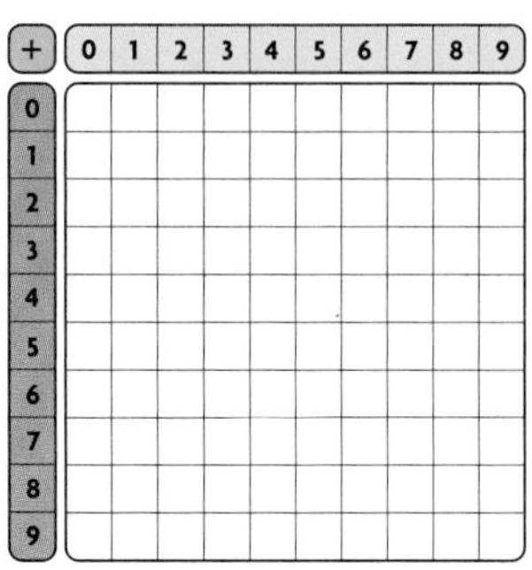

Observe

Jake's baby sister tore his multiplication table into little pieces. Where in the table does this piece belong?

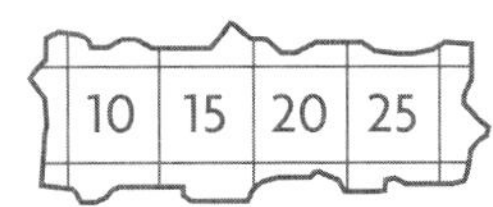

Step 1	Find the pattern. Five is added to each number.
Step 2	Describe the pattern using multiplication. The numbers 10, 15, 20, and 25 are all multiples of 5.
Step 3	Look at the first and last numbers. $10 = \mathbf{2} \times 5$ $25 = \mathbf{5} \times 5$

So, this piece is from row 5 between columns 2 and 5.

Identify

Below are parts of a multiplication table. In which row or column is each part found?

1. 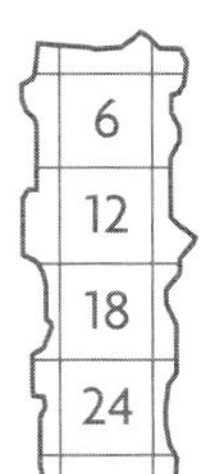

2. 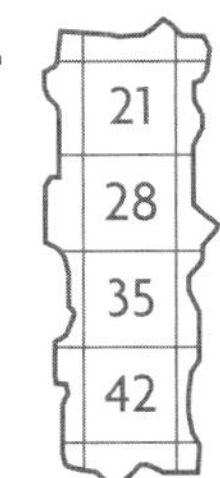

3. 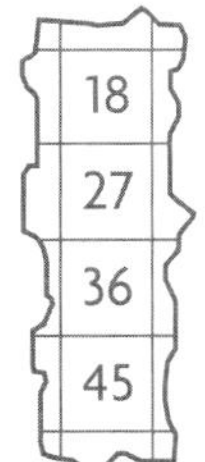

4. 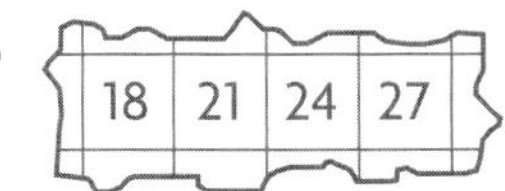

5. 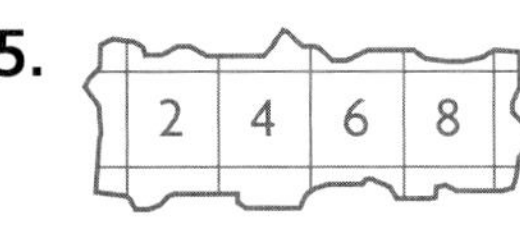

Conclude

WRITE Math ▸ In what part of the table is this piece found? **Explain.**

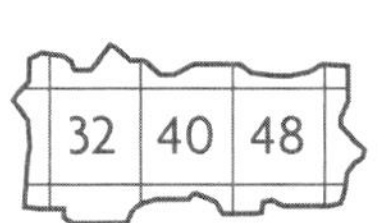

Unit Review/Test
Chapters 9–12

Multiple Choice

1. ■ ■ ■ ■ ■ ■ ■ ■
   ■ ■ ■ ■ ■ ■ ■ ■

   How many squares in all? (TAKS Obj. 2)

   A 14
   B 16
   C 18
   D 20

2. Clarence put 0 books on each of 3 shelves. How many books in all did he put on the shelves? (TAKS Obj. 1)

   F 3
   G 2
   H 1
   J 0

3. Which addition expression represents 3×9? (TAKS Obj. 1)

   A $9 + 9$
   B $9 + 9 + 9$
   C $9 + 9 + 9 + 9$
   D $9 + 9 + 9 + 9 + 9$

4. Tina has $4. Use the table to find how many quarters this is. (TAKS Obj. 2)

Dollars	1	2	3	4
Quarters	4	8	12	■

   F 14 H 18
   G 16 J 20

5. Which number sentence is represented by the counters? (TAKS Obj. 2)

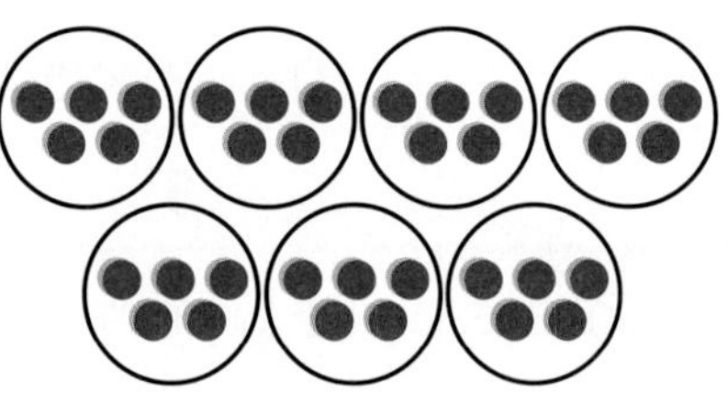

   A $35 \div 6$
   B 9×3
   C 7×5
   D $7 + 5$

6. The graph shows the number of fish in each tank.

Fish Tanks	
Tank 1	🐟 🐟 🐟 🐟 🐟 🐟
Tank 2	🐟 🐟 🐟 🐟 🐟 🐟 🐟 🐟
Tank 3	🐟 🐟 🐟 🐟 🐟
Key: Each 🐟 = 8 fish.	

   How many fish in all are there in Tank 2? (TAKS Obj. 5)

   F 48
   G 52
   H 56
   J 64

GO ONLINE **Technology** Use *Online Assessment.*

7. How many members belong to the Science Club? (TAKS Obj. 5)

Club Members	
Drama	○○○○
Chorus	○○○○○○
Science	○○○○○
Key: Each ○ = 12 members.	

A 48 C 60

B 56 D 64

8. Aunt Ester baked 3 dozen cookies. Which number sentence shows how many cookies Aunt Ester baked? (TAKS Obj. 2)

F $3 \times 12 = 36$ H $3 \times 4 = 12$

G $3 + 12 = 15$ J Not here

9. How many students voted for blue as their favorite color? (TAKS Obj. 5)

Favorite Colors	
green	3 crayons
red	4 crayons
blue	6 crayons
yellow	2 crayons
Key: Each crayon = 5 votes.	

A 10 C 20

B 15 D 30

Short Response

10. Multiply $9 \times (3 \times 4)$. (TAKS Obj. 1)

11. Mr. Ruiz bought 5 sandwiches for \$5 each and 7 desserts for \$3 each. How much did he spend in all? (TAKS Obj. 2)

Extended Response

12. **Explain** how you can find the number of days in 10 weeks. (TAKS Obj. 2)

June						
Sun	Mon	Tue	Wed	Thu	Fri	Sat
1	2	3	4	5	6	7
8	9	10	11	12	13	14
15	16	17	18	19	20	21
22	23	24	25	26	27	28
29	30	31				

13. **Explain** all of the different ways that you can show the product 16 using arrays of counters. (TAKS Obj. 2)

14. **Explain** how to find the total number of flowers you will need to fill 8 vases if each vase holds 7 flowers. (TAKS Obj. 2)

Problem Solving

Texas Animals

Strange Animal Parts

Many animals have 2 eyes, 2 ears, and 1 mouth—just as humans do. However, some animals have unusual numbers of eyes, ears, and even hearts. The following animals all live in Texas.

A Texas burrowing owl has 3 eyelids for each eye.

A greenhouse slug has 4 noses.

An earthworm has 5 hearts.

A bee has 5 eyes.

A praying mantis has 1 ear.

A striped bark scorpion has 12 eyes.

The Texas state butterfly is the monarch butterfly. The monarch butterfly has 4 wings.

FACT · ACTIVITY

Use the facts above to answer the questions. Write a number sentence for each problem.

1. There are 9 slugs. How many noses are there?
2. There are 6 earthworms. How many hearts in all?
3. How many ears do 4 praying mantises have?
4. How many eyelids do 7 Texas burrowing owls have?
5. If a striped bark scorpion has 12 eyes, how many eyes do 3 scorpions have?
6. How many wings are there in a swarm of 7 monarch butterflies?
7. **Pose a Problem** Look at Problems 1 and 2. Write a similar problem about any of the animals shown on this page.

A group of bats is called a *colony*. Many colonies of bats live under the Congress Avenue Bridge in Austin, Texas. Each summer millions of bats make this bridge their home.

Strange Names

Have you ever seen a *gaggle* fly overhead or a *school* in the water? *Gaggle* and *school* are strange names for groups of animals: a *gaggle* of geese, a *school* of fish. You might shiver from fright if you saw some sharks in the water, but did you know that a group of sharks is called a *shiver*? Other strange names include an *army* of frogs, a *band* of gorillas, and a *kindle* of kittens.

FACT • ACTIVITY

Write multiplication sentences to solve.

1. A kitten has 4 paws. How many paws are in a kindle of 8 kittens?
2. A goose has 2 wings. How many wings are in a gaggle of 9 geese?
3. Design an animal that has an unusual number of parts. Think about the number of legs, tails, wings, eyes, noses, ears, or other parts that your animal has.
   - Draw your animal and label its parts.
   - Copy the chart. You may include more parts. Remember, you may choose 0 for some parts.
   - Complete the table to show how many parts there are in 1, 2, and 3 animals.
   - Suppose there are 10 of your animal in a group. Make up a name for the group.

My Animal

Part	Number of Parts		
	In 1 animal	In 2 animals	In 3 animals
eyes			
legs			
tails			
wings			
noses			
ears			

UNIT

5 Division Concepts and Facts

Math on Location

with **Texas Chapter Projects**

1

Each batch of dough is cut into the same number of triangular shapes.

2

The croissants are rolled and placed in rows on baking trays to form an array.

3

The baker divides 18 croissants onto 3 trays to put in the oven to bake.

VOCABULARY POWER

TALK Math

What math do you see in the **Math on Location** photographs? How can you use division to tell how many croissants are in each row?

READ Math

REVIEW VOCABULARY You learned the words below when you learned about division in grade 2. How do these words relate to **Math on Location**?

division the operation that separates objects into equal groups

equal groups the same number of items in each group

WRITE Math

Copy and complete a Semantic Map like the one below. Use Math on Location and what you know about division to fill in the blanks.

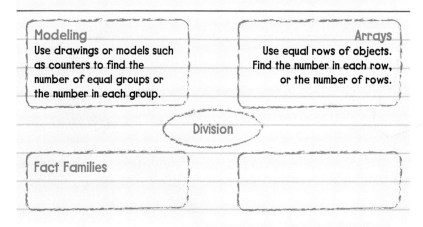

Modeling
Use drawings or models such as counters to find the number of equal groups or the number in each group.

Arrays
Use equal rows of objects. Find the number in each row, or the number of rows.

Division

Fact Families

Technology
Multimedia Math Glossary link at **www.harcourtschool.com/hspmath**

13 Understand Division

The Big Idea Division tells how many groups or how many in each group, is related to repeated subtraction, and is the inverse of multiplication.

Investigate

A skateboard has 4 wheels. Suppose you want to make your own skateboards. Choose a wheel color from the table. Tell how many skateboards you could make using only that wheel color.

Wheels in Skate Shop

Color	Number of Wheels
Red	24
White	40
Black	12
Green	36
Blue	28

Skateboarding began in the 1950s. It was called "sidewalk surfing." In 2006, Texas had 24 public skate parks.

GO ONLINE **Technology** Student pages are available in the Student eBook.

Show What You Know

Check your understanding of important skills needed for success in Chapter 13.

▶ Counting Equal Groups

Complete.

1.

■ groups
■ in each group

2. 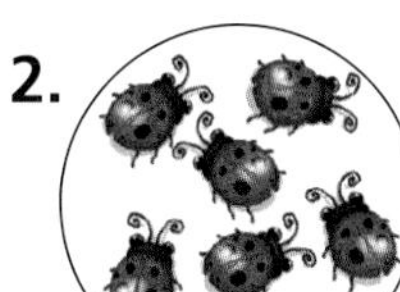

■ groups
■ in each group

3. 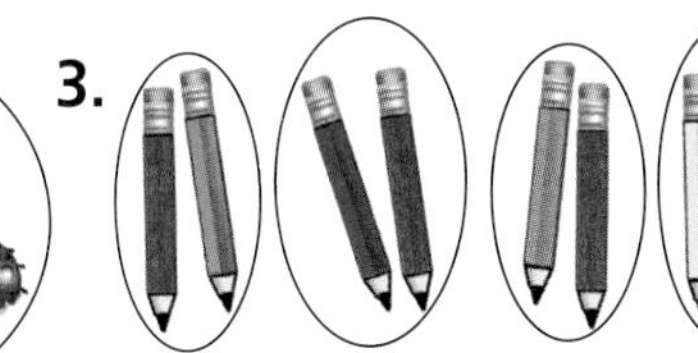

■ groups
■ in each group

4. 

■ groups
■ in each group

5. 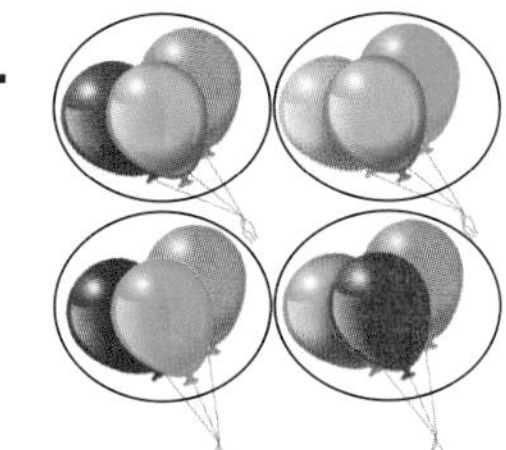

■ groups
■ in each group

6. 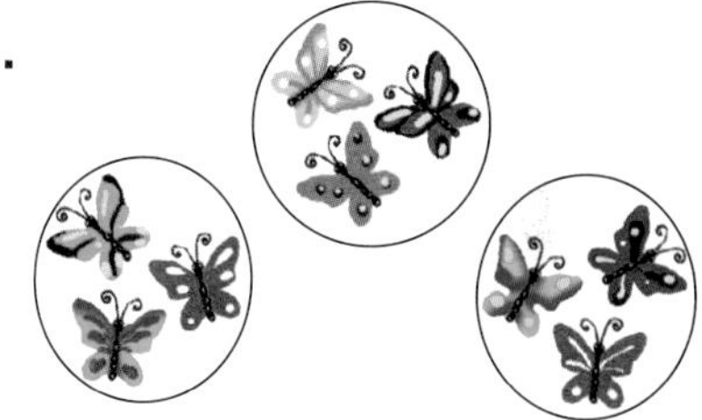

■ groups
■ in each group

▶ Multiplication Facts Through 10

Find the product.

7. $5 \times 3 = $ ■	**8.** ■ $= 6 \times 4$	**9.** $2 \times 8 = $ ■	**10.** $5 \times 6 = $ ■
11. $9 \times 3 = $ ■	**12.** $4 \times 2 = $ ■	**13.** ■ $= 7 \times 7$	**14.** $3 \times 5 = $ ■
15. ■ $= 4 \times 7$	**16.** $8 \times 6 = $ ■	**17.** $9 \times 2 = $ ■	**18.** ■ $= 6 \times 7$

VOCABULARY POWER

CHAPTER VOCABULARY

array
divide
dividend
divisor
fact family
quotient

WARM-UP WORDS

divide To separate into equal groups; the opposite operation of multiplication

fact family A set of related addition and subtraction, or multiplication and division, number sentences

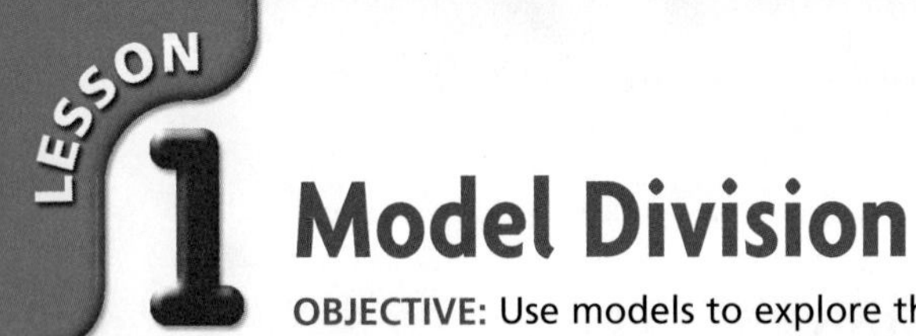

LESSON 1 Model Division

OBJECTIVE: Use models to explore the meaning of division.

Quick Review

1. 2 × 3
2. 5 × 7
3. 4 × 5
4. 3 × 6
5. 7 × 4

Vocabulary

divide

Learn

PROBLEM William has 12 shells. He wants to put the same number of shells in each of 3 boxes. How many shells will be in each box?

When you multiply, you put equal groups together. When you **divide**, you separate into equal groups.

◀ A pink conch shell can be as long as 1 foot!

HANDS ON Activity

Materials ■ counters

Example 1 You can divide to find the number in each group.

Step 1	Step 2	Step 3
Use 12 counters. 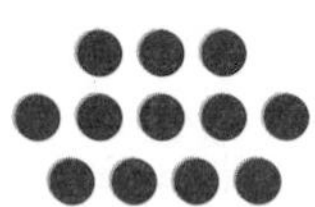	Show 3 groups. Place 1 counter in each group. 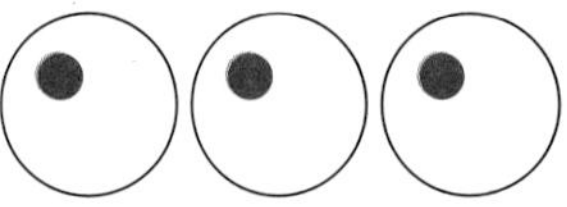	Continue until all 12 counters are used. 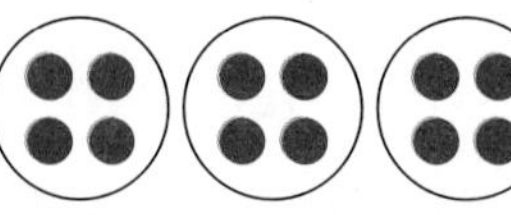

So, there will be 4 shells in each box.

William has decided that he wants to put his 12 shells in groups of 3. How many boxes will he need for his shells?

Example 2 You can divide to find the number of equal groups.

Step 1	Step 2	Step 3
Use 12 counters. 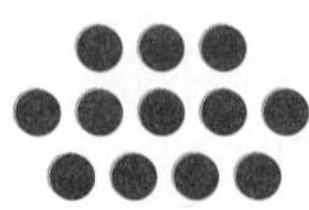	Make 1 group of 3 counters. 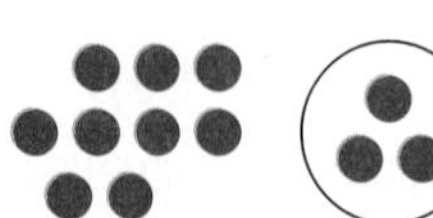	Continue making groups of 3 until all counters are used. 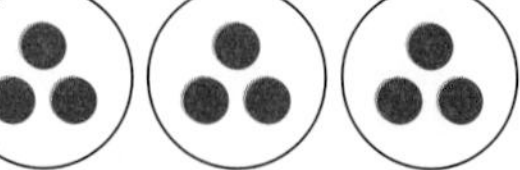 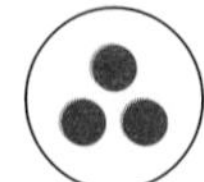 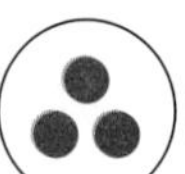  

So, William will need 4 boxes for his shells.

TEKS 3.4C use models to solve division problems and use number sentences to record the solutions. *also* 3.14A, 3.14D, 3.15A, 3.15B

Guided Practice

1. Jon has 8 counters. He wants to put 2 in each group. Draw a picture to show the groups.

Copy and complete the table. Use counters to help.

	Counters	Number of Equal Groups	Number in Each Group
✓2.	10	2	■
✓3.	24	■	4

4. TALK Math **Explain** two ways you could divide 18 counters into equal groups. Draw a picture to show each way.

Independent Practice and Problem Solving

Copy and complete the table. Use counters to help.

	Counters	Number of Equal Groups	Number in Each Group
5.	14	7	■
6.	21	■	3
7.	20	5	■

8. Jackie has 28 stamps. She put an equal number of her stamps on each of 4 pages. How many stamps are on each page?

9. Joe has 25 stamps and Martha has 15 stamps. They put their stamps in the same book. Each page has 5 stamps. How many pages did they fill?

10. WRITE Math Elijah has 16 stamps. He put 4 stamps each on 4 pages. **Explain** another way to arrange his stamps with an equal number of stamps on each page.

Mixed Review and TAKS Prep

11. What is the missing factor?
$6 \times ■ = 48$ (TEKS 3.4A, p. 274)

12. Lee has 3,943 coins. What is the value of the 9 in 3,943? (TEKS 3.1A, p. 12)

13. **TAKS Prep** Zana has 9 rocks. She put 3 rocks in each bag. How many bags did she use in all? (Obj. 1)

A 27 **B** 12 **C** 6 **D** 3

Extra Practice on page 312, Set A

LESSON 2

Relate Division and Subtraction

OBJECTIVE: Relate division to repeated subtraction.

Quick Review

How many are there in all?

1. 2 groups of 5
2. 5 groups of 3
3. 3 groups of 4
4. 4 groups of 2
5. 3 groups of 3

Learn

PROBLEM Sarah and Mandy take a total of 12 newspapers to school for the recycling program. Each girl takes the same number. How many newspapers does each girl take?

Divide. 12 ÷ 2 = ■

ONE WAY **Count back on a number line.**

Start at 12.
Count back by 2s until you reach 0.
Count the number of times you subtract 2.

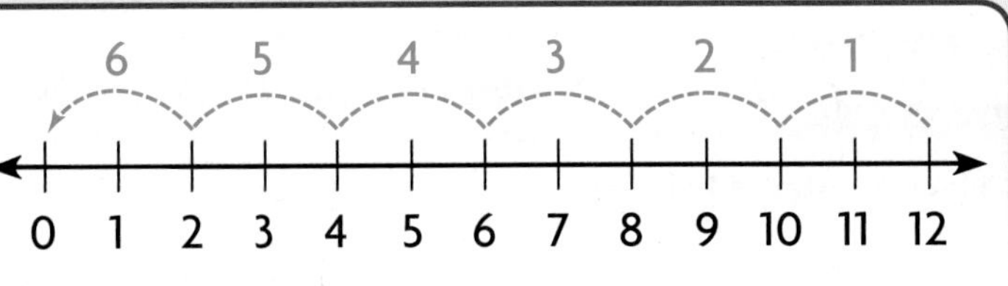

You subtract 2 six times, so each girl takes 6 newspapers.

ANOTHER WAY **Use repeated subtraction.**

Start with 12. Subtract 2 until you reach 0.
Count the number of times you subtract 2.

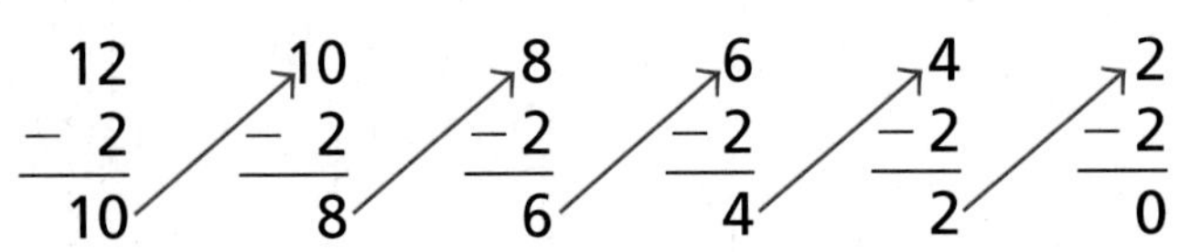

Number of times you subtract 2: 1 2 3 4 5 6

ERROR ALERT

Be sure to keep subtracting until you reach 0 as the answer.

Since you subtract 2 six times, there are 6 groups of 2 in 12.

Write: $12 \div 2 = 6$ or $2\overline{)12}$ with quotient 6 **Read:** Twelve divided by two equals six.

Guided Practice

1. Use the number line to complete the number sentence. 12 ÷ 4 = ■

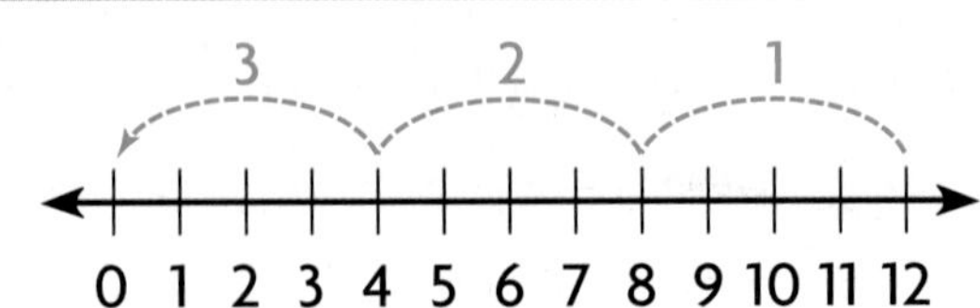

TEKS 3.4C use models to solve division problems and use number sentences to record the solutions. *also* **3.14A, 3.15A, 3.15B**

Use a number line or repeated subtraction to solve.

2. $16 \div 4 = ■$ **3.** $10 \div 5 = ■$ ✓**4.** $3\overline{)21}$ ✓**5.** $8\overline{)32}$

6. TALK Math **Explain** how you can use subtraction to find $18 \div 3$.

Independent Practice and Problem Solving

Write a division sentence for each.

7.

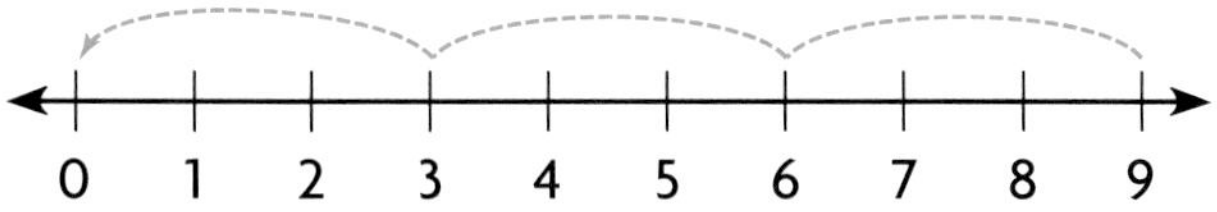

8. $24 - 8 = 16$ → $16 - 8 = 8$ → $8 - 8 = 0$

Use a number line or repeated subtraction to solve.

9. $14 \div 7 = ■$ **10.** $35 \div 5 = ■$ **11.** $27 \div 9 = ■$ **12.** $20 \div 4 = ■$

13. $4\overline{)28}$ **14.** $6\overline{)24}$ **15.** $2\overline{)16}$ **16.** $9\overline{)36}$

USE DATA For 17–19, use the graph.

17. Carl put his box tops in 6 equal piles. How many box tops were in each pile?

18. **Reasoning** Miguel brought an equal number of box tops to school each day for 5 days. Jane also brought an equal number of box tops each day for 5 days. How many box tops did they bring in altogether in 1 day? **Explain.**

19. WRITE Math **What's the Question?** Genna put an equal number of box tops in each of 3 bins. The answer is 5.

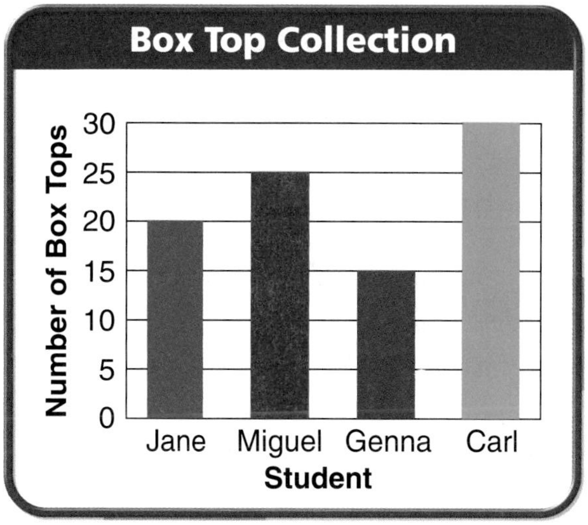

Mixed Review and TAKS Prep

20. Kara has 3 packs of paintbrushes. Each pack has 8 brushes. How many brushes does Kara have? (TEKS 3.4A, p. 230)

21. A figure has 4 vertices and 4 equal sides. What is the figure? (Grade 2 TEKS 2.7A)

22. **TAKS Prep** Mya collected 7 shells each day. She collected 21 shells in all. For how many days did Mya collect shells? (Obj. 1)

A 2 days **C** 4 days

B 3 days **D** 6 days

Extra Practice on page 312, Set B

LESSON HANDS ON

3 Model with Arrays

OBJECTIVE: Model division by using arrays.

Quick Review

1. 3×5
2. 5×7
3. 5×5
4. 4×5
5. 5×6

Investigate

Materials ■ square tiles

You can use arrays to model division and find equal groups.

A Count out 30 tiles. Make an array to find how many groups of 5 are in 30.

B Make a row of 5 tiles.

C Continue to make rows of 5 tiles until all of the tiles have been used.

Draw Conclusions

1. How many groups of 5 are in 30?
2. Explain how you used the tiles to find the number of groups of 5 in 30.
3. **Application** Tell how to use an array to find how many groups of 6 are in 30.

TEKS 3.4C use models to solve division problems and use number sentences to record the solutions. *also* 3.14A, 3.14D, 3.15A, 3.15B

Connect

You can write a division sentence to show what you did.

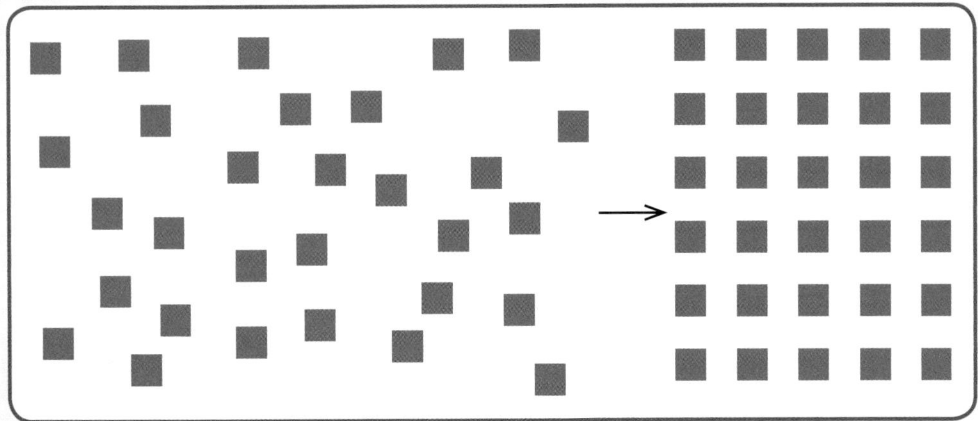

There are 6 rows of 5 tiles in 30.

So, $30 \div 5 = 6$.

- Use 24 tiles. Make an array by placing 6 tiles in each row. Use all of the tiles.
- How many groups of 6 are in 24?
- What division sentence can you write about your array?

TALK Math

How does making an array help you divide?

Practice

Use square tiles to make an array. Solve.

1. How many groups of 3 are in 18?
2. How many groups of 7 are in 28?
3. How many groups of 9 are in 27?
4. How many groups of 8 are in 24?
5. How many groups of 5 are in 20?
6. How many groups of 6 are in 36?

Make an array. Write a division sentence for each one.

7. 16 tiles in 4 groups
8. 21 tiles in 3 groups
9. 24 tiles in 8 groups
10. 14 tiles in 2 groups
11. 25 tiles in 5 groups
12. 12 tiles in 4 groups
13. Reggie made an array with 32 tiles. He placed 8 tiles in each row. How many rows did he make?
14. **WRITE Math** **Explain** how to use an array to find $18 \div 6$.

LESSON 4

ALGEBRA

Multiplication and Division

OBJECTIVE: Relate multiplication and division.

Quick Review

1. 2×7 **2.** 5×6

3. 4×4 **4.** 8×1

5. 9×3

Vocabulary

dividend

divisor

quotient

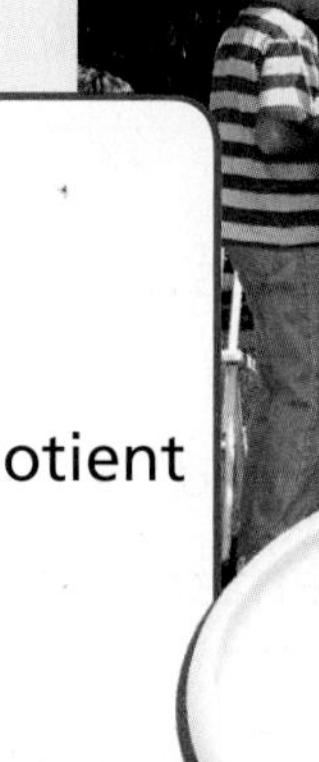

Learn

You can use arrays to understand how multiplication and division are related.

PROBLEM Mark went to the school carnival. He went on the same ride 3 times and used 12 tickets. How many tickets did he need for each ride?

Example Divide. $12 \div 3 = \blacksquare$

Show an array with 12 counters in 3 equal rows. Find how many are in each row.

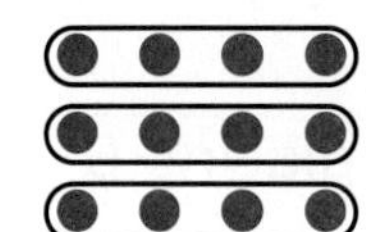

Since $3 \times 4 = 12$, then $12 \div 3 = 4$.

$$\underset{\textbf{dividend}}{12} \div \underset{\textbf{divisor}}{3} = \underset{\textbf{quotient}}{4}$$

divisor → $3\overline{)12}$ ← dividend; 4 ← quotient

So, Mark needed 4 tickets for each ride.

Math Idea

Multiplication and division are opposite, or inverse, operations.

More Examples

A 2 rows of 4 = 8
$8 \div 2 = 4$

B 3 rows of 6 = 18
$18 \div 3 = 6$

Guided Practice

1. What division sentence does the array represent?

Copy and complete.

2.

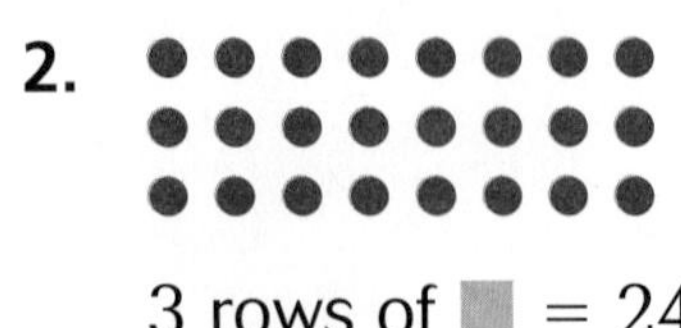

3 rows of $\blacksquare$ = 24
$24 \div 3 = \blacksquare$

✓3. 2 rows of $\blacksquare$ = 12
$12 \div 2 = \blacksquare$

✓4. 3 rows of $\blacksquare$ = 21
$21 \div 3 = \blacksquare$

5. TALK Math **Explain** how you can use an array to find $25 \div 5$.

TEKS 3.4C use models to solve division problems and use number sentences to record the solutions. *also* **3.6C, 3.14A, 3.14D, 3.15A, 3.15B**

Independent Practice and Problem Solving

Copy and complete.

6. ● ● ● ●
● ● ● ●
● ● ● ●
● ● ● ●

4 rows of ■ = 16
$16 \div 4 =$ ■

7. ● ● ● ● ●
● ● ● ● ●
● ● ● ● ●

3 rows of ■ = 15
$15 \div 3 =$ ■

8. ● ● ● ● ● ● ●
● ● ● ● ● ● ●
● ● ● ● ● ● ●
● ● ● ● ● ● ●

4 rows of ■ = 28
$28 \div 4 =$ ■

Complete each number sentence. Draw an array to help.

9. $6 \times$ ■ $= 24$ $24 \div 6 =$ ■

10. $5 \times$ ■ $= 35$ $35 \div 5 =$ ■

11. $8 \times$ ■ $= 32$ $32 \div 8 =$ ■

12. $9 \times$ ■ $= 18$ $18 \div 9 =$ ■

Complete.

13. $3 \times 3 = 27 \div$ ■

14. $16 \div 2 =$ ■ $\times 2$

15. ■ $\times 1 = 25 \div 5$

USE DATA For 16–19, use the signs.

16. Jill has 15 tickets. How many times can she ride the Scooter?

17. Philip bought 8 tickets for the Wildcat ride 3 different times. How many times did he ride the Wildcat?

18. **Reasoning** Joe rode the Scooter 3 times, and Kate rode the Crazy Sub 4 times. Who used more tickets? **Explain.**

19. WRITE Math **Sense or Nonsense** Scott has 13 tickets. He says that to ride the Scooter 4 times, he needs more tickets. Is he correct? **Explain.**

Mixed Review and TAKS Prep

20. There are 6 blue cubes and 3 red cubes in a bag. Are you more likely to pull a blue cube or a red cube? (Grade 2 TEKS 2.11C)

21. A ticket to the zoo costs $4. How much do 9 tickets cost? (TEKS 3.4A, p. 210)

22. **TAKS Prep** At a game booth, there are 32 prizes in 4 equal rows. How many prizes are in each row? (Obj. 1)

A 36 **C** 8
B 28 **D** 6

Extra Practice on page 312, Set C

CD ROM **Technology**
Use Harcourt Mega Math, Ice Station Exploration, *Arctic Algebra*, Level E.

ALGEBRA

Fact Families

OBJECTIVE: Use multiplication and division fact families.

Quick Review

Complete.

1. ■ × 5 = 15
2. 3 × ■ = 15
3. 15 ÷ 5 = ■
4. 5 × ■ = 25
5. 25 ÷ 5 = ■

Vocabulary

fact family

Learn

A **fact family** is a set of related multiplication and division number sentences.

PROBLEM Kim's pack of modeling clay has 2 rows of 5 colors. What is the fact family for 2, 5, and 10?

Activity

Materials ■ square tiles

Step 1

Count the number of rows and the number of colors in each row in the pack of clay.

There are 2 rows with 5 colors in each row.

Step 2

Make an array with 2 rows and 5 columns. Count the total number of tiles.

There are 10 tiles.

Step 3

Write two multiplication sentences and two division sentences that describe the array.

$2 \times 5 = 10$ $10 \div 5 = 2$

$5 \times 2 = 10$ $10 \div 2 = 5$

So, these related number sentences make the fact family for 2, 5, and 10.

Example

The array shows the fact family for 4, 4, and 16.

$4 \times 4 = 16$ $16 \div 4 = 4$

Since both factors are the same, there are only two number sentences in this fact family.

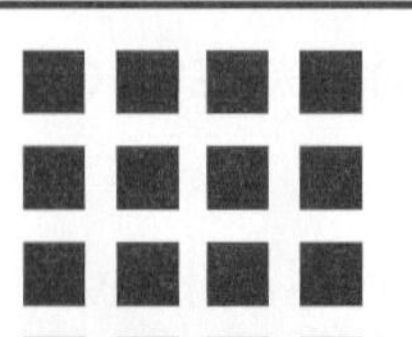

Remember

4	×	4	=	16
↑ factor		↑ factor		↑ product

TEKS 3.6C identify patterns in related multiplication and division sentences (fact families) such as 2 × 3 = 6, 3 × 2 = 6, 6 ÷ 2 = 3, 6 ÷ 3 = 2. *also* **3.4C, 3.14A, 3.14D, 3.15A, 3.15B**

Use a Multiplication Table to Divide

Since division is the opposite of multiplication, you can use a multiplication table to find a quotient or a missing divisor.

Examples

A Find the quotient.

20 ÷ 4 = ■

Think: 4 × ■ = 20

Find the row for the factor 4. Look to the right to find the product 20. Look up to find the missing factor, 5.

4 × 5 = 20
So, 20 ÷ 4 = 5.

B Find the missing divisor.

18 ÷ ■ = 3

Think: ■ × 3 = 18

Find the factor 3 in the top row. Look down to find the product 18. Look left to find the missing factor, 6.

6 × 3 = 18
So, 18 ÷ 6 = 3.

×	0	1	2	3	4	5	6	7
0	0	0	0	0	0	0	0	0
1	0	1	2	3	4	5	6	7
2	0	2	4	6	8	10	12	14
3	0	3	6	9	12	15	18	21
4	0	4	8	12	16	20	24	28
5	0	5	10	15	20	25	30	35
6	0	6	12	18	24	30	36	42
7	0	7	14	21	28	35	42	49

Guided Practice

1. Complete the fact family for this array.

   3 × 8 = 24   24 ÷ 3 = 8

Write the fact family for each array.

2. 

3. 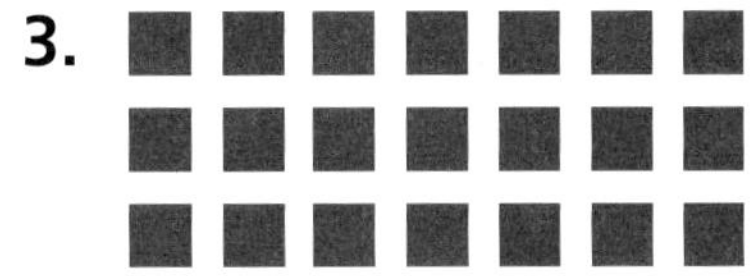

✓4. 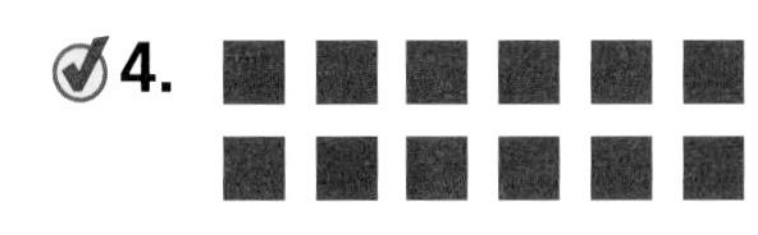

Write the fact family for each set of numbers.

5. 6, 7, 42   6. 2, 3, 6   7. 4, 8, 32   ✓8. 5, 5, 25

9. TALK Math **Explain** how you can use a multiplication table to find the missing divisor in 36 ÷ ■ = 6.

Independent Practice and Problem Solving

Write the fact family for each array.

10.

11. 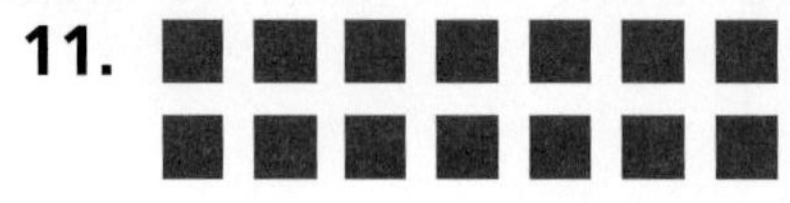

12.

Write the fact family for each set of numbers.

13. 2, 4, 8 **14.** 4, 6, 24 **15.** 3, 3, 9 **16.** 5, 8, 40

Copy and complete each fact family.

17. $4 \times 7 = 28$
$7 \times \blacksquare = 28$
$28 \div \blacksquare = 4$
$28 \div 4 = \blacksquare$

18. $5 \times 6 = \blacksquare$
$6 \times \blacksquare = 30$
$30 \div 6 = \blacksquare$
$30 \div 5 = \blacksquare$

19. $4 \times \blacksquare = 36$
$9 \times \blacksquare = 36$
$36 \div 4 = \blacksquare$
$36 \div 9 = \blacksquare$

20. $\blacksquare \times 9 = 27$
$\blacksquare \times 3 = 27$
$\blacksquare \div 9 = 3$
$27 \div \blacksquare = 9$

Find the quotient or the missing divisor.

21. $20 \div \blacksquare = 5$ **22.** $45 \div 5 = \blacksquare$ **23.** $15 \div 3 = \blacksquare$ **24.** $36 \div \blacksquare = 6$

USE DATA For 25–26, use the table.

Clay Supplies

Item	Number in Package
Clay	12 sections
Clay tool set	11 tools
Glitter dough	36 sections

25. Mrs. Lee divides one package of clay and one package of glitter dough equally among 4 students. How many more glitter dough sections does each student have than clay sections?

26. WRITE Math **What's the Error?** Ty has a package of glitter dough. He says he can give 9 friends 5 equal sections. Describe his error.

27. Pose a Problem Write a division word problem using $35 \div 5 = 7$. Solve your problem.

Mixed Review and TAKS Prep

28. What is the missing factor?
$6 \times \blacksquare = 42$ (TEKS 3.4A, p. 274)

29. Jake has 57 pens and 49 pencils. How many more pens than pencils does he have? (TEKS 3.3B, p. 88)

30. TAKS Prep Which number sentence is not included in the same fact family as $9 \times 4 = 36$? (Obj. 2)

A $4 \times 9 = 36$
B $36 \div 6 = 6$
C $36 \div 4 = 9$
D $36 \div 9 = 4$

 Extra Practice on page 312, Set D

Justify an Answer

Tamara is making a recipe that calls for 15 teaspoons of milk. She doesn't have a teaspoon measure. She knows that 3 teaspoons equal 1 tablespoon. So, she uses 5 tablespoons of milk. How do you know whether she used the right amount of milk?

Jamal wrote this paragraph to justify Tamara's solution to her problem.

I know that a teaspoon is a smaller unit than a tablespoon. First, I use a teaspoon to fill a tablespoon of water. It takes 3 teaspoons of water to fill 1 tablespoon.

Then, I divide 15 by 3 to find out if 5 tablespoons is the correct amount of milk. I use the fact family for 5, 3, and 15 to check my answer.

$5 \times 3 = 15$ $\quad$ $3 \times 5 = 15$

$15 \div 5 = 3$ $\quad$ $15 \div 3 = 5$

I know that Tamara used the right amount of milk because $3 \times 5 = 15$.

Tips

To justify an answer:

- First, check that the information given in the problem is correct.
- Next, check whether the answer given is correct.
- Last, write a sentence to justify the answer, or explain why it is correct.

Problem Solving **Write a paragraph to justify each answer.**

1. Tara says, "I can share 12 crackers evenly with 3 friends."
2. Darin says, "I can share 8 sports cards evenly with 2 friends."

Problem Solving Workshop
Strategy: Write a Number Sentence

OBJECTIVE: Solve problems by using the strategy *write a number sentence.*

Learn the Strategy

Writing a number sentence can help you understand how the numbers in a problem are related.

You can write an addition number sentence.

Joe has 14 crayons. He gets 12 more crayons. Now he has 26 crayons.

$14 + 12 = 26$

14 ↑ crayons Joe has; 12 ↑ crayons Joe got; 26 ↑ crayons Joe has now

You can write a subtraction number sentence.

Kat has 23 shells. She gives 10 shells to her brother. She has 13 shells left.

$23 - 10 = 13$

23 ↑ shells Kat has; 10 ↑ shells Kat gave away; 13 ↑ shells Kat has left

You can write a multiplication number sentence.

April has 4 boxes of books. Each box has 8 books in it. There are 32 books in all.

$4 \times 8 = 32$

4 ↑ boxes April has; 8 ↑ books in each box; 32 ↑ books in all

You can write a division number sentence.

Scott has 40 stickers. There are 8 stickers on each sheet. He has 5 sheets of stickers.

$40 \div 8 = 5$

40 ↑ stickers Scott has; 8 ↑ stickers on each sheet; 5 ↑ sheets of stickers

TALK Math

What question could you ask about each number sentence above?

TEKS 3.14B solve problems that incorporate understanding the problem, making a plan, carrying out the plan, and evaluating the solution for reasonableness. *also* **3.4C, 3.14A, 3.14C, 3.15A, 3.15B, 3.16B**

Use the Strategy

PROBLEM In Michelle's third grade class, the desks are in 5 equal rows. There are 30 desks in all. How many desks are in each row?

Read to Understand

- **Identify the details in the problem.**
- **What information is given?**

Plan

- **What strategy can you use to solve the problem?**
  You can *write a number sentence* to help you solve the problem.

Solve

- **How can you use the strategy to solve the problem?**
  The desks are divided into equal rows.
  This helps you know to use division.
  Write a division sentence. Find the quotient.

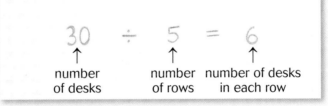

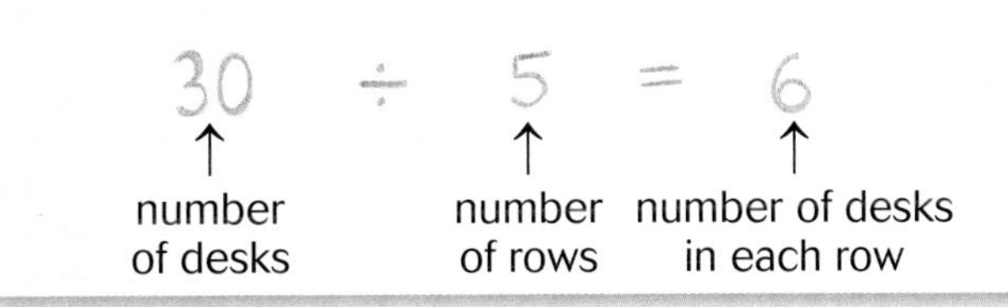

So, there are 6 desks in each row.

Check

- **How can you check your answer?**
- **What other strategy could you use to solve the problem?**

Guided Problem Solving

Read to Understand
Plan
Solve
Check

1. Mrs. Partin gave each student at Jenna's table 5 sheets of paper. She gave out 20 sheets of paper in all. How many students are at Jenna's table?

   First, decide what operation to use. The 20 sheets of paper are divided into equal groups.

   Then, write the number sentence.

   Finally, solve the number sentence.

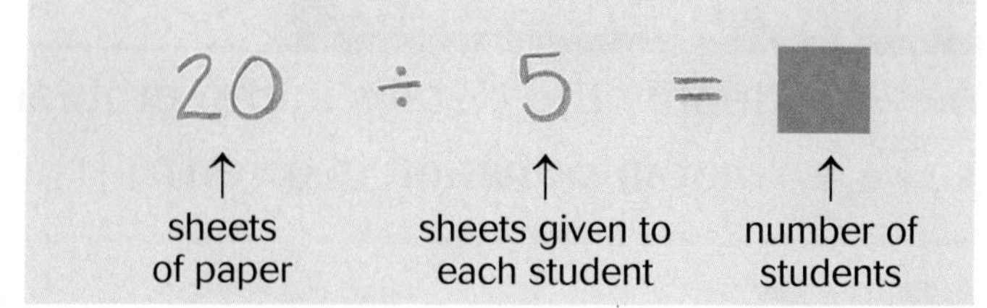

2. **What if** Mrs. Partin gave each student 6 sheets of paper and there were 6 students? How many sheets of paper would she have given out?

3. Jack read for 20 minutes on Monday. He read 15 minutes more on Tuesday than on Monday. For how many minutes did Jack read on Tuesday?

Problem Solving Strategy Practice

For 4–5, choose the number sentence from the box. Solve.

$4 \times 10 = ■$ $10 + 4 = ■$ $27 - 3 = ■$ $27 \div 3 = ■$

4. One eraser costs 3¢. Lizzie spends 27¢ on erasers. How many erasers does Lizzie have?

5. Jeremy has 10 pencils. His teacher gives him 4 more pencils. How many pencils does Jeremy have now?

Write a number sentence to solve.

6. Elizabeth reads for 360 minutes each week. She has read for 215 minutes so far this week. How many more minutes will Elizabeth read this week?

7. Mrs. Vargas has 24 students in her math class. There are 4 tables in her classroom. The same number of students sit at each table. How many students sit at each table?

8. WRITE Math At a store, there are 6 notebooks on each of 7 shelves. There are 5 notebooks on the 8th shelf. How many notebooks are on the shelves altogether? **Explain.**

Mixed Strategy Practice

USE DATA For 9–12, use the table.

9. Mr. Clark buys a pack of pencils for his students. He gives the same number of pencils to 8 students. How many pencils does each student get?

10. **Pose a Problem** Look back at Problem 9. Write a similar problem by changing the number of students.

11. Min bought 3 packs of erasers. She kept 8 erasers and divided the rest of them equally among 4 of her classmates. How many erasers did Min give to each of her 4 classmates? **Explain** your answer.

12. There are blue pencils and red pencils in a pencil pack. There are twice as many red pencils as blue pencils. How many red pencils are there?

13. **Open-Ended** ***FAST FACT*** The first box of Crayola® crayons was sold in 1903 for 5¢. List two different groups of coins you could use to pay for 7 boxes of crayons.

CHALLENGE YOURSELF

The school store has these items for sale:

pencil	**25¢**	**ruler**	**75¢**
marker	**45¢**	**sharpener**	**15¢**
pen	**65¢**	**notebook**	**95¢**

14. Amy spends $1.25 on 3 different items. What items does she buy?

15. Frank buys 4 different items. He pays with three $1 bills, and receives two dimes in change. What items does Frank buy?

Choose a STRATEGY

- Draw a Diagram or Picture
- Make a Model or Act It Out
- Make an Organized List
- Look for a Pattern
- Make a Table or Graph
- Guess and Check
- Work Backward
- Solve a Simpler Problem
- Write an Equation
- Use Logical Reasoning

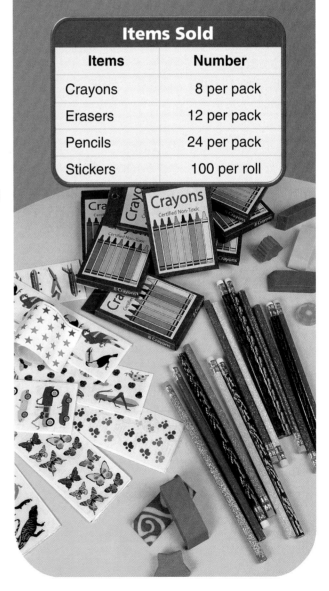

Items Sold

Items	Number
Crayons	8 per pack
Erasers	12 per pack
Pencils	24 per pack
Stickers	100 per roll

Extra Practice

Set A Copy and complete the table. Use counters to help. (pp. 296–297)

	Counters	Number of Equal Groups	Number in Each Group
1.	30	5	■
2.	28	■	7
3.	24	8	■
4.	12	4	■

Set B Write a division sentence for each. (pp. 298–299)

1. 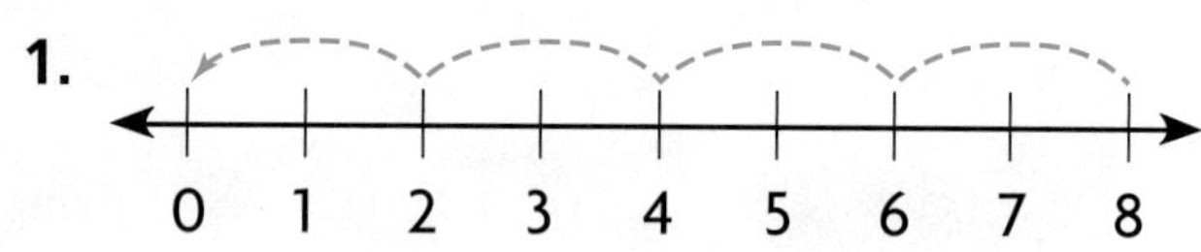

2. 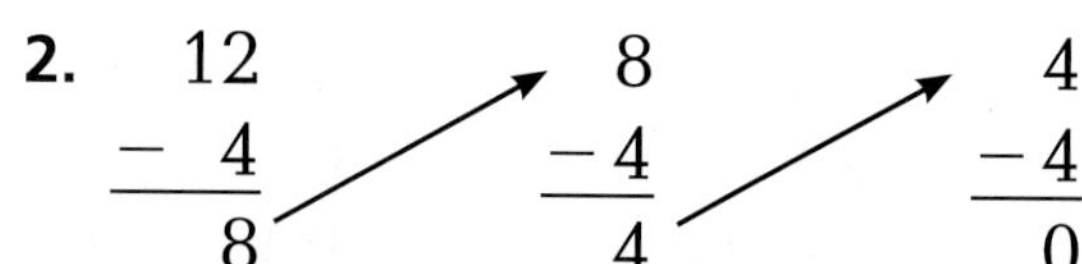

Use a number line or repeated subtraction to solve.

3. $15 \div 3 =$ ■ **4.** $4\overline{)16}$ **5.** $12 \div 2 =$ ■ **6.** $5\overline{)20}$

7. If Desiree can make 6 necklaces in 36 minutes, how long does it take her to make each necklace?

8. Desiree can make 5 bracelets in 25 minutes. How long does it take her to make each bracelet?

Set C Copy and complete. (pp. 302–303)

1.
3 rows of ■ = 12
$12 \div 3 =$ ■

2.
2 rows of ■ = 18
$18 \div 2 =$ ■

3.
3 rows of ■ = 18
$18 \div 3 =$ ■

Complete each number sentence. Draw an array to help.

4. $5 \times$ ■ $= 30$ $30 \div 5 =$ ■ **5.** $8 \times$ ■ $= 40$ $40 \div 8 =$ ■

6. $9 \times$ ■ $= 27$ $27 \div 9 =$ ■ **7.** $6 \times$ ■ $= 36$ $36 \div 6 =$ ■

Set D Write the fact family for each set of numbers. (pp. 304–307)

1. 3, 5, 15 **2.** 4, 7, 28 **3.** 2, 8, 16 **4.** 3, 7, 21

Technology
Use Harcourt Mega Math, Ice Station Exploration, *Arctic Algebra*, Level E.

PRACTICE GAME

All in the Family

Draw Your Cards

2–4 players

Are They a Family?

- Gameboard
- Counter for each player
- Number cards
- Paper and pencils

6 2 12

$2 \times 6 = 12$

$6 \times 2 = 12$

$12 \div 2 = 6$

$12 \div 6 = 2$

9 2 8 3 7 4 6 5

Coming Home

- Players place their counter on any number on the gameboard.
- Each player is dealt 5 number cards. The remaining cards are placed facedown in a pile.
- Player 1 tries to make a fact family, either by using 3 of his or her cards or by using 2 cards and the number on which the counter lies. The player writes down the fact family, and the other players check it.
- Player 1 then discards the cards used, draws cards to replace them, and advances 1 space, clockwise, on the gameboard. It is then the next player's turn.
- If a player cannot make a fact family, he or she exchanges some or all of his or her cards with the cards from the pile, and his or her turn is over.
- The first player to return to his or her start space is the winner.

Chapter 13 Review/Test

Check Vocabulary and Concepts

Choose the best term from the box.

VOCABULARY
divide
divisor
fact family
quotient

1. You __?__ when you separate into equal groups. (TEKS 3.4C, p. 296)
2. A __?__ is a set of related multiplication and division number sentences. (TEKS 3.6C, p. 304)
3. How many times a divisor goes into a dividend is the __?__. (TEKS 3.4C, p. 302)

Check Skills

Copy and complete the table. Use counters to help. (TEKS 3.4C, pp. 296–297)

	Counters	Number of Equal Groups	Number in Each Group
4.	21	3	■
5.	16	■	4
6.	36	9	■

Use a number line or repeated subtraction to solve. (TEKS 3.4C, pp. 298–299)

7. $28 \div 7 = ■$ **8.** $2\overline{)10}$ **9.** $8 \div 4 = ■$ **10.** $7\overline{)35}$

Complete each number sentence. Draw an array to help. (TEKS 3.4C, pp. 302–303)

11. $5 \times ■ = 15$ $15 \div 5 = ■$ **12.** $3 \times ■ = 24$ $24 \div 3 = ■$

13. $6 \times ■ = 42$ $42 \div 6 = ■$ **14.** $6 \times ■ = 30$ $30 \div 6 = ■$

Write the fact family for each set of numbers. (TEKS 3.6C, pp. 304–307)

15. 3, 9, 27 **16.** 3, 4, 12 **17.** 6, 6, 36 **18.** 3, 6, 18

Check Problem Solving

Solve. (TEKS 3.4C, 3.14B, pp. 308–311)

19. Dolly the Clown gave each child 4 balloons. She gave out 36 balloons in all. How many children received balloons?

20. WRITE Math There were 5 students at a table. Each student drew 5 pictures. How many pictures did the students draw in all? **Explain** how you know.

GO ONLINE Technology Use *Online Assessment.*

Enrich • Finding Factor Pairs

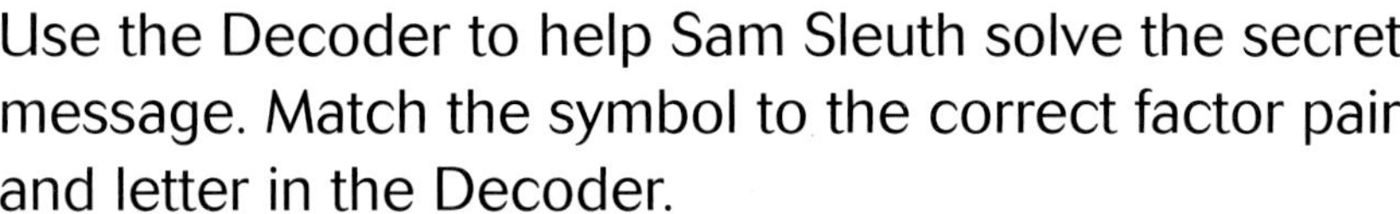

Use the Decoder to help Sam Sleuth solve the secret message. Match the symbol to the correct factor pair and letter in the Decoder.

     ?

DECODER			
4, 5	**A**	4, 6	**G**
6, 7	**R**	2, 6	**W**
3, 8	**M**	2, 9	**N**
4, 9	**E**	3, 6	**I**
5, 7	**X**	3, 7	**S**
3, 9	**H**	2, 4	**T**

The clues used are:

♥ Their product is odd. Their difference is 6.	Δ Their product ends in zero and is less than 30.
∇ Their product equals 21 + 21.	□ Their product is a single digit.
∴ Their product is equal to 18 + 18.	∅ Their product is 18. The larger factor is odd.
ꕤ Their product is between 20 and 25. Their sum is 11.	👍 Their product is equal to 30 − 9.
~ Their product is 18. The smaller factor is odd.	✓ Their product is equal to 16 − 4.
≈ Their product is 24. Both factors are even.	◊ Their product is odd. Their difference is 2.

Receive the Message

A	Read the clue for the first symbol.
B	Find the factor pair that satisfies the clue.
C	Write the letter for the symbol.

Use the Decoder

Solve the rest of the secret message.

Break the Code

WRITE Math ▸ Sam Sleuth sent this message: ∴ ~ ≈ ♥ □ ∴ ∴ ∅. What does it mean? **Explain** how you know.

Getting Ready for the TAKS

Chapters 1–13

Number, Operation, and Quantitative Reasoning (TAKS Obj. 1)

1. There were 1,457 people at a play. What is the value of the 4 in 1,457?

   A 4

   B 40

   C 400

   D 4,000

Eliminate choices.

See item 2. Since you need to subtract to find the answer, you can eliminate the answer choices that are greater than 312. Then subtract carefully, remembering to regroup.

2. Katie and Juan are reading books. Katie has read 312 pages in her book. Juan has read 259 pages in his book. How many more pages has Katie read than Juan?

   F 571

   G 153

   H 147

   J Not here

3. WRITE Math **Explain** how to use the number line to find $12 \div 3$.

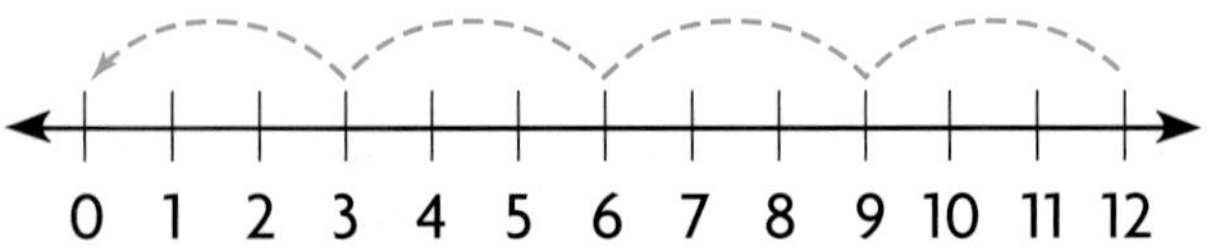

Patterns, Relationships, and Algebraic Thinking (TAKS Obj. 2)

4. Spiders have 8 legs. Marcy wants to find out how many legs are on 5 spiders. Use the table below to find the answer.

Spiders	1	2	3	4	5
Legs	8	16	24	32	■

   A 36

   B 38

   C 40

   D 42

5. Which number sentence is in the same fact family as $4 \times 8 = 32$?

   F $32 \div 8 = 4$

   G $8 \div 4 = 2$

   H $4 \times 4 = 16$

   J $4 \times 2 = 8$

6. WRITE Math Sammy wrote the pattern below.

   4, 7, 6, 9, 8, 11, 10, 13

   Write a rule for Sammy's pattern. **Explain** how to find the next number in his pattern.

Geometry and Spatial Reasoning (TAKS Obj. 3)

7. Which figure is a cone?

A 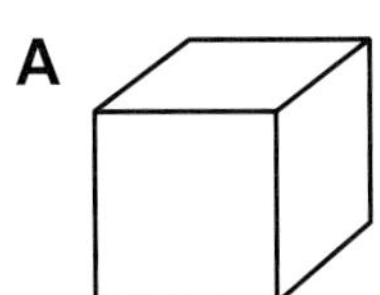

B 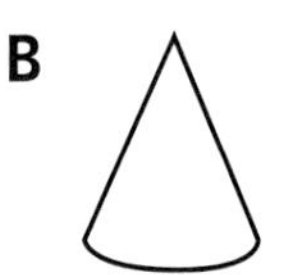

C 

D 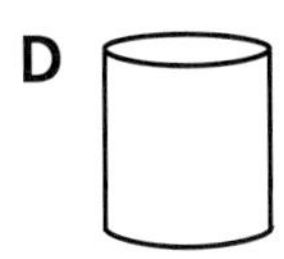

8. How many faces does a cube have?

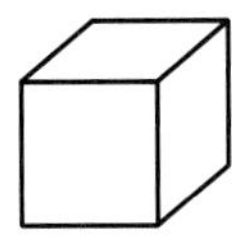

F 3 H 6

G 4 J 8

9. **WRITE Math** Are the two figures below congruent? **Explain** how you know.

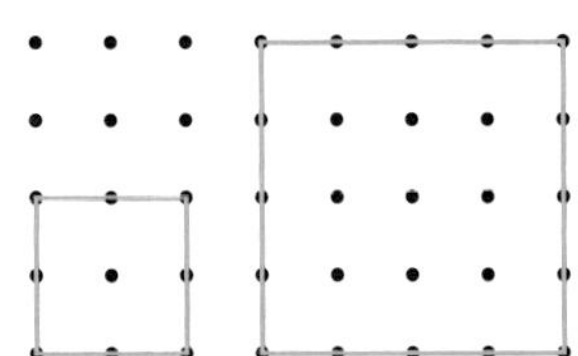

Probability and Statistics (TAKS Obj. 5)

10. How many more points does Drake need to score to equal the number of points Tio scored?

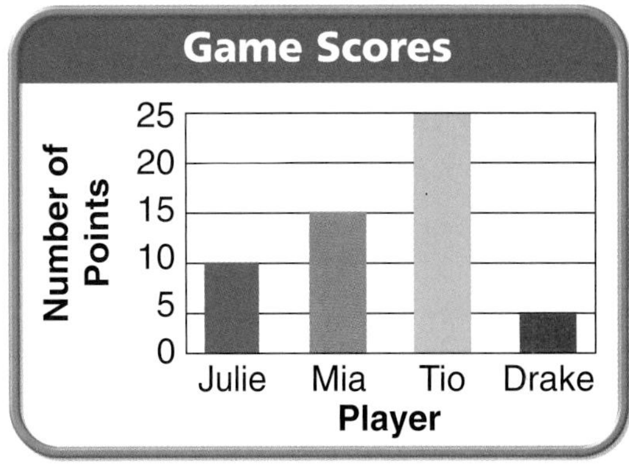

A 10 C 20

B 15 D 30

11. On which color is the spinner most likely to stop?

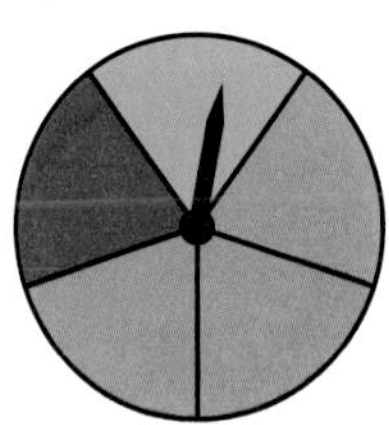

F Blue H Red

G Green J Yellow

12. **WRITE Math** Tina made a pictograph to show how many books she owns.

Each = 10 books.

How many books does stand for? **Explain**.

14 Division Facts

The Big Idea The primary strategy for learning division facts is using a related multiplication fact.

Investigate

A hot-air balloon carries passengers in a basket. The size of the basket determines the number of passengers. Pick a balloon from the pictograph. How many balloons would be needed for all the students in your class to take a hot-air balloon ride?

Hot-Air Balloon Rides

Balloon A	🎈🎈
Balloon B	🎈
Balloon C	🎈🎈🎈🎈🎈
Balloon D	🎈🎈🎈

Key: Each 🎈 = 2 passengers.

TEXAS FAST FACT

Hot-air balloons take flight each year on Labor Day at the Big Bend Balloon Bash in Alpine, Texas. Hot-air balloons can fly because hot air rises and cold air sinks.

Technology
Student pages are available in the Student eBook.

Show What You Know

Check your understanding of important skills needed for success in Chapter 14.

▶ Arrays

Complete.

1. ■ ■ ■ ■ ■ ■
■ ■ ■ ■ ■ ■
■ ■ ■ ■ ■ ■

3 rows of ■ = 18
18 ÷ 3 = ■

2. ■ ■ ■ ■
■ ■ ■ ■

2 rows of ■ = 8
8 ÷ 2 = ■

3. ■ ■ ■
■ ■ ■
■ ■ ■
■ ■ ■

4 rows of ■ = 12
12 ÷ 4 = ■

4. ■ ■ ■ ■ ■
■ ■ ■ ■ ■
■ ■ ■ ■ ■
■ ■ ■ ■ ■

4 rows of ■ = 20
20 ÷ 4 = ■

5. ■ ■ ■ ■ ■ ■ ■
■ ■ ■ ■ ■ ■ ■

2 rows of ■ = 14
14 ÷ 2 = ■

6. ■ ■ ■ ■
■ ■ ■ ■
■ ■ ■ ■

3 rows of ■ = 12
12 ÷ 3 = ■

▶ Multiplication and Division Fact Families

Write the fact family.

7. 4, 6, 24 **8.** 3, 5, 15 **9.** 3, 8, 24 **10.** 5, 5, 25

11. 4, 9, 36 **12.** 8, 9, 72 **13.** 2, 4, 8 **14.** 6, 7, 42

VOCABULARY POWER

CHAPTER VOCABULARY

divide
dividend
divisor
fact family
quotient

WARM-UP WORDS

dividend The number that is to be divided in a division problem

divisor The number that divides the dividend

quotient The number, not including the remainder, that results from division

Divide by 2 and 5

OBJECTIVE: Divide by 2 and 5.

Quick Review

1. ■ × 2 = 10
2. 5 × ■ = 15
3. 3 × ■ = 6
4. ■ × 2 = 18
5. 5 × ■ = 25

Learn

PROBLEM Mrs. Benson needs feeders for 12 hummingbirds. If there will be 2 birds at each feeder, how many feeders does she need?

12 ÷ 2 = ■ (dividend ↑ 12, divisor ↑ 2, quotient ↑ ■)

divisor → $2\overline{)12}$ ← dividend; ■ ← quotient

▲ A hummingbird can beat its wings as many as 80 times per second and can fly at a speed of 25 miles per hour!

Example 1 Divide. 12 ÷ 2 = ■

ONE WAY **Count back on a number line.**

Start at 12. Count back by 2s until you reach 0. Count the number of times you subtract 2.

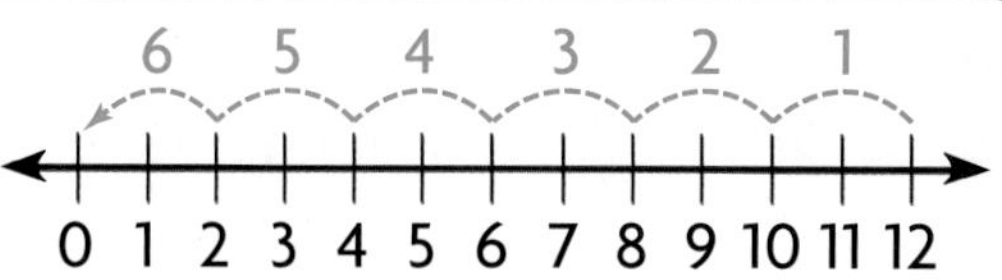

You subtract 2 six times. So, Mrs. Benson needs 6 feeders.

ANOTHER WAY **Use a related multiplication fact.**

12 ÷ 2 = ■ Think: ■ × 2 = 12
6 × 2 = 12

So, 12 ÷ 2 = 6, or $2\overline{)12}$ with quotient 6.

Example 2 Divide. 20 ÷ 5 = ■

ONE WAY **Count back on a number line.**

Start at 20. Count back by 5s until you reach 0. Count the number of times you subtract 5.

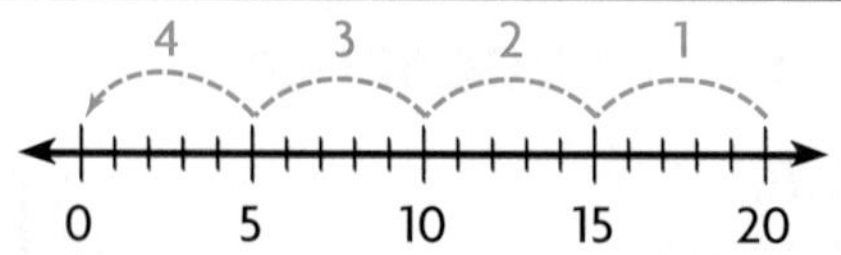

You subtract 5 four times.

ANOTHER WAY **Use a related multiplication fact.**

20 ÷ 5 = ■ Think: ■ × 5 = 20
4 × 5 = 20

So, 20 ÷ 5 = 4, or $5\overline{)20}$ with quotient 4.

TEKS 3.4C use models to solve division problems and use number sentences to record the solutions. *also* **3.6C, 3.14A, 3.15A, 3.15B, 3.16A**

Guided Practice

1. Use the number line to find $25 \div 5$.

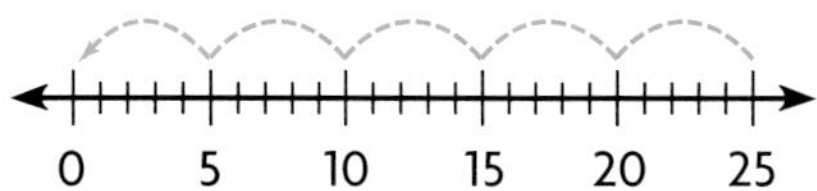

Find each quotient.

2. $16 \div 2 = \blacksquare$
3. $\blacksquare = 30 \div 5$
4. $20 \div 2 = \blacksquare$
5. $\blacksquare = 15 \div 5$
6. **TALK Math** **Explain** how $5 \times 8 = 40$ can help you find $40 \div 5$.

Independent Practice and Problem Solving

Find each quotient.

7. $6 \div 2 = \blacksquare$
8. $\blacksquare = 35 \div 5$
9. $10 \div 5 = \blacksquare$
10. $\blacksquare = 18 \div 2$
11. $\blacksquare = 45 \div 5$
12. $\blacksquare = 10 \div 2$
13. $8 \div 2 = \blacksquare$
14. $5 \div 5 = \blacksquare$
15. $5\overline{)15}$
16. $2\overline{)16}$
17. $5\overline{)35}$
18. $2\overline{)2}$

Algebra Copy and complete each table.

19.

÷	25	30	35	40
5	■	■	■	■

20.

÷	12	14	16	18
2	■	■	■	■

USE DATA For 21–22, use the table.

21. The total mass of 2 hummingbirds of the same type is 8 grams. Which type of hummingbird are they? Write a division sentence to show the answer.

Hummingbirds

Type	Mass in Grams
Magnificent	7
Rubythroat	3
Anna's	4

22. **WRITE Math** Five hummingbirds of the same type have a total mass of 15 grams. What type are they? **Explain** how to find the answer.

Mixed Review and TAKS Prep

23. What is 5×7? (TEKS 3.4B, p. 254)
24. What is the missing number?
$3 \times 8 = \blacksquare \times 3$ (TEKS 3.4B, p. 278)
25. **TAKS Prep** Jo sees the same number of birds each hour for 2 hours. She sees 16 birds in all. How many birds does Jo see each hour? (Obj. 1)

A 6 **B** 7 **C** 8 **D** 9

Extra Practice on page 332, Set A

LESSON 2

Divide by 3 and 4

OBJECTIVE: Divide by 3 and 4.

Quick Review

1. ■ × 3 = 18
2. 4 × ■ = 12
3. 6 × ■ = 24
4. ■ × 9 = 36
5. 3 × ■ = 21

Learn

PROBLEM For field day, 15 students have signed up for the relay race. Each relay team needs 3 students. How many teams can be made?

Example 1 Divide. 15 ÷ 3 = ■

ONE WAY **Draw a picture.**

Draw 15 counters in groups of 3.
Count the number of equal groups.
There are 5 groups of 3.
So, 5 teams can be made.

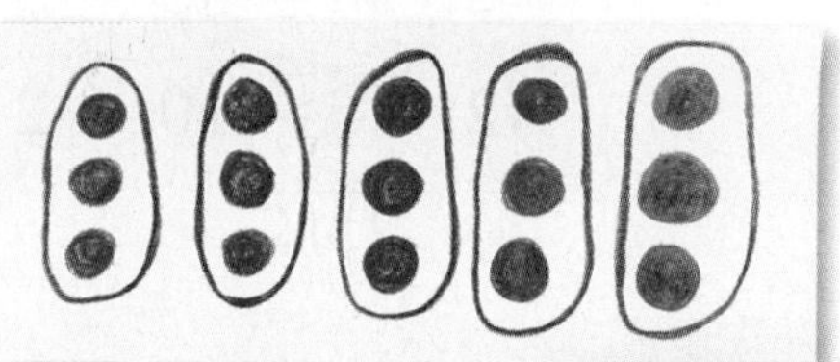

ANOTHER WAY **Use a related multiplication fact.**

15 ÷ 3 = ■ Think: ■ × 3 = 15
5 × 3 = 15 So, 15 ÷ 3 = 5, or $3\overline{)15}$ with quotient 5.

Math Idea
You can divide to find the number of equal groups or to find how many are in each group.

Example 2 Divide. 12 ÷ 4 = ■

ONE WAY **Draw a picture.**

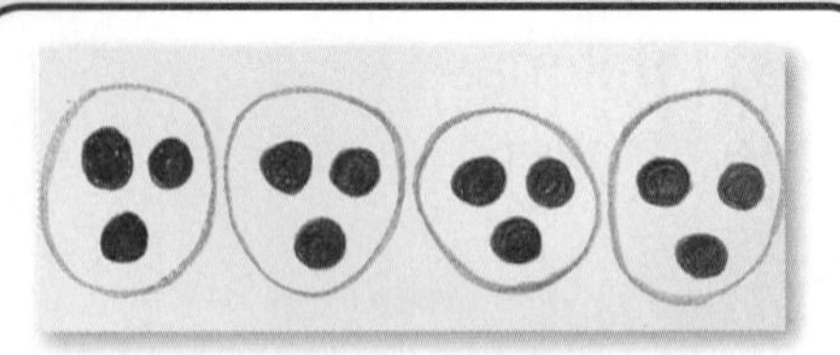

There are 3 counters in each group.

ANOTHER WAY **Use a related multiplication fact.**

Think: 4 × ■ = 12
4 × 3 = 12
So, 12 ÷ 4 = 3, or $4\overline{)12}$ with quotient 3.

Guided Practice

1. Use the picture to find 21 ÷ 3 = ■.

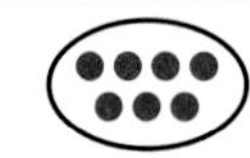 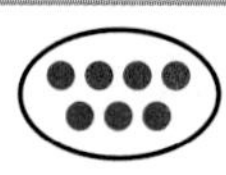 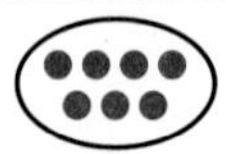

TEKS 3.4C use models to solve division problems and use number sentences to record the solutions. *also* 3.6C, 3.14A, 3.15A, 3.15B, 3.16A

Find each quotient.

2. $9 \div 3 = $ ■ **3.** $28 \div 4 = $ ■ **4.** $32 \div 4 = $ ■ **5.** $24 \div 3 = $ ■

6. TALK Math **Explain** how you can use multiplication to find $20 \div 4$.

Independent Practice and Problem Solving

Find each quotient.

7. $30 \div 3 = $ ■ **8.** $8 \div 4 = $ ■ **9.** ■ $= 27 \div 3$ **10.** $16 \div 4 = $ ■

11. $24 \div 4 = $ ■ **12.** ■ $= 35 \div 5$ **13.** $6 \div 3 = $ ■ **14.** ■ $= 14 \div 2$

15. $3\overline{)12}$ **16.** $4\overline{)36}$ **17.** $5\overline{)20}$ **18.** $3\overline{)18}$

Algebra Copy and complete each table.

19.

÷	6	9	12	15
3	■	■	■	■

20.

÷	20	24	28	32
4	■	■	■	■

USE DATA For 21–22, use the table.

21. Reasoning Students doing the beanbag toss and the jump-rope race competed in groups of 3. How many more groups participated in the jump-rope race than in the beanbag toss? **Explain** how you know.

22. What if students ran the relay race in groups of 4? Write a number sentence to show the number of groups that would have competed.

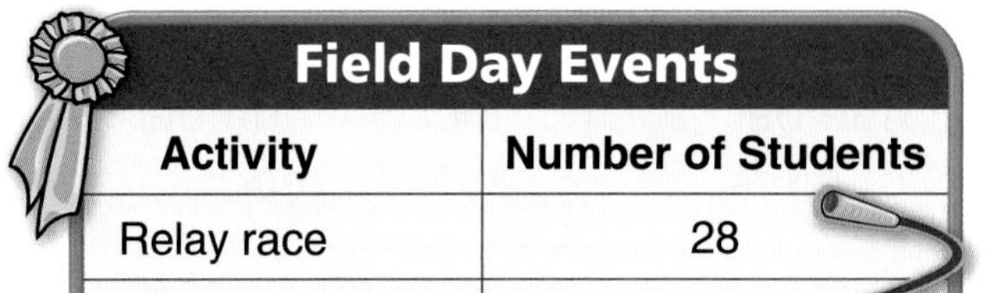

Field Day Events

Activity	Number of Students
Relay race	28
Beanbag toss	18
Jump-rope race	27

23. WRITE Math **What's the Question?** Cara put 36 sports cards into 4 equal piles. The answer is 9 sports cards.

Mixed Review and TAKS Prep

24. Lee used 35 beads to make 5 bracelets. How many beads did she use for each bracelet?
(TEKS 3.4C, p. 320)

25. What is the sum of 297 and 582?
(TEKS 3.3B, p. 66)

26. TAKS Prep Carlos has 24 pretzels. He puts 4 pretzels in each bag. How many bags does Carlos fill? (Obj. 1)

A 4 **B** 5 **C** 6 **D** 7

Extra Practice on page 332, Set B

LESSON 3

Division Rules for 1 and 0

OBJECTIVE: Divide using the rules for 1 and 0.

Quick Review

1. $6 \times \blacksquare = 6$
2. $\blacksquare \times 9 = 0$
3. $1 \times \blacksquare = 3$
4. $8 \times \blacksquare = 0$
5. $\blacksquare \times 1 = 5$

Learn

These division rules can help you divide with 1 and 0.

RULE A: Any number divided by 1 equals that number.

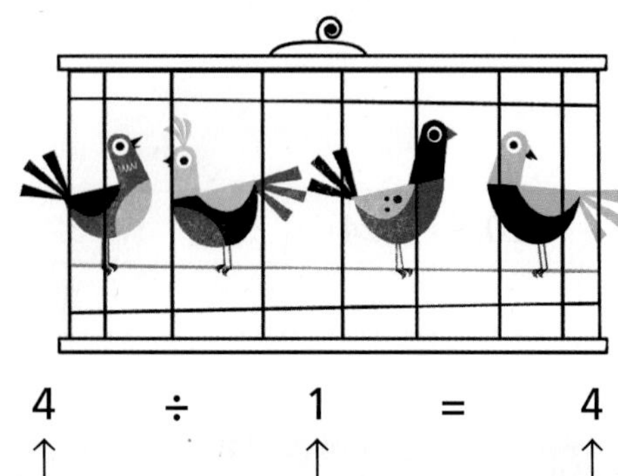

4	÷	1	=	4
↑		↑		↑
number of birds		number of cages		number in each cage

If there is only 1 cage, then all of the birds must go in that cage.

RULE B: Any number (except 0) divided by itself equals 1.

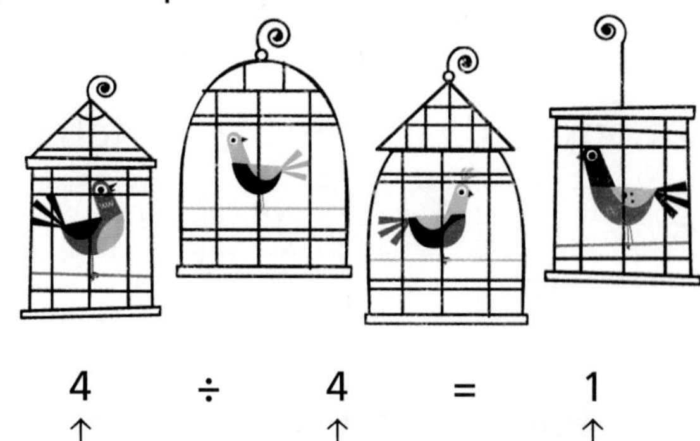

4	÷	4	=	1
↑		↑		↑
number of birds		number of cages		number in each cage

If there are the same number of birds and cages, then 1 bird goes in each cage.

RULE C: Zero divided by any number (except 0) equals 0.

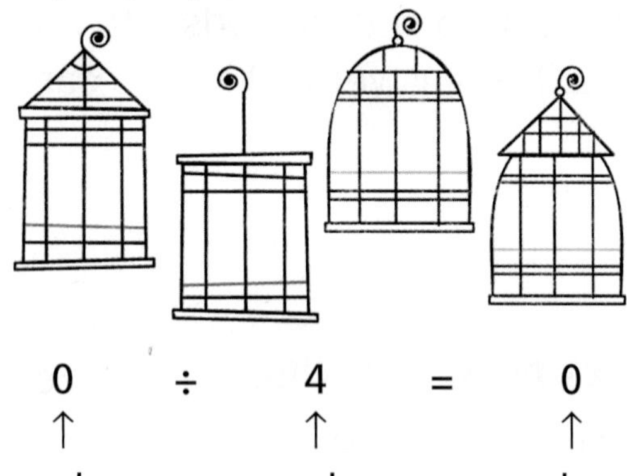

0	÷	4	=	0
↑		↑		↑
number of birds		number of cages		number in each cage

If there are 0 birds and 4 cages, there will not be any birds in the cages.

RULE D: You cannot divide by 0.

If there are 0 cages, then you cannot separate the birds into equal groups. Dividing by 0 is not possible.

TEKS 3.4C use models to solve division problems and use number sentences to record the solutions. *also* **3.14A, 3.15A, 3.15B, 3.16A**

Guided Practice

1. Use the picture to find $3 \div 3 = \blacksquare$.

Find each quotient.

2. $7 \div 1 = \blacksquare$
3. $2 \div 2 = \blacksquare$
4. $0 \div 5 = \blacksquare$
5. $6 \div 6 = \blacksquare$
6. TALK Math **Explain** why it is easy to find $9 \div 1$. Solve.

Independent Practice and Problem Solving

Find each quotient.

7. $0 \div 8 = \blacksquare$
8. $5 \div 5 = \blacksquare$
9. $\blacksquare = 2 \div 1$
10. $0 \div 7 = \blacksquare$
11. $6 \div 1 = \blacksquare$
12. $\blacksquare = 25 \div 5$
13. $\blacksquare = 0 \div 10$
14. $18 \div 3 = \blacksquare$
15. $14 \div 2 = \blacksquare$
16. $\blacksquare = 9 \div 9$
17. $32 \div 4 = \blacksquare$
18. $\blacksquare = 8 \div 1$
19. $4\overline{)24}$
20. $5\overline{)10}$
21. $3\overline{)0}$
22. $10\overline{)10}$

Algebra **Compare. Write <, >, or = for each ●.**

23. $7 \div 7$ ● $7 \div 1$
24. 9×1 ● $9 \div 1$
25. $2 \div 2$ ● $0 \div 2$

26. Angie has 7 parakeets. She put 4 of them in a cage. She let 3 friends hold the other parakeets. How many parakeets did each friend get to hold?

27. **Pose a Problem** Look back at Problem 26. Change the number of parakeets and friends so you can use the division sentence $6 \div 6 = 1$.

28. ***FAST FACT*** There are more than 340 different types of parrots. Mary has 5 different parrots. She gives each parrot 1 grape. How many grapes does she give to her parrots?

29. WRITE Math Suppose a zoo has 59 birds in each of 59 cages. Use what you know to find the number of birds in each cage. **Explain** your answer.

Mixed Review and TAKS Prep

30. A flower shop sold 795 flowers. What is the value of the 9? (TEKS 3.1A, p.10)

31. Use a related multiplication fact to find $18 \div 3 = \blacksquare$. (TEKS, 3.6C, p. 304)

32. **TAKS Prep** Farmer Joe has 4 stables. There is 1 horse in each stable. How many horses are there? (Obj. 1)

A 0 **B** 1 **C** 2 **D** 4

Extra Practice on page 332, Set C

ALGEBRA

Practice the Facts

OBJECTIVE: Practice division facts through 5 using various strategies.

Quick Review

1. $4 \times \blacksquare = 32$
2. $\blacksquare \times 7 = 21$
3. $\blacksquare \times 5 = 10$
4. $2 \times \blacksquare = 12$
5. $1 \times \blacksquare = 9$

Learn

PROBLEM Tory made cottonball snowmen for her friends. She glued 3 cottonballs together to make each snowman. She used a total of 24 cottonballs. How many snowmen did Tory make?

Divide. $24 \div 3 = \blacksquare$

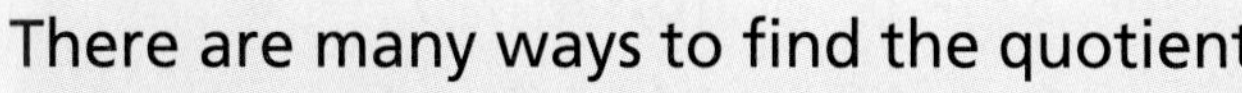

There are many ways to find the quotient.

A Draw a picture.

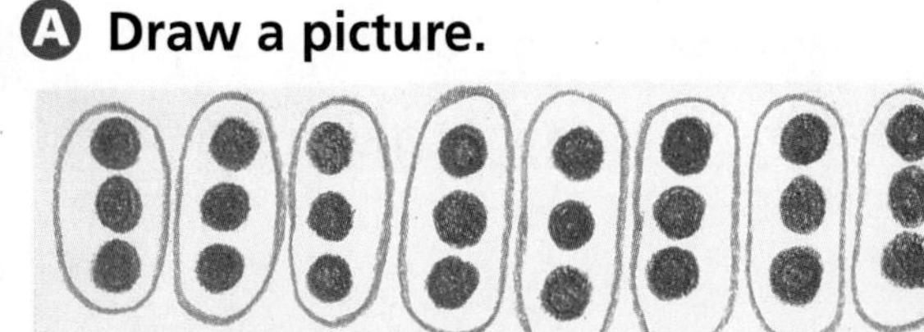

There are 8 groups of 3.
So, $24 \div 3 = 8$.

B Count back on a number line.

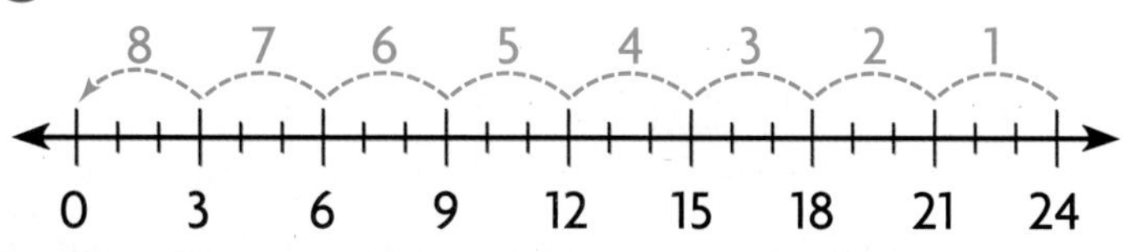

You subtract 3 eight times.
So, $24 \div 3 = 8$.

ERROR ALERT

Be sure to count back the same number of spaces each time you subtract on the number line.

C Use an array.

Make an array with 24 tiles.
Place 3 tiles in each row.
Count the number of rows.
There are 8 rows of 3 tiles.

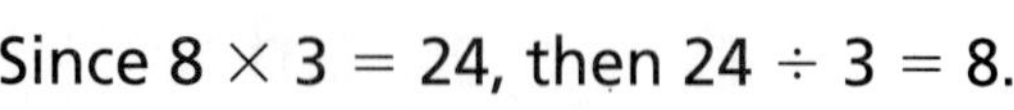

Since $8 \times 3 = 24$, then $24 \div 3 = 8$.

D Use a fact family.

$3 \times 8 = 24$ $\quad$ $24 \div 8 = 3$

$8 \times 3 = 24$ $\quad$ $24 \div 3 = 8$

So, $24 \div 3 = 8$.

TEKS 3.4C use models to solve division problems and use number sentences to record the solutions. *also* **3.6C, 3.14A, 3.14D, 3.15A, 3.15B**

E Use a multiplication table.

Think of a related multiplication fact.

Think: 3 × ■ = 24

Find the row for the factor 3.
Look right to find the product 24.
Look up to find the missing factor, 8.

Since 3 × 8 = 24, then 24 ÷ 3 = 8.
So, Tory made 8 snowmen.

×	0	1	2	3	4	5	6	7	8	9
0	0	0	0	0	0	0	0	0	0	0
1	0	1	2	3	4	5	6	7	8	9
2	0	2	4	6	8	10	12	14	16	18
3	0	3	6	9	12	15	18	21	24	27
4	0	4	8	12	16	20	24	28	32	36
5	0	5	10	15	20	25	30	35	40	45
6	0	6	12	18	24	30	36	42	48	54
7	0	7	14	21	28	35	42	49	56	63
8	0	8	16	24	32	40	48	56	64	72
9	0	9	18	27	36	45	54	63	72	81

Guided Practice

1. Use the array to find 10 ÷ 5. 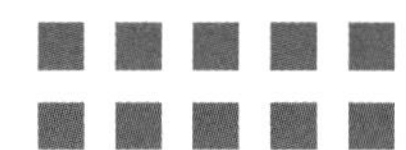

Write a division sentence for each.

2. 

3. 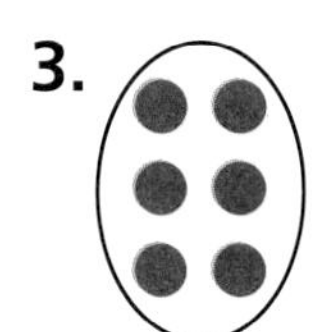 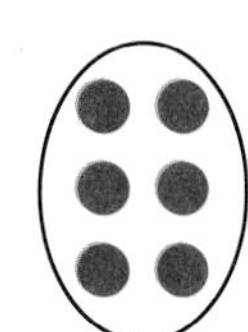 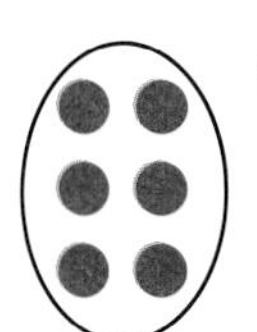

✓4. 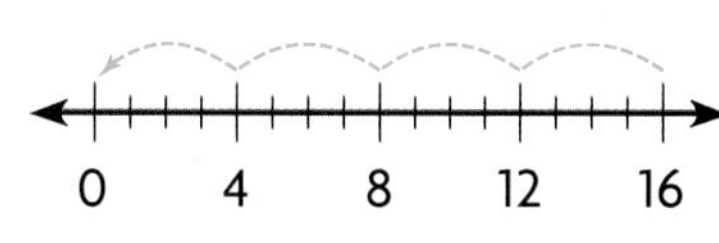

Use models to find each missing factor and quotient.

5. 5 × ■ = 30   30 ÷ 5 = ■

✓6. 1 × ■ = 7   7 ÷ 1 = ■

7. 2 × ■ = 16   16 ÷ 2 = ■

8. 4 × ■ = 32   32 ÷ 4 = ■

9. TALK Math **Explain** two ways to find 15 ÷ 3.

Independent Practice and Problem Solving

Write a division sentence for each.

10. 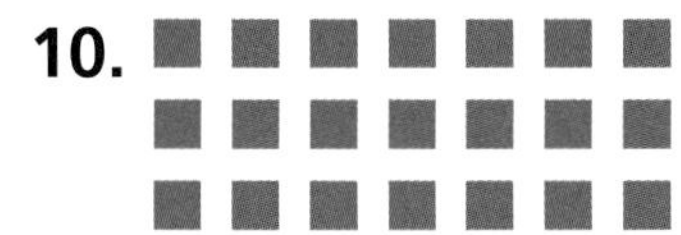

11. 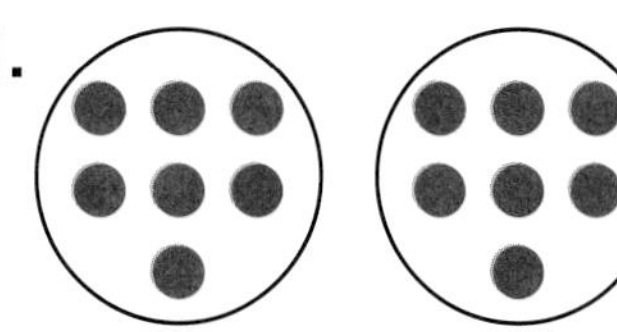

12. 

Extra Practice on page 332, Set D

Use models to find each missing factor and quotient.

13. $4 \times ■ = 24$ $24 \div 4 = ■$ **14.** $5 \times ■ = 40$ $40 \div 5 = ■$

15. $5 \times ■ = 0$ $0 \div 5 = ■$ **16.** $2 \times ■ = 8$ $8 \div 2 = ■$

Find each quotient.

17. $4 \div 4 = ■$ **18.** $27 \div 3 = ■$ **19.** $■ = 25 \div 5$ **20.** $6 \div 1 = ■$

21. $■ = 10 \div 2$ **22.** $36 \div 4 = ■$ **23.** $0 \div 8 = ■$ **24.** $■ = 18 \div 3$

25. $5\overline{)45}$ **26.** $1\overline{)3}$ **27.** $4\overline{)28}$ **28.** $2\overline{)14}$

29. $2\overline{)18}$ **30.** $3\overline{)24}$ **31.** $5\overline{)20}$ **32.** $2\overline{)0}$

Compare. Write <, >, or = for each ●.

33. $30 \div 5$ ● 2×3 **34.** $21 \div 3$ ● $18 \div 2$ **35.** 4×2 ● $7 \div 1$

Write +, −, ×, or ÷ for each ●.

36. 14 ● $2 = 6 \times 2$ **37.** $12 \div 4 = 27$ ● 9 **38.** $21 \div 3 = 5$ ● 2

39. Mary wants to make 8 snowmen. Each snowman gets 2 bead eyes. If bead eyes come in packs of 4, how many packs does Mary need?

40. Robert has 30 buttons. How many snowmen can he decorate if he wants each snowman to have 5 buttons?

41. **Reasoning** Martin has several boxes that hold 6 jars of paint each. Can 25 jars of paint fit in 4 of his boxes? **Explain** how you know.

42. WRITE Math **What's the Error?** Kim drew 3 equal groups of 9 to model $24 \div 3$. Describe her error. Draw a picture to model the division sentence.

Mixed Review and TAKS Prep

43. Find the product. $6 \times 6 = ■$ (TEKS 3.4B, p. 232)

44. The tallest snowman ever made was 113 feet tall. The scarf he wore was 7 feet longer than the height. How long was the scarf? (TEKS 3.3B, p. 66)

45. Round 439 to the nearest hundred. (TEKS 3.5A, p. 40)

46. **TAKS Prep** Which division sentence is related to $6 \times 3 = 18$? (Obj. 1)

A $6 \div 3 = 2$ **C** $18 \div 3 = 6$

B $12 \div 6 = 2$ **D** $18 \div 2 = 9$

CD ROM **Technology**
Use Harcourt Mega Math, The Number Games, *Up, Up, and Array,* Level E.

Pottery Class

Reading Skill **Visualize**

Pottery is one of the oldest arts. To make pottery, clay is molded and hardened with heat. You can learn to make and decorate your own pottery. The Mother Earth Clay Art Center, in Sunnyvale, California, offers pottery classes for children and adults.

The Oakland Museum of California has a collection of crafts and pottery created by local artists. This picture shows one pottery piece displayed in the museum.

A pottery studio has 6 pottery wheels for use by 12 students. How many students will share each wheel?

When you visualize something, you picture it in your mind. You can visualize the information given in a problem to help you solve it. Follow the steps below.

STEP 1 Make a list of models that could be used to help solve the problem, and then picture the models in your mind.

STEP 2 Think about which model best shows the problem.

STEP 3 Picture the problem in your mind.

Models
Groups of objects
Number line
Array
Multiplication table

Problem Solving **Visualize to understand the problem.**

1. Solve the problem above.
2. The students in the beginner pottery class made 4 pots each. Altogether, the class members made 24 pots. How many students are in the beginner pottery class?

Problem Solving Workshop
Skill: Choose the Operation

OBJECTIVE: Solve problems by using the skill *choose the operation.*

Read to Understand
Plan
Solve
Check

Use the Skill

PROBLEM Miss Kent's class went to the science center to visit the new water and animal exhibits.

Sometimes, you need to decide which operation to use to solve a problem.

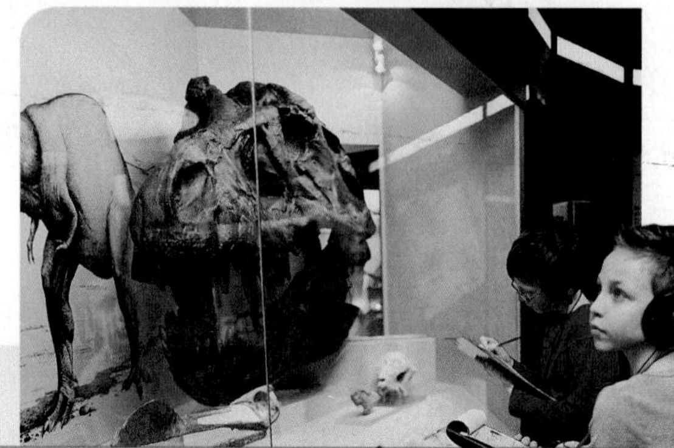

Examples

A Add to join groups of different sizes.
The water exhibit has 26 displays, and the animal exhibit has 18 displays. How many displays are in both exhibits?

$$\begin{array}{r} 26 \\ +\,18 \\ \hline 44 \end{array}$$

26 ← water displays
+ 18 ← animal displays
44 ← total number of displays

B Subtract to find the number left or to compare amounts.
Three of the 26 displays in the water exhibit were closed. How many were open?

26 ← total water displays
− 3 ← closed displays
23 ← open displays

C Multiply to join equal groups.
The gift shop has world map puzzle books for $8 each. What is the cost of 5 puzzle books?

$5 \times \$8 = \$40$

5 ↑ number of books; $8 ↑ cost of one book; $40 ↑ total cost

D Divide to separate into equal groups or to find the number in each group.
The 24 students were separated into 4 equal groups. How many were in each group?

$24 \div 4 = 6$

24 ↑ number of students; 4 ↑ number of groups; 6 ↑ students in each group

Think and Discuss

Choose the operation. Write a number sentence. Then solve.

a. The Davis family spent $30 for 5 tickets to the ocean show. How much did each ticket cost?

b. There were 24 students and 13 adults on the bus for the science center trip. How many people rode on the bus?

TEKS 3.3B select addition or subtraction and use the operation to solve problems involving whole numbers through 999. *also* **3.4B, 3.4C, 3.14A, 3.14B, 3.14C, 3.15A, 3.15B, 3.16B**

Guided Problem Solving

Solve.

1. The show about the ocean was 17 minutes long, and the show about dolphins was 32 minutes long. How much longer was the dolphin show than the ocean show?

   Which operation can you use to compare amounts? Write a number sentence and solve.

2. **What if** Problem 1 asked you to find the total time of the two shows? What operation would you use? Write a number sentence and solve.

3. T-shirts are sold for $9 each at the gift shop. What is the cost of 3 T-shirts?

Mixed Applications

4. There are 45 books in the gift shop. There are an equal number of books on each of 5 shelves. How many books are on each shelf?

5. There are 54 fourth graders and 62 third graders who will enter projects in the science fair. Each project will be set up on its own table. How many tables are needed?

USE DATA For 6–8, use the table.

6. After visiting the science center, Miss Kent's class made this table about water use. In two days, how much water would a family of 4 use for brushing teeth in the morning and at bedtime?

7. Jonas took a bath, and his sister took a shower. How much more water did Jonas use than his sister?

8. WRITE Math Mr. Foster washed his clothes, washed his car, and ran the dishwasher. How much water did he use? **Explain** how you found your answer.

Water Use

Activity	Amount in Gallons
Brush teeth	1
Wash clothes	30
Take a shower	30
Take a bath	40
Wash car	20
Run dishwasher	15

Extra Practice

Set A Find each quotient. (pp. 320–321)

1. $6 \div 2 = ■$
2. $■ = 25 \div 5$
3. $18 \div 2 = ■$
4. $■ = 40 \div 5$
5. $5\overline{)30}$
6. $2\overline{)12}$
7. $5\overline{)15}$
8. $2\overline{)4}$
9. Gina bought movie tickets for $20. Each ticket cost $5. How many tickets did she buy?
10. Carl placed a total of 14 chairs in 2 equal rows. How many chairs were in each row?

Set B Find each quotient. (pp. 322–323)

1. $■ = 21 \div 3$
2. $28 \div 4 = ■$
3. $■ = 18 \div 3$
4. $36 \div 4 = ■$
5. $4\overline{)12}$
6. $3\overline{)24}$
7. $4\overline{)32}$
8. $3\overline{)9}$

Set C Find each quotient. (pp. 324–325)

1. $3 \div 1 = ■$
2. $■ = 0 \div 9$
3. $■ = 5 \div 1$
4. $7 \div 7 = ■$
5. $4\overline{)0}$
6. $5\overline{)5}$
7. $2\overline{)0}$
8. $1\overline{)9}$
9. Dena has 3 fish. She divides them equally among 3 fishbowls. How many fish are in each bowl?
10. Steve has 4 flowers. He puts all of his flowers in 1 vase. How many flowers are in the vase?

Set D Write a division sentence for each. (pp. 326–329)

1. 
2. 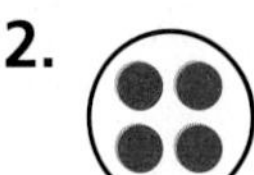  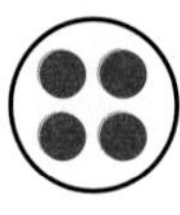
3. 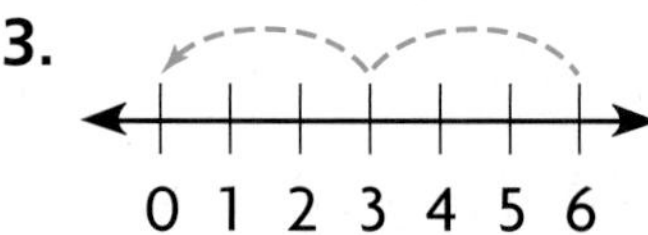

Find each missing factor and quotient.

4. $5 \times ■ = 45 \quad 45 \div 5 = ■$
5. $1 \times ■ = 6 \quad 6 \div 1 = ■$

Find each quotient.

6. $8 \div 2 = ■$
7. $35 \div 5 = ■$
8. $0 \div 7 = ■$
9. $16 \div 2 = ■$
10. $9\overline{)9}$
11. $3\overline{)15}$
12. $1\overline{)8}$
13. $4\overline{)24}$

Technology
Use Harcourt Mega Math, The Number Games, *Up, Up, and Array*, Levels A, E.

PRACTICE GAME

Division Cover-Up

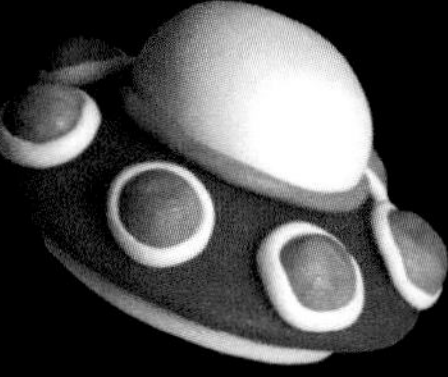

Shuffle!
2 players

Draw!
- Division fact cards
- 10 counters for each player

1	27	14	6	15	5
21	8	7	32	12	2
16	0	18	30	10	24
9	3	45	35	4	36
40	4	28	50	8	3

Cover Them Up!

- Players shuffle the division fact cards and place them facedown in a pile.
- Player 1 draws the card from the top of the pile and says the number that is missing from the division number sentence on that card.
- Player 1 finds the missing number on the gameboard and places a counter on it.
- Players take turns. If a player cannot place a counter on the gameboard because the number is already covered, that player's turn ends.
- The first player to place all 10 of his or her counters on the gameboard wins the game.

Chapter 14 Review/Test

Check Concepts

Write a division sentence for each. (TEKS 3.4C, pp. 326–329)

1.

2. 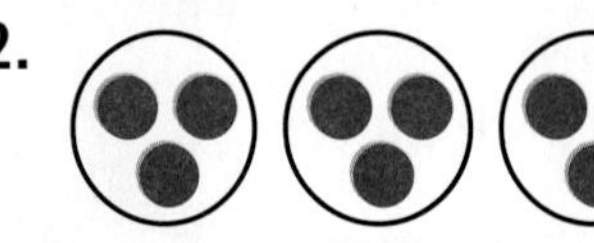

3. 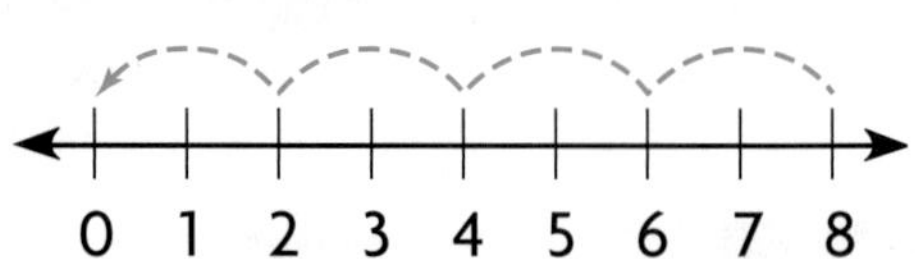

Check Skills

Find each quotient. (TEKS 3.4C, pp. 320–321, 322–323, 324–325, 326–329)

4. $14 \div 2 = ■$	**5.** $8 \div 8 = ■$	**6.** $20 \div 5 = ■$	**7.** $■ = 0 \div 3$
8. $5 \div 1 = ■$	**9.** $■ = 20 \div 2$	**10.** $12 \div 3 = ■$	**11.** $16 \div 4 = ■$
12. $■ = 30 \div 5$	**13.** $24 \div 3 = ■$	**14.** $■ = 6 \div 6$	**15.** $12 \div 2 = ■$
16. $4\overline{)36}$	**17.** $6\overline{)0}$	**18.** $5\overline{)45}$	**19.** $3\overline{)6}$
20. $5\overline{)25}$	**21.** $4\overline{)28}$	**22.** $1\overline{)9}$	**23.** $2\overline{)18}$

Find each missing factor and quotient. (TEKS 3.4C, pp. 326–329)

24. $4 \times ■ = 8$ $\quad 8 \div 4 = ■$

25. $3 \times ■ = 27$ $\quad 27 \div 3 = ■$

26. $1 \times ■ = 7$ $\quad 7 \div 1 = ■$

27. $2 \times ■ = 10$ $\quad 10 \div 2 = ■$

Check Problem Solving

Solve. (TEKS 3.3B, 3.14A, pp. 330–331)

28. Mark put all of his shirts in 4 equal stacks. There are 6 shirts in each stack. How many shirts does Mark have altogether?

29. Beverly has 6 apples, 8 oranges, and 12 bananas. How many pieces of fruit does Beverly have in all?

30. WRITE Math Mike scored 18 points in the flag football game. He scored only touchdowns, and each touchdown he made scored 3 points. How many touchdowns did Mike make? **Explain** how you know which operation to use to solve the problem.

Enrich • Odd and Even

Beat the Odds

Marco and his brother choose pairs of numbers at random and guess if their products are odd or even. What is the best guess for Marco—will most of the products be odd or even?

Make Your Guess

Marco made a table to decide.

Step 1 Find the product of each example.

Step 2 Determine if each product is even or odd.

NUMBERS	EXAMPLE	PRODUCT	ODD OR EVEN?
odd × odd	3 × 9	27	odd
even × even	4 × 8	32	even
odd × even	5 × 8	40	even
even × odd	2 × 7	14	even

Step 3 Make a conclusion based on the table results.
Three of the four possibilities result in an even product.

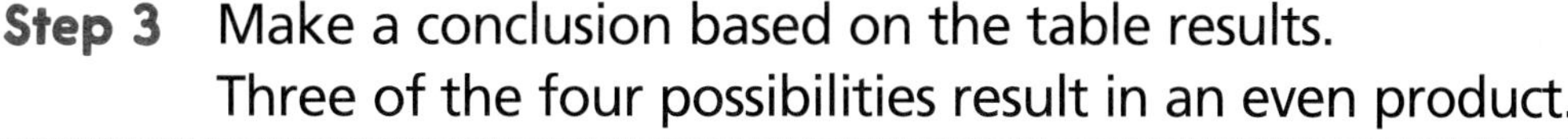

So, Marco should guess that the product will usually be even.

Pick a Number

Complete the table.

	NUMBERS	EXAMPLE	QUOTIENT	ODD OR EVEN?
1.	odd ÷ odd	21 ÷ 3		
2.	odd ÷ odd	35 ÷ 5		
3.	even ÷ even	10 ÷ 2		
4.	even ÷ even	24 ÷ 4		
5.	even ÷ odd	20 ÷ 5		
6.	even ÷ odd	18 ÷ 3		

And the Winner Is

WRITE Math ▸ Make a conclusion based on the table results. **Explain** how you reached that conclusion.

Getting Ready for the TAKS
Chapters 1–14

Number, Operation, and Quantitative Reasoning (TAKS Obj. 1)

1. Sarah is setting tables for a party. She puts the same number of plates on each of 5 tables. There are 40 plates in all. How many plates are on each table?

   A 6

   B 7

   C 8

   D 9

Look for important words.

See item 2. Key words can help you solve a problem. The word *altogether* indicates that you should find a total. Since there are two numbers that are different, find the total by adding.

2. There are 346 books on the first shelf in a library. There are 299 books on the second shelf. How many books are on both shelves altogether?

   F 535 H 635

   G 545 J 645

3. WRITE Math **Explain** how you can use the counters to find $20 \div 5$.

  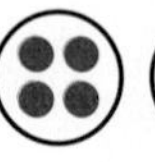  

Patterns, Relationships, and Algebraic Thinking (TAKS Obj. 2)

4. Which number completes the fact family?

   $■ \times 9 = 63$ $63 \div ■ = 9$

   $9 \times ■ = 63$ $63 \div 9 = ■$

   A 6

   B 7

   C 8

   D 9

5. Which number is missing in the pattern below?

   98, 85, 72, 59, 46, 33, ■

   F 22

   G 21

   H 20

   J 19

6. WRITE Math **Explain** how the arrays show the Commutative Property of Multiplication.

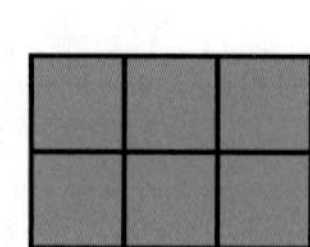 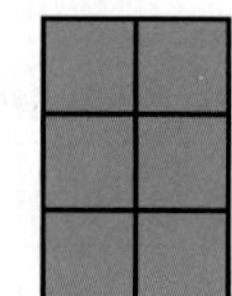

Measurement (TAKS Obj. 4)

7. Which figure has an area of 15 square units?

A 

B 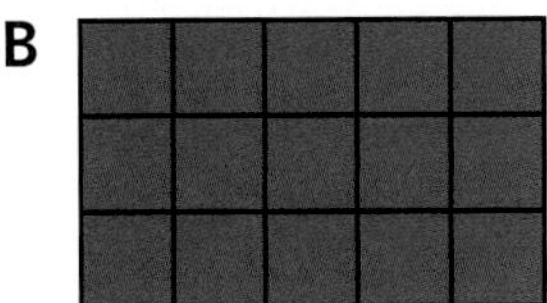

C 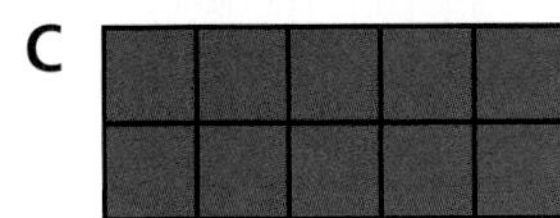

D 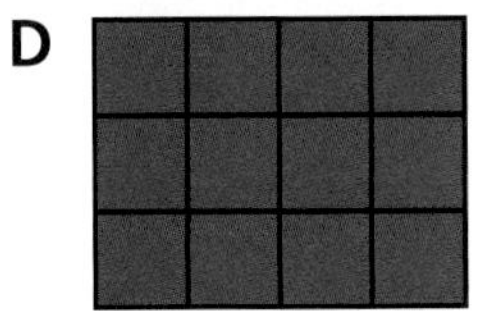

8. Which temperature does the thermometer show?

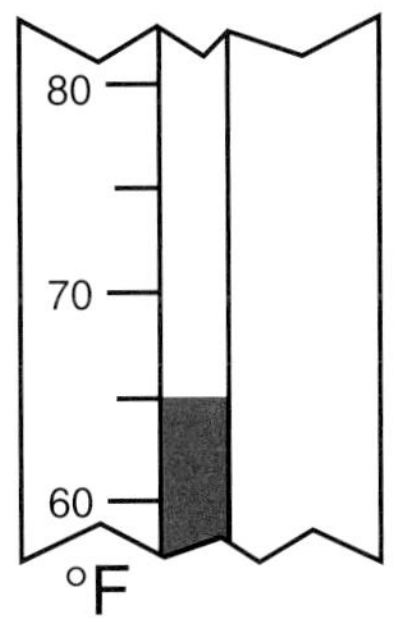

F 70°F

G 65°F

H 60°F

J Not here

9. **WRITE Math** A paper clip is about 1 inch long. **Explain** how you could use a paper clip to measure the length of your pencil.

Probability and Statistics (TAKS Obj. 5)

10. Jerry pulls a marble out of the bag without looking. Which color marble is he most likely to pull?

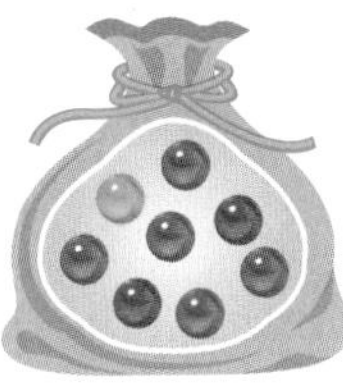

A Green

B Yellow

C Red

D Blue

11. How many letters did Thomas send?

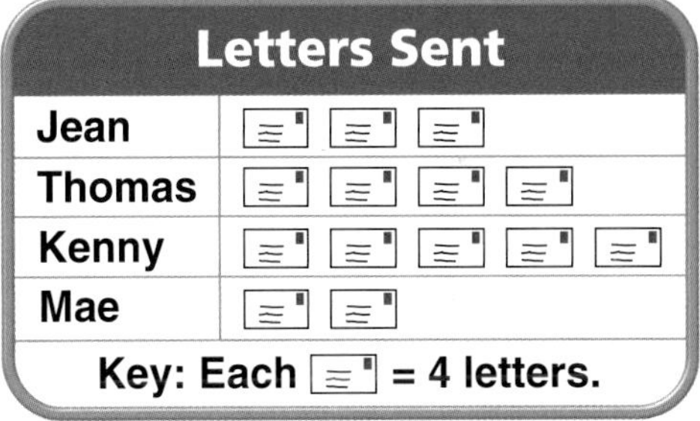

Letters Sent	
Jean	✉ ✉ ✉
Thomas	✉ ✉ ✉ ✉
Kenny	✉ ✉ ✉ ✉ ✉
Mae	✉ ✉
Key: Each ✉ = 4 letters.	

F 4 **H** 16

G 12 **J** 20

12. **WRITE Math** A bar graph shows the number of students in each grade at Faber School. The bars for third grade and fourth grade are the same height. What does this mean? **Explain**.

15 Facts Through 12

The Big Idea Fluency with division facts is based upon using patterns and the inverse relationship to recall quotients.

There are over 350 breeds of horses. The American paint horse is a popular breed in Texas. These horses are about 64 inches tall and weigh over 1,000 pounds.

Investigate

The table shows the number of hours each week that a horse spends doing different activities. How many hours does a horse spend each day doing each activity? (Hint: 1 week = 7 days) Compare this to the amount of time you spend doing each activity.

Horse Activities

Activity	Number of Hours Each Week
Eating	84
Sleeping	21
Exercise and Other Activities	63

Technology
Student pages are available in the Student eBook.

Show What You Know

Check your understanding of important skills needed for success in Chapter 15.

▶ Missing Factors

Find the missing factor.

1. $4 \times ■ = 32$ **2.** $18 = ■ \times 3$ **3.** $■ \times 9 = 54$ **4.** $49 = 7 \times ■$

▶ Multiplication Facts Through 12

Find the product.

5. $7 \times 5 = ■$ **6.** $4 \times 11 = ■$ **7.** $■ = 12 \times 3$ **8.** $■ = 10 \times 8$

9. $11 \times 8 = ■$ **10.** $■ = 4 \times 12$ **11.** $5 \times 9 = ■$ **12.** $■ = 12 \times 7$

▶ Multiplication Properties

Use the properties of multiplication to help you find each product.

13. $6 \times 8 = ■$ $8 \times 6 = ■$ **14.** $(3 \times 2) \times 4 = ■$ $3 \times (2 \times 4) = ■$

15. $7 \times 1 = ■$ **16.** $0 \times 12 = ■$

▶ Division Facts Through 5

Find the quotient.

17. $28 \div 4 = ■$ **18.** $12 \div 3 = ■$ **19.** $■ = 30 \div 5$ **20.** $8 \div 1 = ■$

21. $■ = 18 \div 2$ **22.** $20 \div 4 = ■$ **23.** $27 \div 3 = ■$ **24.** $40 \div 5 = ■$

VOCABULARY POWER

CHAPTER VOCABULARY

array
divide
dividend
divisor
fact family
quotient

WARM-UP WORDS

divide To separate into equal groups; the opposite operation of multiplication

quotient The number, not including the remainder, that results from division

Divide by 6

OBJECTIVE: Divide by 6.

Quick Review

1. ■ × 6 = 6
2. 6 × ■ = 24
3. 3 × ■ = 18
4. ■ × 6 = 54
5. 7 × ■ = 42

Learn

PROBLEM Ms. Moore needs to buy 30 juice boxes for the class picnic. Juice boxes come in packs of 6. How many packs does she need to buy?

Divide. $30 \div 6 = $ ■ $\quad 6\overline{)30}$ (quotient: ■)

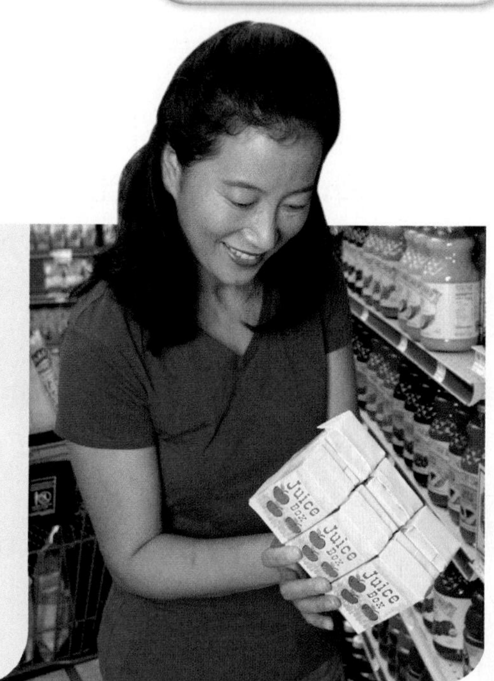

ONE WAY **Use counters.**

Use 30 counters.
Make groups of 6 until all counters are used.
Count the number of groups.

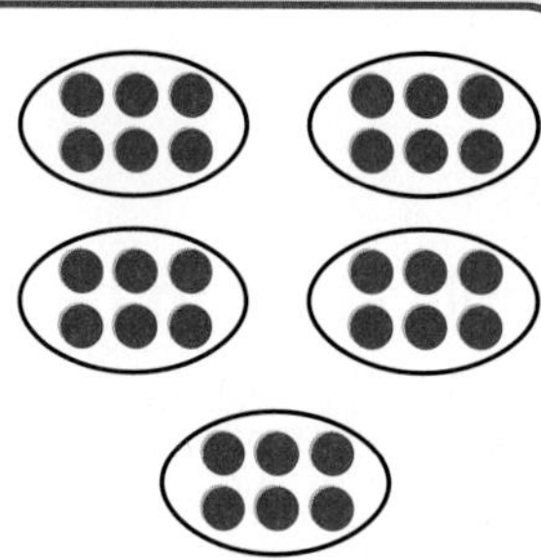

There are 5 groups of 6 counters.

So, Ms. Moore needs to buy 5 packs of juice.

OTHER WAYS

A **Use a related multiplication fact.**

Think: ■ × 6 = 30
5 × 6 = 30

So, 30 ÷ 6 = 5, or $6\overline{)30}$ with quotient 5.

B **Use factors.**

3 × 2 = 6
(3 and 2: factors; 6: product)

Since 3 and 2 are factors of 6, you can divide by 6 using 3 and then 2.

30 ÷ 3 = 10 10 ÷ 2 = 5
So, 30 ÷ 6 = 5.

- How can you solve 24 ÷ 6 by using the factors 3 and 2?

Guided Practice

1. Use the model to find 18 ÷ 6.

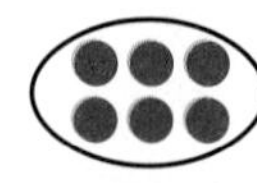 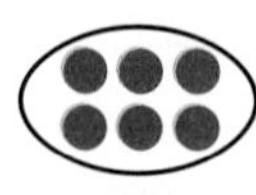 

TEKS 3.4C use models to solve division problems and use number sentences to record the solutions. *also* 3.14A, 3.14D, 3.15A, 3.15B, 3.16A

Find each missing factor and quotient.

2. $6 \times ■ = 36$ $36 \div 6 = ■$
3. $6 \times ■ = 12$ $12 \div 6 = ■$
4. $6 \times ■ = 6$ $6 \div 6 = ■$
5. $6 \times ■ = 42$ $42 \div 6 = ■$
6. TALK Math Explain how $6 \times 9 = 54$ helps you find $54 \div 6$.

Independent Practice and Problem Solving

Find each missing factor and quotient.

7. $6 \times ■ = 30$ $30 \div 6 = ■$
8. $6 \times ■ = 48$ $48 \div 6 = ■$
9. $6 \times ■ = 18$ $18 \div 6 = ■$
10. $6 \times ■ = 24$ $24 \div 6 = ■$

Find each quotient.

11. $12 \div 6 = ■$
12. $■ = 6 \div 2$
13. $■ = 42 \div 6$
14. $15 \div 5 = ■$
15. $■ = 60 \div 6$
16. $20 \div 4 = ■$
17. $7 \div 1 = ■$
18. $■ = 54 \div 6$
19. $4\overline{)28}$
20. $6\overline{)36}$
21. $6\overline{)0}$
22. $3\overline{)21}$

Algebra Find the missing number.

23. $6 \div ■ = 6$
24. $27 \div ■ = 9$
25. $16 \div ■ = 8$
26. $42 \div ■ = 7$

27. Ms. Moore bought a bag of 12 apples for the class picnic. How many apples can each of 6 students have if they each get the same number?

28. There are 30 students in a relay race at the picnic. The students are divided into 6 equal teams. How many students are on each team?

29. **Reasoning** Cody baked 24 muffins. He ate 6 of them. How many muffins does he have left? How many can he give to each of 6 friends if they each get the same number? **Explain**.

30. WRITE Math **What's the Error?** Mary has 36 stickers to give to 6 friends. She says she can give each friend only 5 stickers. Use a division sentence to describe Mary's error.

Mixed Review and TAKS Prep

31. What is the missing number?
$7 \times 8 = 8 \times ■$ (TEKS 3.4B, p. 278)

32. What is 8,024 written in expanded form? (TEKS 3.1A, p. 12)

33. **TAKS Prep** The same number of students are at each of 6 tables. There are 48 students in all. How many students are at each table? (Obj. 1)

A 9 **B** 8 **C** 7 **D** 6

on page 356, Set A

LESSON 2

Divide by 7 and 8

OBJECTIVE: Divide by 7 and 8.

Quick Review

1. ■ × 7 = 21
2. 3 × ■ = 24
3. 2 × ■ = 14
4. ■ × 7 = 42
5. 8 × ■ = 16

Learn

PROBLEM Firewood is sold in bundles of 7 logs. Steve has 28 logs. How many bundles of firewood can he make?

Example 1 Divide. 28 ÷ 7 = ■

ONE WAY Make an array.

Use 28 tiles. Make rows of 7 tiles until all tiles are used. Count the number of rows.

There are 4 rows of 7 tiles.

ANOTHER WAY Use a related multiplication fact.

Think: ■ × 7 = 28

4 × 7 = 28

So, 28 ÷ 7 = 4, or $7\overline{)28}$ with quotient 4.

So, Steve can make 4 bundles of firewood.

Example 2 Divide. 32 ÷ 8 = ■

ONE WAY Make an array.

Use 32 tiles. Make rows of 8 tiles until all tiles are used. Count the number of rows.

There are 4 rows of 8 tiles.

ANOTHER WAY Use a related multiplication fact.

Think: ■ × 8 = 32

4 × 8 = 32

So, 32 ÷ 8 = 4, or $8\overline{)32}$ with quotient 4.

Guided Practice

1. Use the array to find 14 ÷ 7 = ■.

Find each missing factor and quotient.

2. 7 × ■ = 35   35 ÷ 7 = ■
3. 8 × ■ = 48   48 ÷ 8 = ■
4. 8 × ■ = 56   56 ÷ 8 = ■
5. 7 × ■ = 63   63 ÷ 7 = ■
6. TALK Math **Explain** how you can use an array to find 24 ÷ 8 = ■.

TEKS 3.4C use models to solve division problems and use number sentences to record the solutions. *also* 3.14A, 3.14C, 3.14D, 3.15A, 3.15B, 3.16A

Independent Practice and Problem Solving

Find each missing factor and quotient.

7. $8 \times ■ = 40$ $40 \div 8 = ■$

8. $7 \times ■ = 49$ $49 \div 7 = ■$

9. $7 \times ■ = 7$ $7 \div 7 = ■$

10. $8 \times ■ = 64$ $64 \div 8 = ■$

Find each quotient.

11. $21 \div 7 = ■$

12. $■ = 8 \div 8$

13. $18 \div 2 = ■$

14. $■ = 25 \div 5$

15. $24 \div 6 = ■$

16. $■ = 15 \div 3$

17. $■ = 16 \div 8$

18. $56 \div 7 = ■$

19. $■ = 36 \div 4$

20. $70 \div 7 = ■$

21. $■ = 6 \div 1$

22. $72 \div 8 = ■$

23. $8\overline{)80}$

24. $5\overline{)40}$

25. $7\overline{)14}$

26. $6\overline{)54}$

Algebra **Copy and complete each table.**

27.

÷	48	56	64	72
8	■	■	■	■

28.

÷	35	42	49	56
7	■	■	■	■

USE DATA **For 29–31, use the table.**

Tent Sizes

Type	Number of People
Columbia	10
Vista	8
Condor	7
Gamma 450	5

29. **Reasoning** There are 58 people camping at Zoe's family reunion. They have Columbia tents and Vista tents. How many of each type of tent do they need to sleep 58 people? **Explain.**

30. **Pose a Problem** Look back at Problem 29. Write a similar problem by changing the number of people and the types of tents used.

31. **WRITE Math** There are 42 people going camping. How many Condor tents do they need? **Explain.**

Mixed Review and TAKS Prep

32. A Columbia tent costs $286. Mrs. Kent has $177. How much more money does she need to buy the tent? (TEKS 3.3B, p. 92)

33. There are 30 tents set up in groups with 5 tents in each group. How many groups are there? (TEKS 3.4C, p. 320)

34. **TAKS Prep** There are 24 benches in 8 equal rows at a picnic area. How many benches are in each row? (Obj. 1)

A 32 **C** 4

B 16 **D** 3

Extra Practice on page 356, Set B

Problem Solving Workshop
Strategy: Work Backward

OBJECTIVE: Solve problems by using the strategy *work backward*.

Learn the Strategy

When you know the final amount, you can work backward to solve a problem.

You can use subtraction and addition.

Zach paid $1.70 for lunch. Then his mom gave him $5.00. Now, Zach has $7.50. How much money did Zach have to start?

So, Zach had $4.20 to start.

Begin with the final amount of money.

Subtract the money Zach's mom gave him.

$7.50	−	$5.00	=	$2.50
↑		↑		↑
final amount		money from mom		money after lunch

Add the amount Zach spent on lunch.

$2.50	+	$1.70	=	$4.20
↑		↑		↑
money after lunch		money spent on lunch		money to start

You can use addition and multiplication.

Troy cuts a board in 2 equal pieces. Then he cuts 4 inches off one piece. The piece is now 6 inches long. What was the length of the original board?

So, the board was 20 inches long.

Begin with the final length of the board.

Add the number of inches Troy cut off.

6	+	4	=	10
↑		↑		↑
final length		inches cut off		length of one piece

Multiply to find the length of the original board.

10	×	2	=	20
↑		↑		↑
length of one piece		number of pieces		length of board

TALK Math

In the last problem, why did you use multiplication when you worked backward?

TEKS 3.14C select or develop an appropriate problem-solving plan or strategy, including drawing a picture, looking for a pattern, systematic guessing and checking, acting it out, making a table, working a simpler problem, or working backwards to solve a problem. *also* **3.14A, 3.14B, 3.15A, 3.15B, 3.16B**

Use the Strategy

PROBLEM Chad bought 4 packs of T-shirts. He gave 5 T-shirts to his brother. Now Chad has 19 shirts. How many T-shirts were in each pack?

Read to Understand
Plan
Solve
Check

Read to Understand

- **What information is given?**
- **How can you sequence the information?**

Plan

- **What strategy can you use to solve the problem?**
  You can work backward to help you solve the problem.

Solve

- **How can you use the strategy to solve the problem?**
  Work backward from the number of T-shirts Chad has now.

  Begin with the final number of T-shirts. Add the number of T-shirts Chad gave away.

19	+	5	=	24
↑		↑		↑
final number of T-shirts		T-shirts given away		T-shirts in 4 packs

Then divide to find the number of T-shirts in each pack.

24	÷	4	=	6
↑		↑		↑
T-shirts in 4 packs		number of packs		number in each pack

So, each pack had 6 T-shirts.

Check

- **How can you check your answer?**

Guided Problem Solving

Read to Understand
Plan
Solve
Check

1. Mac collects Matchbox® cars. He bought 4 packs of cars. Then his friend gave him 9 cars. Now Mac has 21 cars. How many cars are in each pack?

   Work backward from the total number of cars Mac has now.

   First, subtract the cars Mac's friend gave him.

21	−	9	=	12
↑		↑		↑
total cars		cars given to Mac		cars in 4 packs

   Then, divide to find the number of cars in each pack.

12	÷	4	=	■
↑		↑		↑
cars in 4 packs		number of packs		number in each pack

2. **What if** Mac bought 8 packs of cars and then his friend gave him 3 cars? If Mac has 19 cars now, how many cars are in each pack?

3. Ryan collects model cars. He gave half of his model car collection to a friend. Then he bought 6 more cars. Now Ryan has 14 cars. How many cars did Ryan have to start?

Problem Solving Strategy Practice

USE DATA For 4–6, use the table. Work backward to solve.

4. After lunch, 16 bracelets were sold. Then 2 bracelets were returned. How many bracelets were sold before lunch?

5. During the day, 9 customers each bought the same number of key chains. Then 9 more key chains were sold. How many key chains did each of the 9 customers buy?

6. WRITE Math First, Jan bought half of the total number of one item shown in the table. Then she bought 2 craft books. She bought 12 items in all. Which item did she buy first? **Explain.**

Items Sold in One Day

Item	Number
bracelets	25
craft books	30
key chains	45
model car kits	20

Mixed Strategy Practice

USE DATA For 7–10, use the table.

7. Tim and Erica have eaten at all of the restaurants. Tim's restaurants are all different from Erica's. He has eaten at 10 more of the restaurants than Erica. How many restaurants has Tim eaten at?

8. ***FAST FACT*** The Mall of America is the largest mall in the United States. Suppose there are 6 food stores on each level of the mall. How many levels would there be?

9. **Pose a Problem** Look back at Problem 8. Write a similar problem by using a different fact from the table and changing the number on each level.

10. **Open-Ended** Mark visited every food store. He visited the same number of food stores each day. List 3 different ways he could have done this.

11. Rose saw a movie, shopped in a store, and ate at a restaurant. She did not see the movie first. She shopped last. In what order did Rose do these activities?

12. Mr. Acosta went to the same number of stores each day for 4 days. On the fifth day, he went to 10 stores. He visited 34 stores in all. How many stores did he visit each of the 4 days?

Choose a STRATEGY

- Draw a Diagram or Picture
- Make a Model or Act It Out
- Make an Organized List
- Look for a Pattern
- Make a Table or Graph
- Guess and Check
- Work Backward
- Solve a Simpler Problem
- Write an Equation
- Use Logical Reasoning

Mall of America Facts	
Stores	520
Restaurants	50
Food stores	36
Movie screens	14

CHALLENGE YOURSELF

A store sells pants for $12. The store also gives shoppers one free shirt for each $9 shirt they buy.

13. Dillon paid $30 for pants and shirts. How many pairs of pants did he buy? How many shirts did he get?

14. Pants usually sell for $16. Anna saved a total of $8 on her pants. She received 3 free shirts. How much did Anna spend?

LESSON 4

Divide by 9 and 10

OBJECTIVE: Divide by 9 and 10.

Quick Review

1. 2 × ■ = 20
2. ■ × 10 = 50
3. 9 × ■ = 36
4. ■ × 7 = 70
5. 6 × ■ = 54

Learn

PROBLEM Mateo's class goes to the aquarium. They have 45 minutes to visit 9 exhibits. How much time can they spend at each exhibit if they spend the same amount of time at each one?

▲ The Georgia Aquarium has more than 100,000 animals.

Example 1 Divide. 45 ÷ 9 = ■ $9\overline{)45}$ (quotient ■)

ONE WAY **Use repeated subtraction.**

Start with 45. Subtract 9 until you reach 0.

	45 − 9 = 36	36 − 9 = 27	27 − 9 = 18	18 − 9 = 9	9 − 9 = 0
Number of times you subtract 9:	1	2	3	4	5

You subtract 9 five times.

ANOTHER WAY **Use a related multiplication fact.**

45 ÷ 9 = ■ Think: ■ × 9 = 45
5 × 9 = 45

So, 45 ÷ 9 = 5, or $9\overline{)45}$ = 5.

So, Mateo's class can spend 5 minutes at each exhibit.

Example 2 Divide. 40 ÷ 10 = ■

ONE WAY **Use repeated subtraction.**

Start with 40. Subtract 10 until you reach 0.

40 − 10 = 30	30 − 10 = 20	20 − 10 = 10	10 − 10 = 0
1	2	3	4

Count the number of times you subtract 10. You subtract 10 four times.

ANOTHER WAY **Use a related multiplication fact.**

40 ÷ 10 = ■

Think: ■ × 10 = 40
4 × 10 = 40

So, 40 ÷ 10 = 4, or $10\overline{)40}$ = 4.

TEKS 3.4C use models to solve division problems and use number sentences to record the solutions. *also* 3.14A, 3.14C, 3.15A, 3.15B, 3.16A

Guided Practice

1. Use the related multiplication fact to find $27 \div 9$. $9 \times 3 = 27$

Find each quotient.

2. $80 \div 10 = ■$
3. $36 \div 9 = ■$
4. $63 \div 9 = ■$
5. $30 \div 10 = ■$
6. TALK Math **Explain** how to use repeated subtraction to find $60 \div 10$.

Independent Practice and Problem Solving

Find each quotient.

7. $18 \div 9 = ■$
8. $■ = 30 \div 5$
9. $50 \div 10 = ■$
10. $■ = 81 \div 9$
11. $■ = 20 \div 10$
12. $9 \div 9 = ■$
13. $■ = 12 \div 6$
14. $28 \div 7 = ■$
15. $4\overline{)32}$
16. $9\overline{)72}$
17. $10\overline{)10}$
18. $8\overline{)56}$

Algebra Copy and complete each table.

19.

÷	36	45	54	63
9	■	■	■	■

20.

÷	70	80	90	100
10	■	■	■	■

USE DATA For 21–23, use the table.

21. Which jellyfish is four times the length of the sea wasp?
22. A marlin can be 87 inches long. This is 6 inches more than 9 times the length of which jellyfish?
23. WRITE Math **What's the Question?** A striped bass is 45 inches long. The answer is sea wasp. What is the question?

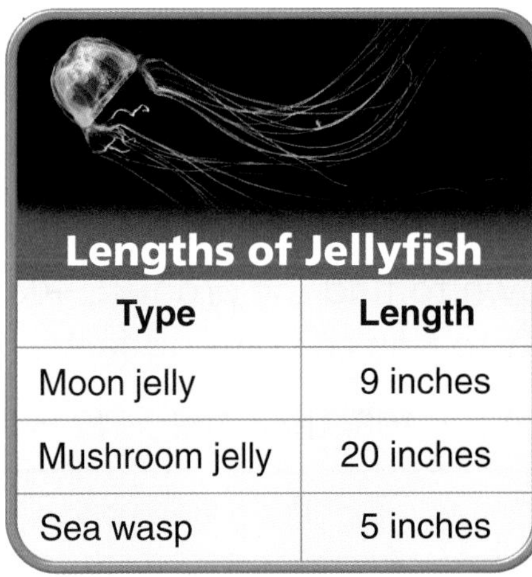

Lengths of Jellyfish

Type	Length
Moon jelly	9 inches
Mushroom jelly	20 inches
Sea wasp	5 inches

Mixed Review and TAKS Prep

24. What is the quotient? $45 \div 5 = ■$ (TEKS 3.4C, p. 320)
25. Compare the numbers. Write <, >, or =. 3,346 ● 3,374 (TEKS 3.1B, p. 30)
26. **TAKS Prep** Fifty people form 10 equal lines. How many people are in each line? (Obj. 1)

A 500 **B** 50 **C** 5 **D** 1

LESSON 5

Divide by 11 and 12

OBJECTIVE: Divide by 11 and 12.

Quick Review

1. 12 × ■ = 24
2. ■ × 11 = 55
3. 2 × ■ = 22
4. ■ × 12 = 72
5. 10 × ■ = 120

Learn

PROBLEM Kenny collects model cars. Each shelf in his room can hold 11 cars. Kenny has 44 cars. How many shelves will Kenny use to display his cars?

Example 1 **Divide.** 44 ÷ 11 = ■

Think of a related multiplication fact.

Think: ■ × 11 = 44

- Find the factor 11 in the top row.
- Look down to find the product, 44.
- Look left to find the missing factor, 4.

Since 4 × 11 = 44, then 44 ÷ 11 = 4.

So, Kenny will use 4 shelves.

Example 2 **Divide.** 108 ÷ 12 = ■

Think of a related multiplication fact.

Think: ■ × 12 = 108

- Find the factor 12 in the top row.
- Look down to find the product, 108.
- Look left to find the missing factor, 9.

Since 9 × 12 = 108, then 108 ÷ 12 = 9.

×	0	1	2	3	4	5	6	7	8	9	10	11	12
0	0	0	0	0	0	0	0	0	0	0	0	0	0
1	0	1	2	3	4	5	6	7	8	9	10	11	12
2	0	2	4	6	8	10	12	14	16	18	20	22	24
3	0	3	6	9	12	15	18	21	24	27	30	33	36
4	0	4	8	12	16	20	24	28	32	36	40	44	48
5	0	5	10	15	20	25	30	35	40	45	50	55	60
6	0	6	12	18	24	30	36	42	48	54	60	66	72
7	0	7	14	21	28	35	42	49	56	63	70	77	84
8	0	8	16	24	32	40	48	56	64	72	80	88	96
9	0	9	18	27	36	45	54	63	72	81	90	99	108
10	0	10	20	30	40	50	60	70	80	90	100	110	120
11	0	11	22	33	44	55	66	77	88	99	110	121	132
12	0	12	24	36	48	60	72	84	96	108	120	132	144

Guided Practice

1. Use the multiplication table to find 88 ÷ 11.

Find each missing factor and quotient.

2. 11 × ■ = 55 55 ÷ 11 = ■
3. 12 × ■ = 24 24 ÷ 12 = ■
4. 12 × ■ = 48 48 ÷ 12 = ■
5. 11 × ■ = 99 99 ÷ 11 = ■
6. TALK Math **Explain** how to use multiplication to find 84 ÷ 12 = ■.

TEKS 3.4C use models to solve division problems and use number sentences to record the solutions. *also* 3.14A, 3.15A, 3.15B, 3.16A

Independent Practice and Problem Solving

Find each missing factor and quotient.

7. $11 \times ■ = 77$ $77 \div 11 = ■$
8. $11 \times ■ = 33$ $33 \div 11 = ■$
9. $12 \times ■ = 96$ $96 \div 12 = ■$
10. $12 \times ■ = 132$ $132 \div 12 = ■$

Find each quotient.

11. $22 \div 11 = ■$
12. $■ = 49 \div 7$
13. $120 \div 12 = ■$
14. $■ = 16 \div 4$
15. $■ = 35 \div 5$
16. $144 \div 12 = ■$
17. $■ = 54 \div 9$
18. $66 \div 11 = ■$
19. $27 \div 3 = ■$
20. $■ = 11 \div 11$
21. $■ = 48 \div 6$
22. $60 \div 12 = ■$
23. $12\overline{)36}$
24. $10\overline{)50}$
25. $11\overline{)132}$
26. $8\overline{)56}$

Algebra Copy and complete each table.

27.

÷	72	84	96	108
12	■	■	■	■

28.

÷	88	99	110	121
11	■	■	■	■

USE DATA For 29–31, use the table.

Model Car Prices

Type	Cost
1932 Ford Phaeton	$12
1958 Triumph TR	$11
1951 Chevy Bel Air	$10

29. Mr. Jacob spent $55 on 5 of the same type of car. What type did he buy?

30. **Reasoning** Bob bought 2 Ford Phaetons and 3 of another type of car. He spent $54 in all. What was the other type of car Bob bought? **Explain.**

31. **WRITE Math** Jeff has $36. His favorite model car is the Ford Phaeton. How many Ford Phaetons can Jeff buy? **Explain.**

Mixed Review and TAKS Prep

32. Vinny has 12 model trains on each of 4 tracks. How many model trains does Vinny have in all? (TEKS 3.4B, p. 260)

33. What are the missing numbers in the pattern? (TEKS 3.6A, p. 182)

    433, 438, 443, 448, ■, 458, ■

34. **TAKS Prep** There are 72 cars at a car show. There are 12 cars in each show area. How many show areas are there? (Obj. 1)

    A 4 **B** 6 **C** 60 **D** 84

Extra Practice on page 356, Set D

ALGEBRA

Practice the Facts

OBJECTIVE: Practice division facts through 12 using various strategies.

Quick Review

1. ■ × 6 = 36
2. 4 × ■ = 44
3. 9 × ■ = 72
4. ■ × 7 = 28
5. 8 × ■ = 24

Learn

PROBLEM Kareem visited his grandfather in Texas for the summer. They went hiking in the mountains 21 times in 7 weeks. They hiked the same number of times each week. How many times did they go hiking each week?

▲ The Davis Mountains are the largest mountain chain in the state of Texas.

Divide. 21 ÷ 7 = ■

A Use counters.

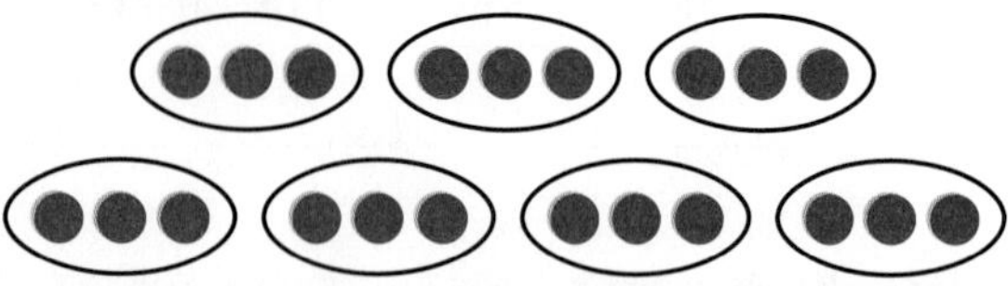

There are 3 counters in each of 7 groups.

So, 21 ÷ 7 = 3.

B Use a fact family.

Fact Family for 3, 7, and 21

factor		factor		product	dividend		divisor		quotient
3	×	7	=	21	21	÷	7	=	3
7	×	3	=	21	21	÷	3	=	7

So, 21 ÷ 7 = 3.

C Use repeated subtraction.

$$\begin{array}{r}21\\-\ 7\\\hline 14\end{array}\quad\rightarrow\quad\begin{array}{r}14\\-\ 7\\\hline 7\end{array}\quad\rightarrow\quad\begin{array}{r}7\\-7\\\hline 0\end{array}$$

1 2 3

You subtract 7 three times.

D Use an array.

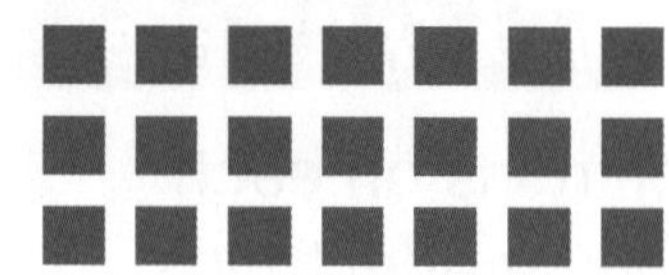

There are 3 rows of 7 tiles.
Since 3 × 7 = 21, then 21 ÷ 7 = 3.

So, Kareem and his grandfather went hiking 3 times each week.

TEKS 3.4C use models to solve division problems and use number sentences to record the solutions. *also* **3.6C, 3.14A, 3.14D, 3.15A, 3.15B**

E **Use a multiplication table.**

Think of a related multiplication fact.

Think: $7 \times \square = 21$

Find the row for the factor 7.
Look right to find the product, 21.
Look up to find the missing factor, 3.

Since $7 \times 3 = 21$, then $21 \div 7 = 3$.

×	0	1	2	3	4	5	6	7	8	9	10	11	12
0	0	0	0	0	0	0	0	0	0	0	0	0	0
1	0	1	2	3	4	5	6	7	8	9	10	11	12
2	0	2	4	6	8	10	12	14	16	18	20	22	24
3	0	3	6	9	12	15	18	21	24	27	30	33	36
4	0	4	8	12	16	20	24	28	32	36	40	44	48
5	0	5	10	15	20	25	30	35	40	45	50	55	60
6	0	6	12	18	24	30	36	42	48	54	60	66	72
7	0	7	14	21	28	35	42	49	56	63	70	77	84
8	0	8	16	24	32	40	48	56	64	72	80	88	96
9	0	9	18	27	36	45	54	63	72	81	90	99	108
10	0	10	20	30	40	50	60	70	80	90	100	110	120
11	0	11	22	33	44	55	66	77	88	99	110	121	132
12	0	12	24	36	48	60	72	84	96	108	120	132	144

Guided Practice

1. Use the array to find $24 \div 12$.

Write a division sentence for each.

2.

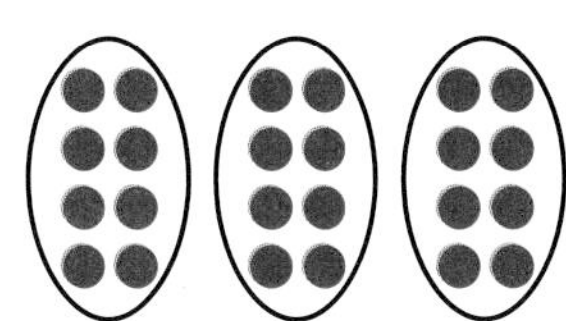

3.

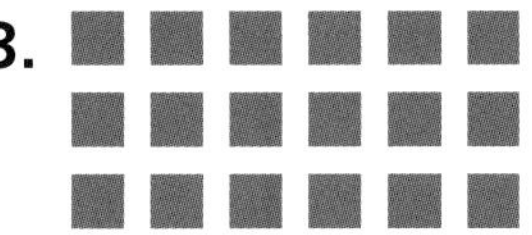

✓4. $36 - 12 = 24$; $24 - 12 = 12$; $12 - 12 = 0$

Use models to find each missing factor and quotient.

5. $9 \times \square = 63$ $\quad 63 \div 9 = \square$

✓6. $6 \times \square = 36$ $\quad 36 \div 6 = \square$

7. $10 \times \square = 80$ $\quad 80 \div 10 = \square$

8. $8 \times \square = 72$ $\quad 72 \div 8 = \square$

9. TALK Math **Explain** how to find $108 \div 9$ two different ways.

Independent Practice and Problem Solving

Write a division sentence for each.

10.

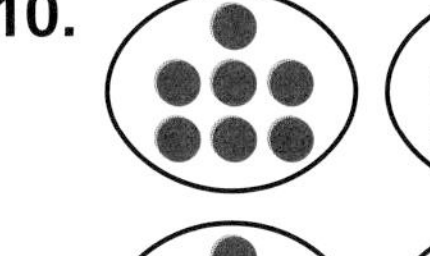

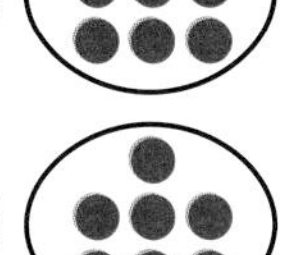

11. $33 - 11 = 22$; $22 - 11 = 11$; $11 - 11 = 0$

12.

Extra Practice on page 356, Set E

Use models to find each missing factor and quotient.

13. $11 \times ■ = 66$ $66 \div 11 = ■$ **14.** $9 \times ■ = 45$ $45 \div 9 = ■$

15. $12 \times ■ = 132$ $132 \div 12 = ■$ **16.** $10 \times ■ = 100$ $100 \div 10 = ■$

Find each quotient.

17. $80 \div 8 = ■$ **18.** $■ = 30 \div 6$ **19.** $63 \div 7 = ■$ **20.** $■ = 32 \div 4$

21. $45 \div 5 = ■$ **22.** $50 \div 10 = ■$ **23.** $■ = 88 \div 11$ **24.** $27 \div 9 = ■$

25. $■ = 96 \div 12$ **26.** $■ = 121 \div 11$ **27.** $10 \div 2 = ■$ **28.** $48 \div 6 = ■$

29. $7\overline{)42}$ **30.** $3\overline{)21}$ **31.** $8\overline{)56}$ **32.** $10\overline{)60}$

Compare. Write <, >, or = for each ●.

33. $49 \div 7$ ● $35 \div 5$ **34.** $100 - 16$ ● 9×9 **35.** $96 \div 8$ ● $4 + 9$

36. $49 + 12$ ● 11×6 **37.** $120 \div 12$ ● $23 - 13$ **38.** 6×7 ● 4×10

Write +, −, ×, or ÷ for each ●.

39. 3 ● 3 = $72 \div 8$ **40.** 9 ● 2 = $63 \div 9$ **41.** 10×3 = 6 ● 5

USE DATA For 42–44, use the table.

42. Hannah likes to visit the Davis Mountains. During her visits, she saw 4 equal groups of deer eating grass. How many deer were in each group?

43. The number of horned lizards Hannah saw is 9 times the number Manuel saw during his visits. How many horned lizards did Manuel see?

44. WRITE Math When Todd visited the Davis Mountains, he saw half as many elk and half as many deer as Hannah saw. How many elk and deer did Todd see in all? **Explain** your answer.

Animals Hannah Saw in the Davis Mountains

Animal	Number
Rattlesnakes	14
Deer	12
Horned lizards	45
Quails	42
Elk	18

45. Reasoning Hannah took 60 photos of animals. She put 4 photos in a picture frame and put the rest in her photo album. Each page in the album holds 8 photos. How many pages did Hannah fill? **Explain.**

CD ROM Technology
Use Harcourt Mega Math, The Number Games, *Up, Up, and Array*, Levels H, T.

Mixed Review and TAKS Prep

46. Guadalupe Peak is a mountain in Texas. It is 8,749 feet high. Write 8,749 in expanded form. (TEKS 3.1A, p. 12)

47. TAKS Prep There are 80 miles of trails on a mountain. Each trail is 10 miles long. How many trails are there? (Obj. 1)

A 8 **B** 10 **C** 70 **D** 90

48. Gabe walked 3 miles each day for a total of 27 miles. What multiplication fact can you use to find the number of days Gabe walked? Solve. (TEKS 3.6C, p. 322)

49. TAKS Prep What is $42 \div 7$? (Obj. 1)

A 8 **B** 7 **C** 6 **D** 5

Problem Solving and Reasoning

MENTAL MATH You can use *near facts* to help you find quotients for division problems that do not come out evenly.

Example Rosa wants to share 25 cookies equally among 4 friends. How many cookies should each friend get?

Divide. $25 \div 4 = \blacksquare$

To find the quotient, look for a *near fact*. A near fact for this problem is a multiplication fact with 4 as a factor and a product as close to 25 as possible without going over.

Think: $4 \times 5 = 20$ (too low)
$4 \times 6 = 24$ (close)
$4 \times 7 = 28$ (too high)

Since $4 \times 6 = 24$ gives the closest product without going over, the quotient is 6. Since $25 - 24 = 1$, 1 is left over.

So, each friend should get 6 cookies. There will be 1 cookie left over.

Use near facts to solve. Write the near fact you used.

1. Mrs. Hart wants to put 33 desks in 4 equal rows. How many desks will be in each row? How many desks will be left?
2. Keisha has 47 plates. She sets tables with 5 plates each. How many tables can she set? How many plates will she have left over?

Extra Practice

Set A Find each missing factor and quotient. (pp. 340–341)

1. $6 \times ■ = 36$ $\quad 36 \div 6 = ■$
2. $6 \times ■ = 54$ $\quad 54 \div 6 = ■$

Find each quotient.

3. $12 \div 6 = ■$
4. $■ = 42 \div 6$
5. $30 \div 6 = ■$
6. $■ = 24 \div 6$
7. $6\overline{)48}$
8. $6\overline{)6}$
9. $6\overline{)60}$
10. $6\overline{)18}$

Set B Find each missing factor and quotient. (pp. 342–343)

1. $7 \times ■ = 28$ $\quad 28 \div 7 = ■$
2. $8 \times ■ = 40$ $\quad 40 \div 8 = ■$

Find each quotient.

3. $■ = 56 \div 7$
4. $16 \div 8 = ■$
5. $■ = 72 \div 8$
6. $21 \div 7 = ■$
7. $8\overline{)48}$
8. $7\overline{)35}$
9. $8\overline{)32}$
10. $7\overline{)63}$

Set C Find each quotient. (pp. 348–349)

1. $70 \div 10 = ■$
2. $■ = 27 \div 9$
3. $■ = 50 \div 10$
4. $81 \div 9 = ■$
5. $9\overline{)54}$
6. $10\overline{)20}$
7. $10\overline{)100}$
8. $9\overline{)36}$

Set D Find each quotient. (pp. 350–351)

1. $■ = 55 \div 11$
2. $60 \div 12 = ■$
3. $24 \div 12 = ■$
4. $■ = 88 \div 11$
5. $12\overline{)108}$
6. $11\overline{)22}$
7. $11\overline{)110}$
8. $12\overline{)84}$
9. Mr. Jones divided 33 children into 11 equal groups. How many children were in each group?
10. Marie has 72 CDs. She has them arranged in stacks of 12. How many stacks of CDs does she have?

Set E Write a division sentence for each. (pp. 352–355)

1. $\begin{array}{r} 24 \\ -\ 8 \\ \hline 16 \end{array} \nearrow \begin{array}{r} 16 \\ -\ 8 \\ \hline 8 \end{array} \nearrow \begin{array}{r} 8 \\ -\ 8 \\ \hline 0 \end{array}$

2. 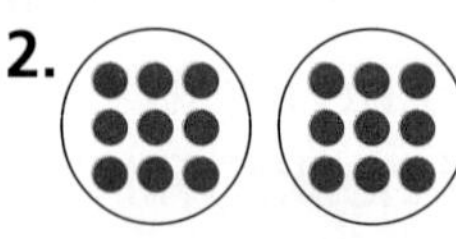

3. 

Technology
Use Harcourt Mega Math, The Number Games, *Up, Up, and Array*, Levels F, G, H.

TECHNOLOGY CONNECTION

Calculator: Division Facts (TEKS 3.4C, 3.14D, 3.15A)

Use a Calculator for Division

Ms. Andrews bought 56 new books for her class library. There are 7 shelves on her bookshelf. If she puts the same number of books on each shelf, how many will go on each shelf?

Write a number sentence for the word problem. $56 \div 7 = \blacksquare$

Use a calculator to solve.

    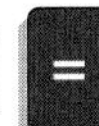 

So, Ms. Andrews can put 8 books on each shelf.

What if Ms. Andrews bought 58 books? How many books would go on each shelf? How many would be left over?

A calculator gives the remainder as a decimal. A remainder is the amount left over when a number cannot be divided evenly.

To find out how many books are left over, use a *near fact*.

So, Ms. Andrews can put 8 books on each shelf and have 2 left over.

Try It

Use a calculator to divide.

1. $63 \div 7 = \blacksquare$ **2.** $60 \div 12 = \blacksquare$ **3.** $54 \div 9 = \blacksquare$ **4.** $48 \div 6 = \blacksquare$

Use a calculator to divide. Then use a *near fact* to find the remainder.

5. $32 \div 5 = \blacksquare$ remainder $\blacksquare$

6. $65 \div 9 = \blacksquare$ remainder $\blacksquare$

7. $76 \div 8 = \blacksquare$ remainder $\blacksquare$

8. $68 \div 11 = \blacksquare$ remainder $\blacksquare$

 Chapter 15 Review/Test

Check Concepts

Write a division sentence for each. (TEKS 3.4C, pp. 352–355)

1. 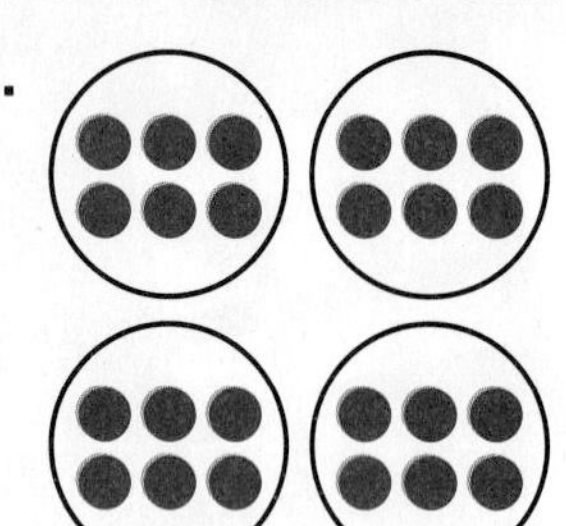

2. 

3. 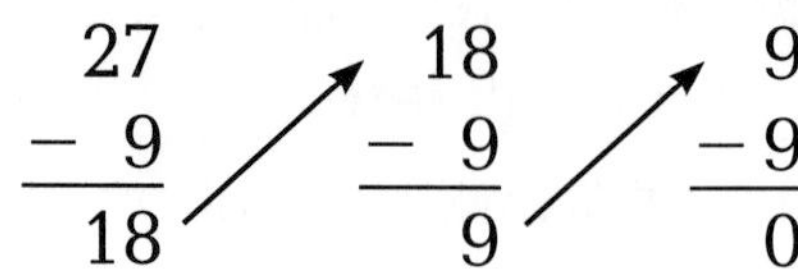

Check Skills

Find each missing factor and quotient. (TEKS 3.4C, pp. 340–341, 342–343, 348–349, 350–351, 352–355)

4. $6 \times ■ = 48$ $48 \div 6 = ■$
5. $10 \times ■ = 80$ $80 \div 10 = ■$
6. $12 \times ■ = 84$ $84 \div 12 = ■$
7. $5 \times ■ = 35$ $35 \div 5 = ■$

Find each quotient. (TEKS 3.4C, pp. 340–341, 342–343, 348–349, 350–351, 352–355)

8. $56 \div 7 = ■$
9. $27 \div 9 = ■$
10. $20 \div 10 = ■$
11. $12 \div 4 = ■$
12. $110 \div 11 = ■$
13. $■ = 32 \div 8$
14. $18 \div 3 = ■$
15. $0 \div 2 = ■$
16. $36 \div 6 = ■$
17. $28 \div 4 = ■$
18. $72 \div 12 = ■$
19. $■ = 90 \div 10$
20. $■ = 9 \div 9$
21. $64 \div 8 = ■$
22. $54 \div 6 = ■$
23. $5 \div 1 = ■$
24. $7\overline{)49}$
25. $9\overline{)36}$
26. $11\overline{)77}$
27. $5\overline{)40}$

Check Problem Solving

Solve. (TEKS 3.14C, pp. 344–347)

28. Tim bought 3 packs of baseball cards. He gave 4 cards to his friend. Now Tim has 14 cards. How many cards were in each pack?

29. Mary gave half of her markers to a friend. Then she bought 8 more markers. Now Mary has 21 markers. How many markers did she have to start?

30. WRITE Math Katrina baked 4 batches of cookies with the same amount of cookies in each batch. The extra cookie dough made 6 more cookies. Katrina made 54 cookies in all. How many cookies were in each batch? **Explain** how you know.

GO ONLINE **Technology** Use *Online Assessment.*

Enrich • What's in a Shape?

Hide and Seek

Each shape hides a number. Seek out the number that each shape stands for. Find the value of each shape.

♥ × ♥ = 25   20 ÷ ⬟ = ♥

Count

Step 1	Solve the first equation. ♥ × ♥ = 25, so a number times itself is 25.
Step 2	Find the value. Since 5 × 5 = 25, then the value of ♥ is 5.
Step 3	Use the value of ♥ to solve the second equation. 20 ÷ ⬟ = ♥, so 20 ÷ ⬟ = 5
Step 4	Find the value. Since 20 ÷ 4 = 5, then the value of ⬟ is 4.

So, ♥ = 5 and ⬟ = 4.

Hide

Find the value of each shape.

1. 9 ÷ ▲ = ▲   **2.** 36 ÷ ● = ●   **3.** 4 ÷ ◆ = ◆

4. ▲ × ● = 18   **5.** ● × ◆ = ■   **6.** ■ ÷ ▲ = ⬟

7. ♥ × 1 = ♥   **8.** 30 ÷ ♥ = ●   **9.** ⬟ × ▲ = ■

Seek

WRITE Math Tell what values the shapes in this equation could have. **Explain** how you know. ⏷ × ⬢ = 18

Unit Review/Test
Chapters 13–15

Multiple Choice

1. Which division sentence is represented by this array? (TAKS Obj. 1)

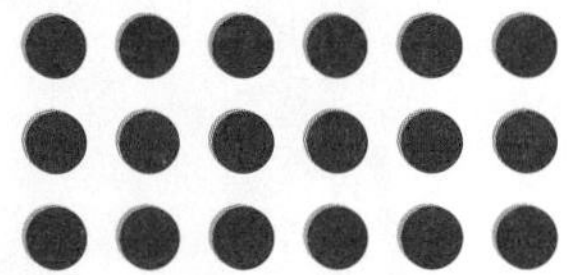

A $18 \div 2 = 9$

B $18 \div 3 = 6$

C $24 \div 3 = 8$

D $24 \div 6 = 4$

2. Which number makes this number sentence true? (TAKS Obj. 2)

$$54 \div \blacksquare = 9$$

F 8

G 7

H 6

J 5

3. Which number sentence is in the same fact family as $32 \div 8 = 4$? (TAKS Obj. 2)

A $8 \times 5 = 40$

B $4 \times 8 = 32$

C $24 \div 8 = 3$

D $8 \div 4 = 2$

4. Luis has 20 model cars. He puts 5 cars on each shelf. How many shelves does he use? (TAKS Obj. 1)

F 2

G 3

H 4

J 5

5. A pet shop has 108 goldfish. There are 12 goldfish in each fish tank. How many fish tanks have goldfish? (TAKS Obj. 1)

A 6

B 7

C 8

D 9

6. Which division sentence is represented by the following? (TAKS Obj. 1)

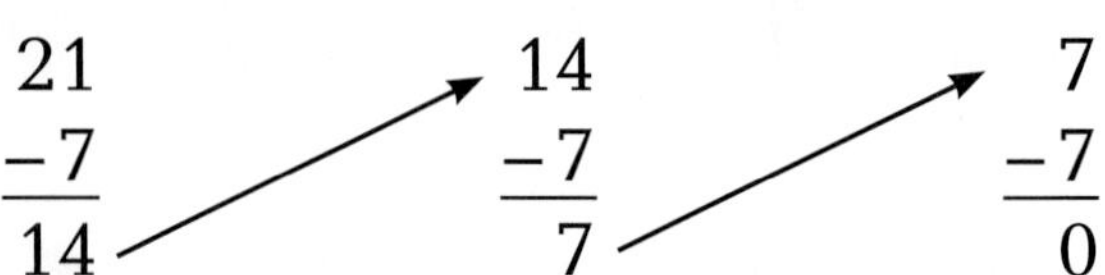

F $7 \div 1 = 7$

G $14 \div 2 = 7$

H $28 \div 7 = 4$

J $21 \div 7 = 3$

7. Which number is missing from the table? (TAKS Obj. 1)

÷	16	■	24	28
4	4	5	6	7

A 21

B 20

C 19

D 18

8. Melissa spent $40 on tickets to the school play. She bought 8 tickets. Each ticket cost the same amount. What was the cost of each ticket? (TAKS Obj. 1)

F $8

G $6

H $5

J Not here

9. The school store has 80 pencils in boxes. Each box holds 10 pencils. How many boxes of pencils does the store have? (TAKS Obj. 1)

A 7

B 8

C 9

D 10

Short Response

10. What number makes this number sentence true? (TAKS Obj. 2)

$$77 \div \blacksquare = 7$$

11. Sammy picked 24 apples and gave the same number of apples to each of 3 friends. How many apples did he give to each friend? (TAKS Obj. 1)

12. Write a division sentence for the array. (TAKS Obj. 1)

Extended Response

13. Darrin picked 63 strawberries. He wants to divide them equally among 9 friends. **Explain** how to use repeated subtraction to find how many strawberries Darrin will give to each of his friends. (TAKS Obj. 1)

14. Aimee baked 36 cookies. She wants to divide them equally among 6 bags. How many cookies will go in each bag? **Explain** how to use a related multiplication fact to find the answer. (TAKS Obj. 2)

Problem Solving

The Wheel Is a Big Deal

The first pedaled bicycle was invented in Scotland in 1839. Today, bicycles are used all over the world.

Around the Wheel

Think about the wheel. Without it, almost no one could travel anywhere. Buses, trains, cars, skateboards, and even planes and space shuttles use wheels.

FACT·ACTIVITY

Vehicles with Different Numbers of Wheels

	Vehicle	Number of Wheels
	unicycle	1
	bicycle	2
	tricycle	3
	car	4
	space shuttle	6
	tractor trailer	18

School teams are making models of vehicles with a given number of wheels. Use the table to answer the questions.

1. Team A has 22 wheels. How many bicycles can they make?
2. Team B has 48 wheels. How many space shuttles can they make?
3. Team A wants to make cars instead of bicycles. How many cars can they make? What can they make with the extra wheels?
4. Make your own vehicle.
   - Invent a new vehicle that uses 7 wheels.
   - Draw your vehicle and name it.
   - How many of these new vehicles could you make if you had 21 wheels?

ALMANAC Fact

The Texas Department of Transportation has used old tires to build more than 2,500 miles of roads and landing strips for airplanes.

REUSING TIRED TIRES

Trucks, motorcycles, and cars all use tires. These tires are strong, but they do wear out. What happens to old tires? Ground-up tires can be used to make roads, playground surfaces, and jogging tracks. Some tires are even made into park benches and waste containers. Whole tires can be used to make playground equipment.

FACT·ACTIVITY

Climbing Wall
9 tires

Tunnel
5 tires

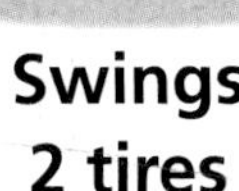

Swings
2 tires

Sandbox
1 tire

Some Texas playgrounds use tires for swings, tunnels, and climbing walls. Use the data from the playground pictures to answer the questions.

1. How many tires are needed for this playground?
2. How many climbing walls can be made from 63 tires?
3. WRITE Math Are 19 tires enough to make 4 tire tunnels? Explain.
4. It takes 6 tires to make the tunnel and sandbox combined. How many sets of these can be made from 30 tires?

UNIT 6

Geometry

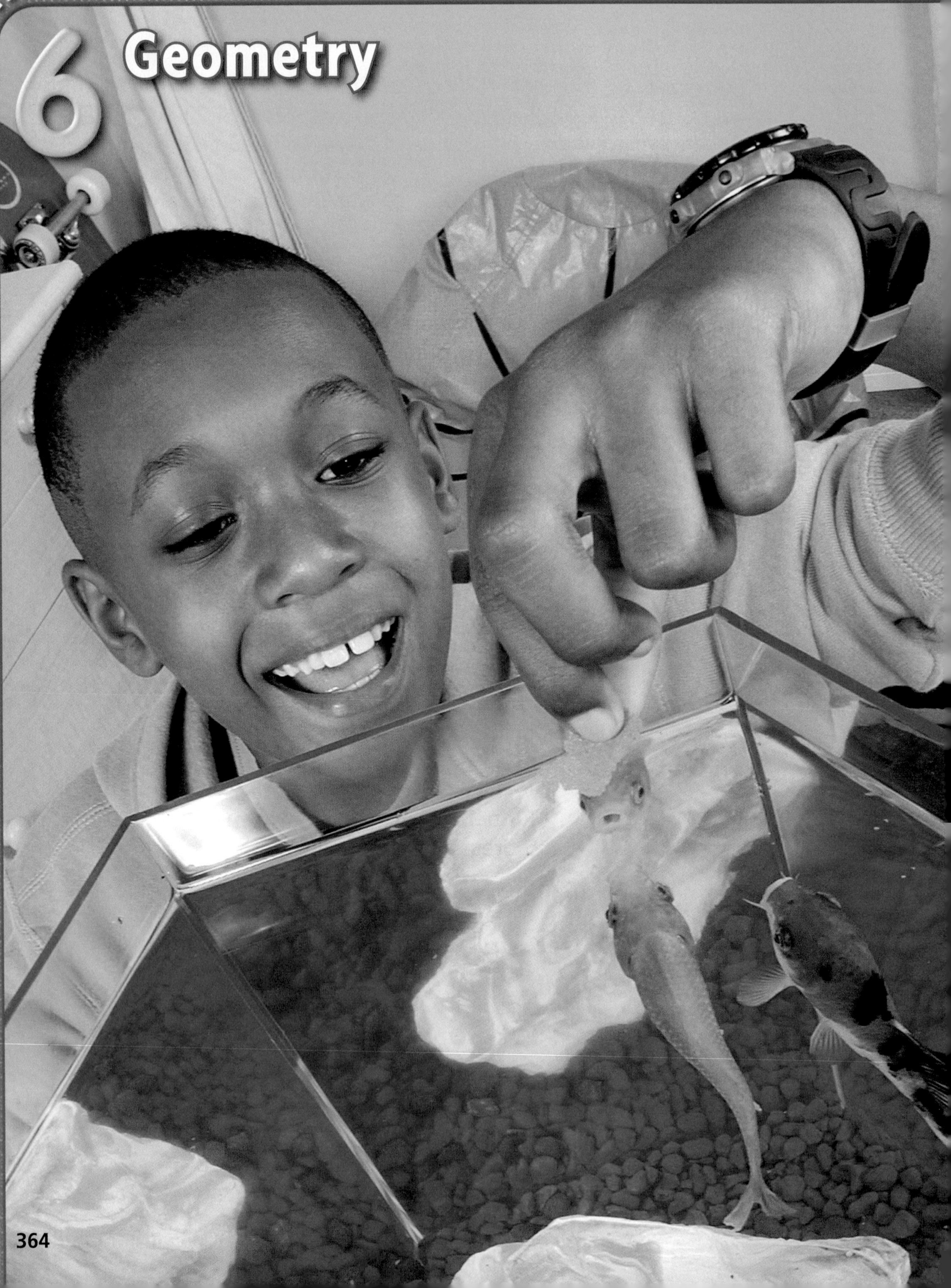

Math on Location

with **Texas Chapter Projects**

1

Fresh or saltwater aquariums of all shapes and sizes bring nature into a home or office.

2

This large tank, a rectangular prism, will hold 32,000 pounds of water. It needs thick acrylic faces!

3

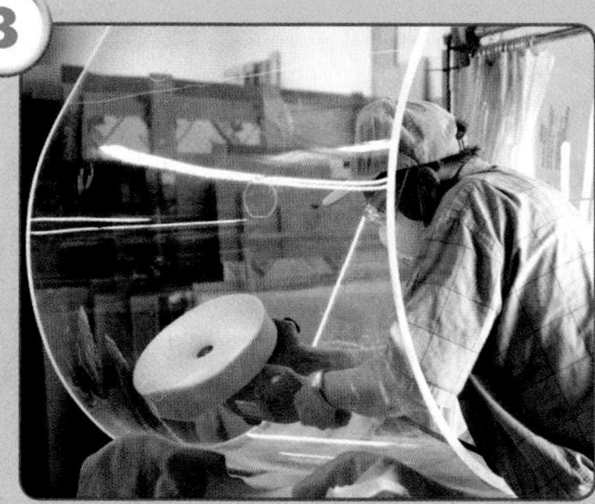

Some customers want curved-shaped aquariums like the half-cylinder surface that is being polished.

VOCABULARY POWER

TALK Math

What math ideas do you see in the **Math on Location** photographs? How many faces does the large rectangular tank have?

READ Math

REVIEW VOCABULARY You learned the words below when you learned about geometry last year. How do these words relate to **Math on Location**?

rectangle ▭

square ▢

solid figure a figure such as a sphere, a cube, a rectangular prism, a cylinder, a cone, or a pyramid

WRITE Math

Copy and complete a Degree of Meaning Grid like the one below. Use what you know about geometry.

General	Less General	Specific	More Specific
Plane figure	Lines	Line segment	Yarn
	Quadrilateral	Square	Napkin
Solid figure			

Technology
Multimedia Math Glossary link at
www.harcourtschool.com/hspmath

16 2-Dimensional Figures

The Big Idea Two-dimensional figures can be classified according to their geometric properties.

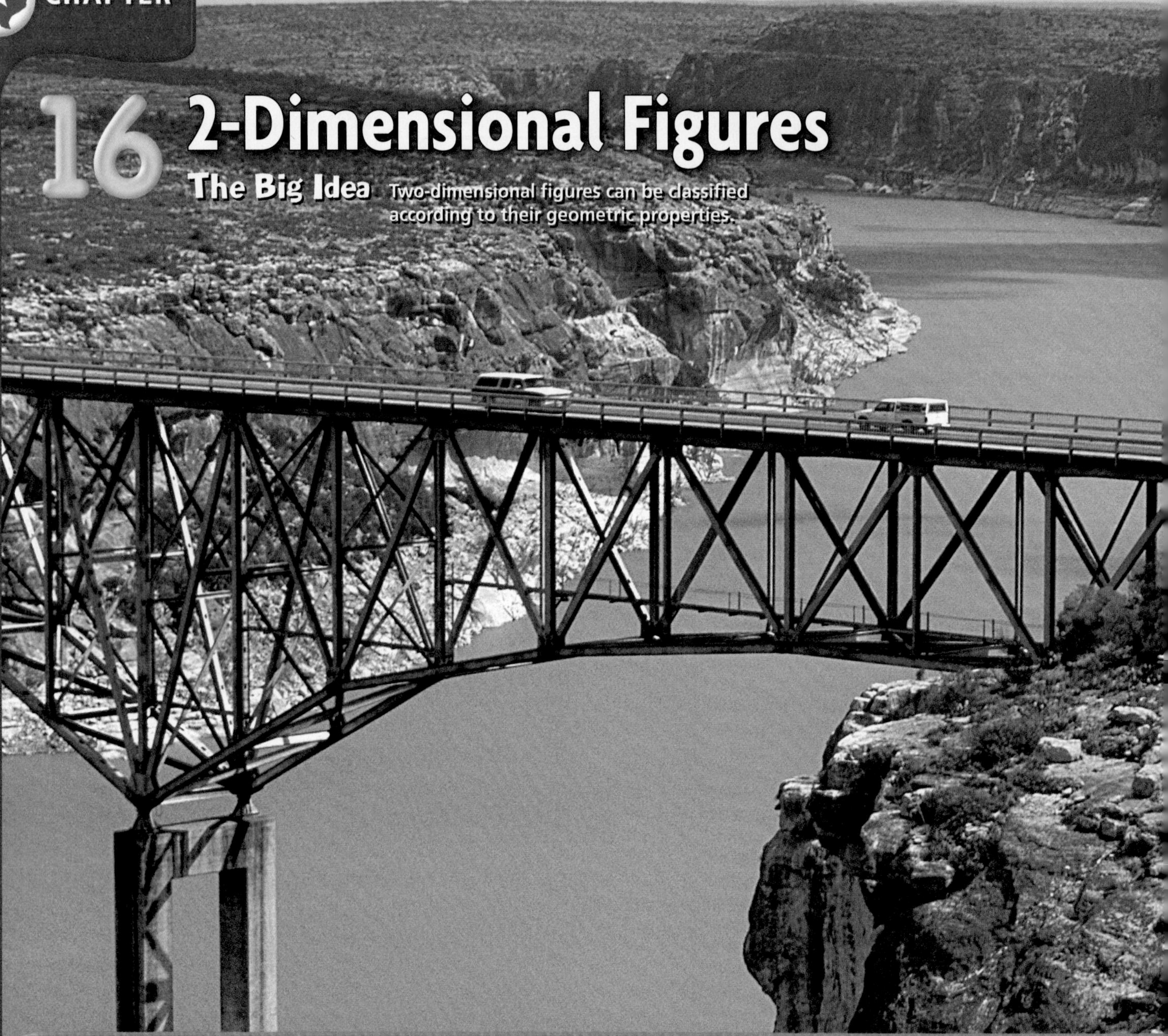

Investigate

The Pecos River Bridge is north of Del Rio, Texas. It is made of reinforced concrete and steel, and it was completed in 1959. Make a list of 2-dimensional figures you see on the bridge.

The Pecos River Bridge is the tallest highway bridge in Texas. It is 273 feet high and 1,310 feet long.

Technology
Student pages are available in the Student eBook.

Show What You Know

Check your understanding of important skills needed for success in Chapter 16.

▶ Plane Figures

Name each figure.

1. 

2. 

3. 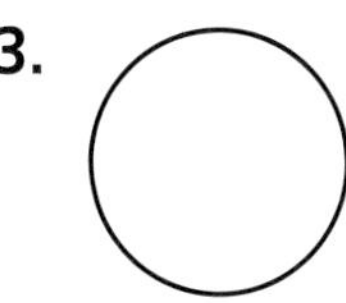

4. 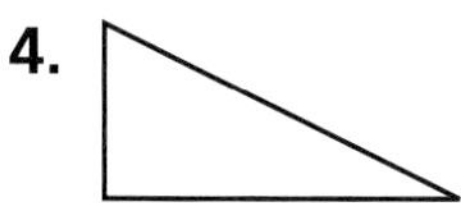

5. 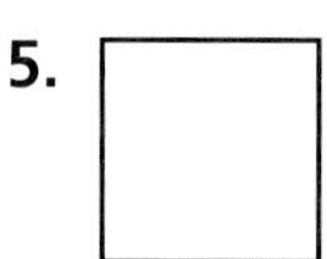

6. 

▶ Sides and Vertices

Tell the number of sides and vertices in each figure.

7.

8. 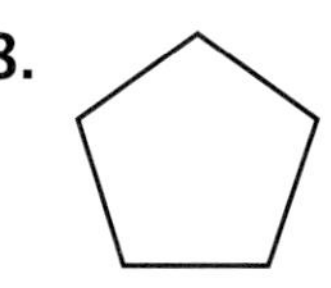

9. 

10.

VOCABULARY POWER

CHAPTER VOCABULARY

acute angle
acute triangle
angle
center
circle
diameter
equilateral triangle
hexagon
intersecting lines
isosceles triangle
line
line segment
obtuse angle
obtuse triangle
octagon
parallel lines
parallelogram
pentagon
perpendicular lines
plane figure
quadrilateral
radius
ray
rhombus
right angle
right triangle
scalene triangle
trapezoid
triangle
Two-dimensional figures
Venn diagram
vertex

WARM-UP WORDS

ray A part of a line with one endpoint, that is straight and continues in one direction

line A straight path extending in both directions with no endpoints

line segment A part of a line that includes two points, called endpoints, and all of the points between them

LESSON 1

Line Segments and Angles

OBJECTIVE: Identify points, lines, line segments, rays, and angles.

Quick Review

Write the number of sides.

1.

2.

3.

4.

5. 

Vocabulary

line **line segment** **ray** **angle** **vertex** **right angle** **acute angle** **obtuse angle**

Learn

PROBLEM Carmen drew this figure. What math words can you use to describe the figure?

The words below can help you describe figures.

line
- is straight
- continues in both directions
- does not end

line segment
- is straight
- is part of a line
- has 2 endpoints

ray
- is straight
- is part of a line
- has 1 endpoint
- continues in one direction

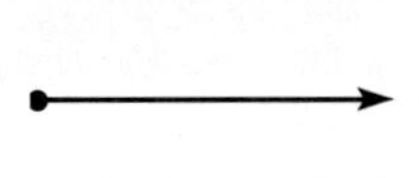

Angles

An **angle** is formed by two rays that share an endpoint. The shared endpoint is called a **vertex**. The plural of *vertex* is *vertices*.

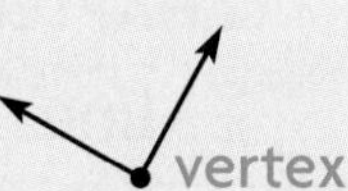

A **right angle** is a special angle that forms a square corner.

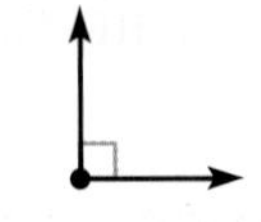

An **acute angle** is less than a right angle.

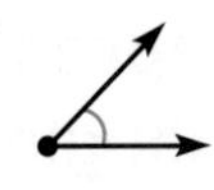

An **obtuse angle** is greater than a right angle.

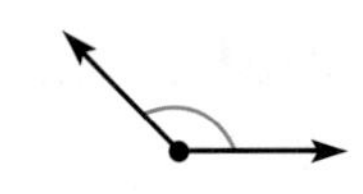

So, the 4 sides of Carmen's figure are line segments. There are 4 right angles and 4 vertices.

- How are lines and line segments alike? How are they different?

3.8 Identify, classify, and describe two- and three-dimensional geometric figures by their attributes. The student compares two-dimensional figures, three-dimensional figures, or both by their attributes using formal geometry vocabulary. *also* **3.14A, 3.14D, 3,15A, 3.15B**

Activity

Materials ■ straw, paper, pencil

- Bend a straw in half. Then open it up to model an angle.
- Use the corner of a sheet of paper to tell whether the angle formed is a right angle. The angle is a right angle if it matches the corner of the paper.
- Open and close the straw to make other angles. Trace the angles, and label them *right, acute,* or *obtuse.*

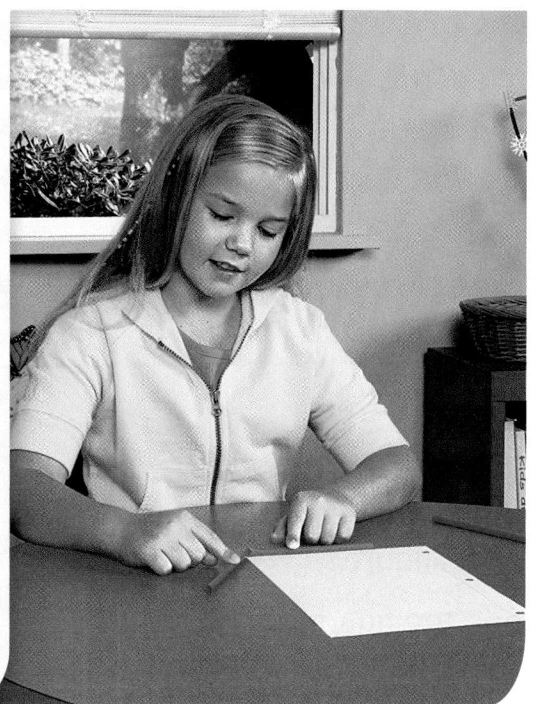

Guided Practice

1. How many line segments are in this figure? 

Tell whether each is a *line, line segment,* or *ray*.

2\.

3\.

4\.

Use the corner of a sheet of paper to tell whether each angle is *right, acute,* or *obtuse*.

5\. 

6\. 

7\. 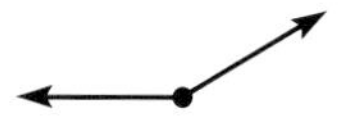

8\. 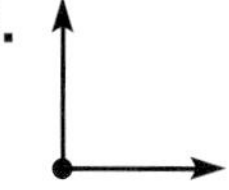

9\. TALK Math **Explain** the difference between a ray and a line segment.

Independent Practice and Problem Solving

Tell whether each is a *line*, *line segment*, or *ray*.

10.

11.

12.

Use the corner of a sheet of paper to tell whether each angle is *right*, *acute*, or *obtuse*.

13.

14.

15. 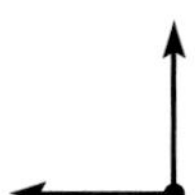

16. 

17. What math words can you use to describe this figure?

18. Katie made the figure on the right on her geoboard. How many angles does Katie's figure have? Tell how many are right, acute, and obtuse.

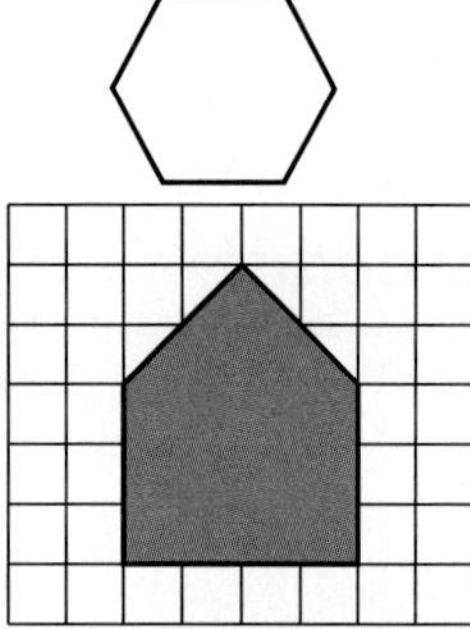

19. **FAST FACT** The first pocket watch was invented in 1524. What time is shown? What type of angle do the hands form?

20. **WRITE Math** **What's the Error?** Zoey says this angle is an acute angle. Is she correct? **Explain.**

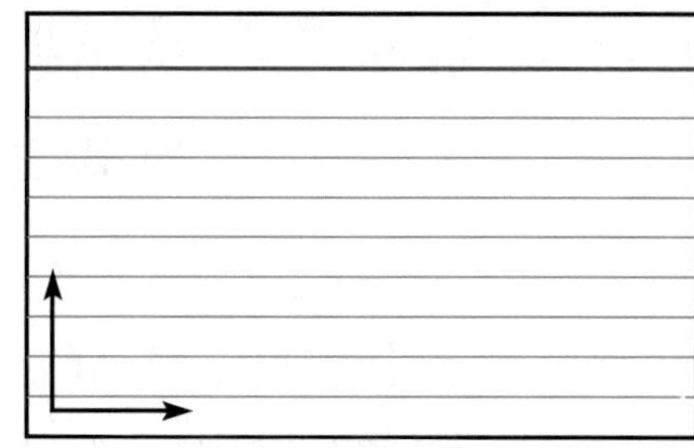

Mixed Review and TAKS Prep

21. Bruce has 8 bags of marbles. Each bag has the same number of marbles, and there are a total of 56 marbles. How many marbles are in each bag? (TEKS 3.4C, p. 342)

22. Drama club members sold 985 tickets for 3 shows. They sold 287 tickets on Thursday and 215 tickets on Friday. How many tickets did they sell on Saturday? (TEKS 3.3B, pp. 66, 92)

23. **TAKS Prep** Which shows a ray? (Obj. 3)

A

B

C

D

Extra Practice on page 388, Set A

Write to Explain

One way to explain two different things is to write about ways they are alike and ways they are different. In doing so, you compare the things.

Allen is learning about line segments, rays, and angles. He compares two angles by explaining how they are alike and how they are different.

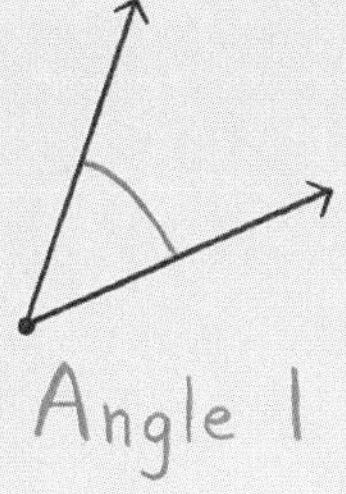

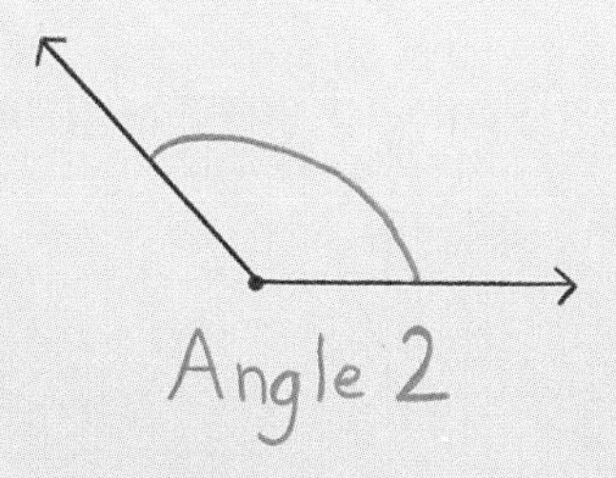

The two angles are alike. They are both made of two rays that share one endpoint.

The two angles are different. The angles are different sizes. Angle 1 is an acute angle. It is smaller than a right angle. Angle 2 is an obtuse angle. It is larger than a right angle.

Tips

To compare two drawings:

- First, describe the ways the drawings are alike.
- Then, describe the ways the drawings are different.
- Use correct definitions of math words.

Problem Solving **Write a paragraph to explain how the drawings are alike and how they are different.**

1. 

2. 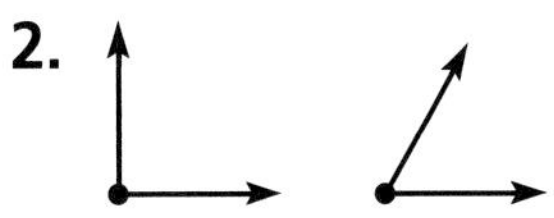

LESSON 2

Types of Lines

OBJECTIVE: Identify and classify lines as intersecting, perpendicular, or parallel.

Quick Review

Name each figure.

1.
2.
3.
4.
5.

Vocabulary

intersecting lines
perpendicular lines
parallel lines

Learn

PROBLEM What kinds of line segments are in this figure?

There are different ways to describe lines and line segments.

Types of Lines

Lines that cross are **intersecting lines**. Intersecting lines form angles.

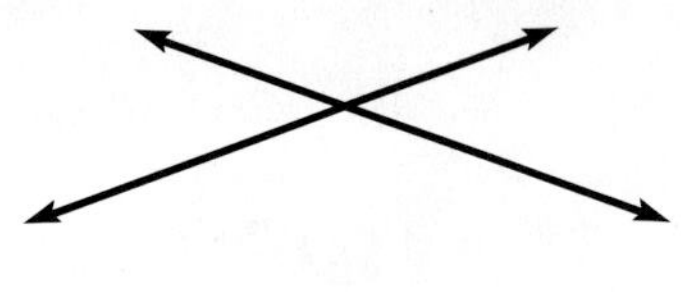

Intersecting lines that cross to form right angles are **perpendicular lines**.

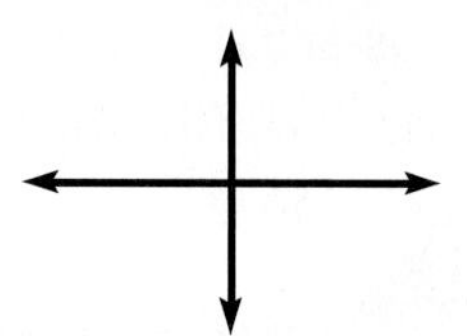

Lines that appear never to cross are **parallel lines**. They are always the same distance apart. They do not form any angles.

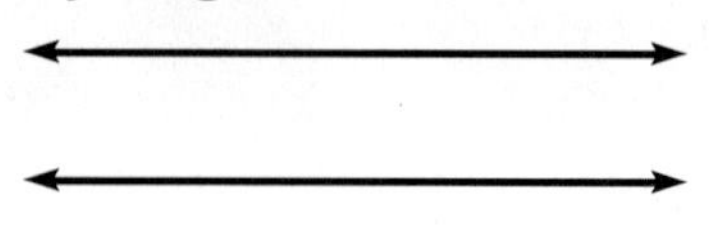

Types of Line Segments

The yellow and blue line segments meet. So, they form an angle.

The red and blue line segments meet at a right angle. So, they are perpendicular.

The green and blue line segments never cross. They are always the same distance apart. So, they appear to be parallel.

3.8 The student is expected to identify, classify, and describe two- and three-dimensional geometric figures by their attributes. The student compares two-dimensional figures, three-dimensional figures, or both by their attributes using formal geometry vocabulary. *also* **3.14A, 3.14D, 3.15A, 3.15B**

Guided Practice

1. The lines cross to form an angle. Are they perpendicular lines or intersecting lines?

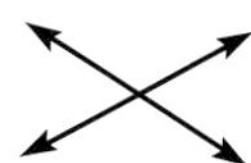

Describe the red line segments. Tell if the line segments appear to be *perpendicular* or *parallel*.

2. 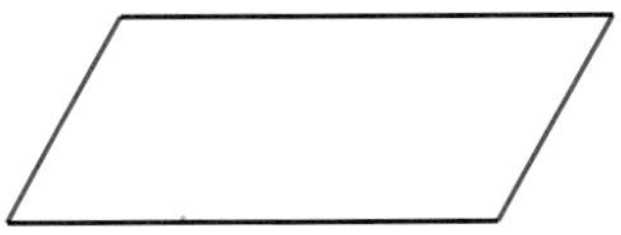

✓3. 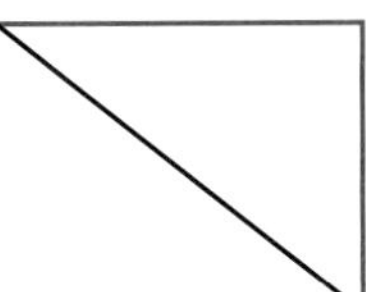

✓4. 

5. TALK Math **Explain** the difference between parallel lines and perpendicular lines.

Independent Practice and Problem Solving

Describe the lines. Tell if the lines appear to be *intersecting, perpendicular,* or *parallel*.

6. 

7. 

8. 

Describe the red line segments. Tell if the line segments appear to be *perpendicular* or *parallel*.

9. 

10. 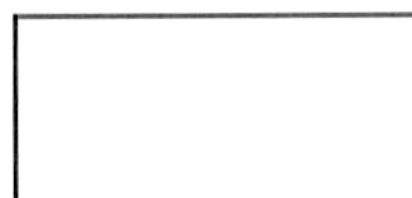

11. 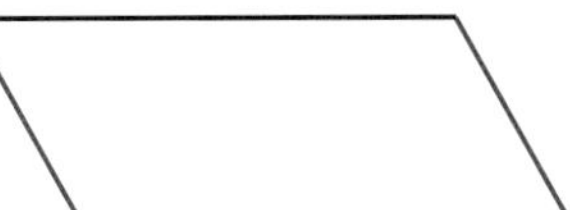

12. Use a ruler to draw pairs of intersecting, parallel, and perpendicular lines. Label each pair of lines and describe the angles.

13. WRITE Math **What's the Error?** Katie says the lines below appear to be parallel. **Explain** her error.

Mixed Review and TAKS Prep

14. What operation sign makes this number sentence true? $12 \bullet 4 = 3$ (TEKS 3.4C, p. 330)

15. Name this angle. (TEKS 3.8, p. 369)

16. **TAKS Prep** How can you describe the red line segments? (Obj. 3)

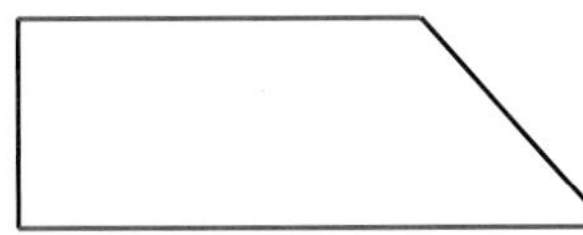

A intersecting **C** perpendicular
B right **D** parallel

LESSON 3

Identify 2-Dimensional Figures

OBJECTIVE: Identify, classify, and describe 2-dimensional figures.

Quick Review

Write the number of angles in each.

1. □
2. ▽
3. △
4. ○
5. ▭

Vocabulary

plane figure
two-dimensional figures
quadrilateral
pentagon
hexagon
octagon

Learn

A **plane figure** is a figure on a flat surface. It is formed by lines that are curved, straight, or both. Plane figures have length and width, and they are also called **two-dimensional figures**.

The number of sides and vertices a figure has helps you name it.

triangle
3 sides
3 vertices

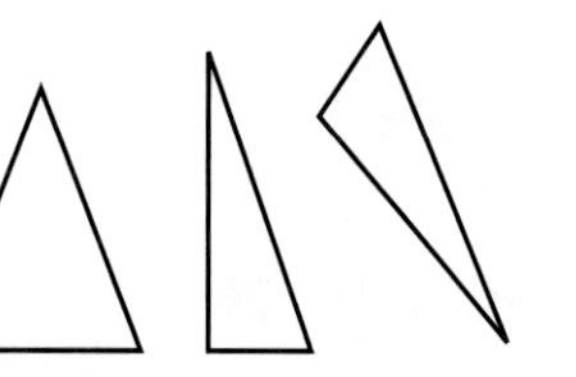

quadrilateral
4 sides
4 vertices

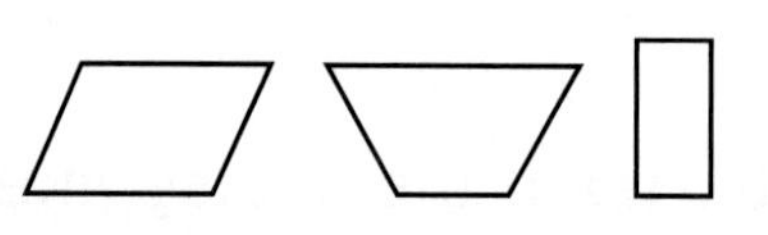

pentagon
5 sides
5 vertices

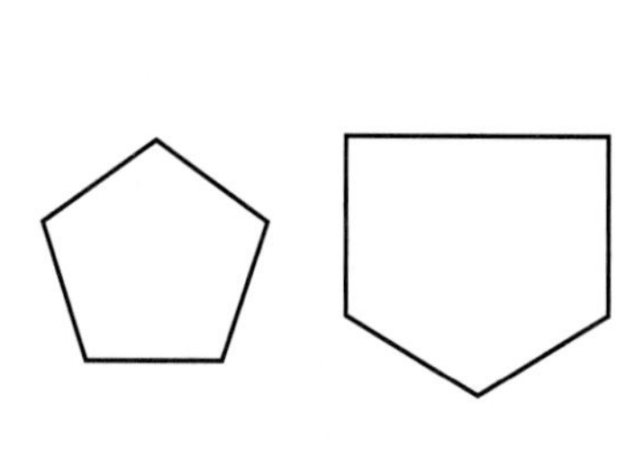

hexagon
6 sides
6 vertices

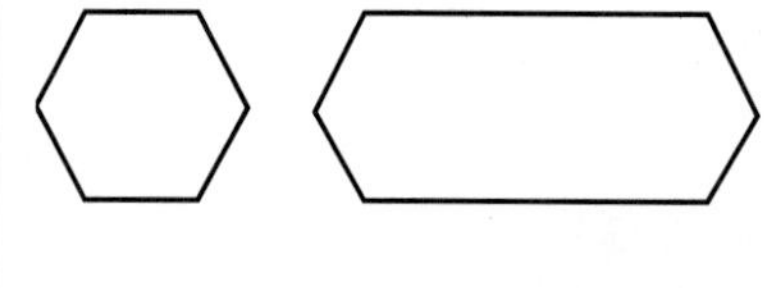

octagon
8 sides
8 vertices

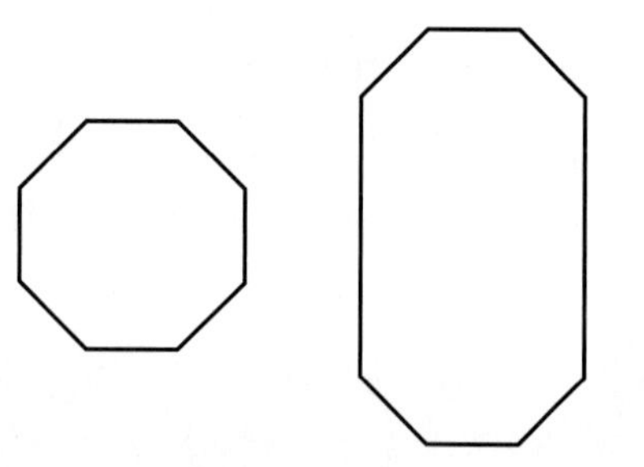

- What do you notice about the number of sides and the number of vertices in each of the figures shown above?

3.8 Identify, classify, and describe two- and three-dimensional geometric figures by their attributes. The student compares two-dimensional figures, three-dimensional figures, or both by their attributes using formal geometry vocabulary. *also* **3.14A, 3.14D, 3.15A, 3.15B, 3.16A**

Guided Practice

1. Tell if this figure is a two-dimensional figure. Write *yes* or *no*.

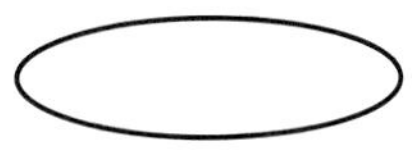

Name each figure. Tell how many sides.

2. 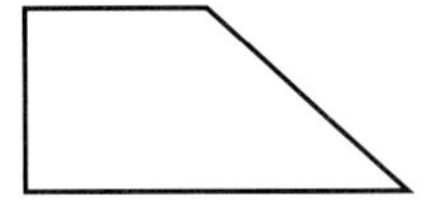

3. 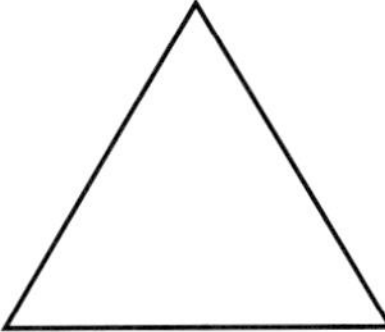

4. 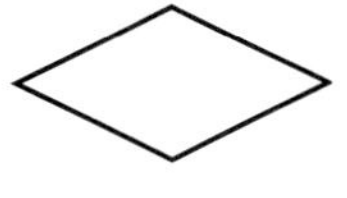

5. 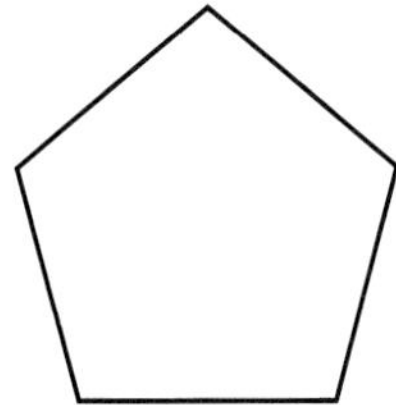

6. TALK Math **Explain** how you can describe a pentagon.

Independent Practice and Problem Solving

Name each figure. Tell how many sides.

7. 

8. 

9. 

10. 

11. Draw a figure with 4 sides and 4 vertices. Then name the figure.

12. Val has 25 craft sticks. She glues some sticks together to make 6 separate triangles. How many sticks does she have left?

For 13–14, use Figures A–E.

13. WRITE Math Are Figures *A–E* all two-dimensional figures? **Explain** why or why not.

14. Which figures have vertices?

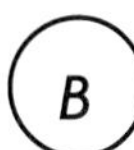

Mixed Review and TAKS Prep

15. Is this angle right, acute, or obtuse? (TEKS 3.8, p. 368)

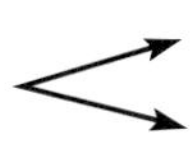

16. Write the fact family for 7, 6, and 42. (TEKS 3.6C, p. 304)

17. **TAKS Prep** How many sides does a pentagon have? (Obj. 3)

A 4 **B** 5 **C** 6 **D** 8

Extra Practice on page 388, Set C

Triangles

OBJECTIVE: Identify, describe, and classify triangles.

Quick Review

Does the angle appear to be a right angle? Write *yes*, or *no*.

1. 2. 3.

4. 5.

Vocabulary

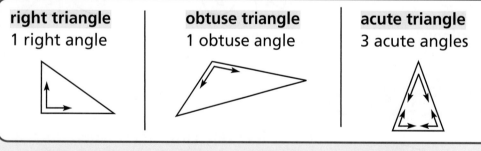

equilateral triangle
isosceles triangle
scalene triangle
right triangle
obtuse triangle
acute triangle

Learn

PROBLEM The sculpture in the photo is called Moondog. The artist used triangles and other plane figures. Name the types of triangles outlined in the sculpture.

ONE WAY You can identify triangles by their equal sides.

equilateral triangle
3 equal sides

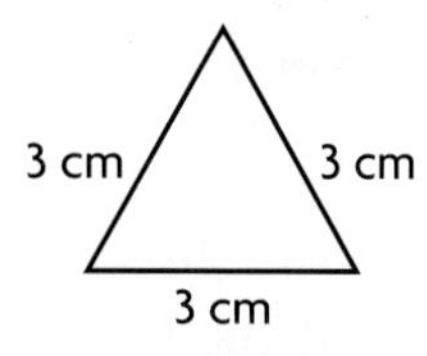

isosceles triangle
2 equal sides

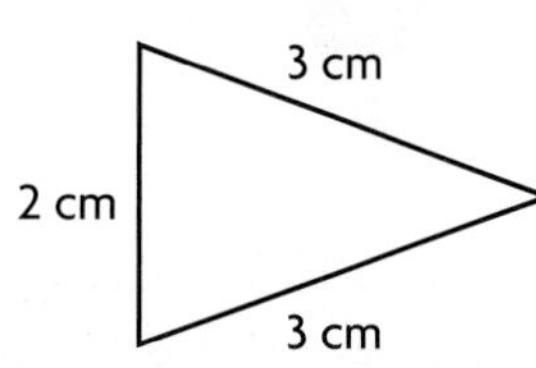

scalene triangle
0 equal sides

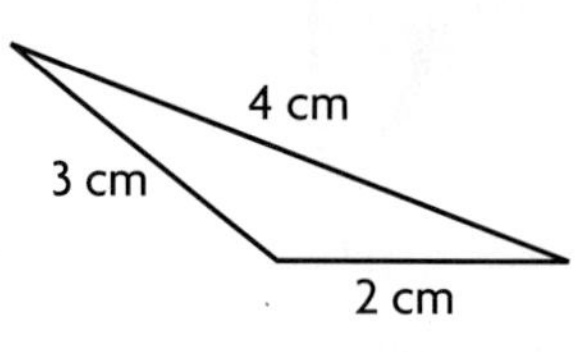

So, the red and white triangles are equilateral triangles, the yellow, purple, and green triangles are isosceles triangles, and the blue triangles are scalene triangles.

▲ The sculpture *Moondog*, by Tony Smith, is at the National Gallery of Art in Washington, D.C.

ANOTHER WAY You can identify triangles by their angles.

right triangle
1 right angle

obtuse triangle
1 obtuse angle

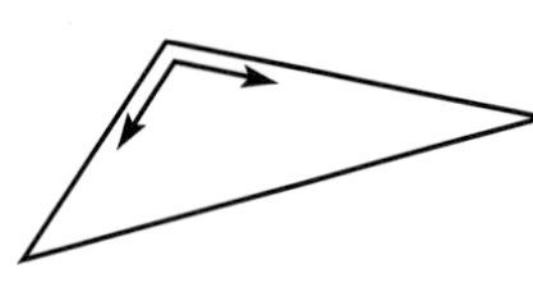

acute triangle
3 acute angles

- Which triangles in the sculpture are right triangles?
- Can a right triangle also be an isosceles triangle? **Explain.**

Remember

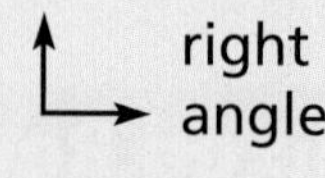
right angle

obtuse angle

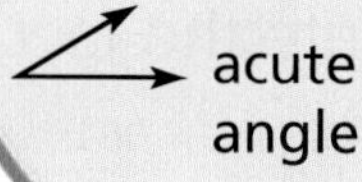
acute angle

3.8 The student is expected to identify, classify, and describe two- and three-dimensional geometric figures by their attributes. The student compares two-dimensional figures, three-dimensional figures, or both by their attributes using formal geometry vocabulary. *also* **3.14A, 3.14D, 3.15A, 3.15B**

Guided Practice

1. Identify each triangle.
Write *equilateral, isosceles,* or *scalene.*
Think: How many equal sides does each triangle have?

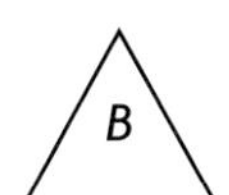

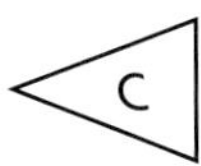

Identify each triangle. Write *right, obtuse,* or *acute.*

2. 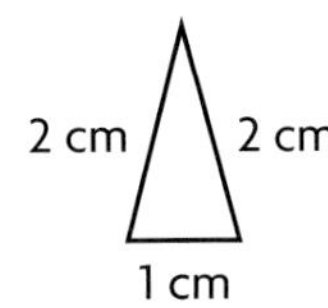

3. 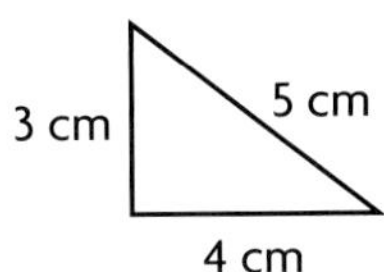

4. 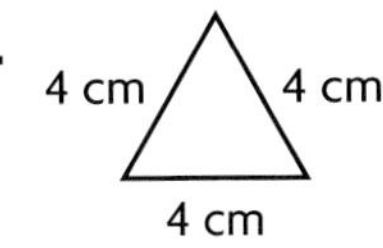

5. 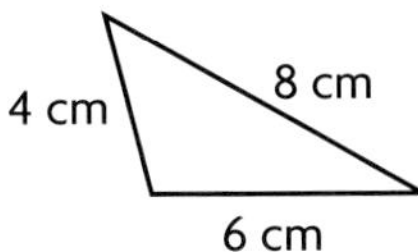

6. TALK Math **Explain** why a triangle can be both equilateral and acute.

Independent Practice and Problem Solving

Identify each triangle. Write *equilateral, isosceles,* or *scalene.*

7. 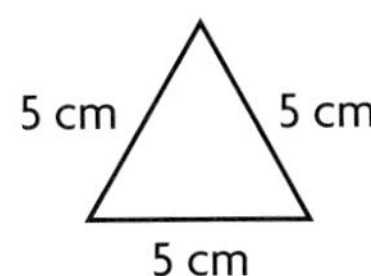

8. 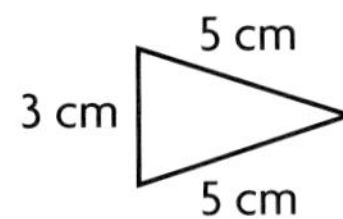

9. 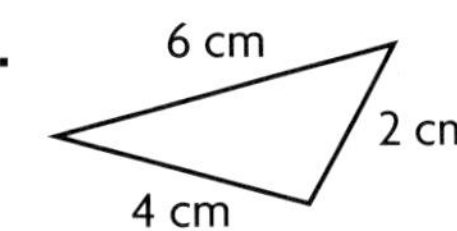

10. 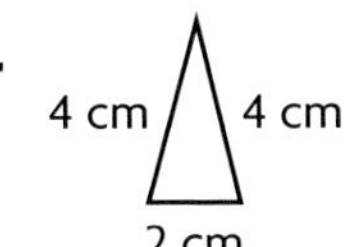

Identify each triangle. Write *right, obtuse,* or *acute.*

11. 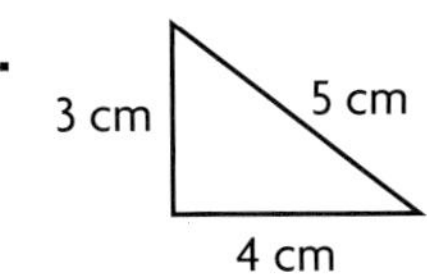

12. 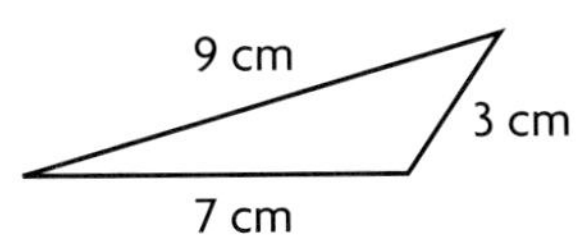

13. 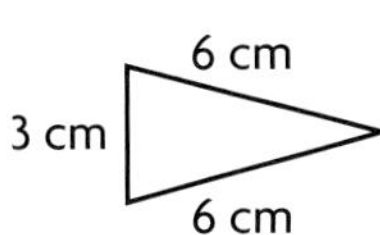

14. 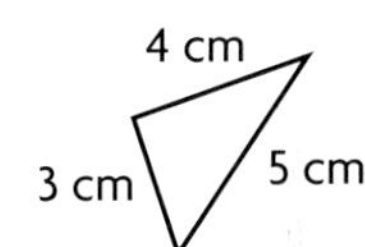

15. Two of my sides are 5 inches long. My third side is shorter. All of my angles are less than a right angle. What kind of triangle am I?

16. WRITE Math How are an equilateral triangle and a scalene triangle alike? How are they different? **Explain.**

Mixed Review and TAKS Prep

17. Aaron drew a plane figure with 5 sides and 5 angles. Name the figure Aaron drew. (TEKS 3.8, p. 374)

18. Which amount is greater– 5 quarters or $1.15? (TEKS 3.1C, p. 114)

19. **TAKS Prep** Which correctly names this triangle? (Obj. 3)

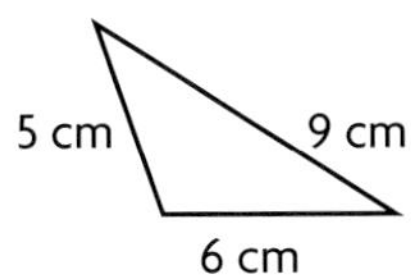

A scalene and obtuse

B isosceles and acute

C scalene and acute

D isosceles and obtuse

Extra Practice on page 389, Set D

LESSON 5

Quadrilaterals

OBJECTIVE: Identify, describe, and classify quadrilaterals.

Quick Review

Write the number of sides each has.

1.

2.

3.

4.

5. 

Vocabulary

rhombus **parallelogram**

trapezoid **Venn diagram**

Learn

PROBLEM Lynn's aunt sent her this postcard of the Eiffel Tower, in Paris, France. What type of quadrilateral do you see in the tower?

▲ The Eiffel Tower is 984 feet high. From the top you can see the city of Paris.

Some quadrilaterals are named by their sides and their angles.

Examples

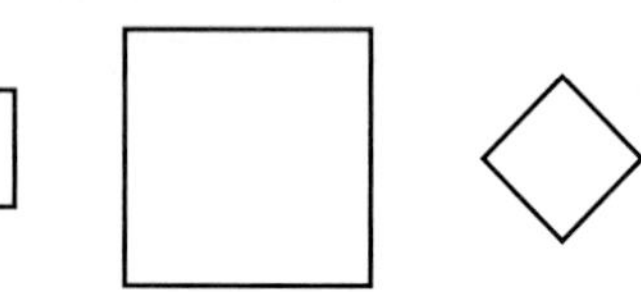

Square
- 2 pairs of parallel sides
- 4 equal sides
- 4 right angles

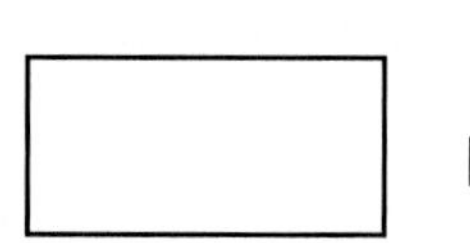

Rectangle
- 2 pairs of parallel sides
- 2 pairs of equal sides
- 4 right angles

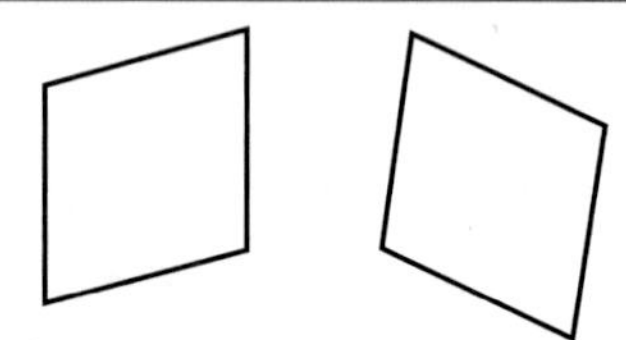

Rhombus
- 2 pairs of parallel sides
- 4 equal sides

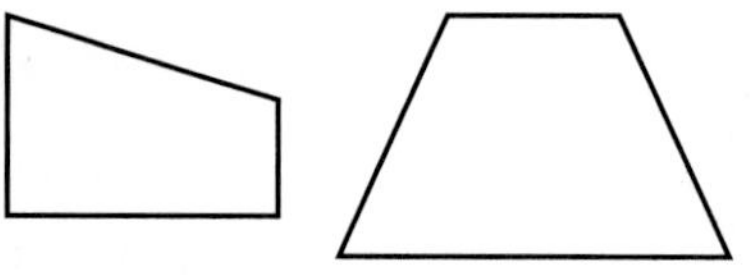

Trapezoid
- exactly 1 pair of parallel sides
- lengths of sides may not be the same
- sizes of angles may not be the same

The quadrilateral in the tower has 1 pair of parallel sides.

So, the quadrilateral in the Eiffel Tower is a trapezoid.

- What types of angles are in the trapezoid?

3.8 The student is expected to identify, classify, and describe two- and three-dimensional geometric figures by their attributes. The student compares two-dimensional figures, three-dimensional figures, or both by their attributes using formal geometry vocabulary. *also* **3.14A, 3.14D, 3.15A, 3.15B, 3.16B**

Parallelograms

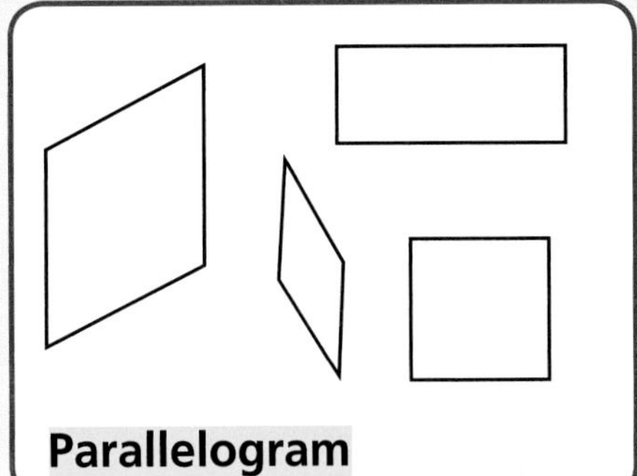

- 2 pairs of parallel sides
- 2 pairs of equal sides

- Explain why a trapezoid is not a parallelogram.
- Explain why a square is also a parallelogram, a rectangle, a quadrilateral, and a rhombus.

Guided Practice

Look at the quadrilateral at the right.

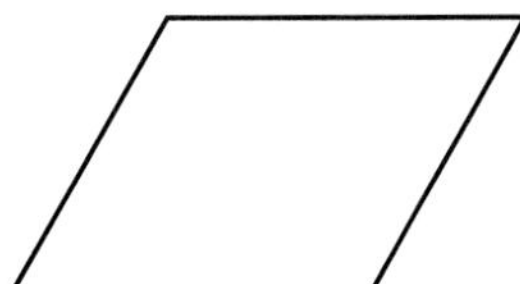

1. How many pairs of sides are parallel?
2. How many pairs of sides are equal?
3. Name the quadrilateral.

Write as many names for each quadrilateral as you can.

4.

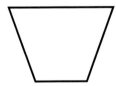

5.

✓6.

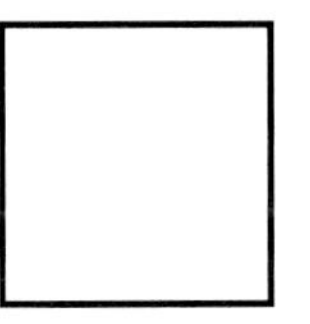

7.

8.

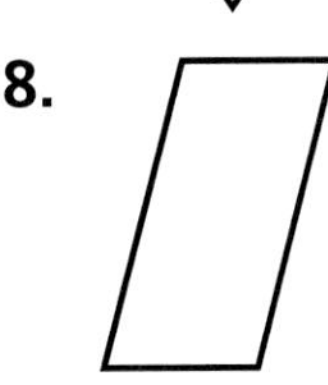

✓9.

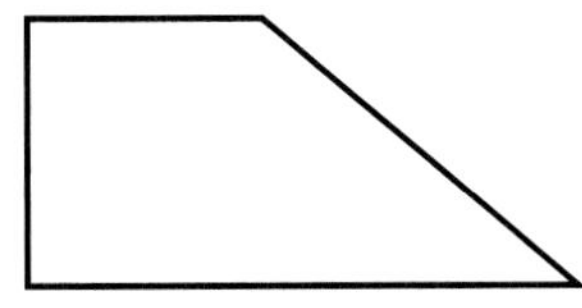

10. TALK Math **Describe** a square by its sides and by its angles.

Independent Practice and Problem Solving

Write as many names for each quadrilateral as you can.

11.

12.

13.

14. 

15. 

16. 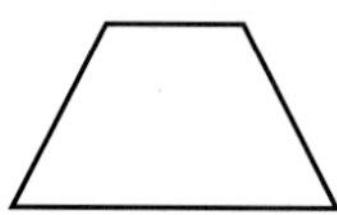

For 17–20, use the quadrilaterals at the right.

17. Which quadrilaterals have 4 right angles?

18. Which quadrilaterals have 2 pairs of parallel sides?

19. Which quadrilaterals have no right angles?

20. How are quadrilateral B and quadrilateral C alike? How are they different?

A B C D E

21. Describe the quadrilaterals you see in the flag of France at the right.

22. Below is a diagram of Jay's bedroom. His bedroom is a rectangle. What is the length of the side labeled *s*?

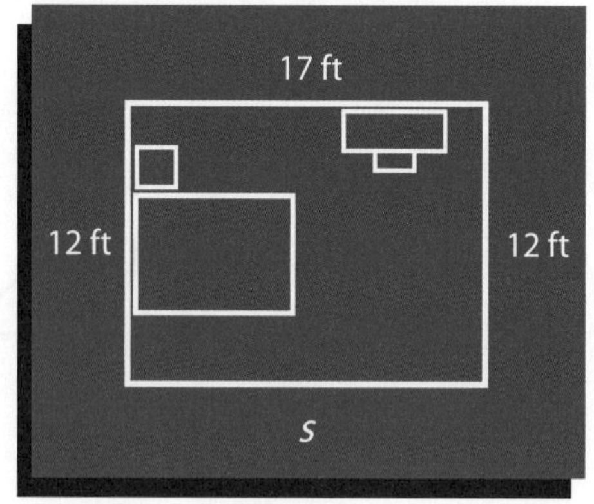

23. I am a quadrilateral with 1 pair of parallel sides. My sides may not be the same length. What figure am I?

24. I have 2 pairs of parallel sides and 2 pairs of equal sides. What figure am I?

25. **Reasoning** Describe how a rhombus is like a square and how it is different.

26. WRITE Math **Sense or Nonsense** Joe said all parallelograms have 4 equal sides. Does Joe's statement make sense? **Explain.**

CD ROM **Technology**
Use Harcourt Mega Math, Ice Station Exploration, *Polar Planes*, Level G.

 Extra Practice on page 389, Set E

Mixed Review and TAKS Prep

27. Chris, Lee, and Jill played a computer game. Chris scored 6,852 points. Lee scored 6,781 points, and Jill scored 6,917 points. Write the scores in order from least to greatest. (TEKS 3.1B, p. 36)

28. Name this triangle by its sides. (TEKS 3.8, p. 376)

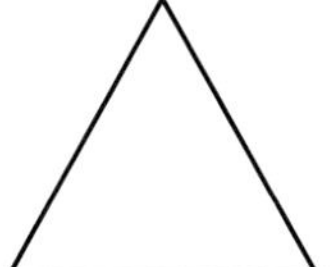

29. **TAKS Prep** What figure has 2 pairs of parallel sides, no right angles, and 4 equal sides? (Obj. 3)

30. **TAKS Prep** Rita glued craft sticks together to make this shape. Which best describes the quadrilateral Rita made? (Obj. 3)

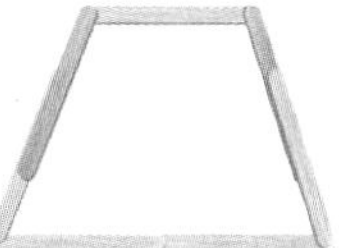

A parallelogram
B rectangle
C rhombus
D trapezoid

Problem Solving and Reasoning

VISUAL THINKING A **Venn diagram** shows how sets of things are related. Look at the Venn diagram below. One set has figures that are rectangles. The other set has figures that are rhombuses. The figures inside the area where the sets overlap are both rectangles and rhombuses.

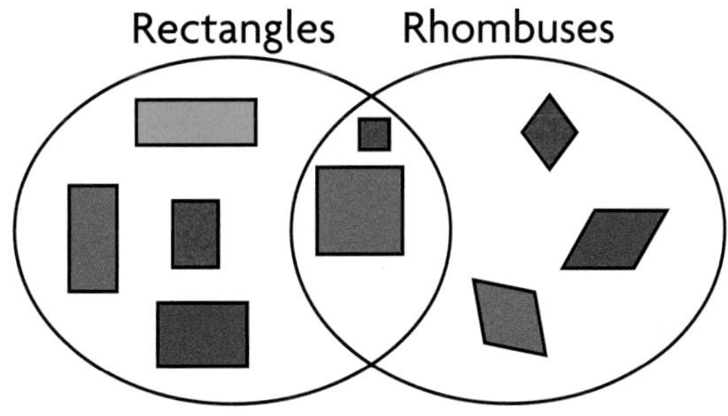

Use the Venn diagram.

1. How many rectangles are there?
2. How many rhombuses are there?
3. How many figures are both rectangles and rhombuses?
4. What type of quadrilateral is in both sets?
5. Where in the Venn diagram would you put this figure?

LESSON HANDS ON

6 Circles

OBJECTIVE: Identify and draw the parts of a circle.

Quick Review

Name each figure.

1. 2. 3. 4. 5.

Vocabulary

center radius

A circle is a closed plane figure made of points that are the same distance from the center. The **center** is the point in the middle of a circle.

Investigate

Materials ■ large and small paper clips, 2 pencils, ruler

A Draw a point on a sheet of paper.

B Place a pencil in each end of a small paper clip. Place one pencil on the point. Move the other pencil around to draw a circle.

C Repeat the steps with a large paper clip.

Draw Conclusions

1. How are the circles you drew alike? How are they different?
2. Why do you think they are different?
3. **Analysis** If you used a giant paper clip to draw a circle, how would the circle compare to the first two circles you drew? Explain.

The pencil on the point should not move when you draw your circle.

3.8 The student is expected to identify, classify, and describe two- and three-dimensional geometric figures by their attributes. The student compares two-dimensional figures, three-dimensional figures, or both by their attributes using formal geometry vocabulary. *also* **3.14A, 3.14D, 3.15A, 3.15B**

Connect

A **radius** is a line segment. Its endpoints are the center of the circle and any point on the circle.

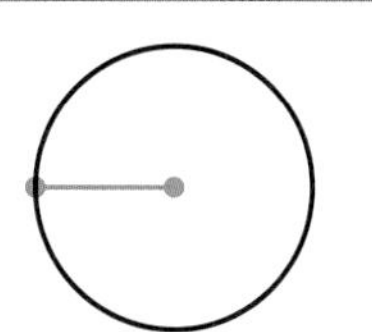

TALK Math

When you draw a circle using a paper clip, how does the length of the paper clip compare to the length of the radius?

Practice

1. Which figures are circles?

2. In which circle is the radius drawn in blue?

3. In which circle is the center drawn in blue?

A

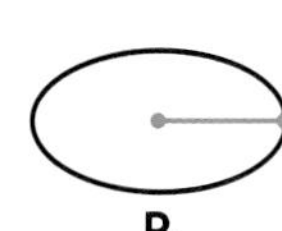
B

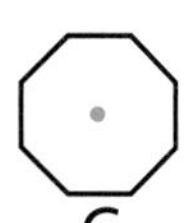
C

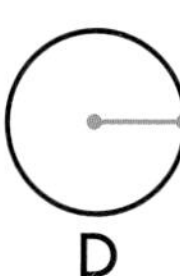
D

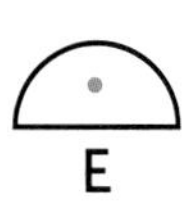
E

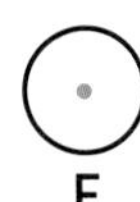
F

Name the blue part in each circle.

4. 

5. 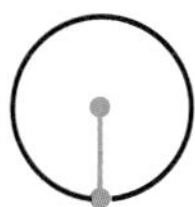

6. 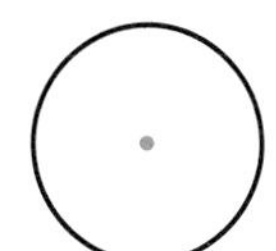

7. 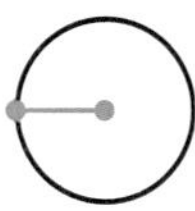

8. **WRITE Math** Cindy and Reggie drew the figures at the right. How are their figures alike? How are they different?

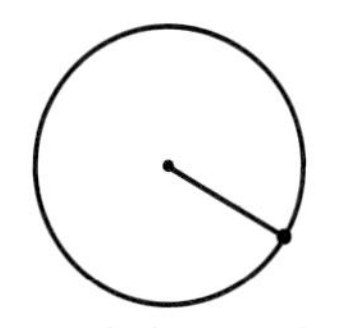
Cindy's circle

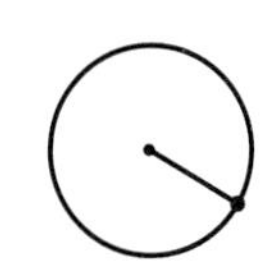
Reggie's circle

LESSON 7 Compare 2-Dimensional Figures

OBJECTIVE: Compare attributes of 2-dimensional figures.

Quick Review

Tell how many sides each figure has.

1. triangle
2. pentagon
3. octagon
4. hexagon
5. rectangle

Learn

PROBLEM Robert drew these two figures. What math words can he use to compare them?

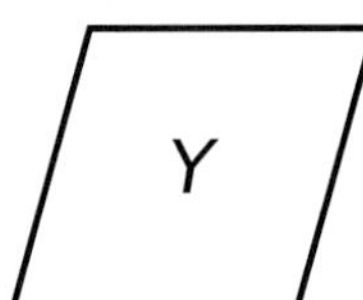

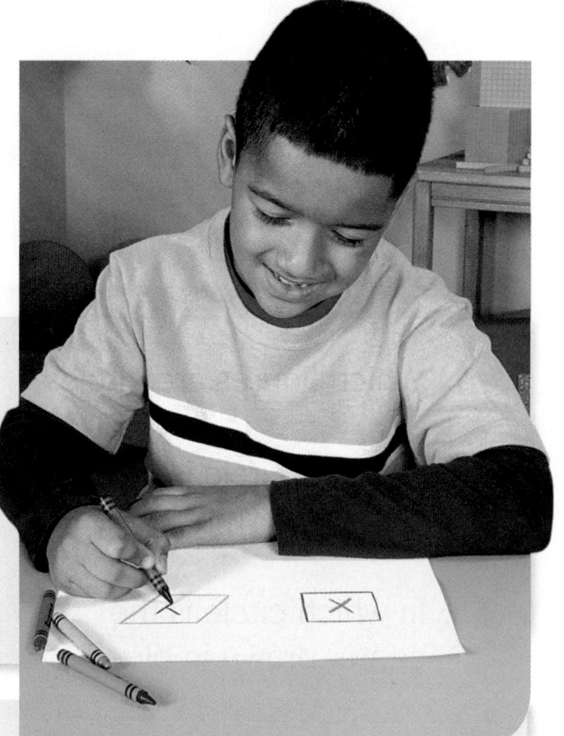

ONE WAY **Compare the number of sides and vertices.**

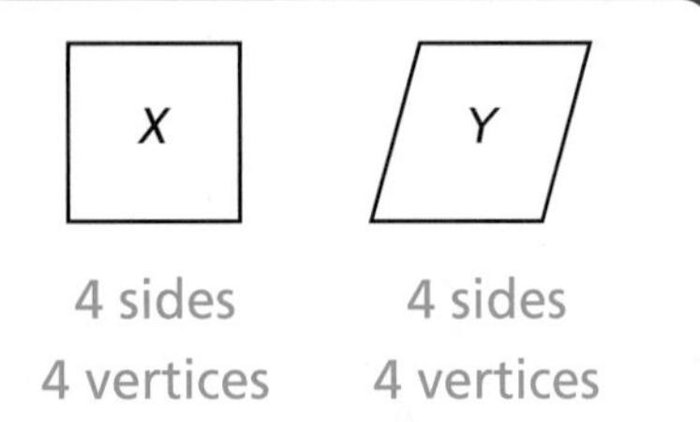

OTHER WAYS

A **Compare the types of angles.**

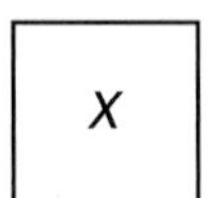

4 right angles

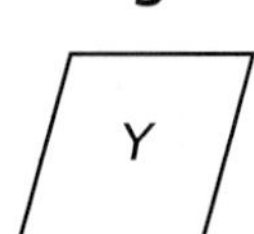

2 acute angles
2 obtuse angles

B **Compare the number of parallel sides.**

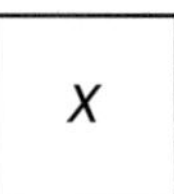

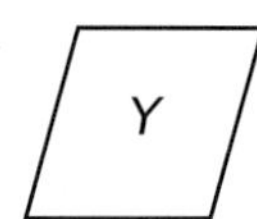

Both figures have opposite sides that are parallel.
Both figures have 2 pairs of parallel sides.

So, plane figures can be compared by the number of sides and vertices, by the types of angles, and by the number of parallel sides.

- How are figures *X* and *Y* alike? How are they different?

3.8 The student is expected to identify, classify, and describe two- and three-dimensional geometric figures by their attributes. The student compares two-dimensional figures, three-dimensional figures, or both by their attributes using formal geometry vocabulary. *also* **3.14A, 3.15A, 3.15B**

Guided Practice

1. Name the figures. Which has more sides? Which has parallel sides?

For 2–4, compare the figures at the right.

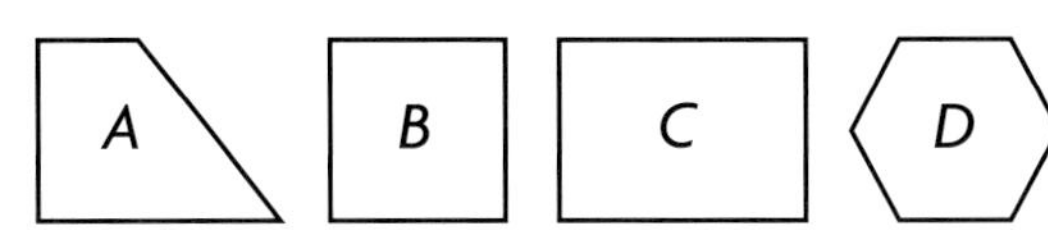

2. Which figures have parallel sides?
3. Which figures have 4 sides?
4. Which figures have right angles?
5. TALK Math **Explain** how a right triangle and a rectangle are alike by describing their angles.

Independent Practice and Problem Solving

For 6–9, compare the figures at the right.

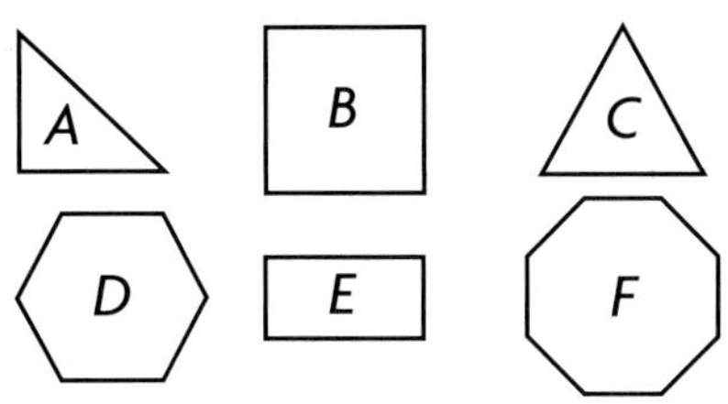

6. Which figures have 4 sides?
7. Which figures have 6 or more angles?
8. Which figures have parallel sides?
9. Which figures have at least 1 right angle?
10. WRITE Math **Explain** how a square and a rectangle are alike and how they are different.
11. **Reasoning** Jade drew 2 plane figures. The first had 2 more sides than the second. The second had 4 right angles. Draw and name the plane figures.

Mixed Review and TAKS Prep

12. Two lines intersect and form right angles. Are the lines parallel or perpendicular? (TEKS 3.8, P. 372)
13. Mason counted the square tiles on the floor. He counted 9 rows of 8 tiles. How many tiles did he count in all? (TEKS 3.4B, P. 250)
14. **TAKS Prep** How are the figures alike? (Obj. 3)

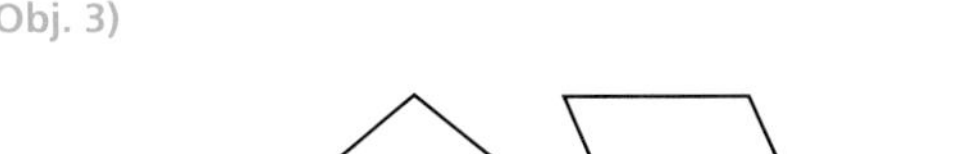

A Both have 4 right angles.

B Both have 4 acute angles.

C Both have 4 obtuse angles.

D Both have 2 acute angles and 2 obtuse angles.

Extra Practice on page 389, Set F

Problem Solving Workshop
Strategy: Draw a Diagram

OBJECTIVE: Solve problems by using the strategy *draw a diagram*.

Read to Understand
Plan
Solve
Check

Use the Strategy

PROBLEM In art class, Harry used 11 figures to make this train. How can you sort the figures Harry used?

Read to Understand

- **Classify and categorize the figures Harry used.**
- **What information is given?**

Plan

- **What strategy can you use to solve the problem?**
  You can draw a diagram to sort the figures Harry used.

Solve

- **How can you use the strategy to solve the problem?**

Draw a Venn diagram. A Venn diagram shows how sets of things are related.

Draw one circle, and label it *Quadrilaterals*.

Draw another circle that overlaps the first circle. Label this circle *Blue*.

Sort the figures into the two circles.

The figures inside the area where the circles overlap are both blue and quadrilaterals.

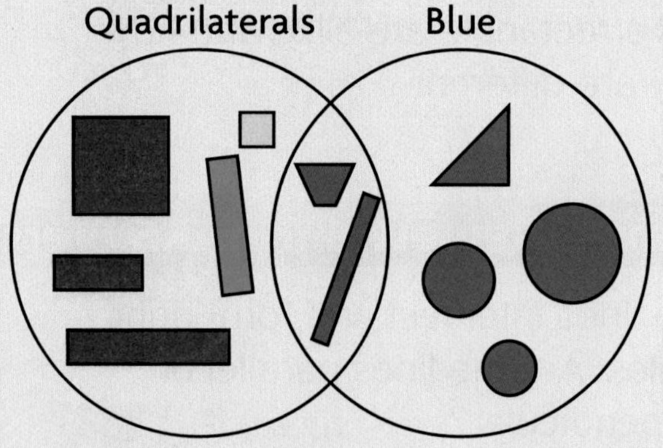

Check

- **What other strategy could you use?**

3.8 Identify, classify, and describe two- and three-dimensional geometric figures by their attributes. The student compares two-dimensional figures, three-dimensional figures, or both by their attributes using formal geometry vocabulary. *also* **3.14A, 3.14B, 3.14C, 3.14D, 3.15A, 3.15B**

Guided Problem Solving

1. Georgia used these figures to make a picture.

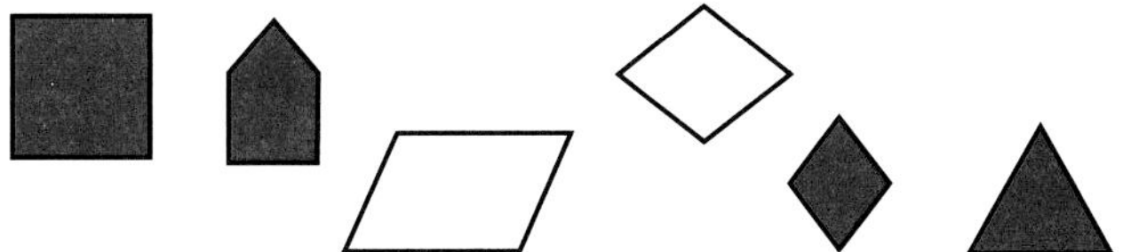

How are the figures alike, and how are they different?

Parallelograms Red

First, draw a Venn diagram with two overlapping circles.

Next, sort the figures.

Last, tell how the figures are alike and how they are different.

2. **What if** Georgia added this figure to her picture?

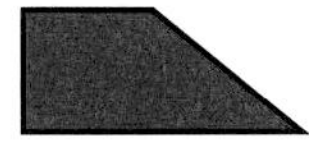

Where should it be placed in the Venn diagram?

3. Copy the Venn diagram, showing multiples of 2 and 3. Complete the diagram, using the numbers through 24.

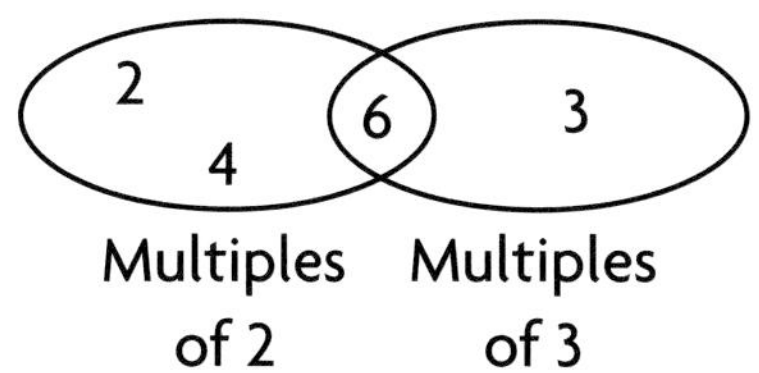

What do the numbers in the overlapping section represent?

Mixed Strategy Practice

USE DATA For 4–6, use the Venn diagram.

4. The Venn diagram shows the figures Cory used to make a picture. How many quadrilaterals with right angles did he use?

5. How many red figures have right angles but are not quadrilaterals?

6. WRITE Math **Explain** what the figures in the overlapping section represent.

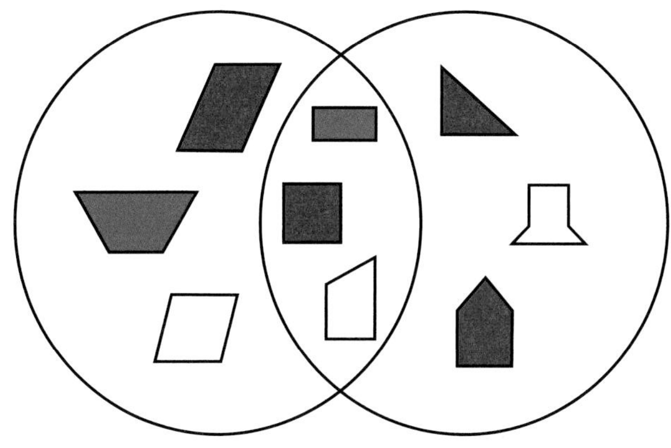

7. **Reasoning** Twenty pictures were entered in an art contest. The pictures were done with either paint or chalk. There were 8 more done with paint than with chalk. How many were done with paint and how many were done with chalk?

Choose a STRATEGY

- Draw a Diagram or Picture
- Make a Model or Act It Out
- Make an Organized List
- Look for a Pattern
- Make a Table or Graph
- Guess and Check
- Work Backward
- Solve a Simpler Problem
- Write an Equation
- Use Logical Reasoning

Extra Practice

Set A Tell whether each is a *line, line segment,* or *ray.* (pp. 368–371)

1. 
2. 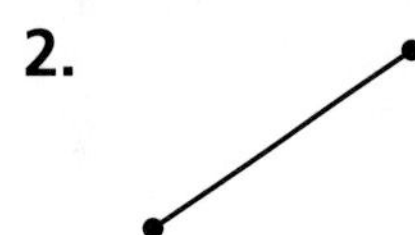
3. 
4. 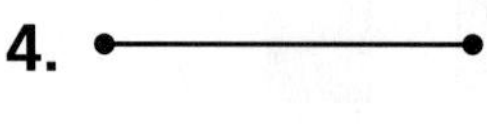

Use the corner of a sheet of paper to tell whether each angle is *right, acute,* or *obtuse.*

5. 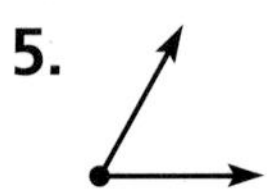
6. 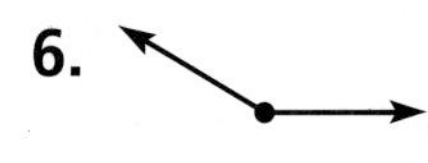
7. 
8.

Set B Describe the lines. Write *intersecting, perpendicular,* or *parallel.* (pp. 372–373)

1. 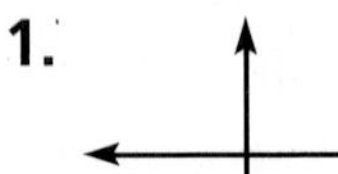
2. 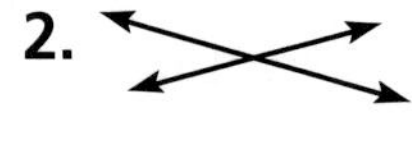
3. 

Set C Tell if each figure is a 2-dimensional figure. Write *yes* or *no.* (pp. 374–375)

1. 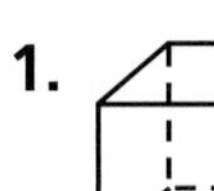 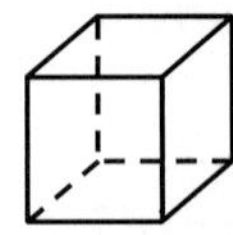
2. 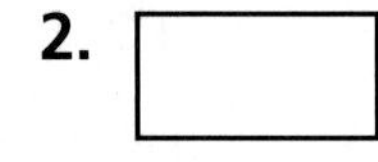
3. 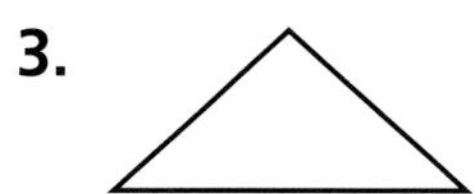
4. 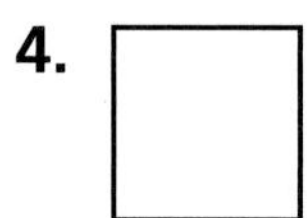

Name each figure. Tell how many sides.

5. 

6. 
7. 

8. 

9. Which figures have vertices?

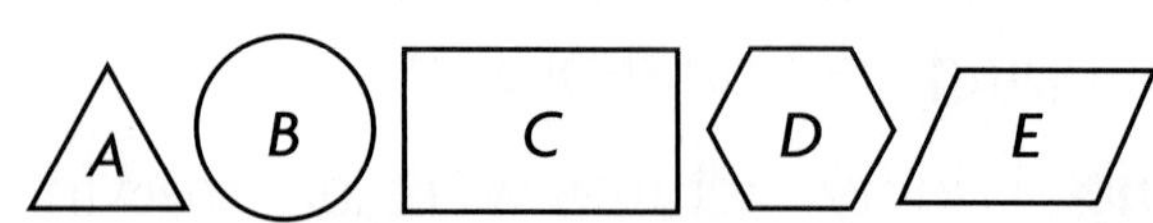

CD ROM Technology
Use Harcourt Mega Math, Ice Station Exploration, *Polar Planes*, Levels A–C, E–G.

Set D Identify each triangle. Write *equilateral*, *isosceles*, or *scalene*. (pp. 376–377)

1. 2. 3. 4.

Identify each triangle. Write *right*, *obtuse*, or *acute*.

5. 6. 7. 8.

Set E Write as many names for each quadrilateral as you can. (pp. 378–381)

1. 2. 3. 4.

For 5–6, use the quadrilaterals below.

A B C D E

5. Which quadrilaterals have no right angles?

6. How are quadrilateral B and quadrilateral D alike? How are they different?

Set F For 1–4, use the figures at the right. (pp. 384–385)

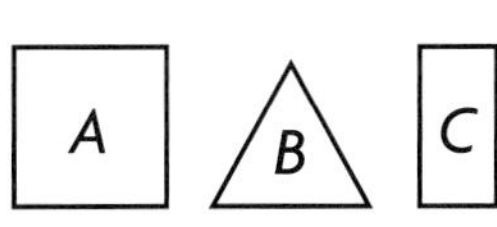

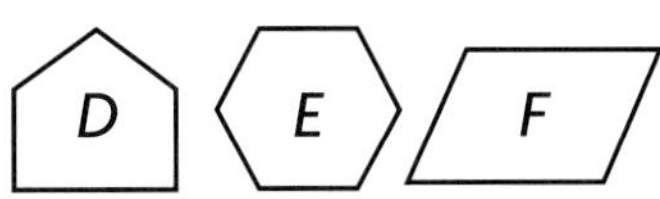

1. Which figures have 4 sides?
2. Which figures have no right angles?
3. Which figures have at least one right angle?
4. Which figures have parallel sides?

Chapter 16 Review/Test

Check Vocabulary and Concepts

Choose the best term from the box.

VOCABULARY
equilateral triangle
isosceles triangle
parallelogram
right angle

1. A __?__ is a special angle that forms a square corner. (TEKS 3.8, p. 369)
2. An __?__ is a triangle with 3 equal sides. (TEKS 3.8, p. 376)
3. A __?__ is a quadrilateral with 2 pairs of equal and parallel sides. (TEKS 3.8, p. 378)

Check Skills

Identify each figure. Tell how many sides. (TEKS 3.8, pp. 374–375)

4. 
5. 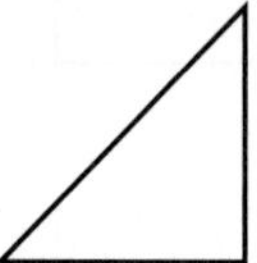
6. 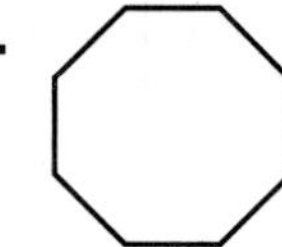
7. 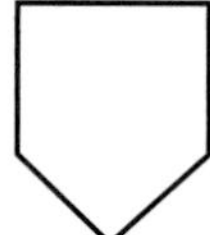

Identify each triangle. Write *equilateral*, *isosceles*, or *scalene*. (TEKS 3.8, pp. 376–377)

8. 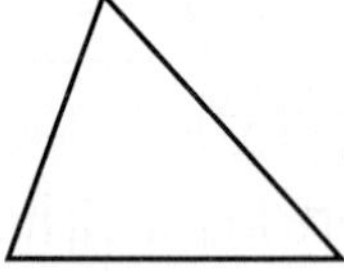
9. 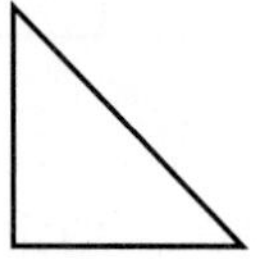
10. 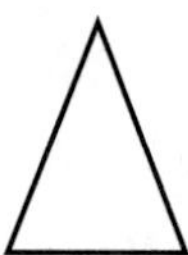
11. 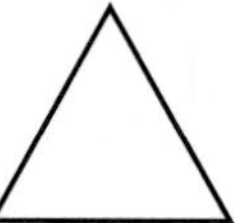

Check Problem Solving

Solve. (TEKS 3.8, 3.14C, pp. 386–387)

12. The Venn diagram shows the figures Ethan used to make a picture. How many red quadrilaterals did he use?

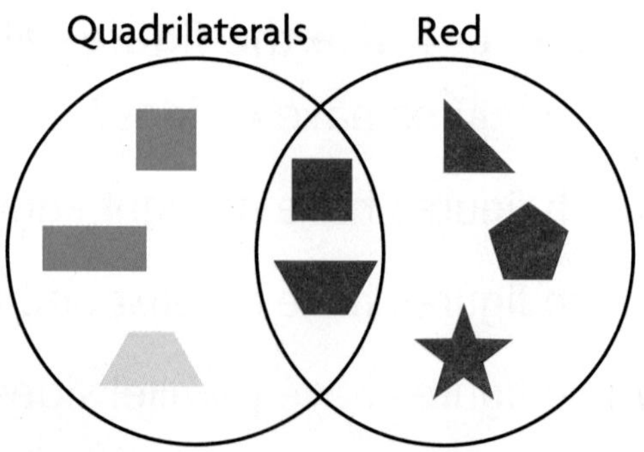

13. WRITE Math Ethan added this figure to his picture. **Explain** where it should be placed in the Venn diagram.

GO ONLINE **Technology** Use *Online Assessment.*

Enrich • Tessellations
Make a Pattern

Some geometric figures can form a tessellation. A **tessellation** is a repeating pattern made of a closed plane figure that covers a surface with no overlapping or empty space.

▲ ***Sun and Moon*** **by M.C. Escher**

Twist It

Will the figures below form a tessellation?

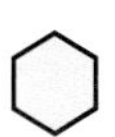  

Step 1 Repeat the figure in a row, as close together as possible without overlapping.

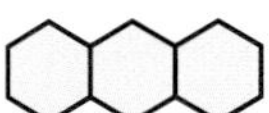  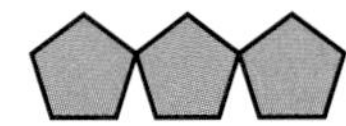

Step 2 Place a second row on top of the first.

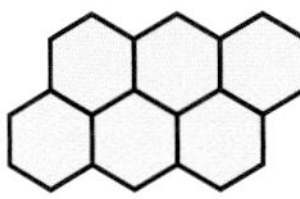 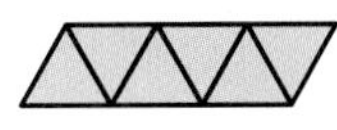 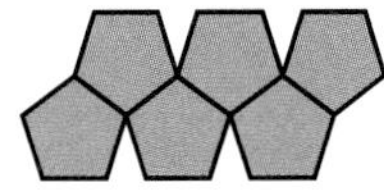

Step 3 Add more rows. If there is no empty space, the figure has formed a tessellation.

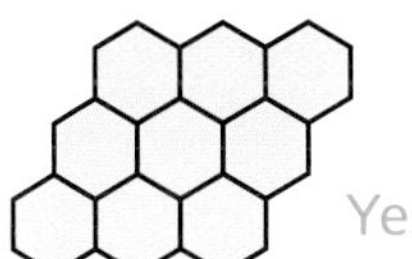

Yes

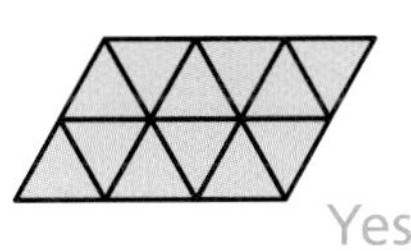

Yes

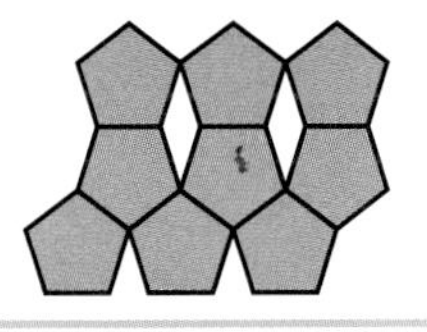

No

So, the hexagon and triangle will form a tessellation, but the pentagon will not.

Turn It

Tell if each figure will form a tessellation. Write *yes* or *no*.

1. 

2. 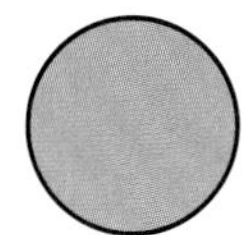

3. 

4. 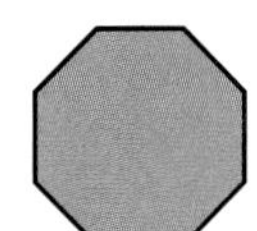

Draw It

WRITE Math ▸ Is this figure a tessellation? **Explain.**

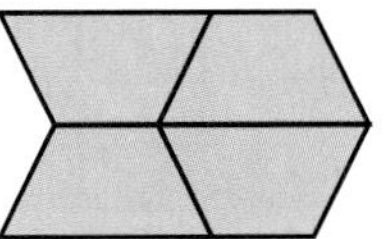

Getting Ready for the TAKS
Chapters 1–16

Number, Operation, and Quantitative Reasoning (TAKS Obj. 1)

1. Joan flew 908 miles to visit her grandmother. What is 908 rounded to the nearest hundred?

A 910

B 908

C 900

D 800

Understand the problem.

See item 2. Read the question again. What are you asked to find? Look in the problem for the information you need to answer the question.

2. Bill is putting his stamps in an album. There are 8 stamps on each page. Bill has filled 7 pages. How many stamps does Bill have?

F 1

G 15

H 48

J 56

3. WRITE Math **Explain** how this array models $6 \times 9 = 54$.

Patterns, Relationships, and Algebraic Thinking (TAKS Obj. 2)

4. Look at the table. How many wheels do 4 wagons have?

Number of Wagons	Number of Wheels
1	4
2	8
3	12
4	■

A 8

B 16

C 20

D 22

5. Which number completes the fact family?

$4 \times ■ = 32$ $\quad ■ \times 4 = 32$

$32 \div 4 = ■$ $\quad 32 \div ■ = 4$

F 4

G 8

H 9

J 32

6. WRITE Math **Explain** how knowing $(2 \times 4) \times 8 = 64$ helps you find $2 \times (4 \times 8)$.

Geometry and Spatial Reasoning (TAKS Obj. 3)

7. Look at the shape below. Which does NOT describe the shape?

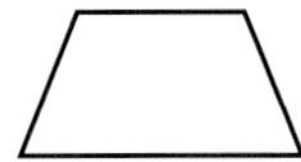

A It is a rhombus.

B It is a trapezoid.

C It is a polygon.

D It is a quadrilateral.

8. Which plane figure has more sides than this figure?

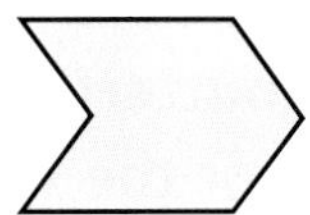

F Triangle

G Quadrilateral

H Hexagon

J Octagon

9. WRITE Math **Explain** how parallel lines are different than perpendicular lines.

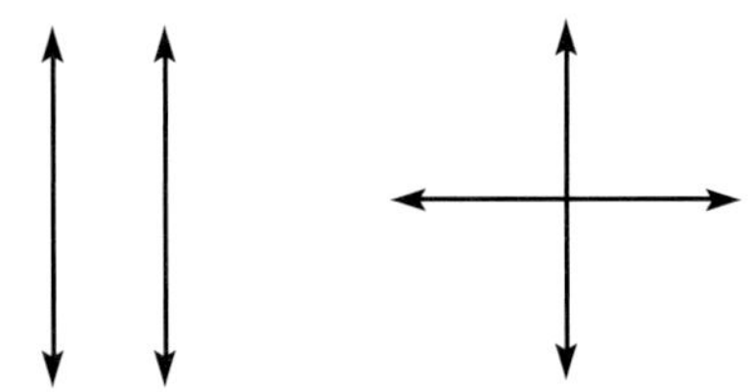

Probability and Statistics (TAKS Obj. 5)

10. A tally table shows 卌 卌 卌 || for the number of students who rode bikes to school. How many students rode bikes?

A 20 **C** 15

B 17 **D** Not here

11. The graph shows some of the activities Jason did during the day. How many more hours did Jason spend sleeping than reading?

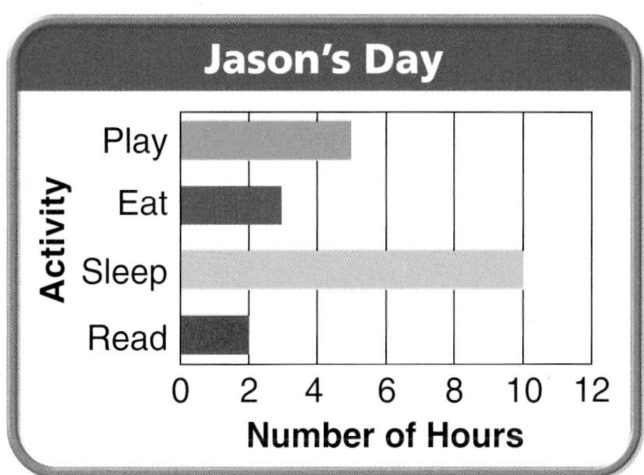

F 2 hours **H** 10 hours

G 8 hours **J** 12 hours

12. WRITE Math Rosanna picks a card from the cards shown. Is she more likely or less likely to pick an *A* than a *B*? **Explain** how you know.

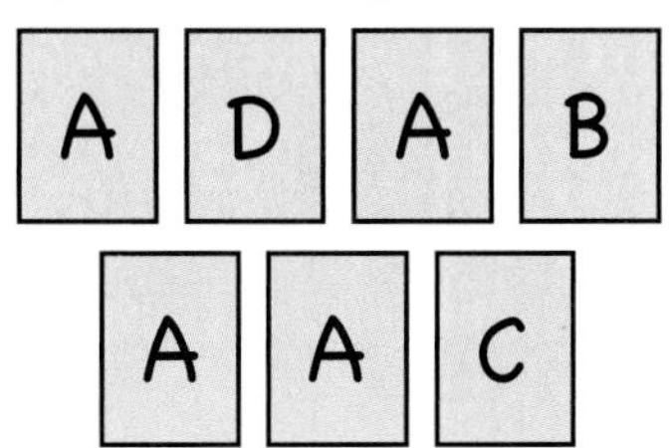

17 Congruence and Symmetry

The Big Idea Two-dimensional figures can be classified according to their geometric properties.

The Texas state insect is the monarch butterfly. Monarch butterflies fly south for the winter. They travel from the northern United States, through Texas, and into Mexico.

Investigate

All butterflies are symmetrical. Their left and right wings have the same designs and colors. Look at the drawings. Which cannot be true butterflies? How do you know?

Technology
Student pages are available in the Student eBook.

Show What You Know

Check your understanding of important skills needed for success in Chapter 17.

▶ Same Size, Same Shape

Tell whether the figures are the same size and shape. Write *yes* or *no*.

1. 

2. 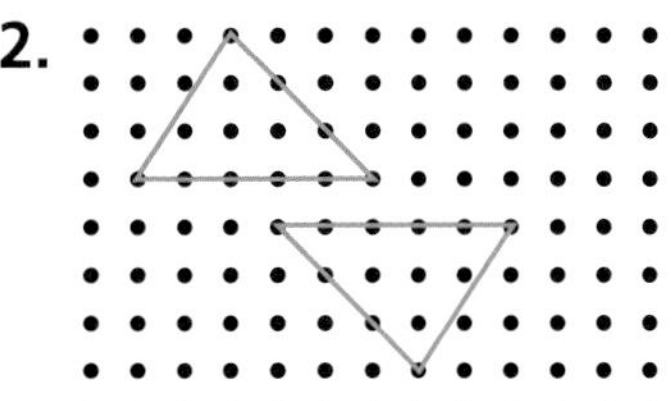

3. 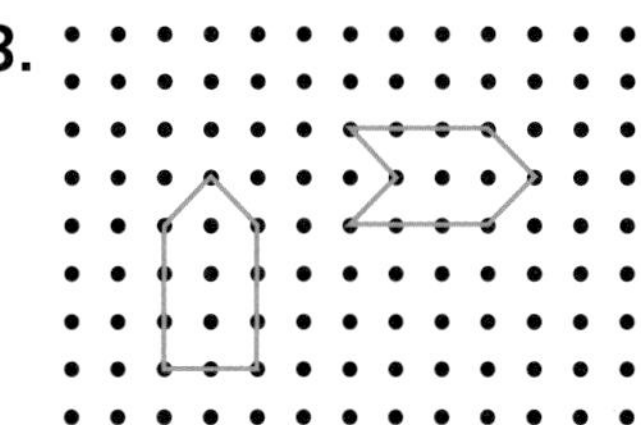

4. 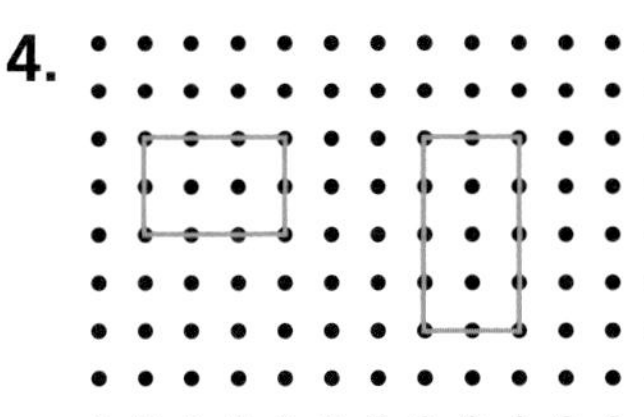

5. 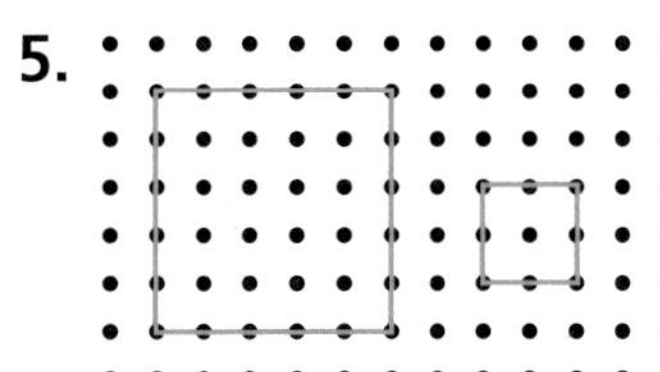

6. 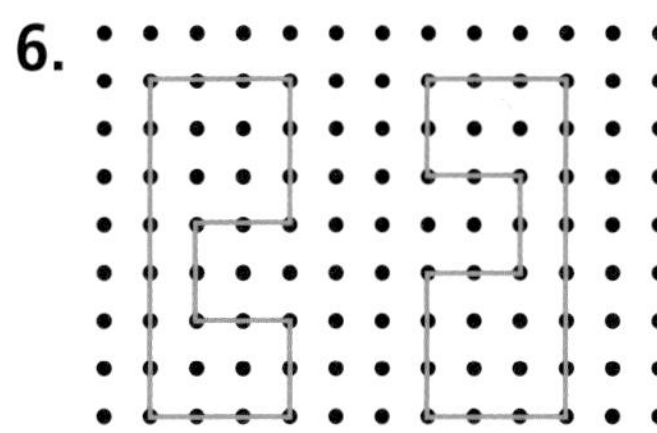

7. 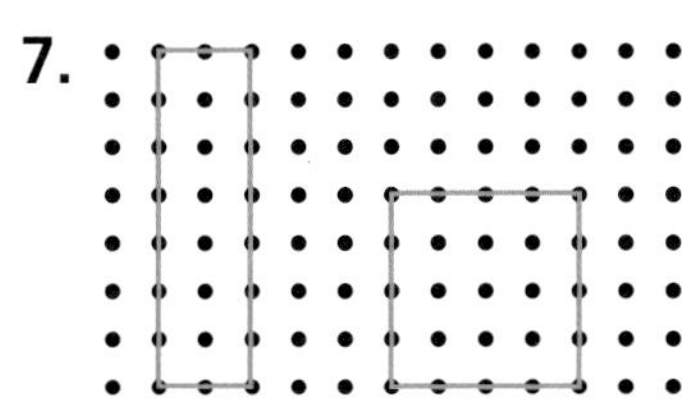

8. 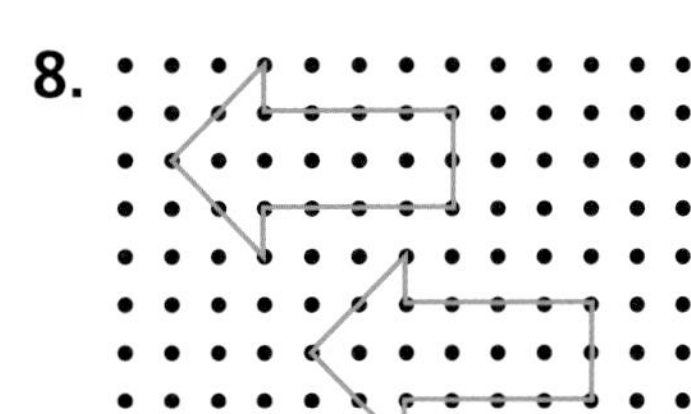

9. 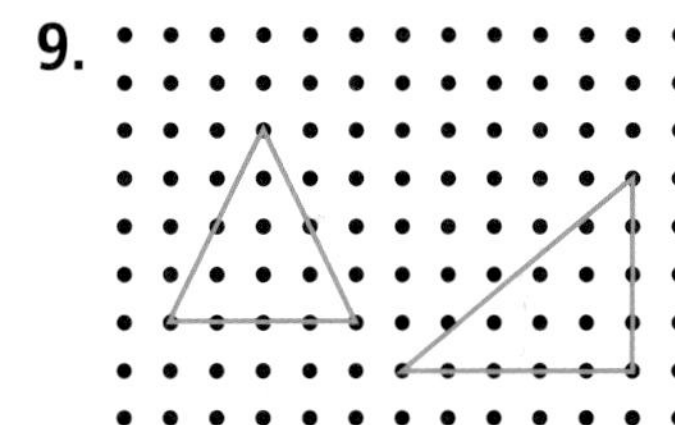

VOCABULARY POWER

CHAPTER VOCABULARY

congruent
line of symmetry
symmetry

WARM-UP WORDS

congruent Figures that have the same size and shape

symmetry A figure has symmetry if it can be folded along a line so that the two parts match exactly.

line of symmetry An imaginary line on a figure that when the figure is folded on this line, the two parts match exactly

LESSON 1 Congruent Figures

OBJECTIVE: Identify 2-dimensional congruent figures.

Quick Review

Name 4 plane figures in this picture.

Vocabulary

congruent

Learn

Figures with the same size and shape are **congruent**. Congruent figures can be in different positions.

These pairs appear to be congruent.	These pairs do not appear to be congruent.	
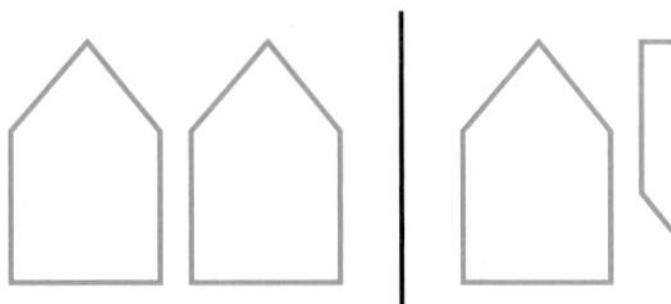	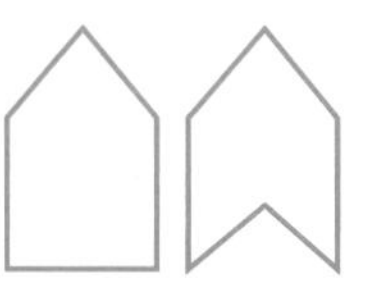	
Same size, same shape	Same size, not the same shape	Same shape, not the same size

PROBLEM Molly pasted a red hexagon on one side of her scrapbook cover. She wants to decorate the back of her scrapbook with a congruent figure. Which figure should she use?

HANDS ON

Activity **Materials** ■ tracing paper

Use tracing paper to identify the congruent figure.

- Trace and cut out Molly's figure, the red hexagon.
- Place your tracing over Figure 1. Do the figures appear to be congruent?

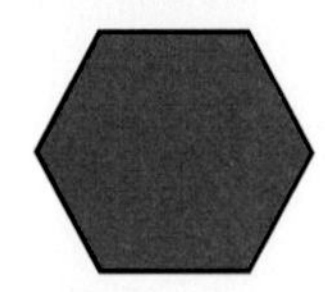		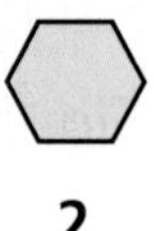	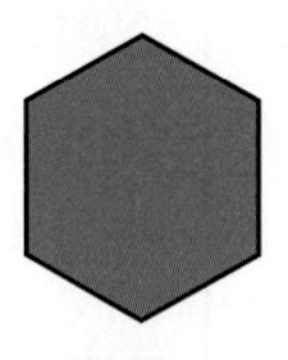
Molly's hexagon	1	2	3

- Place it over Figures 2 and 3. Do they appear to be congruent?

So, Molly should use Figure 3, the blue hexagon, because it appears to be congruent to her red hexagon.

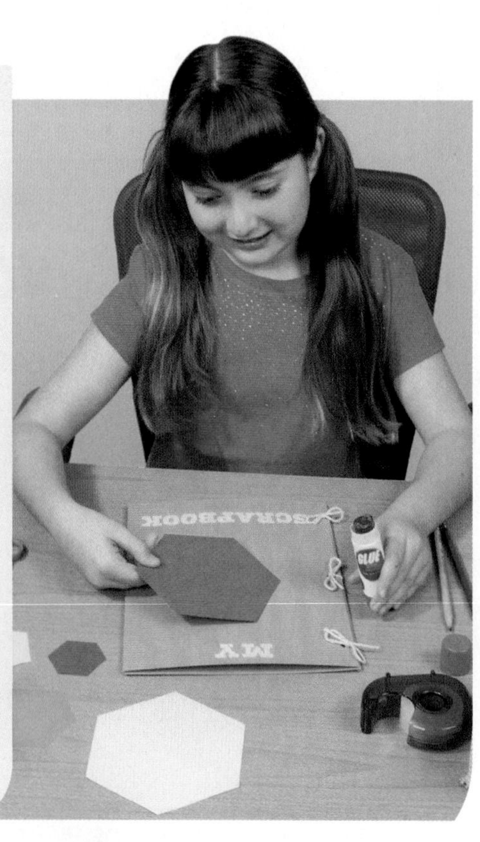

TEKS 3.9A identify congruent two-dimensional figures. *also* **3.8A, 3.14A, 3.14D, 3.15A, 3.15B, 3.16A, 3.16B**

Guided Practice

1. Trace triangle A. Which triangle appears to be the same size and shape as A?

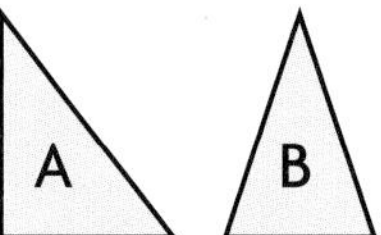

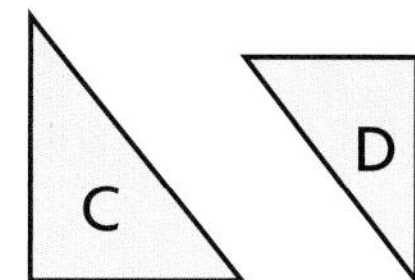

Trace and cut out each pair of figures. Tell if the figures appear to be congruent. Write *yes* or *no*.

2. 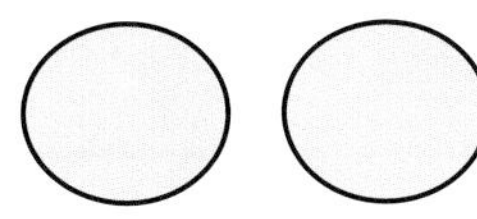

3. 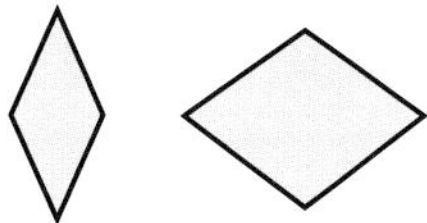

4. 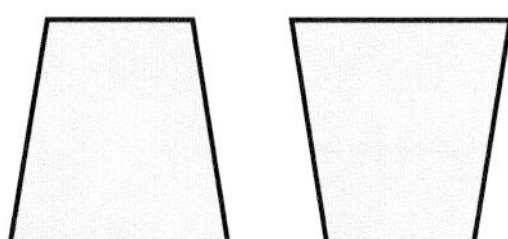

5. TALK Math **Explain** how to tell if two figures appear to be congruent.

Independent Practice and Problem Solving

Trace and cut out each pair of figures. Tell if the figures appear to be congruent. Write *yes* or *no*.

6. 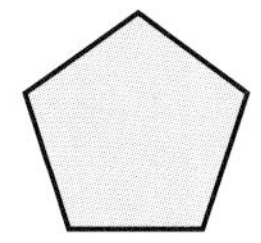 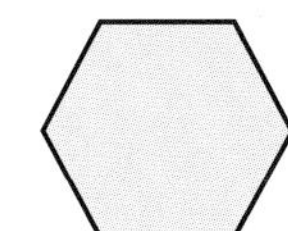

7. 

8. 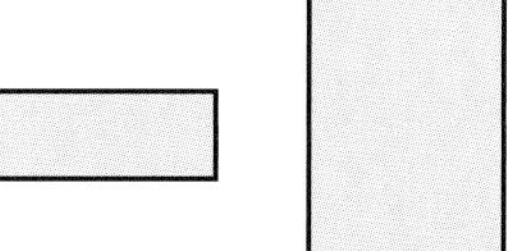

For 9–11, use the figures in the chart.

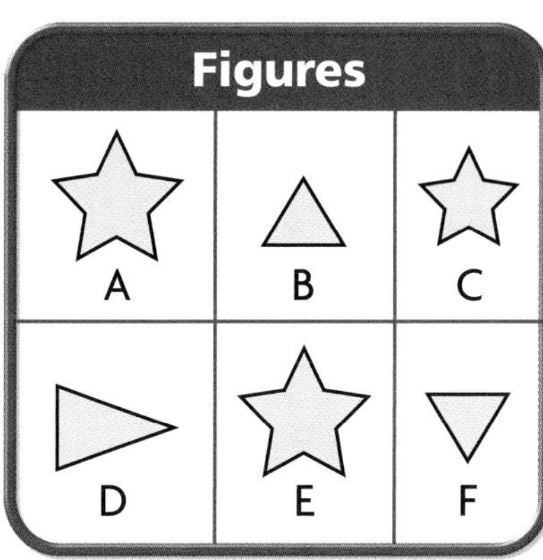

9. Johnny used two congruent star figures for his picture. Which figures did he use?

10. One of the figures in Mae's picture is triangle F. Which figure appears to be congruent to triangle F?

11. WRITE Math Look at stars A and C. Do they appear to be congruent? **Explain**.

Mixed Review and TAKS Prep

12. The picture on the wall of Jill's school has 2,039 figures in it. Write the number 2,039 in expanded form.
(TEKS 3.1A, p. 12)

13. A figure has 4 equal sides and 4 right angles. What is the figure?
(TEKS 3.8A, p. 378)

14. **TAKS Prep** Which figure appears to be congruent to this figure?
(Obj. 3)

A 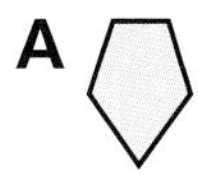 B  C  D 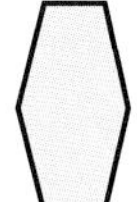

Extra Practice on page 408, Set A

Problem Solving Workshop
Strategy: Make a Model

OBJECTIVE: Use the strategy *make a model* to solve problems.

Learn the Strategy

Making models can help you solve problems. You can use many different kinds of models.

You can use base-ten blocks.

There were 45 people at a play on Tuesday. There were 32 people at the play on Wednesday.

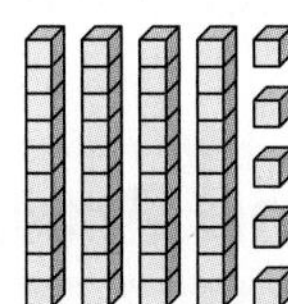

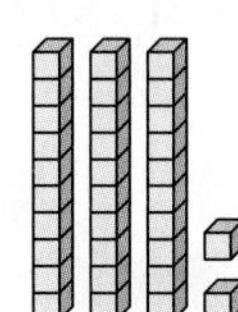

You can use square tiles.

There are 5 rows of desks with 6 desks in each row.

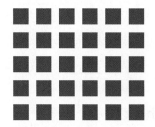

You can use counters.

Kara has 28 flowers. She puts 4 flowers in each vase.

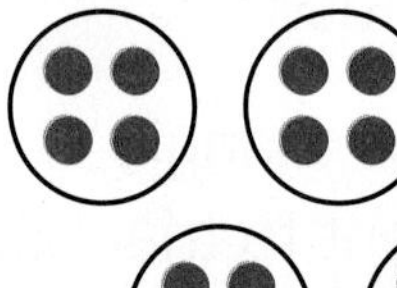

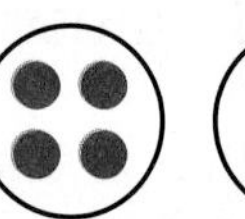

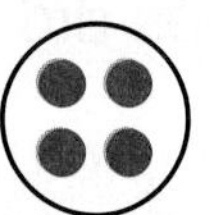

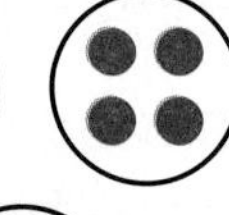

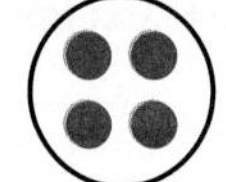

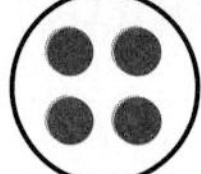

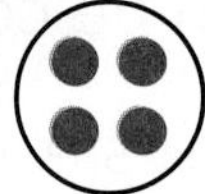

You can use pattern blocks.

Ben is tiling his floor. He uses triangles and squares to make a border.

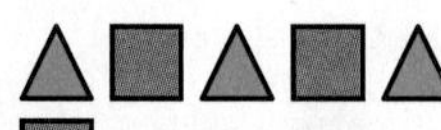

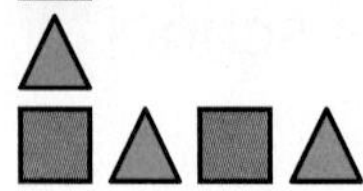

TALK Math

What problem can be solved by using each of the models shown?

TEKS 3.9A identify congruent two-dimensional figures. *also* 3.8A, 3.14A, 3.14B, 3.14C, 3.14D, 3.15A, 3.15B, 3.16A, 3.16B

Use the Strategy

PROBLEM Mr. Miller is making a path in his garden by using stones that are shaped like hexagons. He needs one more stone to complete the path. How can he use the stone shapes below to make the last stepping stone?

Read to Understand

- **Visualize a hexagon.**
- **What information is given?**

Plan

- **What strategy can you use to solve the problem?**
  You can *make a model.*

Solve

- **How can you use the strategy to solve the problem?**
  Use pattern blocks to model the problem. Use the yellow hexagon, the green triangles, and the red trapezoid to model the stones.

  Arrange the pattern blocks to make a hexagon.

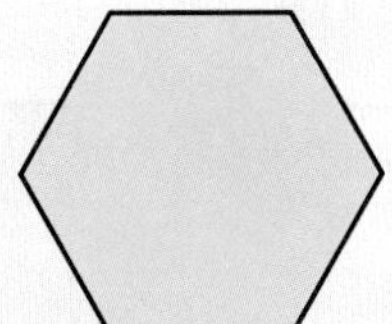

hexagon stone

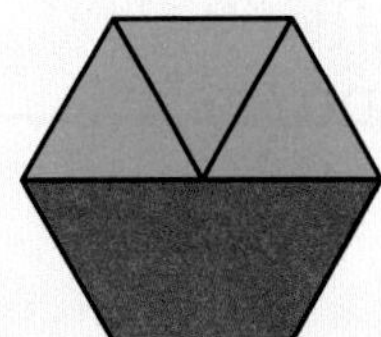

pieces of stone

So, 3 triangles and 1 trapezoid can be put together to make a hexagon.

Check

- **How do you know your answer is correct?**

Guided Problem Solving

1. Jillian is making a pattern. What pieces are missing from her pattern?

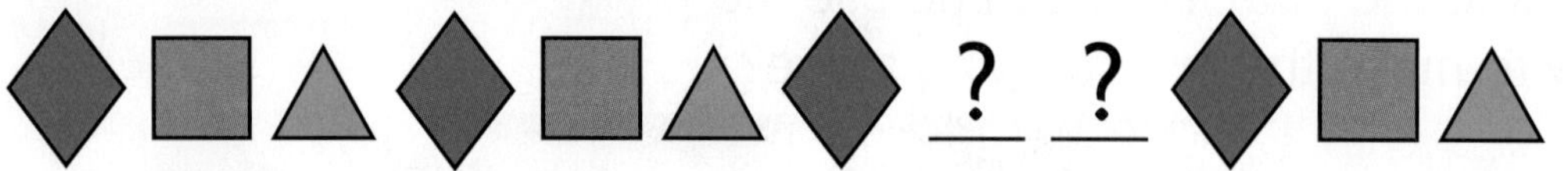

First, decide what model to use.
You can use pattern blocks to make the design.

Then, use the blocks to fill in the missing pieces.
Explain how you completed the pattern.

2. What if Jillian added 1 hexagon after each triangle? How many hexagons would be in her design?

3. Hunter uses square tiles to make an array with 4 rows and 3 columns. How many square tiles does he use?

Problem Solving Strategy Practice

Make a model to solve.

4. Two apples are the same size. Jenna ate $\frac{1}{2}$ of an apple. Caitlin ate $\frac{1}{3}$ of an apple. Who ate the larger part?

5. Mary has 4 packages of 6 napkins. She puts the same number of napkins on each of 3 tables. How many napkins does Mary put on each table?

6. Ashley is making a photo album. Each page holds 6 photos. There are 12 pages. How many photos can her album hold?

7. Mrs. Parker bought 48 muffins. There are 8 muffins in each box. How many boxes are there?

8. John used 1 hexagon and 2 triangles to make this rhombus. What other pattern blocks can be used to make a rhombus congruent to this one?

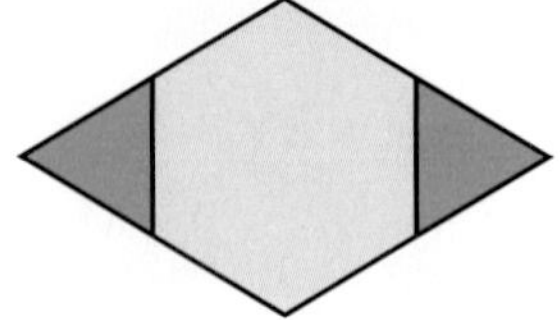

9. WRITE Math Mike uses 5 pattern blocks to make a shape congruent to this one. Which pattern blocks does he use? **Explain.**

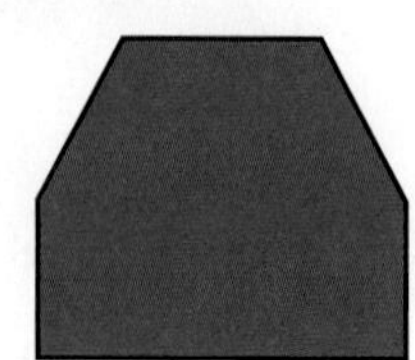

Mixed Strategy Practice

USE DATA For 10–12, use the table.

10. Tina buys 9 pattern-block stamp kits. How many stamps does Tina have in all?

11. There are 2 sorting circles in each bag. How many bags of sorting circles are in 1 kit?

12. There are 4 different kinds of activity cards in a kit. How many of each kind of card are there if there are the same number of each kind?

13. Sierra picked a square, a rhombus, and a triangle from the pattern blocks. The block she picked first did not have 4 sides. She did not pick the square last. In what order did Sierra pick the blocks?

14. **Pose a Problem** Look back at problem 13. Write a similar problem using a trapezoid, a rectangle, and a square. **Explain** the answer.

15. **Open-Ended** Draw a Venn diagram to sort the figures pictured below.

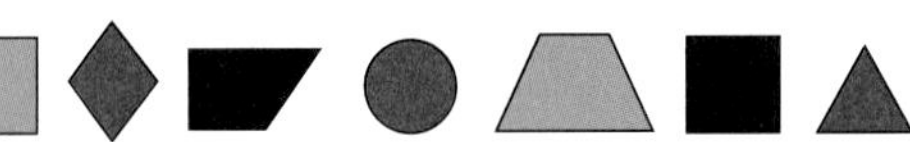

16. Marti traced pattern blocks to make a design. The pattern unit is *green triangle, green triangle, blue rhombus*. What is the eighth block in her pattern?

Choose a STRATEGY

- Draw a Diagram or Picture
- Make a Model or Act It Out
- Make an Organized List
- Look for a Pattern
- Make a Table or Graph
- Guess and Check
- Work Backward
- Solve a Simpler Problem
- Write an Equation
- Use Logical Reasoning

Math Kit

Item	Number in Each Kit
Pattern blocks	100
Activity cards	36
Pattern-block stamps	6
Sorting circles	12

CHALLENGE YOURSELF

Texas has 8 Block's School Supplies stores. Each store has 95 pattern-block stamp kits for sale.

17. Two schools each bought 28 pattern-block stamp kits from one store in September. Then one school returned 17 stamp kits. How many pattern-block stamp kits were in stock after the kits were returned?

18. Each pattern-block stamp kit costs \$9. On Tuesday, two stores each sold 5 kits, and four stores each sold 3 kits. How much money was paid for the kits on Tuesday?

LESSON 3

Symmetry

OBJECTIVE: Identify figures that have a line of symmetry.

Quick Review

Which two figures appear to be congruent?

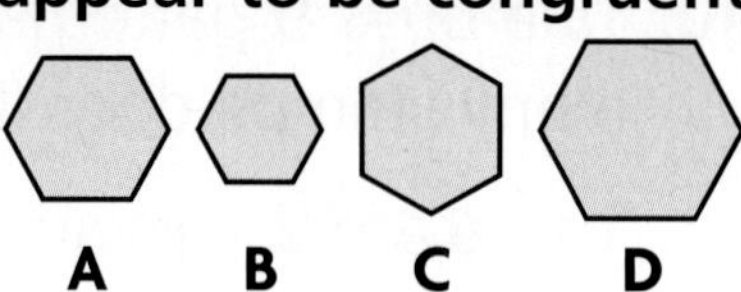

Vocabulary

symmetry

line of symmetry

A figure has **symmetry** if it can be folded in half so that the halves match exactly.

These figures appear to have a line of symmetry.

These figures do not appear to have a line of symmetry.

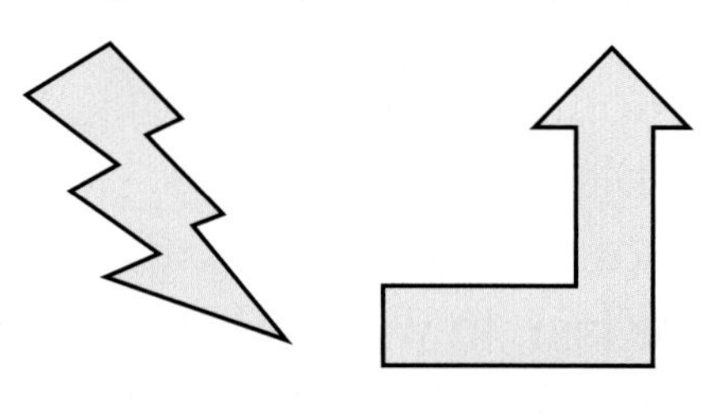

The line that divides a figure into two congruent parts is the **line of symmetry**.

Activity

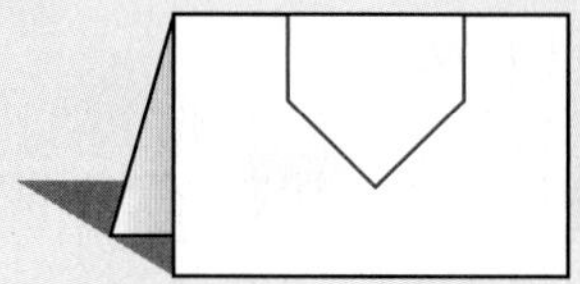

Materials ■ paper, scissors, crayon or marker

You can fold paper to explore symmetry.

- Fold a sheet of paper in half.
- Draw a figure that begins and ends on the fold. Cut out the figure with the paper still folded.
- Unfold the figure, and draw a line on the fold.
- Do the halves match exactly? Explain.

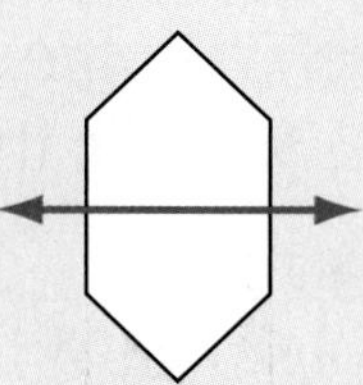

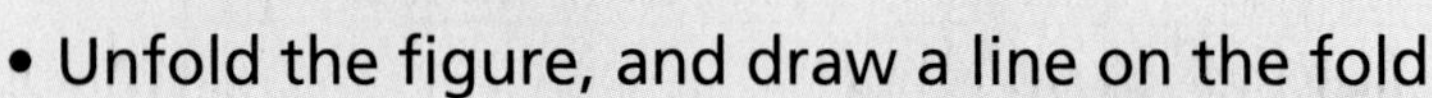

Guided Practice

1. Does the blue line appear to be a line of symmetry? **Explain.**
   Think: Do the halves match exactly?

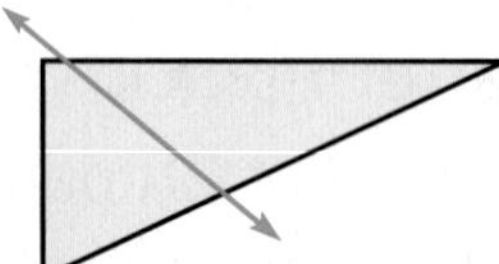

TEKS 3.9C Identify lines of symmetry in two-dimensional geometric figures. *also* 3.9A, 3.9B, 3.14A, 3.14D, 3.15A, 3.15B, 3.16A

Tell if the blue line appears to be a line of symmetry. Write *yes* or *no*.

2. 

3. 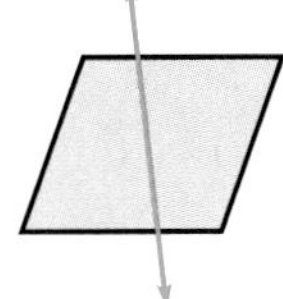

4. 

5. 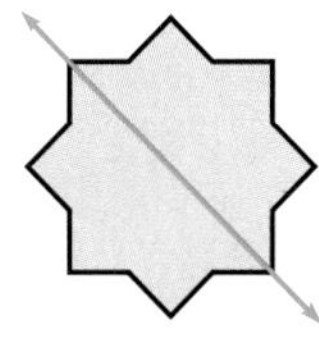

6. TALK Math **Explain** how you can fold paper to find a line of symmetry.

Independent Practice and Problem Solving

Tell if the blue line appears to be a line of symmetry. Write *yes* or *no*.

7. 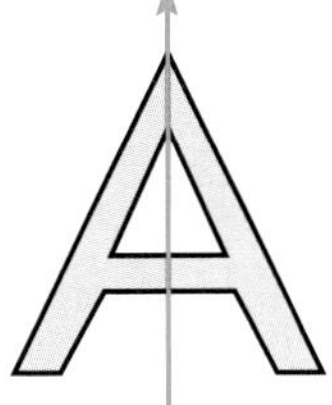

8. 

9. 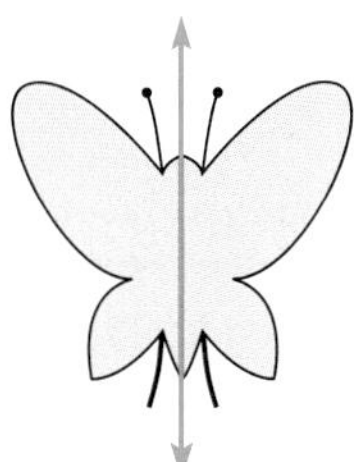

10. 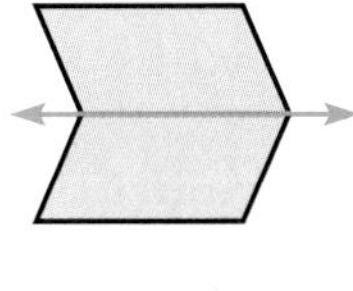

11. **Reasoning** Trace and cut out the figure below. Fold it to find a line of symmetry. **Explain** how you know your line shows symmetry.

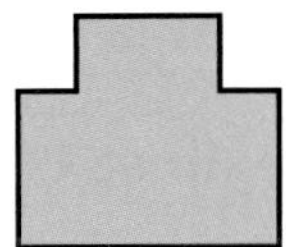

12. WRITE Math **What's the Error?** Julia says that the figure below shows a line of symmetry. Describe her error.

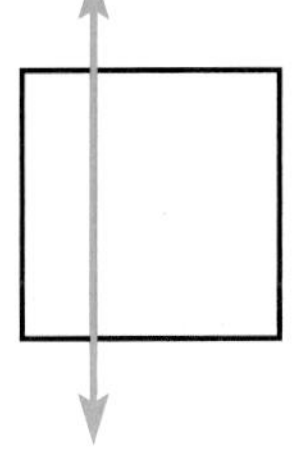

Mixed Review and TAKS Prep

13. A Favorite Drinks tally table shows 𝍸 𝍸 ||| next to *Juice*. How many voted for juice? (TEKS 3.13A, p. 164)

14. Are the lines parallel or perpendicular? (TEKS 3.8A, p. 372)

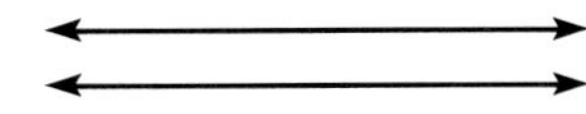

15. **TAKS Prep** Which line does not appear to be a line of symmetry? (Obj. 3)

A 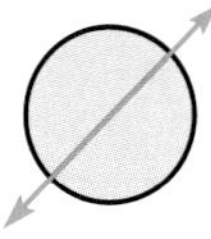

C 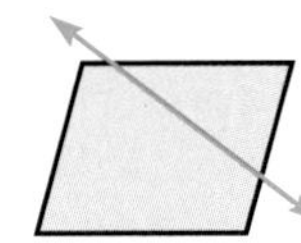

B 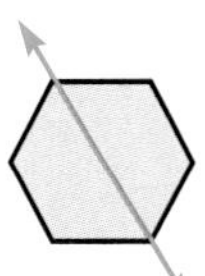

D 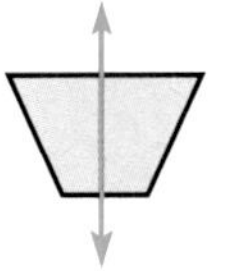

Technology
CD ROM Use Harcourt Mega Math, Ice Station Exploration, *Polar Planes*, Level K.

Extra Practice on page 408, Set B

Lines of Symmetry

OBJECTIVE: Identify and draw lines of symmetry in plane figures.

Quick Review

Tell if the blue line appears to be a line of symmetry. Write *yes* or *no*.

a. 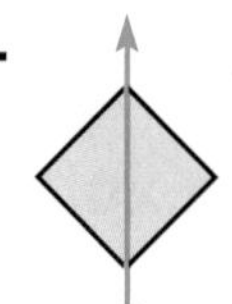

b.  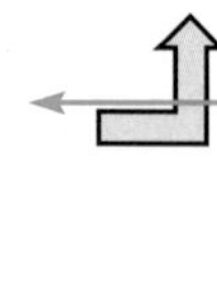

c. 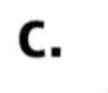 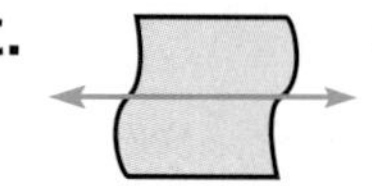

d. 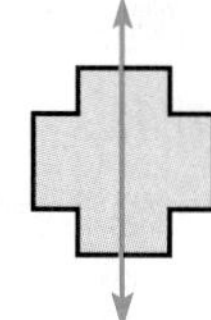

Learn

Some figures appear to have one or more lines of symmetry. Some figures have no lines of symmetry.

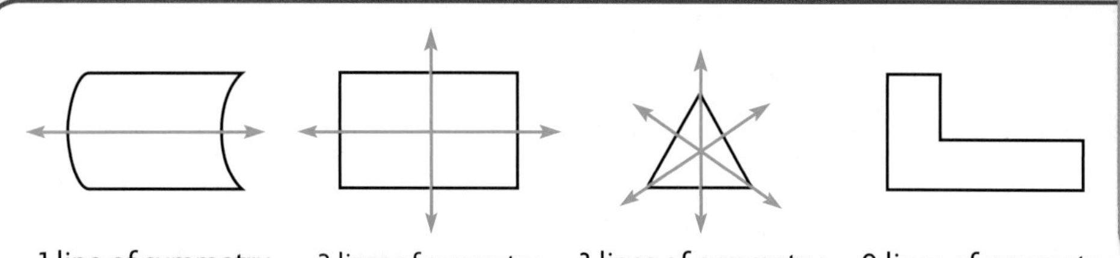

Some letters and numbers appear to have lines of symmetry.

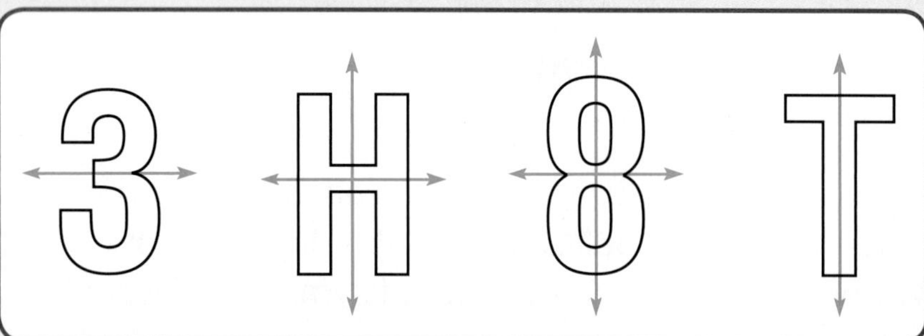

- Which other letters or numbers have more than 1 line of symmetry?

ERROR ALERT

Make sure that both halves of the figure match, or are congruent, when you draw lines of symmetry.

Guided Practice

1. Which of these letters appear to have more than 1 line of symmetry? Trace the letters, and draw the lines of symmetry.

Trace each figure. Then draw the line or lines of symmetry.

2. 

3. 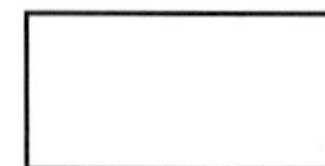

4. 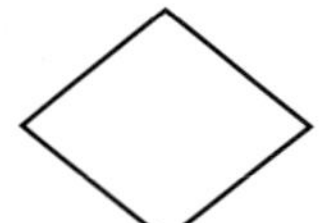

5. 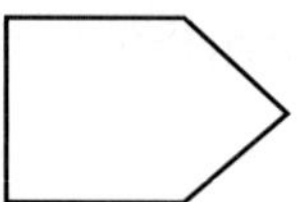

6. TALK Math Trace and cut out this figure. **Explain** how you can find all the lines of symmetry.

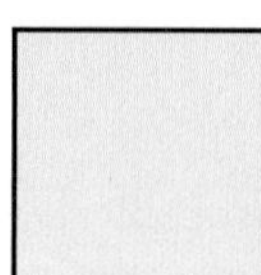

TEKS 3.9C identify lines of symmetry in two-dimensional geometric figures. *also* **3.9A, 3.9B, 3.14A, 3.15A, 3.15B, 3.16A, 3.16B**

Independent Practice and Problem Solving

Trace each figure. Then draw the line or lines of symmetry.

7. 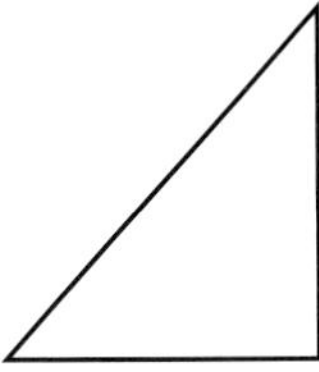

8. 

9. 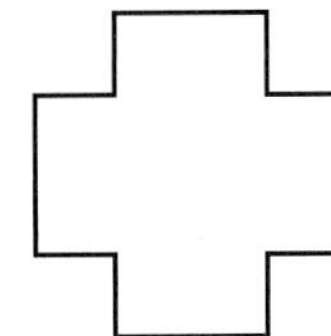

10. 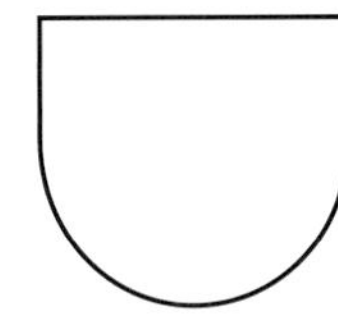

Decide if each figure appears to have 0 lines, 1 line, or more than 1 line of symmetry. Write *0, 1, or more than 1*.

11. 

12. 

13. 

14. 

For 15–16, use shapes A–C.

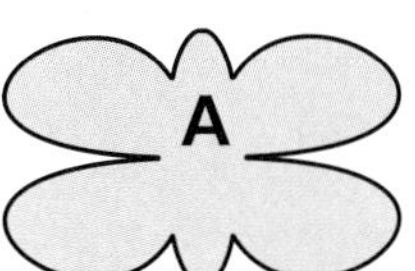

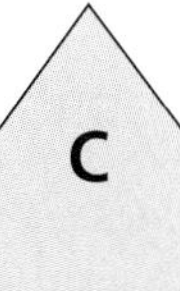

15. Gillian is making a book cover. She drew a figure on it that has 2 lines of symmetry. Which figure did she draw?

16. **FAST FACT** • Geometry A nonagon is a polygon with 9 sides. Which of Gillian's book cover shapes is a nonagon? How many lines of symmetry does it have?

17. **WRITE Math** **Sense or Nonsense** Sienna says that the pattern block she traced has only 1 line of symmetry. Does her statement make sense? **Explain.**

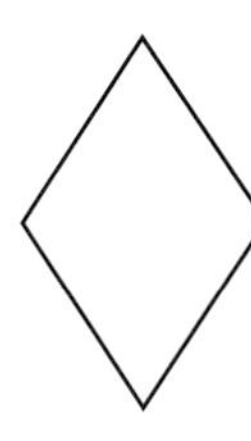

Mixed Review and TAKS Prep

18. Max drew a figure that is congruent to a hexagon. How many sides does his figure have? (TEKS 3.9A, p. 396)

19. Which division number sentences are in the same fact family as $2 \times 8 = 16$? (TEKS 3.6C, p. 304)

20. **TAKS Prep** Which letters appear to have only 1 line of symmetry? (Obj. 3)

A K and X **C** B and O

B X and O **D** K and B

Extra Practice on page 408, Set C

Technology Use Harcourt Mega Math, Ice Station Exploration, *Polar Planes*, Level J.

LESSON 5

Draw Symmetric Figures

OBJECTIVE: Draw 2-dimensional figures with lines of symmetry.

Quick Review

Does the blue line appear to be a line of symmetry? Write *yes* or *no*.

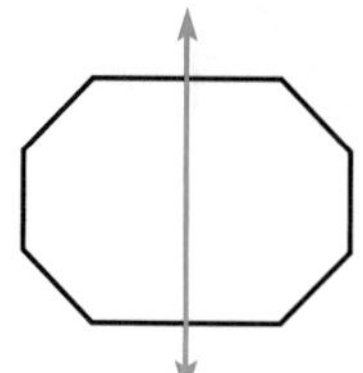

Learn

Figures with symmetry can be folded in half so that the halves match exactly.

Activity **Materials** ■ dot paper, ruler

Use dot paper to draw figures with symmetry.

- Fold a sheet of dot paper in half, and draw a figure along the fold.
- Unfold the paper, and complete the other half to make a figure with a line of symmetry.
- Repeat the activity by drawing another figure.
- Does your figure have any other lines of symmetry? How can you check?

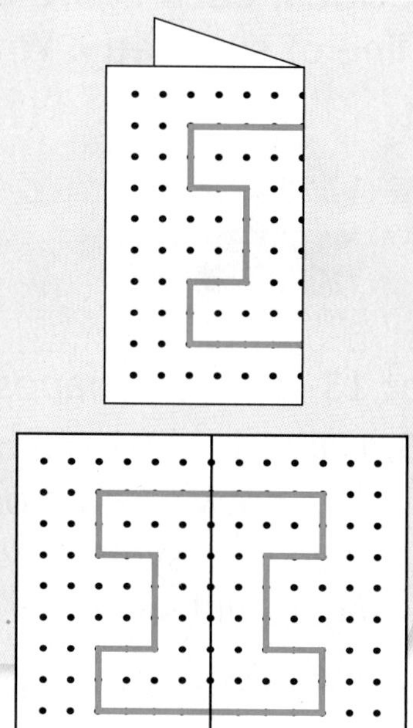

Guided Practice

1. The folded paper shows half of a figure with a line of symmetry. Tell how to draw the other half.

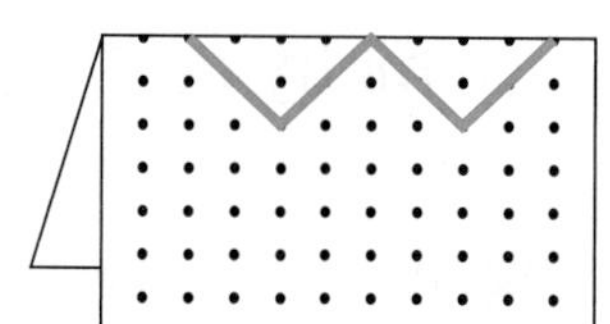

Copy each figure on dot paper. Complete the drawing so each has a line of symmetry.

2. 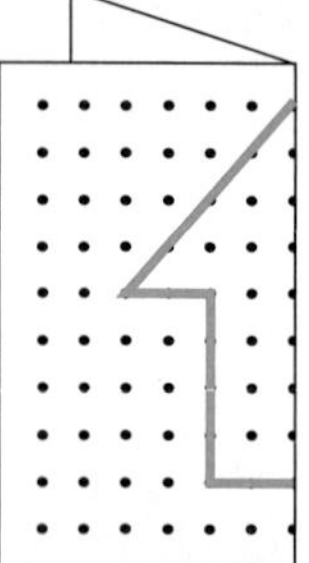

3. 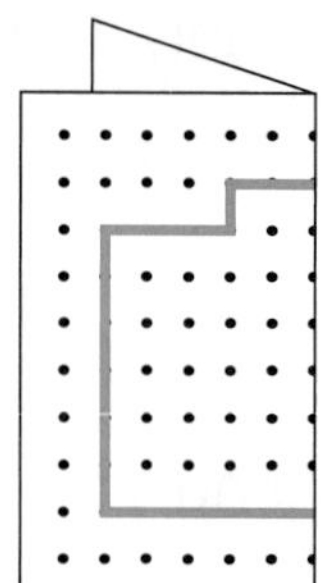

✓4. 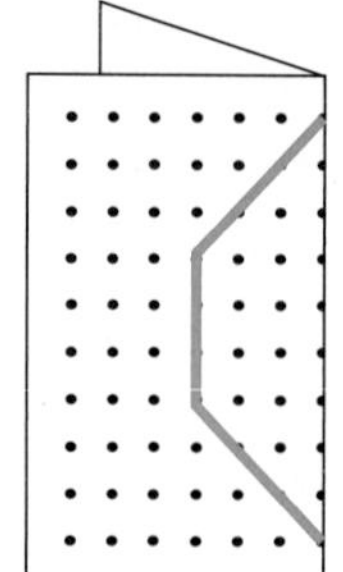

✓5. 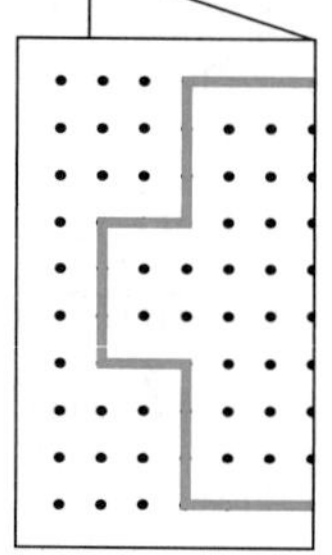

6. TALK Math **Explain** how you know if a figure you drew has a line of symmetry.

TEKS 3.9B create two-dimensional figures with lines of symmetry using concrete models and technology. *also* **3.9A, 3.9C, 3.14A, 3.14D, 3.15A, 3.15B**

Independent Practice and Problem Solving

Copy each figure on dot paper. Complete the design so each has a line of symmetry.

7. 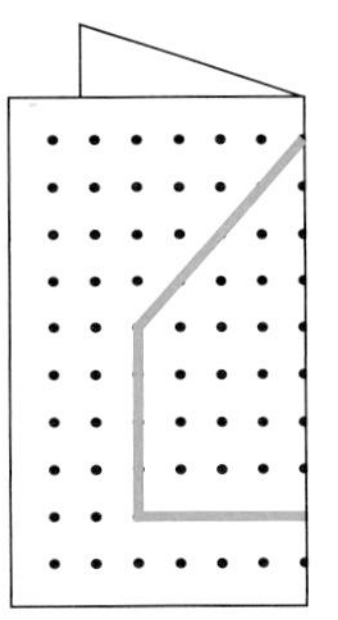

8. 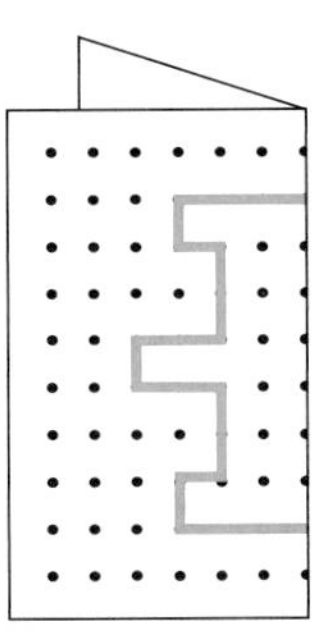

9. 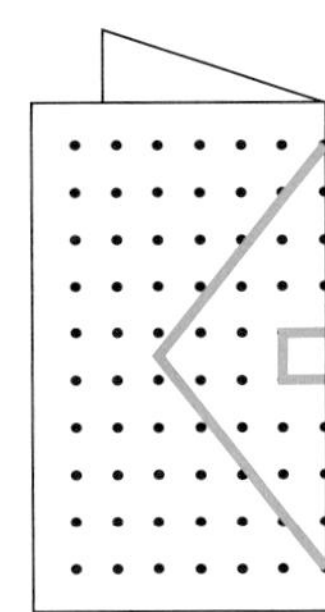

10. 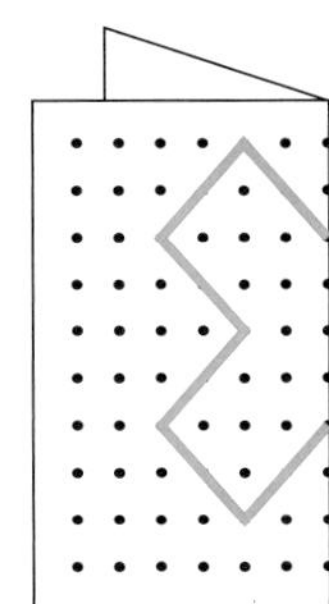

For 11–12, use the hexagons.

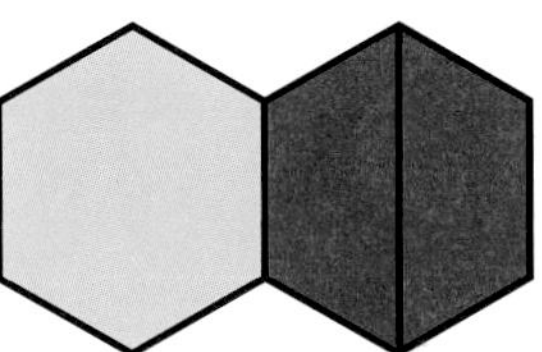

11. Trace these combined figures. How many lines of symmetry does your figure appear to have?

12. WRITE Math ▸ Ben traced a yellow hexagon to the right of the red trapezoids. There are no gaps between the two figures. Is the number of lines of symmetry the same? **Explain**.

13. **Reasoning** Trace this circle. Does it have more than one line of symmetry? How do you know?

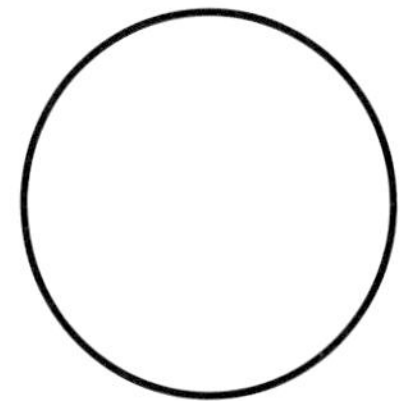

Mixed Review and TAKS Prep

14. Joni is eating lunch. Is it more likely to be 1:00 A.M. or 1:00 P.M.? (TEKS 3.12B, p. 140)

15. Three friends each have 4 hexagons and 3 triangles. How many figures in all do they have? (TEKS 3.4A, p. 276)

16. **TAKS Prep** Which line appears to be a line of symmetry? (Obj. 3)

A 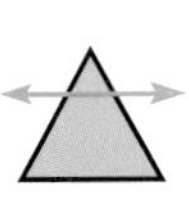

C 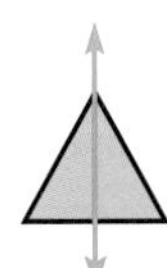

B 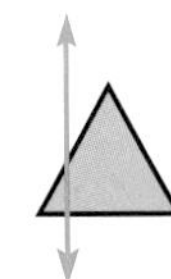

D 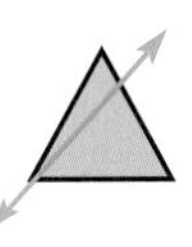

Extra Practice on page 408, Set D

Extra Practice

Set A Trace and cut out each pair of figures. Tell if the figures appear to be congruent. Write *yes* or *no*. (pp. 396–397)

1. 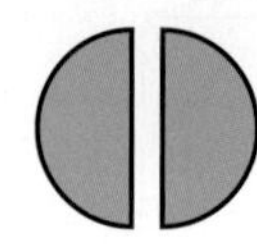
2. 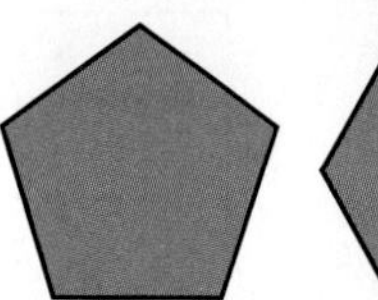
3. 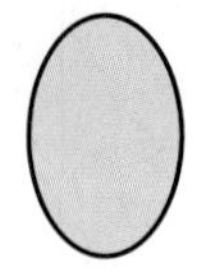 

Set B Tell if the blue line appears to be a line of symmetry. Write *yes* or *no*. (pp. 402–403)

1. 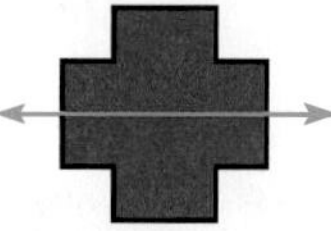
2. 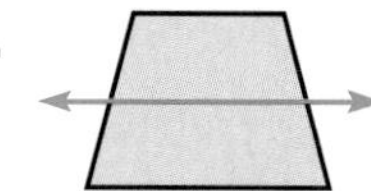
3. 
4. 

Set C Trace each figure. Then draw the line or lines of symmetry. (pp. 404–405)

1. 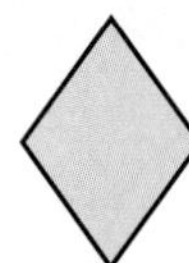
2. 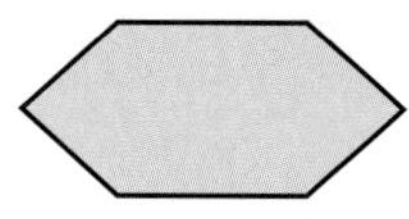
3. 
4. 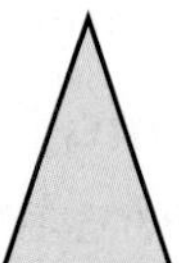

Decide if each figure appears to have **0**, **1**, or more than **1** line of symmetry. Write *0*, *1*, or *more than 1*.

5. 
6. 
7. 
8. 

Set D Trace each figure. Complete the design so each has a line of symmetry. (pp. 406–407)

1. 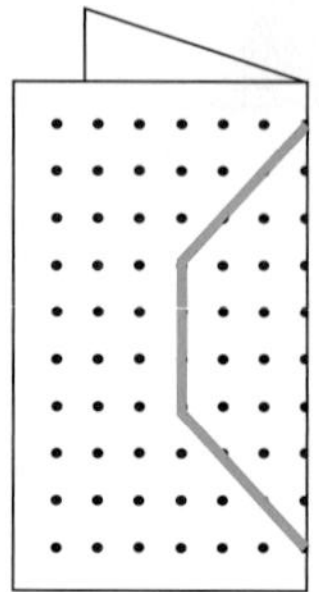
2. 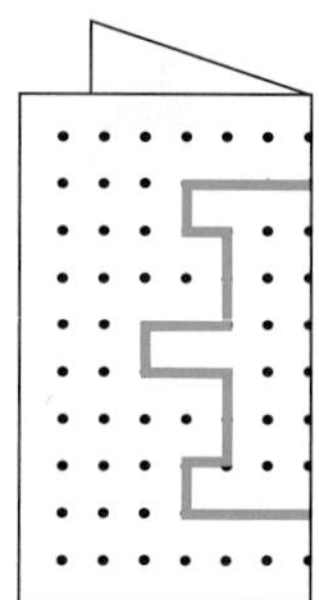
3. 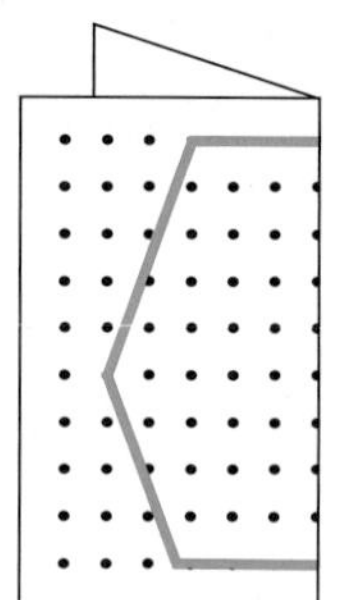
4. 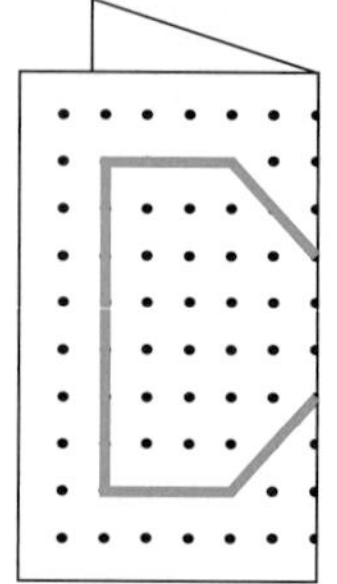

CD ROM **Technology**
Use Harcourt Mega Math, Ice Station Exploration, *Polar Planes*, Levels H, J, K.

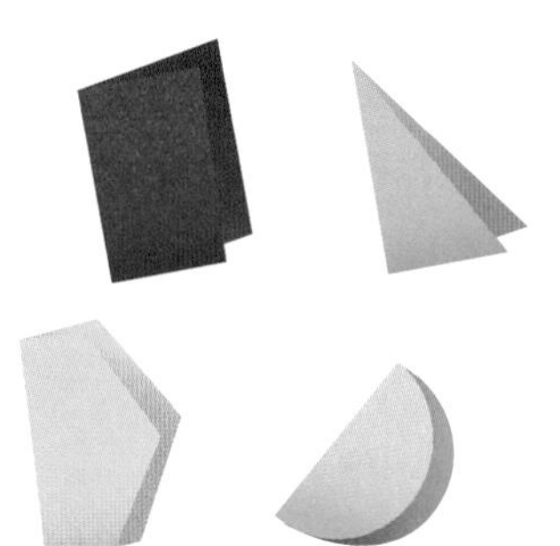

*i*Tools: Geometry (TEKS 3.9C, 3.14D)

Find out If a Plane Figure has Symmetry

Jane made invitations for her party. She used figures that had lines of symmetry and then folded them to make cards.

Step 1	Click on *Geometry*. Then click on *Plane Figures* in the *Activities* menu. Now click on the second tab at the bottom.
Step 2	Click on the square to place it on the grid.
Step 3	Click on the arrows at the top of the screen to make the sentence true. Then click on *Check*.
Step 4	Click on *Line of Symmetry*. Click on the arrows to place the line of symmetry. Then click on *Check*.

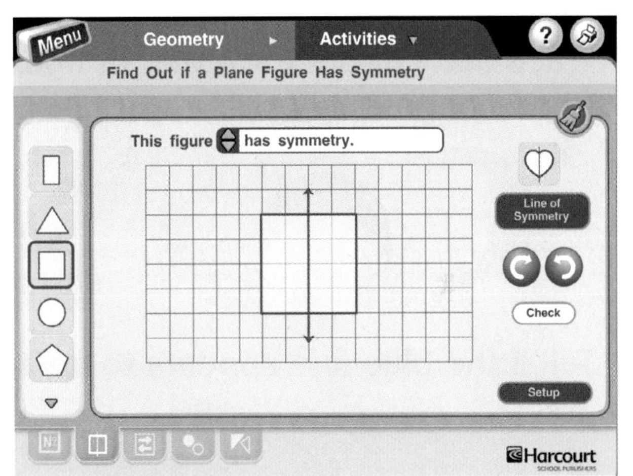

Click on the broom to clear the workspace.

Try It

1. Look at the figures on the left of the screen. Find a figure that has 2 lines of symmetry. Then find a figure with more than 2 lines of symmetry.
2. Click on the arrow below the figures. Find a figure that has no lines of symmetry.
3. **Explore More** How many lines of symmetry does the hexagon have? Use the *i*Tool to show the lines of symmetry, and then draw what you see. **Explain** the lines of symmetry.

Technology
*i*Tools available online or on CD-ROM

Chapter 17 Review/Test

Check Vocabulary and Concepts

Choose the best term from the box.

1. Figures with the same size and shape are _?_. (TEKS 3.9A, p. 396)
2. A figure has _?_ if it can be folded in half so that the halves match exactly. (TEKS 3.9C, p. 402)

VOCABULARY
congruent
line of symmetry
symmetry

Check Skills

Trace and cut out each pair of figures. Tell if the figures appear to be congruent. Write *yes* or *no*. (TEKS 3.9A, pp. 396–397)

3. 

4. 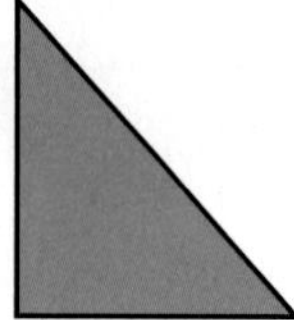

5. 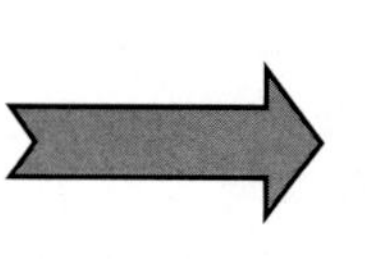

Tell if the blue line appears to be a line of symmetry. Write *yes* or *no*. (TEKS 3.9C, pp. 402–403)

6. 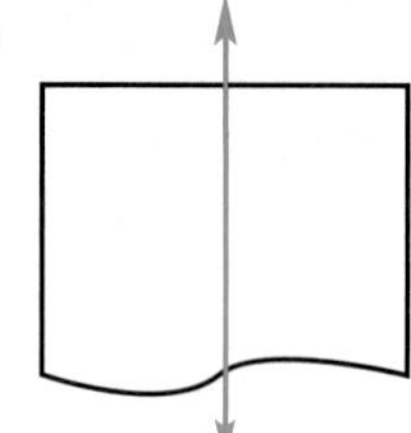

7. 

8. 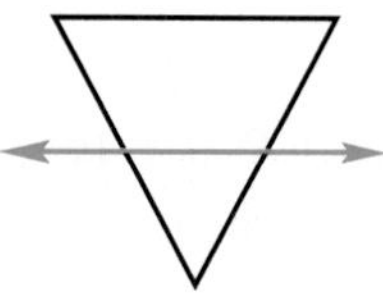

9. 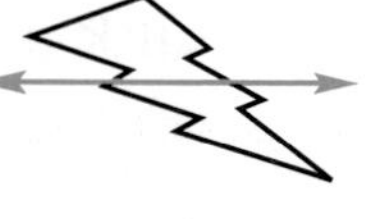

Trace each figure. Then draw the line or lines of symmetry. (TEKS 3.9C, pp. 404–405)

10. 

11. 

12. 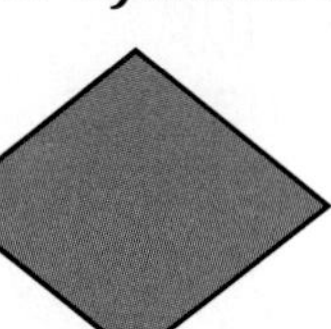

13. U

Check Problem Solving

Make a model to solve. (TEKS 3.8, pp. 398–401)

14. Mrs. Thompson baked 4 apple pies. Each pie is cut into 8 slices. How many pieces of pie are there?

15. WRITE Math Bailey used 2 triangles and 2 trapezoids to make this rhombus. What other pattern blocks can be used to make a rhombus congruent to this one? **Explain**.

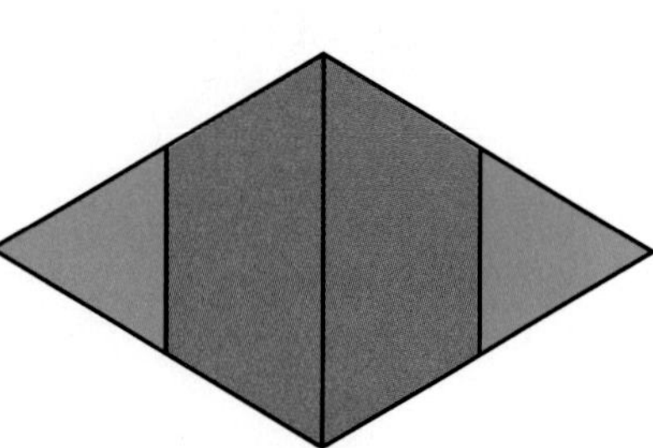

GO ONLINE **Technology** Use *Online Assessment*.

Enrich • Rotations

How Do They Turn?

Angles are measured in **degrees**. The rotation, or turn, of an object is named by the angle the object turns. To show how a figure rotates, follow the blue side.

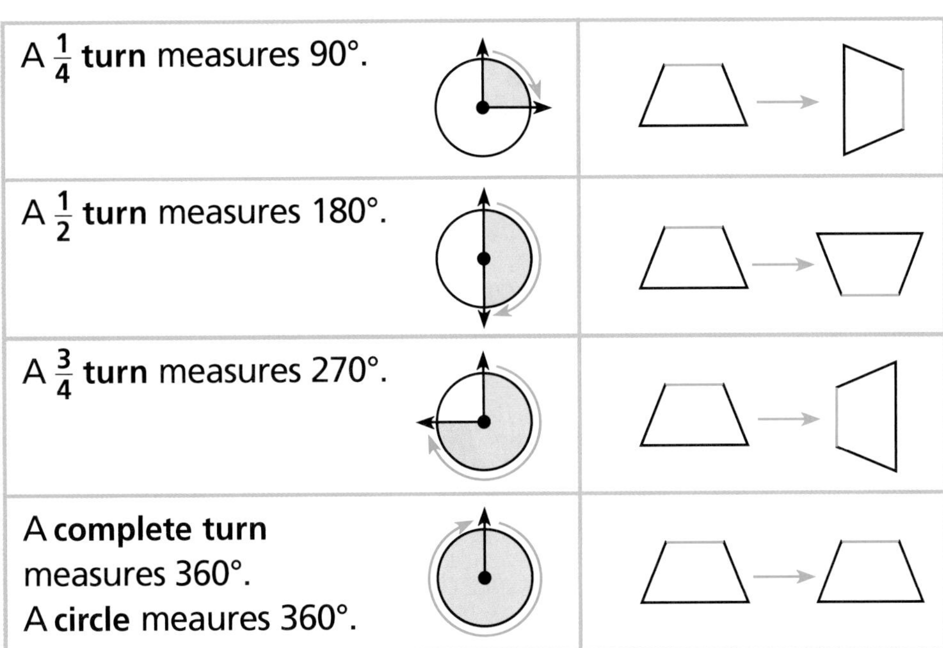

A $\frac{1}{4}$ **turn** measures 90°.	
A $\frac{1}{2}$ **turn** measures 180°.	
A $\frac{3}{4}$ **turn** measures 270°.	
A **complete turn** measures 360°. A **circle** meaures 360°.	

Figures rotate clockwise or counterclockwise.

A **clockwise** rotation is when an object moves in the same direction that the hands on a clock move. 	A **counterclockwise** rotation is when an object moves in the opposite direction that the hands on a clock move. 

Examples

Tell if the objects have turned 90°, 180°, or 360°.

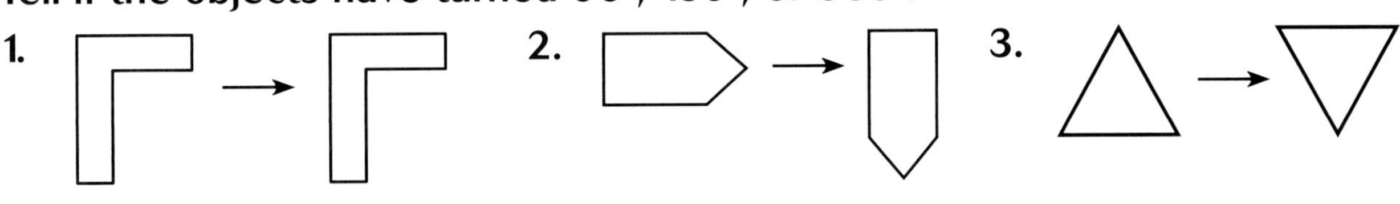

Try It

WRITE Math Marty read from 1:00 P.M. to 1:30 P.M. Did the minute hand turn 90°, 180°, or 270°? **Explain.**

Getting Ready for the TAKS

Chapters 1–17

Number, Operation, and Quantitative Reasoning (TAKS Obj. 1)

1. At *Beads and Things*, there are 447 wooden beads. There are 600 glass beads. How many more glass beads than wooden beads are there?

   A 47
   B 153
   C 247
   D 1,047

Test Tip **Check your work.**

See item 2. It is important to check your answer after you have solved a problem. You can use multiplication to check division. To check problem 2, multiply your answer by 10.

2. It takes Eli 10 minutes to read a page in his book. Eli reads for 90 minutes. How many pages does he read?

   F 900
   G 100
   H 80
   J 9

3. **WRITE Math** Ben has 2 half dollars, 1 quarter, 5 dimes, and 6 pennies in his bank. How much money does Ben have? **Explain** how you know.

Patterns, Relationships, and Algebraic Thinking (TAKS Obj. 2)

4. What related multiplication fact can help you find $132 \div 11$?

   A $10 \times 11 = 110$
   B $11 \times 1 = 11$
   C $66 \times 2 = 132$
   D $12 \times 11 = 132$

5. Which shape comes next in the pattern?

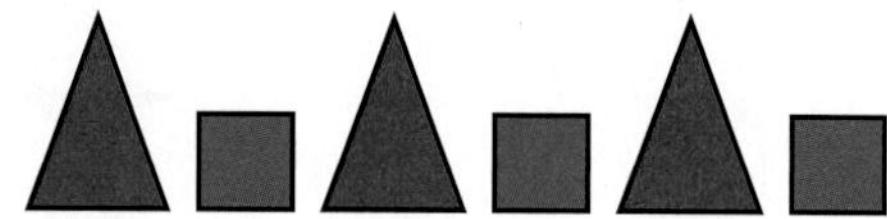

   F blue triangle
   G red triangle
   H blue square
   J red square

6. How many wheels do 4 wagons have?

Wagons	1	2	3	4
Wheels	4	8	12	■

   A 16
   B 15
   C 14
   D 13

7. **WRITE Math** How can you use a fact family to find $32 \div 8$? **Explain** your answer.

Geometry and Spatial Reasoning (TAKS Obj. 3)

8. Which figure appears to be congruent to Figure A?

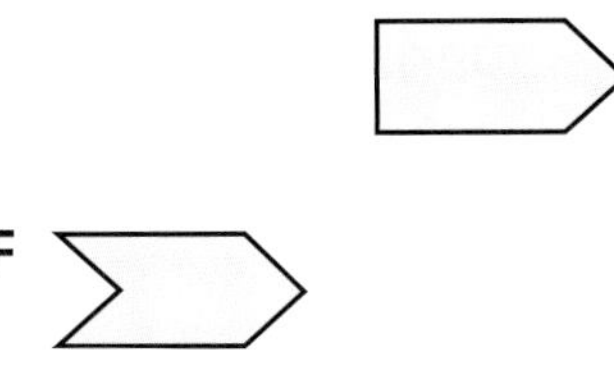

F

G

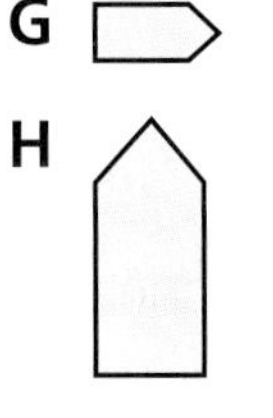

H

J

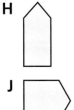

9. How many right angles are in a square?

A 1

B 2

C 3

D 4

10. WRITE Math How many lines of symmetry does this figure appear to have? Use a drawing to help you **explain**.

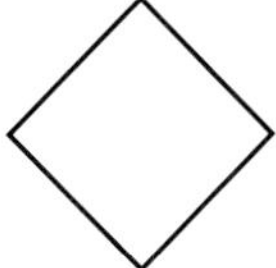

Probability and Statistics (TAKS Obj. 5)

11. The pictograph shows the number of trading cards Maria's friends have. Maria has 30 cards. How many symbols are needed to show this on the graph?

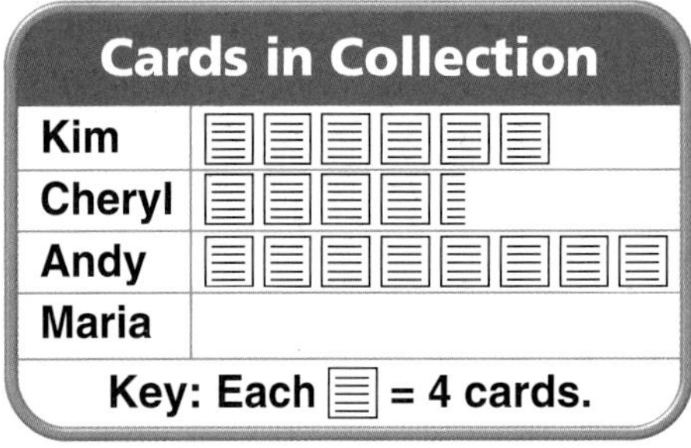

Cards in Collection
Kim
Cheryl
Andy
Maria
Key: Each = 4 cards.

F 6

G $7\frac{1}{2}$

H 8

J Not here

12. WRITE Math The graph shows the insects Stephen saw on a walk. How many insects did Stephen see in all? **Explain** how you know.

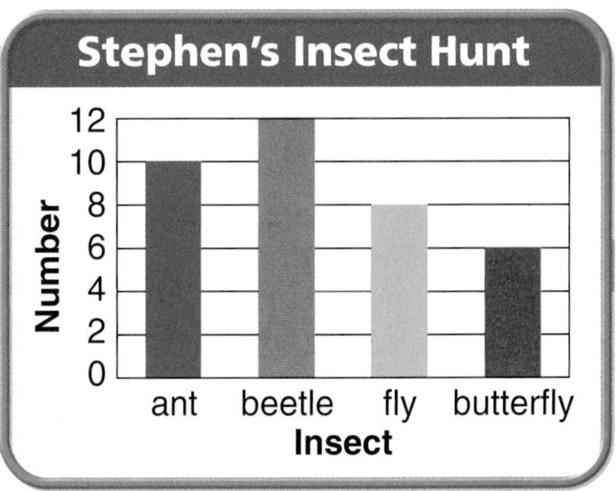

18 3-Dimensional Figures

The Big Idea Three-dimensional figures can be classified according to their geometric properties.

At Moody Gardens® in Galveston, Texas, there are three pyramids—the Discovery Pyramid®, the Aquarium Pyramid®, and the Rainforest Pyramid®.

Investigate

Here is a walkway in the Aquarium Pyramid®. The walkway is in the shape of a cylinder. Can you think of items in your classroom or around your house that are shaped like pyramids or cylinders? Make a list.

GO ONLINE **Technology**
Student pages are available in the Student eBook.

Show What You Know

Check your understanding of important skills needed for success in Chapter 18.

Solid Figures

Choose the best term from the box.

cone
cube
cylinder
pyramid
rectangular prism
sphere

1. 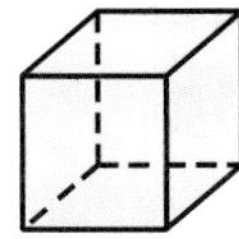

2. 

3. 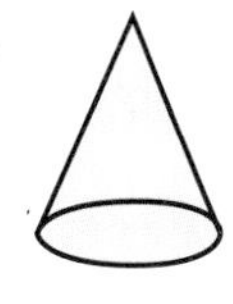

4. 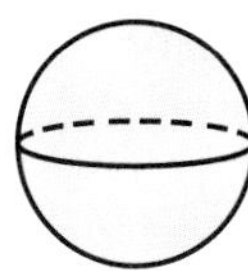

5. 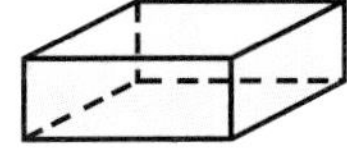

6. 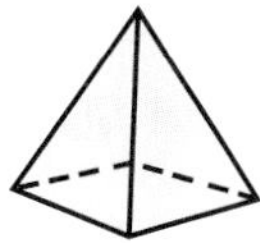

Name the solid figure that each object looks like.

7. 

8. 

9. 

10. 

VOCABULARY POWER

CHAPTER VOCABULARY

cone
cube
cylinder
edge
face
rectangular prism
sphere
square pyramid
three-dimensional figure
triangular prism
vertex

WARM-UP WORDS

three-dimensional figure A figure having length, width, and height

rectangular prism A solid figure with six faces that are all rectangles

cube A solid figure with six congruent square faces

LESSON 1

Identify 3-Dimensional Figures

OBJECTIVE: Identify, describe, and classify three-dimensional figures.

Quick Review

Name each plane figure.

1. □ 2. △

3. ▭ 4. ○

5. 

Vocabulary

three-dimensional figure
rectangular prism
triangular prism
cube
cylinder
cone
sphere
square pyramid

Learn

Three-dimensional figures have length, width, and height. They are also called solid figures.

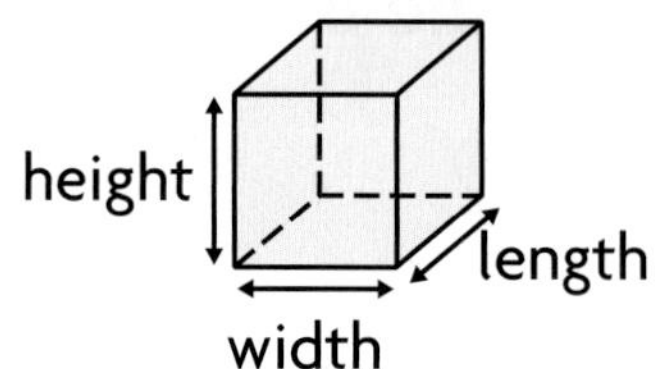

PROBLEM Jodie's grandmother gave her a charm bracelet. Which charm on her bracelet is shaped like a sphere?

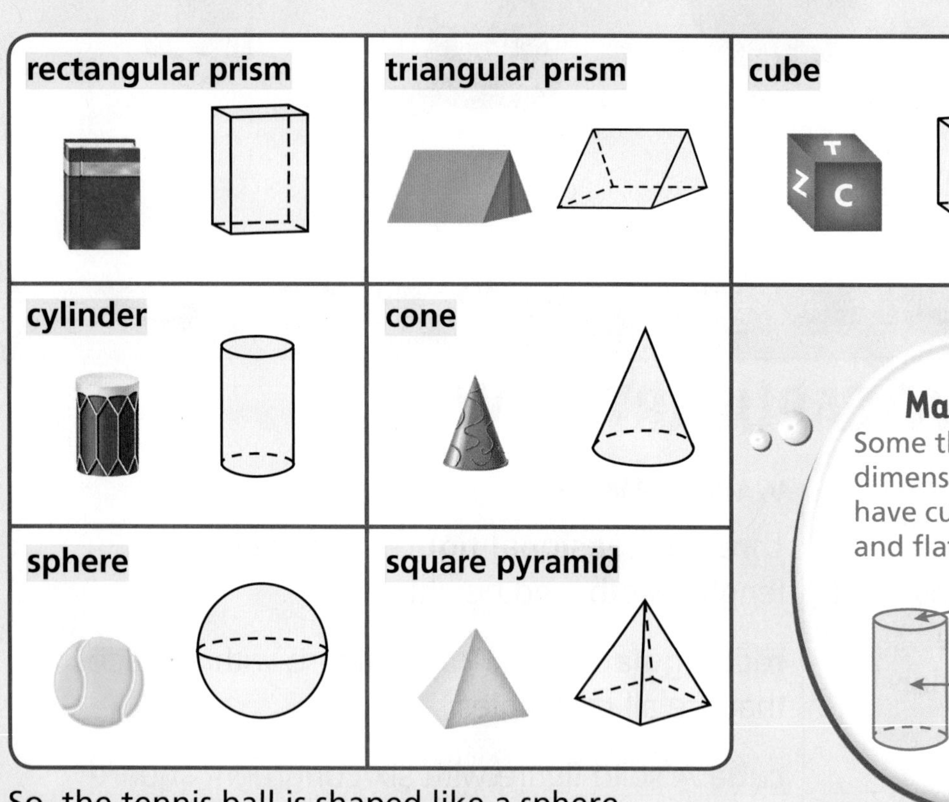

Math Idea

Some three-dimensional figures have curved surfaces and flat surfaces.

flat surface
curved surface

So, the tennis ball is shaped like a sphere.

- Which charm is shaped like a rectangular prism?

TEKS 3.8 The student is expected to identify, classify, and describe, two- and three-dimensional geometric figures by their attributes. The student compares two-dimensional figures, three-dimensional figures, or both by their attributes using formal geometric vocabulary. *also* **3.14A, 3.14D, 3.15A, 3.15B, 3.16B**

Guided Practice

1. Are the surfaces of your math book flat or curved?

Name the solid figure that each object is shaped like.

2. 

3. 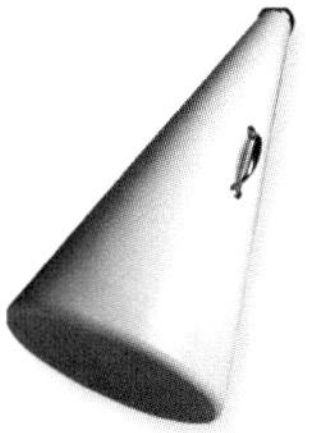

4. 

5. 

6. **TALK Math** **Explain** how a sphere, a cylinder, and a cone are alike.

Independent Practice and Problem Solving

Name the solid figure that each object is shaped like.

7. 

8. 

9. 

10. 

11. 

12. 

13. 

14. 

Name each solid figure.

15. 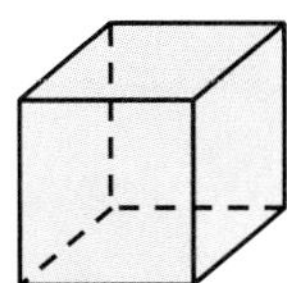

16. 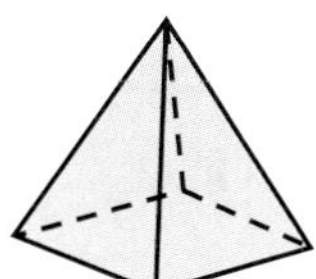

17. 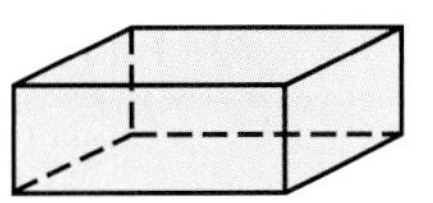

18. 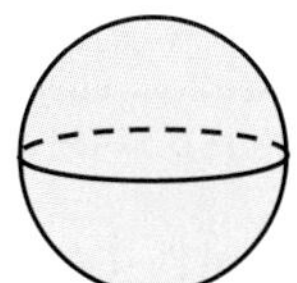

19. ***FAST FACT*** Earth is the third planet from the sun and the fifth-largest planet in our solar system. What three-dimensional figure is shaped like Earth?

Extra Practice on page 426, Set A

20. Mrs. Selnik placed these items on the table for a picnic. Melinda chose the item that was in the shape of a cylinder. Which item did Melinda choose?

For 21–24, use the model.

21. Tony built this model using different solid figures. What solid figures are the red blocks?

22. How many square pyramids did Tony use to make his model?

23. How many more cylinders are in Tony's model than cubes?

24. How many rectangular prisms did Tony use to make his model?

25. Rick built a tower using 7 rectangular prisms, 4 cylinders, 8 cubes, and 1 square pyramid. Half of the figures were blue and half were red. How many figures were blue?

26.  WRITE Math **What's the Error?** Paige said that this cardboard box is a cube. Describe her error and name the figure.

Mixed Review and TAKS Prep

27. Raina bought 5 charms for her bracelet. Each charm cost $9. How much did she spend? (TEKS 3.4B, p. 228)

28. How many lines of symmetry does this figure appear to have? (TEKS 3.9C, p. 404)

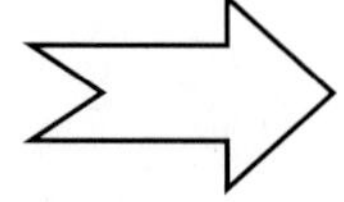

29. **TAKS Prep** Which best describes the shape of a can of paint? (Obj. 3)

A cone

B rectangular prism

C cylinder

D square pyramid

The Art of Origami

Classify and Categorize

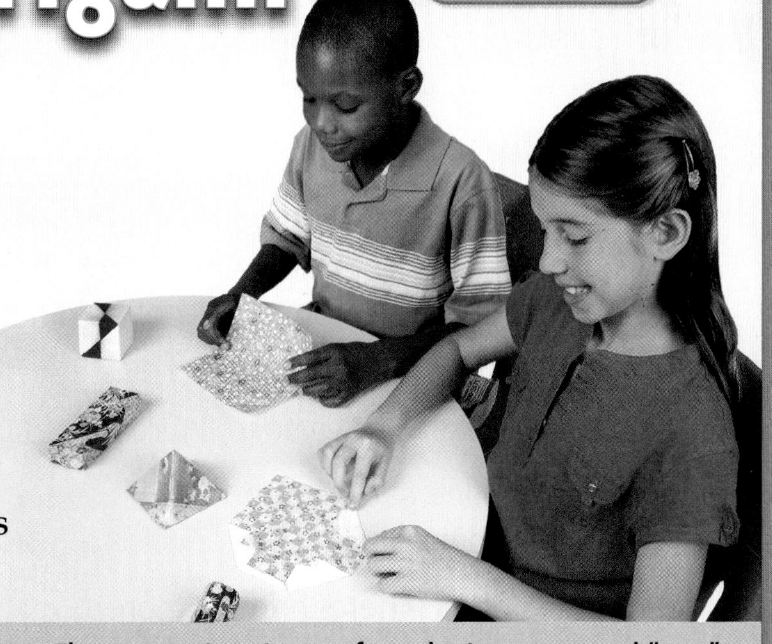

Origami is the art of folding paper. The only material needed is paper. Some people can make models of animals and geometric shapes. Look at the origami models below.

When you classify 3-dimensional figures, you organize them into groups by what they have in common.

▲ The name *origami* comes from the Japanese word "oru," which means to fold, and "kami," which means paper.

Figures that stack	Figures that roll	Figures with flat surfaces	Figures with curved surfaces	Figures with right angles	Figures with no right angles
cylinder rectangular prism cube	cylinder cone sphere	rectangular prism square pyramid cube	cylinder cone sphere	rectangular prism square pyramid cube	cylinder cone sphere

Problem Solving **Use *classify and categorize* to solve.**

1. What do the cube and the square pyramid have in common?
2. Teresa sorted the solid figures shown below into two groups. Tell two ways Teresa could classify the models. Which models would you place in each category?

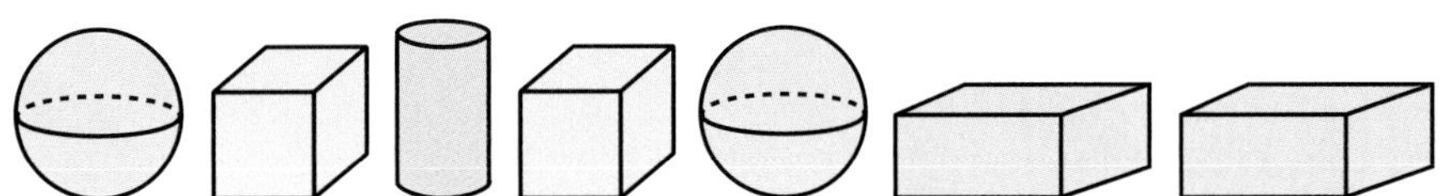

LESSON 2

Faces, Edges, and Vertices

OBJECTIVE: Identify faces, edges, and vertices in solid figures.

Quick Review

Name each solid figure.

1. 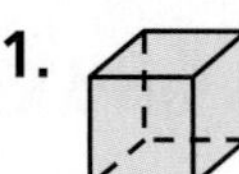
2. 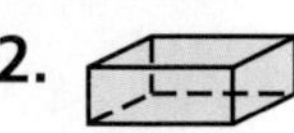
3. 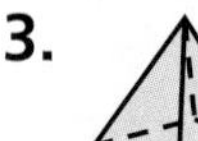
4.  
5. 

Vocabulary

face edge vertex

Learn

PROBLEM Alex is building a birdhouse. The bottom part is in the shape of a cube. He painted each face of the house a different color. How many colors did he use?

A **face** is a flat surface of a solid figure.

An **edge** is the line segment formed where two faces meet.

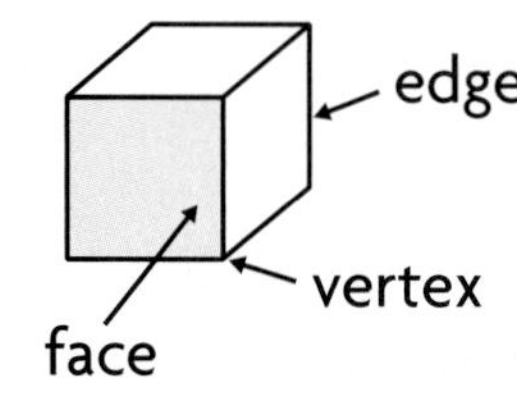

A **vertex** is a point where three or more edges meet. The plural of *vertex* is *vertices*.

Activity

Materials ■ solid figures (cube, square pyramid, rectangular prism), paper, crayons

- Trace the faces of a cube. Name the plane figures.
- Count the numbers of faces, edges, and vertices. Record the numbers in a table.

Name of Figure	Shapes of Faces	Names of Faces	Number of		
			Faces	Edges	Vertices
cube	□ □ □ □ □ □	6 squares	6	12	8

A cube has 6 faces. So, Alex used 6 different colors.

- Repeat the steps for a square pyramid and a rectangular prism.

TEKS 3.8 The student is expected to identify, classify, and describe, two- and three- dimensional geometric figures by their attributes. The student compares two-dimensional figures, three-dimentional figures, or both by their attributes using formal geometry vocabulary. *also* **3.14A, 3.14D, 3.15A, 3.15B**

Guided Practice

1. How many faces does a square pyramid have?

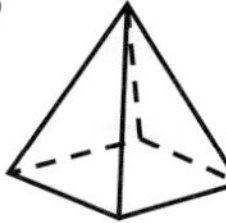

For 2-3, name the solid figure. Then tell how many faces, edges, and vertices.

2. 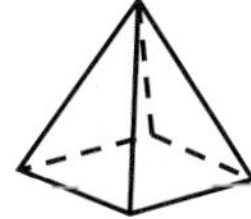

3. 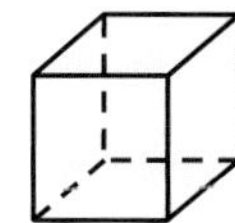

4. TALK Math **Explain** the difference between an edge and a vertex.

Independent Practice and Problem Solving

For 5–6, use the figure.

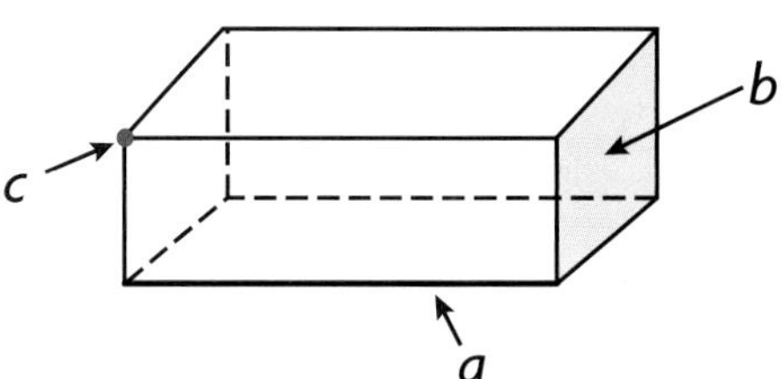

5. Name the solid figure. Then tell how many faces, edges, and vertices.
6. Which part of the figure is a face? Write *a*, *b*, or *c*.

Name the solid figure that has the faces shown.

7. 

8.

9. I am a solid figure with 5 faces. One of my faces is a quadrilateral. Four of my faces meet at one vertex. What figure am I?

10. WRITE Math **Explain** how a cube and a square are alike and how they are different.

Mixed Review and TAKS Prep

11. What solid figure is shaped like a soup can? (TEKS 3.8, p. 416)

12. How much is one $5 bill, 5 quarters, 3 dimes, 3 nickels and 2 pennies? (TEKS 3.1C, p. 110)

13. **TAKS Prep** Which solid figure has an edge shaded red? (Obj. 3)

A 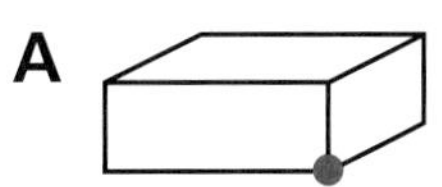

C 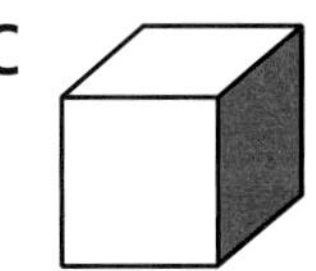

B 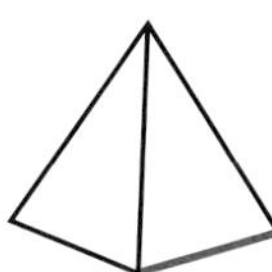

D 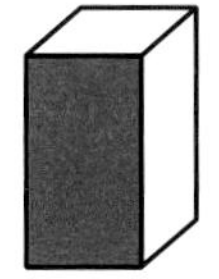

Extra Practice on page 426, Set B

CD ROM **Technology**
Use Harcourt Mega Math, Ice Station Exploration, *Frozen Solids*, Level G.

Problem Solving Workshop
Skill: Identify Relationships

OBJECTIVE: Solve problems by using the skill *identify relationships.*

Read to Understand
Plan
Solve
Check

Use the Skill

PROBLEM Trisha traced the face of a solid figure to make this design. Which solid figure did she use?

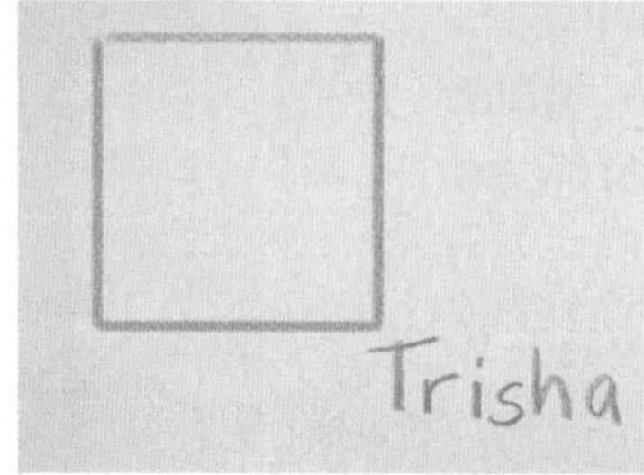

You can identify solid figures by looking at the different views.

A circle can be • the bottom view of a cone • the top or bottom view of a cylinder • any view of a sphere 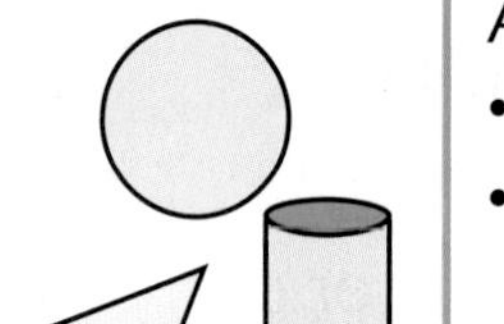	A square can be • any view of a cube • the top, bottom, or side view of a rectangular prism • the bottom view of a square pyramid  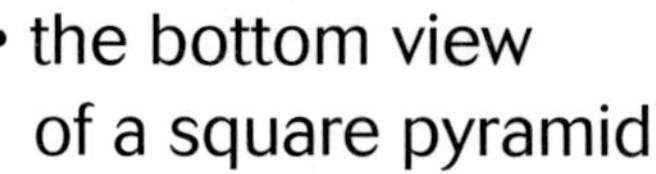
A rectangle can be • the top, bottom, or side view of a rectangular prism  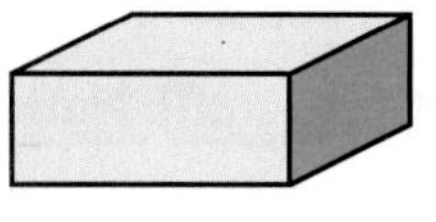	A triangle can be • the side view of a square pyramid 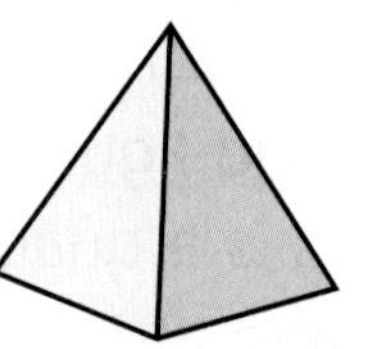

So, Trisha could have used a cube, a square pyramid, or a rectangular prism.

Think and Discuss

Use plane and solid figures to solve.

a. Natalie has a wooden block shaped like a square pyramid. If you look at the bottom view of her block, what plane figure would you see?

b. Eileen pressed a solid figure into clay. It left the outline of a triangle. What solid figure did she use?

c. Karl made this design. Which solid figures could he have traced?

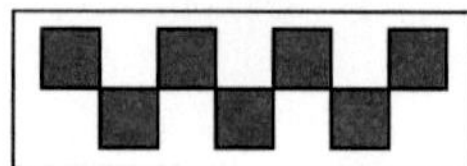

TEKS 3.8 The student is expected to identify, classify, and describe two- and three-dimensional geometric figures by their attributes. The student compares two-dimensional figures, three-dimensional figures, or both by their attributes using formal geometry vocabulary. *also* **3.14A, 3.14C, 3.14D, 3.15A, 3.15B, 3.16B**

Guided Problem Solving

Solve.

1. Jannelle used a sponge to paint a border of circles around a picture frame. She has three different sponges in the shapes of a cylinder, a cube, and a rectangular prism. Which sponge did she use to make the border?

   Think about the three solid figures from different views.

   Which figure has a circle as the top, bottom, or side view?

   Now solve the problem.

2. **What if** Jannelle made a border of squares? Which sponge could she have used?

3. Casey made a sponge paint border of triangles around a poster. Was his sponge in the shape of a cylinder, a sphere, or a square pyramid?

Mixed Applications

For 4–7, use the pictures.

4. Matt bought an item at the store. He said that if you look at the item from the side, it looks like a rectangle. Which item could Matt have bought?

5. Martin bought some items. He paid with a $20 bill. He got $3 in change. Which items could Martin have bought?

6. **WRITE Math** Mrs. Garrett bought 6 cans of peanuts and 2 boxes of crayons. Find the total amount she spent.

7. **Pose a Problem** Look at Problem 6. Write a similar problem by changing the items that Mrs. Garrett bought.

8. On Saturday 482 people visited an aquariam. On Sunday 621 people visited the aquariam. How many more people visited the aquarium on Sunday?

9. **WRITE Math** Nick painted a fence for 75 minutes in the morning and 90 minutes in the afternoon. How many minutes in all did Nick spend painting? How many hours and minutes? **Explain.**

LESSON 4 Compare 3-Dimensional Figures

OBJECTIVE: Compare three-dimensional figures.

Quick Review

Name each figure.

1. 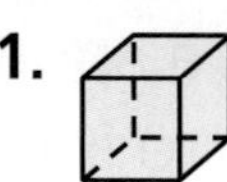
2. 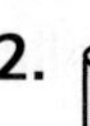 
3.  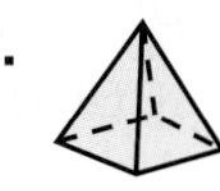
4. 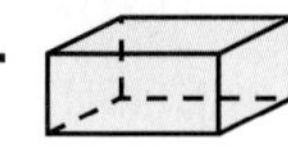
5. 

Learn

PROBLEM Oscar and Mikah are making a piñata in art class. Oscar's piece of the piñata is shaped like a cube. Mikah's piece of the piñata is shaped like a square pyramid. How are the two figures alike?

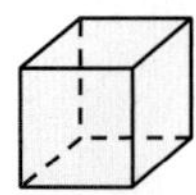 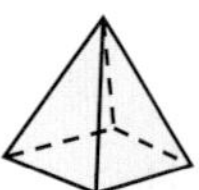

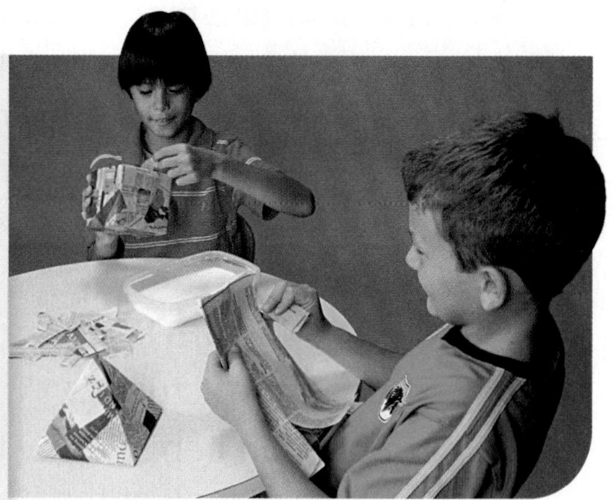

Examples

You can compare three-dimensional figures by the numbers of faces, edges, and vertices. You can also compare the shapes of the faces.

Solid Figure	Faces	Edges	Vertices
cube	6 • squares	12	8
square pyramid	5 • 1 square • 4 triangles	8	5
rectangular prism	6 • rectangles	12	8
triangular prism	5 • 2 triangles • 3 rectangles	9	6

So, a cube and a square pyramid are alike because they both have faces that are squares.

Math Idea

Some solid figures have curved surfaces and no faces.

sphere

cylinder cone

TEKS 3.8 The student is expected to identify, classify, and describe two- and three-dimensional geometric figures by their attributes. The student compares two-dimensional figures, three-dimensional figures, or both by their attributes using formal geometry vocabulary. *also* **3.14A, 3.14D, 3.15A, 3.15B**

Guided Practice

1. Which solid figure has more faces? How many more?

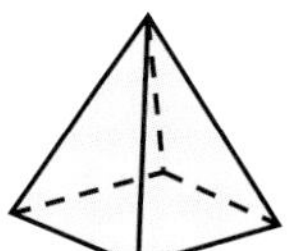 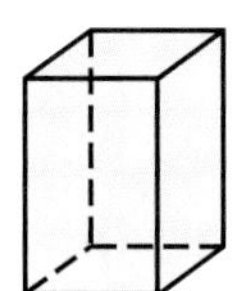

Compare the figures. Tell one way they are alike or different.

2. 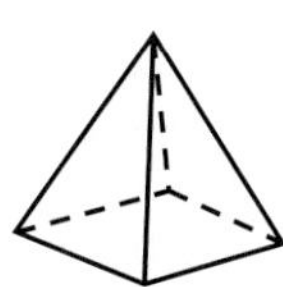 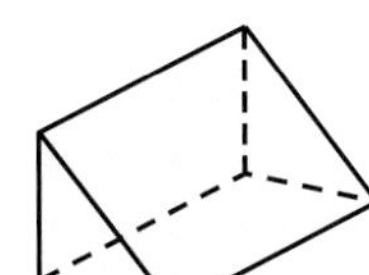

3. 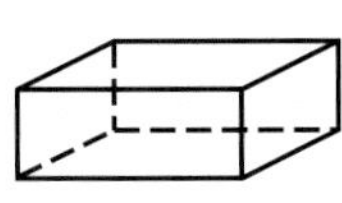 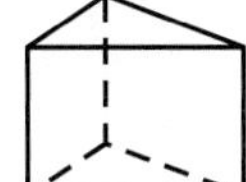

 4. 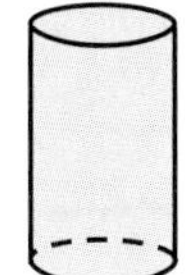 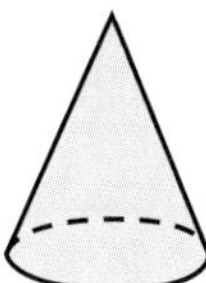

5. TALK Math **Explain** how a cube and a rectangular prism are different.

Independent Practice and Problem Solving

Compare the figures. Tell one way they are alike or different.

6. 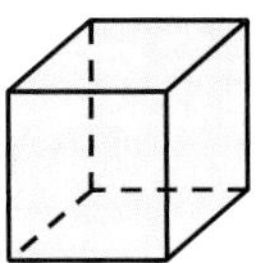 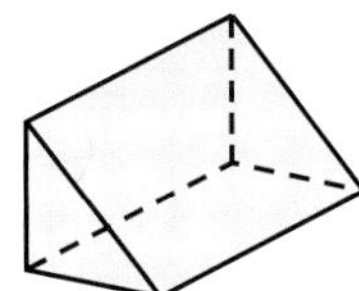

7. 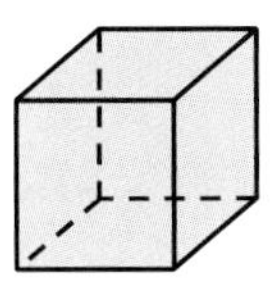 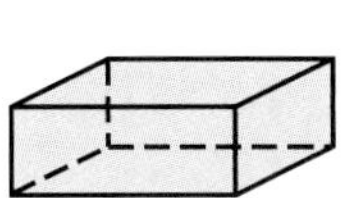

8. 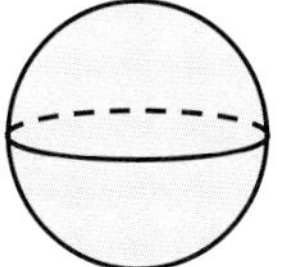 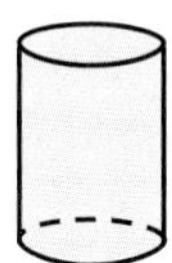

For 9–10, identify each figure.

9. I have 6 faces that are rectangles. What figure am I?

10. I have 5 faces. Three of my faces are rectangles. What figure am I?

11. What solid figures have curved surfaces?

12. WRITE Math How are a cube and a rectangular prism the same? **Explain**.

Mixed Review and TAKS Prep

13. Nick has a model of a cube. What shape are the faces? (TEKS 3.8, p. 420)

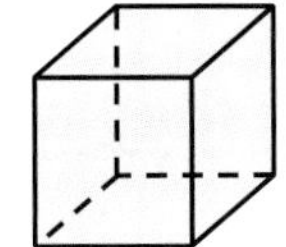

14. Draw the next two figures in this pattern. (TEKS 3.6A, p. 182)

        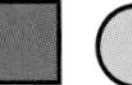 

15. **TAKS Prep** How are a square pyramid and a triangular prism alike? (Obj. 3)

A Both have 8 edges.

B Both have 6 faces.

C Both have at least one face that is a triangle.

D Both have curved surfaces.

Extra Practice on page 426, Set C

Extra Practice

Set A Name the solid figure that each object is shaped like. (pp. 416–419)

1. 

2. 

3. 

4. 

For 5–6, use the model. (pp. 416–419)

5. Kara built this model with blocks. What solid figures are the green blocks? What color are the tall cylinders?
6. How many more square pyramids than rectangular prisms did she use?

Set B Name the solid figure. Then tell how many faces, edges, and vertices. (pp. 420–421)

1. 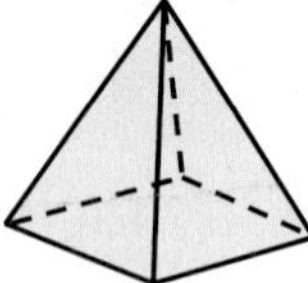

2. 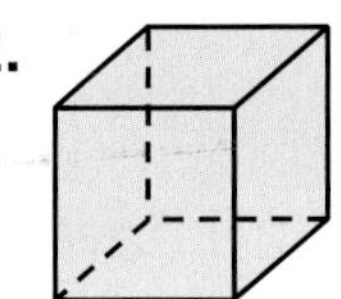

3. 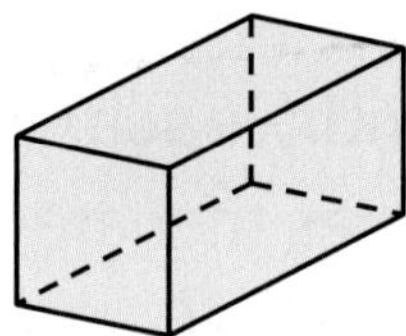

Name the solid figure that has the faces shown. (pp. 422–423)

4. 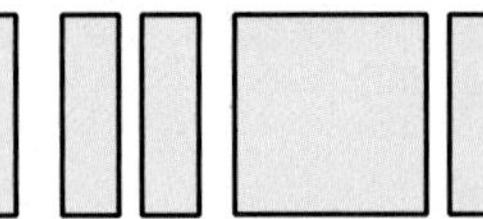

5. 

Set C Compare the figures. Tell one way they are alike or different. (pp. 424–425)

1. 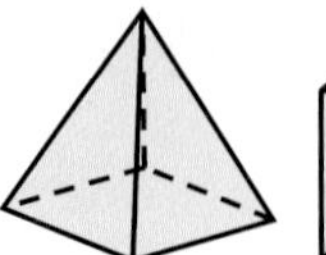

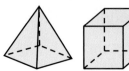

2. 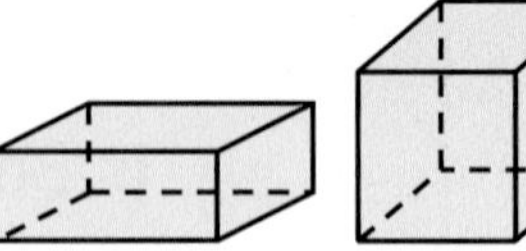

3. 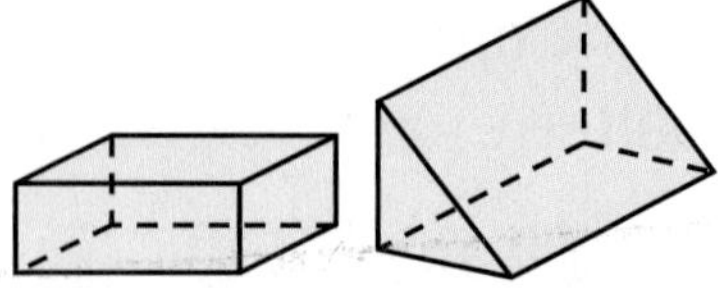

For 4–5, identify each figure. (pp. 426–427)

4. I have 12 edges. All of my faces are the same size and shape.
5. I have 9 edges. Two of my faces are triangles.

Technology
Use Harcourt Mega Math, Ice Station Exploration, *Frozen Solids*, Levels A, G.

PRACTICE GAME

Rolling Figures

Shake!
2–4 players

Rattle!
- Gameboard
- 2 solid figures cubes
- Game card, crayon or pencil, and counter for each player

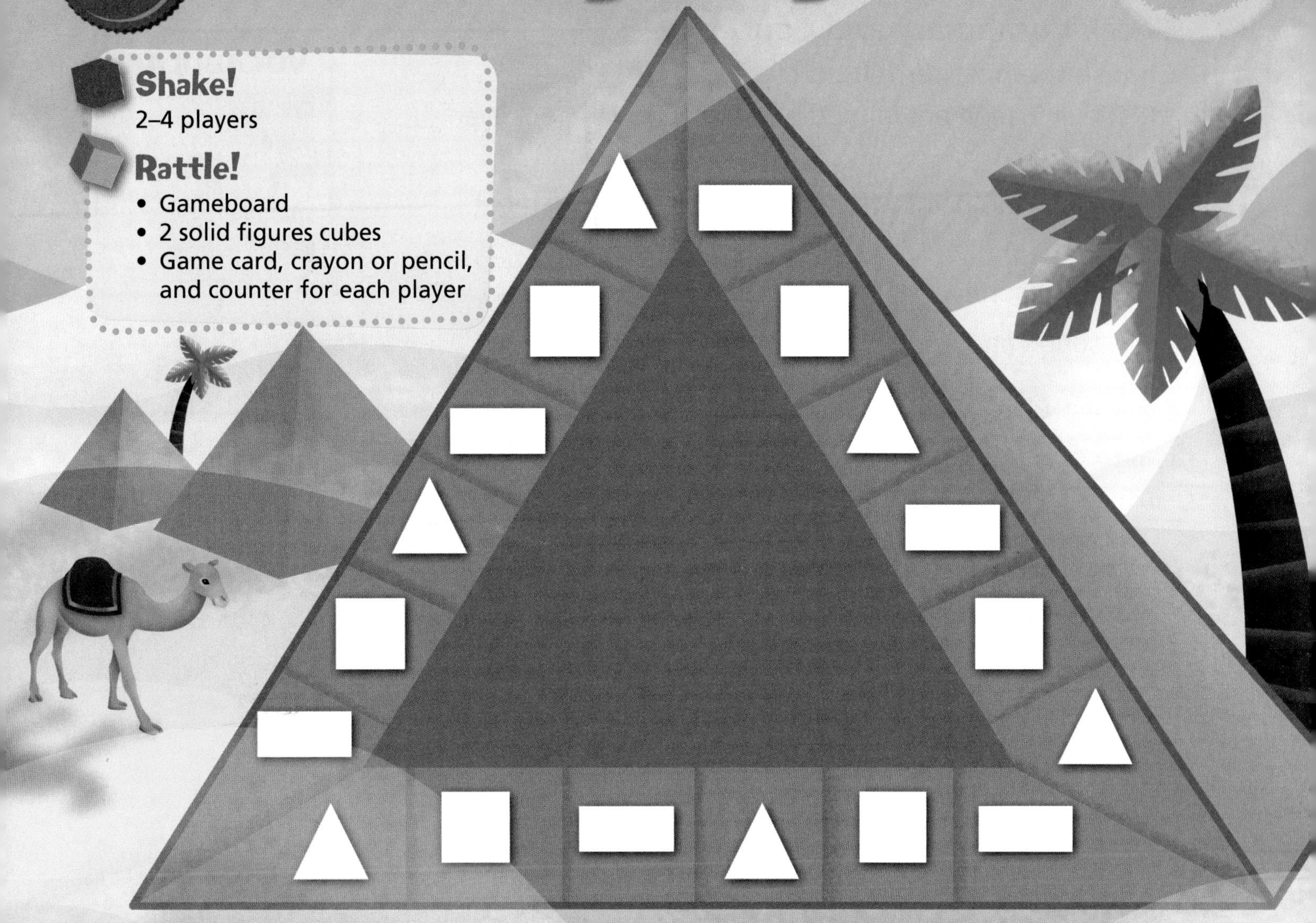

Roll!

- Each player places a counter on any space on the gameboard.
- The first player rolls both solid figures cubes and then tells whether the two figures that land faceup can be combined.
- If the two figures can be combined, Player 1 shades a face on his or her game card that matches the face on which the counter lies. Player 1 then moves 1 space in any direction.
- Player 2 follows the same steps as Player 1. If the rolled figures cannot be combined, it is the next player's turn.
- The game continues as players roll the cubes, shade faces, and move around the gameboard.
- The first player to shade all the faces of any solid figure on his or her game card wins.

Chapter 18 Review/Test

Check Vocabulary and Concepts

Choose the best term from the box.

VOCABULARY
cylinder
edge
face
sphere
vertex

1. The line segment formed where two faces meet is an __?__. (TEKS 3.8, p. 420)
2. A __?__ is the point where three or more edges meet. (TEKS 3.8, p. 420)
3. The flat surface of a solid figure is a __?__. (TEKS 3.8, p. 420)
4. A soup can has the shape of a __?__. (TEKS 3.8, p. 416)

Check Skills

Name the solid figure that each object is shaped like. (TEKS 3.8, pp. 418–421)

5. 

6. 

7. 

8. 

Name the solid figure. Then tell how many faces, edges, and vertices. (TEKS 3.8, pp. 420–421)

9. 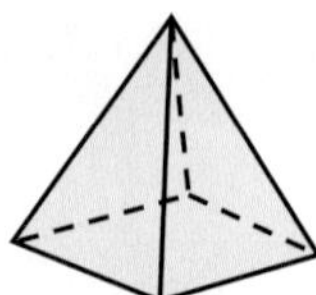

10. 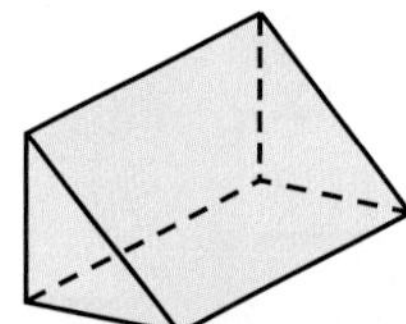

11. 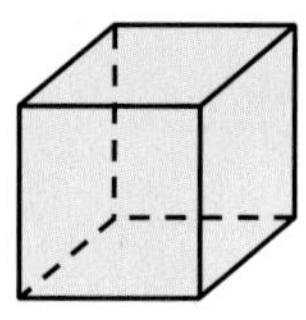

Name the solid figure that has the faces shown. (TEKS 3.8, pp. 420–421)

12. 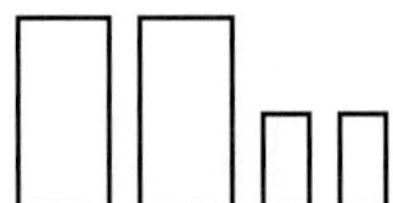

13. 

Check Problem Solving

Solve. (TEKS 3.15A, pp. 424–425)

14. Denise made this pattern by pressing the faces of a solid figure into clay. What could the figure have been?

15. WRITE Math Jennita has 2 cubes, 2 rectangular prisms, and 1 square pyramid. She is painting them all blue. How many faces in all will she paint? **Explain** how you found the answer by writing number sentences.

GO ONLINE **Technology** Use *Online Assessment.*

Enrich • Congruent Solid Figures

Building Blocks

▲ The small plastic Lego® bricks were invented in Denmark. There is a LEGOLAND® Park in Carlsbad, California.

Chantal and Miguel each made a solid figure with cubes. Are the two solid figures congruent?

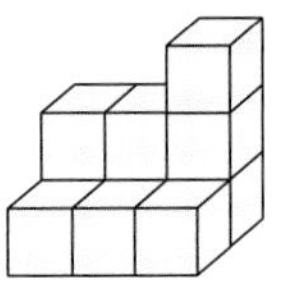

Chantal

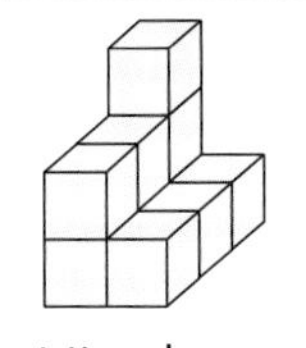

Miguel

Frame It Up

Two figures are congruent if they have exactly the same shape and size. Look at each layer of the figures to tell if they are congruent.

Step 1 Make a table to compare the figures.

Step 2 Find the number of cubes in each row.

Step 3 Find the number of cubes in the layer.

	NUMBER OF CUBES	CHANTAL'S FIGURE	NUMBER OF CUBES	MIGUEL'S FIGURE
Layer 1	6	2 rows of 3 cubes	6	2 rows of 3 cubes
Layer 2	3	1 row of 3 cubes	3	1 row of 3 cubes
Layer 3	1	1 cube	1	1 cube

Step 4 Compare the sizes and shapes of the figures at each layer. If all of the sizes and shapes are the same, then the figures are congruent.

So Chantal's figure is congruent to Miguel's figure.

Fill It In

Are the solid figures congruent?

1. 

2. 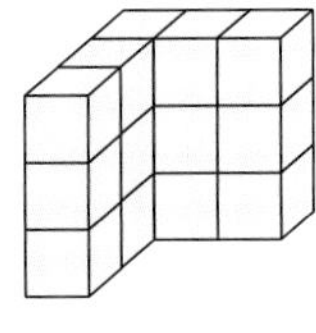

3. 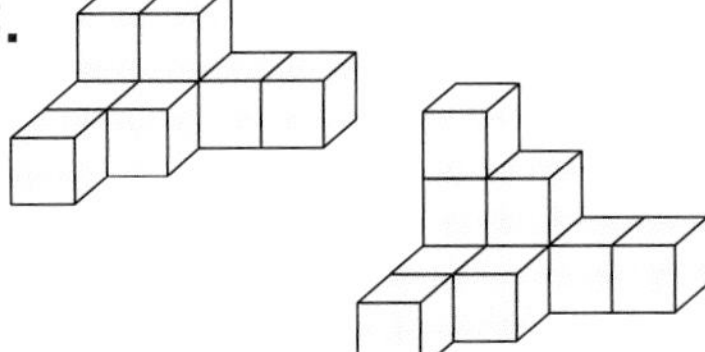

Finish It Out

WRITE Math ▸ Use cubes to build a figure congruent to the one shown. **Explain** how you know they are congruent.

Unit Review/Test
Chapters 16–18

Multiple Choice

1. Which does NOT describe this figure? (TAKS Obj. 3)

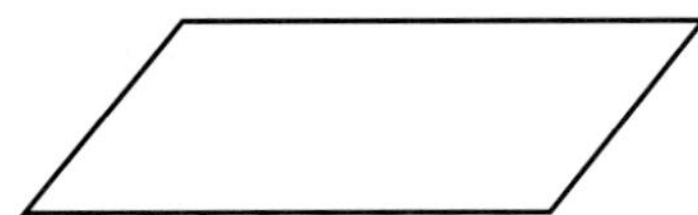

A Parallelogram

B Quadrilateral

C Rectangle

D Polygon

2. Which figure has the fewest number of sides? (TAKS Obj. 3)

F Hexagon

G Triangle

H Quadrilateral

J Pentagon

3. How many lines of symmetry does this figure appear to have? (TAKS Obj. 3)

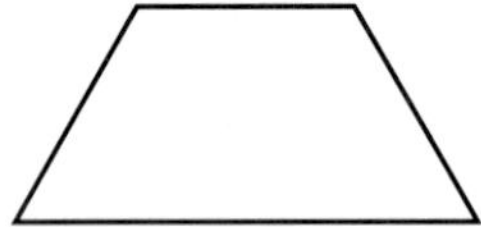

A 1

B 2

C 4

D Not here

4. Which figure has 5 vertices? (TAKS Obj. 3)

F 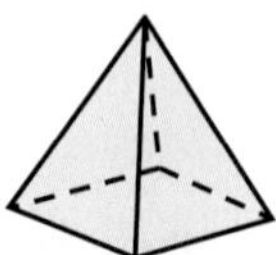

H 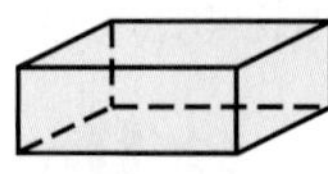

G 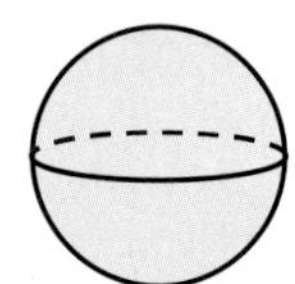

J 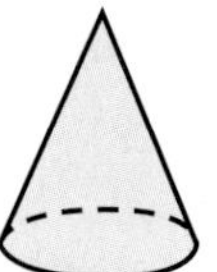

5. Which pair of lines is parallel? (TAKS Obj. 3)

A 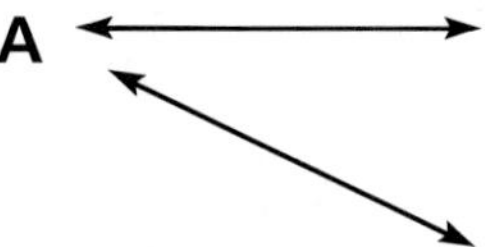

C

B 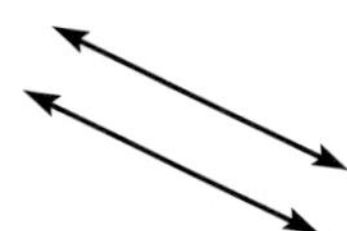

D 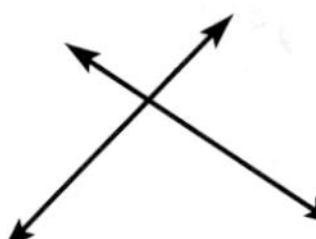

6. Which pair of figures appears to be congruent? (TAKS Obj. 3)

F 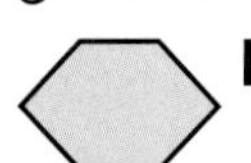

H 

G 

J 

GO ONLINE Technology Use *Online Assessment.*

7. Vinny cut a board so that it is shaped like an equilateral triangle. Which is true about the board? (TAKS Obj. 3)

A It has one right angle.

B All three sides are congruent.

C It has one obtuse angle.

D Only two sides are congruent.

8. Which figure best describes the can of soup? (TAKS Obj. 3)

F Cylinder

G Cone

H Sphere

J Square pyramid

9. Which completes the design so it has a line of symmetry? (TAKS Obj. 3)

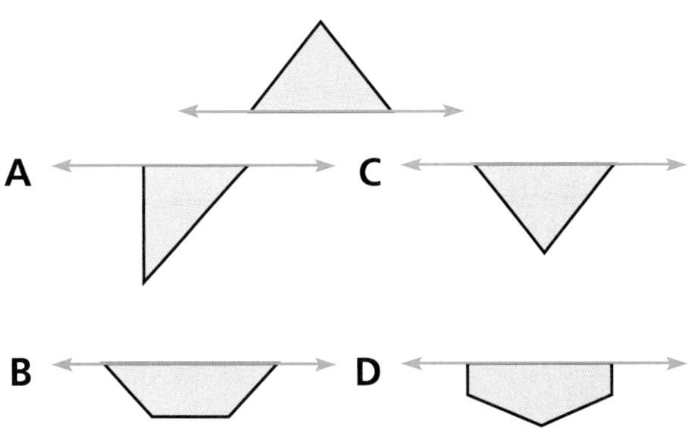

10. Which statement best describes congruent figures? (TAKS Obj. 3)

F They are not the same shape.

G They are the same size and color.

H They are the same shape and size.

J They are not the same size.

Short Response

11. Which figure has more faces, a cube or a square pyramid? (TAKS Obj. 3)

12. Annemarie drew the figure below. Does the blue line appear to be a line of symmetry? (TAKS Obj. 3)

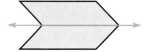

13. Cathy drew the plane figure below. What kind of plane figure is it? (TAKS Obj. 3)

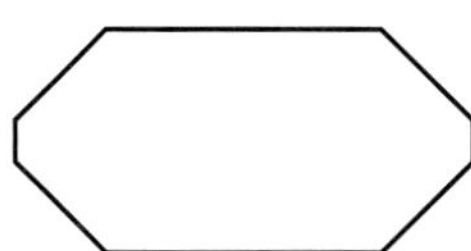

Extended Response WRITE Math

14. A box has 6 faces. The faces of the box are all squares. What figure is the box? **Explain.** (TAKS Obj. 3)

Texas

Problem Solving

Native American Culture

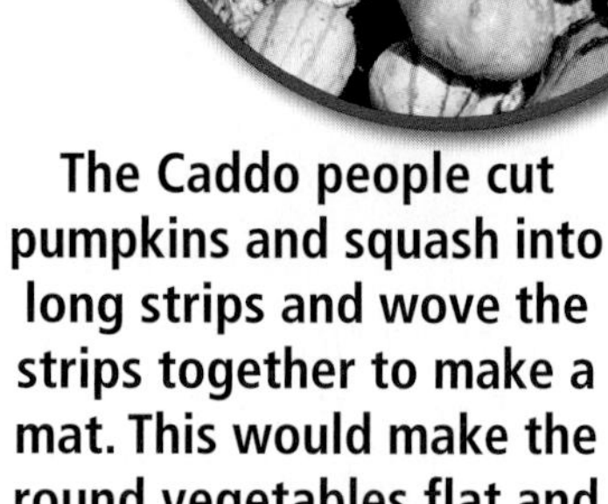

The Caddo people cut pumpkins and squash into long strips and wove the strips together to make a mat. This would make the round vegetables flat and easier to store.

Food Symmetry

The Caddo people lived in East Texas. They were farmers, hunters, and builders. They made pottery and carved wood. They grew many types of plants including corn, pumpkins, squash, beans, and sunflowers. Parts of the plants were used for food.

FACT·ACTIVITY

Look at the pictures to answer the questions.

1. Which lines appear to be a line of symmetry?

A 
B 
C 
D 

2. How can you draw a bean that is congruent to the bean below?

3. How many lines of symmetry does this squash appear to have?

Useful Caddo Objects

Many objects made by the Caddo people are in museums. Some objects were for everyday use. Others were for decoration or for special occasions. Often these objects tell us a lot about the Caddo people.

ALMANAC Fact

Caddo houses were made of grass with domed roofs. Some were large enough to hold 30 people! It took one day to build a house, because the whole village worked together.

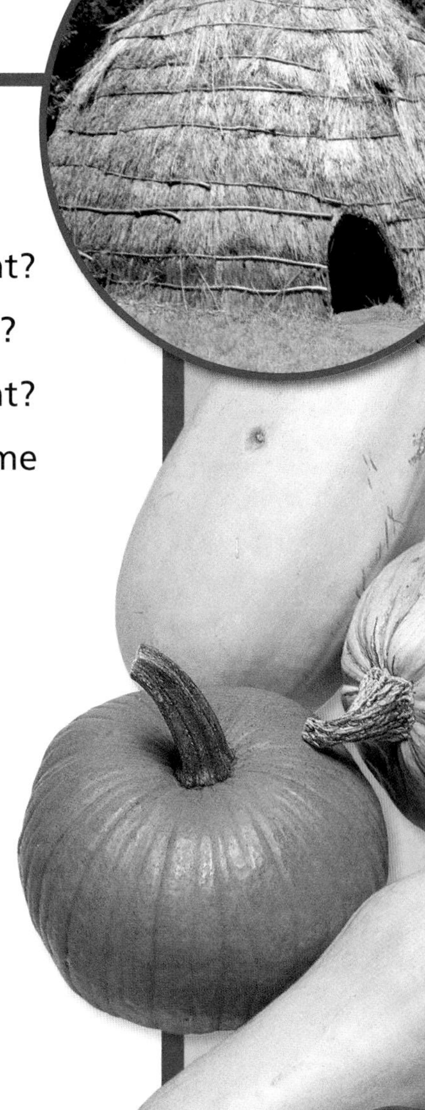

FACT·ACTIVITY

Pictures of Caddo objects can be congruent, even if they have moved.

1. Object A shows a turn. Are the objects congruent?
2. Object B shows a flip. Are the objects congruent?
3. Object C shows a slide. Are the objects congruent?
4. Draw 2 congruent objects that are not in the same position.

A

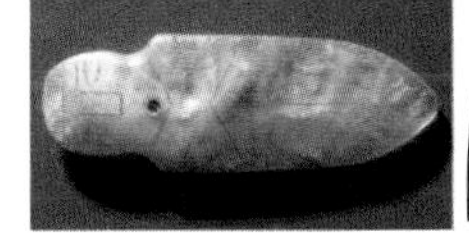

B

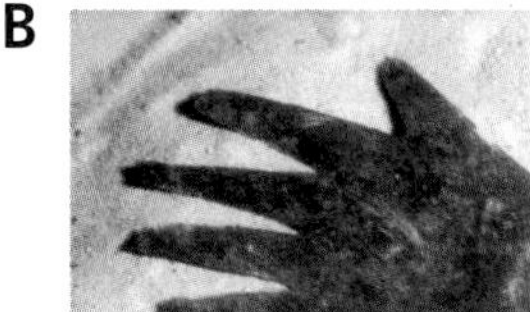

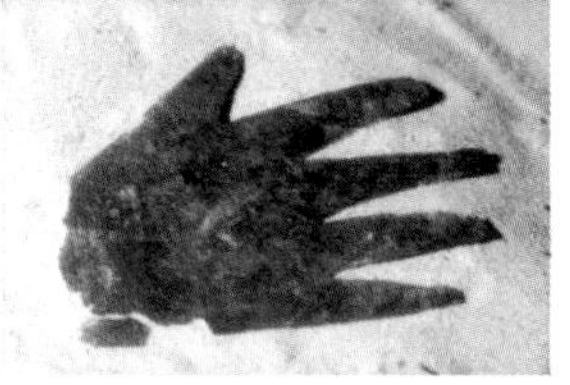

C

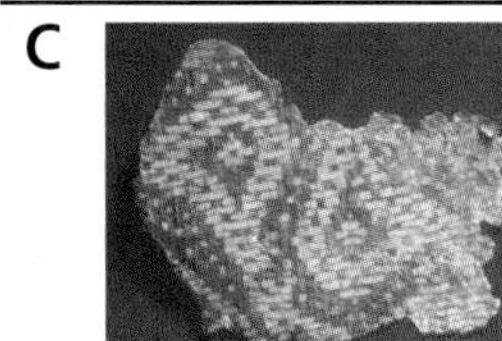

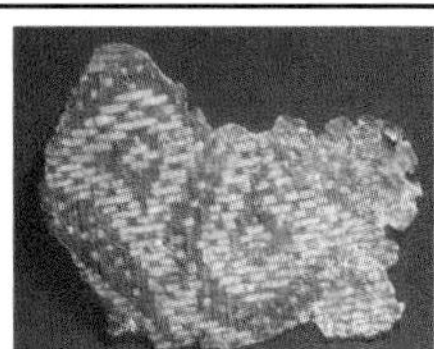

UNIT 7 Measurement

Math on Location

with **Texas Chapter Projects**

1

Daily chores at the zoo include cutting, measuring, and mixing food that keeps the animals healthy.

2

The sea lion on the scale weighs 180 pounds; it swims in a tank of over 1,000 gallons of water.

3

The cougar was measured to make sure its living space was large enough for it to move about easily.

VOCABULARY POWER

TALK Math

What math is being used in the **Math on Location** photographs? How can you find the weight of the sea lion in ounces?

READ Math

REVIEW VOCABULARY You learned the words below when you learned about measurement last year. How do these words relate to **Math on Location**?

gallon a customary unit for measuring capacity

kilogram a metric unit for measuring mass

ounce a customary unit for measuring weight

WRITE Math

Copy a Magic Square like the one below. Use what you know about measurement to start filling in the square. Complete the square as you study measurement in this unit.

A	B	C
D	E	F
G	H	I

A. liter
B. kilometer
C. quart
D. yard
E. kilogram
F. gallon
G. pint
H. foot
I. meter

1. equals 12 inches
2. equals 1,000 milliliters
3. equals 4 quarts
4. equals 2 pints
5. equals 1,000 grams
6. equals 2 cups
7. equals 3 feet
8. equals 100 cm
9. equals 1,000 meters

Technology
Multimedia Math Glossary link at **www.harcourtschool.com/hspmath**

19 Customary Measurement

The Big Idea Measurement involves a comparison of an attribute of an object or situation with a unit that describes that attribute.

Investigate

Limestone formations in a cave that build up from the ground are called stalagmites. The graph shows the heights of some stalagmites. Make a list of other objects that are about the same height as each stalagmite.

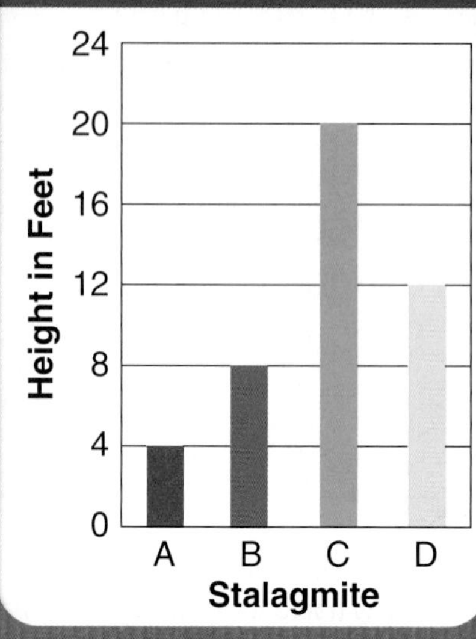

TEXAS FAST FACT

Natural Bridge Caverns is the largest known cavern system in Texas. The largest underground room, the Hall of the Mountain Kings, is 350 feet long, 100 feet wide, and 100 feet high.

GO ONLINE **Technology** Student pages are available in the Student eBook.

Show What You Know

Check your understanding of important skills needed for success in Chapter 19.

▶ Use a Customary Ruler

Use an inch ruler to measure.

1.

2. 

3.

4. 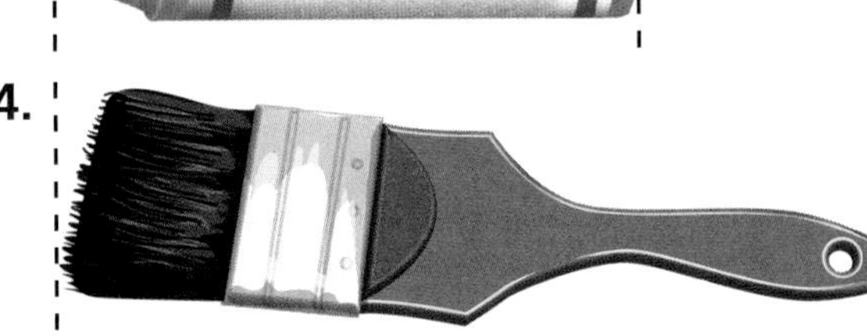

▶ Measure to the Nearest Inch

Use an inch ruler to measure to the nearest inch.

5.

6.

7.

8.

VOCABULARY POWER

CHAPTER VOCABULARY

capacity
cup (c)
degrees Fahrenheit (°F)
foot (ft)
gallon (gal)
inch (in.)
length
mile (mi)
ounce (oz)
pint (pt)
pound (lb)
quart (qt)
weight
yard (yd)

WARM-UP WORDS

length The measure of something from end to end

foot (ft) A customary unit used to measure length or distance; 1 foot = 12 inches

yard (yd) A customary unit for measuring length or distance; 1 yard = 3 feet

LESSON 1 HANDS ON

Compare Attributes

OBJECTIVE: Compare objects by capacity, length, and weight.

Quick Review

Which piece of yarn is the longest?

A

B

C

You can compare objects by how much they hold, how long they are, and how heavy they are.

Investigate

Materials ■ 2 different-sized containers, water, crayon, pencil, ruler, notebook

A **Compare capacity.**
Fill one container with water.
Then pour this water into a second container.
Does the water fill the second container?
Is there water left in the first container?
Which container holds more?

B **Compare length.**
Place a crayon on your desk.
Place a pencil beside it.
Compare the 2 objects.
Which object is longer?

C **Compare weight.**
Hold a ruler in one hand.
Hold a notebook in your other hand.
Compare the 2 objects.
Which object is heavier?

Draw Conclusions

1. Is a large object always heavier than a small object? Give an example.
2. Do you think that a taller container always holds more than a shorter container? **Explain.**
3. **Synthesis** Besides their lengths, what else can you compare about the crayon and the pencil? **Explain.**

TEKS 3.11 The student directly compares the attributes of length, area, weight/mass, and capacity, and uses comparative language to solve problems and answer questions. The student selects and uses standard units to describe length, area, capacity/volume, and weight/mass. *also* **3.14A, 3.14D, 3.15A, 3.15B**

Connect

Sometimes pictures can help you compare objects.

Which holds more?	Which is longer?	Which is heavier?

The washtub holds more.	The pair of scissors is longer.	The backpack is heavier.

TALK Math

How do you know the pair of scissors is longer?

Practice

Compare.

1. Which is shorter?

2. Which is heavier?

✓ **3.** Which holds less?

4. Draw an object in your classroom that is heavier than a paintbrush. **Explain** your choice.

✓ **5.** Draw an object in your classroom that is longer than your shoe. **Explain** your choice.

6. Find three objects in your classroom. Compare their lengths. Write the objects in order from shortest to longest.

7. **WRITE Math** How can you find out whether a container will hold more than a drinking glass holds? **Explain**.

LESSON

2 Length

OBJECTIVE: Introduce customary units of length.

Quick Review

Which is longer?

Vocabulary

length	**foot (ft)**
yard (yd)	**mile (mi)**

Learn

Length is the measurement of distance between two points. Customary units used to measure length and distance are inch (in.), **foot (ft)**, **yard (yd)**, and **mile (mi)**.

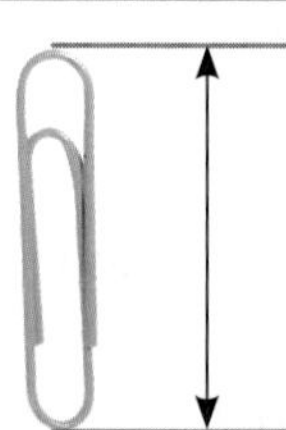

A small paper clip is about 1 inch long.

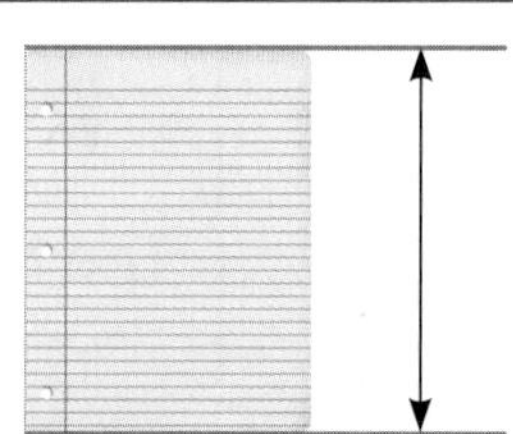

A sheet of notebook paper is about 1 foot long.

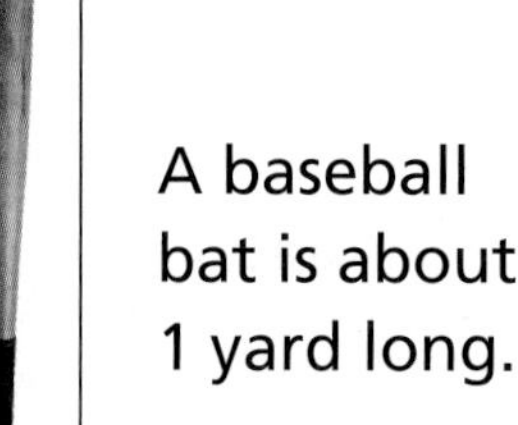

A baseball bat is about 1 yard long.

It takes about 20 minutes to walk 1 mile.

This chart shows how customary units of length are related.

Customary Units of Length
12 inches = 1 foot
3 feet = 36 inches = 1 yard
5,280 feet = 1 mile

Guided Practice

1. Would you measure the length of a pencil in inches or feet? **Think:** Is a pencil longer or shorter than a sheet of notebook paper?

Choose the unit you would use to measure each. Write *inch*, *foot*, *yard*, or *mile*.

2. 

3. 

4. 

5. TALK Math **Explain** what unit you would use to measure the length of your classroom.

TEKS 3.11A use linear measurement tools to estimate and measure lengths using standard units. *also* 3.14A, 3.14D, 3.15A, 3.15B

Independent Practice and Problem Solving

Choose the unit you would use to measure each. Write *inch*, *foot*, *yard*, or *mile*.

6. 

7. 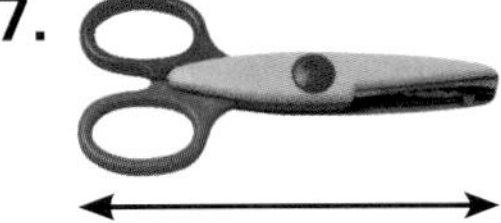

8. 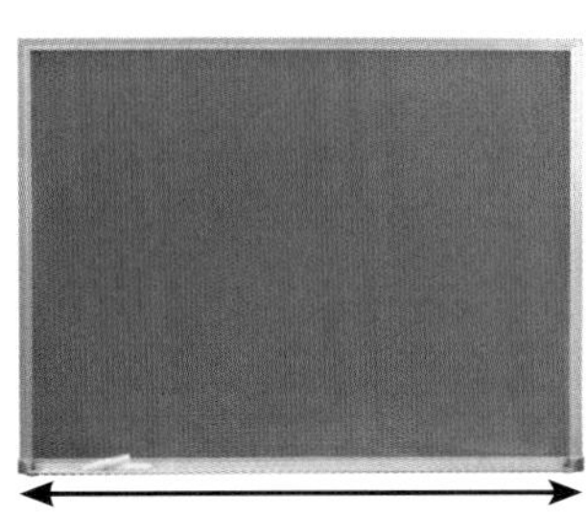

9. length of a one dollar bill

10. distance between two towns

11. length of a kitchen table

12. Annie is going to walk to her friend's house. Her friend lives 3 houses away. What unit best measures how far Annie will have to walk?

13. **Reasoning** Jack is 2 weeks old. Andy is 12 years old. What unit would you use to measure how tall Jack is? Would you use the same unit to measure how tall Andy is? **Explain**.

14. Toni saw a giraffe at the zoo. What unit should Toni use to give the height of the giraffe?

15. **WRITE Math** Madison visits her grandmother in another city. Does she travel 100 feet, 100 yards, or 100 miles? **Explain** your answer.

Mixed Review and TAKS Prep

16. There are 3 tennis balls in each of 5 cans. How many tennis balls are there in all? (TEKS 3.4B, p. 228)

17. What shape comes next in this pattern? (TEKS 3.6A, p. 182)

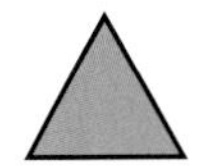  

18. **TAKS Prep** Kenny uses a large piece of poster board to draw a picture. About how long is the posterboard? (Obj. 4)

A 20 inches **C** 20 yards
B 20 feet **D** 20 miles

Extra Practice on page 458, Set A

LESSON 3

Estimate and Measure Inches

OBJECTIVE: Estimate and measure length to the nearest inch and half inch.

Quick Review

Choose the unit you would use to measure the length of each. Write *inch, foot, yard,* or *mile.*

1. skateboard
2. banana
3. distance between 2 cities
4. picture frame
5. your bed

Learn

You can use an inch ruler to measure the length of an object to the nearest inch and nearest half inch.

Measure to the Nearest Inch

Activity **Materials** ■ inch ruler

Step 1

Copy the table.

Length of Yarn		
Color	**Estimate**	**Measure**
red		
blue		
orange		
purple		
green		

Step 2

Estimate the length of the piece of red yarn. Record your estimate in your table.

Step 3

Use a ruler. Measure the length of the red yarn to the nearest inch. Record your measurement in your table.

Step 4

Repeat Steps 2 and 3 for the blue, orange, purple, and green yarn.

- Which piece of yarn is 2 inches longer than the shortest piece of yarn?

Remember

Always be sure that the left end of the object you are measuring is lined up with the 0 mark on the ruler.

TEKS 3.11A use linear measurement tools to estimate and measure lengths using standard units. *also* **3.14A, 3.14D, 3.15A, 3.15B, 3.16B**

Measure to the Nearest Half Inch

You can also measure to the nearest half inch.

Examples

What is the length of each object to the nearest half inch?

A

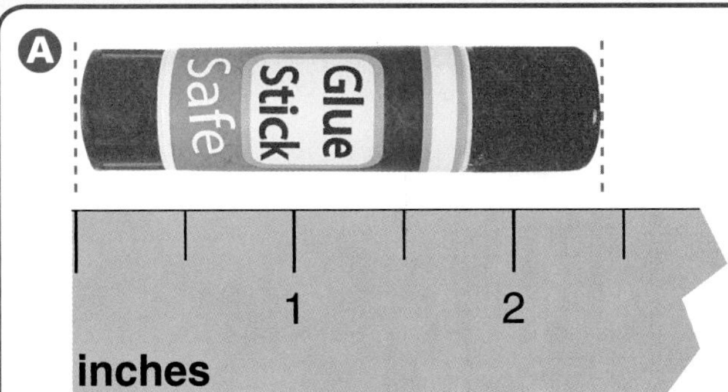

The left end of the glue stick is lined up with the 0 mark on the ruler.

The $\frac{1}{2}$ inch mark that is closest to the right end of the glue stick is $2\frac{1}{2}$.

So, the length of the glue stick to the nearest half inch is $2\frac{1}{2}$ inches.

B

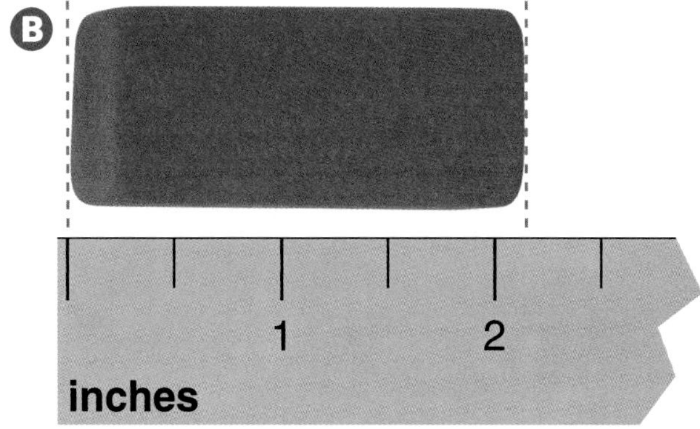

The left end of the eraser is lined up with the 0 mark on the ruler.

The $\frac{1}{2}$ inch mark that is closest to the right end of the eraser is 2.

So, the length of the eraser to the nearest half inch is 2 inches.

Guided Practice

1. Is the key $1\frac{1}{2}$ inches, 2 inches, or $2\frac{1}{2}$ inches long?

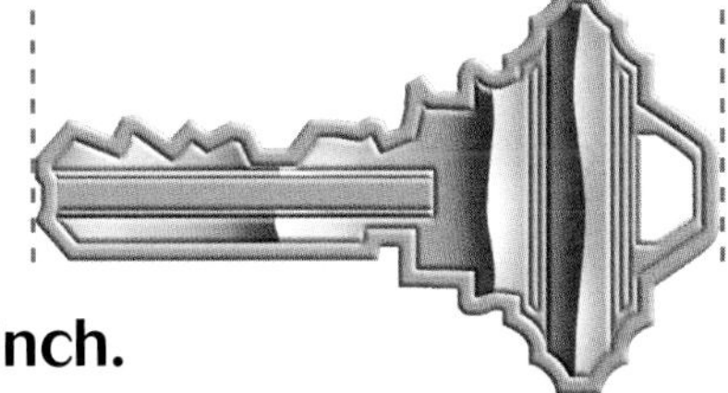

Measure the length to the nearest inch.

2. 

Measure the length to the nearest half inch.

3. 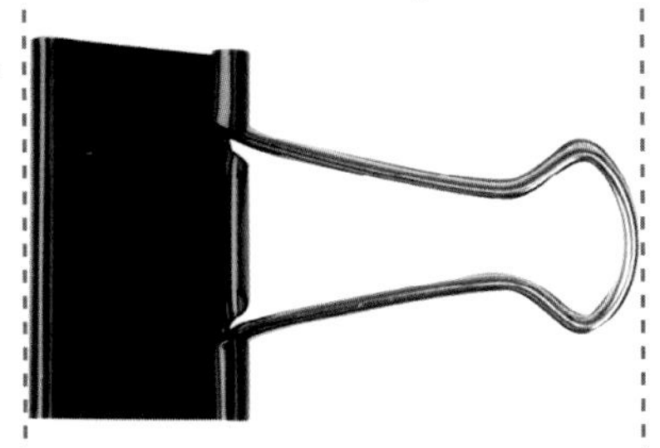

4. 

5. **TALK Math** **Explain** how you measured the shell to the nearest half inch.

Independent Practice and Problem Solving

Measure the length to the nearest inch.

6. 

7. 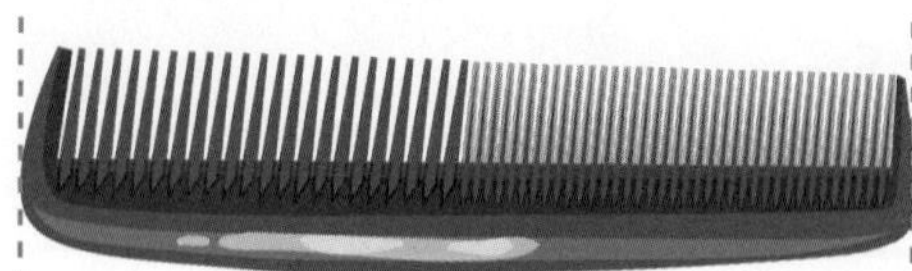

Measure the length to the nearest half inch.

8. 

9. 

10. 

Use a ruler. Draw a line for each length.

11. 3 inches
12. $4\frac{1}{2}$ inches
13. 5 inches
14. $6\frac{1}{2}$ inches

15. Emily is measuring her hairbrush. It is $7\frac{1}{2}$ inches long. Between which two inch marks is the end of the hairbrush?

16. **WRITE Math** **What's the Error?** Joni said this piece of ribbon is 3 inches long. Describe her error.

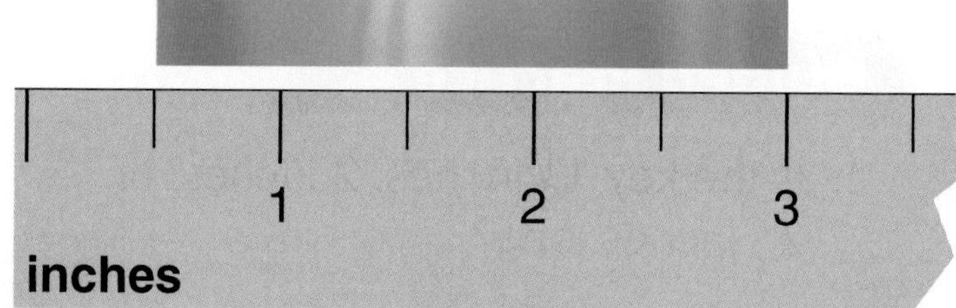

17. Find two different-sized objects in your desk. Measure the length of each object to the nearest half inch. Use < or > to compare the measurements.

Mixed Review and TAKS Prep

18. Is a football about 1 foot or 1 yard long? (TEKS 3.11A, p. 440)

19. Mary spent $4.25 on a notebook and $5.15 on some trading cards. She paid with a $10 bill. How much change did she receive? (TEKS 3.1C, p. 120)

20. **TAKS Prep** What is the length of the bandage to the nearest half inch? (Obj. 4)

A $1\frac{1}{2}$ inches
B 2 inches
C $2\frac{1}{2}$ inches
D 3 inches

Technology
Use Harcourt Mega Math, Ice Station Exploration, *Linear Lab*, Levels C and D.

 Extra Practice on page 458, Set B

Describe an Error

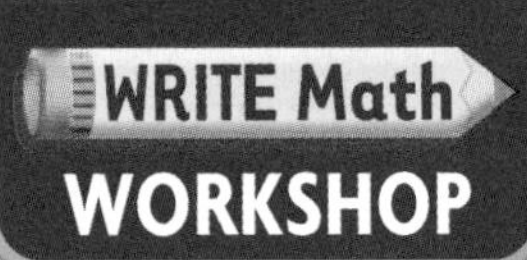

Matthew says, "The length of the pencil is 4 inches to the nearest half inch." What error did Matthew make? This is how Sonia described Matthew's error.

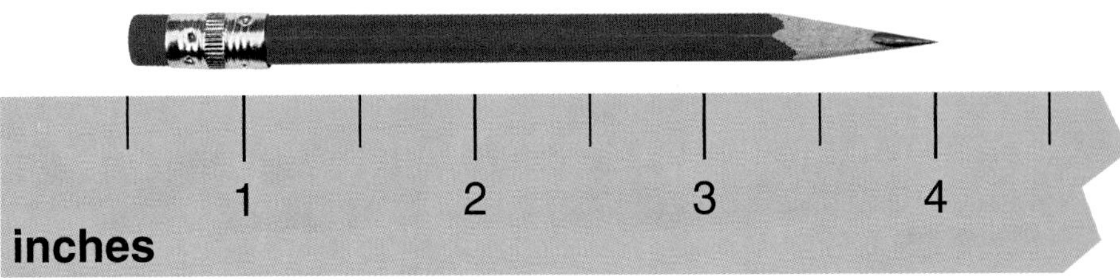

Matthew did not line up the left end of the pencil with the zero mark of the ruler. He lined it up with the $\frac{1}{2}$ inch mark. The point of the pencil is close to the 4-inch mark, so Matthew said the length of the pencil is 4 inches to the nearest half inch.

Matthew should line up the left end of the pencil with the zero mark of the ruler. Then the point of the pencil will be close to the $3\frac{1}{2}$ inch mark.

The length of the pencil is $3\frac{1}{2}$ inches to the nearest half inch.

Tips

To describe an error:

- First, tell what error you think was made.
- Next, explain how you think the error was made.
- Finally, describe how to correct the error.
- State the correct answer in the last sentence.

Problem Solving Describe the error. Explain how to correct the error and give the correct answer.

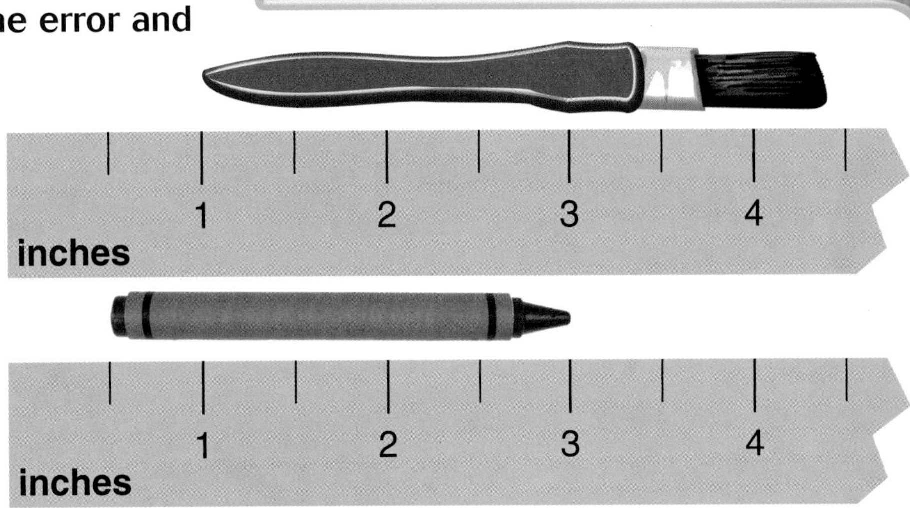

1. To the nearest half inch, what is the length of the paintbrush?

   Answer: $4\frac{1}{2}$ inches

2. To the nearest half inch, what is the length of the crayon?

   Answer: 3 inches

LESSON 4 HANDS ON

Estimate and Measure Feet and Yards

OBJECTIVE: Estimate and measure length to the nearest foot and yard.

Quick Review

Is your math book about 8 feet, 8 inches, or 8 yards wide?

You can use a ruler or yardstick to measure longer lengths.

Investigate

Materials ■ inch ruler and yardstick

A Make a table like the one at the right.

B Estimate the length of your desk, and record your estimate in the table. Think: What unit should you use?

C Measure the length of your desk, and record the measurement in your table.

D Repeat Steps B and C for 2 other objects in your classroom. Some examples are the length of the teacher's desk, the height of the door, and the width of a window.

Length of Classroom Objects

Object	Estimate	Measure
desk		

Draw Conclusions

1. When did you use a yardstick instead of a ruler to measure an object?
2. How does the length of your desk compare with another object you measured?
3. **Evaluation** If you know about how long 1 foot is, how does that help you estimate the length of an object 1 yard long? **Explain.**

TEKS 3.11A use linear measurement tools to estimate and measure lengths using standard units. *also* **3.14A, 3.14D, 3.15A, 3.15B, 3.16A**

Connect

Objects that are longer than 12 inches can be measured using a combination of units.

Suppose the length of your desk is 16 inches. You can write the length of the desk in inches or in feet and inches.

16 inches = ■ foot ■ inches

Think: 12 inches = 1 foot

16 inches = 12 inches + 4 inches

So, 16 inches = 1 foot 4 inches.

Table of Measures
1 foot = 12 inches
1 yard = 3 feet
1 yard = 36 inches

TALK Math

Explain how to write 40 inches as a combination of yards and inches.

Practice

Choose the better unit of measure.

1. the width of a small window

   3 feet or 3 yards

2. the length of a car

   9 feet or 9 yards

3. the height of a bookcase

   4 feet or 4 yards

4. the length of a bathtub

   2 feet or 2 yards

Use the Table of Measures. Write the length in feet and inches or in yards and feet.

5. 28 inches = ■ feet ■ inches
6. 7 feet = ■ yards ■ feet
7. 10 feet = ■ yards ■ feet
8. 42 inches = ■ feet ■ inches

Algebra Compare. Write <, >, or = for each ●.

9. 4 feet ● 30 inches
10. 70 inches ● 2 yards
11. 24 inches ● 2 feet
12. Karl is building a pen for his rabbit. He needs 8 feet of wire. He has 2 yards of wire. Does he have enough wire to build the pen? **Explain.**
13. **WRITE Math** **What's the Error?** Mary said the length of the soccer field is 100 feet. Describe her error.

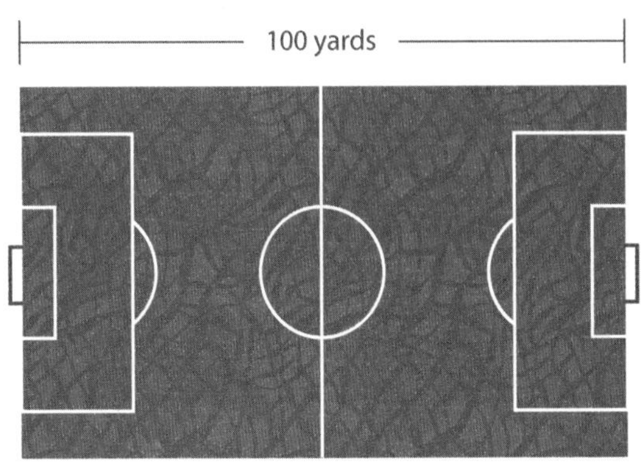

LESSON HANDS ON

5 Capacity

OBJECTIVE: Estimate and measure capacity.

Quick Review

Which container holds more?

Vocabulary

capacity cup (c)
pint (pt) quart (qt)
gallon (gal)

Capacity is the amount a container will hold. Customary units used to measure capacity are **cup (c)**, **pint (pt)**, **quart (qt)**, and **gallon (gal)**.

 1 cup (c)	 1 pint (pt)	 1 quart (qt)	 1 gallon (gal)

Investigate

Materials ■ cup, pint, quart, and gallon containers; water

A Make a table like the one at the right.

B Estimate the number of cups it will take to fill the pint container. Record your estimate.

C Fill a cup and pour it into the pint container. Repeat until the pint container is full.

D Record the number of cups it took to fill the pint container.

E Repeat Steps B–D for the quart and gallon containers.

Number of Cups		
	Estimate	Measure
Cups in a pint		
Cups in a quart		
Cups in a gallon		

E

Draw Conclusions

1. How do your measurements compare to your estimates?
2. How many cups are in a pint? a quart? a gallon?
3. **Synthesis** Which unit would you use to measure the amount of water needed to fill an aquarium? **Explain.**

TEKS 3.11E identify concrete models that approximate standard units for capacity and use them to measure capacity. *also* **3.14A, 3.14D, 3.15A, 3.15B, 3.16A, 3.16B**

Connect

TALK Math

Explain how you can find the number of cups in 3 pints 1 cup.

How are cups, pints, quarts, and gallons related?

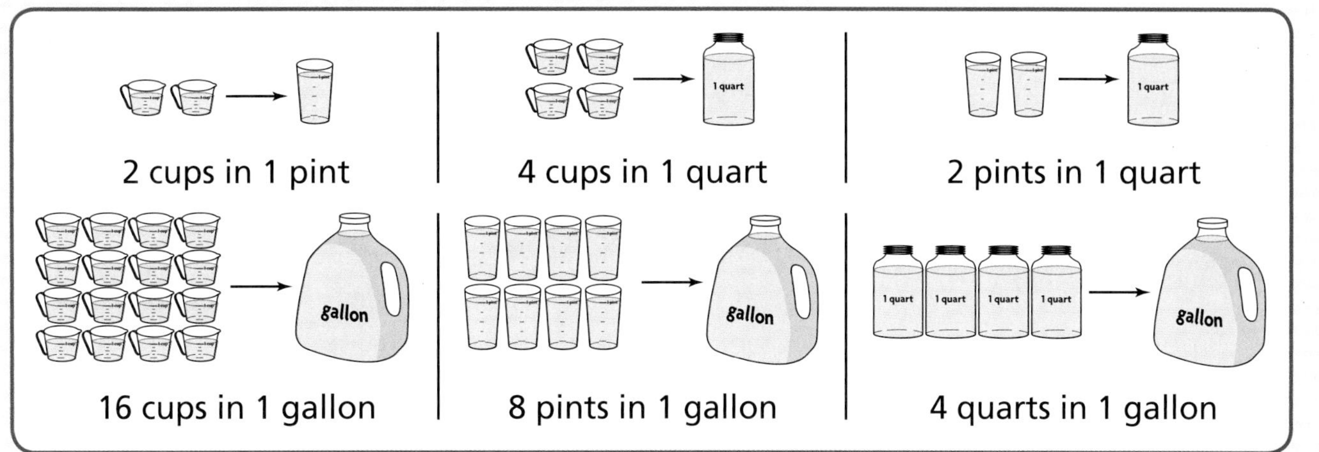

Practice

Choose the unit you would use to measure the capacity of each. Write *cup, pint, quart,* or *gallon*.

1.  **2.**  **3.**  ✓**4.** 

Tell how the units are related.

5. 8 cups = ■ pints **6.** 6 pints = ■ quarts ✓**7.** 2 gallons = ■ quarts

Algebra Compare. Write <, >, or = for each ●.

8. 2 gallons ● 7 quarts **9.** 3 cups ● 2 pints **10.** 1 quart ● 5 cups

11. Find a container in the classroom that holds about 2 pints. Draw the container.

12. Write these amounts in order from greatest to least: 2 quarts, 6 pints, 10 cups.

13. WRITE Math **What's the Error?** Connor says it takes 8 cups to fill a 1-gallon container. Is he correct? **Explain.**

6 Weight

OBJECTIVE: Estimate and measure weight.

Quick Review

Which object is heavier?

1. a backpack or a plate?
2. a donut or a glass of milk?
3. a baseball or a feather?
4. a book or a postcard?
5. a wristwatch or a TV?

Vocabulary

weight
ounce (oz)
pound (lb)

Weight is the measurement of how heavy an object is. Customary units used to measure weight are **ounce (oz)** and **pound (lb)**.

9 pennies weigh about 1 ounce.

144 pennies weigh about 1 pound.

Investigate

Materials ■ balance, pennies, classroom objects

A Place 9 pennies on one side of a balance. Find objects that you think weigh about 1 ounce. Weigh the objects. Write whether they weigh more than, less than, or the same as 1 ounce.

B Place 144 pennies on one side of a balance. Find objects that you think weigh about 1 pound. Weigh the objects. Write whether they weigh more than, less than, or the same as 1 pound.

Draw Conclusions

1. How does the weight of your notebook compare with the weight of your pencil?
2. **Analysis** How can you use the weight of 144 pennies to help you estimate the weight of a notebook? **Explain.**

TEKS 3.11D identify concrete models that approximate standard units of weight/mass and use them to measure weight/mass. *also* **3.14A, 3.14D, 3.15A, 3.15B, 3.16A, 3.16B**

Connect

You can use a scale to measure heavier objects. Estimate the weight of each object in pounds. Then use a scale to measure to the nearest pound.

- tape dispenser
- bottle of water
- box of crayons
- pencil box

Customary Units of Weight
1 pound = 16 ounces

Explain how to write 18 ounces as a combination of pounds and ounces.

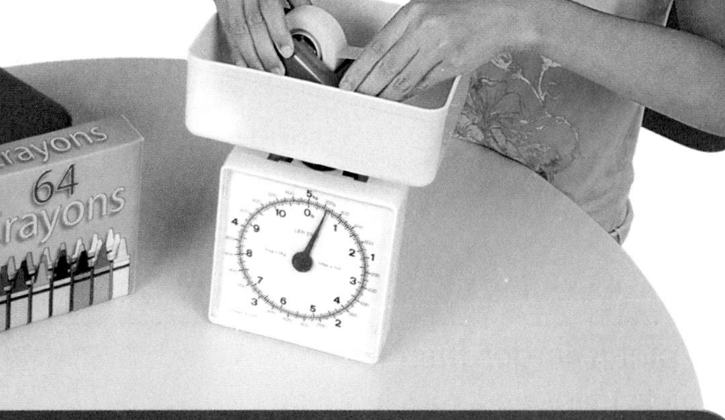

Practice

Choose the unit you would use to weigh each. Write *ounce* or *pound*.

1. 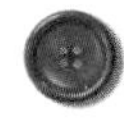

2. 

3. 

✓4. 

Find two objects in the classroom to match each weight. Draw them and label their weight.

5. about 2 pounds
6. about 3 ounces
✓7. about 8 ounces

Algebra Compare. Write <, >, or = for each ●.

8. 10 ounces ● 1 pound
9. 21 ounces ● 1 pound
10. 15 ounces ● 1 pound

11. **FAST FACT** A dram is a customary unit of measure smaller than an ounce. There are 16 drams in 1 ounce. How many drams are in 2 ounces? **Explain.**

12. **WRITE Math** **Sense or Nonsense** Hank says that 20 ounces is the same as 1 pound 4 ounces. Does his statement make sense? **Explain.**

Problem Solving Workshop
Skill: Choose a Unit

OBJECTIVE: Solve problems by using the skill *choose a unit.*

Read to Understand
Plan
Solve
Check

Read to Understand

PROBLEM Ian's class is setting up a freshwater fish tank. What customary unit would Ian use to measure the capacity of the tank?

Remember how customary units of capacity are related.

A pint is larger than a cup.
Think: there are 2 cups in 1 pint.

A quart is larger than a pint.
Think: there are 2 pints in 1 quart.

A gallon is larger than a quart.
Think: there are 4 quarts in 1 gallon.

So, Ian would use gallons to measure the capacity of the fish tank.

Table of Measures
Length
12 inches = 1 foot
3 feet = 1 yard
Capacity
2 cups = 1 pint
4 cups = 1 quart
2 pints = 1 quart
8 pints = 1 gallon
4 quarts = 1 gallon
Weight
16 ounces = 1 pound

Think and Discuss

Choose the better unit of measure.

a. Marianna measures the length of a black swordtail fish in the classroom fish tank. Is the length closer to 2 inches or 2 feet?

b. It takes Ned 12 minutes to drive from his house to the store. Is the distance he travels about 7 yards or 7 miles?

c. Ben likes to watch the pandas at the zoo. Is the weight of an adult panda measured in ounces or pounds?

TALK Math

How can you decide which unit is better to measure the weight of an object?

TEKS 3.11E identify concrete models that approximate standard units for capacity and use them to measure capacity. *also* **3.11A, 3.11D, 3.14A, 3.14C, 3.15A, 3.15B, 3.16A, 3.16B**

Guided Problem Solving

1. About 2 cars, end to end, will fit in Beth's driveway. What customary unit of length should Beth use to measure the length of her driveway?

   Think of the units of length.

   Which unit would be best to measure the length of a car?

   Which unit would be the best to measure a distance that is about 2 car lengths long?

   Solve the problem.

2. **What if** Beth helps her dad build a small birdhouse? What customary unit of length could they use to estimate the amount of wood they would need?

3. Mary enjoys drinking cocoa in the morning. Does her mug hold about 2 cups or 2 quarts?

Mixed Applications

4. Which unit would you use to measure the amount of water in a bathtub?

5. A bathtub is twice as long as Kia's dog. Kia's dog is 3 feet long. How many yards long is the bathtub?

For 6–8, use the items pictured.

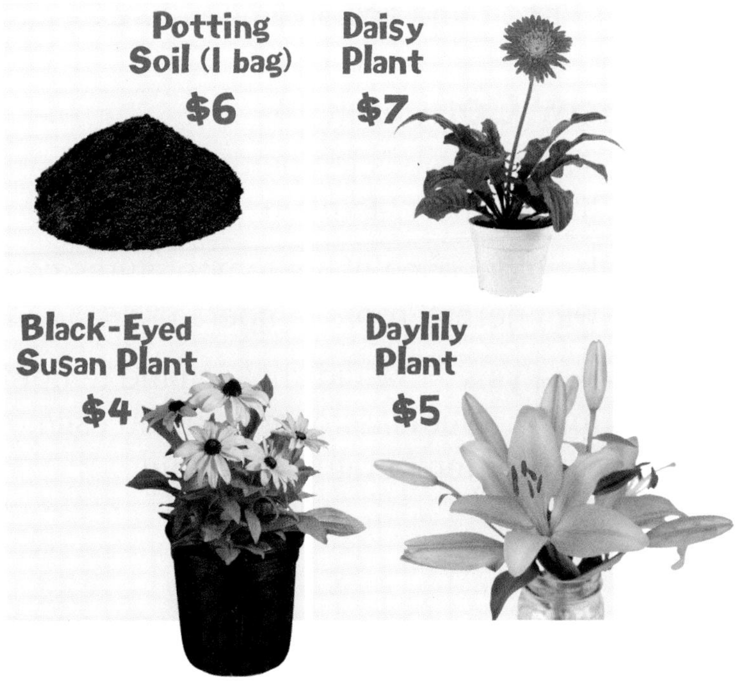

6. Mike bought 2 bags of potting soil and 3 daylily plants. How much did he spend?

7. Which would cost more, 4 black-eyed Susan plants or 3 daisy plants? How much more?

8. Joe has $10. Name two combinations of items he could buy.

9. 

Judy bought 24 daisy plants. She wants to plant them in 4 equal rows. How many daisies will be in each row? **Explain** your answer by drawing an array.

LESSON HANDS ON

8 Fahrenheit Temperature

OBJECTIVE: Estimate and measure temperature in degrees Fahrenheit.

Quick Review

Which is colder?

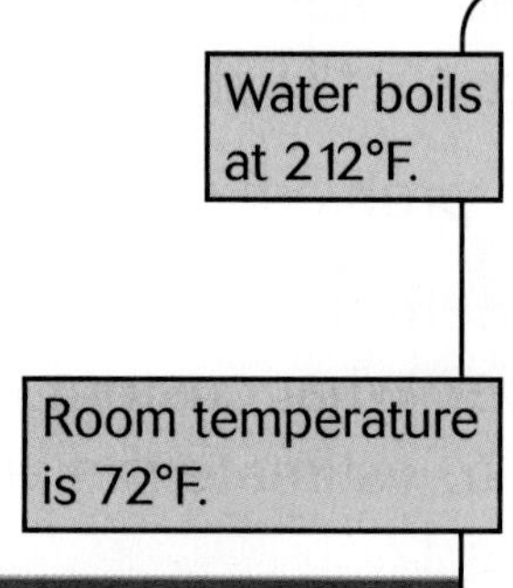

Vocabulary

degrees Fahrenheit (°F)

Temperature is the measure of how hot or cold something is. **Degrees Fahrenheit (°F)** are customary units of temperature.

To read a thermometer, find the number closest to the top of the red bar. Use the scale along the side like a number line. On the thermometer at the right, each line on the scale stands for 1 degree. The top of the red bar is at 67°F. The temperature shown is 67°F.

Write: 67°F Read: sixty-seven degrees Fahrenheit

Water boils at 212°F.

Room temperature is 72°F.

Water freezes at 32°F.

220, 215, 210, 100, 95, 90, 85, 80, 75, 70, 65, 60, 55, 50, 45, 40, 35, 30, 25, 20, 15, 10, 5, 0, −5, −10

°F

Investigate

Materials ■ Fahrenheit thermometer

A Estimate what you think the outdoor temperature will be, in degrees Fahrenheit, 3 times during the day. Record your estimates.

B Use a Fahrenheit thermometer to measure the outdoor temperature at the listed times. Record the actual temperature.

Draw Conclusions

1. At what time is temperature the coolest? the warmest? **Explain**.
2. How did each of the temperatures compare with normal room temperature?
3. **Analysis** How did knowing the temperature inside your classroom help you estimate the outside temperature? **Explain**.

TEKS 3.12A use a thermometer to measure temperature. *also* **3.14A, 3.14D, 3.15A, 3.15B**

Connect

Below are outside activities you might do at 20°F, 90°F, and 75°F.

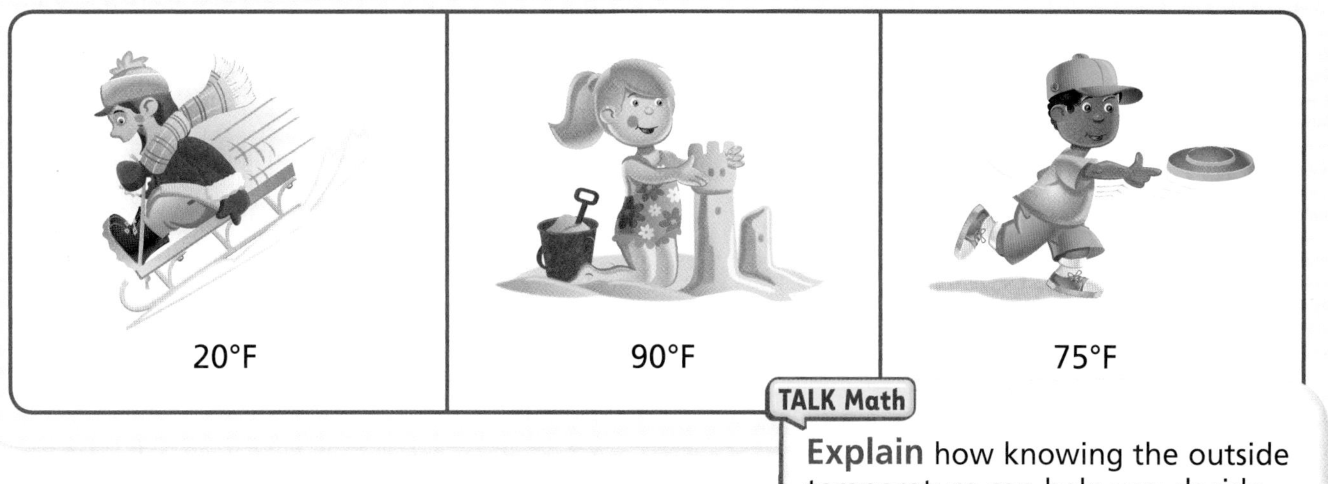

TALK Math

Explain how knowing the outside temperature can help you decide what clothes to wear.

Practice

Write each temperature in °F.

1. 50 40 30 °F

2.
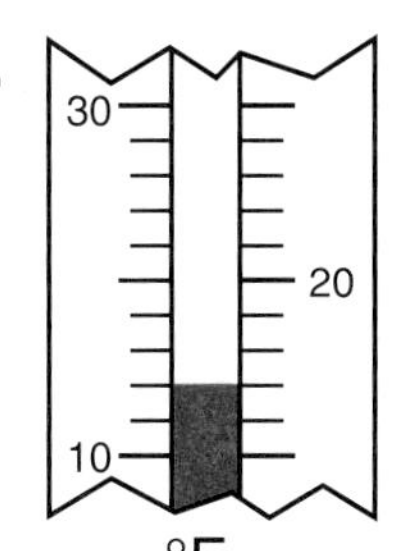

°F

3.
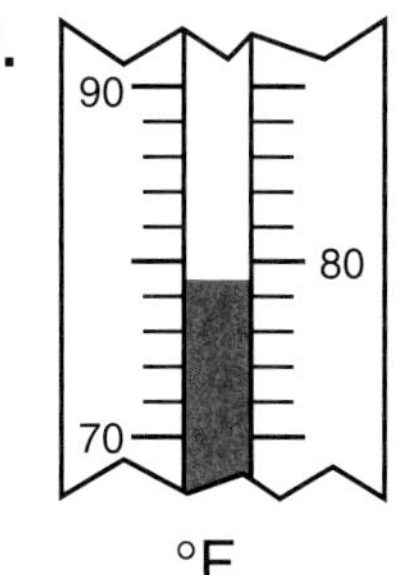

°F

4.
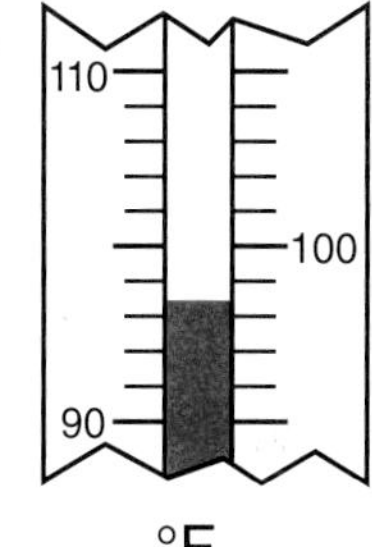

°F

Choose the better temperature for each activity.

5.

50°F or 80°F

6.

75°F or 105°F

7.

23°F or 53°F

8.

90°F or 30°F

9. **WRITE Math** Kenny's father is building a fire in the fireplace. About what temperature might it be outside? **Explain**.

10. It is 85°F outside. What is an activity that Paige might do at this temperature? What clothes do you think she might wear?

LESSON 9 Use a Thermometer

OBJECTIVE: Solve problems by using a thermometer.

Quick Review

What temperature does the thermometer show?

70, 60, 50 °F

Learn

PROBLEM The thermometer below shows the temperature in Corpus Christi, Texas, at noon. The weather forecast says the temperature will be about 16 degrees cooler by midnight. What is the temperature likely to be at midnight?

You can use a thermometer and what you know about adding and subtracting to solve problems about temperature.

110, 100, 90 °F

Look at the thermometer. The red bar ends at the line between 96°F and 98°F, so the temperature is 97°F at noon.

It will be about 16 degrees cooler at midnight, so subtract.

$$97 - 16 = 81$$

So, the temperature at midnight is likely to be 81°F.

Activity **Materials** ■ Fahrenheit thermometer

Use a thermometer to explore how temperature changes.

Step 1

Make a table like the one at the right.

Step 2

Record the outside temperature once each hour.

Hourly Temperature	
Time	**Temperature in °F**

- At what time was the temperature the highest? the lowest?
- What was the difference between the highest and lowest temperatures?

Guided Practice

1. The thermometer shows the temperature at 9:00 A.M. The temperature will be about 8 degrees warmer at 2:00 P.M. What is the temperature likely to be at 2:00 P.M?

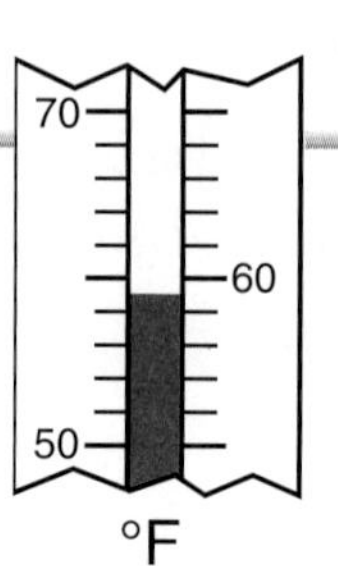

TEKS 3.12A use a thermometer to measure temperature. *also* 3.14A, 3.14D, 3.15A, 3.15B

Use the thermometers. Find the difference in temperatures.

2.

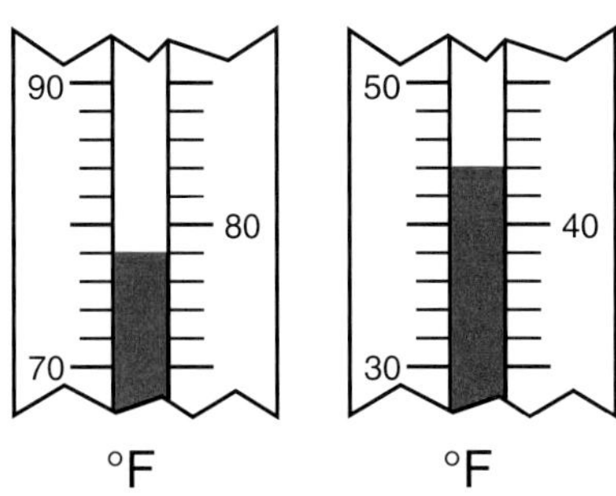

3.

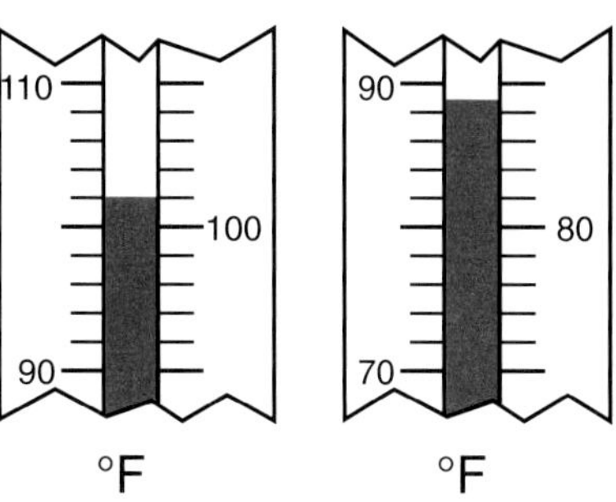

4. **TALK Math** **Explain** how you found the difference in temperatures in Exercise 2.

Independent Practice and Problem Solving

Use the thermometers. Find the difference in temperatures.

5.

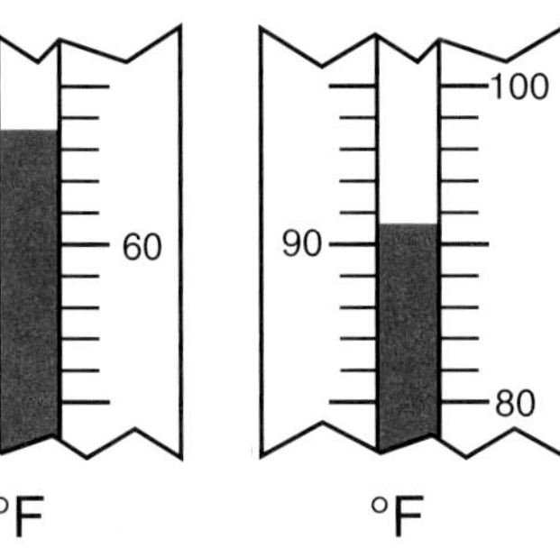

6.

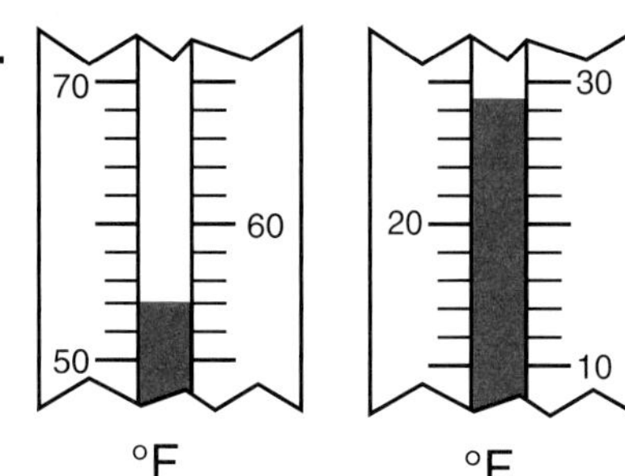

For 7–8, use the thermometers.

7. The temperature rose 10°F from 8:00 A.M. to 9:00 A.M. What was the temperature at 9:00 A.M.?

8. **WRITE Math** What was the change in temperature between 8:00 A.M. and 2:00 P.M.? At which time was the temperature cooler? **Explain.**

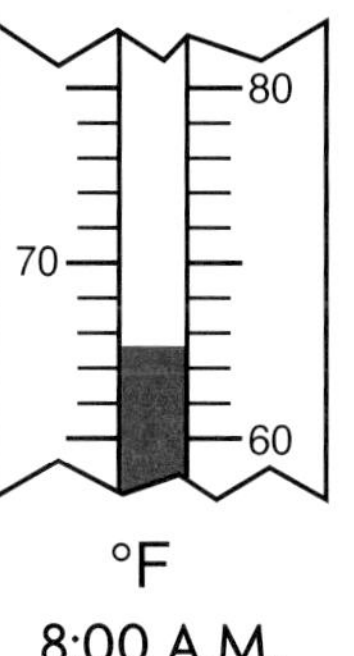

8:00 A.M.

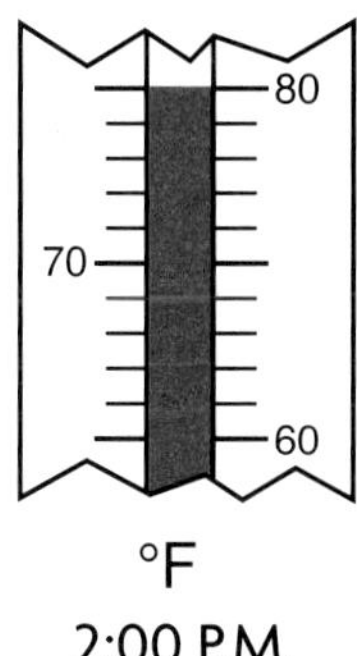

2:00 P.M.

Mixed Review and TAKS Prep

9. Rory's bedroom is 3 yards 2 feet long. How many feet long is it? (TEKS 3.11A, p. 446)

10. There were 478 people at a soccer game. What is 478 rounded to the nearest ten? (TEKS 3.5A, p. 38)

11. **TAKS Prep** The temperature is 40°F. It will be about 12°F cooler by 8:00 P.M. What will the temperature likely be at 8:00 P.M.? (Obj. 4)

A 28°F **B** 38°F **C** 52°F **D** 60°F

Extra Practice on page 458, Set C

Extra Practice

Set A **Choose the unit you would use to measure each. Write *inch, foot, yard,* or *mile.*** (pp. 440–441)

1. 

2. 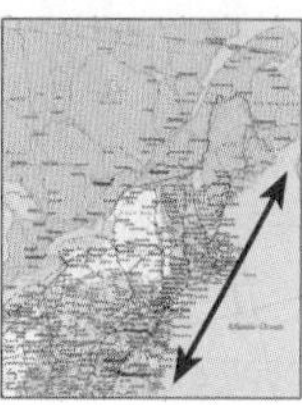

3. 

4. Helena is going to measure her kitten to see how much he has grown. What unit should she use?

Set B **Measure the length to the nearest inch.** (pp. 442–445)

1.

Measure the length to the nearest half inch.

2. 

3. 

Set C **Use the thermometers. Find the difference in temperatures.** (pp. 456–457)

1. 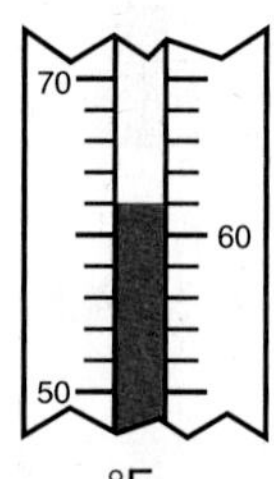

2. 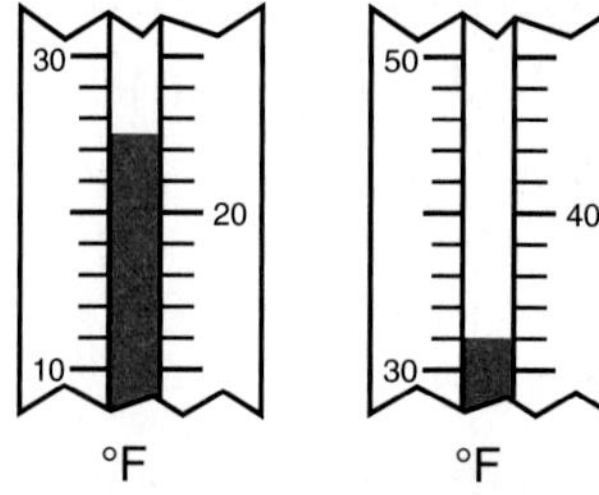

3. 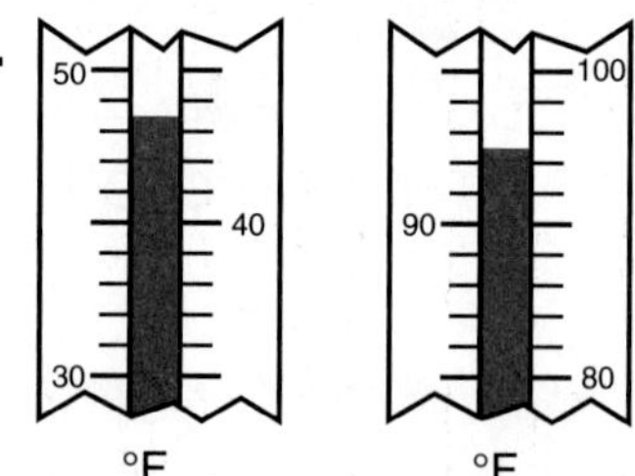

4. The temperature at 8:00 P.M. was 15°F cooler than the temperature at 2:00 P.M. What was the temperature at 8:00 P.M.?

5. What was the change in temperature between 8:00 P.M. and 11:00 P.M.?

2:00 P.M. 11:00 P.M.

Technology

Use Harcourt Mega Math, The Number Game, *Tiny's Think Tank*, Levels N, O, P.

TECHNOLOGY CONNECTION

iTools: Measurement (TEKS 3.11D, 3.14D)

Sam has 1 apple. Diane has 1 box of raisins. Do their items have the same mass? If not, who should add more items? How many more?

Step 1
Click on *Measurement*.

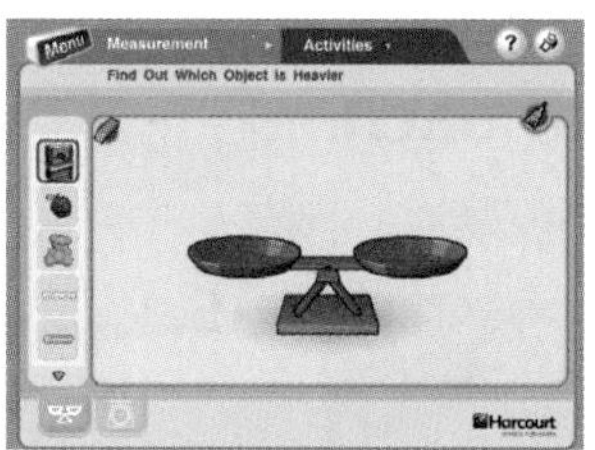

Step 2
Click on the apple then on one side of the balance. Click on the box of raisins then the other side of the balance.

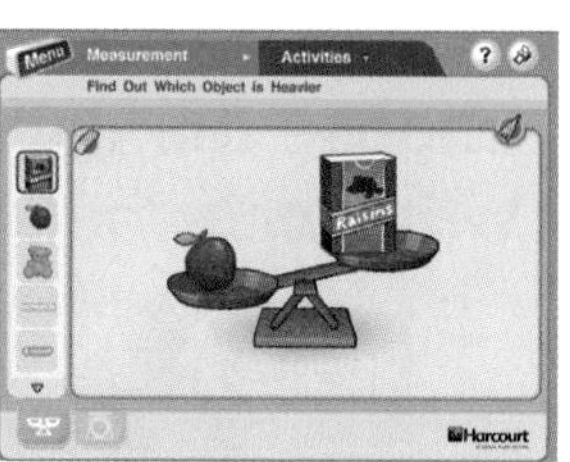

Step 3
If the balance is not level, keep clicking to add items until the balance is level.

So, the items do not have the same mass. Diane should add 3 boxes of raisins. Click on the broom to clear the workspace.

Try It

Follow the steps above to compare.

1. 2 bears
   2 connecting cubes
2. 4 footballs
   2 bowling balls
3. 2 glue bottles
   3 crayon boxes
4. 1 pumpkin
   10 strawberries
5. 2 rulers
   2 erasers
6. 4 folders
   1 notebook
7. **Explore More** Erin needs 12 ounces of nuts to make a recipe. She also has oranges that she knows are 4 ounces each. **Explain** how to use the balance to get 12 ounces of nuts.

GO ONLINE **Technology**
iTools available online or on CD-ROM

Chapter 19 Review/Test

Check Concepts

Solve.

1. Would you choose a cup, pint, quart, or gallon to measure the amount of juice in a glass? (TEKS 3.11E, pp. 448–449)
2. Which weighs more, a baseball or a crayon? (TEKS 3.11D, pp. 450–451)

Check Skills

Choose the unit you would use to measure each. Write *inch*, *foot*, *yard*, or *mile*. (TEKS 3.11A, pp. 440–441)

3. 

4. 

5. 

Measure to the nearest half inch. (TEKS 3.11A, pp. 442–445)

6. 

7. 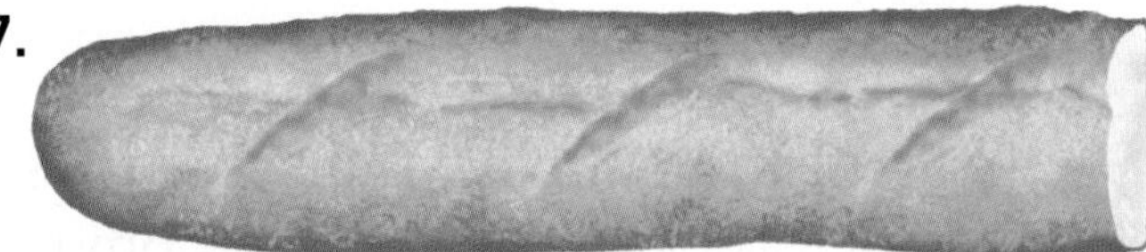

8. 

Check Problem Solving

Solve. (TEKS 3.14A, 3.15A, pp. 452–453)

9. Christina's garden has 6 rows of corn, with 10 plants in each row. What unit of length should she use to measure the corn section of her garden?

10. WRITE Math Christina's mother is preparing 12 ears of corn. Should she put the corn in a pot that holds 3 cups or 3 gallons of water? **Explain**.

GO ONLINE **Technology** Use *Online Assessment.*

Enrich • Mixed Units of Length

Mixing Measures

Some measurements can be written as mixed units. The length 20 inches can be written in feet and inches. There are 12 inches in 1 foot, so 20 inches = 12 inches + 8 inches = 1 foot 8 inches.

You can add mixed units of length.

Example

Add 2 feet 10 inches to 2 feet 8 inches.

Step 1	Find the total number of inches.	2 feet 8 inches + 2 feet 10 inches 18 inches
Step 2	Regroup the inches as feet and inches. 18 inches = 12 inches + 6 inches = 1 foot 6 inches	
Step 3	Add the feet. Then add the regrouped inches.	4 feet + 1 foot 6 inches 5 feet 6 inches

So, 2 feet 10 inches + 2 feet 8 inches = 5 feet 6 inches.

Practice

Add the mixed units of length.

1. 17 inches + 23 inches

2. 3 feet 7 inches + 2 feet 9 inches

3. 1 foot 9 inches + 1 foot 4 inches

4. 20 inches, 15 inches + 21 inches

5. 2 feet 8 inches, 10 inches + 1 foot 6 inches

6. 2 feet 8 inches, 2 feet 6 inches + 2 feet 5 inches

Wrap Up

WRITE Math Michael is 5 feet 6 inches tall. Write this measurement in yards, feet, and inches. **Explain.**

Getting Ready for the TAKS
Chapters 1–19

Number, Operation, and Quantitative Reasoning (TAKS Obj. 1)

1. There are 204 people in the band. There are 289 people in the choir. Which shows the BEST estimate of how many more people are in the choir than in the band?

   A 400
   B 100
   C 50
   D 0

Test Tip **Choose the answer.**

See item 2. Order the numbers from greatest to least mentally. Then compare your list with the answers given. If your answer does not match any of the answers given, carefully solve the problem again.

2. One of Liz's books has 347 pages. Another book has 299 pages. A third book has 390 pages. Which lists the number of pages in order from greatest to least?

   F 299; 347; 390
   G 347; 390; 299
   H 390; 299; 347
   J 390; 347; 299

3. **WRITE Math** How can this picture help you find 5×8? **Explain.**

Patterns, Relationships, and Algebraic Thinking (TAKS Obj. 2)

4. What is the pattern unit in this number pattern?

   2, 0, 1, 4, 2, 0, 1, 4, 2, 0, 1, 4

   A 0, 1, 4, 2
   B 2, 0, 1, 4
   C 2, 0, 1
   D 1, 4, 0, 2

5. How many players are on 5 teams?

Teams	1	2	3	4	5
Players	5	10	15	20	■

   F 10
   G 15
   H 20
   J Not here

6. **WRITE Math** What is a rule for the number pattern below? **Explain.**

   77, 66, 55, 44, 33

Measurement (TAKS Obj. 4)

7. Marisa used inches to measure an object. Which object did she measure?

A

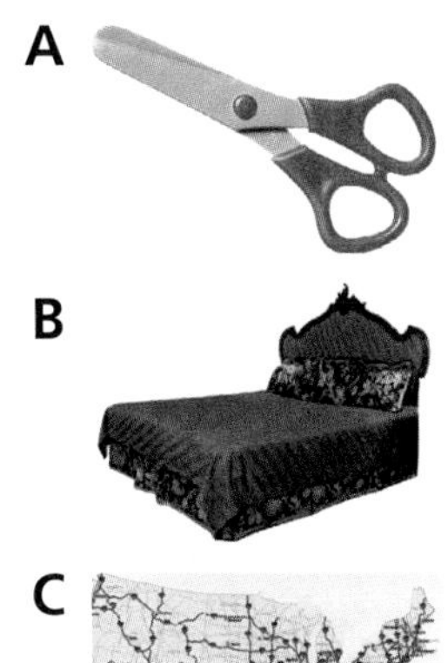

B

C

D

8. What temperature does the thermometer show?

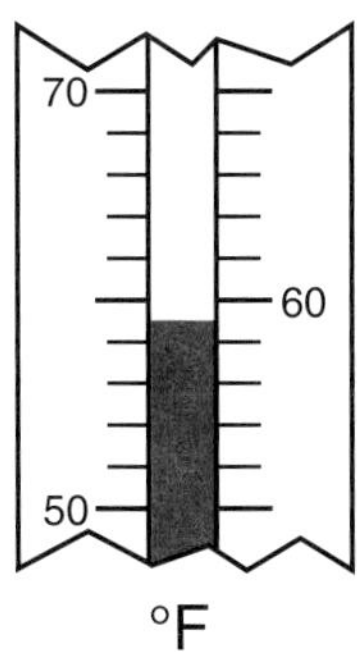

F 51°F H 59°F

G 54°F J 61°F

9. WRITE Math Would the height of the desk be 28 inches or 28 feet? **Explain**.

Probability and Statistics (TAKS Obj. 5)

10. Billy and Eric use this spinner to play a game. Which color are they more likely to spin?

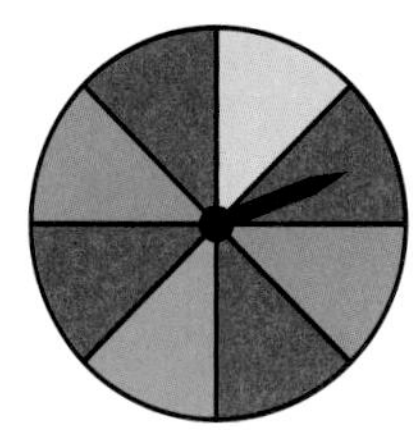

A yellow

B blue

C green

D red

11. John made a pictograph to show how many people played winter sports. He used the key: Each = 8 people. The pictograph shows next to ice skating. How many people ice skate?

F 36 H 44

G 40 J 48

12. WRITE Math John wants to make a bar graph from the data in his pictograph. The bars for ice skating and skiing are the same length. **Explain** what this means.

20 Metric (SI) Measurement

The Big Idea Measurement involves a comparison of an attribute of an object or situation with a unit that has the same attribute.

The state lizard of Texas is the Texas horned lizard. These lizards are about 7 cm long. Horned lizards sometimes are difficult to see because of their tan color.

Investigate

There are many species of lizards. Select a lizard from the chart and compare it to the length of a Texas horned lizard. Find the difference between the two lengths.

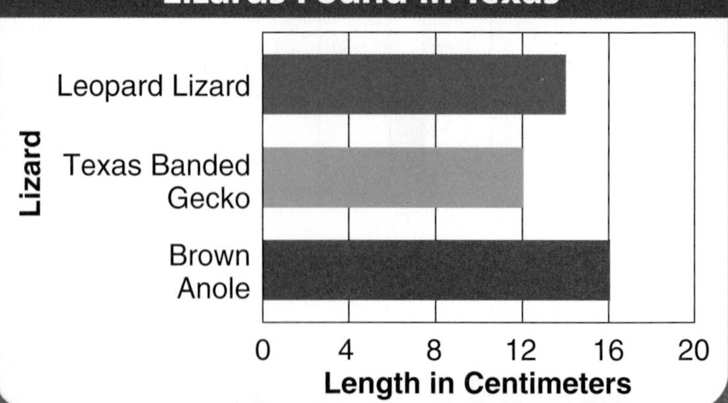

GO ONLINE **Technology** Student pages are available in the Student eBook.

Show What You Know

Check your understanding of important skills needed for success in Chapter 20.

▶ Use a Metric Ruler

Use a centimeter ruler to measure.

1.

2.

3. 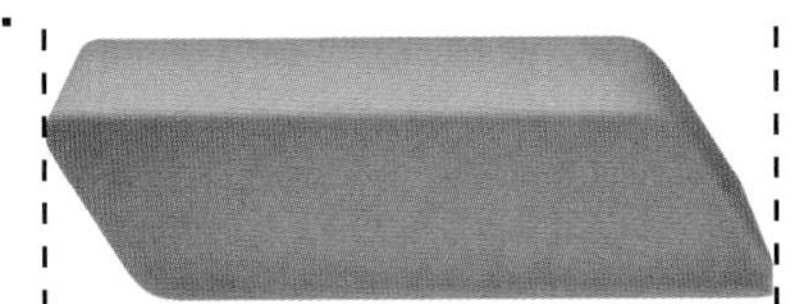

4. 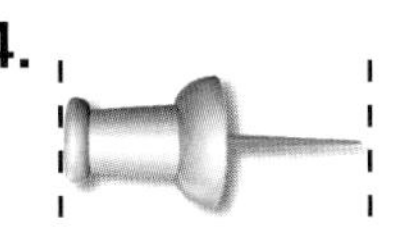

▶ Measure to the Nearest Centimeter

Use a centimeter ruler to measure to the nearest centimeter.

5.

6. 

7.

8.

VOCABULARY POWER

CHAPTER VOCABULARY

centimeter (cm)
decimeter (dm)
gram (g)
kilogram (kg)
kilometer (km)
length
liter (L)
mass
meter (m)
milliliter (mL)

WARM-UP WORDS

centimeter (cm) A metric unit for measuring length or distance

decimeter (dm) A metric unit for measuring length of distance; 1 decimeter = 10 centimeters

meter (m) A metric unit for measuring length of distance; 1 meter = 100 centimeters

LESSON 1 Length

OBJECTIVE: Introduce metric units of length.

Quick Review

Would you use an inch ruler or a yardstick to measure the length of a pencil?

Vocabulary

centimeter (cm)
decimeter (dm)
meter (m)
kilometer (km)

Learn

Metric units used to measure length and distance are **centimeter (cm)**, **decimeter (dm)**, **meter (m)**, and **kilometer (km)**.

PROBLEM Aaron plays basketball in college. Is Aaron about 2 centimeters, 2 decimeters, 2 meters, or 2 kilometers tall?

Measure shorter lengths in centimeters and decimeters.

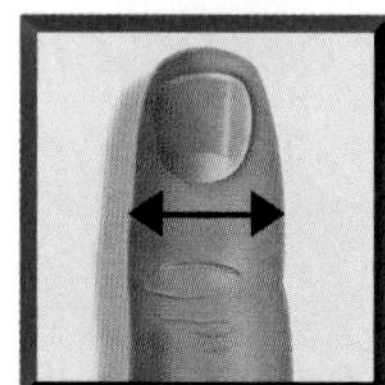

A child's finger is about 1 centimeter wide.

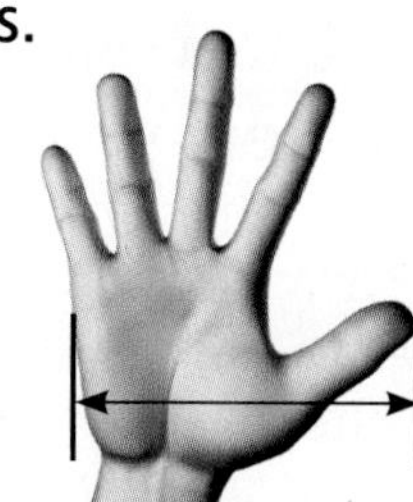

An adult's hand is about 1 decimeter wide.

Measure longer lengths in meters and kilometers.

A doorway is about 1 meter wide.

It takes about 10 minutes to walk 1 kilometer.

So, Aaron is about 2 meters tall.

Guided Practice

1. Would you measure the length of this crayon in centimeters or decimeters?

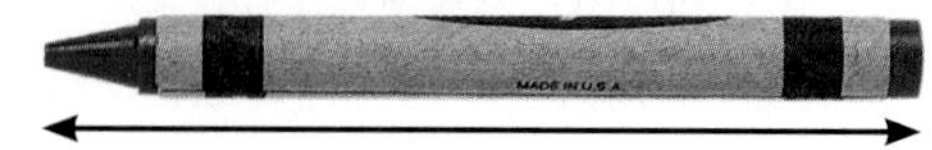

TEKS 3.11A Use linear measurement tools to estimate and measure lengths using standard units. *also* **3.14A, 3.14D, 3.15A, 3.15B, 3.16B**

Choose the unit you would use to measure each. Write *cm*, *m*, or *km*.

2. 

3. 

4. 

5. TALK Math Would you use centimeters or meters to measure the width of your school picture? **Explain.**

Independent Practice and Problem Solving

Choose the unit you would use to measure each. Write *cm*, *m*, or *km*.

6. 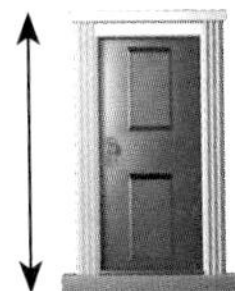

7. 

8. 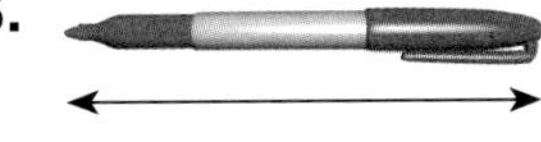

9. distance from your house to school

10. width of a bookshelf

11. height of a mountain

12. Brad walks from his house to the park every afternoon to play basketball. It takes him 20 minutes to get to the park. Is the park 2 dm, 2 m, or 2 km from his house?

13. WRITE Math **What's the Error?** Nancy's plant is about the same width as her front door. She says it is about 1 dm wide. Describe Nancy's error.

 Mixed Review and TAKS Prep

14. Theresa has 5 quarters, 3 dimes, and 5 pennies. How much money does she have? (TEKS 3.1C, p. 110)

15. The temperature is 30°F. Is Eric planting flowers or shoveling snow? (TEKS 3.12A, p. 454)

16. **TAKS Prep** About how long is this shell? (Obj. 4)

A 3 cm **C** 3 m

B 3 dm **D** 3 km

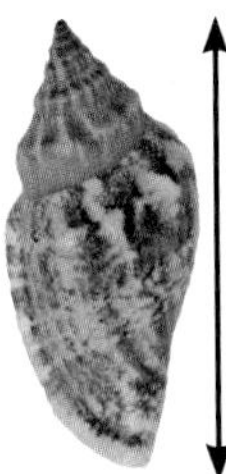

Extra Practice on page 478, Set A

LESSON 2

Centimeters and Decimeters

OBJECTIVE: Estimate and measure length to the nearest centimeter and decimeter.

Quick Review

Would you use *cm*, *m*, or *km* to measure each?

1. width of a penny
2. height of a bookcase
3. distance from one city to another
4. length of a paper clip
5. length of a car

Learn

You can use a centimeter ruler to measure the length of an object to the nearest centimeter and decimeter.

Estimate and measure lengths in centimeters and decimeters.

Activity **Materials** ■ centimeter ruler

Metric Units of Length
10 centimeters = 1 decimeter

Step 1

Copy the table. Choose three objects to measure.

Step 2

Estimate the length of each object in centimeters and decimeters. Record your estimates.

Step 3

Use a centimeter ruler to measure each object to the nearest centimeter and decimeter. Record the measurements.

Length of Objects

Object	Estimate	Measure

- How did your estimates compare to the actual measurements?
- Choose one object you measured. Are there more centimeters or decimeters? Explain.

Remember

To use a ruler:
- line up one end of the object with the zero mark on the ruler.
- find the centimeter mark closest to the object's other end.

Guided Practice

1. To the nearest centimeter and decimeter, how long is the marker? Think: Which centimeter mark is closer to the right end of the marker?

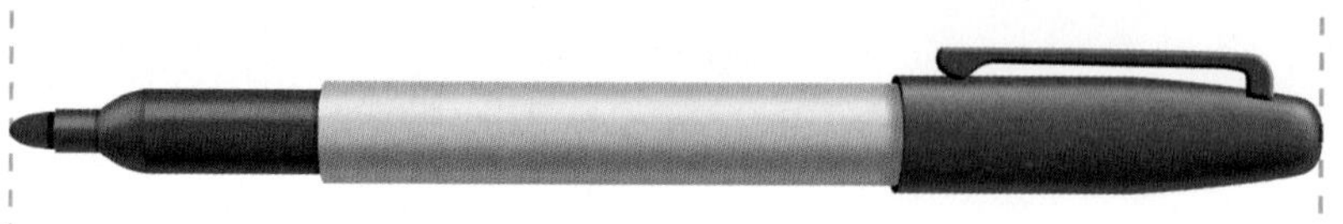

TEKS 3.11A Use linear measurement tools to estimate and measure lengths using standard units. *also* 3.14A, 3.14D, 3.15A, 3.15B, 3.16B

Estimate the length in centimeters. Then use a centimeter ruler to measure to the nearest centimeter.

2. 

3. 

4. 

5. TALK Math **Explain** how you can measure the length of your notebook to the nearest centimeter and decimeter.

Independent Practice and Problem Solving

Estimate the length in centimeters. Then use a centimeter ruler to measure to the nearest centimeter.

6. 

7. 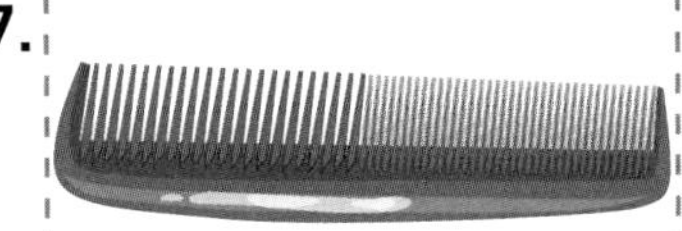

8. 

Choose the better estimate.

9. 

12 cm or 12 dm?

10. 

3 cm or 3 dm?

11. 

15 cm or 15 dm?

12. **Reasoning** Peter is 8 dm tall. Mary is 86 cm tall. Susan is 9 dm tall, and Jack is 84 cm tall. Who is tallest? **Explain.**

13. Suppose you measure your desk in centimeters and then in decimeters. Will there be more centimeters or more decimeters? **Explain.**

14. WRITE Math **Sense or Nonsense?** Justin said that 32 centimeters is the same as 3 decimeters plus 2 centimeters. Do you agree? **Explain.**

Mixed Review and TAKS Prep

15. There are 12 cars on a roller coaster. Each car holds 8 people. How many people does it hold? (TEKS 3.4A, p. 260)

16. Would the length of a playground be about 500 meters or 500 centimeters? (TEKS 3.11A, p. 466)

17. **TAKS Prep** June's book is 40 centimeters long. How many decimeters is that? (Obj. 4)

A 4,000 decimeters
B 400 decimeters
C 40 decimeters
D 4 decimeters

Extra Practice on page 478, Set B

LESSON 3

Meters and Kilometers

OBJECTIVE: Measure longer lengths in meters and kilometers.

Quick Review

1. 10 cm = ■ dm
2. 100 cm = ■ m
3. 10 dm = ■ m
4. 2 m = ■ cm
5. 10 m = ■ dm

Learn

PROBLEM Bobby lives in El Paso, Texas. He and his family drive to San Simeon, California. It takes them about 15 hours. Is the distance about 1,500 meters or 1,500 kilometers?

The window is about 1 meter wide.

It takes about 10 minutes to walk 1 kilometer.

A car can travel about 100 kilometers in 1 hour.

So, it is about 1,500 kilometers from El Paso to San Simeon.

The table shows how metric units of length are related.

- How many kilometers are in 4,000 meters? Explain.

Table of Measures
1 meter = 100 centimeters
1 meter = 10 decimeters
1 kilometer = 1,000 meters

Measure in Meters

Activity **Materials** ■ centimeter grid paper, crayons, tape

Step 1 Use the Table of Measures to find the number of decimeters in 1 meter.

Step 2 Cut enough decimeter strips out of grid paper to make a 1-meter strip.

Step 3 Color each decimeter strip a different color. Tape the strips together so that the edges do not overlap.

Step 4 Estimate the length of your classroom. Then use your meter strip to find the actual measure.

Guided Practice

1. It takes Louis about 20 minutes to walk to school. Does he walk about 2 meters or 2 kilometers?

TEKS 3.11A Use linear measurement tools to estimate and measure lengths using standard units. *also* **3.14A, 3.14D, 3.15A, 3.15B**

Choose the unit you would use to measure each. Write *m* or *km*.

2. length of a driveway

3. length of a soccer field

4. distance from Ohio to Texas

5. TALK Math Are there more meters or kilometers in a distance that is 10 kilometers long? **Explain.**

Independent Practice and Problem Solving

Choose the unit you would use to measure each. Write *m* or *km*.

6.

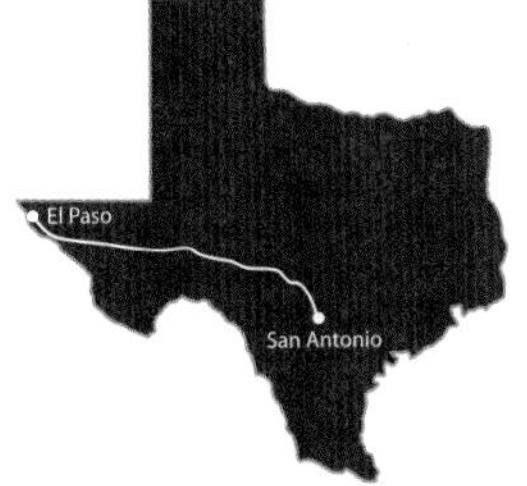

7.

8.

Find two objects in the classroom that have a length that matches the statement. Draw them, and label their length.

9. less than 1 meter

10. greater than 1 meter

11. greater than 5 meters

12. FAST FACT Windsor Castle, near London, England, is the largest castle in the world. The avenue leading up to the castle, called the "Long Walk," is about 5 kilometers long. About how many meters long is it?

13. **Reasoning** Mia and her family hike 5 kilometers around Windsor Castle. Then they hike 3 kilometers around the castle's picnic area. How many meters does the family hike in all? **Explain.**

14. Could one of the rooms in the castle be 15 m or 15 km long? **Explain.**

15. WRITE Math Mia and her family drive about 2 hours from their home to San Francisco, California. About how far do they drive? **Explain.**

Mixed Review and TAKS Prep

16. What is the next number in the pattern?
5,000; 4,000; 3,000; ■ (TEKS 3.6A, p. 182)

17. Write the fact family for 3, 4, and 12. (TEKS 3.6C, p. 304)

18. **TAKS Prep** How many meters are in 3 kilometers? (Obj. 4)

A 3 meters
B 30 meters
C 300 meters
D 3,000 meters

Extra Practice on page 478, Set C

LESSON HANDS ON

4 Capacity

OBJECTIVE: Estimate and measure capacity.

Metric units used to measure capacity are **milliliter (mL)** and **liter (L)**.

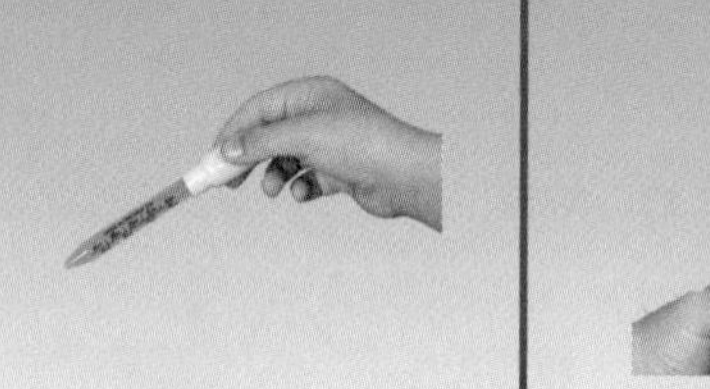 A dropper holds about 1 mL.	 A glass holds about 250 mL.	 A water bottle holds about 1 L.

Quick Review

Which container holds more?

Vocabulary

milliliter (mL) **liter (L)**

Investigate

Materials ■ 250-mL plastic glass, liter container, pitcher

A Make a table like the one at the right to help find the capacity of different containers.

B Estimate the number of milliliters that are in 1 liter. Use the glass. Pour 250 mL of water into the liter container.

C Repeat until the liter container is full. Record how many milliliters you poured.

D Estimate the number of liters it will take to fill the pitcher.

E Pour 1 liter of water into the pitcher. Repeat until the pitcher is full. Record the number of liters you poured.

Find the Capacity

How many:	Estimate	Measure
milliliters in a liter?		
liters in the pitcher?		

B

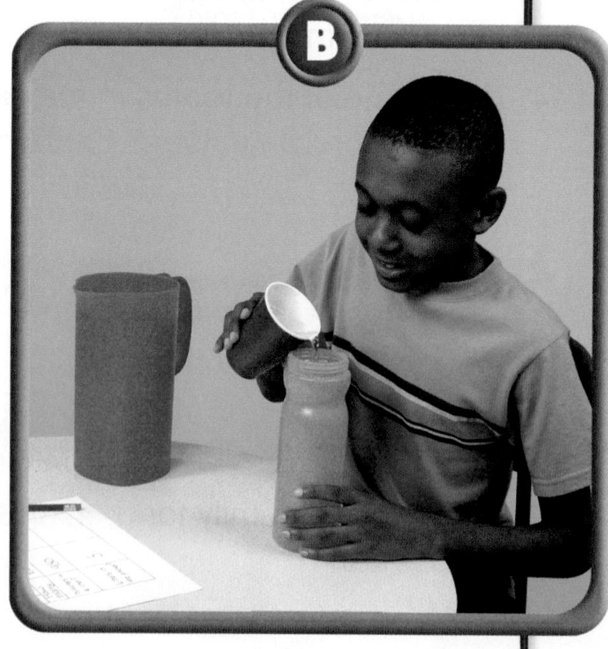

Draw Conclusions

1. How close were your estimates to the actual capacity of your containers?
2. **Evaluation** Suppose you drank a tall glass of orange juice. Did you drink about 4 mL or 400 mL of orange juice? **Explain.**

TEKS 3.11E Identify concrete models that approximate standard units for capacity and use them to measure capacity. *also* **3.14A, 3.14D, 3.15A, 3.15B, 3.16A**

Connect

The table helps you see how liters and milliliters are related.

L	1	2	3	4	5
mL	1,000	2,000	3,000	4,000	5,000

TALK Math

Explain how many milliliters are in 6 liters.

Practice

Choose the unit you would use to measure the capacity of each. Write *mL* or *L*.

1. 

2. 

3. 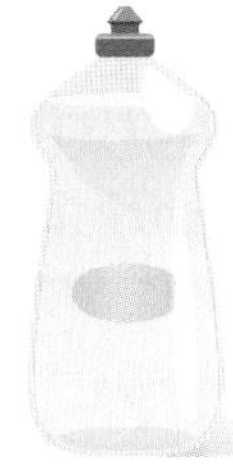

4. 

5. 

✓6. 

Find two containers in the classroom that show each capacity. Draw them and label their capacity.

7. less than 250 mL

8. greater than 1 L

9. greater than 2 L

Algebra Find each missing number.

10. ■ mL = 4 L

11. 12,000 mL = ■ L

✓12. 8 L = ■ mL

13. **Reasoning** Jason made 1 liter of lemonade. He drank 450 milliliters of it. How much lemonade is left now? **Explain** how you got your answer.

14. **WRITE Math** Patrick's aquarium holds 10 L of water. He fills the aquarium using a 500-mL container. How many times will Patrick have to fill his container? **Explain.**

CD ROM Technology
Use Harcourt Mega Math, The Number Games, *Tiny's Think Tank*, Level N.

5 Mass

OBJECTIVE: Estimate and measure mass.

Quick Review

Which is heavier?

Vocabulary

mass gram (g) kilogram (kg)

Mass is the amount of matter in an object. Metric units used to measure mass are **gram (g)** and **kilogram (kg)**.

A small paper clip has a mass of about 1 gram.

A box of 1,000 paper clips has a mass of about 1 kilogram.

Investigate

Materials ■ balance, paper clips, classroom objects

Make a table like the one at the right to help you find the mass of classroom objects.

Mass of Objects		
Object	Estimate	Measure

Ⓐ Estimate the mass of an object. Record it in the table.

Ⓑ Use the balance and paper clips to check. Record the measurement in the table.

Ⓒ Repeat steps A–B for 4 other objects.

Draw Conclusions

1. Look at the objects you used. Which objects have a mass less than 10 grams? Greater than 10 grams?
2. Put the 5 objects in order from least to greatest mass.
3. **Synthesis** Would the total mass of the 5 objects be greater than 1 kilogram or less than 1 kilogram? **Explain.**

TEKS 3.11D Identify concrete models that approximate standard units of weight/mass and use them to measure weight/mass. *also* **3.14A, 3.14D, 3.15A, 3.15B, 3.16A**

Connect

You can use a scale to find the mass of heavier objects in kilograms.

The table helps you see how grams and kilograms are related.

kilograms	1	2	3	4	5
grams	1,000	2,000	3,000	4,000	5,000

TALK Math

Explain which is greater—5,000 grams or 6 kilograms.

Practice

Choose the unit you would use to find the mass of each. Write *gram* or *kilogram*.

1. 

2. 

3. 

✓4. 

Find two objects in the classroom that have a mass that matches the statement. Draw them, and label their mass.

5. less than 50 grams
6. greater than 100 grams
✓7. greater than 1 kilogram

Algebra Find each missing number.

8. ■ g = 8 kg
9. 10,000 g = ■ kg
10. 9 kg = ■ g

11. Archie's cat has a mass of 3 kilograms. How many grams is that?

12. **Reasoning** Do objects of about the same size always have about the same mass? **Explain**.

13. **WRITE Math** Nikia bought 900 grams of apples, 5 kilograms of oranges, and 200 grams of grapes. Write the masses of the fruits in order from least to greatest. **Explain** how you got your answer.

Problem Solving Workshop
Strategy: Compare Strategies

OBJECTIVE: Compare different strategies to solve problems.

Read to Understand
Plan
Solve
Check

PROBLEM Joey has a seashell collection. He has an Australian trumpet shell that is 3 dm long. How many centimeters long is the shell?

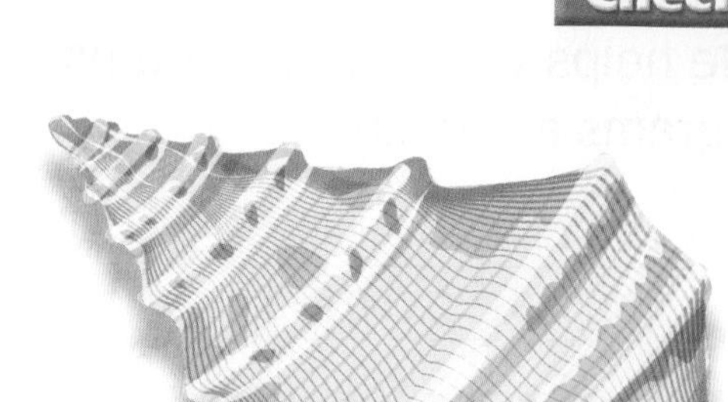

▲ The Australian trumpet shell is one of the largest shells in the world.

Read to Understand

- **Identify the details in the problem.**
- **What information is given?**

Plan

- **What strategy can you use to solve the problem?**

Sometimes you can use more than one strategy to solve a problem. You can *make a table* or *act it out* to help you solve this problem.

Solve

- **How can you use the strategies to solve the problem?**

Make a table.
You know that 1 dm = 10 cm. Use this information to make a table.

dm	1	2	3
cm	10	20	30

Act it out.
Draw a line 3 dm long for the length of the Australian trumpet shell. Then measure the line to the nearest centimeter.

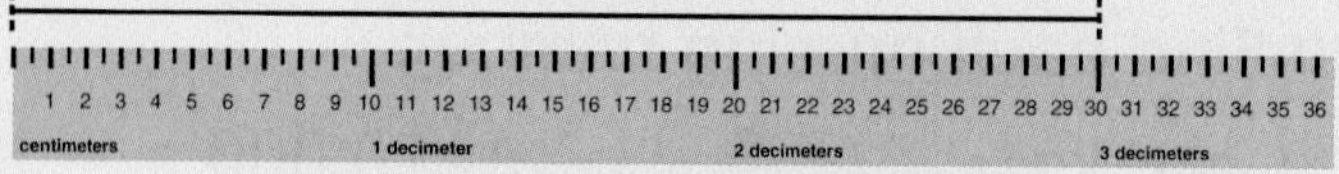

So, the shell is 30 cm long.

Check

- **How can you check your answer?**

TALK Math
Which strategy would you use to solve the problem? **Explain.**

TEKS 3.14C select or develop an appropriate problem-solving plan or strategy, including drawing a picture, looking for a pattern, systematic guessing and checking, acting it out, making a table, working a simpler problem, or working backwards to solve a problem. *also* **3.14A, 3.14B, 3.15A, 3.15B, 3.16B**

Guided Problem Solving

1. Joey's box of shells has a mass of 5,000 grams. What is the mass of the box in kilograms?

   First, decide what strategy to use. You can make a table or act it out.

   Then, use the strategy to solve the problem.

g	1,000	2,000	3,000	4,000	5,000
kg	1	2	3	■	■

   5,000 g = ■ kg

2. **What if** Joey's box of shells has a mass of 8 kilograms? What would the mass of the box be in grams?

3. Mr. Tanner's family room is 6 meters wide. How many decimeters wide is the room?

Choose a STRATEGY

Draw a Diagram or Picture
Make a Model or Act It Out
Make an Organized List
Look for a Pattern
Make a Table or Graph
Guess and Check
Work Backward
Solve a Simpler Problem
Write an Equation
Use Logical Reasoning

Mixed Strategy Practice

For 4–6, use the picture.

4. Is the height of the daisy greater than or less than 1 decimeter?

5. Nina places 6 daisy petals end-to-end. How long is the line of petals? **Explain.**

6. **Pose a Problem** Look back at Problem 5. Write a similar problem by changing the number of petals.

7. Larry plants a poppy, a tulip, and a daisy in a row in his garden. He does not put the poppy or the tulip first. He does not put the tulip next to the daisy. In what order does Larry plant the flowers?

8. Julie plants 1 daisy plant on Monday. She plants 2 daisy plants on Tuesday. She plants 3 daisy plants on Wednesday. If the pattern continues through Friday, how many daisy plants will Julie have planted in all? **Explain.**

Extra Practice

Set A **Choose the unit you would use to measure each. Write *cm*, *m*, or *km*.** (pp. 466–467)

1. 
2. 
3. 

4. height of a drinking glass
5. distance from your home to school
6. length of a skating rink
7. distance from Texas to Florida
8. length of a playground
9. height of a chair

Set B **Estimate the length in centimeters. Then use a centimeter ruler to measure to the nearest centimeter.** (pp. 468–469)

1. 
2. 

3. Is the height of a window 8 cm or 8 dm?
4. Is the length of a safety pin 3 cm or 3 dm?

Set C **Choose the unit you would use to measure each. Write *m* or *km*.** (pp. 470–471)

1. 
2. 
3. 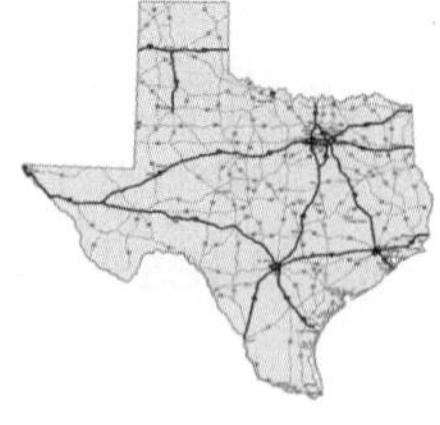

Find 2 objects in the classroom about each length. Draw them and label their lengths. (pp. 470–471)

4. greater than 1 meter
5. less than 1 meter
6. greater than 5 meters

Technology
Use Harcourt Mega Math, Ice Station Exploration, *Linear Lab*, Level H.

PRACTICE GAME

Collect-a-Meter

Roll 'Em! Measure 'Em!

2–4 players

- Gameboard
- Centimeter rulers
- Number cube
- Counter, paper, and pencil for each player
- Action cards

START | ACTION | ACTION | ACTION | START

ACTION | ACTION

ACTION CARDS

START | ACTION | ACTION | START

Collect 'Em!

- Players shuffle the Action cards and place them facedown in the middle of the gameboard.
- Each player places a counter in one of the START corners.
- Player 1 rolls the number cube, moves the number of spaces rolled, measures the picture of the object on the space where he or she lands, and writes the measurement on a score sheet. It is then Player 2's turn.
- When players land on an Action space, they pick an Action card and follow its directions.
- The first player to score a total of 100 centimeters wins.

Chapter 20 Review/Test

Check Concepts

Solve.

1. Which is a greater mass, a gram or a kilogram? (TEKS 3.11D, p. 474)
2. Which is a greater capacity, a liter or a milliliter? (TEKS 3.11E, p. 472)
3. Which is a greater distance, a kilometer or a meter? (TEKS 3.11A, p. 466)

Check Skills

Choose the unit you would use to measure each.
Write *cm*, *m*, or *km*. (TEKS 3.11A, pp. 466–467)

4. length of a driveway
5. height of a tree
6. length of a carrot
7. distance from one room to another
8. distance from one city to another
9. distance from your nose to your mouth

Choose the better estimate. (TEKS 3.11A, pp. 468–469)

10. 

40 cm or 40 dm?

11. 

8 cm or 8 dm?

12. 

3 cm or 3 dm?

Check Problem Solving

Solve. (TEKS 3.14C, pp. 476–477)

13. Ed rides 3,000 meters to get to school. How many kilometers does he ride?
14. Becky's bedroom is 5 meters long. How many decimeters long is her room?
15. WRITE Math Michael's puppy has a mass of 7,000 grams. Pauline's puppy has a mass of 8 kilograms. **Explain** how to find whose puppy has a greater mass.

GO ONLINE **Technology** Use *Online Assessment.*

Enrich • Inches and Centimeters

Compare Units

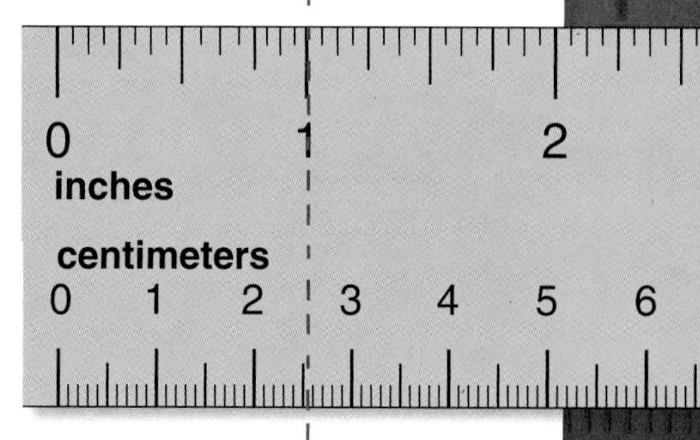

In the United States, we use the customary system of measurement, which includes inches as a unit of measure. Most other countries use the metric system of measurement, which includes centimeters as a unit of measure.

You can use estimates to compare measures using inches and centimeters.

Understand

Look at the ruler.

One inch is about $2\frac{1}{2}$ centimeters.

Five inches is about how many centimeters?

Step 1 Make a table to compare inches and centimeters. 1 inch is about $2\frac{1}{2}$ centimeters.

inches	1	2	3	4	5
centimeters	$2\frac{1}{2}$	5	$7\frac{1}{2}$	10	$12\frac{1}{2}$

Step 2 Find 5 inches in the table and the estimated centimeter measure that matches it.

So, 5 inches is about $12\frac{1}{2}$ centimeters.

Apply

Copy and complete each comparison.

1. 4 inches is about ____ centimeters.
2. 5 centimeters is about ____ inches.
3. $17\frac{1}{2}$ centimeters is about ____ inches.
4. 10 inches is about ____ centimeters.

Explain

WRITE Math **Explain** how to compare centimeters to 1 foot.

Getting Ready for the TAKS
Chapters 1–20

Number, Operation, and Quantitative Reasoning (TAKS Obj. 1)

1. Jackie baked cookies. She put 6 cookies in each of 9 bags. How many cookies in all did she bake?

   A 63 C 45
   B 54 D 15

2. The population of Alaska is about 663,700 people. What is the value of the digit 3 in 663,700?

   F 30
   G 300
   H 3,000
   J Not here

3. Which number is between 3,165 and 3,217?

   A 3,098
   B 3,147
   C 3,185
   D 3,240

4. WRITE Math What division fact does this model show? **Explain** your answer.

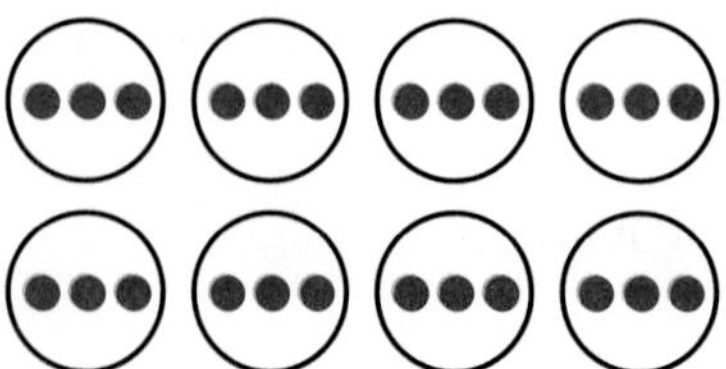

Patterns, Relationships, and Algebraic Thinking (TAKS Obj. 2)

5. Maribele collects coins. If the pattern continues, how many coins will she collect in the fifth month?

Judy's Coins				
Month	1	2	3	4
Coins	6	12	18	24

   F 26 H 30
   G 28 J 32

Test Tip **Decide on a plan.**

See item 6. Make a plan to find the missing number. First, choose a number that completes one of the number sentences. Next, check if it completes the others. Then, find the number in the answers choices. Use the plan to find the answer.

6. Which number completes the fact family?

   $6 \times ■ = 42$ $■ \times 6 = 42$
   $42 \div ■ = 6$ $42 \div 6 = ■$

   A 6 C 8
   B 7 D 36

7. WRITE Math What is a rule in this pattern? **Explain** how you know.

   4, 5, 8, 9, 12, 13, 16

Geometry and Spatial Reasoning (TAKS Obj. 3)

8. Which pair of figures appears to be congruent?

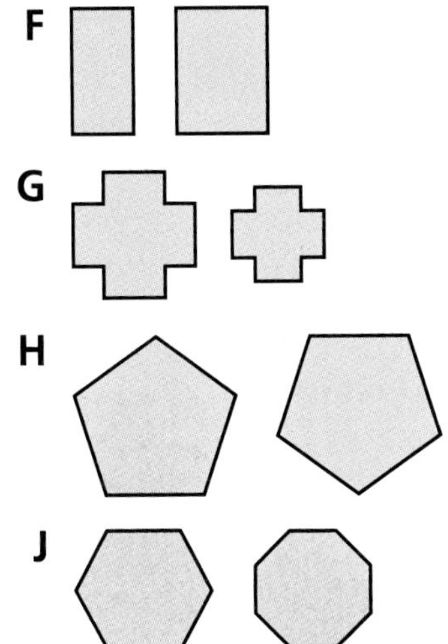

9. Cho drew these figures on the computer. Which figure appears to have a line of symmetry?

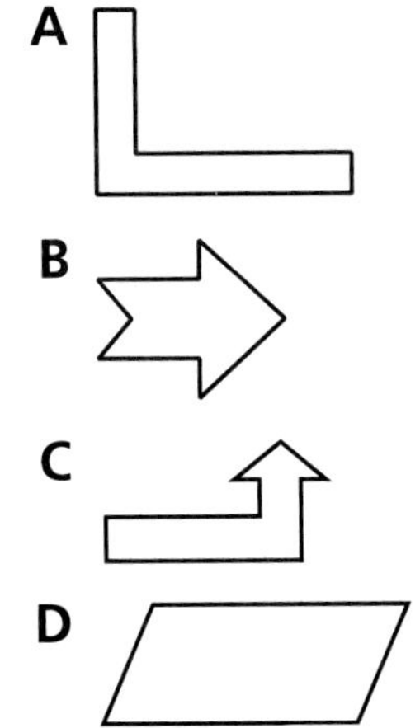

10. WRITE Math What kind of angle is shown? **Explain** how you know.

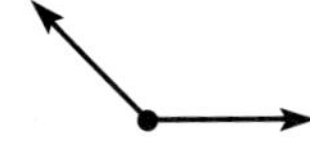

Probability and Statistics (TAKS Obj. 5)

11. How much money did the children earn altogether?

Money Earned	
Mia	**$ $ $**
Jeff	**$ $**
Carol	**$ $ $ $ $**
Key: Each $ = $3.	

F $10

G $12

H $30

J $40

12. Which color tile is more likely to be pulled?

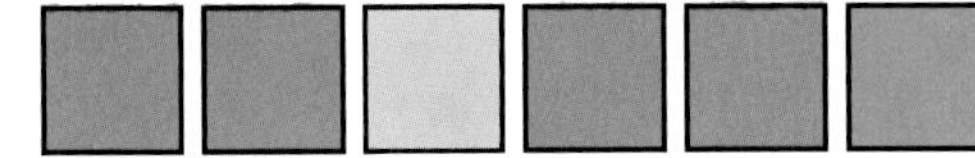

A Yellow

B Blue

C Green

D Not here

13. WRITE Math Judy made a bar graph to show the number of pictures she took each day for a week. The bar for Wednesday ends at 12. What does this mean? **Explain**.

21 Perimeter, Area, and Volume

The Big Idea Attributes of two- and three-dimensional figures can be measured.

Ameriquest Field in Arlington, Texas, is home to the Texas Rangers baseball team. The stadium has enough seats for 49,115 baseball fans to watch a game.

Investigate

A Major League baseball infield is similar to a Little League baseball infield. Look at the two drawings. Describe how the infields are alike and how they are different.

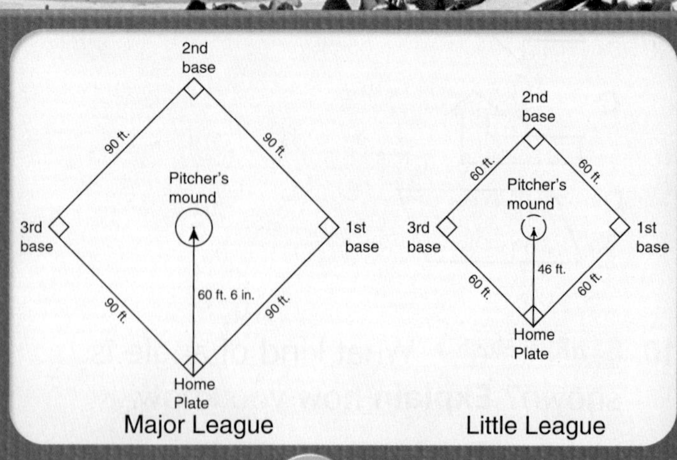

GO ONLINE Technology Student pages are available in the Student eBook.

Show What You Know

Check your understanding of important skills needed for success in Chapter 21.

Column Addition

Find the sum.

1. $\begin{array}{r} 1 \\ 8 \\ 9 \\ +4 \\ \hline \end{array}$ **2.** $\begin{array}{r} 2 \\ 6 \\ 7 \\ +6 \\ \hline \end{array}$ **3.** $\begin{array}{r} 5 \\ 5 \\ 8 \\ +3 \\ \hline \end{array}$ **4.** $\begin{array}{r} 4 \\ 2 \\ 2 \\ +7 \\ \hline \end{array}$

5. $\begin{array}{r} 6 \\ 7 \\ 5 \\ +2 \\ \hline \end{array}$ **6.** $\begin{array}{r} 10 \\ 9 \\ 9 \\ +4 \\ \hline \end{array}$ **7.** $\begin{array}{r} 3 \\ 5 \\ 2 \\ +4 \\ \hline \end{array}$ **8.** $\begin{array}{r} 10 \\ 10 \\ 7 \\ +\ 2 \\ \hline \end{array}$

Multiplication Facts Through 10

Find the product.

9. $3 \times 4 = ■$ **10.** $7 \times 5 = ■$ **11.** $8 \times 2 = ■$ **12.** $6 \times 3 = ■$

13. $1 \times 5 = ■$ **14.** $4 \times 9 = ■$ **15.** $3 \times 2 = ■$ **16.** $5 \times 5 = ■$

17. $\begin{array}{r} 3 \\ \times 8 \\ \hline \end{array}$ **18.** $\begin{array}{r} 5 \\ \times 3 \\ \hline \end{array}$ **19.** $\begin{array}{r} 6 \\ \times 4 \\ \hline \end{array}$ **20.** $\begin{array}{r} 7 \\ \times 9 \\ \hline \end{array}$

VOCABULARY POWER

CHAPTER VOCABULARY

area
cubic unit
perimeter
square unit
volume

WARM-UP WORDS

perimeter The distance around a figure

area The number of square units needed to cover a flat surface

square unit A square with a side length of 1 unit

LESSON HANDS ON

1 Perimeter

OBJECTIVE: Find the perimeter of a figure.

Quick Review

Add.

1. 5 + 3 + 5
2. 2 + 2 + 2 + 2
3. 7 + 3 + 3 + 7
4. 4 + 8 + 2 + 1 + 3
5. 2 + 2 + 1 + 3 + 2

Vocabulary

perimeter

Perimeter is the distance around a figure.

You can use square tiles to measure the perimeter of an index card. Each edge of a square tile has a length of 1 inch.

Investigate

Materials ■ square tiles, index card

Ⓐ Place square tiles around the outside of an index card.

Ⓑ Count the number of square tiles you used.

Ⓒ Record the number of tiles it took to go all the way around the card.

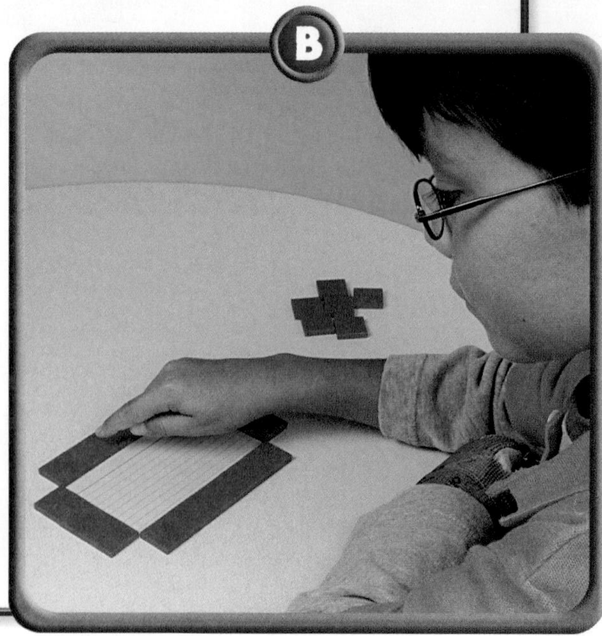

Draw Conclusions

1. How many square tiles did you place around the index card?
2. What is the perimeter of the index card?
3. **Synthesis What if** you traced your notebook and measured the perimeter with square tiles? Would you use more or fewer square tiles than you did to measure the index card? **Explain.**

TEKS 3.11B use standard units to find the perimeter of a shape. *also* 3.14A, 3.14D, 3.15A, 3.15B, 3.16B

Connect

You can count customary or metric units on a grid to find perimeter.

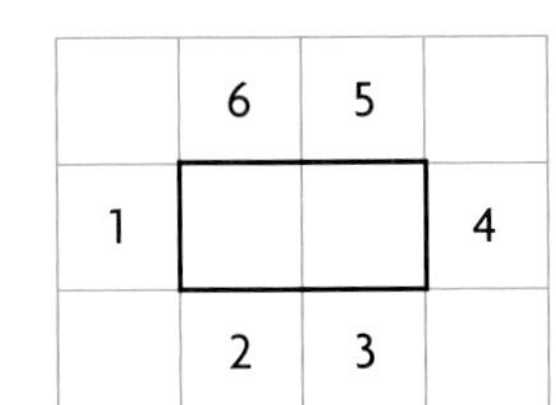

Perimeter = 6 inches

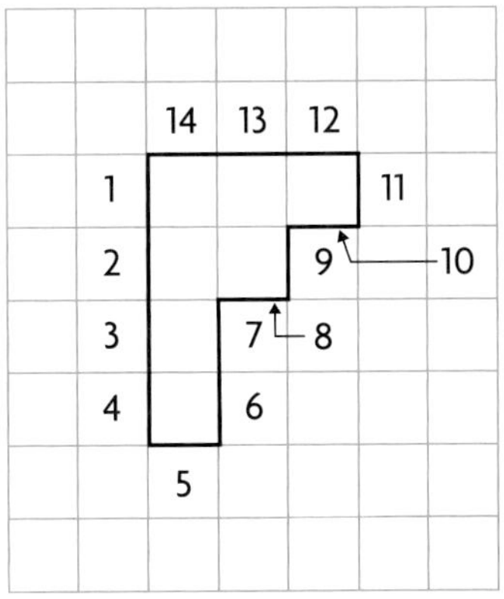

Perimeter = 14 cm

TALK Math

Explain how to find the perimeter of this rectangle.

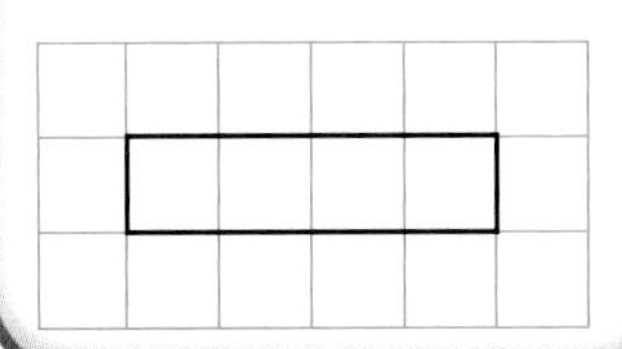

Practice

Find the perimeter of each figure.

1.

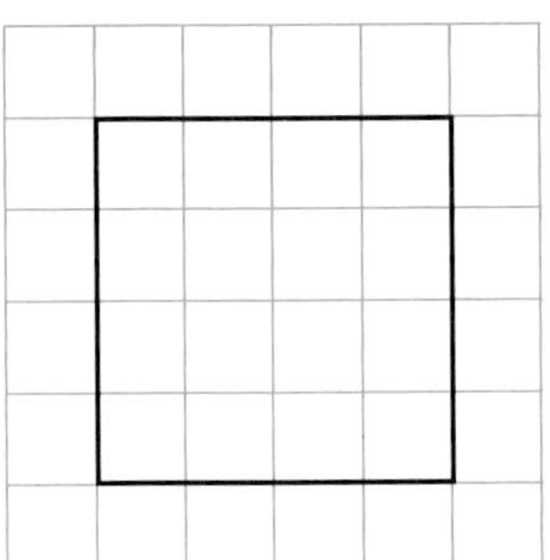

2.

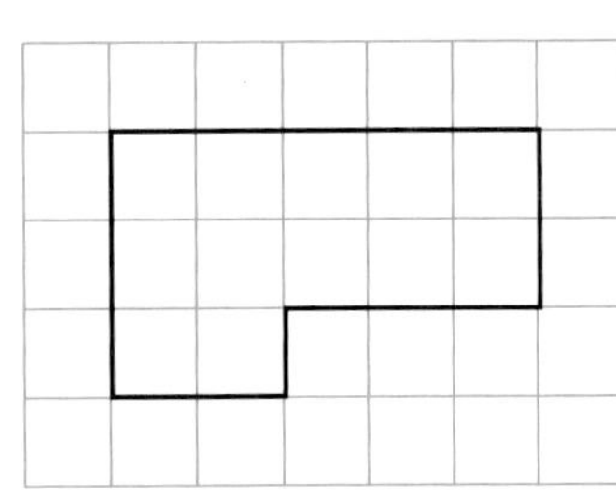

3.

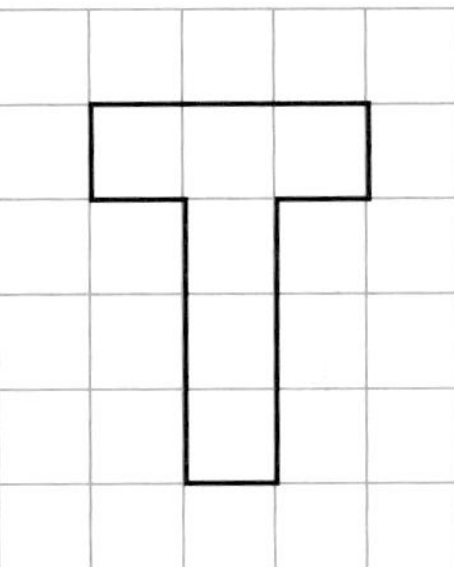

4.

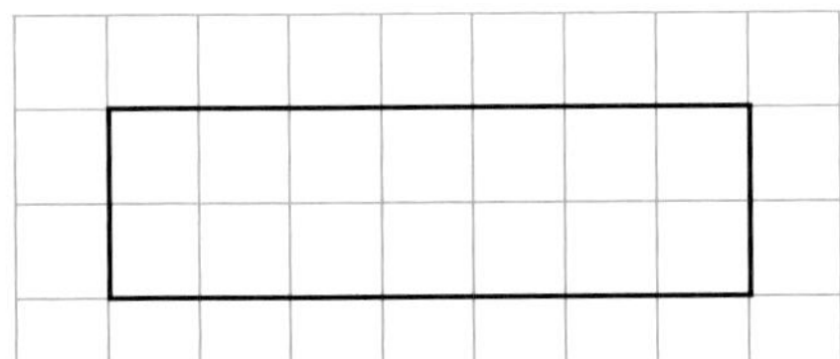

5.

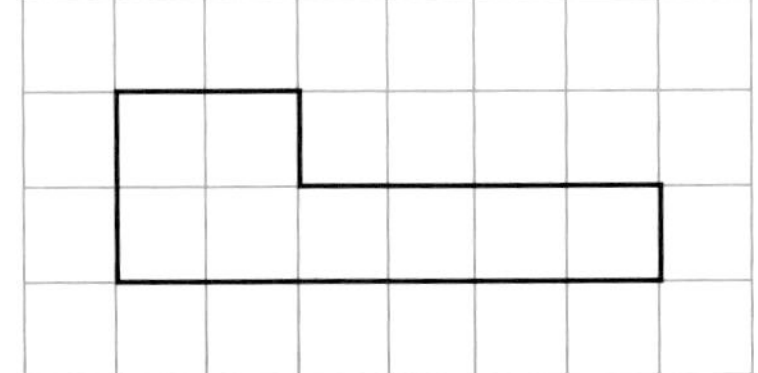

6.

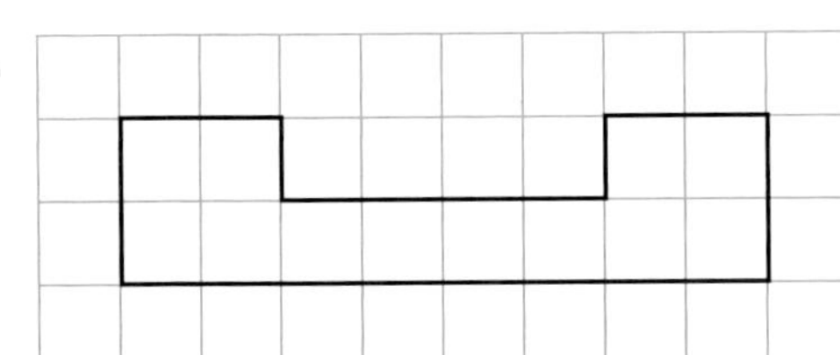

7. **WRITE Math**

What's the Error? Brian said the perimeter of this figure is 8 centimeters. **Explain** his error. Write the correct perimeter.

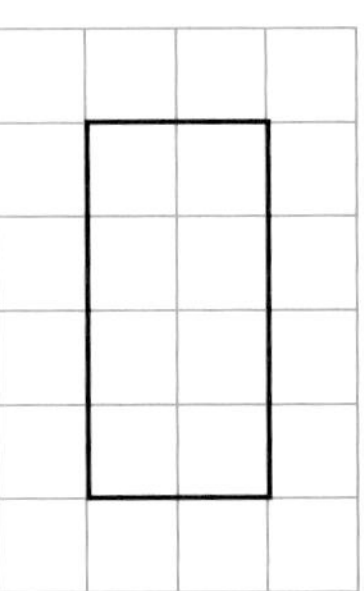

LESSON 2

Estimate and Measure Perimeter

OBJECTIVE: Estimate and measure perimeter.

Quick Review

Find the sum.

1. 8 + 8 + 8 + 8
2. 2 + 3 + 4
3. 1 + 1 + 8 + 3
4. 6 + 6 + 5 + 5
5. 3 + 3 + 1 + 4 + 1

Learn

You can estimate and measure perimeter in standard units, such as inches and centimeters.

Find the perimeter of a notebook.

Activity **Materials** ■ inch ruler

Step 1
Estimate the perimeter of a notebook in inches. Record your estimate.

Step 2
Use an inch ruler to measure the length of each side of the notebook.

Step 3
Add the lengths of the sides.
Record the perimeter.

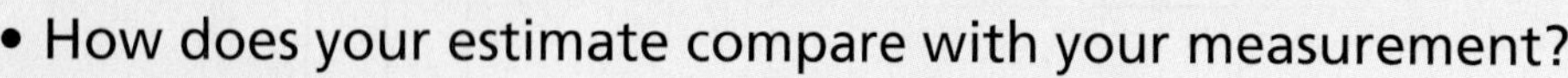
■ inches + ■ inches + ■ inches + ■ inches = ■ inches

- How does your estimate compare with your measurement?

Examples

Use a ruler to find the length of each side in inches.

Add the lengths of the sides:
1 in. + 2 in. + 1 in. + 2 in. = 6 in.
The perimeter is 6 inches.

Use a ruler to find the length of each side in centimeters.

Add the lengths of the sides:
3 cm + 3 cm + 3 cm + 3 cm = 12 cm
The perimeter is 12 centimeters.

TEKS 3.11B use standard units to find the perimeter of a shape. *also* **3.11A, 3.14A, 3.14D, 3.15A, 3.15B, 3.16A**

More Examples

Add the lengths of the sides to find the perimeter.

A

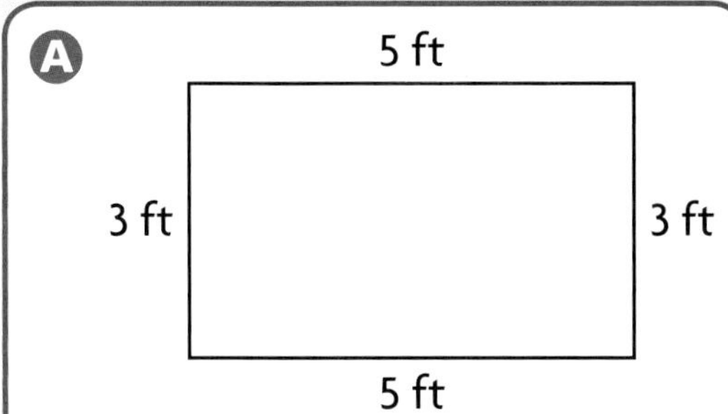

Add the lengths of the sides:
3 ft + 5 ft + 3 ft + 5 ft = 16 ft
The perimeter is 16 feet.

B

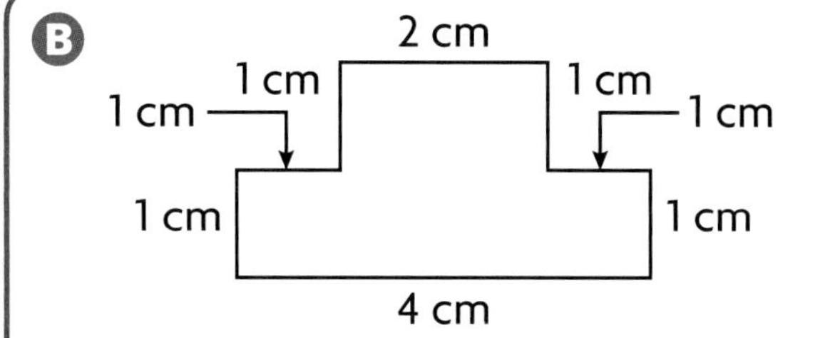

Add the lengths of the sides:
1 cm + 1 cm + 1 cm + 2 cm + 1 cm +
1 cm + 1 cm + 4 cm = 12 cm
The perimeter is 12 centimeters.

- What if you added 1 foot to each side of the rectangle in Example A? How would the perimeter change?

Guided Practice

1. Find the perimeter of the triangle in inches.
   Think: How long is each side?

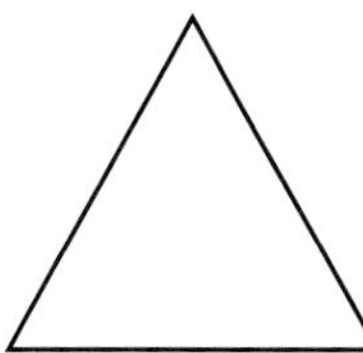

Estimate. Then use a centimeter ruler to find the perimeter.

2. 

3. 

4. 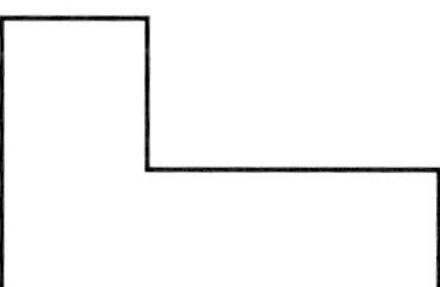

Estimate. Then use an inch ruler to find the perimeter.

5. 

6. 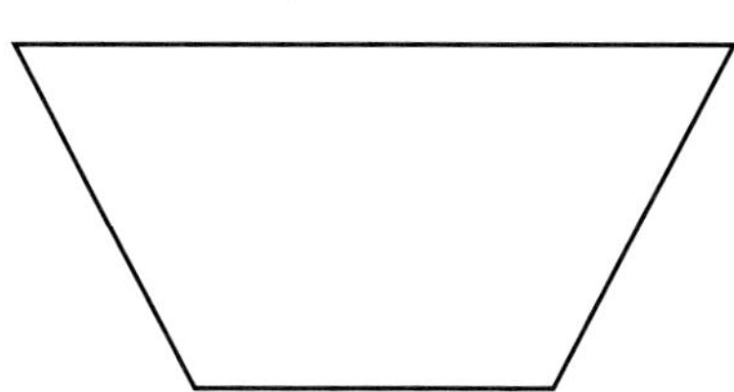

7. TALK Math **Explain** how to find the perimeter of this figure in centimeters.

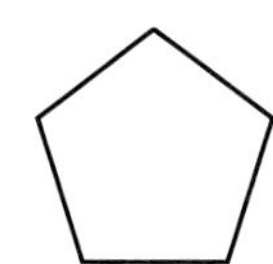

Independent Practice and Problem Solving

Estimate. Then use a centimeter ruler to find the perimeter.

8. 

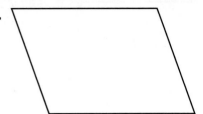

9. 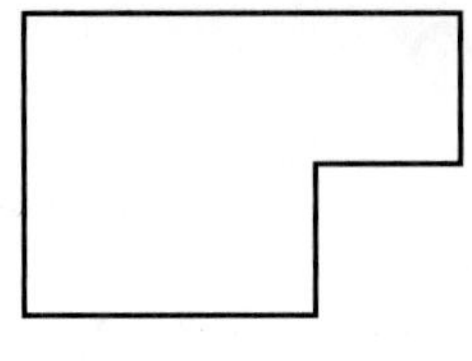

10. 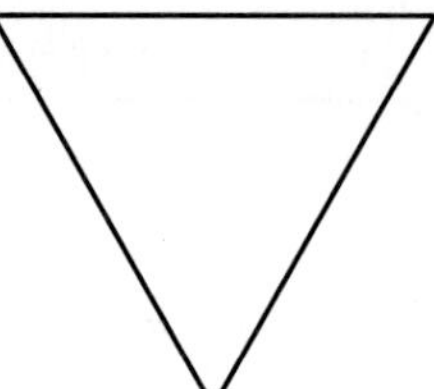

Estimate. Then use an inch ruler to find the perimeter.

11. 

12. 

13. 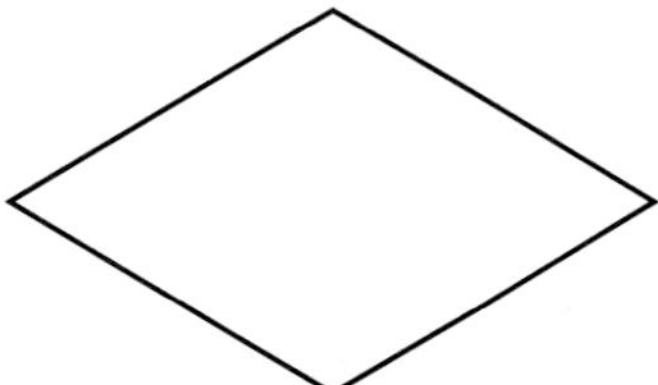

For 14–15, use the photos.

14. Which of the animal photos has a perimeter of 24 inches?

15. How much greater is the perimeter of the bird photo than the perimeter of the cat photo?

16. Lacy is putting a fence around her square garden. Each side of her garden is 3 yards long. The fence costs $5 for each yard. How much will the fence cost?

17. **Open Ended** Use grid paper or a ruler to draw a polygon with a perimeter of 20 cm. Label the length of each side.

18. **WRITE Math** One side of a rectangle is 4 feet long and one side is 10 feet long. What is the perimeter of the rectangle? **Explain**.

Mixed Review and TAKS Prep

19. A quadrilateral has two pairs of parallel sides and four right angles. Name this quadrilateral. (TEKS 3.8, p. 378)

20. Which is the better estimate for the length of a room: 12 in. or 12 ft? (TEKS 3.11A, p. 440)

21. **TAKS Prep** Use your centimeter ruler to find the perimeter of this rectangle. (Obj. 4)

A 8 cm **B** 10 cm **C** 12 cm **D** 16 cm

Technology
Use Harcourt Mega Math, Ice Station Exploration, *Polar Planes*, Level P and *Arctic Algebra*, Level CC.

 Extra Practice on page 502, Set A

Take My Picture

Cause and Effect

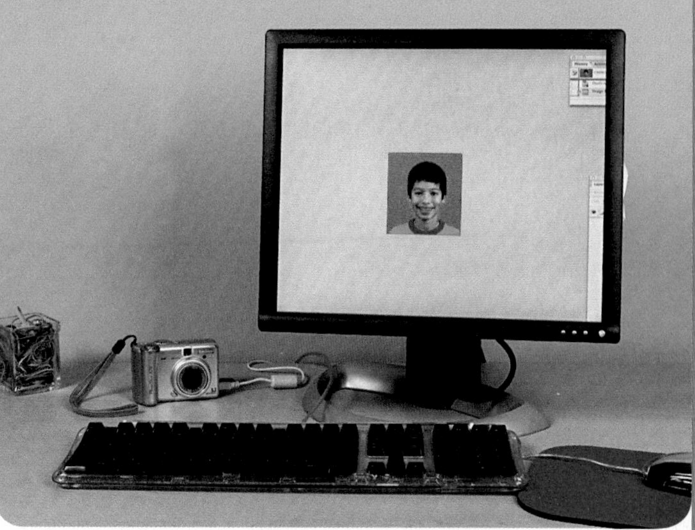

When you take a picture with a digital camera, the picture is stored in the camera's memory. Then you can print your picture later. Before you print the picture, you can choose the size. Look at the photo below. If each side of the photo is increased by 2 inches, how much will the perimeter increase?

Cause and effect is a strategy that can help you understand a problem. A cause is the reason something happens. An effect is the result or outcome.

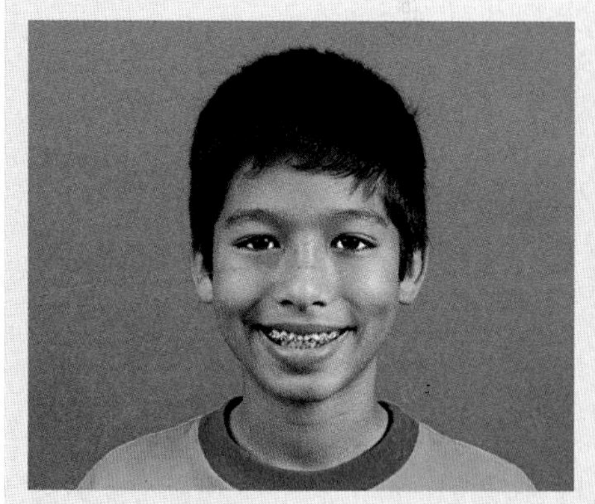

Cause	Effect
Increase each side of the photo by 2 inches.	The perimeter increases.

So, if the length of each side changes, then the perimeter will also change.

Problem Solving Use the information and the strategy to solve the problems.

1. Solve the problem above. What operation did you use to solve the problem?
2. Courtney has a photo of her dog. The photo is 8 inches wide and 10 inches long. She wants to decrease the length of each side by 3 inches and reprint the photo. How will the perimeter change? **Explain**.

LESSON 3 HANDS ON

Area of Plane Figures

OBJECTIVE: Use square units to find the area of two-dimensional surfaces.

Quick Review

Multiply.

1. 4×5
2. 6×3
3. 2×8
4. 5×7
5. 9×9

Vocabulary

area

square unit

Area is the number of square units needed to cover a flat surface.

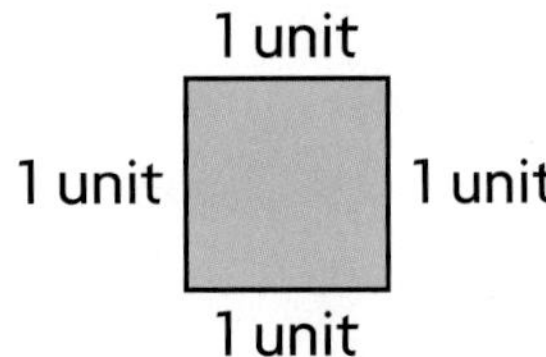

A **square unit** is a square with a side length of 1 unit.

Investigate

Materials ■ square tiles, index card, grid paper

A Estimate how many square tiles it will take to cover an index card.

B Use square tiles to cover the surface of an index card.

C Use grid paper. Draw a picture to show how you covered the index card.

D Count and record the number of tiles you used. This number is the area of the index card in square units.

Draw Conclusions

1. What is the area of the index card?
2. How is finding the area like making an array?
3. **Synthesis** What if you used larger paper squares to cover the surface of your math book? How would the number of paper squares compare to the number of tiles?

TEKS 3.11C use concrete and pictorial models of square units to determine the area of two-dimensional surfaces. *also* **3.14A, 3.14D, 3.15A, 3.15B**

Connect

You can count or multiply square units to find area.

A Count units.

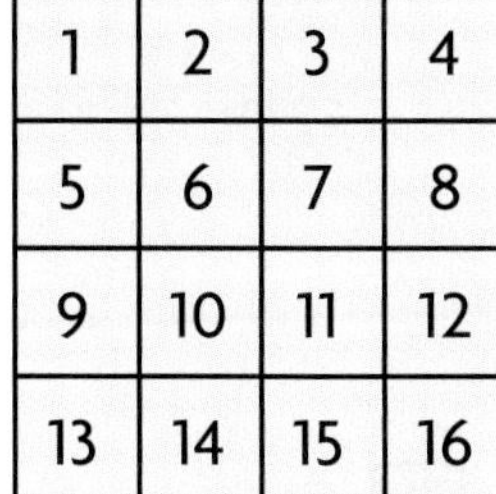

16 square units

1
2 3
4 5 6
7 8 9 10

10 square units

TALK Math

How can you use multiplication to find the area of the figure on the left in A?

B Multiply units.

To find the area of a rectangle, multiply the number of rows by the number in each row.

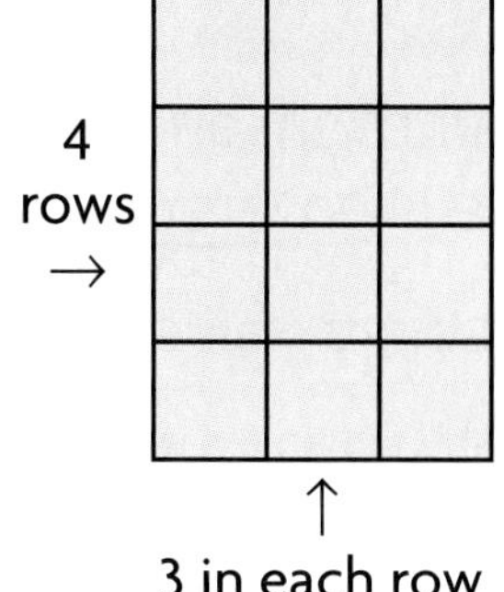

number of rows		number in each row		area
↓		↓		↓
4	×	3	=	12 square units

Practice

Find the area of each figure. Write the answer in square units.

1.

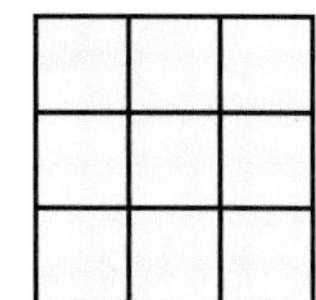

2.

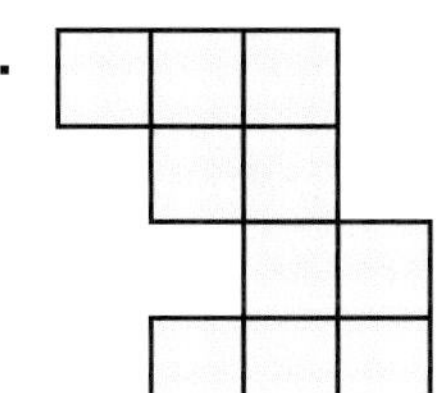

✓3.

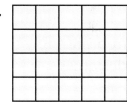

4.

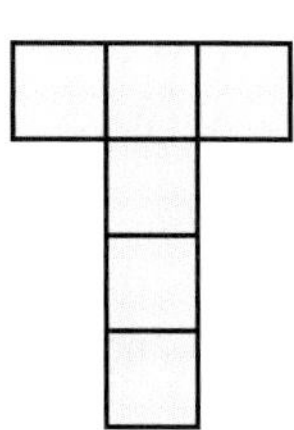

5.

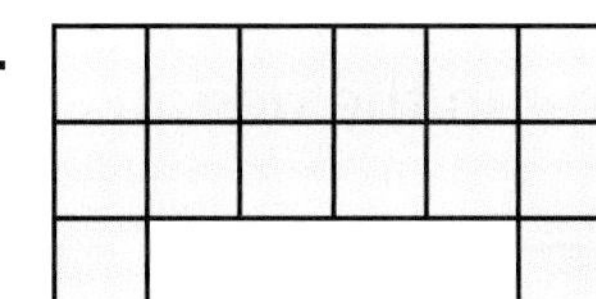

✓6.

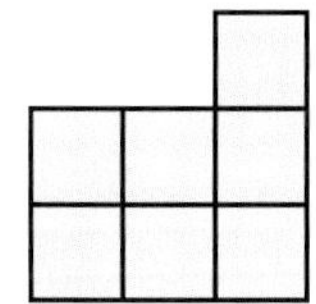

7. **WRITE Math** **Sense or Nonsense** Carly says that if you double the length of each side of this square from 4 units to 8 units, the area will double. Does her statement make sense? **Explain.**

Find Area

OBJECTIVE: Find the area of two-dimensional surfaces.

Quick Review

Add.

1. 9 + 2 **2.** 8 + 3
3. 23 + 1 **4.** 16 + 2
5. 1 + 19

Learn

You can count and multiply units to find area. Sometimes a figure is covered by square units and half square units.

These are half square units.

2 half square units = 1 square unit 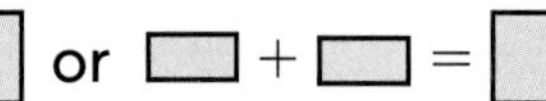

PROBLEM Patty decorated a jewelry box with square tiles. Here is a drawing of the design she made. What is the area of Patty's design?

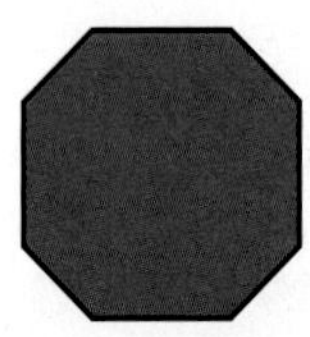

Example

Step 1

Count or multiply to find the number of whole squares in the design.

The design has 12 whole squares.

Step 2

Count the number of half squares in the design.

The design has 4 half squares.

Step 3

Find the total number of squares.

The design has 12 whole squares and 2 more squares.

12 + 2 = 14

So, the area of Patty's design is 14 square units.

- **What if** Patty's design covered 12 whole squares and 3 half squares? What would the area of her design be?

Math Idea
Since 2 half squares equal 1 whole square, then 4 half squares equal 2 whole squares.

TEKS 3.11C use concrete and pictorial models of square units to determine the area of two-dimensional surfaces. *also* **3.14A, 3.14D, 3.15A, 3.15B**

Guided Practice

1. What is the area of this figure?
   Think: How many whole squares are there? How many half squares?

Count or multiply to find the area of each figure. Write the answer in square units.

2. 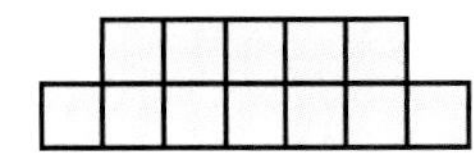

3. 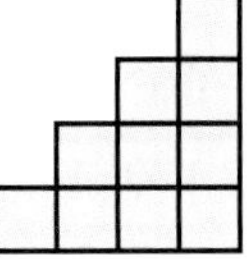

4. 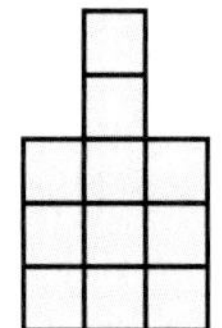

5. TALK Math **Explain** how to find the area of a figure that is covered by whole square units and half square units.

Independent Practice and Problem Solving

Count or multiply to find the area of each figure. Write the answer in square units.

6. 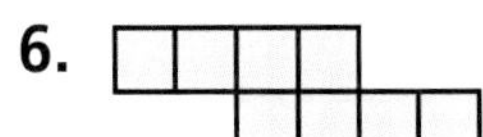

7. 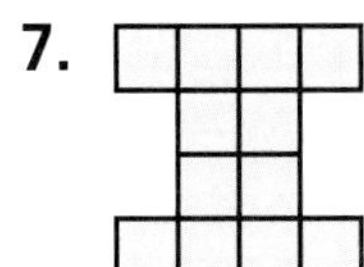

8. 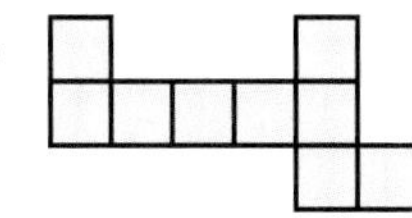

9. Amy made this design. She used 4 half square units. What is the area of Amy's design? **Explain**.

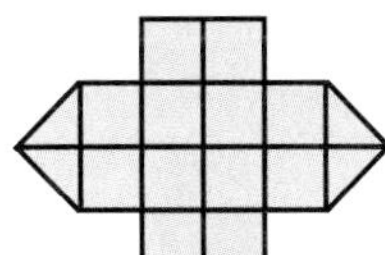

10. WRITE Math The perimeter of Trent's figure is 18 units. What is the area of his figure? **Explain**.

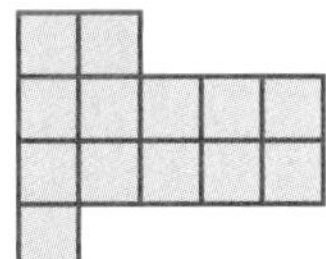

Mixed Review and TAKS Prep

11. There were 683 people at the fair on Friday and 581 people on Saturday. How many people in all came to the fair? (TEKS 3.3B, p. 66)

12. Jade's square pillow is 10 inches on each side. What is the perimeter? (TEKS 3.11B, p. 488)

13. **TAKS Prep** Eve made this design. What is the area of Eve's design? (Obj. 4)

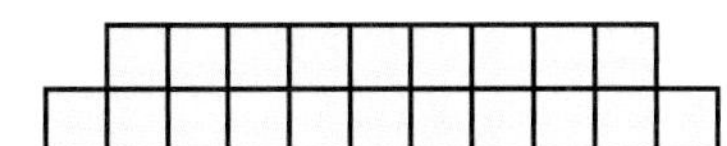

A 20 square units
B 21 square units
C 22 square units
D 24 square units

Extra Practice on page 502, Set B

Relate Perimeter and Area

OBJECTIVE: Explore the relationship between the area and the perimeter of a figure.

Quick Review

Find the perimeter and the area.

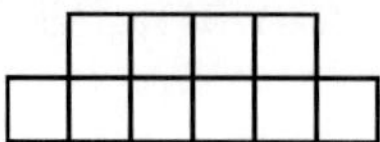

Learn

PROBLEM Cody has 20 feet of wood boards to put around a rectangular sandbox. How long should he make each side so that the area of the sandbox is as large as possible?

Example

Use square tiles. Make all the rectangles you can that have a perimeter of 20. Then find the area of each.

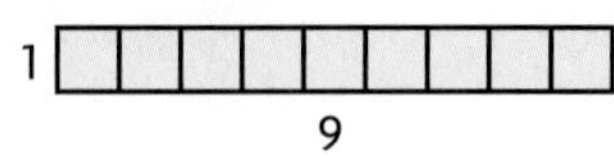

Perimeter: 9 + 1 + 9 + 1 = 20 units
Area: 1 × 9 = 9 square units

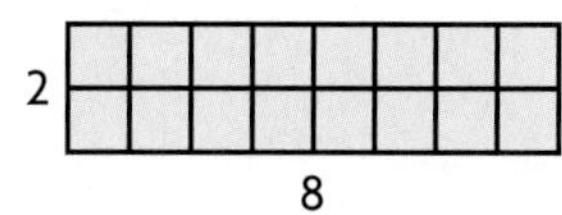

Perimeter: 8 + 2 + 8 + 2 = 20 units
Area: 2 × 8 = 16 square units

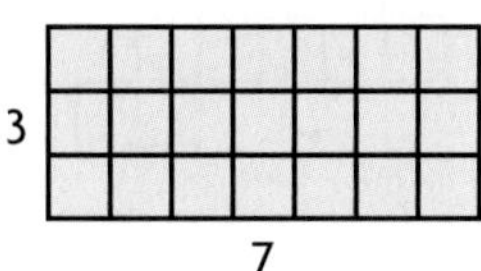

Perimeter: 7 + 3 + 7 + 3 = 20 units
Area: 3 × 7 = 21 square units

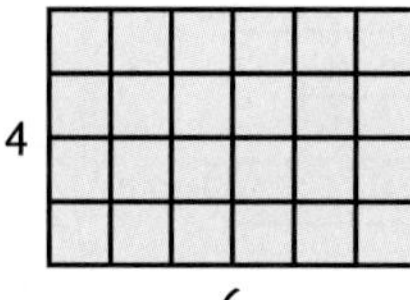

Perimeter: 6 + 4 + 6 + 4 = 20 units
Area: 4 × 6 = 24 square units

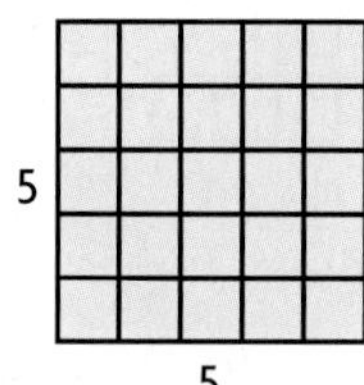

Perimeter: 5 + 5 + 5 + 5 = 20 units
Area: 5 × 5 = 25 square units

Order the areas: 9 < 16 < 21 < 24 < 25
25 square units is the greatest area.

So, to have a sandbox with the largest area possible, Cody should make a square with sides 5 feet long.

More Examples

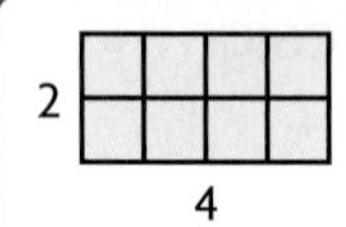

Perimeter:
4 + 2 + 4 + 2 = 12 units
Area:
2 × 4 = 8 square units

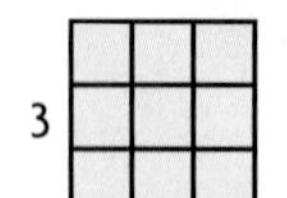

Perimeter:
3 + 3 + 3 + 3 = 12 units
Area:
3 × 3 = 9 square units

- What do you notice about the perimeters and areas of the two figures in More Examples?

TEKS 3.11C use concrete and pictorial models of square units to determine the area of two-dimensional surfaces. *also* **3.11, 3.11B, 3.14A, 3.14D, 3.15A, 3.15B**

Guided Practice

1. Use square tiles. Make a rectangle with the same perimeter as the one on the right. Which figure has the greater area?

For each pair, find the perimeter and the area. Tell which figure has the greater area.

2. 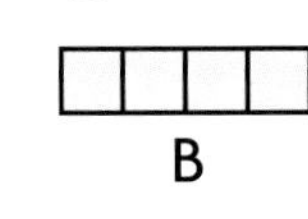

A B

3. 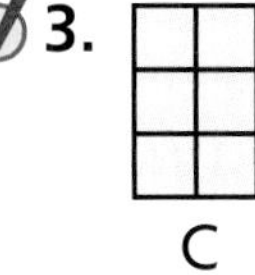

C D

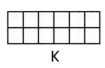

4. TALK Math Figures E and F have the same perimeter. **Explain** which figure has the greater area.

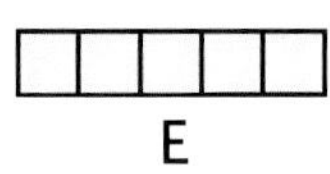

E

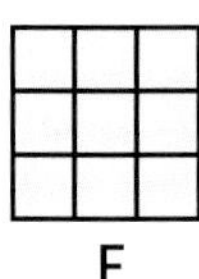

F

Independent Practice and Problem Solving

For each pair, find the perimeter and the area. Tell which figure has the greater area.

5. G

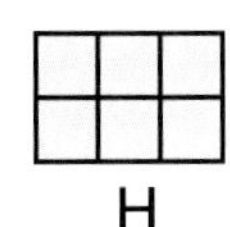

H

6. 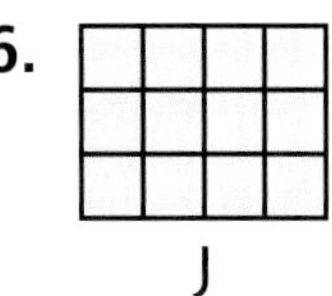

J K

7. Julia made a rectangular flower garden with a perimeter of 16 feet and an area of 15 square feet. What are the lengths of the sides? Draw a picture to show your answer.

8. WRITE Math **What's the Question?** Todd's flower garden is 4 feet wide and 8 feet long. The answer is 32 square feet.

Mixed Review and TAKS Prep

9. A violin has 4 strings. How many strings are on 9 violins? (TEKS 3.4B, p. 210)

10. Ann glued strips of felt around the perimeter of a square picture frame. One side is 5 inches. How many inches of felt did she use? (TEKS 3.11B, p. 488)

11. **TAKS Prep** Which figure has an area of 16 square units and a perimeter of 16 units? (Obj. 4)

A

C

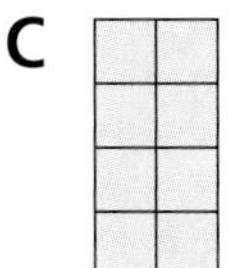

B

D

LESSON 6

Volume

OBJECTIVE: Estimate and find volume.

Quick Review

Multiply.

1. 4×3
2. 2×5
3. 3×2
4. 6×4
5. 5×5

Vocabulary

volume cubic unit

Learn

Volume is the amount of space a solid figure takes up.

A **cubic unit** is used to measure volume. A cubic unit is a cube with a side length of 1 unit.

1 cubic unit

ONE WAY **Count the cubes to find volume.**

HANDS ON

Activity **Materials** ■ small boxes, cubes

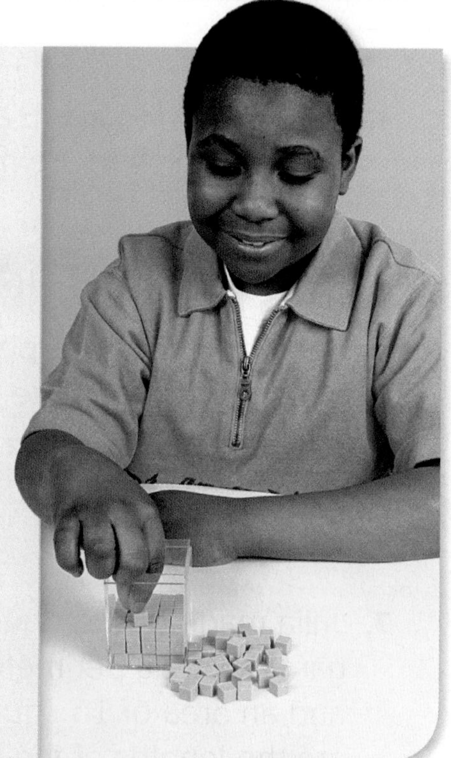

Step 1

Choose a box. Estimate the number of cubes it will take to fill your box. Record your estimate.

Step 2

Count the cubes you use. Place the cubes in rows along the bottom of the box. Continue to make layers of cubes until the box is full.

Step 3

Record how many cubes it took to fill the box. This is the volume of the box in cubic units.

- How does your estimate compare with the actual volume?

ANOTHER WAY **Multiply to find volume.**

When you cannot count each cube, count the number of cubes in the top layer. Then count the number of layers and multiply.

2 layers $\times$ 6 cubes per layer $=$ 12 cubic units

The volume is 12 cubic units.

3 layers $\times$ 8 cubes per layer $=$ 24 cubic units

The volume is 24 cubic units.

TEKS 3.11F use concrete models that approximate cubic units to determine the volume of a given container or other three-dimensional geometric figure. *also* **3.14D, 3.15A, 3.15B, 3.16B**

Guided Practice

1. Find the volume of this solid figure. **Think:** How many layers are there? How many cubes are in each layer?

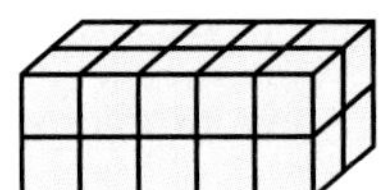

Use cubes to make each solid. Then write the volume in cubic units.

2.

3. 

4.

5. **TALK Math** **Explain** one way you can find the volume of a box that has 3 layers with 6 cubes in each layer.

Independent Practice and Problem Solving

Use cubes to make each solid. Then write the volume in cubic units.

6. 

7. 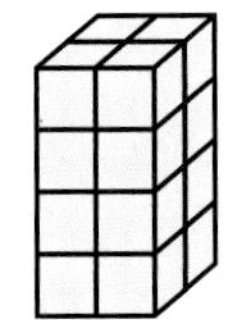

8. 

Find the volume of each solid. Write the volume in cubic units.

9.

10. 

11. 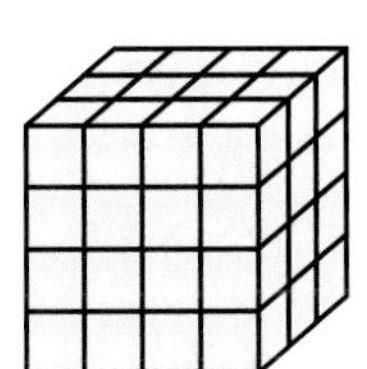

12. Each layer of a prism is 6 cubic units. The volume is 18 cubic units. How many layers are in the prism?

13. **WRITE Math** **What's the Error?** Describe the error. Give the correct answer.

Volume = 6 cubic units

Mixed Review and TAKS Prep

14. If $(4 \times 2) \times 3 = 24$, what is $(2 \times 3) \times 4$? (TEKS 3.4A, p. 268)

15. Find the perimeter and area of this rectangle. (TEKS 3.11B, 3.11C, pp. 504, 508)

16. **TAKS Prep** What is the volume of this solid figure? (Obj. 4)

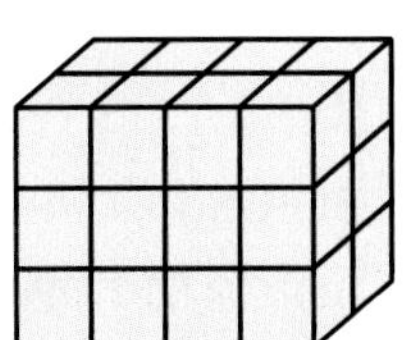

A 9 cubic units

B 12 cubic units

C 24 cubic units

D 36 cubic units

Extra Practice on page 502, Set D

OBJECTIVE: Solve problems by using the skill *use a model.*

Use the Skill

PROBLEM Mr. Davis bought 12 baseballs. The baseballs come in cube-shaped boxes. He wants to put all the baseballs into one large box. Which box can Mr. Davis use to hold the 12 baseballs?

Box A

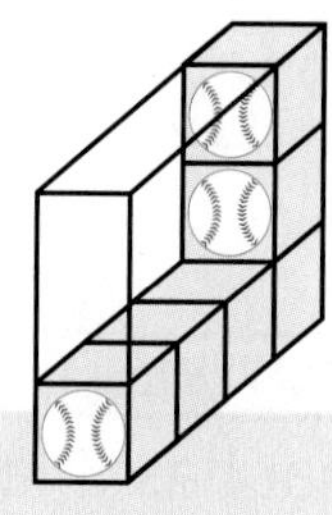

Box B

You can decide whether a box will hold 12 baseballs by using a model.

Make a model of Box A and Box B.
Use a cube to represent each baseball.

Box A	Box B
Place 3 rows of 2 cubes in the first layer. Add a second layer. 	Place 1 row of 4 cubes in the first layer. Add two more layers. 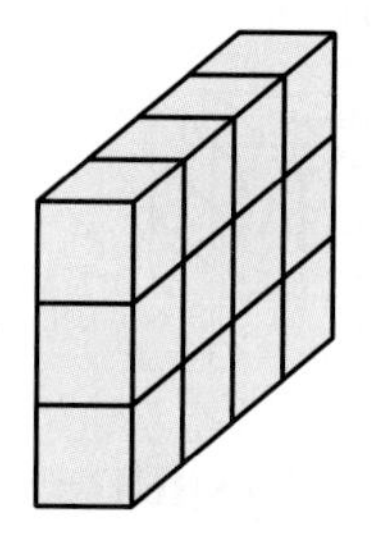
Find the volume: 2 layers × 6 cubes per layer = 12 cubic units	Find the volume: 3 layers × 4 cubes per layer = 12 cubic units

Both containers have a volume of 12 cubic units.

So, Mr. Davis can use Box A or Box B. Both boxes will hold 12 baseballs.

Think and Discuss

Use a model to solve.

a. Lou filled a box with blocks. There are 2 layers. Each layer has 3 rows of 4 blocks. What is the volume of the box?

b. Ryan has two boxes. The red box has 4 layers. Each layer holds 3 rows of 3 cubes. The blue box has 5 layers. Each layer holds 2 rows of 4 cubes. Which box holds more cubes?

c. A box has a volume of 24 cubic units. There are 3 rows with 2 cubes in each row. How many layers does the box have?

TEKS 3.11F use concrete models that approximate cubic units to determine the volume of a given container or other three-dimensional geometric figure. *also* **3.14A, 3.14C, 3.14D, 3.15A, 3.15B, 3.16B**

Guided Problem Solving

Solve.

1. Mrs. Spencer collects teacups. She keeps them in cube-shaped boxes. She wants to pack her teacups in a larger box. There are two different-sized boxes she can use. Which box can hold 36 teacups?

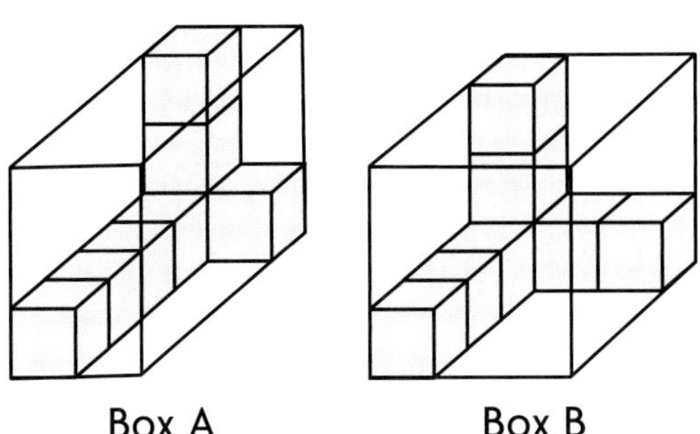

Make a model of each box.
Use a cube to represent each teacup box.
Count the cubes or multiply to find the volume of each box. Solve the problem.

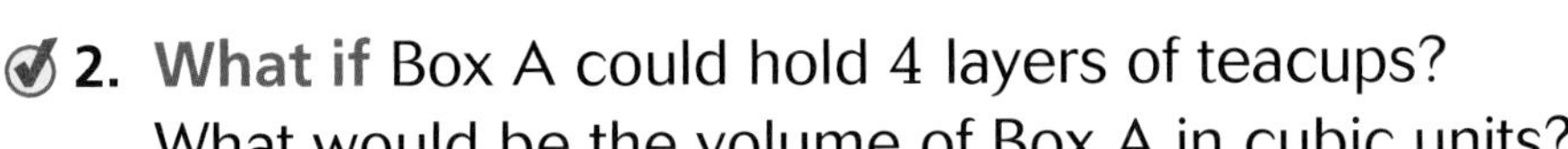

2. **What if** Box A could hold 4 layers of teacups? What would be the volume of Box A in cubic units?

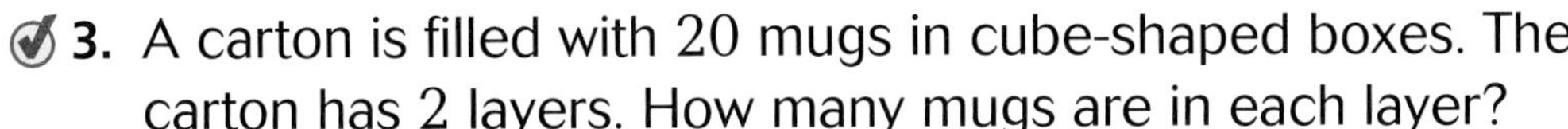

3. A carton is filled with 20 mugs in cube-shaped boxes. The carton has 2 layers. How many mugs are in each layer?

Mixed Applications

USE DATA For 5–6, use the table.

4. Ms. Wagner bought a box full of strawberry yogurt cups. The box has 2 layers. Each layer has 3 rows of 4 cups. How many yogurt cups are in the box?

Strawberry Snacks

Snack	Price
Strawberry yogurt cup	$2.00
Strawberry pie slice	$3.50
Strawberry ice cream cone	$2.75

5. Brandon had $10. He bought 2 slices of strawberry pie and 1 strawberry ice cream cone. How much money does he have left?

6. Tom bought an ice cream cone and a yogurt cup. He did not use any quarters. What bills and coins could he have used?

7. Bryanna is washing her dad's car. Is the temperature about 25°F or about 75°F?

8. Steve traced around the bottom of a solid figure. He drew a circle. Which could he have traced: a square pyramid, a cone, or a cube?

9. Sandy can run 1 mile in 8 minutes. At that speed, about how long will it take Sandy to run a 3-mile race?

10. **WRITE Math** Bob's box has 2 layers with 2 rows of 3 blocks. Tom's box has 3 layers with 2 rows of 2 blocks. Whose box has more blocks? **Explain.**

Extra Practice

Set A Estimate. Then use a centimeter ruler to find the perimeter. (pp. 488–491)

1. 

2.

3.

Set B Count or multiply to find the area of each figure. Write the answer in square units. (pp. 494–495)

1. 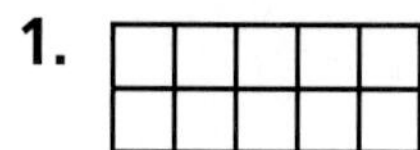

2. 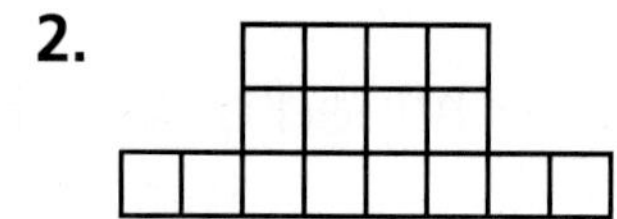

3. 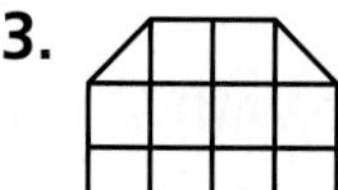

4. A checkboard has 8 rows and 8 columns of red and black squares. What is the area in square units?

5. Aidan put tiles on his bathroom floor. There are four rows of five tiles and two rows of two tiles. What is the area?

Set C For each pair, find the perimeter and the area. Tell which figure has the greater area. (pp. 496–497)

1. 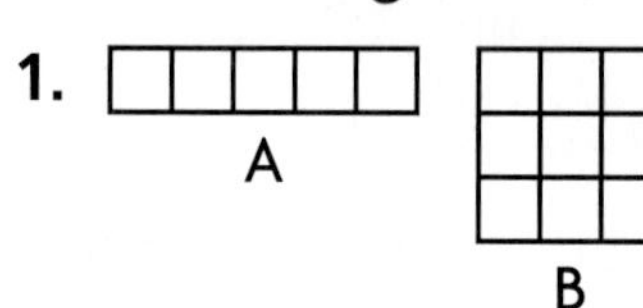

2. 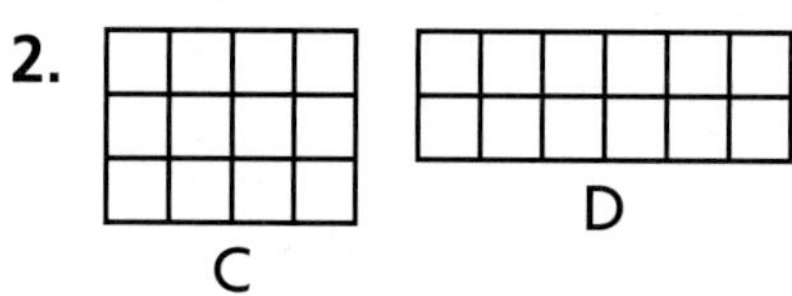

Set D

Find the volume of each solid. Write the volume in cubic units. (pp. 502–503)

1.

2. 

3. 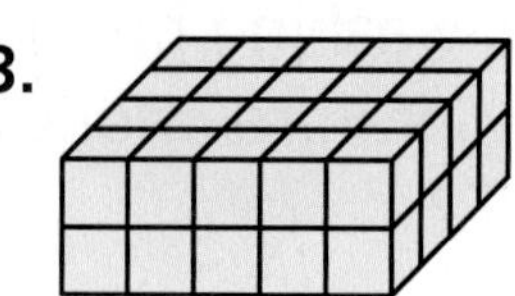

4. Each layer of a prism is 4 cubic units. The volume is 24 cubic units. How many layers are in the prism?

CD ROM **Technology**
Use Harcourt Mega Math, Ice Station Exploration, *Polar Planes*, Levels Q, S.

PRACTICE GAME

Find That Measure

Roll!

3 players

Move!

- game cards
- 1 number cube
- 3 game pieces

Win!

- Each player places a game piece on either the Perimeter, Area, or Volume space on the gameboard.
- Players take turns tossing a number cube and moving clockwise that number of spaces.
- If a player lands on Perimeter, Area, or Volume, he or she draws a game card and finds the perimeter, area, or volume of the figure on the card.
- The other players check the answer. If it is correct, the player keeps the card and gets another turn.
- If the answer is incorrect, the player returns the card to the bottom of the deck, and play passes to the next player.
- The first player to collect one card each from Perimeter, Area, and Volume wins.

Chapter 21 Review/Test

Check Vocabulary and Concepts

Choose the best term from the box.

VOCABULARY
area
perimeter
volume

1. The __?__ is the amount of space a solid figure takes up. (TEKS 3.11F, p. 498)
2. The distance around a figure is the __?__. (TEKS 3.11B, p. 486)

Check Skills

Find the area of each figure. Write the answer in square units.
(TEKS 3.11C, pp. 492–493)

3. 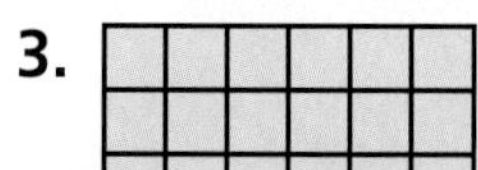

4. 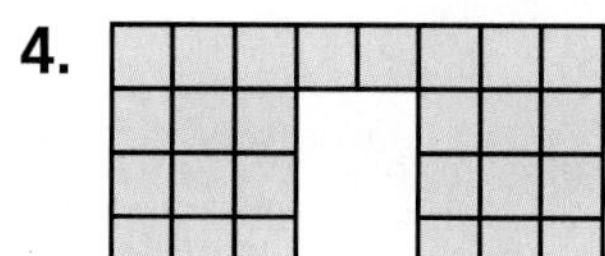

5. 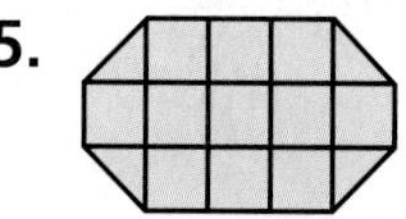

Find the volume of each solid. Write the volume in cubic units.
(TEKS 3.11F, pp. 498–499)

6. 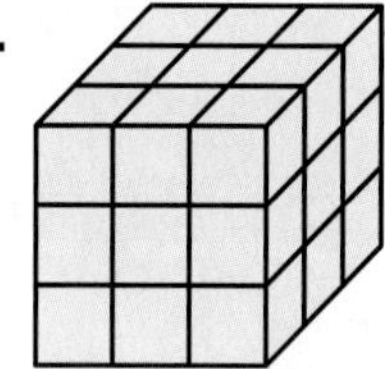

7. 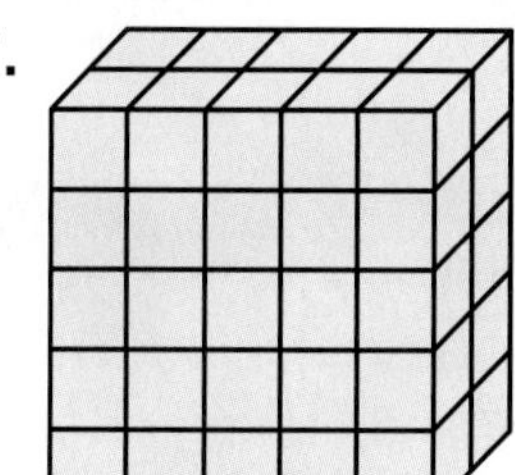

8. 

Check Problem Solving

Solve. (TEKS 3.11F, pp. 504–505)

9. Natasha wants to store her souvenir golf balls in a box. The balls are packaged in cube-shaped boxes. Which of the boxes at the right will hold Natasha's 20 golf balls?

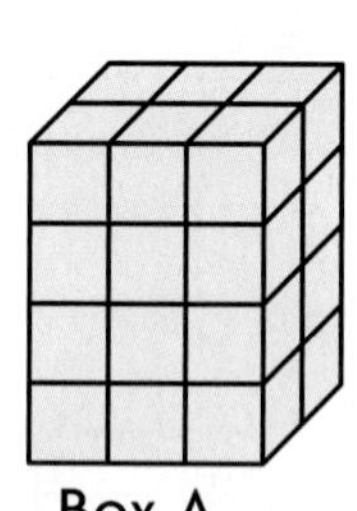
Box A

Box B

10. WRITE Math **Explain** why a box that has 6 layers of 6 cubes will not hold as much as a box that has 4 layers of 10 cubes.

GO ONLINE **Technology** Use *Online Assessment.*

Enrich • Perimeter Patterns

Predicting Perimeters

Look at the square. Its perimeter is 4 cm. You can use connected squares to form a perimeter pattern.

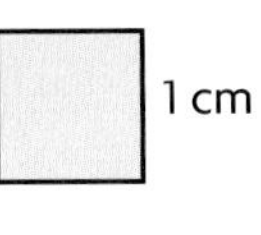

Learn It

Find the perimeter of 6 connected squares by using a pattern.

Step 1 Find the perimeters of the first few shapes.

Perimeter = 4 cm

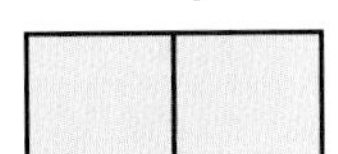

Perimeter = 6 cm

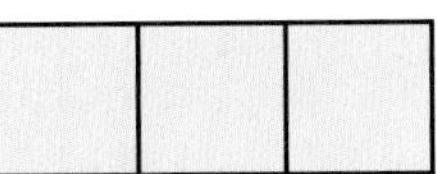

Perimeter = 8 cm

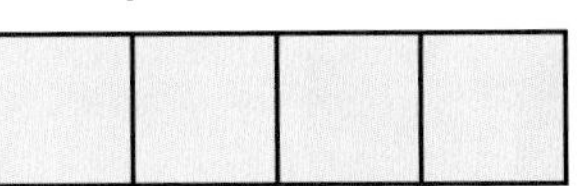

Perimeter = 10 cm

Step 2 Look at the pattern to find the rule.

4, 6, 8, 10 The rule is add 2.

Step 3 Extend the pattern.

$10 + 2 = 12$, so 5 squares have a perimeter of 12 cm.
$12 + 2 = 14$, so 6 squares have a perimeter of 14 cm.

So, 6 connected squares have a perimeter of 14 cm.

Try It

Find a pattern. Then use the rule to find the perimeter of a row of 6 connected shapes.

1.

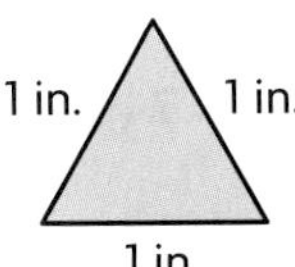

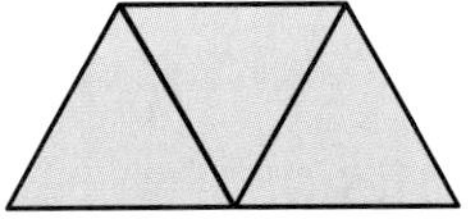

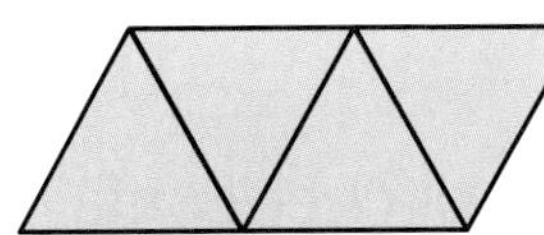

2.

Explain It

WRITE Math Suppose the rectangles in item 2 were turned and the pattern at the right was made. Has the perimeter pattern changed? **Explain** how you know.

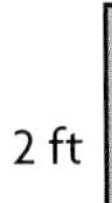

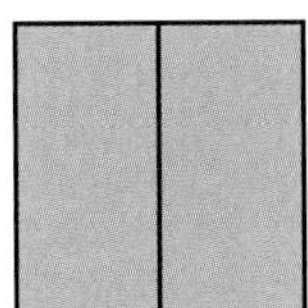

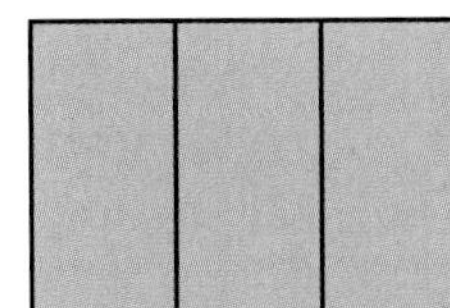

Unit Review/Test
Chapters 19–21

Multiple Choice

1. Which unit would be best to measure the weight of the dog? (TAKS Obj. 4)

A Ounce
C Pound
B Foot
D Yard

2. Which measurement best describes the length of a desk? (TAKS Obj. 4)

F 2 inches
G 2 feet
H 20 feet
J 2 miles

3. Susan's pitcher contains 6 pints of lemonade. How many 1-cup glasses of lemonade can she fill from the pitcher? (TAKS Obj. 4)

A 3
B 6
C 10
D 12

4. Which distance is about 10 kilometers? (TAKS Obj. 4)

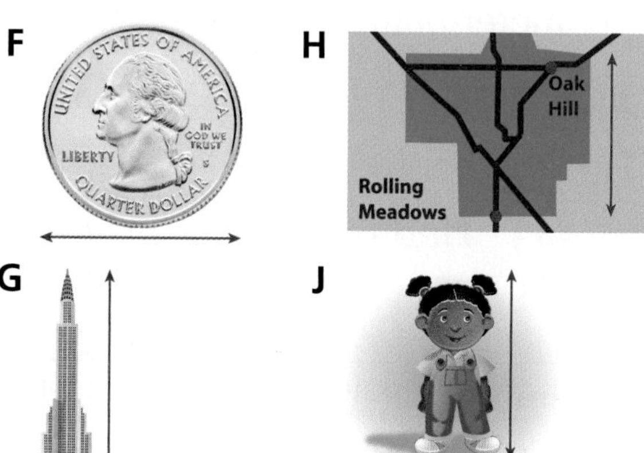

5. Which statement is true? (TAKS Obj. 4)

A 700 cm = 7 m
B 700 cm = 70 m
C 700 cm = 700 m
D 700 cm = 7,000 m

6. What is the perimeter of this figure? (TAKS Obj. 4)

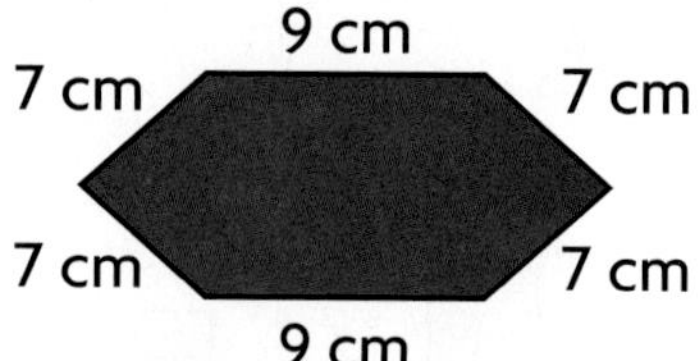

F 63 centimeters
G 49 centimeters
H 46 centimeters
J Not here

GO ONLINE **Technology** Use *Online Assessment.*

7. A statue is 300 decimeters tall. How many meters tall is the statue? (TAKS Obj. 4)

A 3,000 meters

B 300 meters

C 30 meters

D 3 meters

8. What was the change in temperature between 8:00 A.M. and 2:00 P.M.? (TAKS Obj. 4)

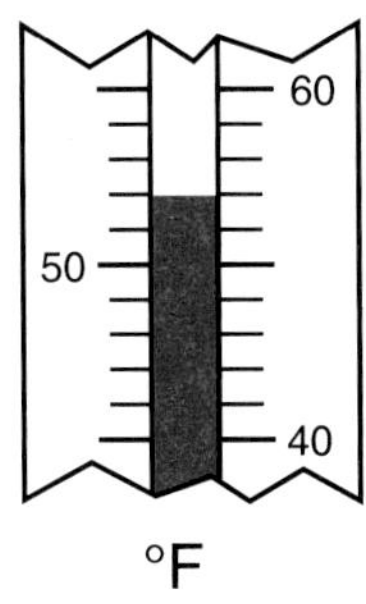

8:00 A.M.

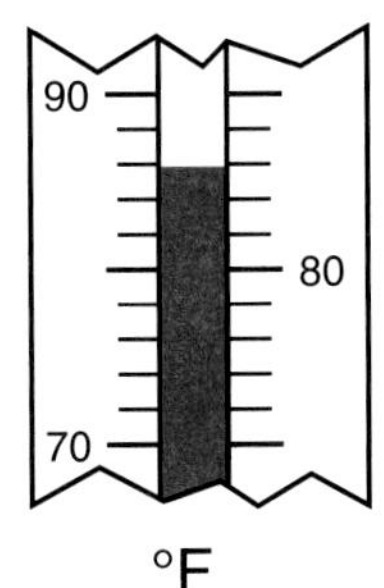

2:00 P.M.

F 140°F

G 86°F

H 54°F

J 32°F

9. What is the area of the figure? (TAKS Obj. 4)

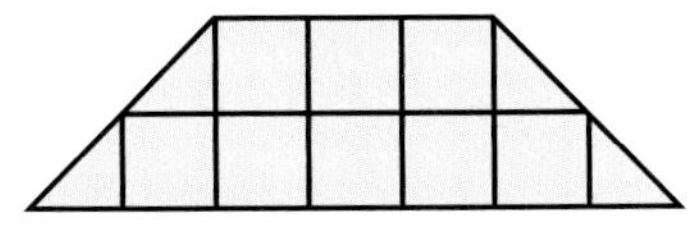

A 10 square units

B 12 square units

C 14 square units

D 20 square units

Short Response

10. Ginny has a ribbon that is 24 feet long. How many yards long is the ribbon? (TAKS Obj. 4)

11. What is the volume of this solid figure? (TAKS Obj. 4)

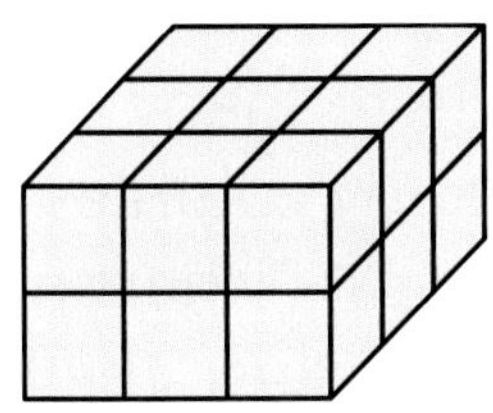

12. Annemarie has 20 cups of juice. Jerry has 6 quarts of juice. Who has more juice? (TAKS Obj. 4)

Extended Response WRITE Math

13. Ted used milliliters to measure the amount of iced tea in a pitcher. Vanessa used liters to measure the same amount. Whose measurement was greater? **Explain**. (TAKS Obj. 4)

14. What is an activity you could do at the temperature shown? **Explain** your answer. (TAKS Obj. 4)

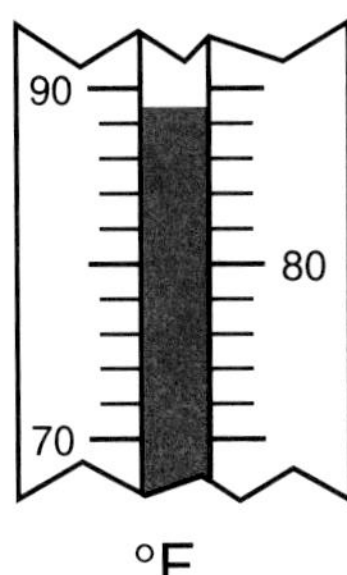

Texas

Problem Solving

Fish Stories

Texas Coral Reefs

The Flower Gardens coral reef is off the coast of Galveston, Texas, in the Gulf of Mexico. It is home to many colorful coral and fish. Coral is formed by colonies of tiny sea animals called coral polyps. Fishers named this reef Flower Gardens because the brightly colored coral looked like flowers below the water.

Some of the fish that live at the Flower Gardens coral reef are shown on these two pages.

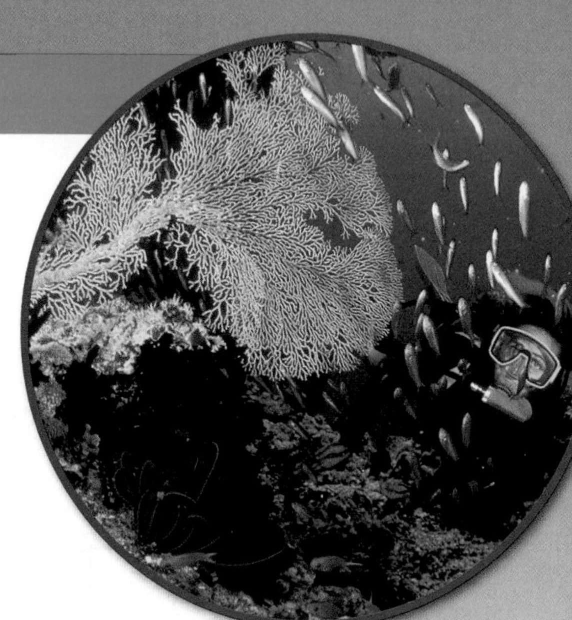

FACT·ACTIVITY

Clown fish

Angelfish

Use a ruler to measure to the nearest centimeter.

1. About how long is the angelfish?
2. About how long is the clown fish?
3. About how much shorter is the clown fish than the angelfish?
4. Choose an object that is about the same length as each of these fish. Measure the objects. How do your measurements compare to the lengths of these fish?

ALMANAC Fact

The Flower Gardens were discovered by fishers over 200 years ago.

You and the Fish

Have you heard people talk about "the fish that got away"? When people tell such "fish stories," they sometimes use their hands and arms to show the length of the fish. It's easier to understand how long something is when you compare it to something familiar, such as the length of your arm span.

The bull shark is about 4 meters long.

FACT·ACTIVITY

For 3–5, use the data on these two pages.

1. Copy the table. Estimate and record each length. Then, with a partner, use a centimeter ruler to measure to the nearest centimeter.

About How Many Centimeters?

Body Unit	Estimate	Actual Measurement
Length of pointer finger		
Length of arm		
Length of foot		

2. How close were your estimates?
3. Which fish is about as long as your pointer finger?
4. Is the length of your foot greater than or less than the length of the clown fish?
5. Is the length of your arm and your partner's arm together greater than or less than the length of the box jellyfish shown at the right?
6. WRITE Math Measure the width of your classroom with a meterstick. Explain how to compare your measurement with the length of the bull shark shown above by writing a number sentence using <, >, or =.

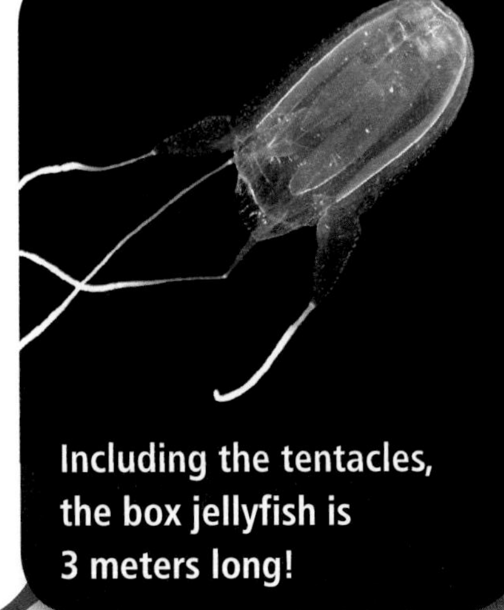
Including the tentacles, the box jellyfish is 3 meters long!

UNIT

8 Fractions, Multiplication, and Probability

Math on Location

with **Texas Chapter Projects**

1

Some gold coins were cut into 4 or 8 equal pieces to make change in colonial times.

2

Today people buy and sell rare coins, which have values much greater than their face value.

3

If you find an old wheat penny or buffalo nickel, you might be able to sell them for more than 1 cent or 5 cents!

VOCABULARY POWER

TALK Math

What math do you see in the **Math on Location** photographs? If a coin was cut into 4 equal pieces, what fraction of the whole coin would each piece represent?

READ Math

REVIEW VOCABULARY You learned the words below when you learned about fractions, multiplication, and probability. How do these words relate to **Math on Location**?

numerator the part of a fraction that is above the fraction bar and tells how many parts are being counted

denominator the part of the fraction that is below the fraction bar and tells how many equal parts are in the whole or in the group

likelihood the chance that something will happen

WRITE Math

Copy and complete a Word Association Map like the one below. Use **Math on Location** and what you know about fractions to complete the map.

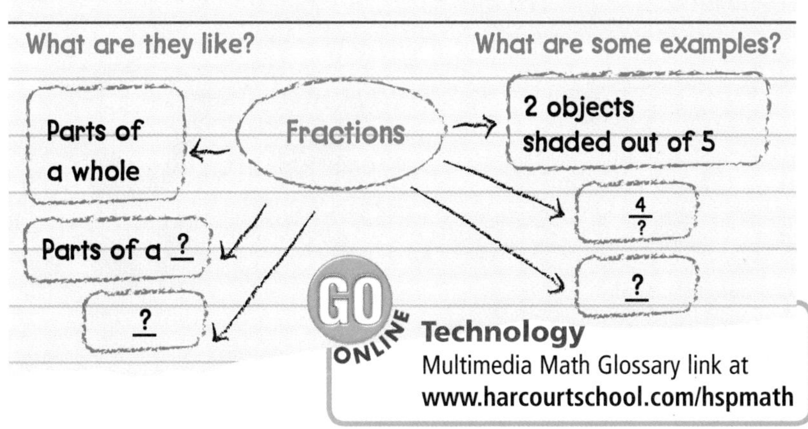

Technology
Multimedia Math Glossary link at www.harcourtschool.com/hspmath

22 Understand Fractions

The Big Idea Fractional parts are equal shares or equal-sized portions of a whole or group and can be expressed in equivalent forms.

Investigate

Sometimes you will see flowers on the prickly pear cactus. The flowers can be yellow, red, or purple. Look at the group of prickly pear cactus flowers below. Use a fraction to describe the colors in the group. Now draw your own cactus with flowers. Write a fraction to describe one of the colors.

TEXAS FAST FACT

The state plant of Texas is the prickly pear cactus. This plant has flat pads that look like large leaves. The pads and the fruit of the plant are often used in recipes.

GO ONLINE **Technology** Student pages are available in the Student eBook.

Show What You Know

Check your understanding of important skills needed for success in Chapter 22.

▶ Parts of a Group

Write the number in each set. Then write the number in each set that are striped.

1. 

2. 

3. 

4. 

5. 

6. 

▶ Parts of a Whole

Write how many equal parts make up the whole figure. Then write how many parts are shaded.

7. 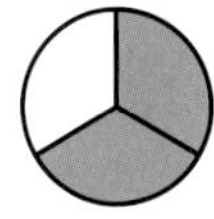

8. 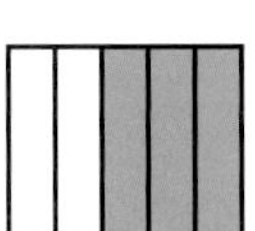

9. 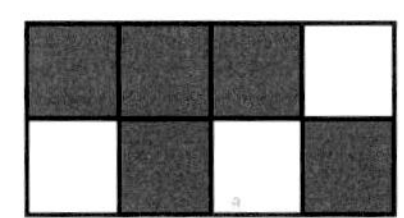

10. 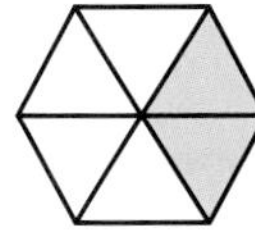

11. 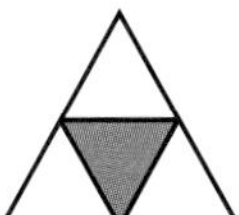

12. 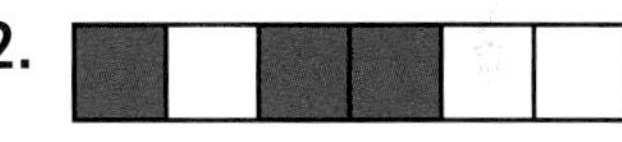

VOCABULARY POWER

CHAPTER VOCABULARY

denominator
equivalent fractions
fraction
numerator
simplest form

WARM-UP WORDS

fraction A number that names part of a whole or part of a group

numerator The part of a fraction above the line, which tells how many parts are being counted

denominator The part of a fraction below the line, which tells how many equal parts there are in the whole or in the group

1 Model Part of a Whole

OBJECTIVE: Read, write, and model fractional parts of a whole.

Quick Review

Tell how many equal parts are in each.

1. 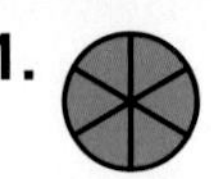
2.
3. 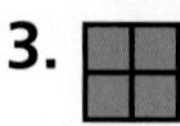
4.
5. 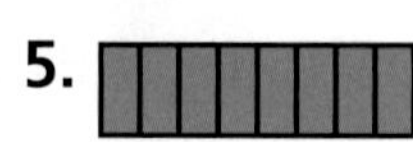

Vocabulary

fraction

numerator

denominator

Learn

PROBLEM The first pizzeria in America opened in New York in 1905. The pizza recipe came from Italy. What fraction of Italy's flag is red?

A **fraction** is a number that names part of a whole or part of a group.

The flag is divided into 3 equal parts, and 1 part is red.

1 red part → $\frac{1}{3}$ ← numerator
3 equal parts in all → ← denominator

Read: one third **Write:** $\frac{1}{3}$

one part out of three equal parts 1 divided by 3

So, $\frac{1}{3}$ of Italy's flag is red.

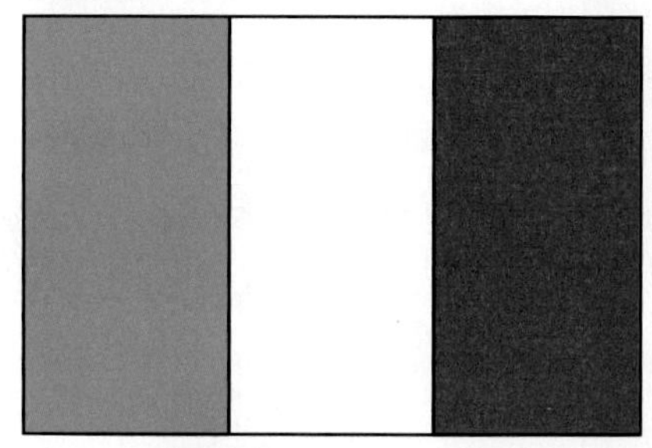

▲ The ingredients of some pizzas—basil, mozzarella, and tomato—show the colors of Italy's flag.

The **numerator** tells how many parts are being counted.

The **denominator** tells how many equal parts are in the whole.

Activity Materials ■ fraction circle pieces

Maria ate 2 out of 6 slices of pizza.
Find the fraction of the pizza that is left.

Step 1

Use fraction circle pieces to model a pizza with 6 equal slices.

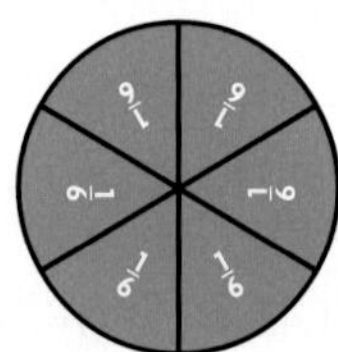

Step 2

Remove 2 of the pieces to show that 2 slices were eaten.

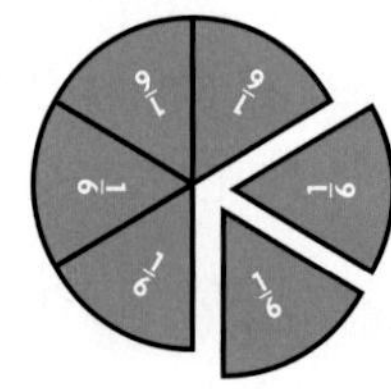

Step 3

Count the number of slices left.

4 slices → $\frac{4}{6}$ ← 6 equal slices in all

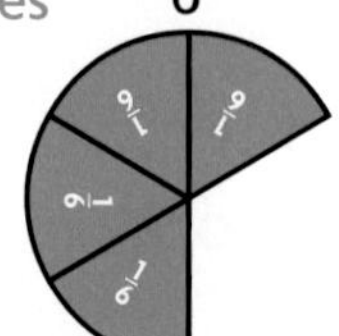

So, $\frac{4}{6}$ of the pizza is left.

TEKS 3.2C use fraction names and symbols to describe fractional parts of whole objects or sets of objects. *also* **3.2A, 3.10, 3.14A, 3.14D, 3.15A, 3.15B**

Examples

A

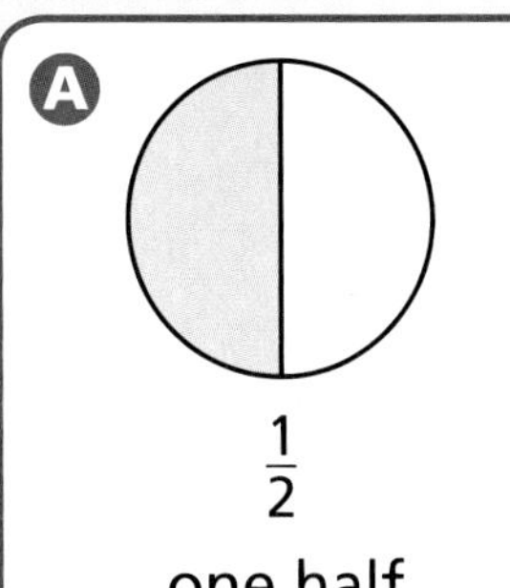

$\frac{1}{2}$

one half

B

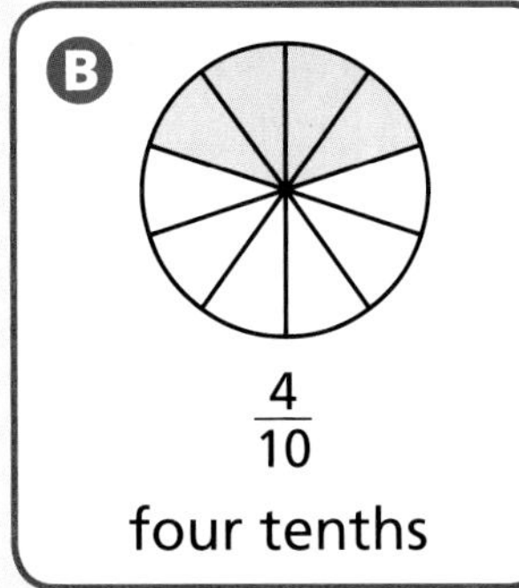

$\frac{4}{10}$

four tenths

C

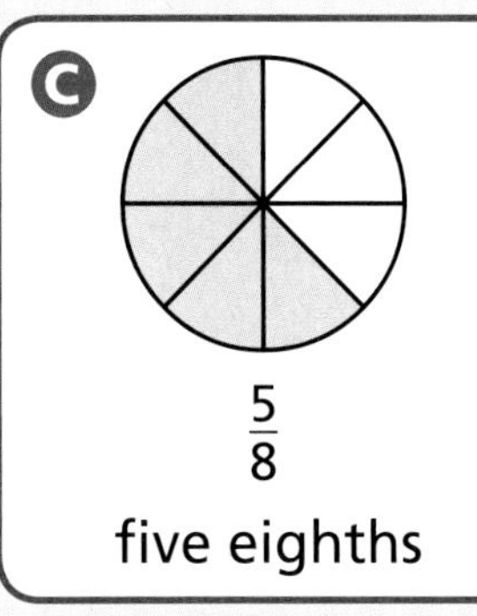

$\frac{5}{8}$

five eighths

D

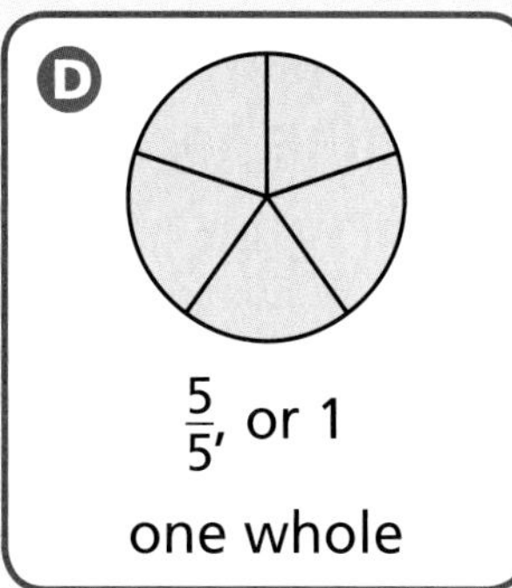

$\frac{5}{5}$, or 1

one whole

A number line can show parts of one whole. The space from one whole number to the next represents one whole. The line can be divided into any number of equal parts.

E This number line shows thirds.

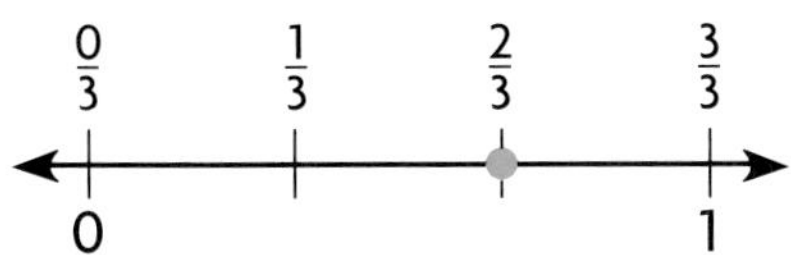

The point shows the location of $\frac{2}{3}$.

F This number line shows fourths.

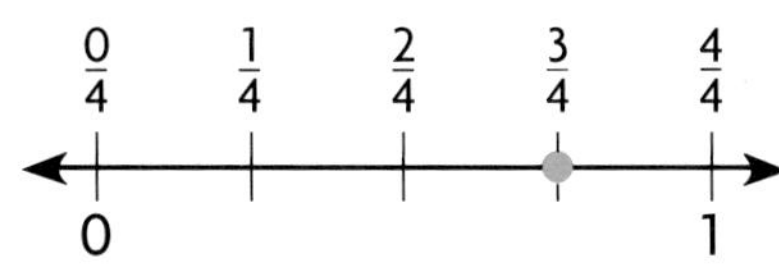

The point shows the location of $\frac{3}{4}$.

Guided Practice

1. This rectangle is divided into how many equal parts?

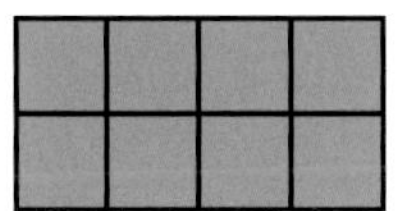

Write a fraction in numbers and in words to name the shaded part.

2. 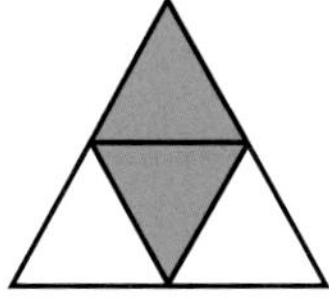

3. 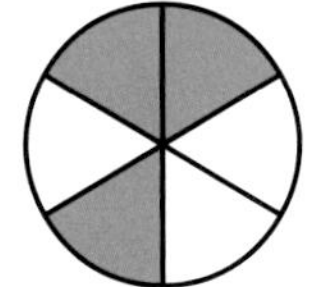

✓4. 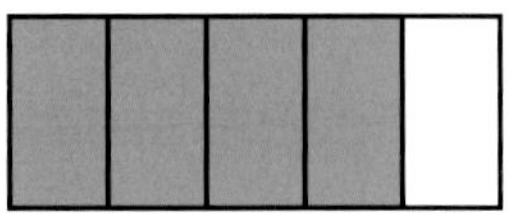

Use fraction circle pieces to make a model of each. Then write the fraction by using numbers.

5. nine twelfths
6. two divided by ten
✓7. seven out of nine

8. TALK Math **Explain** how to write a fraction for the part that is not shaded.

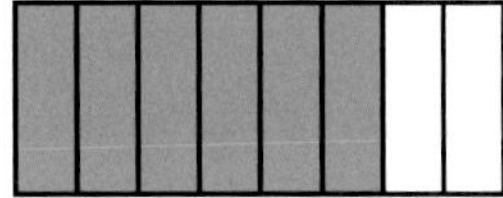

Independent Practice and Problem Solving

Write a fraction in numbers and in words to name the shaded part.

9. 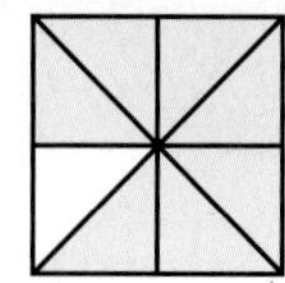

10. 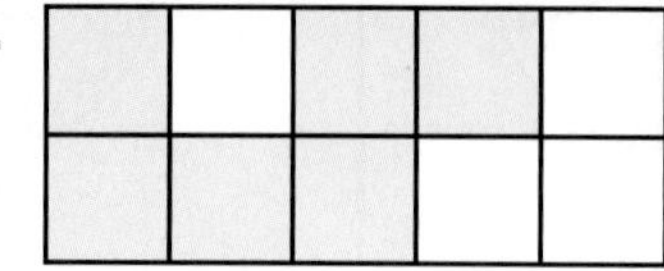

11. 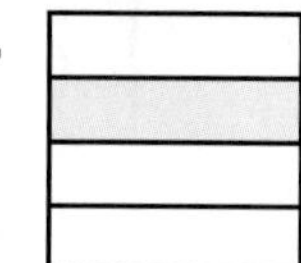

12. 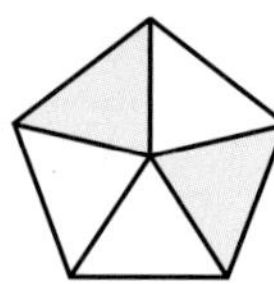

13. 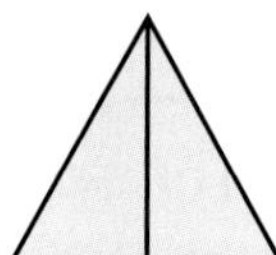

14. 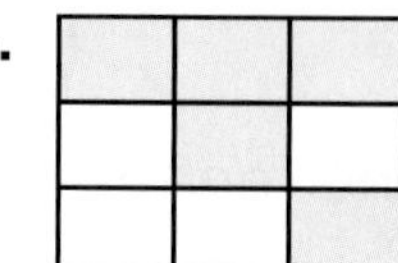

Use fraction circle pieces to make a model of each. Then write the fraction by using numbers.

15. five sixths

16. four out of twelve

17. one divided by three

18. six out of eight

19. two fourths

20. eight tenths

Write a fraction for the shaded part of each figure.

21. 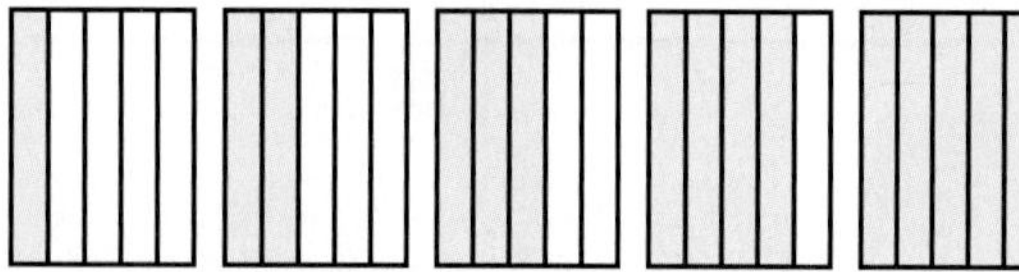

22. 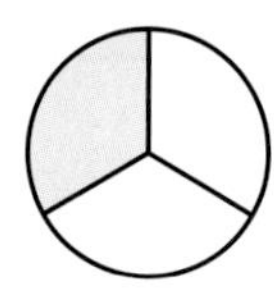 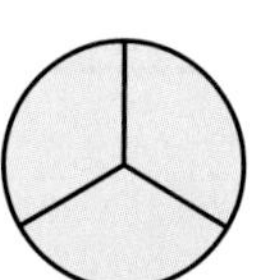

Write a fraction that names each point.

23. 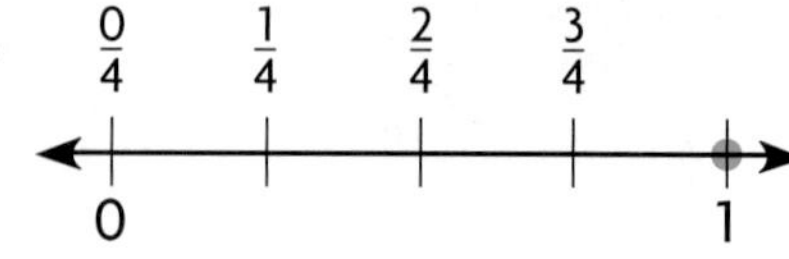

24. 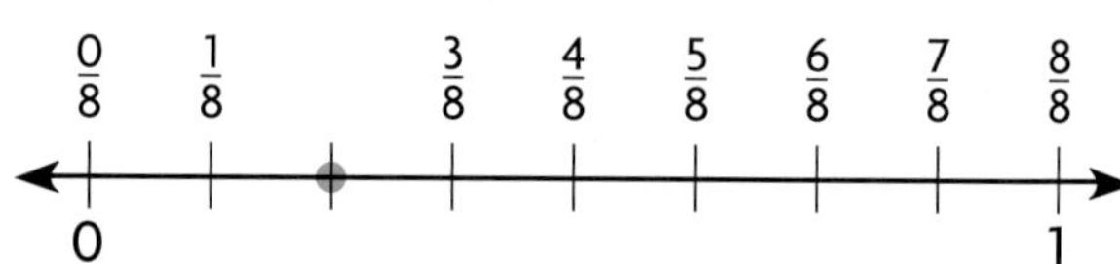

USE DATA For 25–27, use the pizzas.

25. Mrs. Ormond ordered pizza. Each pizza had 8 equal slices. What fraction of the pepperoni pizza is left?

26. What fraction of the cheese pizza is left?

27. **Pose a Problem** Use the picture of the veggie pizza to write a problem that can be answered by using fractions.

Pepperoni

Cheese

Veggie

28. Randy's family ate six eighths of a pizza. Draw a picture to show the amount that Randy's family ate.

CD ROM Technology
Use Harcourt Mega Math, Fraction Action, *Fraction Flare Up*, Level B.

Extra Practice on page 536, Set A

29. **Reasoning** Two pizzas are the same size. The cheese pizza is cut into 6 equal slices. The meat pizza is cut into 8 equal slices. Which pizza has larger slices? **Explain.**

30. 

What's the Error? Kate says that $\frac{2}{3}$ names the shaded part. Describe her error. Write the correct fraction.

Mixed Review and TAKS Prep

31. John said these two figures are congruent. Do you agree? **Explain.** (TEKS 3.9A, p. 396)

32. **TAKS Prep** Write the fraction in numbers and words that names the shaded part. (Obj. 1)

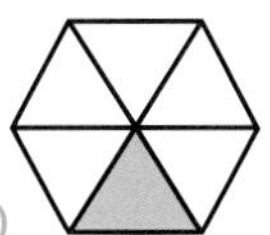

33. What is the volume of this solid? (TEKS 3.11F, p. 498)

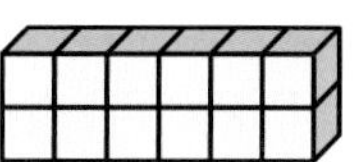

34. **TAKS Prep** What fraction of the figure is blue? (Obj. 1)

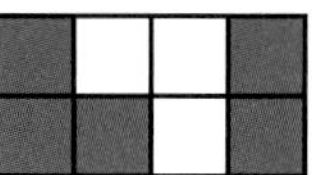

A three fifths
B eight fifths
C three eighths
D five eighths

Problem Solving and Reasoning

The minute hand can divide a clock into equal parts. So, you can use fractions when you tell time.

6:00

6:15

$\frac{1}{4}$, or quarter after 6

6:30

$\frac{1}{2}$, or half past 6

6:45

$\frac{1}{4}$, or quarter to 7

Complete each sentence. Write *one fourth*, *one half*, or *three fourths*.

1. At 6:30, the minute hand has moved ___?___ of the way around the clock.
2. At 6:15, the minute hand has moved ___?___ of the way around the clock.
3. At 6:45, the minute hand has moved ___?___ of the way around the clock.

LESSON 2

Model Part of a Group

OBJECTIVE: Read, write, and model fractional parts of a group.

Quick Review

Name the fraction for each shaded part.

1. 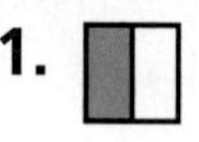 **2.** **3.** 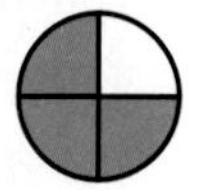

4. 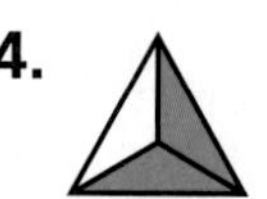 **5.** 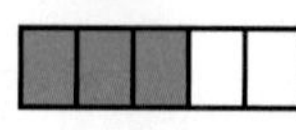

Learn

PROBLEM Jake and Emma each have a collection of marbles. What fraction of each collection is blue?

Jake's marbles	Emma's marbles
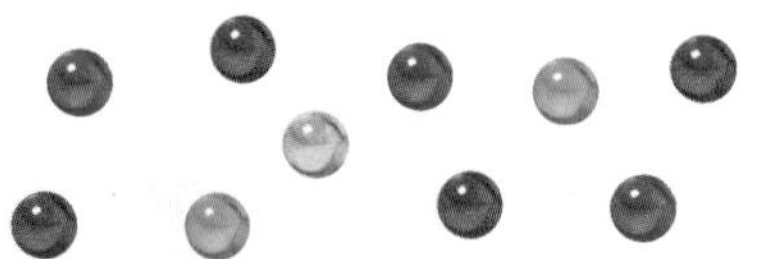	 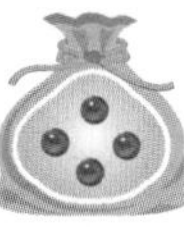 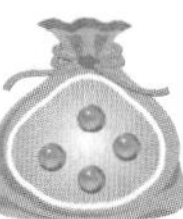 
number of blue marbles → 3 ← numerator total marbles → 10 ← denominator	sets of blue marbles → 1 ← numerator total number of sets → 4 ← denominator
Read: three tenths, or three out of ten	**Read:** one fourth, or one out of four
Write: $\frac{3}{10}$	**Write:** $\frac{1}{4}$
So, $\frac{3}{10}$ of Jake's marbles are blue.	So, $\frac{1}{4}$ of Emma's marbles are blue.

Math Idea
A fraction can name part of a group.

Brian has 8 marbles. Two of them are red. What fraction of Brian's marbles are red? What fraction are not red?

Activity 1 **Materials** ■ two-color counters

Step 1

Use 2 red counters and 6 yellow counters to show the marbles.

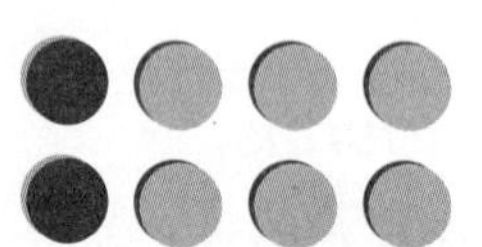

Step 2

Write the fraction of marbles that are red.

$\frac{2}{8}$ ← number of red counters / ← total number of counters

Write the fraction of marbles that are not red.

$\frac{6}{8}$ ← number of yellow counters / ← total number of counters

So, $\frac{2}{8}$ of Brian's marbles are red and $\frac{6}{8}$ are not red.

TEKS 3.2C use fraction names and symbols to describe fractional parts of whole objects or sets of objects.
also **3.2A, 3.14A, 3.14D, 3.15A, 3.15B**

Twelve students signed up to play in a marble tournament. One third of the students who signed up are girls. How many girls will play in the marble tournament?

Find $\frac{1}{3}$ of 12.

▲ The National Marble Tournament is held in Wildwood, New Jersey. It is for children ages 7 to 14.

Activity 2

Materials ■ two-color counters

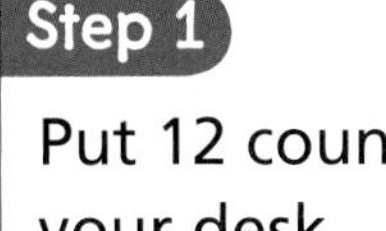

Step 1

Put 12 counters on your desk.

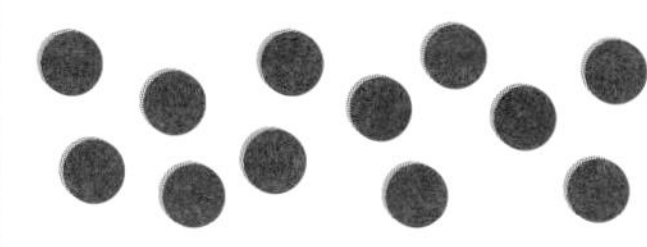

Step 2

Place the counters in 3 equal groups.

Step 3

Count the number in one of the 3 groups.

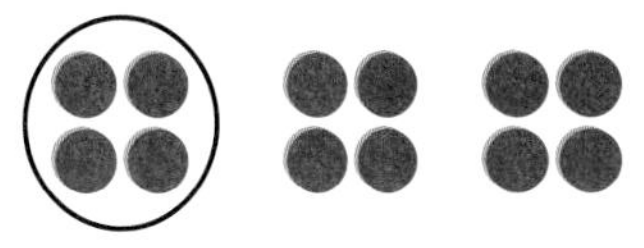

There are 4 counters in one group. $\frac{1}{3}$ of $12 = 4$

So, 4 girls will play in the marble tournament.

What is $\frac{2}{3}$ of 12?

Guided Practice

1. Use the counters to find $\frac{1}{2}$ of 8.

Write a fraction that names the red part of each group.

2.

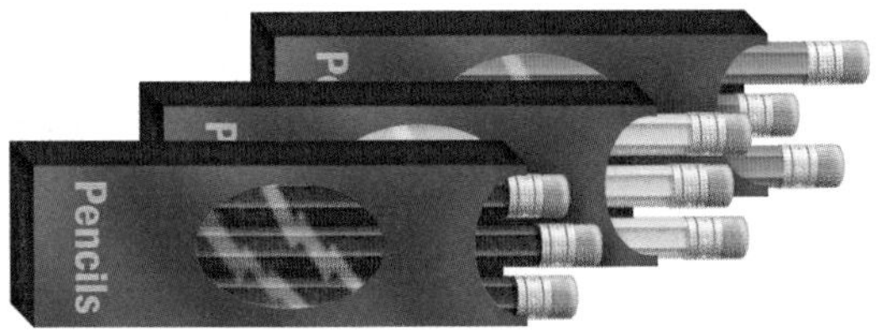

3.

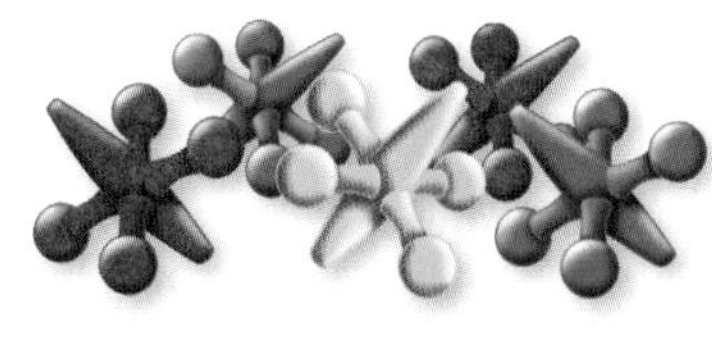

Draw each. Then write a fraction that names the shaded part.

4. Draw 10 squares. Shade 7 squares.

5. Draw 6 triangles. Make 2 equal groups. Shade 1 group.

6. Draw 8 circles. Shade 3 circles.

7. TALK Math **Explain** how to use counters to find $\frac{1}{5}$ of 10.

Independent Practice and Problem Solving

Write a fraction that names the blue part of each group.

8. 

9. 

10. 

11. 

Draw each. Then write a fraction that names the shaded part.

12. Draw 3 circles. Shade 2 circles.

13. Draw 8 triangles. Make 4 equal groups. Shade 2 groups.

14. Draw 4 rectangles. Shade 1 rectangle.

Model each fraction with counters. Then write the fraction in words.

15. $\frac{4}{9}$ **16.** $\frac{1}{5}$ **17.** $\frac{6}{6}$ **18.** $\frac{2}{4}$ **19.** $\frac{5}{8}$

Use counters to solve.

20. $\frac{1}{2}$ of 4 **21.** $\frac{3}{4}$ of 8 **22.** $\frac{1}{3}$ of 9 **23.** $\frac{2}{6}$ of 12 **24.** $\frac{5}{5}$ of 10

USE DATA **For 25–27, use the bar graph.**

25. The bar graph shows the winners of the Smith Elementary School Marble Tournament. How many games were played? What fraction of the games did Scott win?

26. What fraction of the games did Robyn NOT win?

27. **Pose a Problem** Use the data from the bar graph. Write a problem that can be answered by using a fraction to name part of a group.

 Extra Practice on page 536, Set B

28. Kevin has 5 blue pens and 3 red pens. What fraction of Kevin's pens are red?

29. Lori has 10 flowers. Four of those flowers are pink. What fraction of the flowers are NOT pink?

30. Jess has a bag of 12 marbles. Of those marbles, $\frac{4}{12}$ are red, $\frac{3}{12}$ are white, and the rest are green. How many green marbles are in the bag?

31. **WRITE Math** **What's the Question?** A bag has 2 yellow cubes, 3 blue cubes, and 1 white cube. The answer is $\frac{5}{6}$.

Mixed Review and TAKS Prep

32. What fraction of the circle is shaded? (TEKS 3.2C, p. 514)

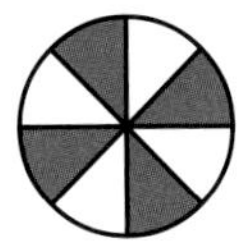

33. **TAKS Prep** A basket is filled with 8 pieces of fruit. Of the pieces of fruit, $\frac{1}{4}$ are apples. How many apples are there? (Obj. 1)

A 1 **B** 2 **C** 4 **D** 6

34. Which is a more reasonable estimate for the weight of a stapler—1 pound or 10 pounds? (TEKS 3.11D, p. 450)

35. **TAKS Prep** What fraction of the coins are pennies? (Obj. 1)

Problem Solving and Reasoning

You can use the models and a pattern to complete the table.

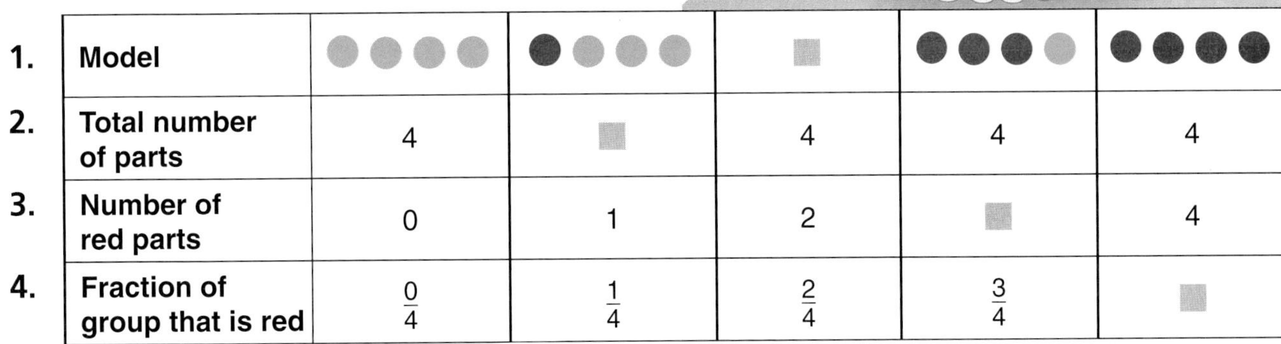

1.	**Model**					
2.	**Total number of parts**	4		4	4	4
3.	**Number of red parts**	0	1	2		4
4.	**Fraction of group that is red**	$\frac{0}{4}$	$\frac{1}{4}$	$\frac{2}{4}$	$\frac{3}{4}$	

LESSON 3

Equivalent Fractions

OBJECTIVE: Model and write equivalent fractions.

Quick Review

Name the fraction for each shaded part.

1.

2. 

3. 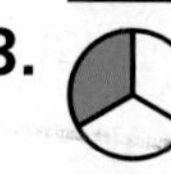

4.

5. 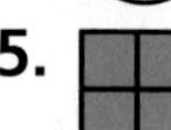

Vocabulary

equivalent fractions

Learn

Two or more fractions that name the same amount are called **equivalent fractions**.

HANDS ON

Activity 1

Materials ■ fraction bars

What is an equivalent fraction for $\frac{1}{4}$?

Step 1

Start with the bar for 1 whole. Line up one $\frac{1}{4}$ fraction bar.

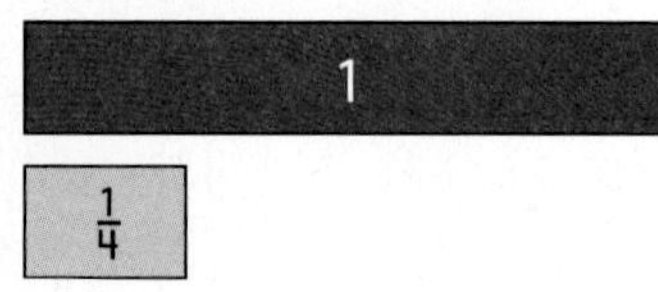

Step 2

Use $\frac{1}{8}$ fraction bars to match the length of the bar for $\frac{1}{4}$.

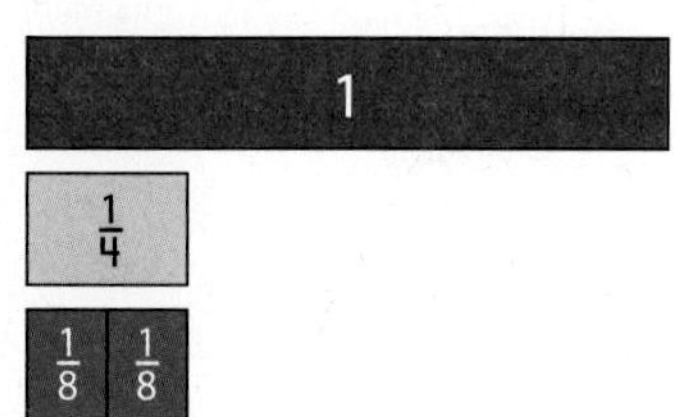

Step 3

Count the number of $\frac{1}{8}$ bars that equal $\frac{1}{4}$. Write the equivalent fraction.

Count: $\frac{1}{8}$, $\frac{2}{8}$

Write: $\frac{1}{4} = \frac{2}{8}$

ERROR ALERT

Be sure that the fraction bars are lined up at the left.

HANDS ON

Activity 2

Materials ■ fraction bars

What is an equivalent fraction for $\frac{2}{5}$?

Step 1

Start with the bar for 1 whole. Line up two $\frac{1}{5}$ bars for $\frac{2}{5}$.

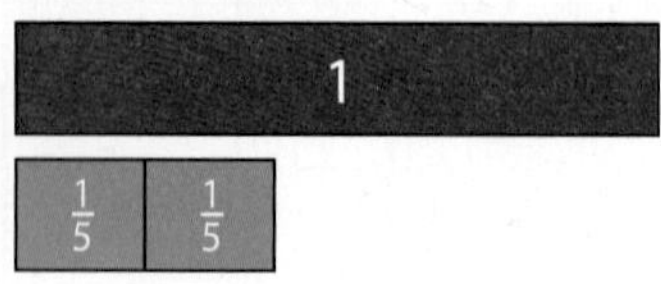

Step 2

Use $\frac{1}{10}$ fraction bars to match the length of the bars for $\frac{2}{5}$.

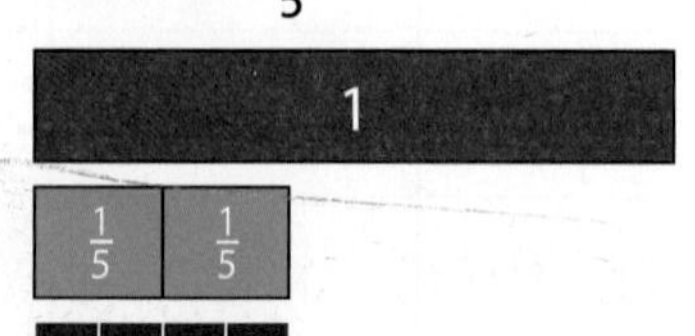

Step 3

Count the number of $\frac{1}{10}$ bars that equal $\frac{2}{5}$. Write the equivalent fraction.

Count: $\frac{1}{10}$, $\frac{2}{10}$, $\frac{3}{10}$, $\frac{4}{10}$

Write: $\frac{2}{5} = \frac{4}{10}$

TEKS 3.2D construct concrete models of equivalent fractions for fractional parts of whole objects. *also* **3.2A, 3.2C, 3.14A, 3.14D, 3.15A, 3.15B**

More Examples

A

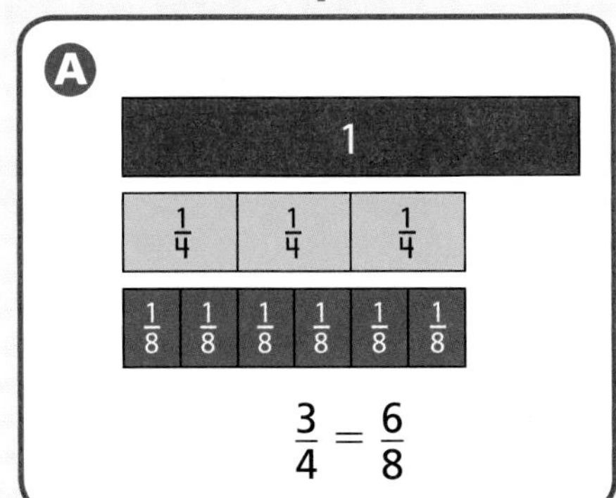

$\frac{3}{4} = \frac{6}{8}$

B

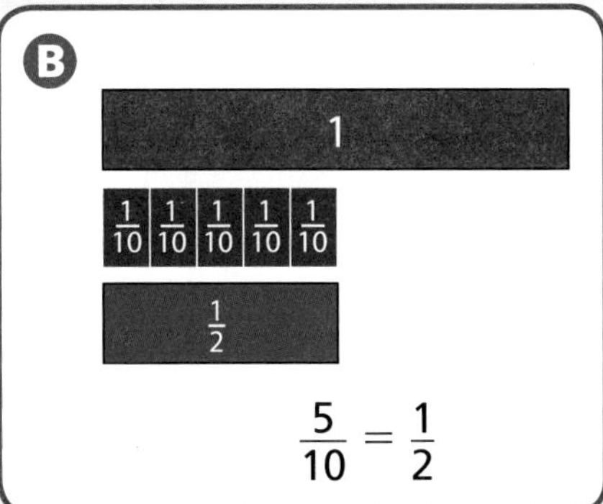

$\frac{5}{10} = \frac{1}{2}$

C

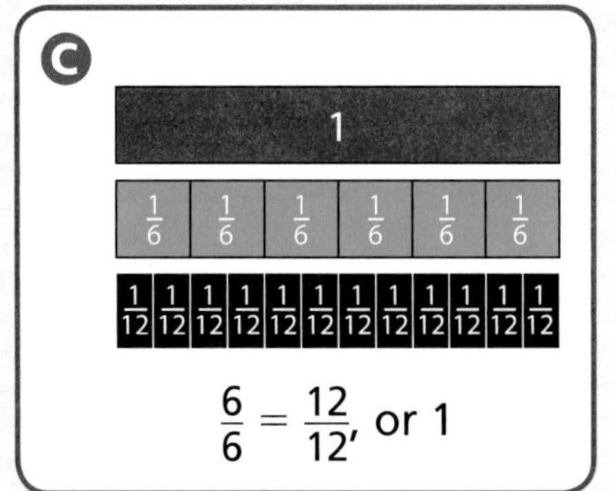

$\frac{6}{6} = \frac{12}{12}$, or 1

Guided Practice

1. What fraction is equivalent to $\frac{2}{3}$?

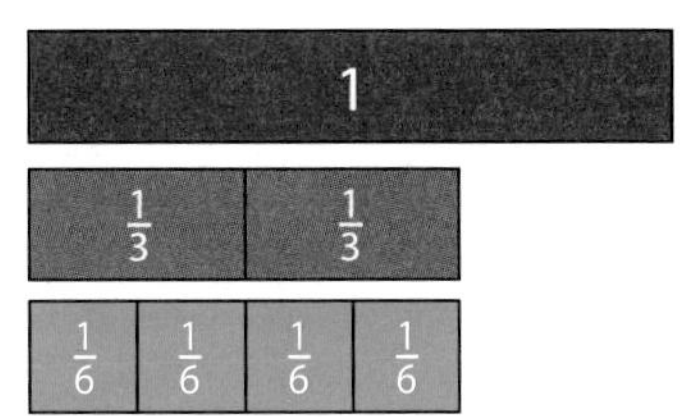

Find an equivalent fraction. Use fraction bars.

2. 1; $\frac{1}{5}$ $\frac{1}{5}$ $\frac{1}{5}$

✓ 3. 1; $\frac{1}{8}$ $\frac{1}{8}$

✓ 4.

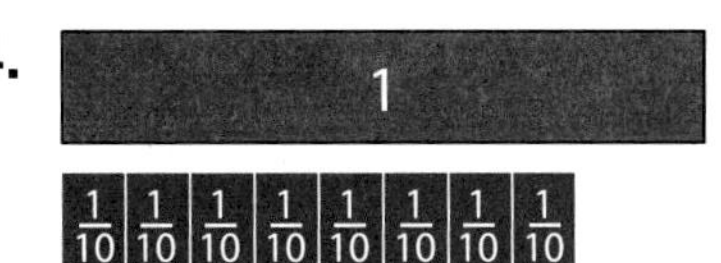

5. **TALK Math** **Explain** how to use fraction bars to find a fraction that is equivalent to $\frac{3}{4}$.

Independent Practice and Problem Solving

Find an equivalent fraction. Use fraction bars.

6. 1; $\frac{1}{4}$ $\frac{1}{4}$

7. 1; $\frac{1}{6}$ $\frac{1}{6}$ $\frac{1}{6}$ $\frac{1}{6}$

8. 1; $\frac{1}{3}$ $\frac{1}{3}$ $\frac{1}{3}$

9. 1; $\frac{1}{12}$ $\frac{1}{12}$ $\frac{1}{12}$

10. 1; $\frac{1}{5}$

11. 1; $\frac{1}{10}$ $\frac{1}{10}$ $\frac{1}{10}$ $\frac{1}{10}$ $\frac{1}{10}$

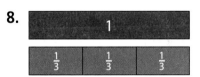

Extra Practice on page 536, Set C

Find the missing numerator. Use fraction bars.

12. 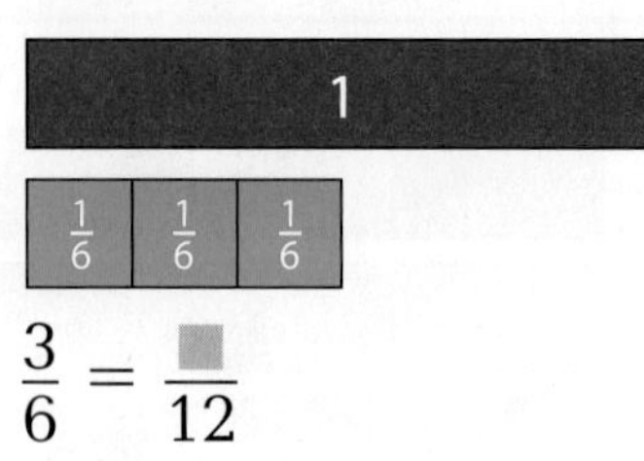

$\frac{3}{6} = \frac{\blacksquare}{12}$

13. 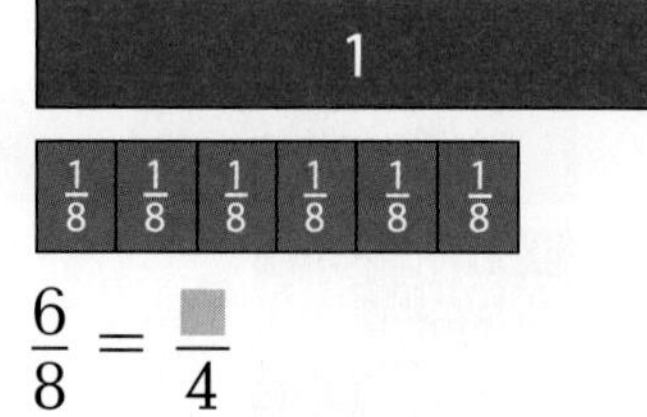

$\frac{6}{8} = \frac{\blacksquare}{4}$

14. 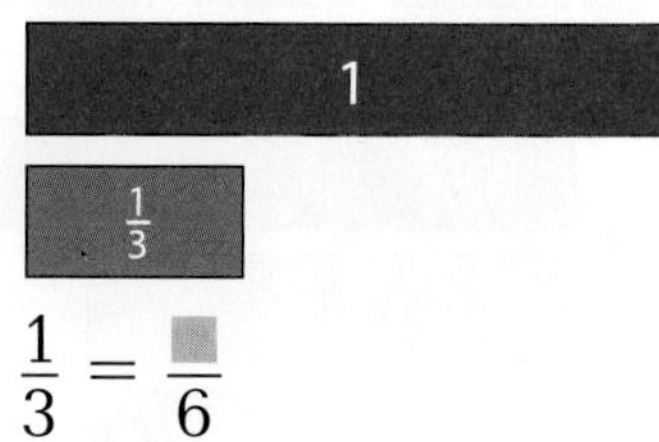

$\frac{1}{3} = \frac{\blacksquare}{6}$

15. $\frac{8}{10} = \frac{\blacksquare}{5}$

16. $\frac{1}{2} = \frac{\blacksquare}{8}$

17. $\frac{4}{12} = \frac{\blacksquare}{3}$

18. $\frac{2}{4} = \frac{\blacksquare}{12}$

19. $\frac{5}{5} = \frac{\blacksquare}{10}$

20. $\frac{4}{8} = \frac{\blacksquare}{2}$

21. Write the fraction that names the shaded part of each. Then tell which fractions are equivalent.

a. 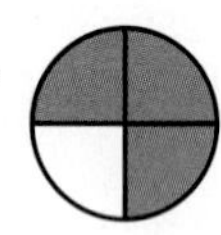 **b.** 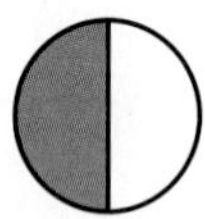 **c.** 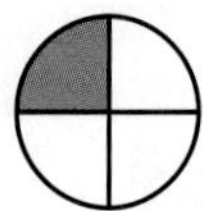 **d.** 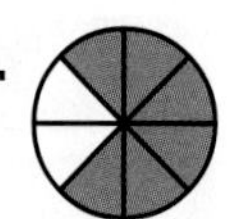 **e.** 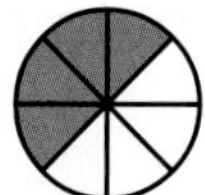

USE DATA For 22–24, use the table.

22. The table shows the lengths of three different types of ants. How many fire ants would it take to equal the length of one carpenter ant?

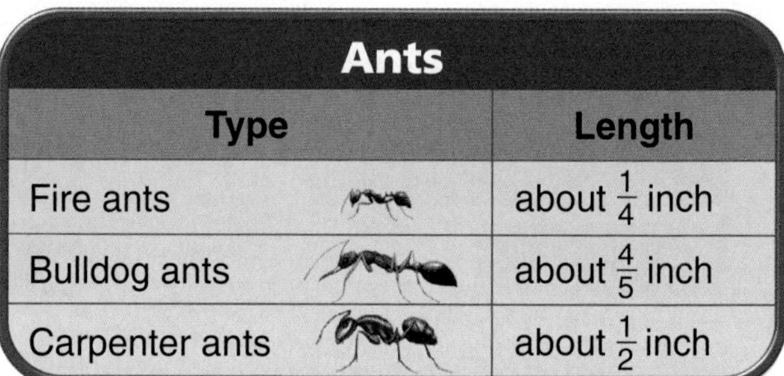

Ants

Type	Length
Fire ants	about $\frac{1}{4}$ inch
Bulldog ants	about $\frac{4}{5}$ inch
Carpenter ants	about $\frac{1}{2}$ inch

23. What fraction is equivalent to the length of a bulldog ant?

24. **Reasoning** Are any of the ants in the table the same length? **Explain.**

25. **WRITE Math** **Sense or Nonsense** Jay cut an orange into 8 equal pieces and ate 4 of the pieces. He says he ate one half of the orange. Does Jay's statement make sense? **Explain.**

Mixed Review and TAKS Prep

26. Erin has 6 striped socks and 2 white socks in a drawer. What fraction of her socks are striped? (TEKS 3.2C, p. 518)

27. Each box of crayons costs $6. What is the cost of 4 boxes of crayons? (TEKS 3.4B, p. 210)

28. **TAKS Prep** What is the missing numerator? $\frac{5}{6} = \frac{\blacksquare}{12}$ (Obj. 1)

A 7 **C** 9

B 8 **D** 10

WRITE Math WORKSHOP

Draw to Explain

Sometimes you can best explain your thinking by drawing a picture or diagram.

Marta wants to find two fractions that are equivalent to $\frac{1}{3}$. She uses crayons and strips of paper to make diagrams of equivalent fractions.

She explains her thinking by describing what she did and showing her drawings.

First, I cut three strips of paper that are the same size. Next, I folded the strips by using different numbers of folds to show $\frac{1}{3}$. I drew lines to show the folds and shaded $\frac{1}{3}$ of each strip.

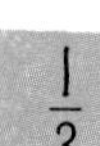

$\frac{1}{3}$	$\frac{1}{3}$	$\frac{1}{3}$

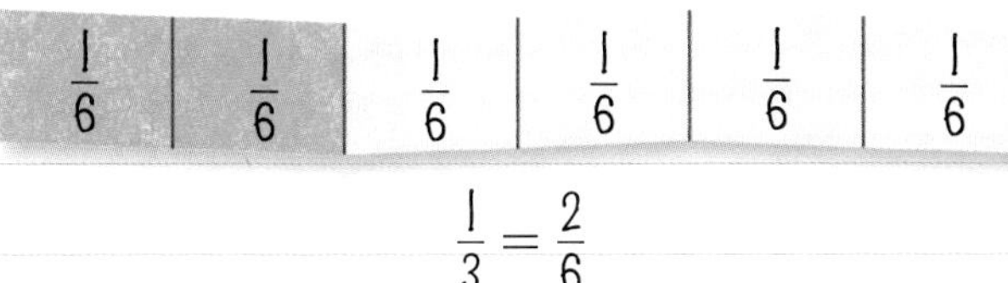

$\frac{1}{6}$	$\frac{1}{6}$	$\frac{1}{6}$	$\frac{1}{6}$	$\frac{1}{6}$	$\frac{1}{6}$

$$\frac{1}{3} = \frac{2}{6}$$

$\frac{1}{12}$	$\frac{1}{12}$	$\frac{1}{12}$	$\frac{1}{12}$	$\frac{1}{12}$	$\frac{1}{12}$	$\frac{1}{12}$	$\frac{1}{12}$	$\frac{1}{12}$	$\frac{1}{12}$	$\frac{1}{12}$	$\frac{1}{12}$

$$\frac{1}{3} = \frac{4}{12}$$

My drawings prove that $\frac{1}{3}$, $\frac{2}{6}$, and $\frac{4}{12}$ are equivalent fractions.

Problem Solving

Fold paper strips to show fractional parts. Draw lines to show the folds. Shade some parts to show the fractions. Then explain what you did. Use your drawings to show your solution.

1. Find an equivalent fraction for $\frac{2}{3}$.
2. Find an equivalent fraction for $\frac{3}{4}$.

LESSON 4

Simplest Form

OBJECTIVE: Model and write fractions in simplest form.

Quick Review

Write an equivalent fraction for each.

1. $\frac{1}{2}$ **2.** $\frac{2}{5}$ **3.** $\frac{1}{3}$

4. $\frac{3}{4}$ **5.** $\frac{1}{6}$

Vocabulary

simplest form

Learn

PROBLEM Mr. Diaz cut lasagna into 10 equal pieces. His family ate $\frac{4}{10}$ of the lasagna. How can you write this fraction in simplest form?

Example 1

Step 1	Step 2
Line up four $\frac{1}{10}$ fraction bars for $\frac{4}{10}$. 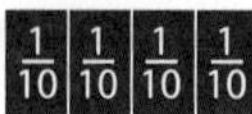	Find the largest fraction bars that are equivalent. 

Two $\frac{1}{5}$ fraction bars are equivalent to four $\frac{1}{10}$ fraction bars.

So, $\frac{4}{10} = \frac{2}{5}$.

A fraction is in **simplest form** when it is modeled with the largest fraction bar or bars possible.

Remember

Equivalent fractions name the same amount.

Example 2

Sue has 9 apples. Of those apples, $\frac{3}{9}$ are red. What is the simplest form of $\frac{3}{9}$? You can use counters to find the answer.

Step 1	Step 2
Use 3 red counters and 6 yellow counters.	Put the counters in the largest equal groups possible. The counters in each group can be only one color.

There are 3 equal groups of counters.

One of the groups is red. So, $\frac{3}{9} = \frac{1}{3}$.

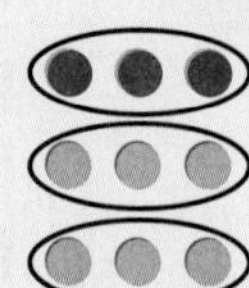

A fraction is in **simplest form** when it is modeled with the largest equal groups possible.

TEKS 3.2B compare fractional parts of whole objects or sets of objects in a problem situation using concrete models. *also* 3.2A, 3.2C, 3.2D, 3.14A, 3.14D, 3.15A, 3.15B

Guided Practice

1. Write $\frac{3}{6}$ in simplest form. $\frac{3}{6} = \frac{■}{■}$

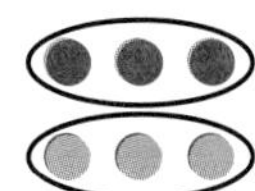

Think: How many groups are red?
How many equal groups?

Write each fraction in simplest form. Use fraction bars or counters.

2. $\frac{2}{8} = \frac{■}{■}$

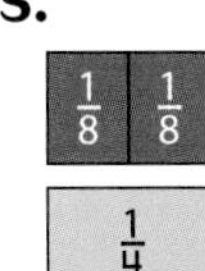

✓3. $\frac{4}{12} = \frac{■}{■}$

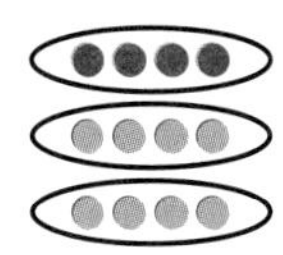

✓4. $\frac{4}{6} = \frac{■}{■}$

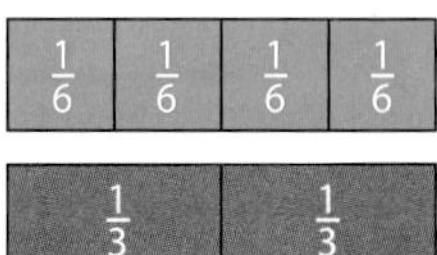

5. TALK Math **Explain** how you know when a fraction is in simplest form.

Independent Practice and Problem Solving

Write each fraction in simplest form. Use fraction bars or counters.

6. $\frac{8}{12} = \frac{■}{■}$

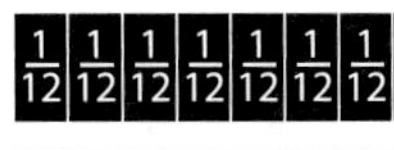

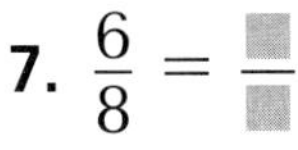

7. $\frac{6}{8} = \frac{■}{■}$

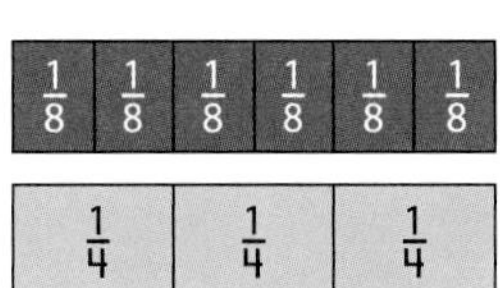

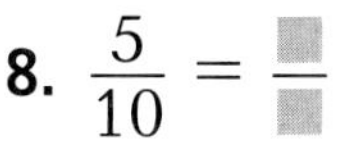

8. $\frac{5}{10} = \frac{■}{■}$

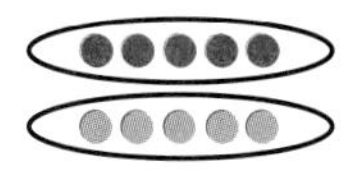

9. $\frac{2}{4}$

10. $\frac{10}{12}$

11. $\frac{2}{6}$

12. $\frac{6}{10}$

13. $\frac{4}{8}$

14. $\frac{6}{9}$

15. Gwen ate 3 out of 12 muffins. What fraction of the muffins are left? Write the fraction in simplest form.

16. Brian read 4 out of 6 pages. What fraction of the pages did he read? Write the fraction in simplest form.

17. WRITE Math What is $\frac{2}{10}$ in simplest form? **Explain** how you got your answer.

Mixed Review and TAKS Prep

18. What number is missing in this pattern? 72, 62, 52, 42, __?__ (TEKS 3.6A, p. 182)

19. Nicki has 3 quarters, 1 dime, and 2 nickels. How much money does she have? (TEKS 3.1C, p. 110)

20. **TAKS Prep** Which fraction is in simplest form? (Obj. 1)

A $\frac{3}{9}$

B $\frac{5}{8}$

C $\frac{3}{12}$

D $\frac{5}{10}$

Extra Practice on page 537, Set D

LESSON

5 Fractions on a Number Line

OBJECTIVE: Locate and name fractions on a number line.

Quick Review

Find the next number in each pattern.

1. 5, 10, 15, ■
2. 6, 9, 12, ■
3. 3, 5, 7, ■
4. 7, 11, 15, ■
5. 2, 8, 14, ■

Learn

PROBLEM This weekend is the town's fun run. The course is 1 mile long. Daniel is posting signs along the course to label each $\frac{1}{4}$ mile. What sign will be at Point a?

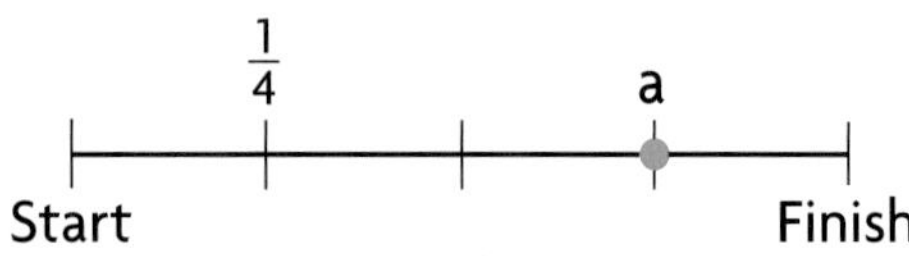

You can use fractions to name points on a number line.

Example

Look at the number of equal parts on the number line. Since there are 4 equal parts, count by fourths and label each point.

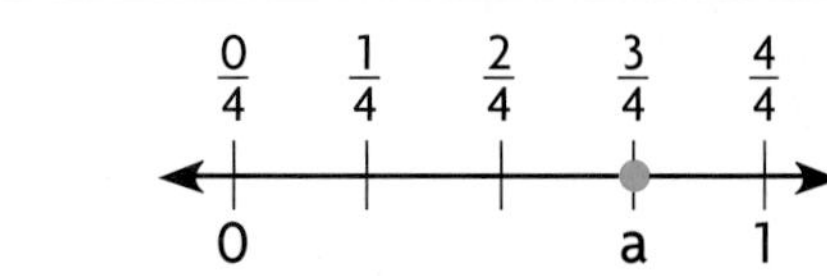

So, the sign at Point a will be $\frac{3}{4}$ mile.

More Examples

A What are the missing fractions?

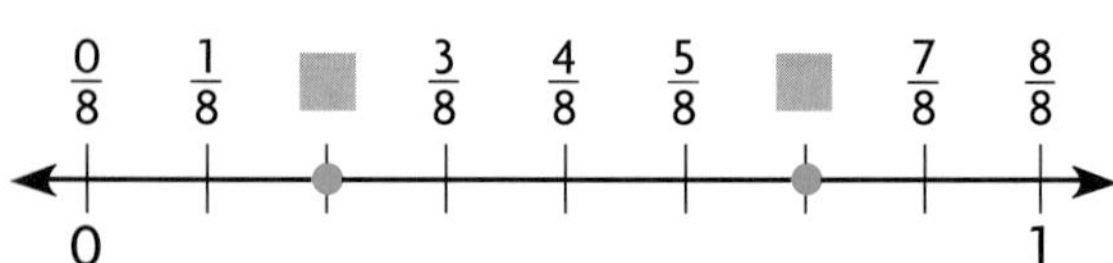

The missing fractions are $\frac{2}{8}$ and $\frac{6}{8}$.

B Which point represents $\frac{5}{6}$?

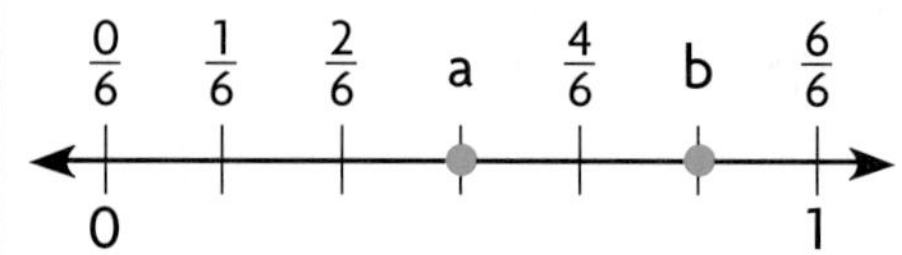

Point b represents $\frac{5}{6}$.

Guided Practice

1. What is the missing fraction?

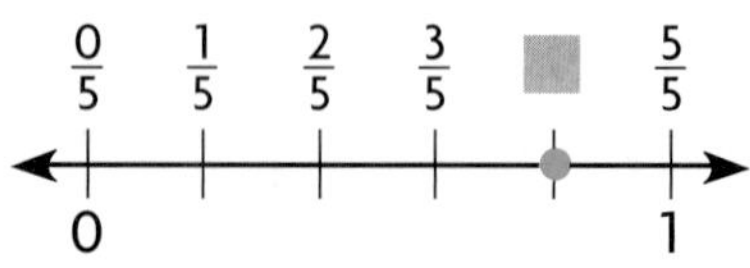

TEKS 3.10 The student is expected to locate and name points on a number line using whole numbers and fractions, including halves and fourths. *also* **3.2C, 3.14A, 3.15A, 3.15B**

Write the missing fractions for each number line.

2. 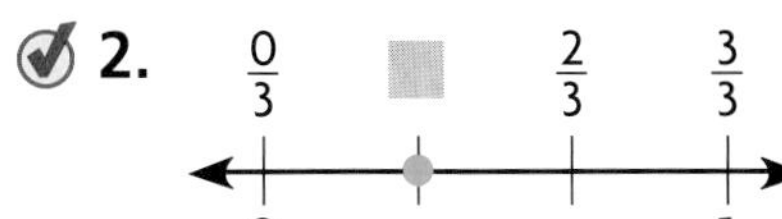

3. 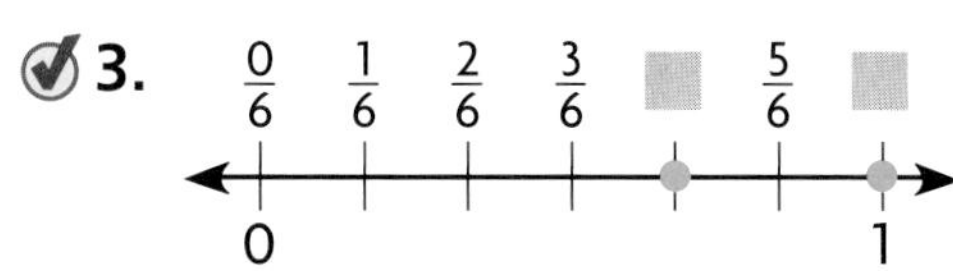

4. TALK Math **Explain** how you can use what you know about numbers to locate a fraction on a number line.

Independent Practice and Problem Solving

Write the missing fractions for each number line.

5. $\frac{0}{9}$ $\frac{1}{9}$ $\frac{2}{9}$ $\frac{3}{9}$ $\frac{4}{9}$ ■ ■ $\frac{7}{9}$ ■ $\frac{9}{9}$ (number line from 0 to 1)

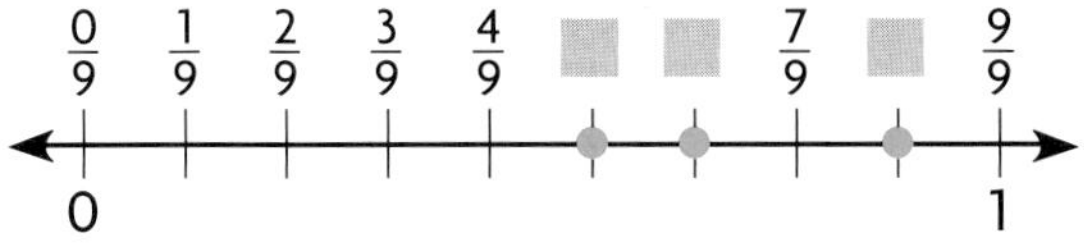

6. 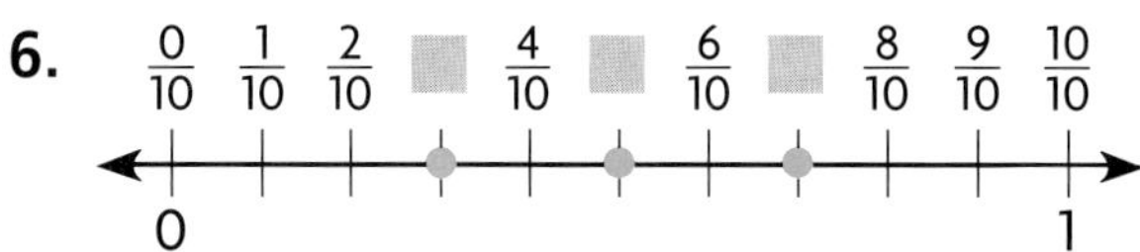

Tell which point represents each fraction.

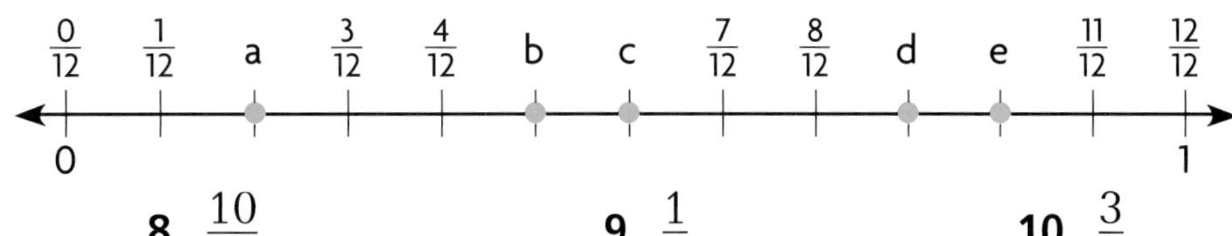

7. $\frac{5}{12}$

8. $\frac{10}{12}$

9. $\frac{1}{2}$

10. $\frac{3}{4}$

For 11–12, use the bracelet.

11. **FAST FACT** Tourmaline is a stone used in jewelry. It is known as the "Rainbow Gemstone" because it comes in many colors. What color is the stone at the $\frac{1}{2}$ mark?

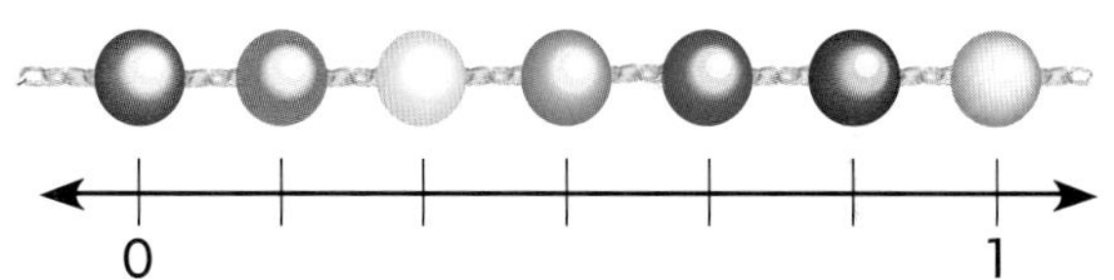

12. Which stone is the same distance from the red and the blue stones? Write a fraction for the location of this stone.

13. WRITE Math Can a point on a number line stand for more than one fraction? **Explain**.

Mixed Review and TAKS Prep

14. Kim has 20 cards. She put the cards in two equal piles. How many cards are in each pile? (TEKS 3.4C, p. 320)

15. Write the number sentences that belong in the same fact family as $3 \times 4 = 12$. (TEKS 3.6C, p. 304)

16. **TAKS Prep** Which point represents $\frac{3}{8}$ on the number line? (Obj. 3)

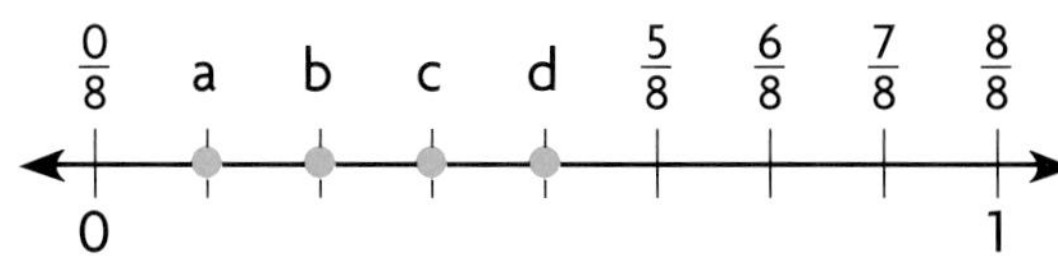

A a **B** b **C** c **D** d

Extra Practice on page 537, Set E

LESSON 6

Compare Fractions

OBJECTIVE: Compare fractions with like and unlike denominators.

Quick Review

Compare. Write <, >, or = for each ●.

1. 52 ● 48

2. 67 ● 68

3. 183 ● 183

4. 2,594 ● 2,549

5. 5,271 ● 5,712

Learn

You can use fraction bars to compare parts of a whole.

Examples

A Compare $\frac{2}{6}$ and $\frac{3}{6}$.

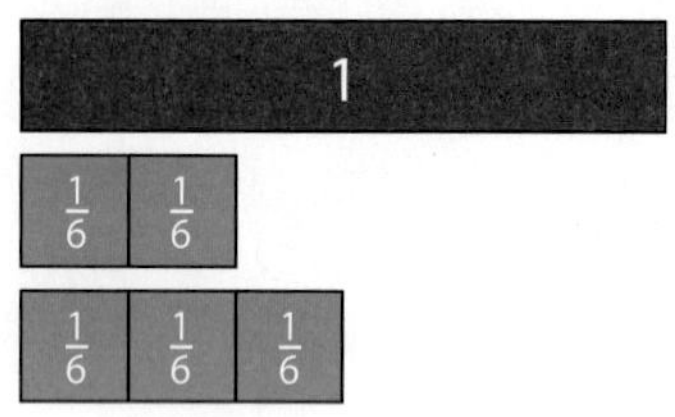

The bars for $\frac{2}{6}$ are shorter than the bars for $\frac{3}{6}$.

So, $\frac{2}{6} < \frac{3}{6}$, or $\frac{3}{6} > \frac{2}{6}$.

B Compare $\frac{2}{6}$ and $\frac{1}{4}$.

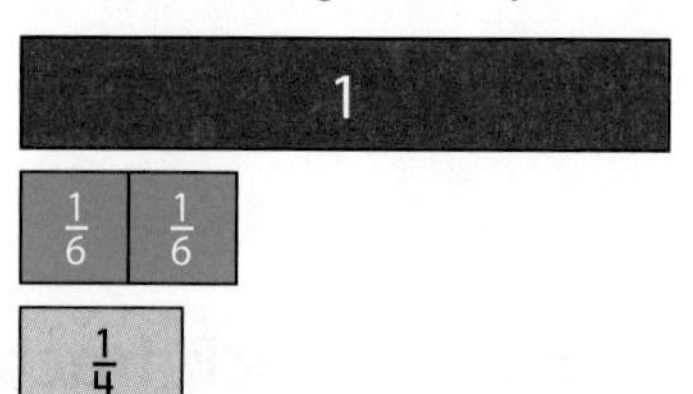

The bars for $\frac{2}{6}$ are longer than the bar for $\frac{1}{4}$.

So, $\frac{2}{6} > \frac{1}{4}$, or $\frac{1}{4} < \frac{2}{6}$.

- In Example A, you compared using fraction bars. What is another way you could compare fractions with the same denominators but different numerators?

- Compare $\frac{1}{4}$ and $\frac{1}{6}$. When the denominator is greater, is the fraction bar longer or shorter? Why?

Remember
$>$ means greater than.
$<$ means less than.

You can use tiles to compare parts of a group.

Examples

A Compare $\frac{3}{4}$ and $\frac{2}{4}$.

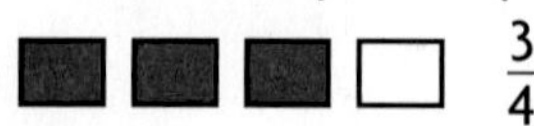 $\frac{3}{4}$

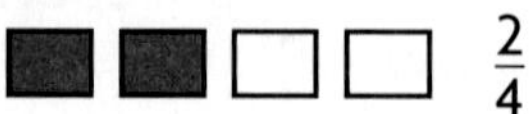 $\frac{2}{4}$

3 red tiles are more than 2 red tiles.

So, $\frac{3}{4} > \frac{2}{4}$, or $\frac{2}{4} < \frac{3}{4}$.

B Compare $\frac{4}{8}$ and $\frac{1}{2}$.

 $\frac{4}{8}$

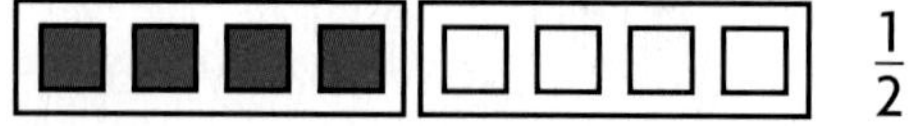 $\frac{1}{2}$

4 blue tiles are the same as 4 blue tiles.

So, $\frac{4}{8} = \frac{1}{2}$.

TEKS 3.2B compare fractional parts of whole objects or sets of objects in a problem situation using concrete models. *also* **3.2A, 3.2C, 3.10, 3.14A, 3.14D, 3.15A, 3.15B**

You can also use a number line to compare fractions.

Examples

A Compare $\frac{2}{5}$ and $\frac{4}{5}$.

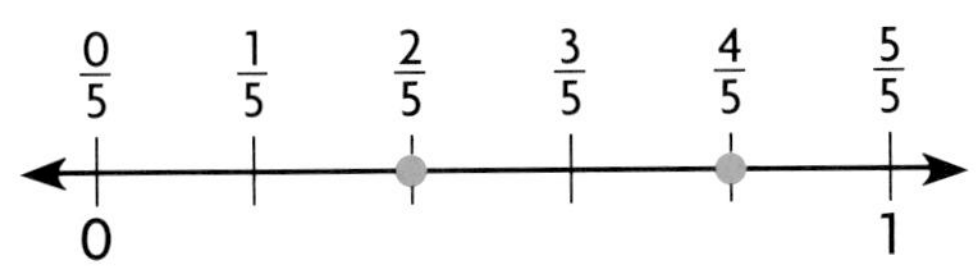

$\frac{4}{5}$ is to the right of $\frac{2}{5}$. It is closer to 1.

So, $\frac{4}{5} > \frac{2}{5}$, or $\frac{2}{5} < \frac{4}{5}$.

B Compare $\frac{3}{6}$ and $\frac{1}{3}$.

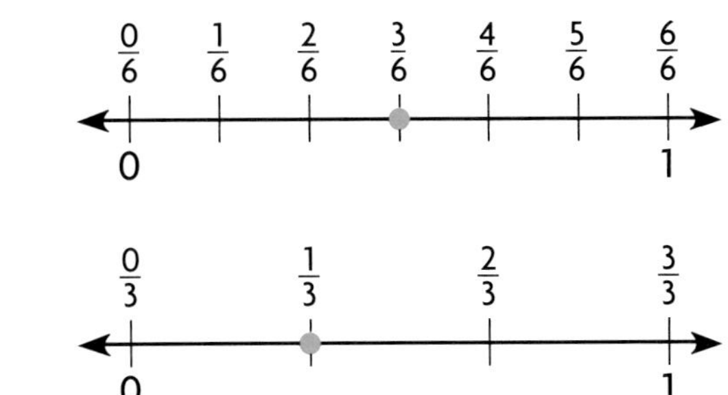

$\frac{1}{3}$ is to the left of $\frac{3}{6}$. It is closer to 0.

So, $\frac{3}{6} > \frac{1}{3}$, or $\frac{1}{3} < \frac{3}{6}$.

Guided Practice

1. Which fraction is greater, $\frac{4}{5}$ or $\frac{5}{8}$?
   Think: The bar for $\frac{4}{5}$ is longer.

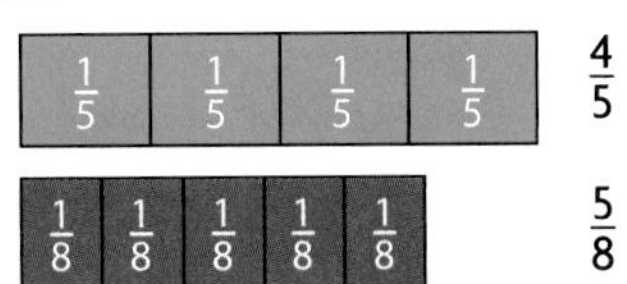

Compare. Write <, >, or = for each ●.

2. $\frac{1}{10}$ $\frac{1}{10}$ $\frac{1}{10}$ $\frac{1}{10}$ $\frac{1}{10}$ $\frac{1}{10}$ $\frac{1}{10}$

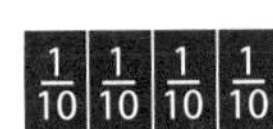

$\frac{7}{10}$ ● $\frac{4}{10}$

3. 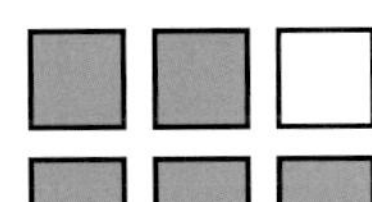

$\frac{2}{3}$ ● $\frac{3}{3}$

4. 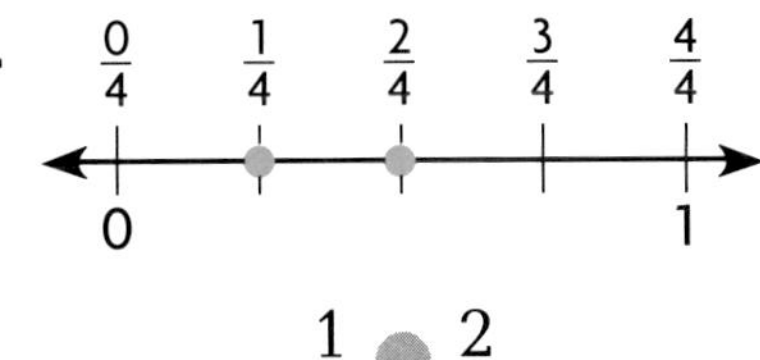

$\frac{1}{4}$ ● $\frac{2}{4}$

5. 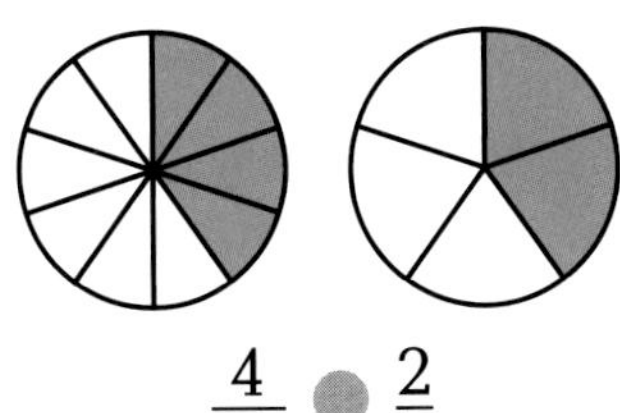

$\frac{4}{10}$ ● $\frac{2}{5}$

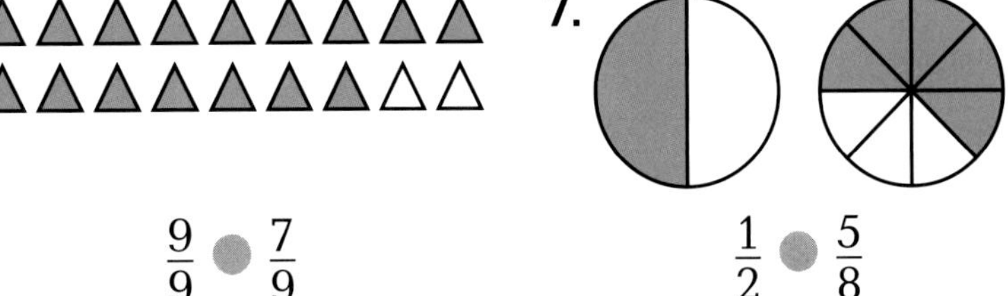

6. $\frac{9}{9}$ ● $\frac{7}{9}$

7. $\frac{1}{2}$ ● $\frac{5}{8}$

8. **TALK Math** **Explain** how to use a number line to compare $\frac{2}{8}$ and $\frac{6}{8}$.

Independent Practice and Problem Solving

Compare. Write <, >, or = for each ●.

9. 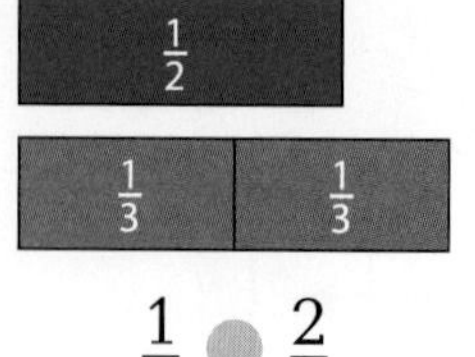

$\frac{1}{2}$ ● $\frac{2}{3}$

10. 

$\frac{3}{12}$ ● $\frac{2}{8}$

11. 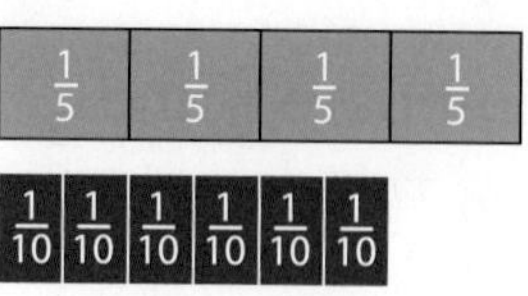

$\frac{4}{5}$ ● $\frac{6}{10}$

12. 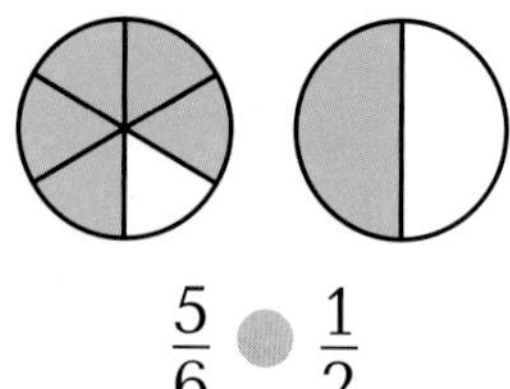

$\frac{5}{6}$ ● $\frac{1}{2}$

13. 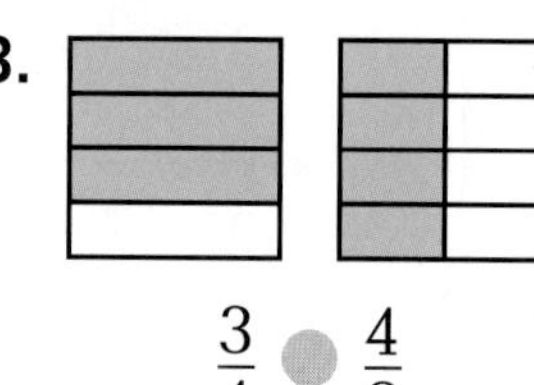

$\frac{3}{4}$ ● $\frac{4}{8}$

14. 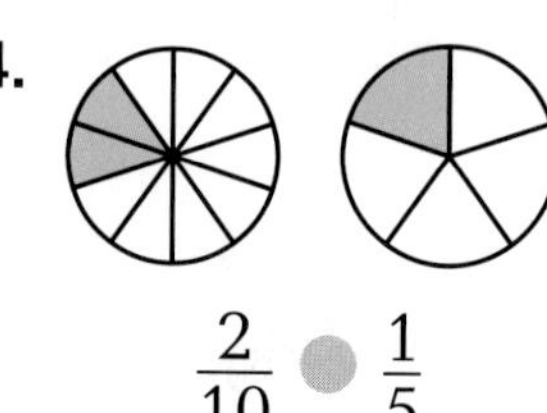

$\frac{2}{10}$ ● $\frac{1}{5}$

15. 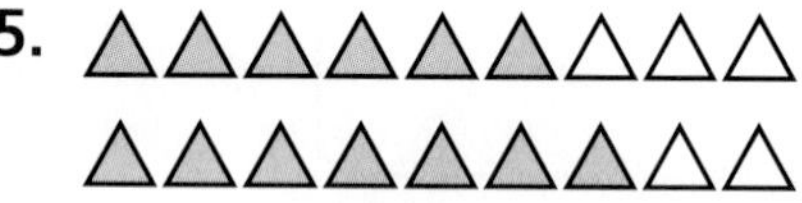

$\frac{6}{9}$ ● $\frac{7}{9}$

16. 
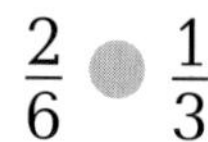

$\frac{2}{6}$ ● $\frac{1}{3}$

17. 

$\frac{3}{5}$ ● $\frac{2}{5}$

18. $\frac{0}{10}$ $\frac{1}{10}$ $\frac{2}{10}$ $\frac{3}{10}$ $\frac{4}{10}$ $\frac{5}{10}$ $\frac{6}{10}$ $\frac{7}{10}$ $\frac{8}{10}$ $\frac{9}{10}$ $\frac{10}{10}$

0 1

$\frac{9}{10}$ ● $\frac{7}{10}$

19. 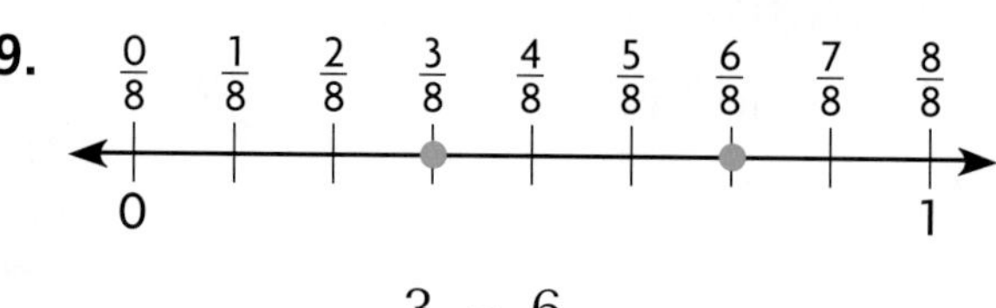

$\frac{3}{8}$ ● $\frac{6}{8}$

Use fraction bars, tiles, or number lines to compare.
Write <, >, or = for each ●.

20. 1 ● $\frac{3}{3}$

21. $\frac{5}{9}$ ● $\frac{10}{12}$

22. $\frac{1}{2}$ ● $\frac{3}{6}$

23. $\frac{1}{4}$ ● $\frac{1}{8}$

For 24–25, use the map.

24. Which pet store is closer to Becky's house, Pet Mart or Super Pet?

25. Becky walked her dog from her house to Super Pet and then from Super Pet to the dog park. Which distance is greater?

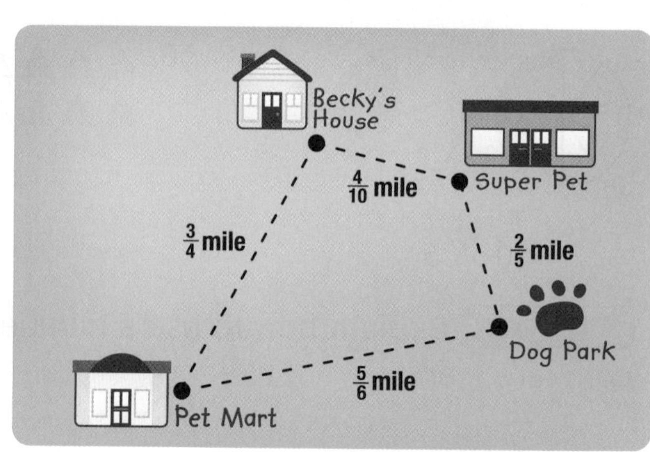

 Extra Practice on page 537, Set F

26. I am greater than $\frac{3}{6}$ and less than $\frac{4}{5}$. My denominator is 4. What fraction am I?

27. I am greater than $\frac{2}{8}$ and less than $\frac{1}{2}$. My denominator is 5. What fraction am I?

28. Jen found a recipe for dog biscuits. She needs $\frac{3}{4}$ cup water and $\frac{1}{2}$ cup powdered milk. Does she need more water or milk?

29. 

Explain how you can compare fractions that have the same denominators. Give an example.

Mixed Review and TAKS Prep

30. One jar of jelly costs \$3. Two jars cost \$6, and three jars cost \$9. What is the cost of 7 jars of jelly? (TEKS 3.6B, p. 184)

31. **TAKS Prep** Which fraction is greater than $\frac{5}{8}$? (Obj. 1)

A $\frac{1}{2}$ **B** $\frac{4}{10}$ **C** $\frac{3}{8}$ **D** $\frac{3}{4}$

32. Find the sum. $486 + 643 = \blacksquare$ (TEKS 3.3B, p. 66)

33. **TAKS Prep** Rick and Jerry are reading the same book. Rick has read $\frac{2}{3}$ of the book, and Jerry has read $\frac{6}{12}$ of the book. Who has read more of the book? (Obj. 1)

MATH POWER Problem Solving and Reasoning

NUMBER SENSE Bobby and Jill went to a pizza restaurant and ordered the pizzas shown. Bobby and Jill each ate $\frac{1}{2}$ of his or her pizza.

1. Did Bobby and Jill eat the same amount of pizza? Explain.
2. One slice of each pizza is $\frac{1}{8}$. Explain why Bobby's and Jill's slices aren't the same size.
3. Which pizza slices do you think cost less? Explain.
4. What if the pizzas were divided into thirds? Would Bobby's slices and Jill's slices be the same size?

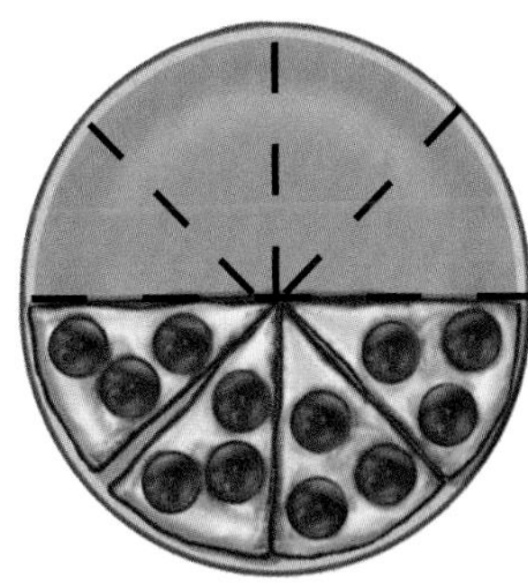

Bobby's pizza

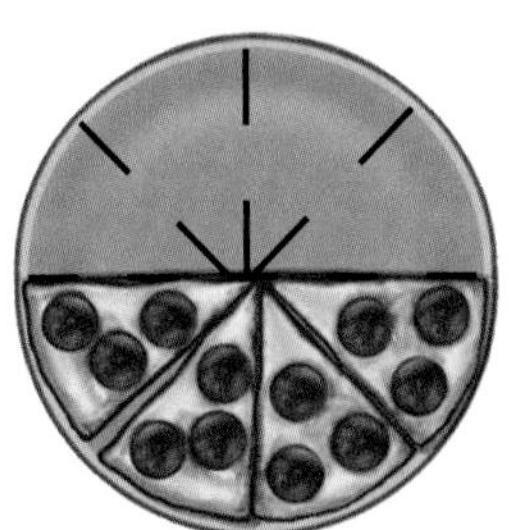

Jill's pizza

Problem Solving Workshop
Strategy: Compare Strategies

OBJECTIVE: Compare different strategies to solve problems.

Use the Strategy

PROBLEM Emma and her friends climbed a rock wall. Emma climbed $\frac{3}{4}$ of the wall, Elijah climbed $\frac{3}{6}$ of the wall, and Martin climbed $\frac{2}{3}$ of the wall. Who climbed the highest?

Read to Understand

- **Visualize the problem.**
- **What information is given?**

Plan

- **What strategy can you use to solve the problem?**

Sometimes you can use more than one strategy to solve a problem. You can *make a model* or *draw a picture* to solve this problem.

Solve

- **How can you use each strategy to solve the problem?**

Make a Model Use fraction bars to model the problem.

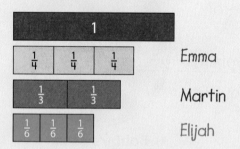

1		
$\frac{1}{4}$	$\frac{1}{4}$	$\frac{1}{4}$	Emma
$\frac{1}{3}$	$\frac{1}{3}$		Martin
$\frac{1}{6}$	$\frac{1}{6}$	$\frac{1}{6}$	Elijah

Compare the lengths.

Draw a Picture Draw and label number lines to model the problem.

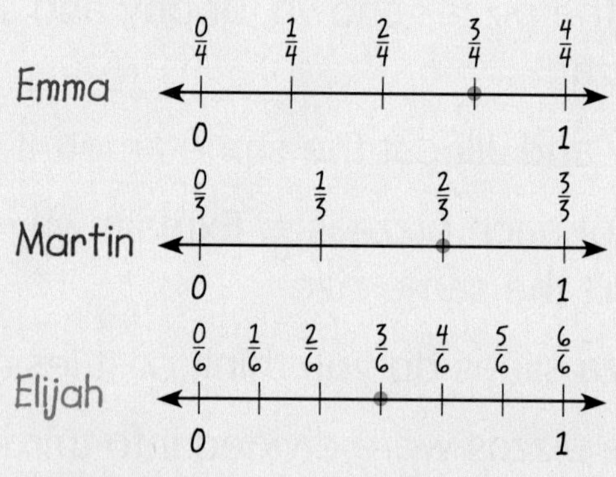

Compare the points.

$\frac{3}{4} > \frac{2}{3} > \frac{3}{6}$ So, Emma climbed the highest.

Check

- **How do you know the answer is correct?**

TEKS 3.14C select or develop an appropriate problem-solving plan or strategy, including drawing a picture, looking for a pattern, systematic guessing and checking, acting it out, making a table, working a simpler problem, or working backwards to solve a problem. *also* **3.2A, 3.2B, 3.2D, 3.14A, 3.14B, 3.14D, 3.15A, 3.15B, 3.16B**

Guided Problem Solving

1. Tracy and Kim ran on the track to see who could run farther without stopping. Tracy ran $\frac{4}{5}$ mile and Kim ran $\frac{8}{10}$ mile. Who ran farther?

   First, decide which strategy to use.

   Then, compare the fractions.

   Finally, find the greater fraction.

   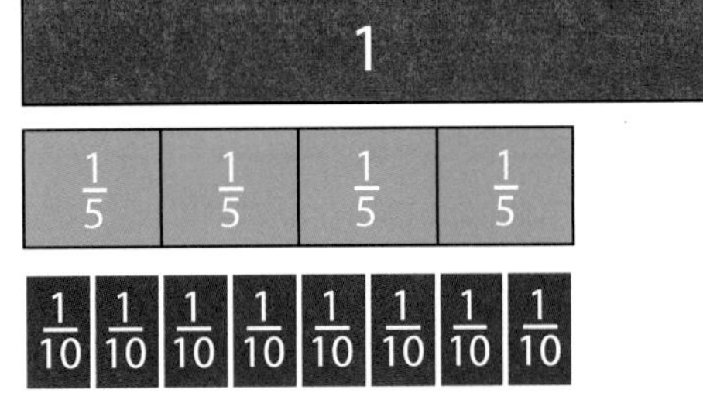

   $\frac{4}{5} \bullet \frac{8}{10}$

2. **What if** Cara ran on the track, too, and she ran $\frac{9}{10}$ mile? Who would have run the farthest?

3. Lewis made a wax candle at the carnival. He made $\frac{2}{8}$ of it blue, $\frac{1}{2}$ of it green, and $\frac{1}{4}$ of it yellow. Which color did he use the most?

Choose a STRATEGY

- Draw a Diagram or Picture
- Make a Model or Act It Out
- Make an Organized List
- Look for a Pattern
- Make a Table or Graph
- Guess and Check
- Work Backward
- Solve a Simpler Problem
- Write an Equation
- Use Logical Reasoning

Mixed Strategy Practice

USE DATA For 4–5, use the table.

4. For the Frisbee toss, players get 12 chances to toss Frisbees through a tire. Who threw the most Frisbees through the tire?

5. Who threw the fewest Frisbees through the tire? Write the fraction for that person in words.

6. Malia, Andy, and Jenna are in line for popcorn. Jenna is not first. Malia is last. In what position in line is Andy?

7. Joe and Mark did the balloon toss. Joe caught the balloon 3 more times than Mark. Together they caught the balloon 29 times. How many times did Mark catch the balloon?

8. WRITE Math Each team ran 1 lap in a relay race. Byron ran $\frac{1}{4}$ of a lap. Each person on his team ran the same distance. How many runners were on Byron's team? **Explain.**

Frisbee® Toss

Name of Player	Fraction Thrown Through Tire
Lisa	$\frac{4}{12}$
Suri	$\frac{5}{6}$
Patrick	$\frac{3}{4}$

Extra Practice

Set A Write a fraction in numbers and in words to name the shaded part. (pp. 514–517)

1. 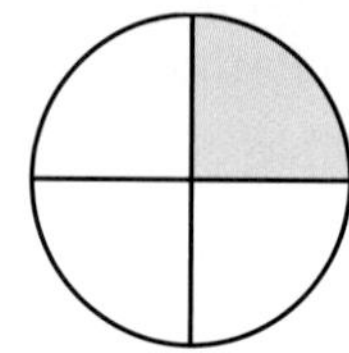

2. 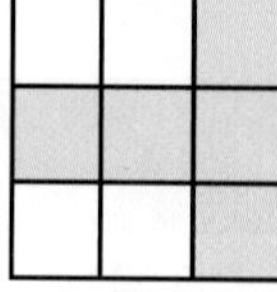

3. 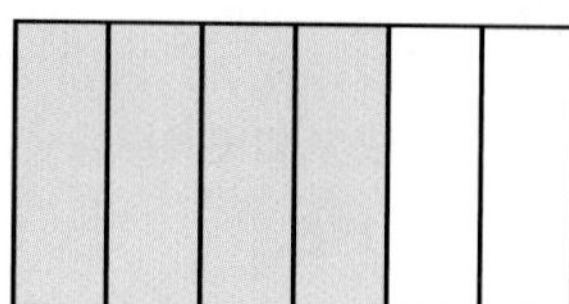

Write a fraction that names each point.

4. 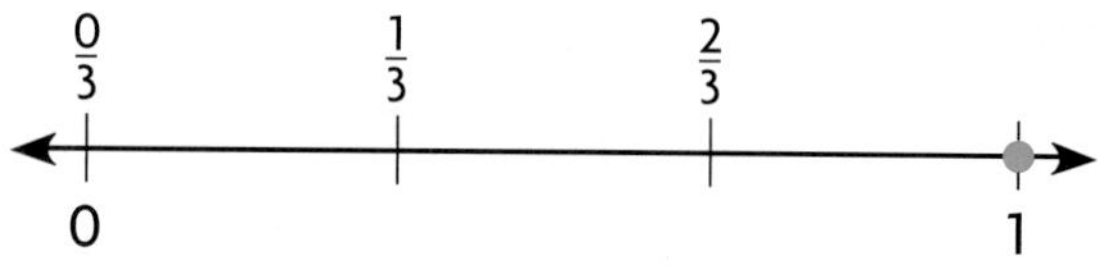

5. 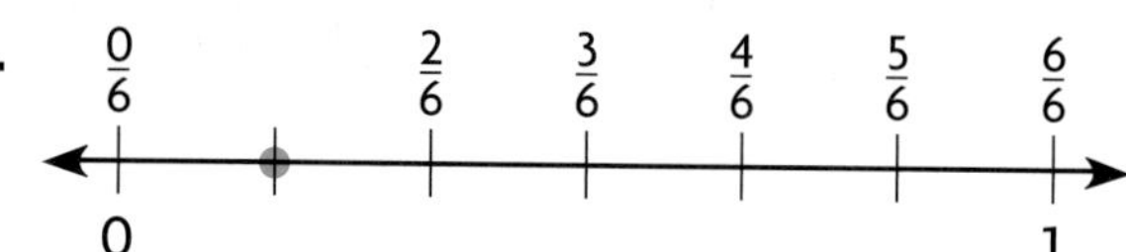

Set B Write a fraction that names the red part of each group. (pp. 518–521)

1. 

2. 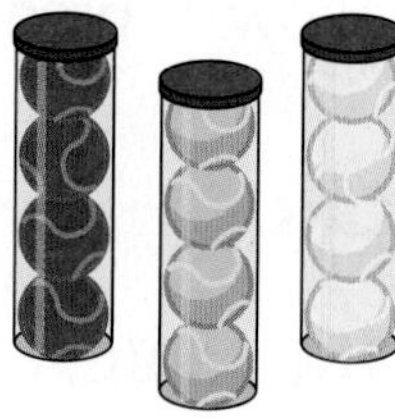

Draw each. Then write a fraction that names the shaded part.

3. Draw 4 squares.
   Shade 3 squares.

4. Draw 6 triangles.
   Make 3 groups.
   Shade 1 group.

5. Draw 10 circles.
   Shade 7 circles.

Set C Find an equivalent fraction. Use fraction bars. (pp. 522–525)

1.

1	
$\frac{1}{6}$	$\frac{1}{6}$

2. 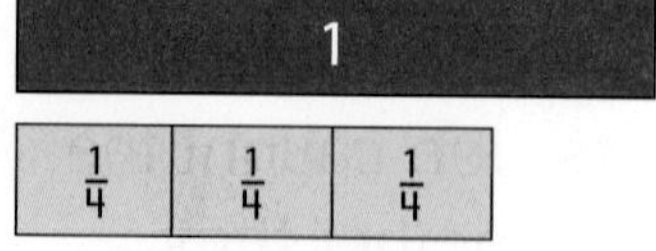

3. 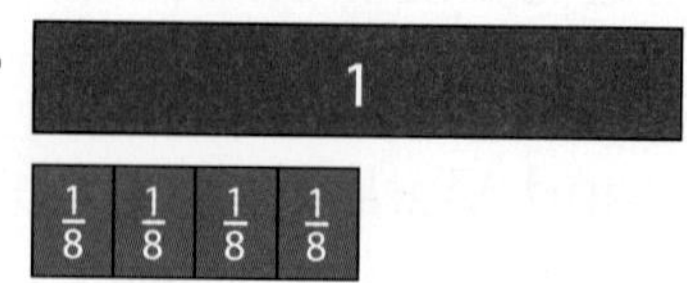

CD ROM **Technology**
Use Harcourt Mega Math, Fraction Action, *Fraction Flare Up*, Levels B–F.

Set D Write each fraction in simplest form. Use fraction bars or counters. (pp. 526–527)

1. $\frac{6}{10} = \frac{\blacksquare}{\blacksquare}$

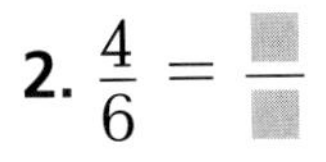

2. $\frac{4}{6} = \frac{\blacksquare}{\blacksquare}$

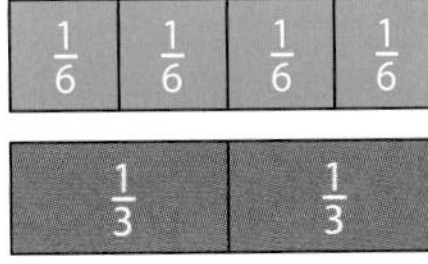

3. $\frac{4}{8} = \frac{\blacksquare}{\blacksquare}$

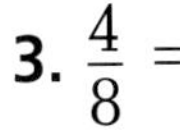

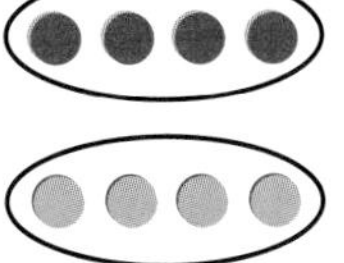

4. Maria ate 2 out of 12 cookies. What fraction of the cookies are left? Write the fraction in simplest form.

5. Patrick ate 4 out of 10 orange slices. What fraction of the slices did he eat? Write the fraction in simplest form.

Set E Write the missing fractions for each number line. (pp. 528–529)

1.

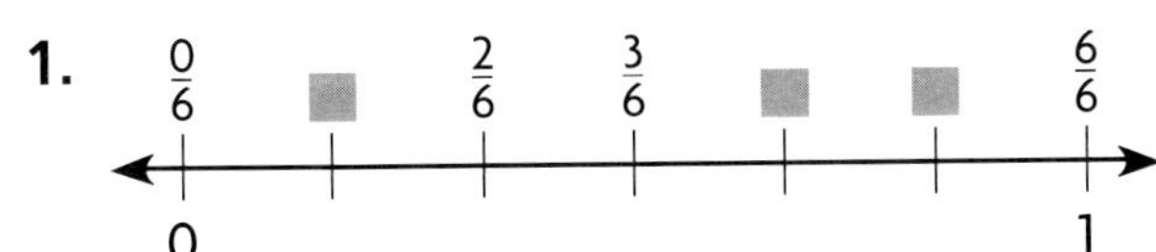

2.

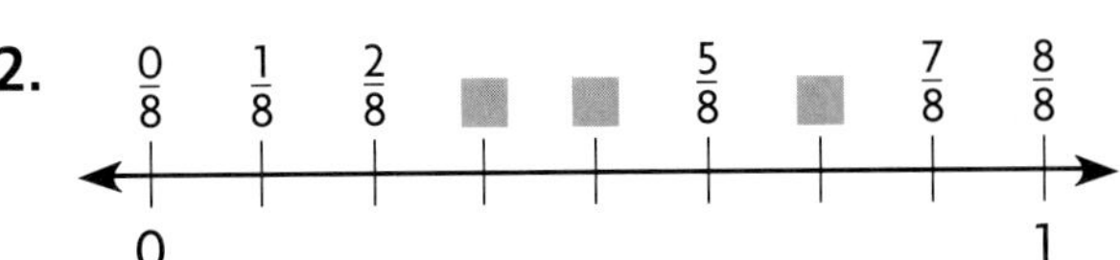

Tell which point represents each fraction.

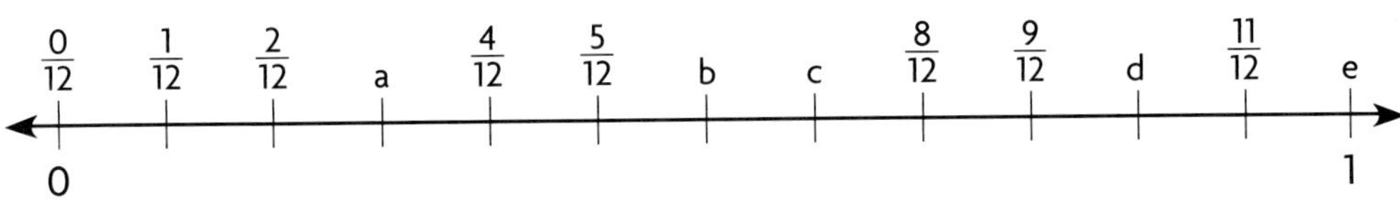

3. $\frac{7}{12}$

4. $\frac{6}{12}$

5. $\frac{1}{4}$

6. $\frac{5}{6}$

Set F Compare. Write <, >, or = for each ●. (pp. 530–533)

1.

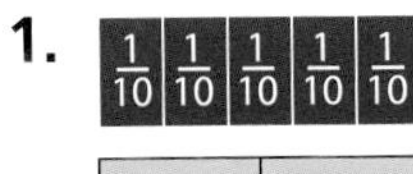

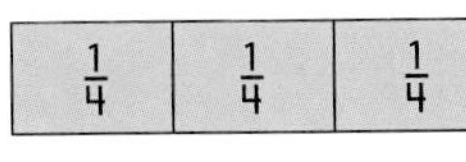

$\frac{5}{10}$ ● $\frac{3}{4}$

2.

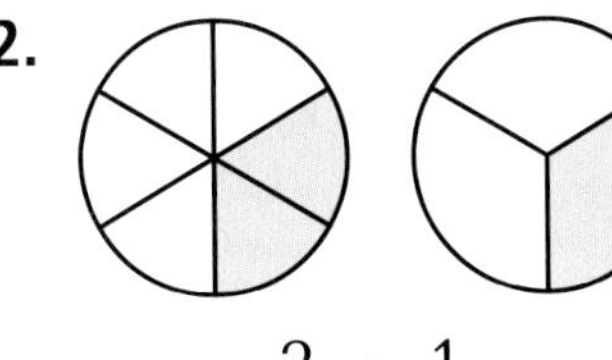

$\frac{2}{6}$ ● $\frac{1}{3}$

3.

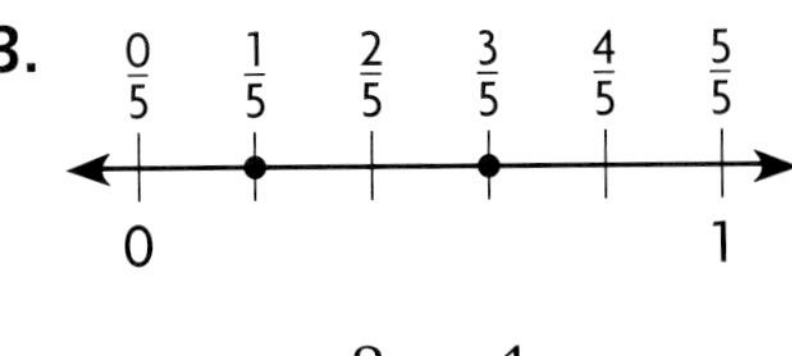

$\frac{3}{5}$ ● $\frac{1}{5}$

4. Car A and Car B have gas tanks that are the same size. Car A's tank is $\frac{3}{6}$ full. Car B's tank is $\frac{2}{3}$ full. Which car has more gasoline?

5. Keisha lives $\frac{6}{8}$ mile from school. Roberto lives $\frac{5}{10}$ mile from school. Who lives closer to school?

Chapter 22 Review/Test

Check Vocabulary and Concepts

Choose the best term from the box.

VOCABULARY
denominator
equivalent fractions
fraction
numerator

1. The _?_ tells how many parts are being counted. (TEKS 3.2C, p. 514)
2. Two or more fractions that name the same amount are called _?_. (TEKS 3.2D, p. 522)
3. The _?_ tells how many equal parts are in the whole or in the group. (TEKS 3.2C, p. 514)

Check Skills

Write a fraction in numbers and in words to name the blue part. (TEKS 3.2C, pp. 514–517, 518–521)

4. 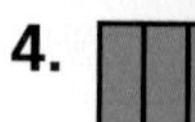 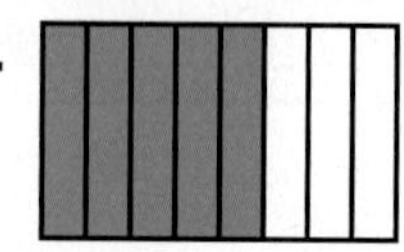

5. 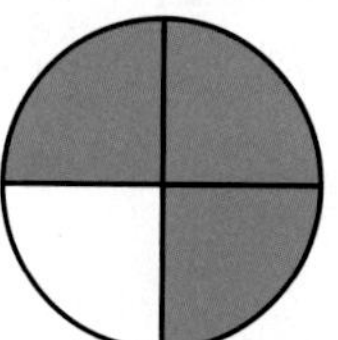

6. 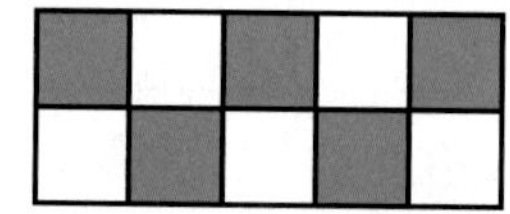

7.    

8.  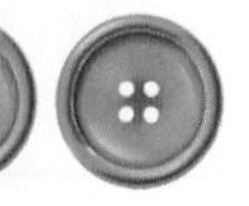    

Write each fraction in simplest form. (TEKS 3.2B, pp. 526–527)

9. $\frac{4}{10}$ 10. $\frac{3}{9}$ 11. $\frac{2}{4}$ 12. $\frac{9}{12}$ 13. $\frac{4}{6}$ 14. $\frac{6}{8}$

Compare. Write <, >, or = for each ●. (TEKS 3.2B, pp. 530–533)

15. $\frac{1}{2}$ ● $\frac{3}{4}$ 16. $\frac{2}{3}$ ● $\frac{4}{5}$ 17. $\frac{6}{10}$ ● $\frac{3}{5}$ 18. $\frac{6}{8}$ ● $\frac{6}{12}$

Check Problem Solving

Solve. (TEKS 3.2B, 3.14C, pp. 534–535)

19. Colby, Fred, and Jim ran for six minutes. Colby ran $\frac{4}{6}$ mile, Fred ran $\frac{8}{10}$ mile, and Jim ran $\frac{8}{12}$ mile. Who ran the farthest?

20. **WRITE Math** Amy ate $\frac{3}{8}$ of a pizza and Sue ate $\frac{2}{4}$ of it. Who ate more pizza? **Explain** how you know.

GO ONLINE **Technology** Use *Online Assessment.*

Enrich • Add Like Fractions

Going for a Walk

Ivan walked $\frac{1}{10}$ of a mile to his friend's house. Together, they walked $\frac{3}{10}$ of a mile to the store. How far did Ivan walk?

Step One

To find how far Ivan walked, add the fractions. Fractions that have the same denominator are called **like fractions**. Add like fractions by adding the numerators. The denominator stays the same.

Step 1 Add the numerators. Keep the denominator the same.	$\frac{1}{10} + \frac{3}{10} = \frac{4}{10}$
Step 2 Simplify the fraction by finding the largest fraction bars that are equivalent to $\frac{4}{10}$.	

So, Ivan walked $\frac{2}{5}$ of a mile.

Step Two

Find the sum. Write the answer in simplest form.

1. $\frac{5}{8} + \frac{1}{8}$ **2.** $\frac{2}{12} + \frac{4}{12}$ **3.** $\frac{3}{5} + \frac{1}{5}$ **4.** $\frac{2}{6} + \frac{2}{6}$

5. $\frac{3}{10} + \frac{5}{10}$ **6.** $\frac{1}{4} + \frac{2}{4}$ **7.** $\frac{4}{12} + \frac{3}{12}$ **8.** $\frac{1}{8} + \frac{1}{8}$

Step Three

WRITE Math Richie walked $\frac{2}{5}$ of a mile to school. He walked the same distance home. How long was Richie's walk to and from school? **Explain** how you found your answer.

Getting Ready for the TAKS

Chapters 1–22

Number, Operation, and Quantitative Reasoning (TAKS Obj. 1)

1. Which fraction names the shaded part?

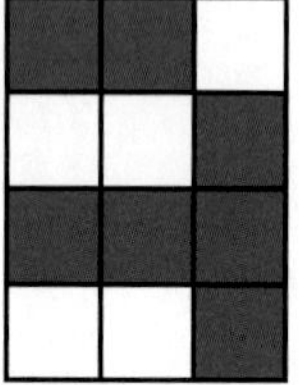

A $\frac{1}{7}$

B $\frac{5}{12}$

C $\frac{7}{12}$

D $\frac{7}{10}$

2. Charlie bought 6 packs of notepads. There were 10 notepads in each pack. How many notepads did Charlie buy?

F 4

G 16

H 54

J 60

3. WRITE Math What is $\frac{4}{6}$ written in simplest form? **Explain** your answer.

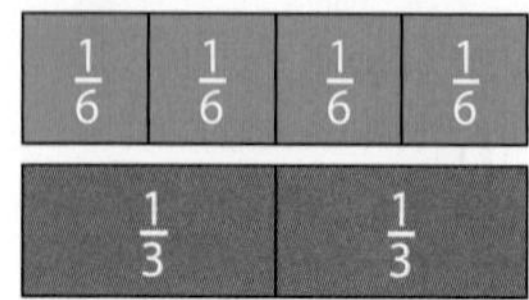

Patterns, Relationships, and Algebraic Thinking (TAKS Obj. 2)

4. Which number sentence is in the same fact family as $27 \div 9 = 3$?

A $9 \div 3 = 3$

B $3 \times 3 = 9$

C $3 \times 9 = 27$

D Not here

Check your work.

See item 5. To check your work, place your answer in the table. Then make sure your number continues the pattern in the table.

5. Which number will complete the table below?

Cars	5	6	7	8	9
Wheels	20	24	28	32	■

F 40

G 38

H 36

J 34

6. WRITE Math **Explain** how you can use a related multiplication fact to find $49 \div 7$.

Measurement (TAKS Obj. 4)

7. Which time is shown on the clock?

A 4:54

B 4:56

C 4:58

D 5:56

8. Which unit would you use to measure the amount of water in the bathtub?

F Cup

G Pint

H Quart

J Gallon

9. WRITE Math What is the area of this figure? **Explain** how you found your answer.

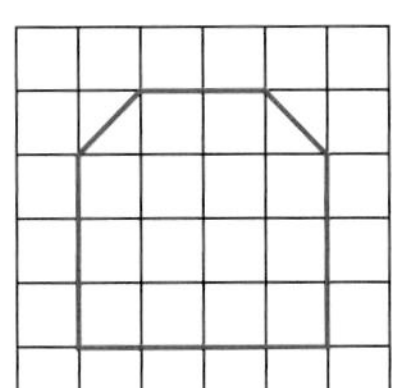

Probability and Statistics (TAKS Obj. 5)

10. How many more books did Julie read than Stephen?

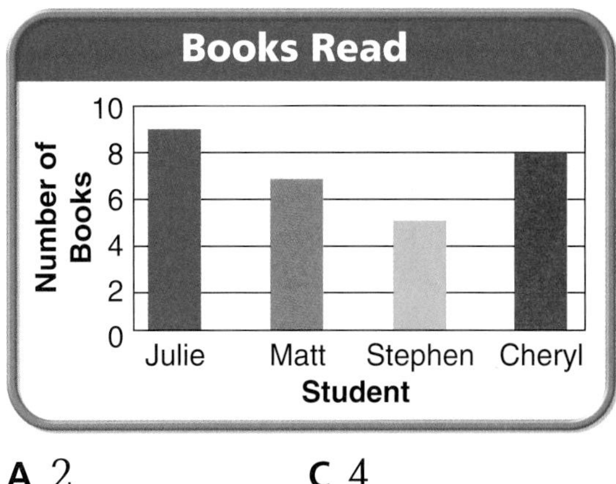

A 2

B 3

C 4

D 5

11. Kenny pulls a marble out of the bag without looking. Which color marble is he least likely to pull?

F Green

G Blue

H Red

J Yellow

12. WRITE Math Jennifer made a pictograph showing her classmates' favorite colors. The key for the graph is: Each [symbol] = 6 students. How many symbols should she use to show that 15 students chose red as their favorite color? **Explain**.

23 Multiply by 1 Digit

The Big Idea Multiplication of multi-digit whole numbers is based on place value and the basic multiplication facts.

Investigate

Cowboy boots come in many different styles. Choose a boot from the advertisement. Tell how much it would cost you to buy boots for yourself and three friends.

TEXAS FAST FACT

The largest cowboy boots ever made were by Nevena Christi in El Paso, Texas. The boots measured over $4\frac{1}{2}$ feet tall!

GO ONLINE **Technology** Student pages are available in the Student eBook.

Show What You Know

Check your understanding of important skills needed for success in Chapter 23.

▶ Regroup Ones as Tens

Find the sum.

1. $\begin{array}{r} 7 \\ +9 \\ \hline \end{array}$ **2.** $\begin{array}{r} 15 \\ +\ 8 \\ \hline \end{array}$ **3.** $\begin{array}{r} 19 \\ +34 \\ \hline \end{array}$ **4.** $\begin{array}{r} 36 \\ +27 \\ \hline \end{array}$

5. $\begin{array}{r} 23 \\ +17 \\ \hline \end{array}$ **6.** $\begin{array}{r} 29 \\ +11 \\ \hline \end{array}$ **7.** $\begin{array}{r} 35 \\ +37 \\ \hline \end{array}$ **8.** $\begin{array}{r} 52 \\ +68 \\ \hline \end{array}$

9. $78 + 65 = ■$ **10.** $47 + 39 = ■$ **11.** $56 + 5 = ■$ **12.** $33 + 8 = ■$

▶ Multiplication Facts through 10

Find the product.

13. $4 \times 5 = ■$ **14.** $3 \times 9 = ■$ **15.** $6 \times 6 = ■$ **16.** $8 \times 7 = ■$

17. $\begin{array}{r} 9 \\ \times 5 \\ \hline \end{array}$ **18.** $\begin{array}{r} 4 \\ \times 2 \\ \hline \end{array}$ **19.** $\begin{array}{r} 7 \\ \times 6 \\ \hline \end{array}$ **20.** $\begin{array}{r} 6 \\ \times 8 \\ \hline \end{array}$

21. $\begin{array}{r} 3 \\ \times 4 \\ \hline \end{array}$ **22.** $\begin{array}{r} 5 \\ \times 7 \\ \hline \end{array}$ **23.** $\begin{array}{r} 8 \\ \times 4 \\ \hline \end{array}$ **24.** $\begin{array}{r} 9 \\ \times 7 \\ \hline \end{array}$

VOCABULARY POWER

CHAPTER VOCABULARY

array
estimate
factor
product

WARM-UP WORDS

factor A number that is multiplied by another number to find a product

product The answer in a multiplication problem

estimate A number close to an exact amount

LESSON 1 HANDS ON

Arrays with Tens and Ones

OBJECTIVE: Model multiplication using arrays with base-ten blocks.

Quick Review

1. $5 \times 7 = \blacksquare$
2. $8 \times 3 = \blacksquare$
3. $\blacksquare = 4 \times 4$
4. $10 \times 9 = \blacksquare$
5. $\blacksquare = 2 \times 6$

Molly has a bookcase with 3 shelves. There are 14 books on each shelf. How many books are there in all?

Multiply. 3×14

Investigate

Materials ■ base-ten blocks

A Use base-ten blocks to model 3×14.

- There are 2 parts to the array. How can you describe each part?

B Multiply each part of the array. Multiply the tens and record that product. Then, multiply the ones and record that product.

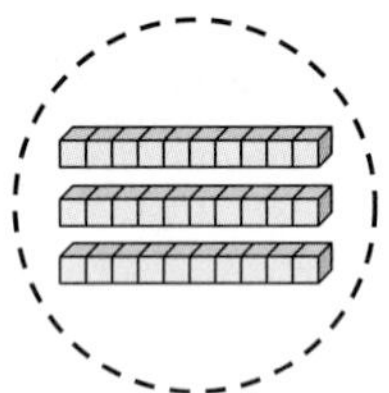

$3 \times 10 = 30$

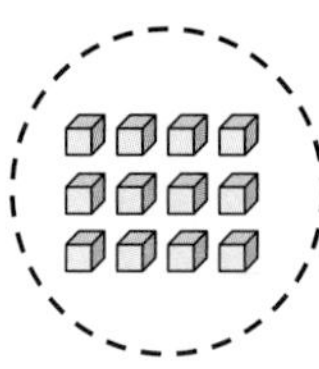

$3 \times 4 = 12$

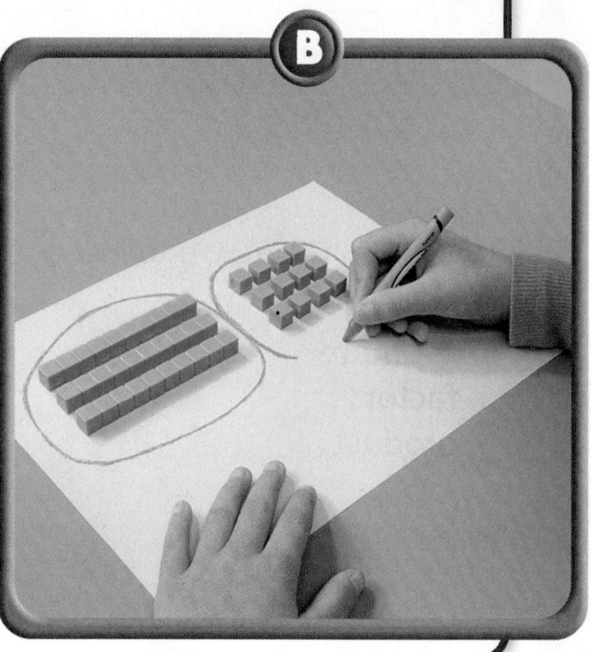

C Find the sum of the products.

D Now use base-ten blocks to model 2×16. Multiply the tens and ones. Find the product.

Draw Conclusions

1. Describe the array you made to model 2×16.
2. How would you change the 2×16 array to model 2×26?
3. **Comprehension** One way to model 18 is 1 ten 8 ones. How can knowing this help you find 4×18?

TEKS 3.4B Solve and record multiplication problems (up to two digits times one digit). *also* 3.6B, 3.14A, 3.14D, 3.15A, 3.15B

Connect

You can draw arrays on grid paper to model multiplication.

Draw an array to model 3×14.

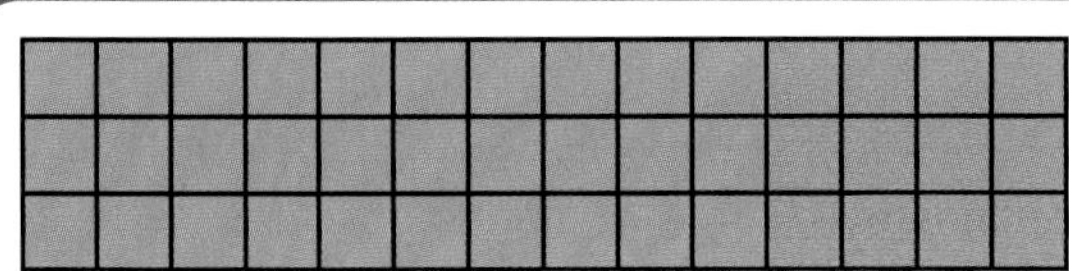

3 rows of 10	3 rows of 4
Multiply the tens.	Multiply the ones.
$3 \times 10 = 30$	$3 \times 4 = 12$

Add. $30 + 12 = 42$

So, $3 \times 14 = 42$.

TALK Math

Explain how to use an array to find 4×17.

Practice

Find the product. Show your multiplication and addition.

1. $3 \times 16 = ■$

2. $5 \times 13 = ■$

3. $4 \times 22 = ■$

4.

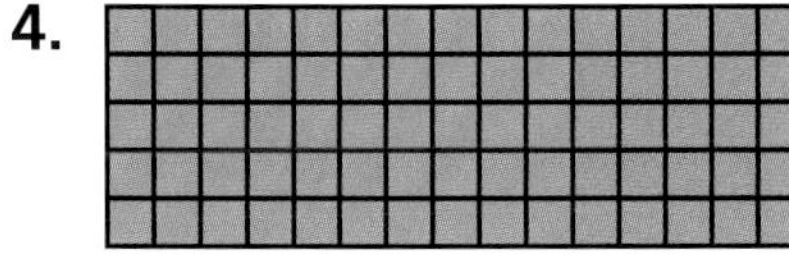

$5 \times 15 = ■$

5.

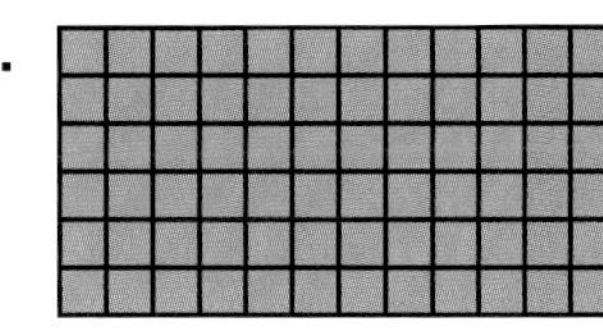

$6 \times 12 = ■$

✓6.

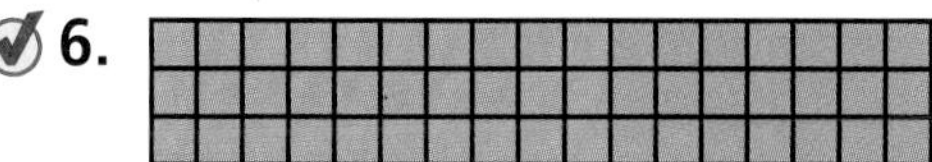

$3 \times 17 = ■$

Use base-ten blocks or grid paper to find each product.

7. $4 \times 25 = ■$ **8.** $3 \times 18 = ■$ **9.** $5 \times 21 = ■$ **✓10.** $4 \times 34 = ■$

11. **Reasoning** The product of two numbers is 48. The sum of the two numbers is 16. What are the two numbers?

12. **WRITE Math** **Explain** how to use base-ten blocks to find the product 5×19.

Model 2-Digit Multiplication

OBJECTIVE: Model 2-digit multiplication with base-ten blocks using place value (partial products) and regrouping.

Quick Review

1. $5 \times 20 =$ ■
2. $7 \times 10 =$ ■
3. $9 \times 60 =$ ■
4. $8 \times 30 =$ ■
5. $3 \times 40 =$ ■

Learn

PROBLEM Sam has 3 boxes of crayons. Each box holds 24 crayons. How many crayons does Sam have in all?

You can model the problem using base-ten blocks. Multiply. 3×24

ONE WAY **Use place value.**

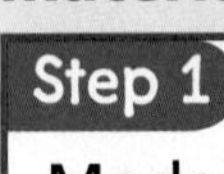

Activity 1

Materials ■ base-ten blocks

Step 1
Model 3 groups of 24. Multiply the ones.

	T	O	
	2	4	
×		3	
	1	2	(3 × 4 ones)

Step 2
Multiply the tens.

	T	O	
	2	4	
×		3	
	1	2	(3 × 4 ones)
	6	0	(3 × 2 tens)

Step 3
Add to find the product.

	T	O
	2	4
×		3
	1	2
+	6	0
	7	2

So, Sam has 72 crayons in all.

More Examples

A
```
    17
  ×  4
    28 (4 × 7 ones)
  + 40 (4 × 1 ten)
    68
```

B
```
     39
   ×  5
     45 (5 × 9 ones)
  + 150 (5 × 3 tens)
    195
```

C
```
     61
   ×  7
      7 (7 × 1 one)
  + 420 (7 × 6 tens)
    427
```

• Why is 4×1 ten recorded as 40 and not 4?

TEKS 3.4B Solve and record multiplication problems (up to two digits times one digit). *also* 3.14A, 3.14D, 3.15A, 3.15B

ANOTHER WAY **Use regrouping.**

Activity 2

Materials: base-ten blocks

Step 1

Use base-ten blocks to model 3 groups of 24.

Step 2

Multiply the ones. $3 \times 4 = 12$ ones
Regroup 12 ones as 1 ten 2 ones.

	T	O
	1	
	2	4
×		3
		2

Step 3

Multiply the tens. 3×2 tens $= 6$ tens.
Add the regrouped ten. 6 tens + 1 ten = 7 tens.

	T	O
	1	
	2	4
×		3
	7	2

More Examples

A
$$\begin{array}{r} {}^{1}\\ 32 \\ \times\ 7 \\ \hline 224 \end{array}$$

B
$$\begin{array}{r} {}^{3}\\ 47 \\ \times\ 5 \\ \hline 235 \end{array}$$

C
$$\begin{array}{r} {}^{2}\\ 58 \\ \times\ 3 \\ \hline 174 \end{array}$$

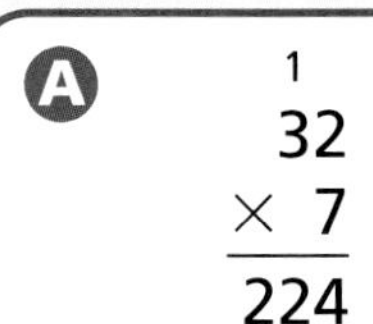

Guided Practice

1. What is 2×30?

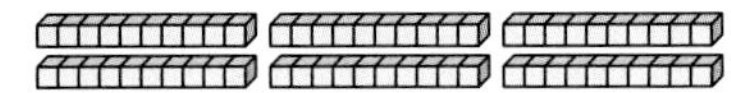

Find the product. Use place value or regrouping.

2. $\begin{array}{r} 16 \\ \times\ 4 \\ \hline \end{array}$

✓3. $\begin{array}{r} 27 \\ \times\ 3 \\ \hline \end{array}$

✓4. $\begin{array}{r} 39 \\ \times\ 2 \\ \hline \end{array}$

5. **TALK Math** Find 3×45 using both place value and regrouping. Tell how the methods are alike and different.

Independent Practice and Problem Solving

Find the product. Use place value or regrouping.

6. $\begin{array}{r} 25 \\ \times\ 3 \\ \hline \end{array}$

7. $\begin{array}{r} 17 \\ \times\ 4 \\ \hline \end{array}$

8. $\begin{array}{r} 32 \\ \times\ 2 \\ \hline \end{array}$

Multiply. You may wish to use base-ten blocks to help you.

9. $\begin{array}{r} 23 \\ \times\ 6 \\ \hline \end{array}$

10. $\begin{array}{r} 39 \\ \times\ 2 \\ \hline \end{array}$

11. $\begin{array}{r} 45 \\ \times\ 3 \\ \hline \end{array}$

12. $\begin{array}{r} 26 \\ \times\ 4 \\ \hline \end{array}$

13. $\begin{array}{r} 31 \\ \times\ 4 \\ \hline \end{array}$

14. $\begin{array}{r} 16 \\ \times\ 5 \\ \hline \end{array}$

15. $\begin{array}{r} 41 \\ \times\ 3 \\ \hline \end{array}$

16. $\begin{array}{r} 18 \\ \times\ 3 \\ \hline \end{array}$

17. $\begin{array}{r} 52 \\ \times\ 5 \\ \hline \end{array}$

18. $\begin{array}{r} 17 \\ \times\ 3 \\ \hline \end{array}$

19. $\begin{array}{r} 14 \\ \times\ 8 \\ \hline \end{array}$

20. $\begin{array}{r} 21 \\ \times\ 5 \\ \hline \end{array}$

Algebra Use base-ten blocks to find the missing factor.

21. $3 \times \blacksquare = 93$

22. $\blacksquare \times 13 = 52$

23. $\blacksquare \times 24 = 72$

24. $5 \times \blacksquare = 80$

USE DATA For 25–26, use the bar graph.

25. The bar graph shows the supplies in the art room. There are 16 pencils in each box. How many pencils are in all of the boxes?

26. **Reasoning** There are 20 tubes of paint in each box. If each tube of paint costs $4, how much did the paint cost altogether?

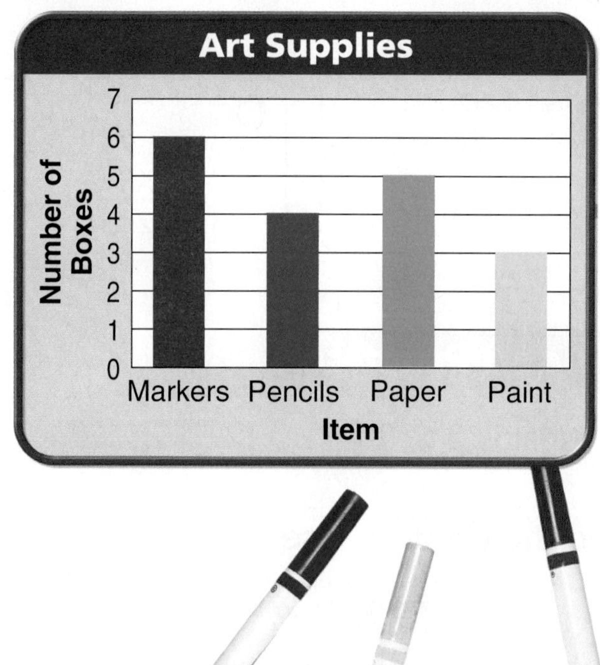

27. **FAST FACT** The first box of crayons was sold in 1903 and had the same 8 colors that are in an 8-count box today. If Holly has 13 of these boxes, how many crayons does she have?

28. **WRITE Math** **Sense or Nonsense** Kate multiplied a two-digit number by a one-digit number. She says the product is a four-digit number. Does this make sense? **Explain.**

 Extra Practice on page 558, Set A

Mixed Review and TAKS Prep

29. Draw an array to model 3×14. Then find the product. (TEKS 3.4B, p. 544)

30. Write the largest 3-digit number possible using the digits 2, 1, and 9 once each. (TEKS 3.1A, p. 10)

31. **TAKS Prep** Freddy's cat sleeps 13 hours a day. How many hours does his cat sleep in a week? (Hint: 1 week = 7 days) (Obj. 1)

32. **TAKS Prep** A third grade class went on a field trip to the science center. There were 26 students in each of 3 groups. How many students went on the field trip? (Obj. 1)

A 29 students

B 68 students

C 78 students

D 84 students

Problem Solving and Reasoning

Lattice multiplication uses basic multiplication facts and a grid to find a product.

Find 8×64.

A Draw 1 row of 2 squares with a diagonal line in each square. Then write the factors as shown

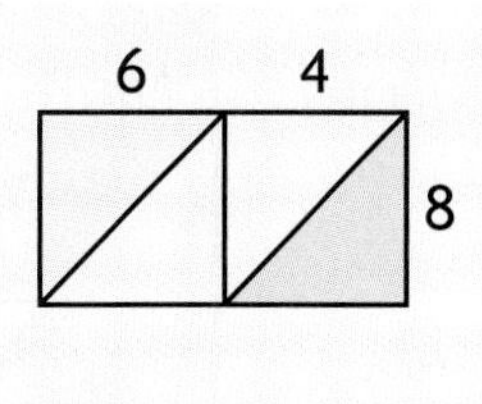

B Multiply each pair of digits.

$8 \times 4 = 32$
$8 \times 6 = 48$

Write each product as shown.

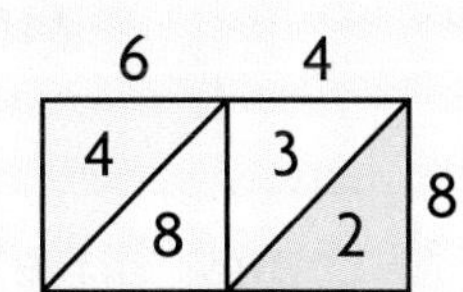

C Start at the right. Add the digits in each diagonal. Regroup if needed.

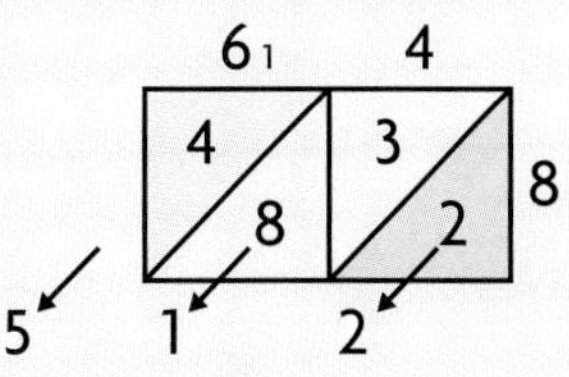

So, $8 \times 64 = 512$.

Use lattice multiplication to find each product.

1. $9 \times 72 =$ ▇ **2.** $7 \times 38 =$ ▇ **3.** $8 \times 47 =$ ▇ **4.** $6 \times 53 =$ ▇

Multiply 2-Digit Numbers

OBJECTIVE: Multiply 2-digit numbers using an algorithm.

Quick Review

1. 9×8
2. 3×12
3. 7×5
4. 2×6
5. 4×10

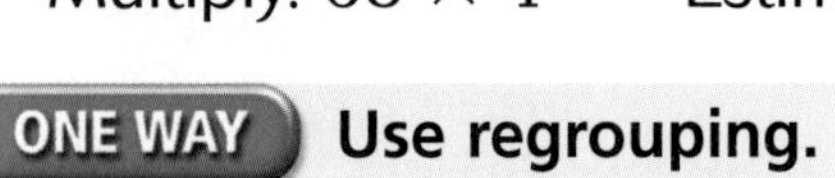

PROBLEM The cafeteria has 68 tables. Each table has 4 chairs. How many chairs are in the cafeteria?

Multiply. 68×4 Estimate. $70 \times 4 = 280$

ONE WAY Use regrouping.

Step 1

Multiply the ones.
4×8 ones = 32 ones
Regroup 32 ones as 3 tens 2 ones.

$$\begin{array}{r} {}^{3} \\ 68 \\ \times\ 4 \\ \hline 2 \end{array}$$

Step 2

Multiply the tens.
4×6 tens = 24 tens
24 tens + 3 tens = 27 tens
Regroup 27 tens as 2 hundreds 7 tens.

$$\begin{array}{r} {}^{3} \\ 68 \\ \times\ 4 \\ \hline 272 \end{array}$$

ANOTHER WAY Use place value.

Step 1

Multiply the ones. Record.

$$\begin{array}{r} 68 \\ \times\ 4 \\ \hline 32 \end{array} \quad (4 \times 8 = 32)$$

Step 2

Multiply the tens. Record.

$$\begin{array}{r} 68 \\ \times\ 4 \\ \hline 32 \\ 240 \end{array} \quad (4 \times 60 = 240)$$

Step 3

Add the products.

$$\begin{array}{r} 68 \\ \times\ 4 \\ \hline 32 \\ +240 \\ \hline 272 \end{array}$$

So, the cafeteria has 272 chairs. Since 272 is close to the estimate, 280, the answer is reasonable.

Guided Practice

1. What is 5×4 tens?

Find each product.

2. $\begin{array}{r} 52 \\ \times\ 6 \\ \hline \end{array}$
3. $\begin{array}{r} 32 \\ \times\ 3 \\ \hline \end{array}$
4. $\begin{array}{r} 71 \\ \times\ 8 \\ \hline \end{array}$
5. $\begin{array}{r} 28 \\ \times\ 3 \\ \hline \end{array}$

6. **TALK Math** **Explain** how to find 7×54.

TEKS 3.4B solve and record multiplication problems (up to two digits times one digit). *also* **3.14A, 3.15A, 3.15B, 3.16B**

Independent Practice and Problem Solving

Find each product.

7. 24×3 8. 76×8 9. 45×6 10. 19×5 11. 37×4

12. 37×9 13. 93×3 14. 31×7 15. 82×4 16. 63×7

17. 98×5 18. 56×7 19. 9×44 20. 3×76

Algebra Find the missing factor.

21. $12 \times ■ = 36$ 22. $■ \times 4 = 44$ 23. $16 \times ■ = 64$ 24. $■ \times 3 = 63$

USE DATA For 25–26, use the bar graph.

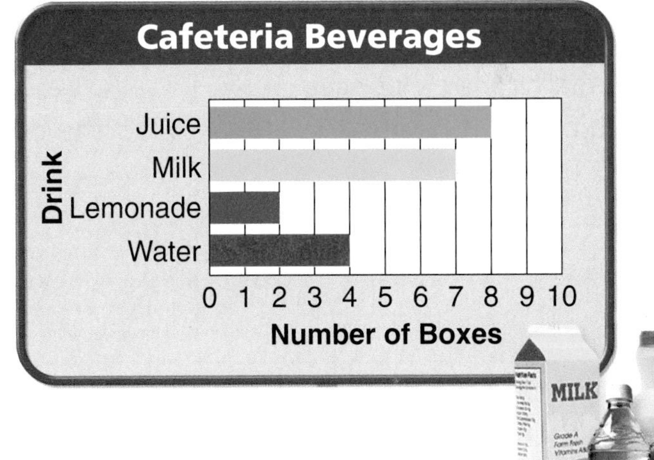

25. A box holds 48 cartons of milk. How many cartons of milk does the cafeteria have in all?

26. **Reasoning** If a box holds 32 bottles of juice and 64 bottles of water, does the cafeteria have more bottles of juice or water? **Explain**.

27. The cafeteria sold 58 bottles of lemonade. If one box holds 36 bottles, how many bottles of lemonade are left?

28. **WRITE Math** **What's the Question?** There are 24 bags of pretzels in each box. The answer is 72 bags.

Mixed Review and TAKS Prep

29. What is the next number in this pattern? 6, 11, 16, 21, ■ (TEKS 3.6A, p. 182)

30. Nina uses 14 inches of ribbon to make a bow. How much ribbon will she need to make 3 bows? (TEKS 3.4B, p. 546)

31. **TAKS Prep** Jamie rented three movies. Each movie is 97 minutes long. How long will it take Jamie to watch all three movies? (Obj. 1)

A 237 minutes **C** 291 minutes

B 271 minutes **D** 480 minutes

Technology
CD ROM Use Harcourt Mega Math, The Number Games, *Up, Up, and Array,* Level K.

Extra Practice on page 558, Set B

Practice 2-Digit Multiplication

OBJECTIVE: Multiply 2-digit by 1-digit numbers with and without regrouping.

Quick Review

1. 6×13 **2.** 7×18
3. 2×24 **4.** 5×15
5. 6×12

Learn

PROBLEM Max loves horseback riding. If he rides his horse 6 hours each week, how many hours a year does he spend horseback riding? (Hint: 1 year = 52 weeks)

Multiply. 52×6 Estimate. $50 \times 6 = 300$

ONE WAY **Use regrouping.**

Step 1	Step 2
Multiply the ones. 6 × 2 ones = 12 ones Regroup if necessary. 12 ones = 1 ten 2 ones $\begin{array}{r} ^{1} \\ 52 \\ \times\ 6 \\ \hline 2 \end{array}$	Multiply the tens. 6 × 5 tens = 30 tens Add the regrouped tens. 30 tens + 1 ten = 31 tens $\begin{array}{r} ^{1} \\ 52 \\ \times\ 6 \\ \hline 312 \end{array}$

Math Idea
There is more than one way to solve a multiplication problem. Choose the method that is easiest for you.

ANOTHER WAY **Use place value.**

Step 1	Step 2	Step 3
Multiply the ones. Record. $\begin{array}{r} 52 \\ \times\ 6 \\ \hline 12 \end{array}$	Multiply the tens. Record. $\begin{array}{r} 52 \\ \times\ 6 \\ \hline 12 \\ 300 \end{array}$	Add the products. $\begin{array}{r} 52 \\ \times\ 6 \\ \hline 12 \\ +300 \\ \hline 312 \end{array}$

So, Max spends 312 hours a year horseback riding. Since 312 is close to the estimate, 300, the answer is reasonable.

More Examples

A
$$\begin{array}{r} 21 \\ \times\ 4 \\ \hline 84 \end{array}$$

B
$$\begin{array}{r} ^{4} \\ 48 \\ \times\ 5 \\ \hline 240 \end{array}$$

C
$$\begin{array}{r} 72 \\ \times\ 3 \\ \hline 6 \\ +210 \\ \hline 216 \end{array}$$

TEKS 3.4B solve and record multiplication problems (up to two digits times one digit). *also* **3.14A, 3.15A, 3.15B, 3.16B**

Guided Practice

1. What is another way to write 64 ones?

Find the product. Use regrouping or place value.

2. $\begin{array}{r} 32 \\ \times\ 3 \\ \hline \end{array}$

3. $\begin{array}{r} 19 \\ \times\ 6 \\ \hline \end{array}$

4. $\begin{array}{r} 45 \\ \times\ 4 \\ \hline \end{array}$

✓5. $\begin{array}{r} 24 \\ \times\ 5 \\ \hline \end{array}$

✓6. $\begin{array}{r} 73 \\ \times\ 8 \\ \hline \end{array}$

7. TALK Math **Explain** how you know when to regroup.

Independent Practice and Problem Solving

Find the product. Use regrouping or place value.

8. $\begin{array}{r} 18 \\ \times\ 7 \\ \hline \end{array}$

9. $\begin{array}{r} 46 \\ \times\ 3 \\ \hline \end{array}$

10. $\begin{array}{r} 27 \\ \times\ 2 \\ \hline \end{array}$

11. $\begin{array}{r} 51 \\ \times\ 3 \\ \hline \end{array}$

12. $\begin{array}{r} 36 \\ \times\ 4 \\ \hline \end{array}$

13. $\begin{array}{r} 34 \\ \times\ 2 \\ \hline \end{array}$

14. $\begin{array}{r} 87 \\ \times\ 5 \\ \hline \end{array}$

15. $\begin{array}{r} 62 \\ \times\ 9 \\ \hline \end{array}$

16. $\begin{array}{r} 72 \\ \times\ 3 \\ \hline \end{array}$

17. $\begin{array}{r} 91 \\ \times\ 5 \\ \hline \end{array}$

18. 59×4
19. 93×5
20. 6×29
21. 2×88
22. 38×5
23. 9×17
24. 3×31
25. 67×8

USE DATA For 26–28, use the pictures.

26. Max's family went to see the rodeo. How much did the family spend on 5 tickets?

27. What is the cost for 27 children to go to the fair if each child also rides a pony?

28. WRITE Math **What's the Error?** Molly says Mr. Trapp will spend $215 on 7 rodeo tickets. Describe her error.

Mixed Review and TAKS Prep

29. What time is shown on the clock?
(TEKS 3.12B, p. 136)

30. Jen has 3 sheets of stickers. There are 40 stickers on each sheet. How many stickers does Jen have?
(TEKS 3.4B, p. 550)

31. **TAKS Prep** A 75-page photo album holds 6 photos on each page. How many photos can fit in the album?
(Obj. 1)

A 420 photos
B 432 photos
C 450 photos
D 720 photos

Extra Practice on page 558, Set C

Problem Solving Workshop
Strategy: Solve a Simpler Problem

OBJECTIVE: Solve problems by using the strategy *solve a simpler problem*.

Learn the Strategy

You can use a simpler problem to help you solve more complex problems. You can either break the problem into simpler parts or you can use estimation to help you solve the problem.

Break into Simpler Parts

Kendra uses beads to make necklaces. The beads come in packages of 75. If Kendra buys 6 packages, how many beads will she have?

Break apart 75 into numbers that are easier to multiply.

Rewrite 75 as 70 + 5.

Multiply each addend by 6.

Add the products.

$$\begin{array}{r} 75 \\ \times\ 6 \\ \hline \end{array} = \begin{array}{r} 70 + 5 \\ \times \quad\quad 6 \\ \hline 30 \leftarrow 6 \times 5 \\ 420 \leftarrow 6 \times 70 \\ \hline 450 \end{array}$$

So, Kendra will have 450 beads.

Use Estimation

Apples cost $0.99 a pound. Grapes cost $0.89 a pound. Pam bought 4 pounds of apples and 3 pounds of grapes. Did she spend more or less than $5 in all?

$0.99 × 4 → $1 × 4 = $4
$0.89 × 3 → $1 × 3 = $3
$4 + $3 = $7
Pam spent about $7.

So, Pam spent more than $5 in all.

TALK Math

Explain how rounding to the nearest dollar makes the second problem simpler to solve.

TEKS 3.14C select or develop an appropriate problem-solving strategy including drawing a picture, looking for a pattern, systematic guessing and checking, acting it out, making a table, working a simpler problem, or working backwards to solve a problem. *also* **3.14A, 3.15A, 3.15B**

Use the Strategy

PROBLEM The students at Lincoln Elementary School are collecting food for the local food pantry. There are 87 third-grade students in the school. Each student brings in 4 cans of food. How many cans do the students collect altogether?

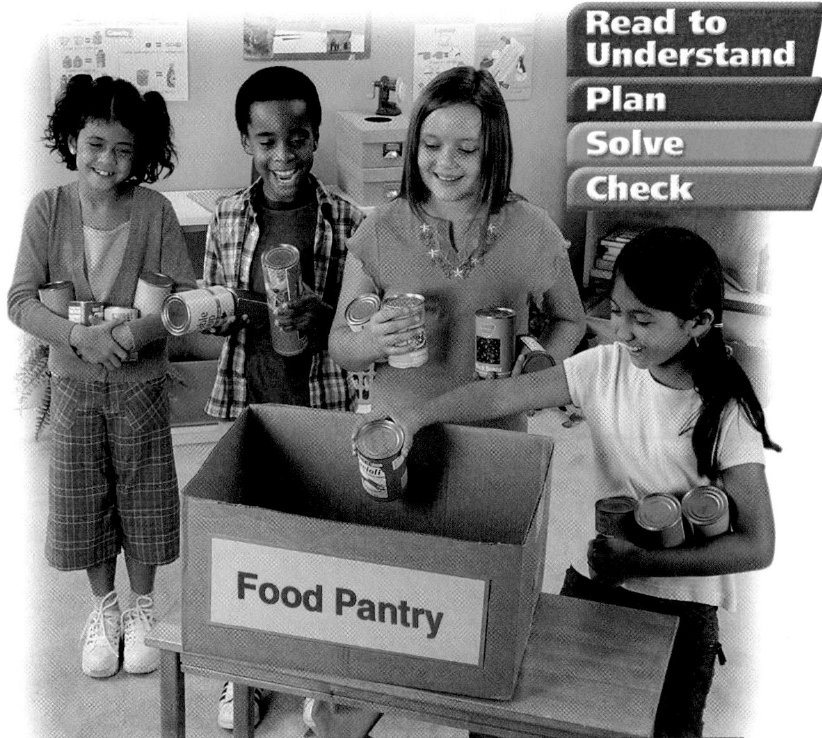

Read to Understand

- **Summarize the problem.**
- **What information is given?**

Plan

- **What strategy can you use to solve the problem?**
  You can solve a simpler problem.

Solve

- **How can you use the strategy to solve the problem?**
  You can find 87×4 by breaking apart 87 into numbers that are easier to multiply.

Rewrite 87 as 80 + 7.

$$\begin{array}{r} 87 \\ \times\ 4 \\ \hline \end{array} = \begin{array}{r} 80 + 7 \\ \times \quad\ \ 4 \\ \hline \end{array}$$

Multiply each addend by 4.

$$\begin{array}{rl} 28 & \leftarrow 4 \times 7 \\ 320 & \leftarrow 4 \times 80 \\ \hline 348 & \end{array}$$

Add the products.

So, the third-grade students collect 348 cans altogether.

Check

- **Look back at the problem. Does the answer make sense for the problem? Explain.**

Guided Problem Solving

1. Ms. Reynolds volunteers at the food pantry. She organizes the donated food items. She puts the canned food on 6 shelves. Each shelf can hold 58 cans of food. How many cans can fit on the 6 shelves?

   First, write a simpler problem.

   Then, multiply.

   $$\begin{array}{r} 58 \\ \times\ 6 \\ \hline \end{array} = \begin{array}{r} 50 + 8 \\ \times \qquad 6 \\ \hline \end{array}$$

   Finally, add the products to find the total number of cans.

2. **What if** there are 8 shelves and each shelf holds 96 cans of food? Describe how you would use a simpler problem to find the total number of cans on the shelves.

3. The recycling center collected 67 bags of aluminum cans in June and 92 bags of aluminum cans in July. If each bag weighed about 3 pounds, how many pounds of aluminum cans did the center collect in the two months?

Problem Solving Strategy Practice

Use a simpler problem to solve.

4. The science club is collecting glass bottles to raise money for a trip to the planetarium. The students get 5 cents for each bottle they collect. So far the club has collected 96 bottles. How much money, in cents, did the club get for the bottles?

5. **Reasoning** The outdoor club hosted a hike-a-thon. Hikers earned 75 points for every $\frac{1}{2}$ mile they hiked. The course was 3 miles long. If Joe hiked the whole course, how many points did he earn?

6. **WRITE Math** The art club is making a paper chain to decorate the gym for a fund-raiser. Each student makes 8 links for the chain. There are 78 students in the art club. How many links will be on the chain? **Explain** how you found the answer.

Mixed Strategy Practice

USE DATA For 7–9, use the poster.

7. The school band held a car wash to raise money for the local animal shelter. If 36 cars, 8 vans, and 21 trucks came to the car wash, how much money did the band raise?
8. **Pose a Problem** Look back at Problem 7. Write a similar problem by changing the numbers of cars, vans, and trucks.
9. **Open-Ended** In the first two hours of the car wash, the band washed both cars and trucks and raised a total of $48. List a possible combination of cars and trucks that the band washed.
10. A green, a red, a white, and a blue car are in line at the car wash. The red car is not last. The white car is in front of the blue car. The blue car is second. Draw a picture to show the order of the cars.

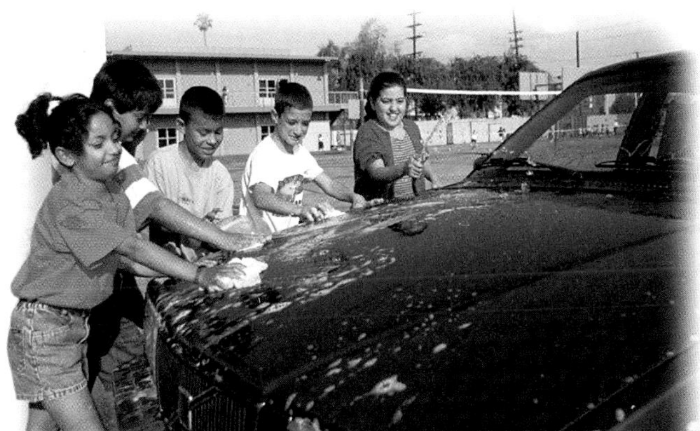

Choose a STRATEGY

- Solve a Simpler Problem
- Draw a Diagram or Picture
- Make a Model or Act It Out
- Make an Organized List
- Make a Table or Graph
- Guess and Check
- Work Backward
- Look for a Pattern
- Write an Equation
- Use Logical Reasoning

Car Wash
SOAP
Friday
2:30 P.M. to 7:00 P.M.
Saturday
9:00 A.M. to 3:00 P.M.
Cars: $3 each
Trucks/Vans: $6 each
All money raised will be donated to the local animal shelter.

CHALLENGE YOURSELF

There are about 5,000 animal shelters nationwide. It costs about $10 a day to care for a cat or dog in a shelter.

11. Vanessa volunteers at her local animal shelter. There are 16 dogs and 24 cats at the shelter. What is the total cost per day to care for the animals?
12. Samuel also volunteers at an animal shelter. At his shelter, there are 12 dogs. Explain how to use a pattern to find the number of dogs nationwide that are in animal shelters if each shelter houses 12 dogs.

Extra Practice

Set A Find the product. Use place value or regrouping. (pp. 546–549)

1. 14×4

2. 31×5

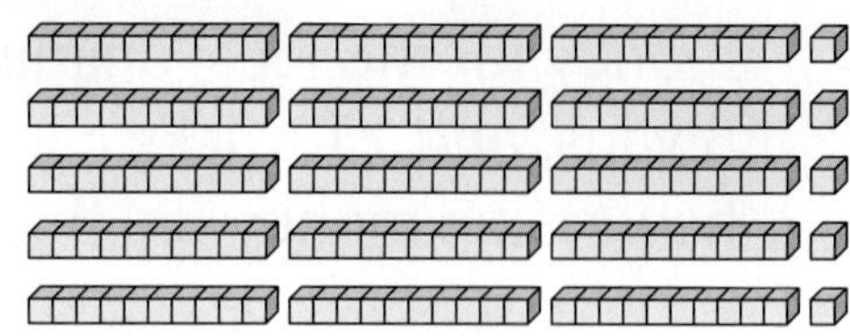

Multiply. You may wish to use base-ten blocks to help you.

3. 43×2
4. 77×5
5. 52×3
6. 40×6
7. 80×9
8. 29×4
9. 36×3
10. 61×2
11. 23×5
12. 68×8

Set B Find each product. (pp. 550–551)

1. 48×6
2. 73×8
3. 62×9
4. 59×4
5. 83×5
6. 34×5
7. 27×4
8. 6×19
9. 3×48
10. Nell is buying ice cream cones for her 4 brothers. If each cone is \$2.59, about how much money does Nell need?
11. Antoine needs to reserve 22 tables for a party. If each table holds 8 people, about how many people are attending the party?

Set C Find the product. Use regrouping or place value. (pp. 552–553)

1. 12×6
2. 44×3
3. 52×9
4. 79×4
5. 87×5
6. 38×5
7. 37×8
8. 59×7
9. 16×5
10. Chuck wrote a short story that was 26 pages long. He had 7 copies of it made. How many pages were copied in all?
11. James has 46 marbles. Mark has 3 times as many marbles. How many marbles does Mark have?

Technology
Use Harcourt Mega Math, The Number Games, *Up, Up, and Array,* Levels I and J.

TECHNOLOGY CONNECTION

Calculator: Multiplication (TEKS 3.4B, 3.14D, 3.15A)

Use a Calculator for Multiplication

The Drama club sold sandwiches at lunch to raise money for a field trip. There were 6 kinds of sandwiches. The club made 45 of each kind. How many sandwiches did they make?

Write a number sentence for the word problem.

$6 \times 45 =$ ■

Use a calculator to solve.

So, the Drama club made 270 sandwiches.

Try It

Use a calculator to multiply. Solve each problem twice to be sure that you have keyed in the correct information.

1. $64 \times 7 =$ ■ **2.** $32 \times 9 =$ ■ **3.** $83 \times 4 =$ ■ **4.** $89 \times 5 =$ ■

5. $55 \times 2 =$ ■ **6.** $49 \times 3 =$ ■ **7.** $53 \times 8 =$ ■ **8.** $77 \times 4 =$ ■

9. $5 \times 42 =$ ■ **10.** $3 \times 29 =$ ■ **11.** $7 \times 91 =$ ■ **12.** $4 \times 52 =$ ■

13. Janet read 9 magazines with 65 pages each during the month of June. How many pages did she read in June?

14. In December, Max read 8 books with 76 pages each. How many pages did he read in December?

15. Angie sold 8 toys for 50¢ each and 6 toys for 75¢ each. How much money, in cents, did she make?

16. **What if** Angie's mother doubled what Angie made? How much money, in cents, does Angie have now?

17. **Explore More** Heather's piano teacher charges $30 for each half hour of lessons. Heather takes two hour-long lessons each month. How much does she pay each month? If her teacher charged $25 for a half-hour lesson and Heather took four half-hour lessons, would she pay more or less each month? **Explain.**

Chapter 23 Review/Test

Check Concepts

1. Explain how you could use base-ten blocks to help you solve 4×12? (TEKS 3.4B, p. 544)
2. What are the steps needed to multiply 6×57? (TEKS 3.4B, p. 550)

Check Skills

Find the product. Use place value or regrouping. (TEKS 3.4B, pp. 546–549)

3. 29×3

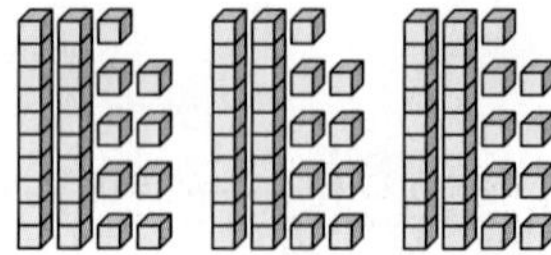

4. 43×2

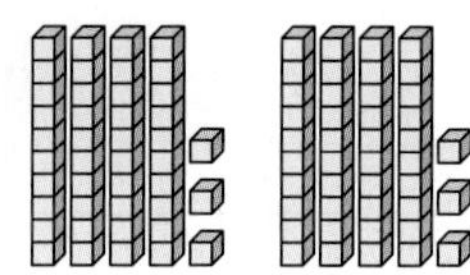

5. 31×4

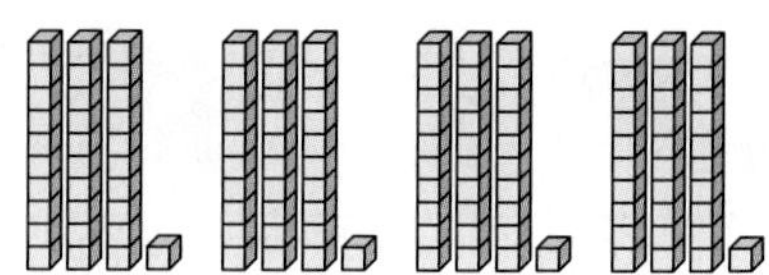

Find each product. (TEKS 3.4B, pp. 550–551, 552–553)

6. 13×3
7. 26×5
8. 49×8
9. 75×9
10. 34×3
11. 19×7
12. 68×6
13. 71×8
14. 58×4
15. 82×2
16. 38×4
17. 51×2
18. 97×6
19. 62×8
20. 83×2
21. 75×4
22. 42×8
23. 84×5

Check Problem Solving

Solve. (TEKS 3.14C, pp. 554–557)

24. At a class trip to the zoo, 37 students and 5 teachers paid \$5 each for admission. How much money did they pay in all for admission to the zoo?

25. WRITE Math Lindsay and Jeff live in towns that each have a population of 8 people per square mile. Lindsay's town is 64 square miles. Jeff's town is 72 square miles. How many people in all live in both towns? **Explain**.

GO ONLINE **Technology** Use *Online Assessment.*

Enrich • How Old Are You?

Time Passages

A person's age is usually given in years. Do you know how many days, hours, or minutes old you are? Use a calculator to find out!

Example

Abby was born on February 8, 1998. How old is she on April 3, 2007 in days, hours, and minutes?

Step 1	Multiply Abby's age in years by 365.	Example: 9 × 365 = 3,285
Step 2	Add the number of days from the birthday to the given date. remaining days in Feb: 20 days in March: 31 days in April: 3	20 + 31 + 3 = 54 3,285 + 54 = 3,339
Step 3	Add one day for each leap year. Leap Years are: . . . 1996, 2000, 2004, and 2008	3,339 + 2 = 3,341
So, Abby is 3,341 days old.		
Step 4	Multiply age in days by 24 hours.	3,341 × 24 = 80,184
So, Abby is 80,184 hours old.		
Step 5	Multiply age in hours by 60 minutes.	80,184 × 60 = 4,811,040
So, Abby is 4,811,040 minutes old.		

Practice

Find each age in years, days, hours, and minutes.

1. Jake's birthday is May 25, 1995. Find his age on January 16, 2006.
2. Elsie's birthday is August 3, 2001. Find her age on September 2, 2008.

Wrap Up

WRITE Math Find your age in days, hours, and minutes. **Explain** how you know.

Getting Ready for the TAKS
Chapters 1–23

Number, Operation, and Quantitative Reasoning (TAKS Obj. 1)

1. Which is a true statement?

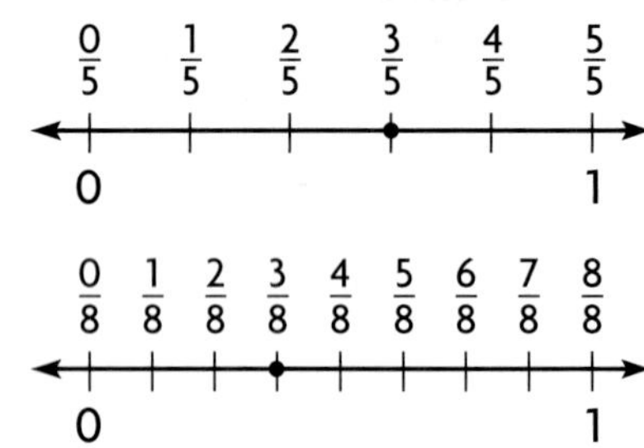

A $\frac{3}{8} > \frac{3}{5}$

B $\frac{3}{5} < \frac{3}{8}$

C $\frac{3}{5} = \frac{3}{8}$

D $\frac{3}{5} > \frac{3}{8}$

Test Tip **Choose the answer.**

See item 2. Multiply to find the answer. If the product does not match one of the answer choices, check your computation.

2. Caroline practiced 9 songs on the piano. She spent 12 minutes playing each song. For how many minutes did Caroline practice?

F 21

G 98

H 108

J 1,080

3. **WRITE Math** There are 65 treats in one bag of dog treats. How many treats are in 8 bags? **Explain** your answer.

Patterns, Relationships, and Algebraic Thinking (TAKS Obj. 2)

4. Which is the next figure in the pattern?

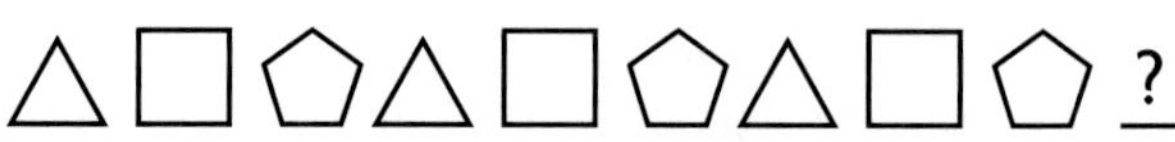

A △

B ⬡

C ⬠

D □

5. Which number sentence is in the same fact family as $72 \div 8 = 9$?

F $8 + 9 = 17$

G $72 - 8 = 64$

H $9 \times 8 = 72$

J $72 \div 12 = 6$

6. **WRITE Math** How many strings are on 6 guitars? **Explain** your answer.

Guitars	1	2	3	4	5	6
Strings	6	12	18	■	■	■

Geometry and Spatial Reasoning (TAKS Obj. 3)

7. Jeremy drew a quadrilateral with all sides the same length. Which figure could Jeremy have drawn?

   A Trapezoid

   B Pentagon

   C Hexagon

   D Not here

8. Which figure appears to have only 1 line of symmetry?

   F 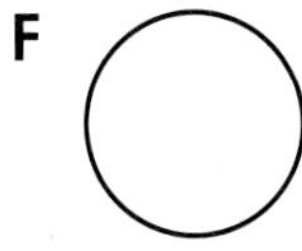

   G 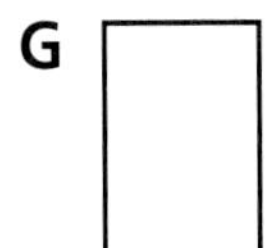

   H 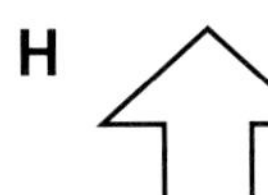

   J 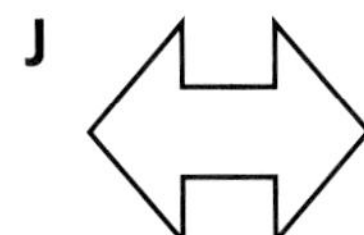

9. **WRITE Math** Which letter shows the location of $\frac{3}{5}$? **Explain** how you know.

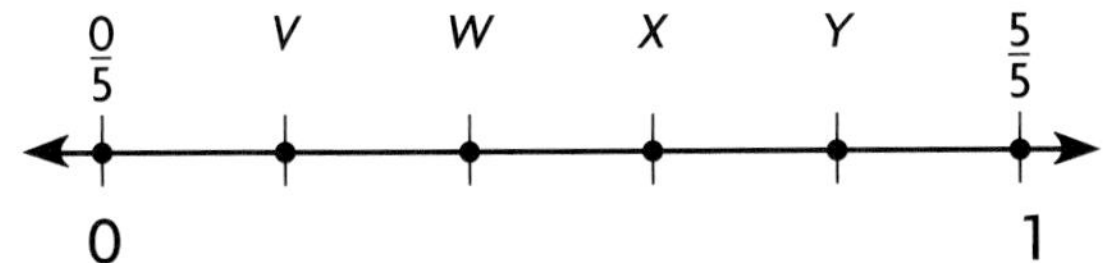

Probability and Statistics (TAKS Obj. 5)

10. How many more books did Mark read than Deb?

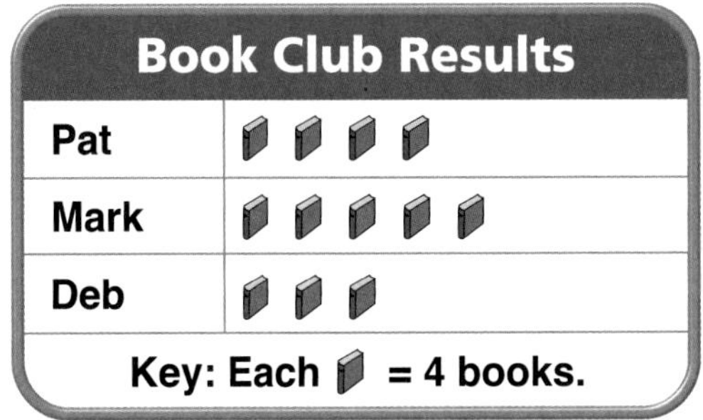

Book Club Results	
Pat	4 book symbols
Mark	5 book symbols
Deb	3 book symbols
Key: Each book = 4 books.	

   A 2 **C** 6

   B 4 **D** 8

11. On which day was the greatest number of books sold?

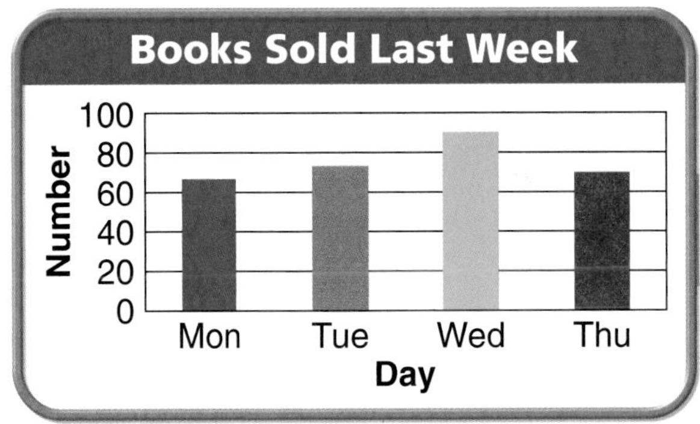

   F Monday **H** Wednesday

   G Tuesday **J** Thursday

12. **WRITE Math** Courtney has 8 blue pencils and 2 red pencils in a drawer. She reaches in the drawer and chooses a pencil without looking. Is she more likely to choose a blue pencil or a red pencil? **Explain**.

CHAPTER

24 Probability

The Big Idea Probability measures the likelihood of events and provides a basis for making predictions.

TEXAS FAST FACT

The first ice cream sundae was made in the late 1800's. In 2005, Texas was the nation's fifth-largest producer of ice cream.

Investigate

Look at the menu. Build your own sundae. Choose 1 ice cream flavor and 1 topping. Make a list to show how many combinations there are. Circle your favorite combination.

Build Your Own Sundae

Ice Cream Flavors	Toppings
Vanilla	Nuts
Chocolate	Sprinkles
Strawberry	Chocolate sauce
	Strawberry sauce

Technology
Student pages are available in the Student eBook.

Show What You Know

Check your understanding of important skills needed for success in Chapter 24.

Read a Tally Table

For 1–4, use the tally table.

1. How many students play baseball?
2. How many students play football?
3. How many students answered the question?
4. How many more students play soccer than basketball?

Which sport do you play?	
Baseball	~~IIII~~ ~~IIII~~ I
Soccer	~~IIII~~ ~~IIII~~ III
Football	~~IIII~~ III
Basketball	~~IIII~~ IIII

Compare Parts of a Whole

For 5–8, write the color shown by the largest part of each spinner.

5. 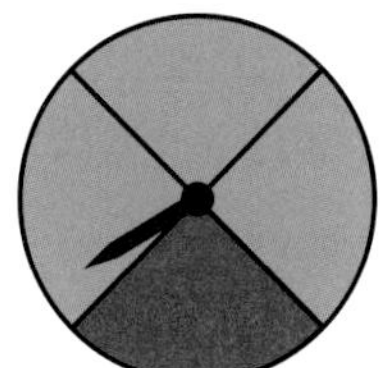
6. 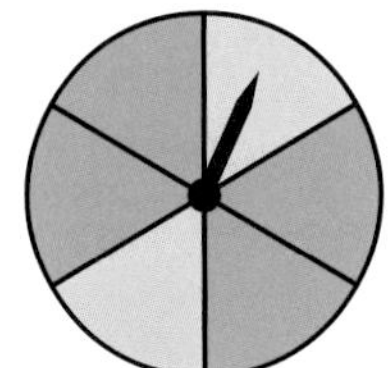
7. 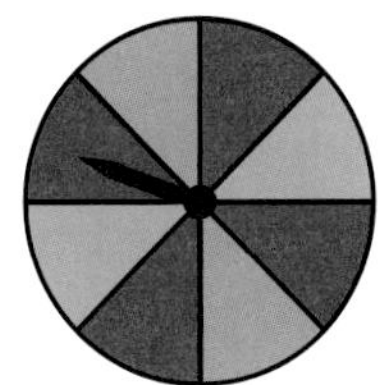
8. 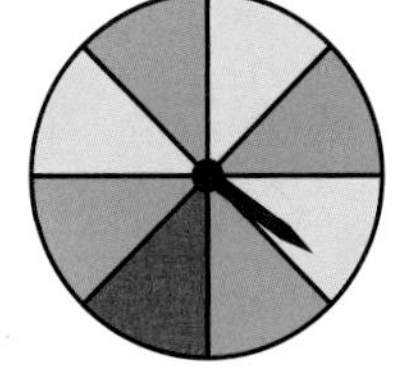

VOCABULARY POWER

CHAPTER VOCABULARY

bar graph
certain
data
equally likely
event
experiment
impossible
less likely
more likely
outcome
predict
probability
tally table

WARM-UP WORDS

event Something that might happen

probability The chance that a given event will occur

more likely An event is more likely if it has a good chance of happening.

Probability: Likelihood of Events

OBJECTIVE: Decide if an event is less likely, more likely, certain, or impossible.

Quick Review

What color marbles can Sarah pull from this bag?

Vocabulary

event	probability
more likely	less likely
impossible	certain

Learn

An **event** is something that might happen. **Probability** is the chance that an event will happen.

PROBLEM Ted is going to pull a marble out of this bag without looking. Is it more likely, less likely, certain, or impossible that Ted will pull a red marble?

Use these examples.

Pulling red is **more likely**. It has a good chance of happening.

Pulling yellow is **less likely**. It does not have a good chance of happening.

Pulling green is **impossible**. It will never happen.

In this bag, pulling red is **certain**. It will always happen.

Ted's bag has more red marbles than blue or yellow marbles.

So, it is more likely that Ted will pull a red marble.

- Is Ted more likely to pull a blue marble or a yellow marble?

Guided Practice

1. Which color marble are you less likely to pull?

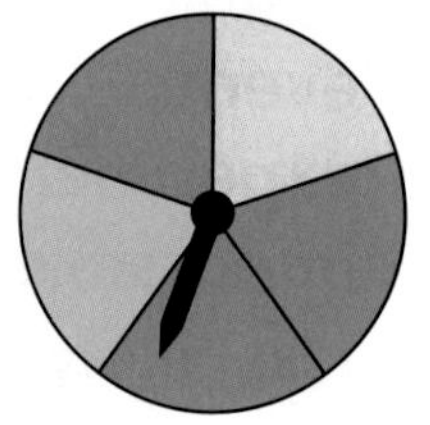

If you spin the pointer one time, tell whether each event is *more likely, less likely, certain,* or *impossible*.

2. The pointer will land on green.
3. The pointer will land on red.
4. The pointer will land on blue.
5. The pointer will land on blue, yellow, or green.
6. TALK Math **Explain** why landing on green is less likely.

TEKS 3.13C use data to describe events as more likely than, less likely than, or equally likely as. *also* **3.14A, 3.14D, 3.15A, 3.15B, 3.16A**

Independent Practice and Problem Solving

If you pull one marble, tell whether each event is *more likely, less likely, certain,* or *impossible*.

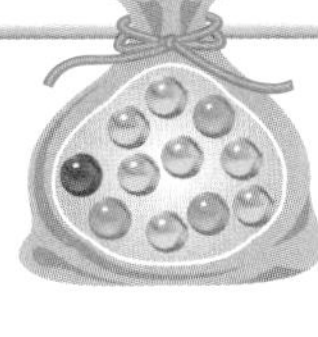

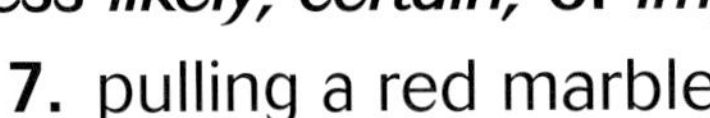

7. pulling a red marble

8. pulling a yellow marble

9. pulling a blue marble

10. pulling a marble

For 11–12, use the spinner.

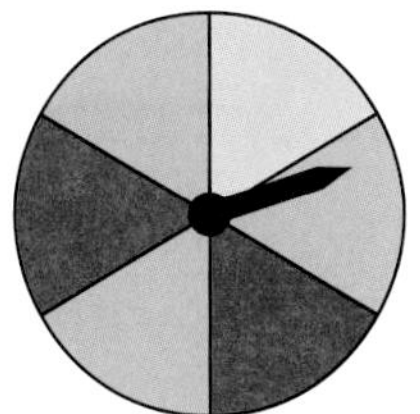

11. Which color are you more likely to spin?

12. Which color are you less likely to spin?

Algebra Find the missing addend.

13. $18 + \blacksquare = 24$

14. $\blacksquare + 79 = 92$

15. $205 + \blacksquare = 472$

USE DATA For 16–19, use the table. Tom pulls one sock from his drawer without looking.

Tom's Socks

Color	Number
Black	14
Brown	12
White	2

16. Is it more likely or less likely that Tom will pull a white sock?

17. Is it certain or impossible that Tom will pull a blue sock?

18. **What if** Tom had 16 more black socks? How many more black socks than brown socks would he have?

19. WRITE Math **What if** Tom had 30 more white socks? **Explain** how your answer to Problem 16 would change.

Mixed Review and TAKS Prep

20. Morgan has 8 books. Each book has 32 pages. How many pages are there in all? (TEKS 3.4B, p. 550)

21. Laura has 20 marbles in her collection. There are 5 green, 4 red, 9 white, and 2 blue marbles. She made a bar graph to show her marble collection. Which color has the shortest bar? (TEKS 3.13A, p. 160)

22. **TAKS Prep** Pulling a green marble from this bag is _?_. (Obj. 5)

A more likely

B less likely

C certain

D impossible

Extra Practice on page 580, Set A

LESSON HANDS ON

2 Possible Outcomes

OBJECTIVE: Find the possible outcomes for simple events.

When you toss a coin, there are two possible results. In probability, a possible result is called an **outcome**.

The possible outcomes in a coin toss are heads up and tails up.

The outcomes *heads up* and *tails up* are **equally likely** because each has the same chance of happening.

Quick Review

Without looking, Roz pulls one marble from the bag. Name a more likely event and an impossible event.

Vocabulary

outcome **equally likely** **predict**

Investigate

Materials ■ coin, tally table

Record the outcomes of tossing a coin. Before the first toss, **predict** the results or tell what you think they will be.

Ⓐ Predict the number of times the coin will land heads up.

Ⓑ Toss the coin 25 times.

Ⓒ Record each outcome in a tally table.

Draw Conclusions

1. How many times did the coin land heads up? tails up?
2. How did your prediction compare to the results?
3. **Synthesis** Would you predict the same number if you were going to toss the coin 25 more times? **Explain**.

TEKS 3.13C Use data to describe events as more likely than, less likely than, or equally likely as. *also* **3.14A, 3.14D, 3.15A, 3.15B, 3.16B**

Connect

You can display the results of the coin toss in a bar graph.

Step 1

Jill tossed a coin 25 times. She recorded the results in a tally table.

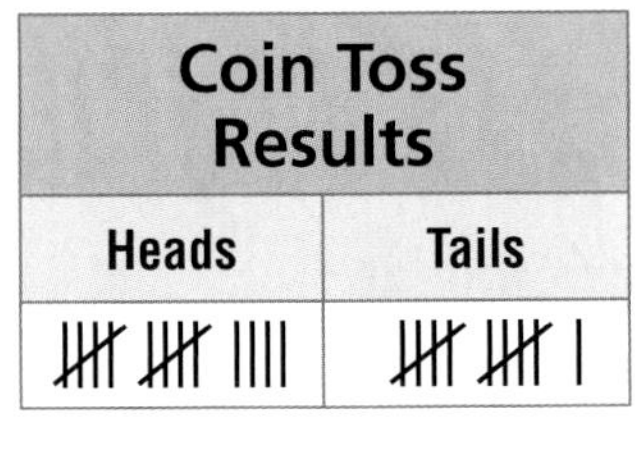

Coin Toss Results	
Heads	**Tails**
卌 卌 ||||	卌 卌	

Step 2

Jill made a bar graph from the data in the tally table.

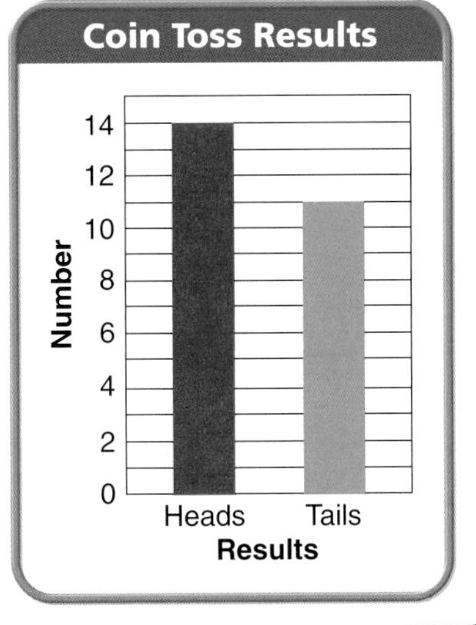

TALK Math

How does the bar graph help you compare Jill's results?

- Why are there 25 tally marks in the tally table?

Practice

For 1–2, list a possible outcome for each.

1. Henry will toss a quarter.

2. Marsha will use the spinner.

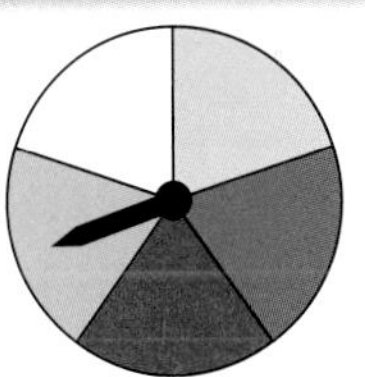

For 3–4, use the bag of marbles.

3. Billy is going to pull 1 marble from the bag. What are the possible outcomes for 1 pull?

4. **WRITE Math** **Sense or Nonsense** Billy says that pulling a red marble is equally likely as pulling a green marble. Does his statement make sense? **Explain.**

5. What are the possible outcomes for tossing a number cube? Which outcomes are equally likely?

6. **Reasoning** Mario drew a spinner with 8 equal sections. Three sections are yellow. Landing on yellow and landing on red are equally likely. How many sections are red? **Explain.**

LESSON 3

Experiments

OBJECTIVE: Conduct probability experiments, record the results, and describe the probability of outcomes.

Quick Review

Name a possible outcome for 1 spin of the pointer.

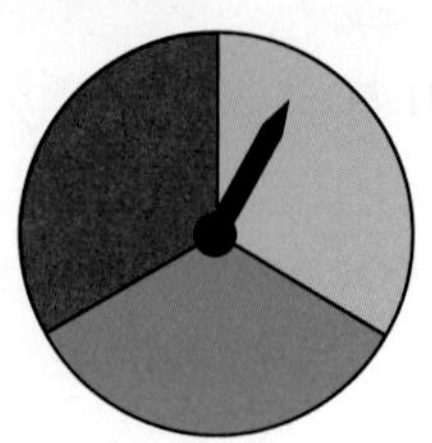

Vocabulary

experiment

Learn

An **experiment** is a test you can do to find out something. You can do probability experiments to explore how likely outcomes are.

Activity

Materials ■ 5-part spinner pattern, crayons, tally table, bar graph pattern

Step 1

Make a spinner that has 5 equal parts. Color the parts yellow, red, green, purple, and blue.

Step 2

Make a tally table. List all the possible outcomes. Spin 20 times. Record the results in the table.

Spinner Experiment	
Color	Tallies
Yellow	
Red	
Green	
Purple	
Blue	

Step 3

Make a bar graph of your data to show the results of your experiment.

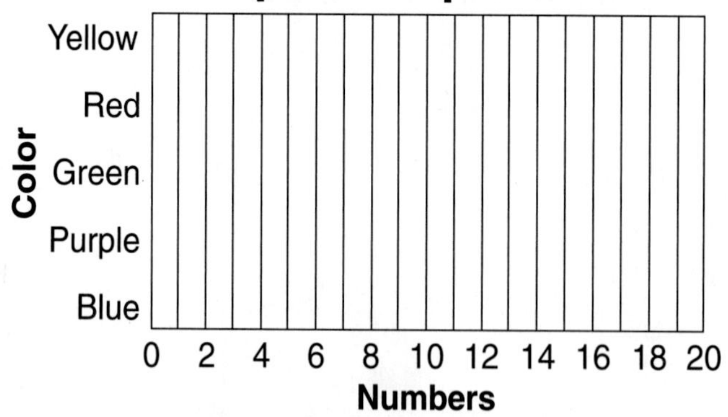

- Did the pointer land on each color about the same number of times? Explain.
- **What if** 2 sections of the spinner were blue? How would the results of your experiment change?

TEKS 3.13C use data to describe events as more likely than, less likely than, or equally likely as. *also* **3.13A, 3.14A, 3.14D, 3.15A, 3.15B**

More About Experiments

Look at Spinner A. There are 5 possible outcomes: green, red, yellow, blue, or purple. Each outcome is equally likely.	Look at Spinner B. There are 5 possible outcomes: yellow, yellow, blue, blue, or green.
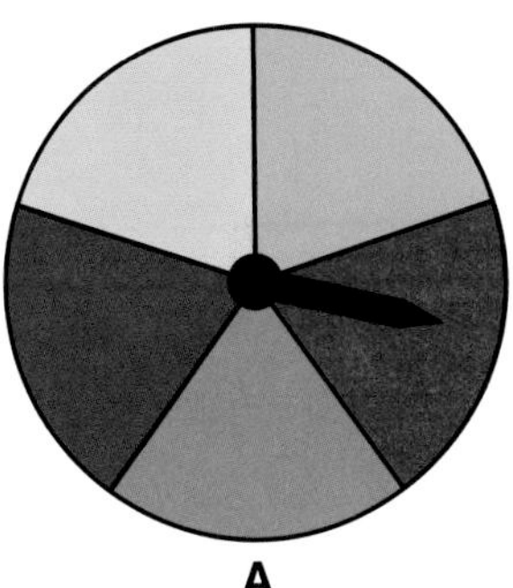 A	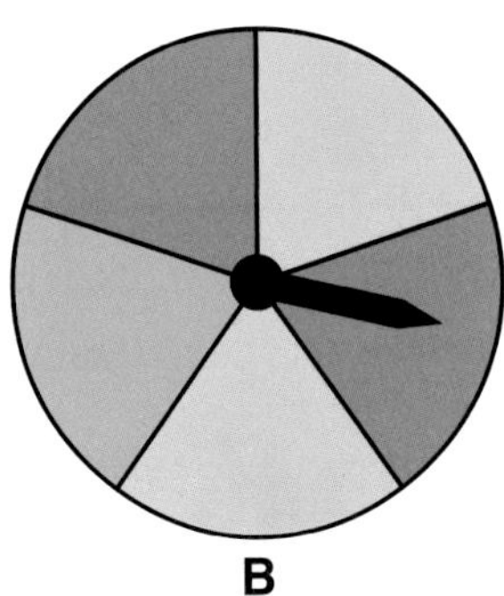 B
The probability of spinning blue is 1 out of 5.	The probability of spinning blue is 2 out of 5.

- For Spinner B, what is the probability of spinning green?
- For Spinner B, which outcomes are equally likely?

Guided Practice

1. In spinner C, which outcome is most likely? Think: Which color is shown most often?

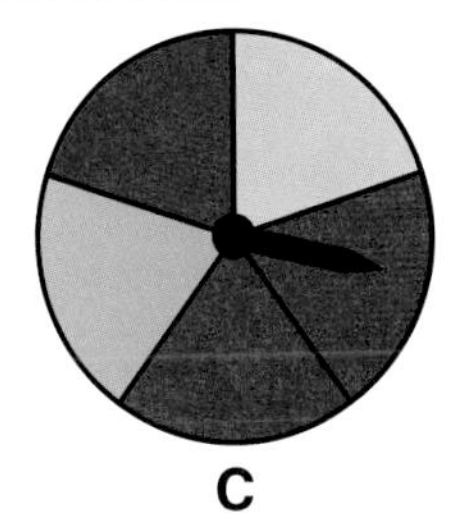

C

For 2–7, use the bags of tiles at the right.

2. For Bag D, which outcomes are equally likely?
3. What are the possible outcomes if you pull 1 tile from Bag D?
4. What are the possible outcomes if you pull 1 tile from Bag E?
5. What is the probability of pulling a green tile from Bag D?
6. What is the probability of pulling a red tile from Bag E?
7. TALK Math **Explain** why the outcomes in Bag E are equally likely.

Bag D

Bag E

Independent Practice and Problem Solving

8. Which outcome is most likely?
9. What is the probability of spinning red?

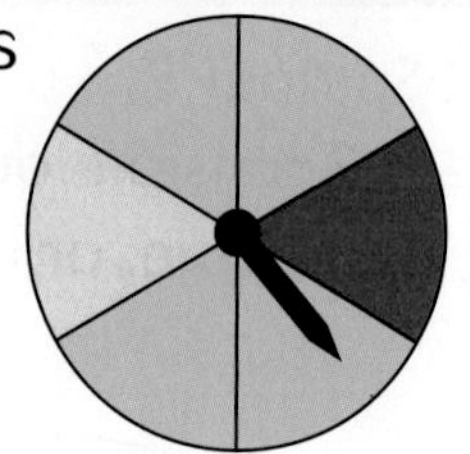

10. Which outcome is least likely?
11. What is the probability of pulling a green tile?

For 12–15, use the bag of marbles.

12. Cheryl is pulling 1 marble from this bag. What are the possible outcomes?
13. Which outcomes are equally likely?
14. What is the probability that Cheryl will pull a red marble?
15. **Pose a Problem** Look back at Problem 14. Write a similar problem by changing the color of the marble.
16. **WRITE Math** There are 6 red, 1 green, 2 blue, and 3 yellow tiles in a bag. **Explain** how to find the probability of pulling a yellow tile.
17. Predict the number of times a coin will land tails up in an experiment. Toss the coin 30 times. Record the outcomes in a table. Then make a bar graph to show the results.
18. ***FAST FACT*** The first machine-made glass marbles were produced in Akron, Ohio, in 1905. How many years ago was that?

Mixed Review and TAKS Prep

19. Is it more likely, less likely, certain, or impossible to pull a red tile from a bag of 1 blue, 2 green, 1 yellow, and 6 red tiles? (TEKS 3.13C, p. 566)
20. Dale bought paper for his printer. The package had 500 sheets of paper. Dale used 112 sheets. How many sheets of paper are left? (TEKS 3.3B, p. 94)
21. **TAKS Prep** What is the probability of pulling a blue tile from this bag? (Obj. 5)

A 1 out of 10

B 2 out of 8

C 4 out of 8

D 4 out of 10

Technology
Use Harcourt Mega Math, Fraction Action, *Last Chance Canyon*, Level D.

 Extra Practice on page 580, Set B

Spinning Around

Make an Inference

The table on the left shows the results of 30 spins on Julie's spinner. The table on the right shows the results of 30 spins on Eve's spinner. What inference can you make about the yellow section of Eve's spinner?

Julie's Results

Color	Times
Orange	5
Yellow	4
Blue	6
Green	6
Red	5
Purple	4

Eve's Results

Color	Times
Orange	5
Yellow	15
Blue	6
Green	0
Red	4
Purple	0

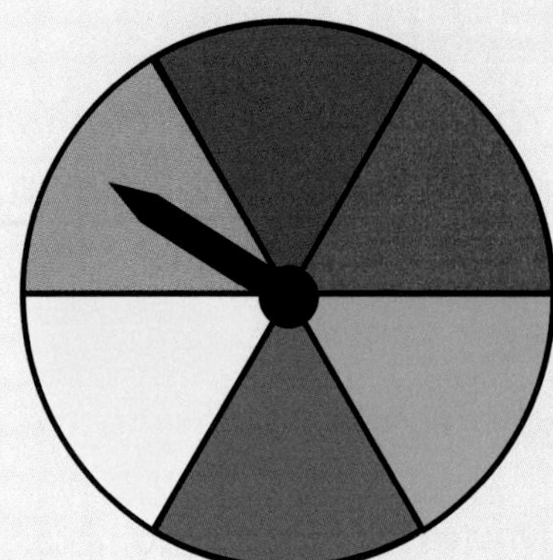
Julie's Spinner

Eve's Spinner

When you make an inference, you develop ideas based on information given in a problem. Use what you know about probability and the data in the table to make an inference about the yellow section of Eve's spinner.

Look at Julie's spinner results. The pointer landed on each color about an equal number of times. Then look at Eve's spinner results. The pointer on Eve's spinner landed on yellow about 3 times more often than it landed on the other colors.

So, you can infer that the yellow section of Eve's spinner is larger than the other sections.

Problem Solving **Make an inference to solve the problems.**

1. How many times did the pointer on Eve's spinner land on purple or green? What inference can you make?

2. How many times did the pointer on Eve's spinner land on orange, blue, or red? What inference can you make? **Explain.**

Predict Future Events

OBJECTIVE: Use the results of experiments to make predictions.

Quick Review

Write the temperature in °F.

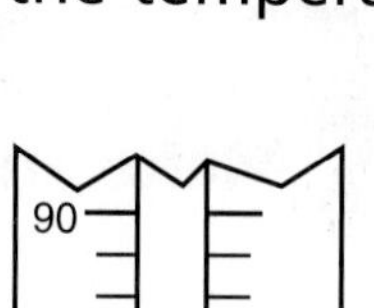

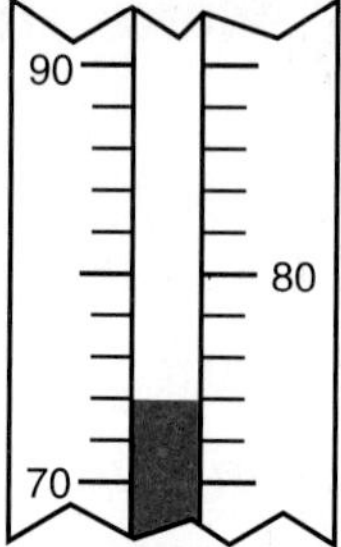

Learn

You can use the results of an experiment to predict what the outcome will be if you do the experiment again.

Activity

Materials ■ thermometer

Step 1

Record the outside temperature at the same time each day for 4 days.

Step 2

Record the results in a table.

Step 3

Use the data to predict the temperature for the fifth day.

Think: Is there one temperature that occurred more often than the other temperatures?

Temperature in °F	
Day 1	
Day 2	
Day 3	
Day 4	
Day 5	

- Record the temperature on the fifth day. How did the temperature on the next day compare to your prediction?

Guided Practice

1. The table shows the results of recording the temperature at the same time for 7 days. Which temperature was recorded most often?

Temperature in °F							
Day	1	2	3	4	5	6	7
Temperature	28	32	30	32	51	32	29

TEKS 3.13C use data to describe events as more likely than, less likely than, or equally likely as. *also* **3.12A, 3.14A, 3.15A, 3.15B, 3.16B**

For 2–4, use the table.

Temperature in °F			
Day 1	60	**Day 6**	64
Day 2	64	**Day 7**	68
Day 3	63	**Day 8**	64
Day 4	64	**Day 9**	66
Day 5	62	**Day 10**	

2. Which temperature was recorded most often?

3. Predict the most likely temperature for Day 10.

4. TALK Math **Explain** how you made your prediction.

Independent Practice and Problem Solving

USE DATA For 5–6, use the bar graph.

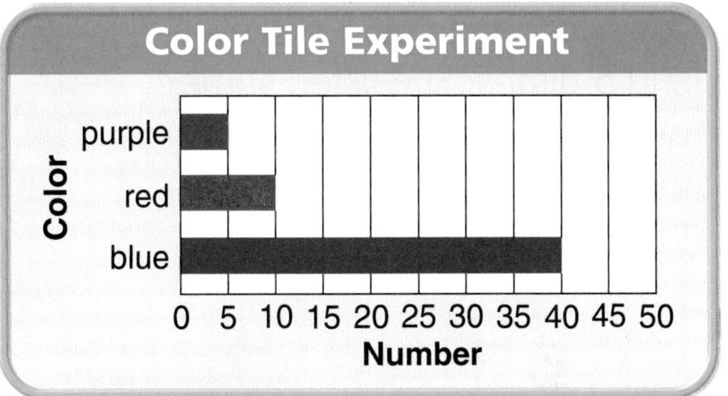

5. How many more times was a blue tile pulled than a purple tile and a red tile combined?

6. WRITE Math **Sense or Nonsense** Molly says that the next tile pulled is most likely to be red. Does Molly's prediction make sense? **Explain.**

7. **Reasoning** A bag contains green and red tiles. There are 7 green tiles. The most likely outcome is pulling a red tile. What do you know about the number of red tiles in the bag?

8. ***FAST FACT*** Liquid-in-glass thermometers are used to measure air and body temperature. The first thermometer was invented by Galileo in 1592. How many years ago was that?

Mixed Review and TAKS Prep

9. Lisa spent $3.28 on pencils. Steven spent $3.82 on crayons. Who spent more money? (TEKS 3.1C, p. 114)

10. Sarah measured the length of her classroom. Which length is reasonable—30 inches, 30 feet, or 30 yards? (TEKS 3.11A, p. 440)

11. **TAKS Prep** The table shows the pulls from a bag of tiles. Predict which color is most likely to be pulled next. (Obj. 5)

Experiment	
Colors	**Tally**
green	𝍸 𝍸
red	|||
blue	𝍸
black	||

A green

B red

C blue

D black

Problem Solving Workshop
Strategy: Make an Organized List

OBJECTIVE: Solve problems by using the strategy *make an organized list.*

Learn the Strategy

You can make an organized list to help solve problems.

Joy has 5 pennies, 5 nickels, and 5 dimes. She listed some of the different ways she can make 20¢.

Ways to make 20¢

20¢ 2 dimes
20¢ 1 dime, 2 nickels
20¢ 1 dime, 1 nickel, 5 pennies
20¢ 3 nickels, 5 pennies
20¢ 4 nickels

Allie is doing a number cube experiment. She found the possible outcomes of 1 toss. Then she listed all the outcomes in order from least to greatest.

Allie

1
2
3
4
5
6

Scott is serving his friends snacks and drinks after school. He listed the possible snack and drink combinations.

pretzels, juice
pretzels, water

popcorn, juice
popcorn, water

chips, juice
chips, water

TALK Math

Look at Scott's list. How many combinations of 1 snack and 1 drink are possible?

TEKS 3.16B justify why an answer is reasonable and explain the solution process. *also* **3.14A, 3.14B, 3.14C, 3.15A, 3.15B**

Use the Strategy

PROBLEM Sonya is having a birthday party. She is planning to serve chocolate cupcakes and yellow cupcakes at her party. Her guests can choose chocolate, vanilla, or strawberry frosting. How many combinations of a cupcake and frosting are there?

Read to Understand

- **Identify the details of the problem.**
- **Is there any information you will not use? If so, what?**

Plan

- **What strategy can you use to solve the problem?** You can make an organized list of the combinations.

Solve

- **How can you use the strategy to solve the problem?**

  Make a list of the possible combinations. Start with one cupcake flavor. Match the cupcake to each frosting flavor.

  Match the other cupcake to each frosting.

  Then, count the combinations.

  So, there are 6 combinations of a cupcake and frosting.

chocolate, chocolate
chocolate, vanilla
chocolate, strawberry

yellow, chocolate
yellow, vanilla
yellow, strawberry

Check

- **Is your answer reasonable? Explain.**

Guided Problem Solving

Read to Understand
Plan
Solve
Check

1. Sonya has prizes for her guests. Each guest will get 1 T-shirt and 1 hat. Sonya has blue, red, and white T-shirts. She has purple, blue, and green hats. How many combinations of 1 T-shirt and 1 hat are there?

   First, start with 1 T-shirt color. Match the T-shirt color to each hat color.

   Next, repeat until you have listed each hat color next to each T-shirt color.

   Finally, count the number of T-shirt and hat combinations.

blue, purple
blue, blue
blue, green

red, purple
red, blue
red, green

white, purple
white, blue
white, green

2. **What if** Sonya also had yellow T-shirts? How would the number of combinations of 1 T-shirt and 1 hat change?

3. Lana's class is having a party. Each student can choose 1 pencil and 1 notebook. There are smiley-face and animal pencils. The notebooks are blue and red. How many combinations of 1 pencil and 1 notebook are there?

Problem Solving Strategy Practice

USE DATA For 4–6, use the table.

Party Prizes		
Balloons	**Bookmarks**	**Trading Cards**
red	ribbon	baseball
white	paper	superhero
blue		

4. There are 3 bags of party prizes. Marty pulls out 1 prize from the balloon bag and 1 prize from the trading-card bag. How many combinations of 1 balloon and 1 trading card are there?

5. Rico pulls out 1 prize from the bookmark bag and 1 prize from the trading card bag. How many combinations of 1 bookmark and 1 trading card are there?

6. WRITE Math Sheree will pull 1 bookmark and 1 balloon. Explain how to find the number of bookmark and balloon combinations there are.

Mixed Strategy Practice

USE DATA For 7–10, use the pictures and prices.

7. Sonya is buying lollipops and yo-yos as party favors. She wants each guest to have one of each. She can buy orange or cherry lollipops and green or blue yo-yos. Make a list to show how many combinations of 1 lollipop and 1 yo-yo Sonya can buy.

8. **WRITE Math** **What's the Question?** Jared had $5.00 to spend at the store. He bought 1 item. The answer is $3.45.

9. **Pose a Problem** Look back at Problem 7. Write a similar problem by adding another color yo-yo.

10. **Open-Ended** Suppose you have $10.00 to spend on party favors. There will be 10 guests, and each guest will receive 2 favors. Choose the favors you would give, and find the total cost.

11. **Reasoning** A party store sold 86 packs of party hats in one day. There were 22 more packs sold in the afternoon than in the morning. How many packs were sold in the morning?

Choose a STRATEGY

- Draw a Diagram or Picture
- Make a Model or Act It Out
- Make an Organized List
- Look for a Pattern
- Make a Table or Graph
- Guess and Check
- Work Backward
- Solve a Simpler Problem
- Write an Equation
- Use Logical Reasoning

CHALLENGE YOURSELF

Ted invited 12 friends to his party. He bought whistles for party favors. Each friend will get 1 whistle. The whistles come in packs of 4 for $2 or packs of 10 for $3.

12. Ted wants to buy the whistles in a way that will cost the least amount of money. Explain how you can find which packs Ted should buy and how many of each pack.

13. Each friend brought Ted a stamp for his collection. Now he has 40 stamps. There are 12 more stamps in his second album than there are in his first album. How many stamps are in each album?

Extra Practice

Set A Tell whether each event is *more likely, less likely, certain,* or *impossible.* (pp. 566–567)

1. pulling a red apple
2. pulling a yellow apple
3. pulling an apple
4. pulling an orange

For 5–6, use the spinner.

5. Which color are you most likely to spin?
6. Which color are you least likely to spin?

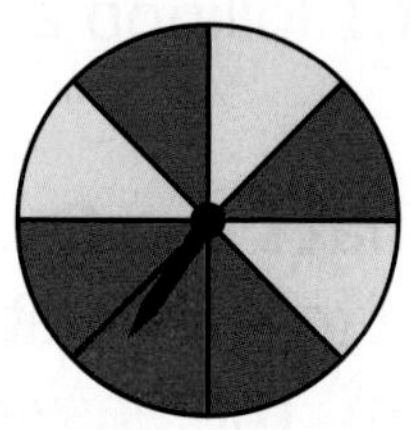

Set B For 1–3, use the spinner. For 4–6, use the bag of tiles. (pp. 570–573)

1. Which outcome is most likely?
2. Which outcomes are equally likely?
3. What is the probability of spinning yellow?

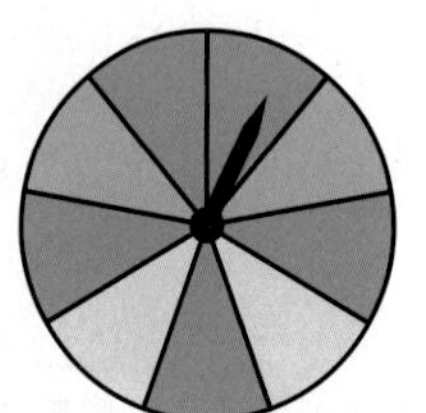

4. Which outcome is most likely?
5. Which outcome is least likely?
6. What is the probability of pulling a red tile?

Set C For 1–2, use the tables. (pp. 574–575)

1. The tally table shows the results of 20 pulls from a bag of marbles. Predict which color marble is most likely to be pulled next. Explain how you made your prediction.

Marble Experiment	
orange	~~||||~~ ~~||||~~ |||
green	||
red	|||
yellow	||

2. The tally table shows the results of a spinner experiment. Predict the most likely outcome of the next spin. Explain your prediction.

Spinner Results	
blue	||
red	|
green	~~||||~~ ~~||||~~ ~~||||~~ ~~||||~~ ~~||||~~ ~~||||~~ ||

Technology
Use Harcourt Mega Math, Fraction Action, *Last Chance Canyon*, Levels A, B, C, D, E.

PRACTICE GAME

Strange Spinners

Going in Circles!

2 players

Round and Round!

- Spinners A, B, and C
- Crayons or colored pencils
- Recording table

Spinner A

Spinner B

Spinner C

Getting Dizzy!

- Each player selects a spinner without letting the other player see it. Players color spinner sections by using 3 different colors.
- Player 1 spins the pointer on his or her spinner 15 times and tells the outcome of each spin. Player 2 records the outcomes in a table.
- Player 2 spins 15 times, and Player 1 records the outcomes.
- Players take turns asking each other questions about their spinners, using the words *certain*, *likely*, *unlikely*, or *impossible*. An example is *Are you certain to spin yellow?*
- The first player to correctly identify the color of each section of the other player's spinner wins.

Chapter 24 Review/Test

Check Vocabulary and Concepts

Choose the best term from the box.

VOCABULARY
experiment
outcome
predict
probability

1. When you __?__ something, you tell what you think the results will be. (TEKS 3.13C, p. 568)
2. __?__ is the chance that an event will happen. (TEKS 3.13C, p. 566)
3. An __?__ is a test you can do to find something out. (TEKS 3.13C, p. 570)

Check Skills

For 4–6, tell whether each event is *more likely, less likely, certain,* or *impossible*. (TEKS 3.13C, pp. 566–567)

4. pulling an orange tile
5. pulling a blue tile
6. pulling a green tile

For 7–9, use the spinner. For 10–12, use the table. (TEKS 3.13C, pp. 570–575)

7. Which outcomes are equally likely?
8. What is the probability of spinning green?
9. What is the probability of spinning yellow?

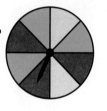

10. Which color marble was pulled most often?
11. How many more times was a blue marble pulled than red?
12. Predict which color marble will be pulled next.

Experiment	
Color	**Tallies**
green	卌
red	||
blue	卌 卌 ||||

Check Problem Solving

Solve. (TEKS 3.16B, pp. 576–579)

13. Eva chooses 1 fruit and 1 drink at a picnic. How many combinations are there of 1 fruit and 1 drink?
14. Dion chooses 1 drink and 1 dessert. How many combinations are there of 1 drink and 1 dessert?

Picnic Snacks		
Fruit	**Drink**	**Dessert**
Apple	Iced tea	Brownie
Orange	Lemonade	Cookie
Banana	Water	

15. **WRITE Math** Tom has 1 fruit and 1 dessert. Explain how to find the number of fruit and dessert combinations he could have.

GO ONLINE **Technology** Use *Online Assessment.*

Enrich • Arrangements

Party Possibilities

Rory is planning her birthday party. Her guests will play games, eat birthday cake, and break a piñata. In how many different ways can Rory plan the order of the 3 activities?

When the order of activities is important, you need an **arrangement**.

Guests Arrive

To solve the problem, select each activity and then combine it with each of the other activities.

Step 1	Choose **games** to be first. Write down all the ways to do the 3 activities with games first.
Step 2	Next, choose **cake** to be first. Write down all the ways to do the 3 activities with cake first.
Step 3	Then, choose the **piñata** to be first. Write down all the ways to do the 3 activities with piñata first.

FIRST	SECOND	THIRD
games	cake	piñata
games	piñata	cake
cake	games	piñata
cake	piñata	games
piñata	cake	games
piñata	games	cake

Now count the ways. The order of activities can be arranged 6 ways.

Play Games

For 1–2, make a chart or list to solve.

1. Paula is arranging her stuffed animals on a shelf. She has a tiger, lion, and an elephant. In how many ways can Paula arrange her animals?

2. Choose 4 numbers from 1 through 9. Using each number once, in how many ways can you arrange the numbers in a 4-digit number?

Open Presents

WRITE Math Jillian and Molly are visiting New York City. They want to visit the places on the list at the right. In how many different ways can they visit the places? **Explain.**

PLACES TO VISIT

Empire State Building
Times Square
Statue of Liberty
Central Park

Unit Review/Test
Chapters 22–24

Multiple Choice

1. Richie, Dominick, Paul, and Ryan are running a race. Richie has run $\frac{3}{4}$ of a lap, Dominick has run $\frac{2}{8}$ of a lap, Paul has run $\frac{2}{4}$ of a lap, and Ryan has run $\frac{6}{12}$ of a lap. Which boy has run the farthest? (TAKS Obj. 1)

   A Richie

   B Dominick

   C Paul

   D Ryan

2. What color balloon are you more likely to pull than red? (TAKS Obj. 5)

   F blue

   G yellow

   H green

   J red

3. The tally table shows the results of pulling cubes from a bag 15 times. Predict which color will be pulled next. (TAKS Obj. 5)

   A red

   B orange

   C purple

   D blue

Cube Experiment

Cube	Number
red	𝍸 ||
orange	|||
purple	||
blue	|||

4. Michelle has 2 jackets and 4 hats. How many combinations of 1 jacket and 1 hat are there? (TAKS Obj. 5)

   F 1

   G 2

   H 6

   J 8

5. There are 37 tables in Tony's Restaurant. There are 4 chairs at each table. How many chairs are in Tony's Restaurant? (TAKS Obj. 1)

   A 148

   B 141

   C 128

   D Not here

6. Tina's scout troop went to the circus. Tickets cost $3 each. There are 13 scouts in Tina's scout troop. How much did their tickets cost in all? (TAKS Obj. 1)

   F $39

   G $49

   H $59

   J $69

GO ONLINE **Technology** Use *Online Assessment.*

7. What is $\frac{2}{5}$ of 10? (TAKS Obj. 1)

A 2

B 4

C 6

D 8

8. What is the probability that the pointer of this spinner will land on green? (TAKS Obj. 5)

F 1 out of 5

G 2 out of 5

H 3 out of 5

J 4 out of 5

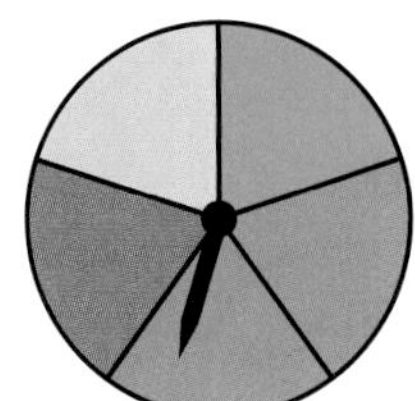

9. What fraction of the circle is shaded? (TAKS Obj. 1)

A one half

B two sixths

C two fourths

D four sixths

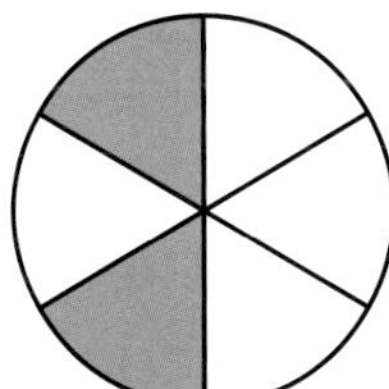

10. Zachary is putting his books onto a bookshelf. The bookshelf has 3 shelves. Each shelf holds 19 books. How many books are there in all? (TAKS Obj. 1)

F 47

G 51

H 54

J 57

Short Response

11. Write the missing fractions for the number line. (TAKS Obj. 1)

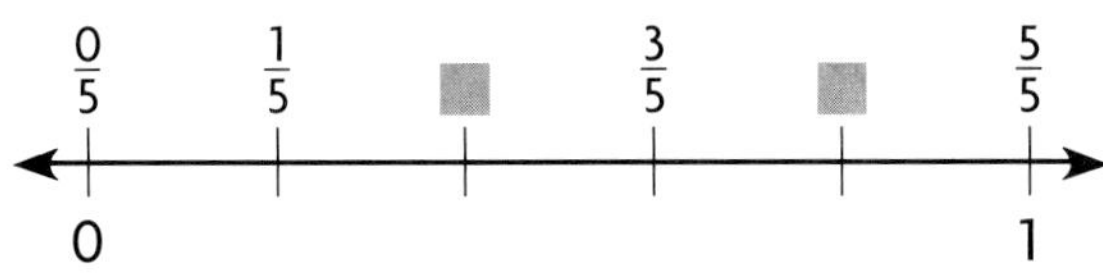

12. What is the product 4×32? (TAKS Obj. 1)

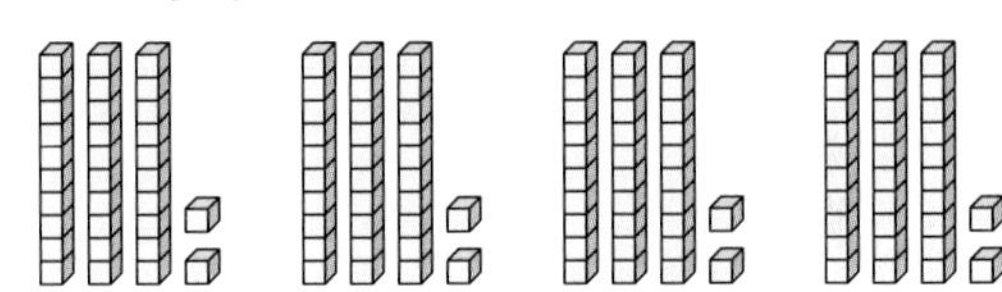

13. Ben pulls one cube from the bag. What are the possible outcomes of 1 pull? (TAKS Obj. 5)

Extended Response

14. What is the missing numerator? **Explain** how you know. (TAKS Obj. 1)

$\frac{4}{6} = \frac{\blacksquare}{12}$

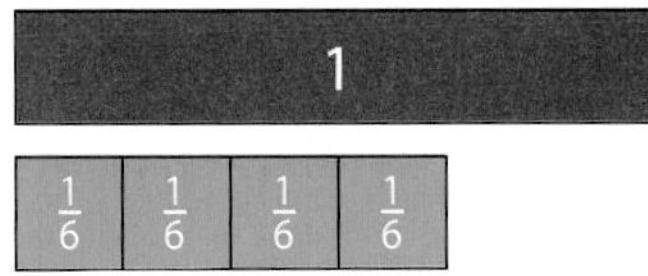

15. There are 28 students in Mrs. McKenna's class. Each student collected 5 shoe boxes. How many shoe boxes are there in all? **Explain** how you found your answer. (TAKS Obj. 1)

Texas

Problem Solving

Hello, World

Ways to Say Hello in Texas

In the United States, about 380 different languages are used, including some signed languages. The six most-used spoken languages in Texas are shown below.

Saying Hello in Texas

FACT·ACTIVITY

Hint: The vowels are A, E, I, O, and U.

For 1–3, use the greetings above.

1. How many of the greetings above begin with the letter *H*? How many greetings are shown in all? Write the fraction for the number of greetings that begin with *H*.
2. What fraction of the letters for the French greeting are vowels?
3. What fraction of the 6 greetings contain the letter *A*?
4. Say hello in your own way.
   - Work with a partner to make up a new word for *hello*.
   - Look at your new word for *hello*. What fraction of the letters are vowels?
   - What other fraction can you write about the letters in your new word?

ALMANAC **Fact**

Texas School for the Deaf was founded in Austin, Texas in 1857. It is the oldest public school in Texas and the first school for the deaf in the state.

SIGN LANGUAGE

Many people who cannot hear or speak use sign language to communicate. American Sign Language uses movements and positions of the hands and arms and expressions on the face. The American Manual Alphabet uses finger spelling.

American Manual Alphabet

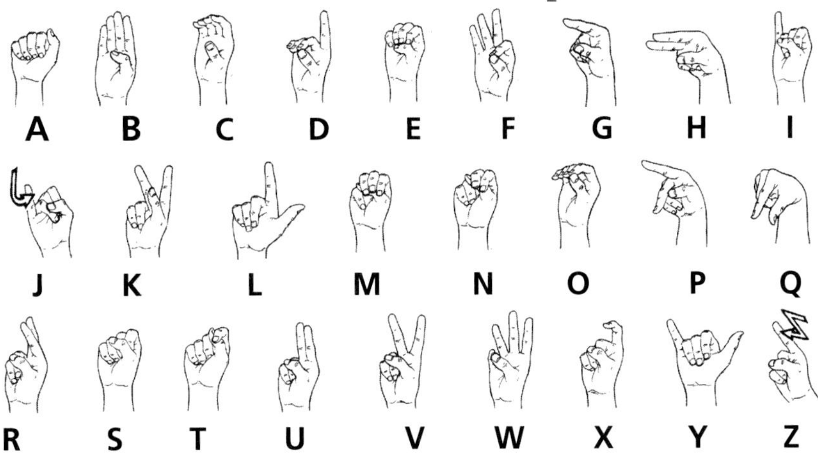

FACT·ACTIVITY

Use the alphabet chart above to help you answer the questions.

1. To sign the letter *F*, what fraction of your fingers on one hand do you have to hold up?
2. Look at the vowels, *A, E, I, O,* and *U*. For which vowel do you hold up $\frac{1}{5}$ of the fingers on your hand? For which vowel do you hold up $\frac{2}{5}$ of your fingers?
3. For what fraction of the letters in *hello* do you need to hold out fingers?
4. WRITE Math **Explain** how you found your answer to Problem 3.

Student Handbook

Review the TEKS

Place Value

TEKS 3.1A use place value to read, write (in symbols and words), and describe the value of whole numbers through 999,999.

Each digit in a number has a value. A place-value chart can help you understand the value of each digit. In the number 456,780, the 5 has a value of 50,000 because it is in the ten-thousands place.

HUNDRED THOUSANDS	TEN THOUSANDS	THOUSANDS	HUNDREDS	TENS	ONES
4	5	6,	7	8	0

Examples

A Write the number 4,506 in word form.

When writing a number in word form, use a comma between the thousands and hundreds places.

four thousand,
five hundred six

B Write the following number in standard form: three hundred twenty thousand, five hundred forty.

There are 3 hundred thousands, 2 ten thousands, 5 hundreds and 4 tens.

320,540

ERROR ALERT

Remember to identify the correct value for each digit.

Try It

Write each number in word form.

1. 2,565
2. 74,406
3. 126,890
4. 650,111

Write each number in standard form.

5. six hundred five

6. two hundred thousand, seventy-three

7. forty-four thousand, twenty-two

8. one thousand, eight hundred seven

9. Read the problem below. **Explain** why C cannot be the correct answer. Then choose the correct answer.

COMMON ERROR

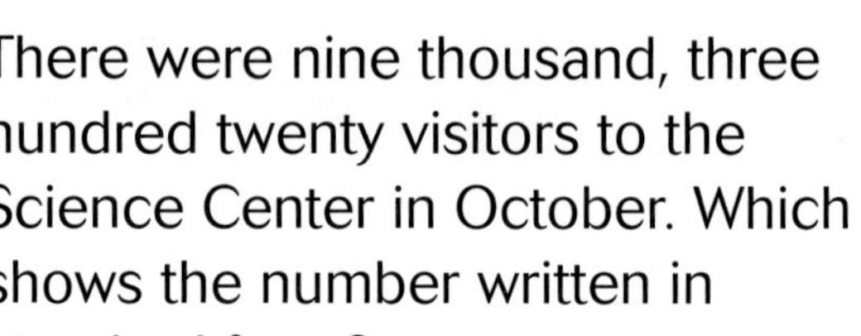

There were nine thousand, three hundred twenty visitors to the Science Center in October. Which shows the number written in standard form?

A 9,320
C 9,302
B 90,302
D 932

Review the TEKS

Compare and Order Numbers

TEKS 3.1B use place value to compare and order whole numbers through 9,999.

Understanding place value can help you compare and order numbers. To compare 6,902 and 6,743, start with the *greatest* place value. Both numbers have a 6 in the thousands place. Look at the digits in the hundreds place. 6,902 is greater than 6,743 because 9 is greater than 7.

Examples

A Which number is greater, 567 or 435?

Compare the digits in the hundreds place first.

567 435

$5 > 4$

So, $567 > 435$.

B Spring Elementary School is voting for class president. There are 261 votes for Connie, 232 votes for Javon, and 268 votes for Gina. Put the number of votes in order from greatest to least.

Since the hundreds digits are the same, compare the tens. If the tens are the same, compare the ones. Then put the numbers in order.

268, 261, 232

ERROR ALERT

Remember to compare digits from left to right.

Try It

Compare. Use $<$, $>$, or $=$ for each ●.

1. 81 ● 85
2. 526 ● 529
3. 772 ● 722
4. 4,237 ● 3,237
5. 3,659 ● 3,596
6. 7,894 ● 7,984

Order the numbers from least to greatest.

7. 14; 18; 12
8. 728; 721; 748
9. 8,593; 8,521; 8,499
10. 1,176; 1,167; 1,178
11. 1,784; 1,144; 1,774

12. Read the problem below. **Explain** why G cannot be the correct answer. Then choose the correct answer.

Store A sold 8,978 books, Store B sold 8,963, Store C sold 3,622, and Store D sold 1,075. Which store sold the most books?

F Store A **H** Store C

G Store B **J** Store D

Review the TEKS

Count Money

TEKS 3.1C determine the value of a collection of coins and bills.

Money amounts are written with whole numbers and decimals. When counting money, the whole numbers represent dollar bills and the decimals represent cents, or coins.

$\$3.00 + \$0.25 + \$0.05 + \$0.04 = \$3.34$

↑ dollars ↑ quarter ↑ nickel ↑ pennies

Examples

A How much money is there in all?

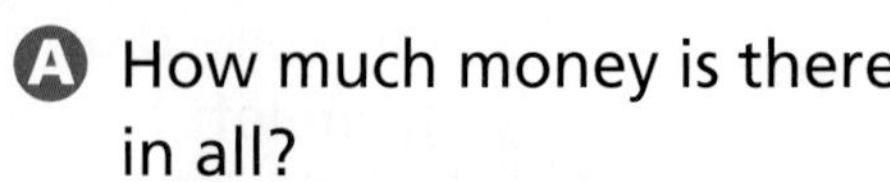

Add the dollars first and then the cents.

$8.00 + $0.25 = $8.25

B Write this amount in words.

$2.00 + $0.25 + $0.50 = $2.75

Two dollars and seventy-five cents.

ERROR ALERT

Remember to put a decimal in the amount to separate the dollars and cents.

Try It

Write each money amount.

1.    

2. 

3.  

4. 

5.   

6. Read the problem below. **Explain** why C cannot be the correct answer. Then choose the correct answer.

How much money is there in all?

A $5.25 **C** $1.25

B $5.35 **D** $0.25

Review the TEKS

Fractions

TEKS 3.2C use fraction names and symbols to describe fractional parts of whole objects or sets of objects.

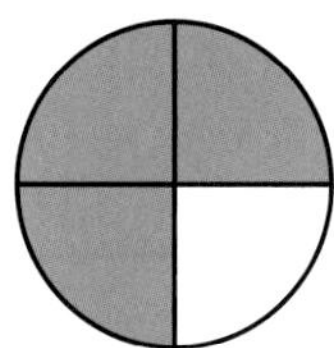

A number that names part of a whole or part of a group is called a fraction. The top number, or **numerator**, tells how many parts are being counted. The bottom number, or **denominator**, tells how many equal parts are in the whole or in the group. The figure to the right shows a circle with four parts. Three parts are shaded. So, $\frac{3}{4}$ of the circle is shaded.

Examples

A What fraction of this pizza is left?

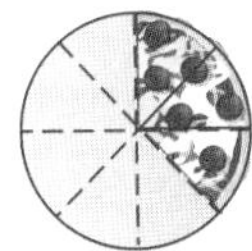

Count the number of slices left. That number is the numerator. Count the number of slices in all. That number is the denominator.

So, $\frac{3}{8}$ of the pizza is left.

B What fraction of the balls are striped?

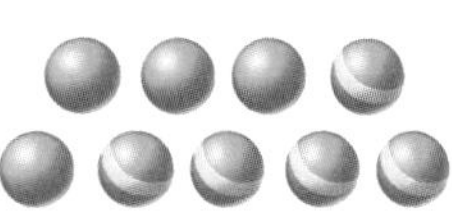

Count the number of striped balls. That number is the numerator. The number of balls in all is the denominator.

So, $\frac{5}{9}$ of the balls are striped.

ERROR ALERT

Think of the denominator as the whole and the numerator as the part that is being counted.

Try It

Answer each question.

1. What fraction of the cookies are round?
2. What fraction of the cookies are triangular?
3. What fraction of the cookies are heart-shaped?

4. Read the problem below. **Explain** why G cannot be the correct answer. Then choose the correct answer.

What fraction of the spinner is blue?

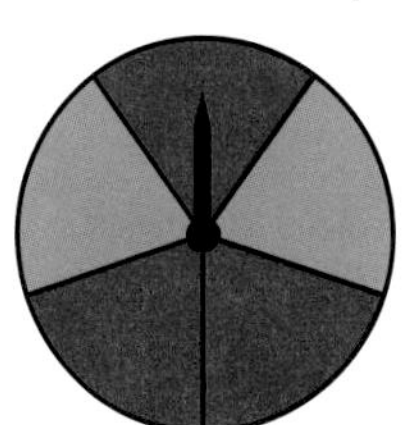

F $\frac{3}{5}$ **G** $\frac{5}{2}$ **H** $\frac{2}{3}$ **J** $\frac{2}{5}$

Review the TEKS

Addition and Subtraction

TEKS 3.3A model addition and subtraction using pictures, words, and numbers.

When adding and subtracting, line up the numbers vertically by place value. Add or subtract one place at a time, starting from the right with the ones, and work your way to the left. Regroup when needed. In the problem below, the sum of the ones is 13, so 10 ones are regrouped as 1 ten.

$$436 + 17 = 453$$

$$\begin{array}{r} \scriptstyle 1 \\ 436 \\ +\ 17 \\ \hline 453 \end{array}$$

Examples

A Randy has 48 comic books. If he buys 22 more, how many comic books will Randy have?

Add 22 comic books to the 48 he already has.

$$\begin{array}{r} \scriptstyle 1 \\ 48 \\ +22 \\ \hline 70 \end{array}$$

B Find 145 − 57.

Subtract 57 from 145.

$$\begin{array}{r} \scriptstyle 13 \\ \scriptstyle 0\ \not{3}\ 15 \\ \not{1}\not{4}\not{5} \\ -\ 57 \\ \hline 88 \end{array}$$

ERROR ALERT

Be sure to add when you see the + sign and subtract when you see the − sign.

Try It

Solve.

1. $\begin{array}{r} 976 \\ -\ 45 \\ \hline \end{array}$

2. $\begin{array}{r} 124 \\ +212 \\ \hline \end{array}$

3. $\begin{array}{r} 232 \\ -\ 23 \\ \hline \end{array}$

4. $\begin{array}{r} 326 \\ +\ 41 \\ \hline \end{array}$

5. 845 − 100

6. 12 + 750

7. 204 + 28

8. 67 + 239

9. 56 − 48

10. 681 − 492

11. 901 − 605

12. 722 + 148

13. Read the problem below. **Explain** why A cannot be the correct answer. Then choose the correct answer.

COMMON ERROR

There are 342 postcards in Isa's collection. Her grandmother gives her 168 more. How many postcards are in Isa's collection in all?

A 174

B 430

C 510

D 644

Review the TEKS

Addition and Subtraction

TEKS 3.3B select addition or subtraction and use the operation to solve problems involving whole numbers through 999.

When reading a word problem, look for key words and information to determine if addition or subtraction should be used. In the problem below, subtraction should be used because a number is being taken away from another number.

$$\begin{array}{r} {\scriptstyle 4\ 13} \\ 2\not{5}\not{3} \\ -\ 38 \\ \hline 215 \end{array}$$

Tyrone has 253 bottle caps in his collection. If he gives 38 of them to his sister, how many bottle caps does he have left?

$$253 - 38 = 215$$

Examples

A Robbie got 128 baseball cards from his brother for his birthday. His sister gave him 137 baseball cards. How many cards did Robbie get in all?

Add 128 and 137.

$$\begin{array}{r} {\scriptstyle 1} \\ 128 \\ +\ 137 \\ \hline 265 \end{array}$$

B Lauren and her mom start out with 317 brownies for the bake sale. If they sell 256, how many brownies will they have left?

Subtract 256 from 317.

$$\begin{array}{r} {\scriptstyle 2\ 11} \\ \not{3}\not{1}7 \\ -\ 256 \\ \hline 61 \end{array}$$

ERROR ALERT

Read the problem carefully to determine if it is an addition or subtraction problem.

Try It

Decide which operation to use. Then solve.

1. Last year, there were 249 booths at the state fair. This year, there will be 57 more booths. How many booths will there be in all?

2. Janet is supposed to pass out 196 flyers for her soccer team. She has passed out 79 of them so far. How many flyers does she have left?

3. Read the problem below. **Explain** why H cannot be the correct answer. Then choose the correct answer.

Michael has 480 stamps in his stamp collection. He sells 75 of them at a garage sale. How many stamps does Michael have left?

F 325 **H** 415

G 405 **J** 505

Review the TEKS

Multiplication

TEKS 3.4B solve and record multiplication problems (up to two digits times one digit).

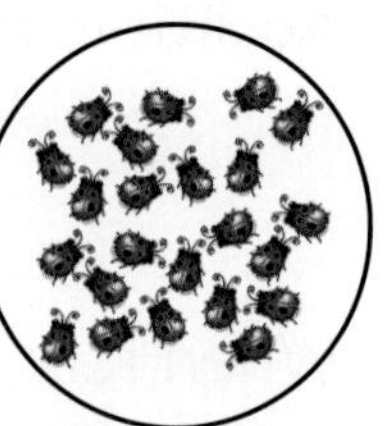

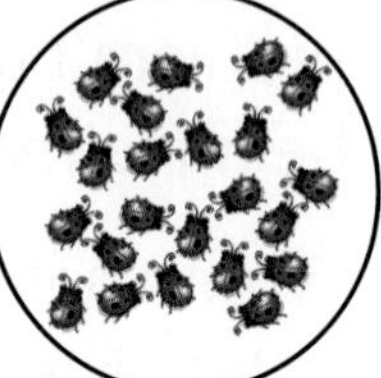

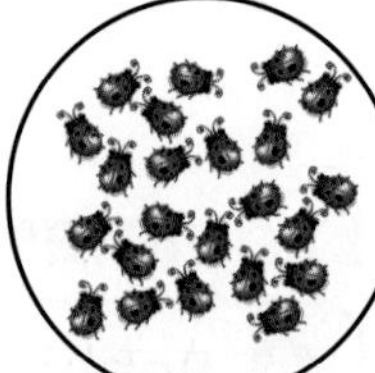

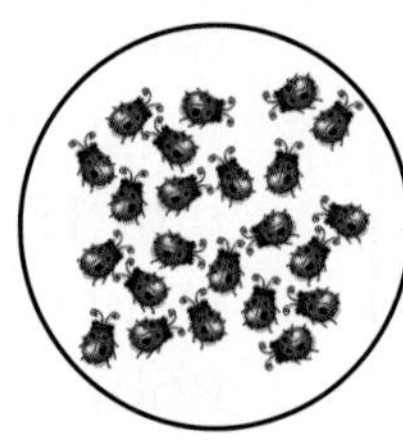

Step 1	Step 2	Step 3
Line up the numbers vertically by place value.	Multiply the ones.	Multiply the tens, and remember to add any regrouped tens.
$\begin{array}{r} 23 \\ \times\ 4 \\ \hline \end{array}$	$\begin{array}{r} {}^{1} \\ 23 \\ \times\ 4 \\ \hline 2 \end{array}$	$\begin{array}{r} {}^{1} \\ 23 \\ \times\ 4 \\ \hline 92 \end{array}$

Examples

A Solve 16 × 6.

$$\begin{array}{r} {}^{3} \\ 16 \\ \times\ 6 \\ \hline 96 \end{array}$$

B Solve 28 × 3.

$$\begin{array}{r} {}^{2} \\ 28 \\ \times\ 3 \\ \hline 84 \end{array}$$

Always multiply starting from the right with the ones. Then work your way left.

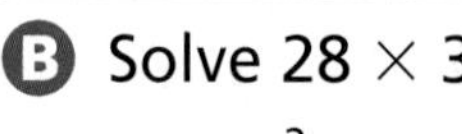

Try It

Solve.

1. $\begin{array}{r} 8 \\ \times 3 \\ \hline \end{array}$

2. $\begin{array}{r} 15 \\ \times\ 7 \\ \hline \end{array}$

3. $\begin{array}{r} 12 \\ \times\ 6 \\ \hline \end{array}$

4. $\begin{array}{r} 33 \\ \times\ 3 \\ \hline \end{array}$

Write vertically and solve.

5. 7 × 13

6. 39 × 2

7. 63 × 5

8. 24 × 3

9. Read the problem below. **Explain** why C cannot be the correct answer. Then choose the correct answer.

Cody needs to make 32 bags of party favors for his sister's birthday party. There need to be 5 balloons in each bag. How many balloons does Cody need in all?

A 50

B 120

C 150

D 160

Review the TEKS

Rounding Whole Numbers

TEKS 3.5A round whole numbers to the nearest ten or hundred to approximate reasonable results in problem situations.

You can round numbers when you do not need an exact answer. To round, first find the place you are rounding to. Then, look at the digit to the right. If the digit is less than 5, the digit being rounded will stay the same. If the digit is 5 or greater, the digit being rounded will increase by 1.

478 rounded to the nearest ten is 480.
478 rounded to the nearest hundred is 500.

Examples

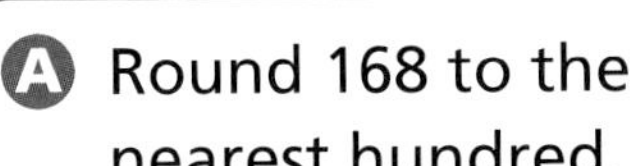

A Round 168 to the nearest hundred.

Look at the tens digit.

$6 > 5$

168 rounds to 200.

B Round 37 to the nearest ten.

Look at the ones digit.

$7 > 5$

37 rounds to 40.

ERROR ALERT

If the digit in the place to the right is 5 or greater, the digit being rounded increases by 1.

Try It

Round to the nearest ten.

1. 15 **2.** 89

3. 109 **4.** 234

5. 27 **6.** 981

Round to the nearest hundred.

7. 116 **8.** 456

9. 795 **10.** 311

11. 98 **12.** 108

13. Read the problem below. **Explain** why G cannot be the correct answer. Then choose the correct answer. **COMMON ERROR**

Which is rounded to the nearest hundred correctly?

F 267 rounds to 250.

G 267 rounds to 200.

H 267 rounds to 300.

J 267 rounds to 260.

Review the TEKS

Estimating

TEKS 3.5B use strategies including rounding and compatible numbers to estimate solutions to addition and subtraction problems.

Rounding and compatible numbers can help you estimate the answer to a problem. Estimating the answer before solving a problem gives you a reasonable idea of what the answer should be.

Examples

A Use rounding to find 27 − 12.

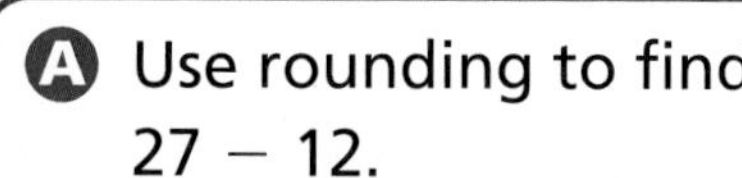

Round to the nearest ten.

$$\begin{array}{rcr} 27 & \rightarrow & 30 \\ -\,12 & \rightarrow & -\,10 \\ \hline & & 20 \end{array}$$

B Use compatible numbers to find 452 + 324.

Find close numbers that are easy to compute mentally.

$$\begin{array}{rcr} 452 & \rightarrow & 450 \\ +\,324 & \rightarrow & +\,325 \\ \hline & & 775 \end{array}$$

ERROR ALERT

If the digit in the place to the right of the place being rounded is 5 or greater, the digit increases by 1.

Try It

Use rounding to estimate.

1. $11 + 22 = ■$
2. $87 - 31 = ■$
3. $\begin{array}{r} 78 \\ -\,56 \\ \hline \end{array}$
4. $\begin{array}{r} 392 \\ +\,225 \\ \hline \end{array}$

Use compatible numbers to estimate.

5. $183 + 219 = ■$
6. $176 - 103 = ■$
7. $\begin{array}{r} 227 \\ +\,521 \\ \hline \end{array}$
8. $\begin{array}{r} 452 \\ -\,295 \\ \hline \end{array}$

9. Read the problem below. **Explain** why C cannot be the correct answer. Then choose the correct answer.

COMMON ERROR

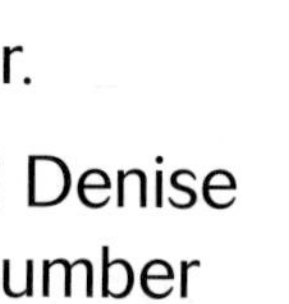

Pete has 279 pennies and Denise has 123 pennies. Which number sentence shows the best estimate of the amount of pennies they have together?

A $200 + 200 = 400$

B $280 + 120 = 400$

C $300 + 200 = 500$

D $200 + 100 = 300$

Review the TEKS

Patterns

TEKS 3.6A identify and extend whole-number and geometric patterns to make predictions and solve problems.

A pattern is an ordered set of numbers or objects. The picture shows a box with four marbles. If each box has 4 marbles, how many marbles are in 3 boxes? Use a pattern. Count by fours 3 times.

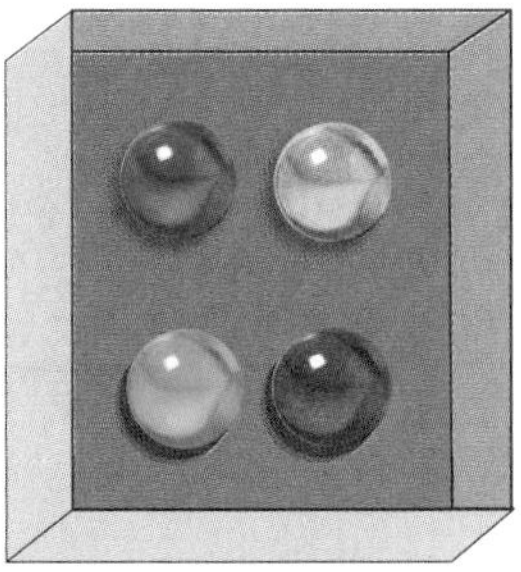

4 marbles in one box, 8 marbles in two boxes, 12 marbles in three boxes.

So, there are 12 marbles in 3 boxes.

Examples

A Tory is making a bracelet. If she continues to use the same pattern, what will be the next three beads?

The pattern unit is striped, solid, polka-dot.

So, the next three beads are polka-dot, striped, and solid.

B Finish the pattern: 6, 12, 18, ■

The numbers increase by 6. The rule is *add 6*.

18 + 6 = 24

So, the next number in the pattern is 24.

ERROR ALERT

Remember to find the pattern unit or rule before solving the problem.

Try It

Write a rule. Then finish the pattern.

1. 5, 10, 15, 20, ■
2. 18, 15, 12, 9, ■, ■
3. 7, 14, ■, 28, 35, ■
4. ○□△○□△○□△ ?

5. Read the problem below. **Explain** why H cannot be the correct answer. Then choose the correct answer.

There are 8 groups of 4 ducks each. What pattern can you use to count them?

F 4, 8, 12, 20, 16, 24, 28, 32

G 8, 16, 24, 32

H 4, 8, 10, 12, 16, 20, 24, 28, 32

J 4, 8, 12, 16, 20, 24, 28, 32

Review the TEKS

Patterns in Multiplication and Division

TEKS 3.6C identify patterns in related multiplication and division sentences (fact families) such as $2 \times 3 = 6$, $3 \times 2 = 6$, $6 \div 2 = 3$, $6 \div 3 = 2$.

A set of related multiplication and division number sentences is called a fact family. Because multiplication and division are opposite operations, you can use related multiplication facts to find quotients or missing divisors in division sentences.

$3 \times 4 = 12$ $\quad$ $12 \div 3 = 4$

$4 \times 3 = 12$ $\quad$ $12 \div 4 = 3$

=

Examples

A Find $9 \times$ ■ $= 18$ and $18 \div$ ■ $= 2$.

Use the fact family to solve.

$9 \times 2 = 18$ and $18 \div 9 = 2$

B Find $20 \div 10 =$ ■ and $10 \times$ ■ $= 20$.

Identify the fact family and solve.

$20 \div 10 = 2$ and $10 \times 2 = 20$

ERROR ALERT

Always use the same 3 numbers when solving fact family problems.

Try It

Use a related fact to solve.

1. $30 \div$ ■ $= 6$
2. $10 \times$ ■ $= 40$
3. $7 \times$ ■ $= 49$
4. $15 \div 3 =$ ■
5. ■ $\times 6 = 54$
6. $3 \times$ ■ $= 24$
7. $40 \div$ ■ $= 8$
8. $10 \times$ ■ $= 90$
9. $4 \times$ ■ $= 32$
10. $42 \div 7 =$ ■
11. ■ $\times 8 = 56$
12. $9 \times$ ■ $= 18$
13. $72 \div$ ■ $= 9$
14. $36 \div 6 =$ ■

15. Read the problem below. **Explain** why D cannot be the correct answer. Then choose the correct answer. **COMMON ERROR**

Which number is missing in the fact family below?
$2 \times 5 = 10$ and $10 \div$ ■ $= 5$.

A 2

B 5

C 10

D 50

Review the TEKS

Tables and Functions

TEKS 3.7A generate a table of paired numbers based on a real-life situation such as insects and legs.

Tables can help you organize information and help you find patterns.

Examples

A If there are 4 birds flying, how many wings are there in all? Make a table to show the pattern.

Number of birds	1	2	3	4
Number of wings	2	4	6	8

So, there are 8 wings.

B Mrs. Foster has 5 tables in her classroom. Each table has 4 legs. How many legs are on 5 tables? Make a table to show the pattern.

Tables	1	2	3	4	5
Legs	4	8	12	16	20

So, 5 tables have 20 legs.

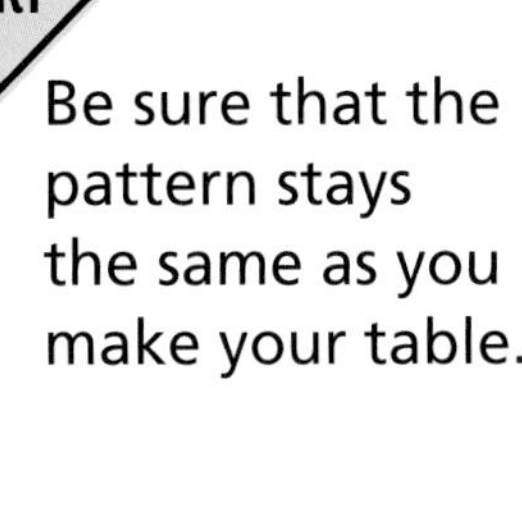

Be sure that the pattern stays the same as you make your table.

Try It

Complete the table.

1. Each child at daycare gets a snack of 10 pretzels. Complete the table to show the pattern.

Child	1	2	3	4	5	6
Pretzels	10	■	30	40	■	■

2. There is a stack of sweaters at the store. Each sweater has 5 buttons. Complete the table to show the pattern.

Sweaters	1	10	20	30
Buttons	5	■	100	■

3. All spiders have 8 legs. Make a table to show how many legs 7 spiders would have.

4. Read the problem below. **Explain** why F cannot be the correct answer. Then choose the correct answer.

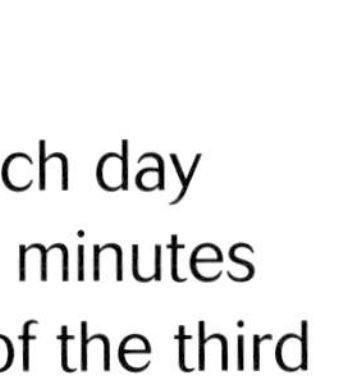

John walks ten minutes each day for seven days. How many minutes has he walked at the end of the third day? Make a table. Then choose an answer.

F 15 minutes

G 30 minutes

H 40 minutes

J 60 minutes

Review the TEKS

Tables and Patterns

TEKS 3.7B identify and describe patterns in a table of related number pairs based on a meaningful problem and extend the table.

Find the pattern and write a rule to understand the relationships between numbers. Writing a rule can help you to extend the table or find missing numbers in the table.

6	9	12	15
2	3	■	5

Pattern: Each number in the top row is divided by 3 to find the number in the bottom row.

Rule: Divide by 3.

To find the missing number, divide 12 by 3. $12 \div 3 = 4$

So, the missing number is 4.

Examples

A What is the rule for this table?

1	3	5	7	9
2	6	10	14	18

The rule is: multiply by 2.

B What is the rule for this table?

10	20	30	40	50
2	4	6	8	10

The rule is: divide by 5.

ERROR ALERT

Use the same rule to find all of the numbers in a table.

Try It

Write a rule. Then copy and complete the table.

1.

Pairs of gloves	3	4	5	6	7
Gloves	6	■	10	12	■

2.

Bottles of water	6	12	18	24	30
Runners	1	2	■	■	5

3. Read the problem below. **Explain** why C cannot be the correct answer. Then choose the correct answer.

COMMON ERROR

Mr. Brown runs 1 mile in 8 minutes. At the same speed, how many miles can he run in 40 minutes?

Miles	1	2	3	4	5
Minutes	8	16	24	32	■

A 4 miles
B 5 miles
C 40 miles
D 320 miles

Review the TEKS

Classifying Two- and Three-Dimensional Figures

TEKS 3.8 The student is expected to identify, classify, and describe two- and three-dimensional geometric figures by their attributes. The student compares two-dimensional figures, three-dimensional figures, or both by their attributes using formal geometry vocabulary.

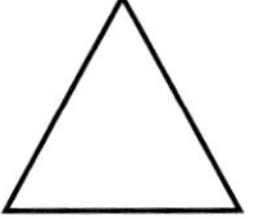

A two-dimensional figure is a figure on a flat surface. Triangles, rectangles, squares, pentagons, and octagons are some examples of two-dimensional figures.

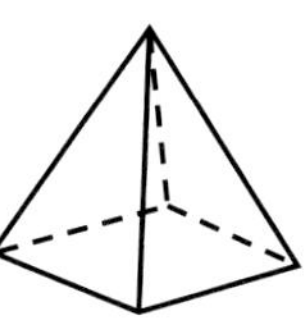

Three-dimensional figures, or solid figures, have length, width, and height. Cubes, spheres, rectangular prisms, cones, square pyramids, and cylinders are some examples of three-dimensional figures.

Examples

A Describe the figure. Think about the number of sides and vertices and the types of angles.

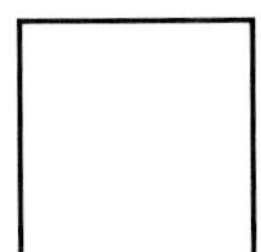

This figure has 4 equal sides, 4 right angles, and 4 vertices. It is two-dimensional. It is a square.

B Describe the figure. Think about how many faces, edges, and vertices it has.

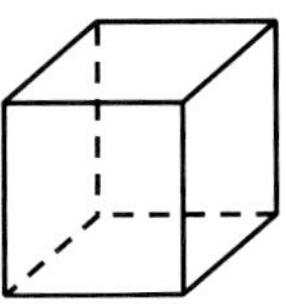

This solid figure has 6 faces that are all squares. It has 8 vertices and 12 edges. It is three-dimensional. It is a cube.

ERROR ALERT

Remember that a three-dimensional figure is a solid, an object you can hold.

Try It

Describe and name each figure.

1.

2.

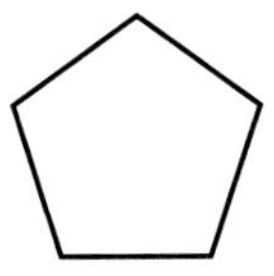

3.

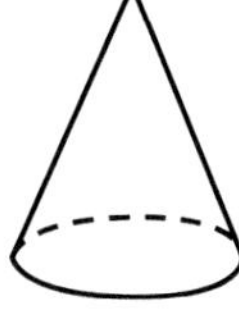

4.

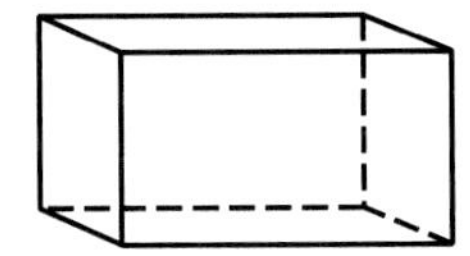

5. Read the problem below. **Explain** why J cannot be the correct answer. Then choose the correct answer.

COMMON ERROR

Which figure is this?

F Triangular prism

G Rectangular prism

H Square pyramid

J Triangle

Review the TEKS

Compare Two- and Three-Dimensional Figures

TEKS 3.8 The student is expected to identify, classify, and describe two- and three-dimensional geometric figures by their attributes. The student compares two-dimensional figures, three-dimensional figures, or both by their attributes using formal geometry vocabulary.

Two-dimensional figures are named by their sides and vertices. Three-dimensional figures are named by their faces, edges, and vertices.

A face of a three-dimensional figure is a flat surface. An edge is a line segment formed where 2 faces meet. A vertex is a point where 3 or more edges meet.

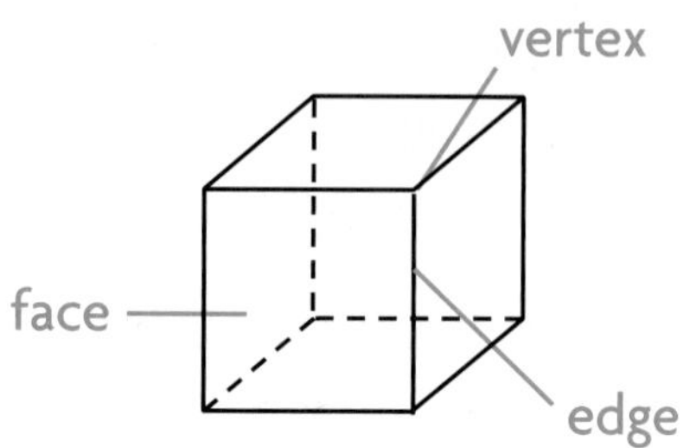

Examples

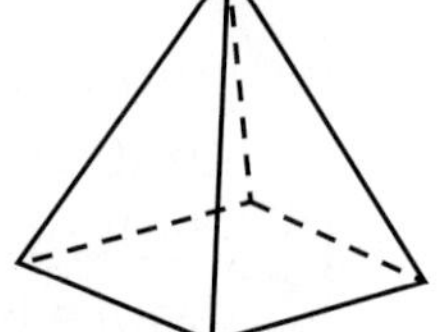

How many faces does the square pyramid have?
5 faces

How would you describe each of the faces?
Four faces are triangles, and one face is a square.

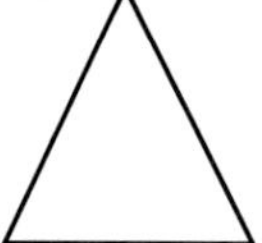

How many sides does the triangle have? 3 sides

How many vertices does the triangle have? 3 vertices

ERROR ALERT

Remember to think about all the hidden faces of a solid figure.

Try It

Look at the figure below.

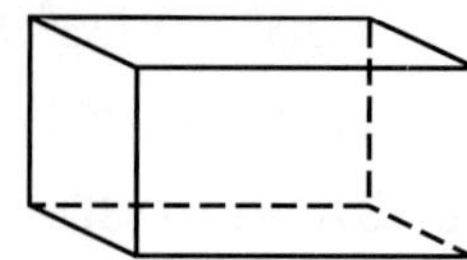

This rectangular prism has:

1. ■ faces
2. ■ vertices
3. ■ edges
4. What two-dimensional figures are found on the prism?

5. Read the problem below. **Explain** why D cannot be the correct answer. Then choose the correct answer. **COMMON ERROR**
What two-dimensional figure forms the top of this cylinder?

A triangle
B square
C circle
D sphere

Review the TEKS

Congruent Figures

TEKS 3.9A identify congruent two-dimensional figures.

Congruent figures have the same size and shape. If you were to trace a figure, cut out the tracing, and place it on top of the figure, their sides and vertices would match.

Examples

A Do these figures appear to be congruent?

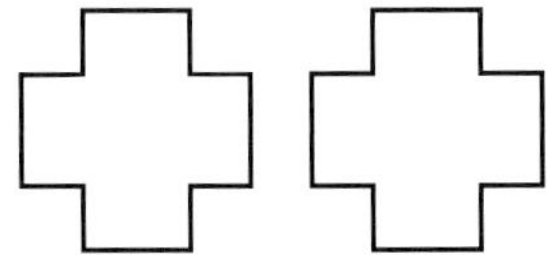

Yes, both figures are the same shape and size.

B Do these figures appear to be congruent?

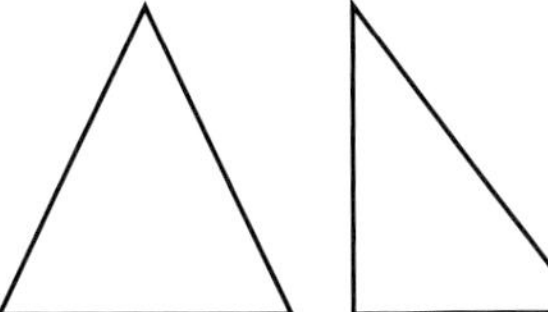

No, the figures are not congruent. They are both triangles, but they are different shapes and sizes.

ERROR ALERT

Remember that even if congruent figures change position, they are still congruent.

Try It

Tell if each pair of figures appears to be congruent. Write *yes* or *no*.

1.

2.

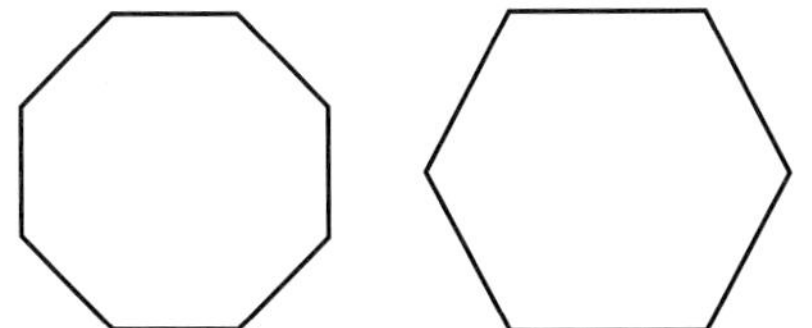

3.

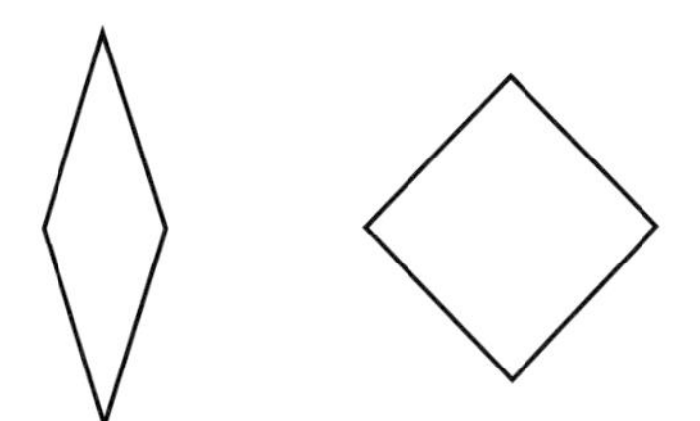

4.

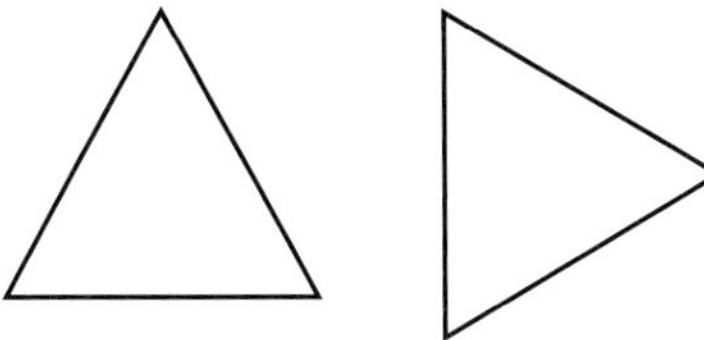

5. Read the problem below. **Explain** why H cannot be the correct answer. Then choose the correct answer.

COMMON ERROR

Which appears to be congruent to this figure?

F

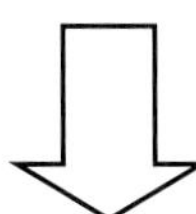

H

G

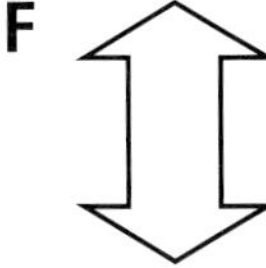

J

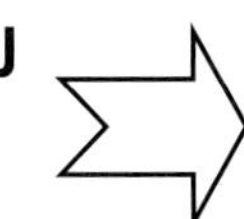

Review the TEKS

Symmetry

TEKS 3.9C Identify lines of symmetry in two-dimensional geometric figures.

A figure has symmetry if it can be folded along a line so that the two halves are congruent. The line is called the **line of symmetry**. Some figures have no line of symmetry, and others have one or more lines of symmetry.

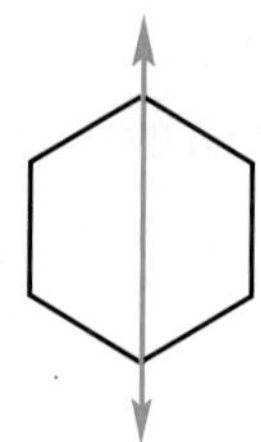

Examples

A Does the blue line appear to be a line of symmetry?

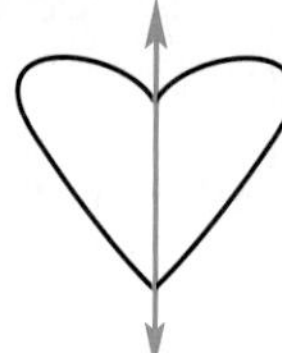

Yes, the figures on both sides of the line appear to be congruent.

B Does the blue line appear to be a line of symmetry?

No, the figures on both sides of the line are not congruent.

ERROR ALERT

The figures on both sides of the fold must have the exact same size and shape.

Try It

Tell if the blue line appears to be a line of symmetry. Write *yes* or *no*.

1. 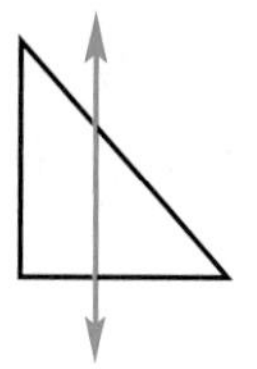

2. 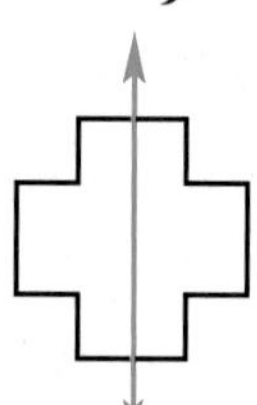

3. 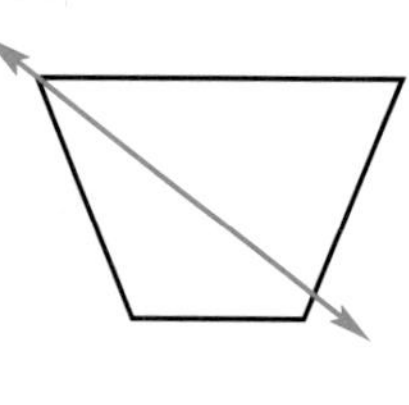

Tell if the figures appear to have 0, 1, or more than 1 line of symmetry.

4. 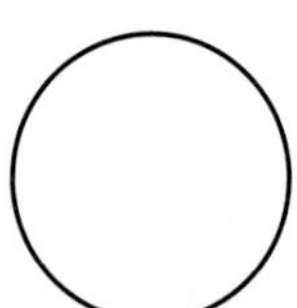

5. 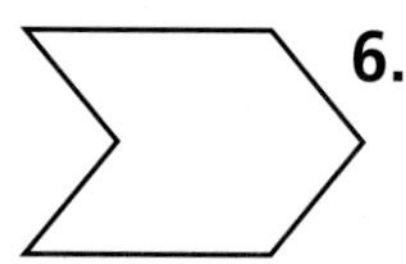

6. 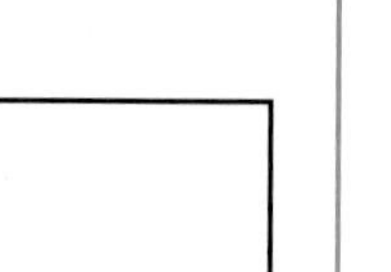

7. Read the problem below. **Explain** why A cannot be the correct answer. Then choose the correct answer.

COMMON ERROR

Which figure or figures show a line of symmetry?

1. 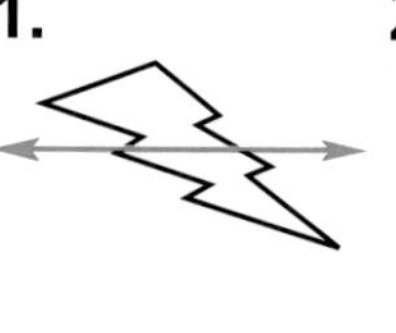

2. 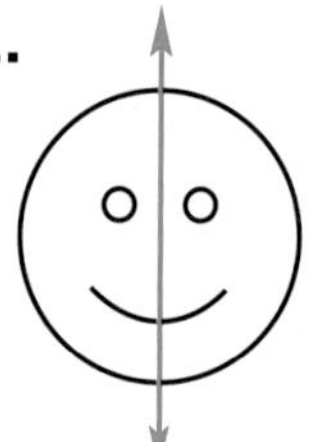

3. 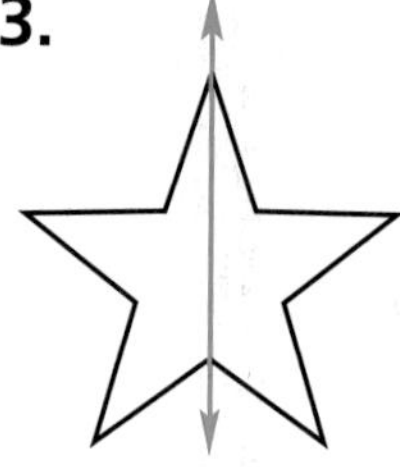

A 1 and 2

B 1 and 3

C 2 and 3

D 1, 2, and 3

Review the TEKS

Perimeter

TEKS 3.11B use standard units to find the perimeter of a shape.

Perimeter is the distance around a shape. Find the perimeter by measuring each side of the shape and adding the lengths of the sides.

Examples

A Find the perimeter.

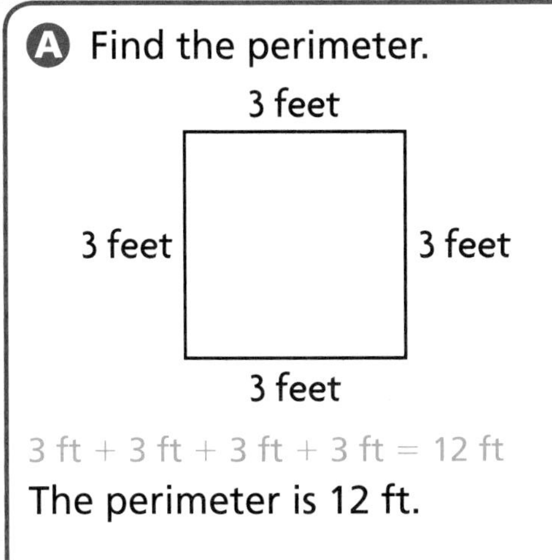

3 ft + 3 ft + 3 ft + 3 ft = 12 ft

The perimeter is 12 ft.

B Find the perimeter.

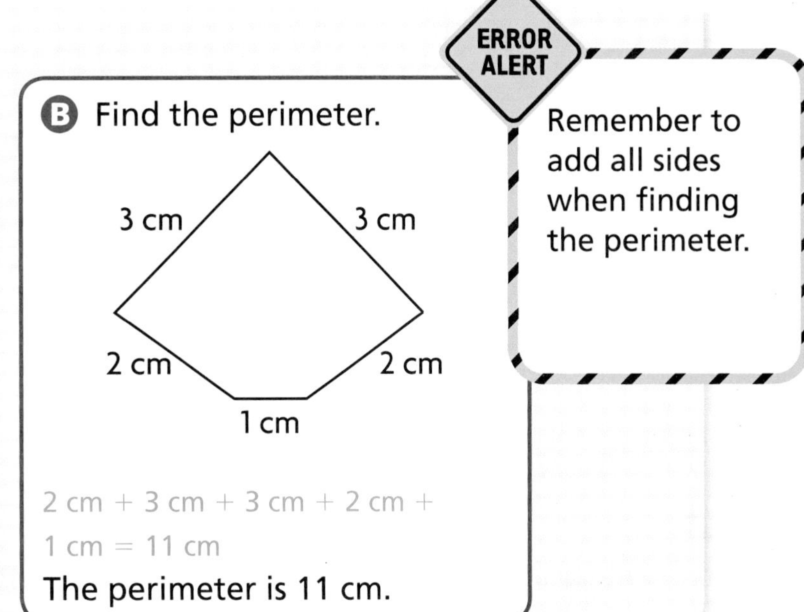

ERROR ALERT
Remember to add all sides when finding the perimeter.
3 cm
3 cm
2 cm
2 cm
1 cm

2 cm + 3 cm + 3 cm + 2 cm + 1 cm = 11 cm

The perimeter is 11 cm.

Try It

Find the perimeter of each figure.

1.

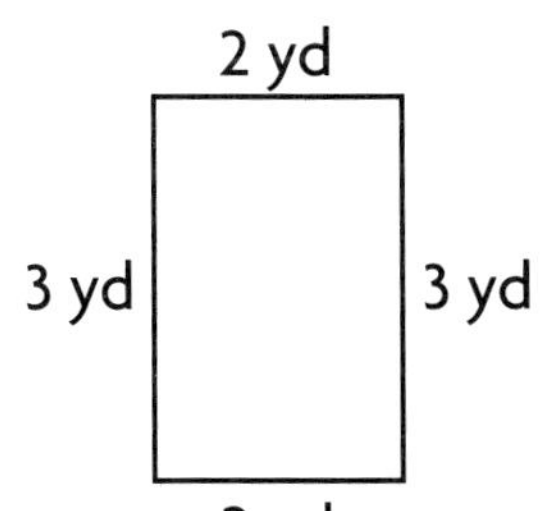

2.

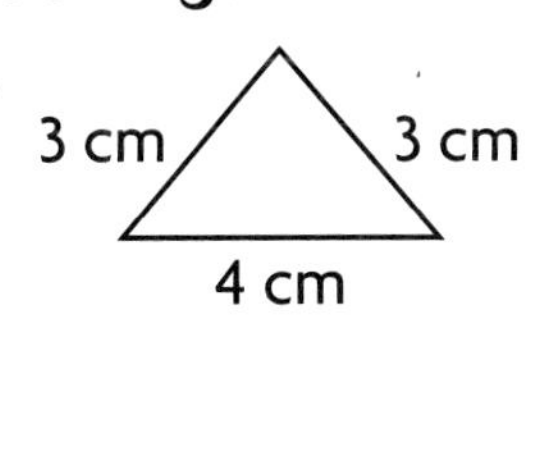

3. **4.**

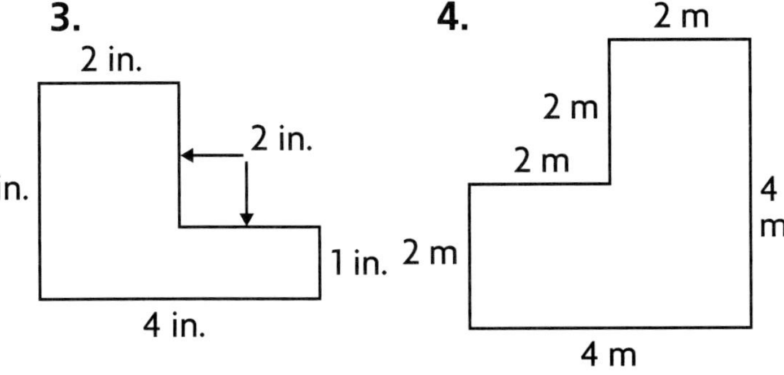

5. Read the problem below. **Explain** why F cannot be the correct answer. Then choose the correct answer.

COMMON ERROR

Each side of Mrs. Brown's square garden measures 10 feet. Which measurements should she use to decide how much fence to buy?

F 10 feet + 10 feet = 20 feet

G 10 feet + 10 feet + 10 feet + 10 feet = 40 feet

H 10 feet + 10 feet + 10 feet = 30 feet

J 10 feet + 10 feet + 10 feet + 10 feet + 10 feet = 50 feet

Review the TEKS

Weight and Mass

TEKS 3.11D identify concrete models that approximate standard units of weight/mass and use them to measure weight/mass.

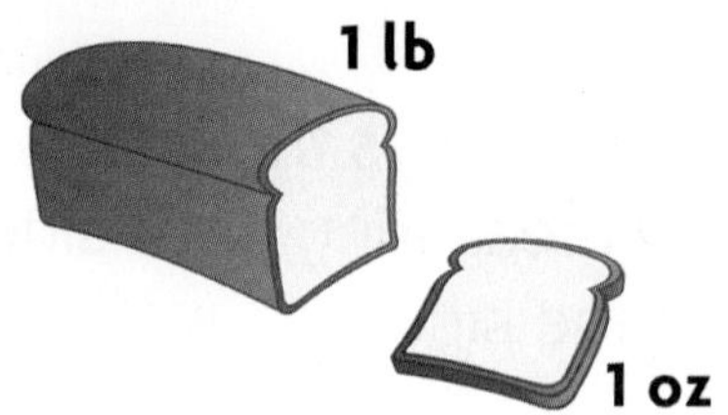

The customary units used to measure weight are ounce (oz) and pound (lb). A slice of bread weighs about 1 ounce. A loaf of bread weighs about 1 pound.

Examples

A Would you use ounces or pounds to estimate the weight of a table?

Pounds; a table weighs more than a loaf of bread.

B Would you use ounces or pounds to estimate the weight of an eraser?

Ounces; the weight of an eraser is much less than a slice of bread.

Try It

Choose the unit you would use to weigh each. Write *ounce* or *pound*.

1. box of paper clips
2. bowling ball
3. golf ball
4. bicycle

Choose the better unit of measure. Write *ounces* or *pounds*.

5. A cat weighs about 10 _?_.
6. A pencil weighs about 1 _?_.

7. Read the problem below. **Explain** why C cannot be the correct answer. Then choose the correct answer.

Mrs. Jones wants to know how much her luggage weighs. Choose the most reasonable weight.

A 20 feet

B 20 pounds

C 20 ounces

D 300 pounds

Review the TEKS

Capacity

TEKS 3.11E identify concrete models that approximate standard units for capacity and use them to measure capacity.

Capacity is the amount a container can hold. Cups, pints, quarts, and gallons are customary units to measure capacity.

1 pint (pt) = 2 cups (c)

1 quart (qt) = 2 pints or 4 cups

1 gallon (gal) = 4 quarts or 8 pints or 16 cups

Examples

A Janine is making fruit punch for a party. Should she buy 4 quarts or 4 cups of orange juice?

4 quarts; 4 cups would not be enough juice.

B Jorge is pouring water into the bird bath outdoors. Would he pour about 1 cup or 1 gallon?

about 1 gallon; the bird bath holds more than 1 cup of water.

ERROR ALERT

When choosing units of capacity, remember how the units are related.

Try It

Choose the better estimate.

1. Hot tub— 200 pints or 200 gallons?
2. Glass of milk— 2 quarts or 2 cups?
3. Jug of milk— 1 gallon or 1 cup?
4. Bird bath— 4 cups or 4 quarts?

Compare. Write <, >, or = for each ●.

5. 2 cups ● 1 pint
6. 2 pints ● 2 quarts
7. 1 gallon ● 2 quarts
8. 1 quart ● 2 cups

9. Read the problem below. **Explain** why F cannot be the correct answer. Then choose the correct answer.

COMMON ERROR

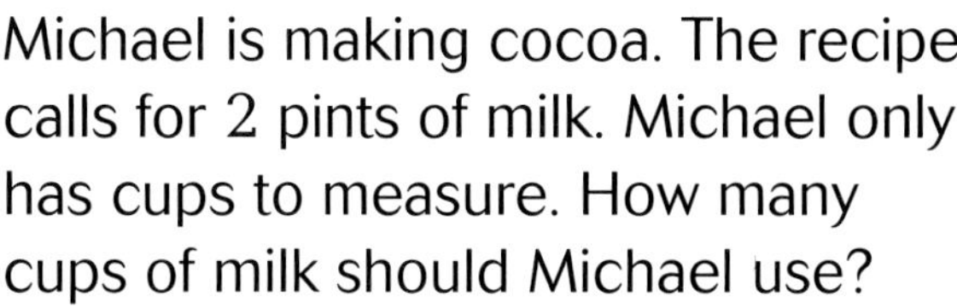

Michael is making cocoa. The recipe calls for 2 pints of milk. Michael only has cups to measure. How many cups of milk should Michael use?

F 2

G 4

H 8

J 16

Review the TEKS

Measure Temperature

TEKS 3.12A use a thermometer to measure temperature.

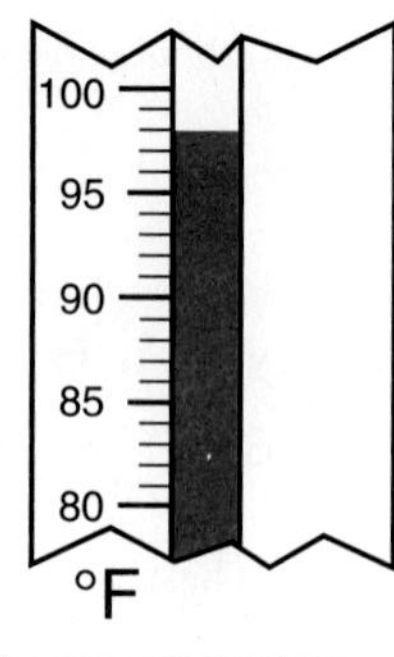

Fahrenheit (°F) is the customary unit to measure temperature. The lines on a thermometer represent degrees. Different thermometers may use different scales. The thermometer on the right reads 98°F.

Examples

A What is the temperature?

90
85
80
75
70
°F

The temperature is two lines past the 70° mark. So the temperature is 72°F.

B What is the temperature?

55
50
45
40
35
°F

The temperature is three lines past the 40° mark. So the temperature is 43°F.

ERROR ALERT

Remember to read the number at the top of the red bar.

Try It

Write the temperature in °F

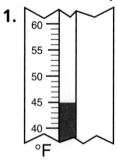

1.

60
55
50
45
40
°F

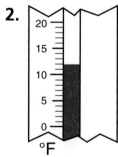

2.

20
15
10
5
0
°F

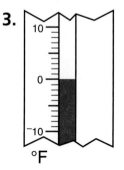

3.

10
0
−10
°F

4.

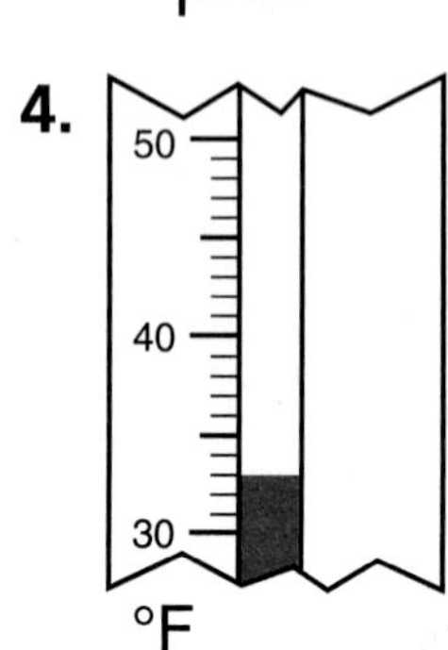

5. Read the problem below. **Explain** why D cannot be the correct answer. Then choose the correct answer.

COMMON ERROR

The thermometer below shows the temperature at an indoor skating rink. What is the temperature?

A 40°F

B 37°F

C 35°F

D 32°F

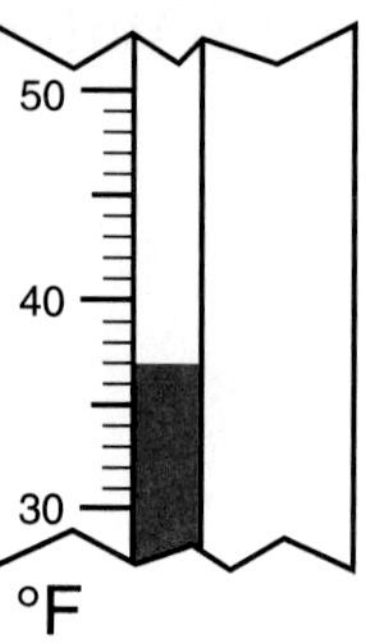

Review the TEKS

Time

TEKS 3.12B tell and write time shown on analog and digital clocks.

Analog and digital clocks show the time in different ways. An analog clock has a hand that shows the hour and a hand that shows the minutes. A digital clock shows the time in digits. The clocks to the right both show 6:23.

Examples

A What time is shown?

The hour is 2, because the hour hand is between the 2 and the 3. To find the number of minutes after the hour, count by fives and ones until you get to where the minute hand is pointing.

2:48

B Read the time on each clock.

Both clocks show the same time. You can read the time as one twenty or 20 minutes after one.

ERROR ALERT

Remember that the hour hand is shorter than the minute hand.

Try It

Write each time. Then write 2 ways to read each time.

1.

2.

3.

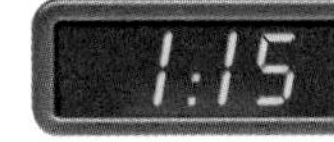

4.

5.

6.

7. Read the problem below. **Explain** why F cannot be the correct answer. Then choose the correct answer.

Sam's music lesson begins at the time shown on the clock below. At what time does Sam's music lesson begin?

F 10:25

G 10:17

H 3:50

J 4:50

Review the TEKS

Pictographs

TEKS 3.13B interpret information from pictographs and bar graphs.

A pictograph is a graph that represents data with pictures. The key tells how many each picture represents.

ERROR ALERT Read the key to learn what number each picture represents.

Examples

A How many monkeys are at the zoo?

Zoo Animals	
Elephants	🐾🐾🐾🐾
Monkeys	🐾🐾🐾🐾🐾
Giraffes	🐾🐾
Key: Each 🐾 = 5 animals.	

Each paw print represents 5 animals. $5 \times 5 = 25$

There are 25 monkeys at the zoo.

B How many students voted for English as their favorite subject?

Favorite Subject	
Math	📘📘📘📘📘
English	📘📘📘📘
Social Studies	📘📘
Science	📘📘📘📘📘
Key: Each 📘 = 4 students.	

Each book represents 4 students. $4 \times 4 = 16$

There were 16 students who voted for English.

Try It

Use the pictograph.

Favorite Fruit	
Apples	☺☺☺
Bananas	☺☺☺☺☺☺☺
Oranges	☺
Grapes	☺☺☺☺☺
Key: Each ☺ = 5 votes.	

1. How many people chose grapes?
2. How many more people chose apples than oranges?

3. Read the problem below. **Explain** why A cannot be the correct answer. Then choose the correct answer.

How many dogs and cats in all are owned by the students in Carl's class?

Family Pets	
Dog	👍👍👍👍👍👍👍👍👍
Cat	👍👍👍👍👍👍
Bird	👍👍👍
Fish	👍👍👍👍
Key: Each 👍 = 2 pets.	

A 15 **B** 20 **C** 30 **D** 44

Review the TEKS

Bar Graphs

TEKS 3.13B interpret information from pictographs and bar graphs.

ERROR ALERT
Remember how to read a bar that ends halfway between 2 lines.

A bar graph uses bars to show data. The number scale helps you find the number that each bar shows.

Example

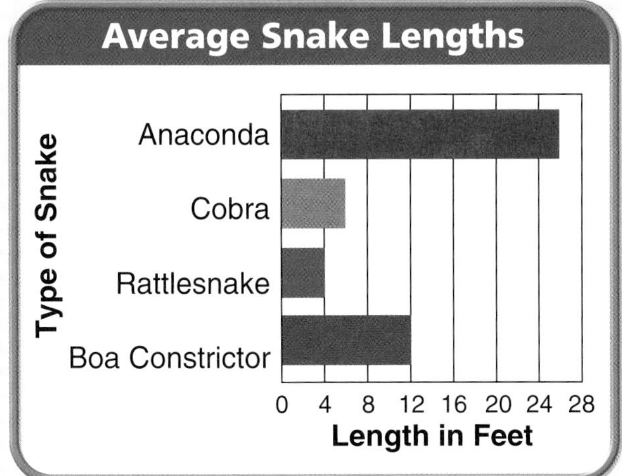

A How much longer is the anaconda than the boa constrictor?

The bar for anaconda is halfway between 24 and 28.

$26 - 12 = 14$

The anaconda is 14 feet longer.

Try It

For 1–3, use the bar graph.

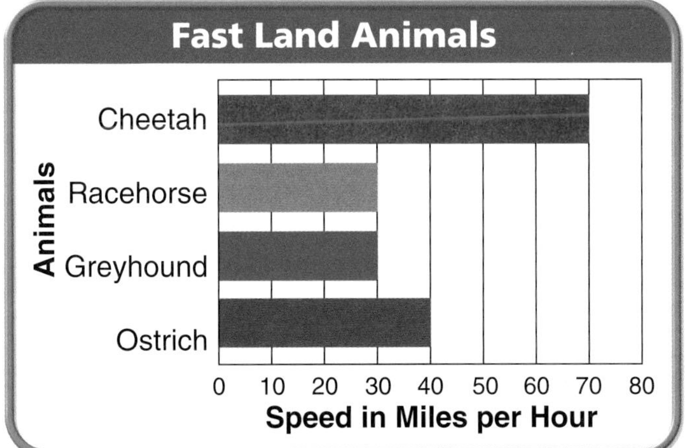

1. How fast can a racehorse run?

2. Which animal is the fastest of the four?

3. Read the problem below. **Explain** why F cannot be the correct answer. Then choose the correct answer.

COMMON ERROR

The bar graph at the left shows information about how fast different animals can run. How much faster is a cheetah than an ostrich?

F 70 miles per hour

G 40 miles per hour

H 30 miles per hour

J 10 miles per hour

Review the TEKS

Probability

TEKS 3.13C use data to describe events as more likely than, less likely than, or equally likely as.

Probability is the chance that an event will happen. An event is more likely if it has a good chance of happening. An event is less likely if it does not have a good chance of happening.

Examples

A Is pulling a red marble more likely than, less likely than, or equally likely as pulling a green marble?

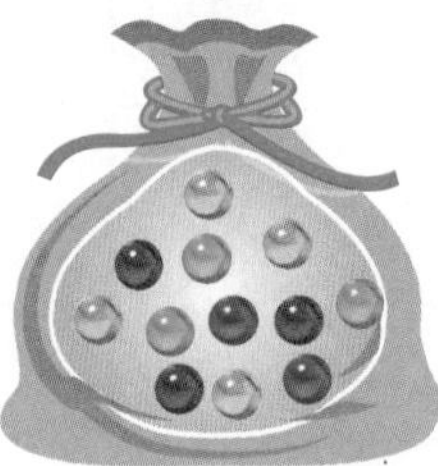

There are the same numbers of red and green marbles, so you have an equally likely chance of pulling red or green.

B What color is the most likely outcome when spinning the pointer?

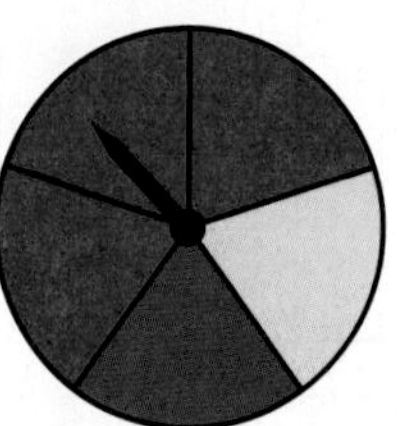

Since three of five sections of the spinner are red, red is the most likely outcome.

ERROR ALERT

Identify the more likely outcome as the one that has the better chance of happening.

Try It

For 1–2, use the spinner.

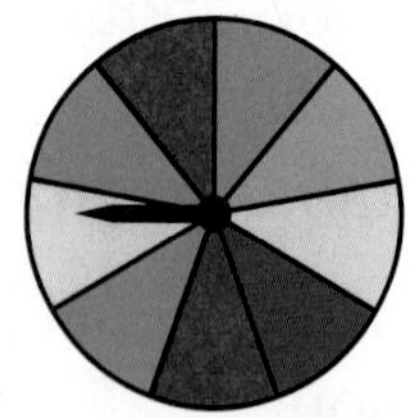

1. What are the possible outcomes for 1 spin of the pointer?
2. Which outcomes are equally likely?

3. Read the problem below. **Explain** why B cannot be the correct answer. Then choose the correct answer.

Justin has a bag with 15 tiles. There are 8 green tiles, 2 red tiles, 2 blue tiles, and 3 yellow tiles. If Justin pulls 1 tile from the bag, which color is he most likely to pull?

A Yellow
B Blue
C Green
D Red

Review the TEKS

Problem Solving

TEKS 3.14 The student applies Grade 3 mathematics to solve problems connected to everyday experiences and activities in and outside of school.

Some word problems have extra information. It is important to reread word problems to identify the information needed to solve each problem.

Read the problem carefully, and ask yourself:

1) What information helps solve this problem?

2) What information is not needed for solving this problem?

ERROR ALERT

Identify what information is needed and what information is not needed when solving word problems.

Examples

A Doug is 63 inches tall and weighs 105 pounds. His brother is 56 inches tall and weighs 93 pounds. What is the combined weight of Doug and his brother? What information is not needed?

Their combined weight is 198 pounds.

Their heights are not needed to solve this problem.

B Dani's heart beats 33 times in thirty seconds. She started walking at 3:45 P.M. Where are the hands on the clock pointing?

The hour hand is between 3 and 4. The minute hand is on the 9.

The information about her heart beat is not needed.

Try It

Solve

1. Purple paint costs $10.50 for a gallon. Red paint costs $9.50 and blue paint costs $11.00. Each gallon covers 80 square feet. How much will 6 gallons of blue paint cost? What information is not needed?

2. Mike has a $10 bill, a $5 bill, and $1.50 in coins. He bought a comic book for $1.23 using the coins. How much change would he get back?

3. Read the problem below. **Explain** why G cannot be the correct answer. Then choose the correct answer.

Heather bought sandals for $23, sneakers for $45, and boots for $53. She bought socks for $10. Which information is NOT needed to find how much she spent in all on shoes?

F sandals for $30 **H** boots for $53

G sneakers for $45 **J** socks for $10

Review the TEKS

Problem Solving

TEKS 3.15 The student communicates about Grade 3 mathematics using informal language.

Look for key words in a problem to help decide which operation is needed to solve the problem. Once you have read a problem, reread the problem and search for key words to guide you. For example:

If you see the word(s)	It usually means
"in all" →	add
"difference" →	subtract
"equal rows" →	multiply
"share equally" →	divide

ERROR ALERT

Look for key words that can help you figure out what operations are needed to solve the problem.

Examples

A Kendall bought 5 roses, 6 daisies, 12 carnations, and 10 petunias. How many flowers did she buy in all?

"In all" suggests adding.

$5 + 6 + 12 + 10 = 33$

She bought 33 flowers in all.

B It takes Marty 15 minutes to walk to school. It takes Wendy 23 minutes to walk to school. What is the difference between the times it takes Marty and Wendy to walk to school?

"Difference" suggests subtraction.

$23 - 15 = 8$

The difference is 8 minutes.

Try It

Solve.

1. Students sat in equal rows of 25 chairs at the school concert. There were 9 full rows. How many students were at the concert?
2. Eric had 243 baseball cards. His grandfather gave him 57 more. His mother gave him 125 more cards. How many cards does Eric have now?
3. Read the problem below. **Explain** why A cannot be the correct answer. Then choose the correct answer.

Mrs. Evans had 65 pumpkin seeds to plant. If she divided them equally among 8 students in the gardening club, how many would be left over?

A 57 **B** 32 **C** 8 **D** 1

Review the TEKS

Problem Solving

TEKS 3.16 The student uses logical reasoning.

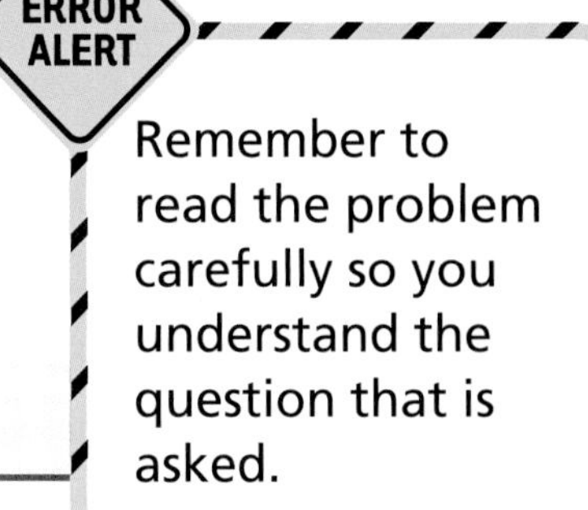

ERROR
ALERT
Remember to read the problem carefully so you understand the question that is asked.

You can use your own words to explain how a math problem is solved.

Examples

A What are the three greatest numbers that can be made using the digits 3, 4, 6, and 7? Each digit must be used only once in each number.

The greatest number would be the digits arranged in order from greatest to least, 7,643. The second greatest number would be 7,634. This number reverses the last two digits. The third greatest number would be 7,463. This number reverses the second and third digits of 7,643.

B Is the quotient of 28 ÷ 7 greater than or less than the quotient of 28 ÷ 4? Explain how you know.

$28 \div 7 = 4$

$28 \div 4 = 7$

$4 < 7$

The quotient of 28 ÷ 7 is less than the quotient of 28 ÷ 4 because $4 < 7$.

Try It

Solve. Explain your answer.

1. Brett has 7 equal rows of stickers. He bought 3 more stickers and now has 45 stickers. How many were in each row before he bought the additional 3?

2. What are the greatest and least numbers that can be made using 1, 3, 5, and 9? Each digit can only be used once in each number. What is the difference between the greatest and least numbers?

3. Read the problem below. **Explain** why F cannot be the correct answer. Then choose the correct answer.

Nathan, Ben, and Marissa each have an aquarium at home. Ben has 18 fish. Marissa has twice as many fish as Ben. Nathan has 7 fewer fish than Marissa. Which shows the number of fish that each person has?

F They have 83 fish in all.

G Nathan 29, Ben 18, Marissa 36

H Nathan 11, Ben 18, Marissa 9

J Ben 18, Marissa 36

Review the TEKS

Problem Solving

TEKS 3.16 The student uses logical reasoning.

When you solve a word problem involving multiplication or division, drawing a picture may help you visualize the problem.

ERROR ALERT

Make sure the picture you dr[a]
matches the information in
problem.

Examples

A Dani had a photo show to display her vacation pictures. She put 20 photographs in 4 equal rows. How many photographs were in each row?

The picture below shows the photos arranged in 4 rows. Each X represents a photo.

XXXXX
XXXXX
XXXXX
XXXXX

From the picture, you can see that there are 5 photographs in each row.

B There are 4 people in Lamont's family. How could they divide 12 pieces of pizza so that everyone gets an equal amount?

Drawing a picture will help you visualize how many pieces of pizza each person will get.

XXX
XXX
XXX
XXX

Each row has 3 Xs. Each family member gets 3 pieces.

Try It

1. Pedro has 60 party favors for the guests that come to his party. He puts an equal number in each of 12 bags. How many party favors are in 2 bags?

2. Julia wants to plant 8 rows of tulips. She has 56 tulip bulbs to plant. How many tulips can go in each of the 8 rows?

3. Read the problem below. **Explain** why A cannot be the correct answer. Then choose the correct answer.

Which fits the picture?

XXX
XXX

A 6 rows of 2 plants each
B 3 books on each of 2 shelves
C 6 cans stacked in a row
D 2 rows of 4 pictures

Review the TEKS

Problem Solving

TEKS 3.16 The student uses logical reasoning.

When solving word problems you can check your answers using inverse operations.

Check addition problems using subtraction. $12 + 3 = 15$ $15 - 3 = 12$

Check multiplication using division. $10 \times 3 = 30$ $30 \div 3 = 10$

Examples

A Randall is 52 inches tall. His sister is 46 inches tall. Randall says that he is seven inches taller than his sister because $52 - 46 = 7$. How could you check if Randall is correct?

Check if Randall is correct by using the inverse operation.

$7 + 46 = 53$, not 52

So, Randall is incorrect.

B Joy is setting up seats for the school assembly. There are 81 students that need to be seated in 9 rows. Joy sets up 9 seats in each row because $81 \div 9 = 9$. Did Joy set up the correct number of seats?

Check with the inverse operation.

$9 \times 9 = 81$

So, Joy is correct.

ERROR ALERT

Use the correct inverse operation when checking your work.

Try It

Solve.

1. Don has \$34 in his bank account. He owes his sister \$12. He says that after he pays his sister he will still have \$23 in his bank account. Is he correct?
2. Andy's soccer team has scored 6 goals in each of the last 8 games. Andy told his friends that his team scored 48 goals in those 8 games. Is Andy correct?
3. Read the problem below. **Explain** why F cannot be the correct answer. Then choose the correct answer.

Kim has 28 books on 4 shelves. How many books are on each shelf?

$$28 \div 4 = \blacksquare$$

Which would you use to check your answer?

F $28 + 4 = 32$ **H** $28 \div 1 = 28$

G $28 - 4 = 24$ **J** $7 \times 4 = 28$

TAKS Test-Taking Strategies

Being a good test taker is like being a good problem solver. When you solve problems, it is good to know strategies for solving. These strategies will help you become a good test taker.

Reading the Problem

• Watch for math terms and other key words.

1. Janice and her family are going to a museum. Her mother and father each pay \$7.95. Janice and her two sisters each pay \$5.95. ESTIMATE how much the whole family pays *in all*.

A \$32 **C** \$35
B \$34 **D** \$37

Notice key words.

The word ESTIMATE tells you that you are not looking for an exact answer. Round each price to the nearest dollar. The words *in all* help you know that you should add or multiply to find the answer. For this problem, you multiply the estimated adult price by 2 and the estimated child price by 3. Then add the products. The answer is **B**.

Key Words

Key words are sometimes in all CAPITAL letters or in a *different kind of type*. This helps you notice them.

Key words that help you understand the problem include: *about, round, estimate, only, best, not, least, most,* and *greatest*.

2. Mrs. Hill has 18 pencils to give to her students. If she gives an equal number to each of her 7 students, how many pencils are left over?

A 2 **C** 4
B 3 **D** 5

Look for key words that tell you what math operation to use.

The words *each* and *left over* help you know that you need to divide. Divide 18 by 7. Each student gets 2 pencils. $7 \times 2 = 14$. There are 4 pencils left over. The answer is **C**.

Key Words—Math Terms

The following key words help you know what math operation to use:

addition *sum, altogether, in all*
subtraction *difference, how much more, how much less*
multiplication *product, altogether, in all*
division *quotient, each, how many, remain, left over*

Also make sure you know exactly what the problem is asking for. For this problem, you divided, but the problem asked for the remainder, not the quotient. If you had given the quotient, you might have answered A.

Reading the Problem

- Pay attention to each detail in the problem.
- Decide what information to use and what information not to use.

3. Craig practices the piano every day except Wednesday. He also skips every other Sunday. In 4 weeks, how many days does he practice?

A 20 **C** 24

B 22 **D** 28

Make sure you do not miss important details.

In 4 weeks, there are 28 (7×4) days. But you need other details: Craig doesn't practice on Wednesdays, so you should multiply 6 days $\times$ 4 weeks. You also have to subtract 2 days because he skips every other Sunday. The answer is **B**.

Important Details

As you read the problem, identify the important details. You need the information that will help you find the answer.

Sometimes small details can make a difference to your answer. In this problem, if you missed the details about when Craig doesn't practice, you might have answered C or D.

4. Brandon took 2 books out of the library on Friday. The first one he read had 185 pages. He read 64 pages of the first book in 3 days. How many pages did he have left of the first book?

A 115 **C** 120

B 118 **D** 121

Don't be distracted by unnecessary information.

In this problem, you don't need to know how many books Brandon took out of the library or how many days it took him to read 64 pages. These are unnecessary details. Subtract the pages he read from the total pages. The answer is **D**.

Sometimes, you will need all the information in a problem. Sometimes, there will be extra information that you don't need. Reread the problem to find out which details you need to solve the problem.

TAKS Test-Taking Strategies

Understanding the Problem

- Make sure you understand graphs, tables, and charts.
- Restate the problem with simpler words or numbers.

5. About how many more days did it rain in June than in August?

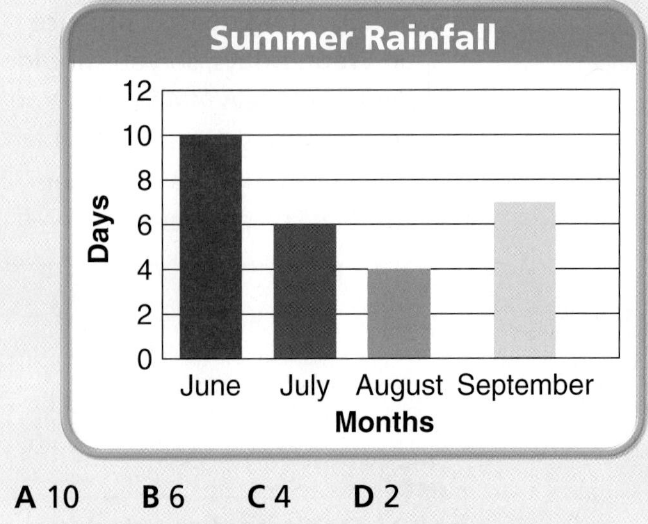

A 10 **B** 6 **C** 4 **D** 2

Understand graphs

Read the labels at the side and bottom of the graph. The side shows the number of days it rained. The bottom shows the months. Follow the labels to see that June had about 10 days of rain. August had about 4 days of rain. The answer is **B**.

Use visual aids

Look at visual aids carefully. Read all the labels to see what is being shown. Then double-check the problem to make sure you answer the right question. In this problem, you have to know which months to look at and what to do with the information you find.

6. Trevor had \$15.00 from doing chores and \$22.00 from his birthday. He spent \$4.50 on a toy and \$6.50 on a book. How much money did he have left?

A \$26.00

B \$32.00

C \$37.00

D \$48.00

Write number sentences. Then solve the problem.

You have to write 3 number sentences in order to solve the problem.

Write a number sentence.

Write number sentences to show what the problem is asking.
\$15.00 + \$22.00 = \$37.00, so Trevor had \$37.00 in all.
\$4.50 + \$6.50 = \$11.00, so he spent \$11.
Subtract to find how much money he has left. The answer is **A**.

Understanding the Problem

- Make sure you solve all the steps in the problem.
- Is there information missing?

7. Suzette has 5 window boxes with 4 plants in each. Keller has 3 window boxes with 5 plants in each. How many more plants does Suzette have than Keller?

A 2 **C** 4

B 3 **D** 5

Solve one step at a time.

Step One Suzette's window boxes: $5 \times 4 = 20$.

Step Two Keller's window boxes: $3 \times 5 = 15$.

Step Three How many more: $20 - 15 = 5$

The answer is **D**.

Solve multi-step problems

Many problems have more than one step for you to solve. Read the problem carefully, and identify the steps. Write the answer to each step.

This problem asks you to find a difference between two numbers. First you have to find out how many plants each person has. Then you can find the difference.

8. Charles wants to build a fence around his garden. The garden is in the shape of a rectangle. It is 20 feet long and half as wide as it is long. How many feet of fence does he need?

A 20 feet **C** 60 feet

B 40 feet **D** 80 feet

Draw a picture.

The problem says the garden is a rectangle and gives one measurement. Draw the rectangle and label the length.

20 feet

The problem tells how to find the other measurement. One-half of 20 is 10. Add another label.

20 feet

10 feet

Since the garden is a rectangle, you know the lengths of the opposite sides.
$20 + 10 + 20 + 10 = 60$

The answer is **C**.

Draw a picture

Pictures make it easier to understand a problem. If the problem doesn't have a picture, you may draw one. Be sure to use the information from the problem when you draw, and double-check your drawing to make sure it matches what you have read.

TAKS Test-Taking Strategies

Understanding the Question

- Identify the question.
- Is the problem asking what information is missing?

9. Kay's class has music lessons on every 4th day in the school term. If a term is 42 days long, how many days are left after the last music lesson?

A 2 **C** 7

B 5 **D** 10

Know what the problem is asking.

At first glance, you might think that this problem is asking how many music lessons are in the term. But the problem asks how many days are left over after the last lesson. The problem is asking for the remainder after you divide. The answer is **A**.

Identify the question

Sometimes the question isn't what you are expecting. Read the problem carefully to identify the question before you answer it.

Watch for answer choices that might seem right if you were answering the wrong question.

10. Chantal was playing bean-bag toss. She hit the 100-point target once and the 50-point target once. She got the rest of her points from hitting the 20-point target. What information do you need in order to tell how many times she hit the 20-point target?

A What the other targets were worth

B Her total score

C How many times she missed

D How many tosses she made in all

Understand what information you need.

Evaluate each answer choice. **A** doesn't help you. **C** and **D** could help you if you knew both. **B** can help you find the answer. Suppose Chantal's total score was 210. The 100-point toss and the 50-point toss total 150 points. That leaves 60 points from the 20-point tosses, or three tosses. The answer is **B**.

Missing information

If a problem asks you what information is missing, look at each answer choice. Ask yourself if that information would help you find the answer.

 TAKS Test-Taking Strategies

Answering the Question

- Estimate the answer.
- Draw a picture or a diagram to help show what information you are being asked to find.

11. 6,276 − 5,382 =

A 469 **C** 894
B 889 **D** 1,215

Estimate when numbers look hard to work with.

Estimate by rounding both numbers to the nearest hundred. Then subtract:

6,300 − 5,400 = 900

Eliminate answers **A** and **D**. Answers **B** and **C** are both reasonable. Subtract the digits in the ones place.

6 − 2 = 4

The answer is **C**.

Use estimation to help find answers

When you see numbers that look hard to work with, start by rounding the numbers to get a reasonable estimate. Eliminate answer choices that aren't reasonable.

If there is more than one reasonable answer, you can start the problem to make your estimate better. In this problem, you only needed to solve for the ones place.

To check your answer, use the original numbers to do the problem.

12. Kay has 3 blue markers and 6 red markers. Edward has 5 blue markers and 4 red markers. If they combine their markers, how many more red than blue markers do they have?

A 2 **C** 6
B 4 **D** 8

Make a chart.

It's easy to get confused when you're working with several numbers. Make a chart to keep track of them.

Kay	Edward	Total
3 blue	5 blue	8 blue
6 red	4 red	10 red

Together, they have 8 blue markers and 10 red markers. The answer is **A**.

Make your own visual aids

You can organize the numbers in a problem by making a visual aid. Often this will help you find the answer more quickly.

 TAKS Test-Taking Strategies

Multiple Choice

- Look at the answer choices one at a time.
- Eliminate choices that are clearly wrong.
- Try answer choices to see which one works in the problem.

13. Amie used a ruler to draw a plane figure. The figure had more than 3 sides but fewer than 6 sides. What was it?

A circle
B triangle
C hexagon
D pentagon

Use the process of elimination.

There are two figures with more than 3 sides but fewer than 6 sides, so you can't tell what figure she drew. Look at each answer choice and decide which ones are clearly wrong:

A Circles have no straight sides. Eliminate **A.**

B Triangles have 3 sides, not more than 3. Eliminate **B.**

C Hexagons have 6 sides, not fewer than 6. Eliminate **C.**

The answer is **D**.

Eliminate answer choices

When starting a problem, decide which answer choices are clearly wrong. This is called *the process of elimination*. In this problem, three of the figures do not fit the description, so you can eliminate those answer choices and choose the remaining answer choice.

You won't always be able to eliminate all the answers except one. The process of elimination can still help you. When you eliminate the answers that are clearly wrong, the correct answer is easier to find.

14. Abbot's Apple Farm sells bags of apples in two sizes. Large bags have 18 apples. Small bags have 7 apples. If there are 15 bags in the cooler and a total of 171 apples, how many bags of each size are there?

A 7 large, 8 small
B 6 large, 9 small
C 7 large, 5 small
D 9 large, 6 small

Test Tip

Try answer choices.

Try each answer choice until you find the right one. Remember, the number of bags must equal 15. Multiply the number of bags times the number of apples in each bag.

A $7 \times 18 = 126$, $8 \times 7 = 56$, $126 + 56 = 182$
Wrong answer

B $6 \times 18 = 108$, $9 \times 7 = 63$, $108 + 63 = 171$
Correct answer

The answer is **B**.

Try answer choices

Sometimes you can quickly find the correct answer by trying each answer choice in the problem. Choose an answer choice and do the math explained in the problem. If it doesn't work, go on to the next answer choice.

Multiple Choice

- Look at each answer choice in the problem. If the correct choice doesn't seem to be there:
  - Check the numbers you used.
  - Check your computations.
  - Use a different math operation.
  - Look for an equivalent number.

15. 8,472 − 3,597 =

A 4,785 **C** 4,875

B 4,874 **D** 4,974

Use a different operation.

Subtract. Then add your answer to the number you originally subtracted to check.

$$\begin{array}{r} 8{,}472 \\ -\,3{,}597 \\ \hline 4{,}875 \end{array} \qquad \begin{array}{r} 4{,}875 \\ +\,3{,}597 \\ \hline 8{,}472 \end{array}$$

If your subtraction is wrong, the addition will not produce the original number. The answer is **C**.

Check your work

It's always a good idea to check your work, using at least one method. If your answer isn't in the answer choices, it's even more important to check your math.

The numbers in this problem are hard to work with, so errors are more likely. The answer choices are similar, so you can't use the process of elimination or estimation to find the answer. Try repeating your math or using a different operation.

- Don't choose NOT HERE until you've checked your work carefully or solved the problem a different way.

16. Charlie buys 3 bags of marbles for $2.95 per bag. How much does he spend in all?

A $7.55 **C** $8.95

B $8.05 **D** NOT HERE

Check your work before choosing NOT HERE.

Multiply 3 × $2.95 and the product is $8.85. This answer is not one of the answer choices. Try adding $2.95 + $2.95 + $2.95. The sum is still $8.85. The answer is **D**.

When to choose NOT HERE

The correct answer will not always appear in the answer choices. If you have carefully checked your work and still don't see your answer, choose NOT HERE. *Never* choose NOT HERE until you've used at least one more method to check your work.

Addition Facts

	K	L	M	N	O	P	Q	R
A	3 + 2	0 + 6	2 + 4	5 + 9	6 + 1	2 + 5	3 + 10	4 + 4
B	8 + 9	0 + 7	3 + 5	9 + 6	6 + 7	2 + 8	3 + 3	7 + 10
C	4 + 6	9 + 0	7 + 8	4 + 10	3 + 7	7 + 7	4 + 2	7 + 5
D	5 + 7	3 + 9	8 + 1	9 + 5	10 + 5	9 + 8	2 + 6	8 + 7
E	7 + 4	0 + 8	3 + 6	6 + 10	5 + 3	2 + 7	8 + 2	9 + 9
F	2 + 3	1 + 7	6 + 8	5 + 2	7 + 3	4 + 8	10 + 10	6 + 6
G	8 + 3	7 + 2	7 + 0	8 + 5	9 + 1	4 + 7	8 + 4	10 + 8
H	7 + 9	5 + 6	8 + 10	6 + 5	8 + 6	9 + 4	0 + 9	7 + 1
I	4 + 3	5 + 5	6 + 4	10 + 2	7 + 6	8 + 0	6 + 9	9 + 2
J	5 + 8	1 + 9	5 + 4	8 + 8	6 + 2	6 + 3	9 + 7	9 + 10

Subtraction Facts

	K	L	M	N	O	P	Q	R
A	9 − 1	10 − 4	7 − 2	6 − 4	20 − 10	7 − 0	8 − 3	13 − 9
B	9 − 9	13 − 4	7 − 1	11 − 5	9 − 7	6 − 3	15 − 10	6 − 2
C	10 − 2	8 − 8	16 − 8	6 − 5	18 − 10	8 − 7	13 − 3	15 − 6
D	11 − 7	9 − 5	12 − 8	8 − 1	15 − 8	18 − 9	14 − 10	9 − 4
E	9 − 2	7 − 7	10 − 3	8 − 5	16 − 9	11 − 9	14 − 8	12 − 6
F	7 − 3	12 − 10	17 − 9	6 − 0	9 − 6	11 − 8	10 − 9	12 − 2
G	15 − 7	8 − 4	13 − 6	7 − 5	11 − 2	12 − 3	14 − 6	11 − 4
H	7 − 6	13 − 5	12 − 9	10 − 5	13 − 8	11 − 3	16 − 10	14 − 7
I	5 − 0	10 − 8	11 − 6	9 − 3	14 − 5	5 − 4	7 − 7	14 − 9
J	15 − 9	9 − 8	13 − 7	8 − 2	7 − 4	13 − 10	10 − 6	16 − 7

Multiplication Facts

	K	L	M	N	O	P	Q	R
A	2 ×7	0 ×6	6 ×6	9 ×2	8 ×3	3 ×4	2 ×8	6 ×1
B	7 ×7	5 ×9	2 ×2	7 ×5	2 ×3	10 ×8	4 ×10	8 ×4
C	4 ×5	5 ×1	7 ×0	6 ×3	3 ×5	6 ×8	7 ×3	9 ×9
D	0 ×9	6 ×4	6 ×10	1 ×6	9 ×8	4 ×4	3 ×2	9 ×3
E	0 ×7	9 ×4	1 ×7	9 ×7	2 ×5	7 ×9	5 ×6	5 ×8
F	4 ×3	6 ×9	1 ×9	7 ×6	7 ×10	6 ×0	2 ×9	10 ×3
G	5 ×3	1 ×5	7 ×1	3 ×8	3 ×6	8 ×10	3 ×9	6 ×7
H	7 ×4	7 ×2	3 ×7	2 ×4	7 ×8	4 ×7	5 ×10	8 ×6
I	4 ×6	5 ×5	5 ×7	3 ×3	9 ×6	8 ×0	4 ×9	8 ×8
J	8 ×9	6 ×2	4 ×8	9 ×5	5 ×4	0 ×5	10 ×6	9 ×10

Division Facts

	K	L	M	N	O	P	Q	R
A	$1\overline{)1}$	$3\overline{)9}$	$2\overline{)6}$	$2\overline{)4}$	$1\overline{)6}$	$3\overline{)12}$	$5\overline{)15}$	$7\overline{)21}$
B	$6\overline{)24}$	$8\overline{)56}$	$5\overline{)40}$	$6\overline{)18}$	$6\overline{)30}$	$7\overline{)42}$	$9\overline{)81}$	$5\overline{)45}$
C	$5\overline{)30}$	$2\overline{)16}$	$3\overline{)21}$	$7\overline{)35}$	$3\overline{)15}$	$9\overline{)9}$	$8\overline{)16}$	$9\overline{)63}$
D	$4\overline{)32}$	$9\overline{)90}$	$4\overline{)8}$	$8\overline{)48}$	$9\overline{)54}$	$3\overline{)18}$	$10\overline{)50}$	$6\overline{)48}$
E	$7\overline{)28}$	$3\overline{)0}$	$5\overline{)20}$	$4\overline{)24}$	$7\overline{)14}$	$3\overline{)6}$	$5\overline{)50}$	$10\overline{)60}$
F	$9\overline{)18}$	$4\overline{)36}$	$5\overline{)25}$	$7\overline{)63}$	$1\overline{)5}$	$8\overline{)32}$	$9\overline{)45}$	$6\overline{)54}$
G	$2\overline{)14}$	$8\overline{)24}$	$4\overline{)4}$	$5\overline{)40}$	$3\overline{)9}$	$4\overline{)12}$	$7\overline{)56}$	$8\overline{)72}$
H	$5\overline{)35}$	$1\overline{)4}$	$8\overline{)64}$	$5\overline{)10}$	$8\overline{)40}$	$2\overline{)12}$	$6\overline{)42}$	$10\overline{)70}$
I	$7\overline{)49}$	$9\overline{)27}$	$10\overline{)90}$	$3\overline{)27}$	$9\overline{)36}$	$4\overline{)20}$	$9\overline{)72}$	$8\overline{)80}$
J	$8\overline{)0}$	$4\overline{)28}$	$2\overline{)10}$	$7\overline{)70}$	$1\overline{)3}$	$10\overline{)80}$	$6\overline{)60}$	$10\overline{)100}$

Table of Measures

METRIC	CUSTOMARY
Length	
1 centimeter (cm) = 10 millimeters (mm)	1 foot (ft) = 12 inches (in.)
1 decimeter (dm) = 10 centimeters	1 yard (yd) = 3 feet, or 36 inches
1 meter (m) = 100 centimeters	1 mile (mi) = 1,760 yards, or 5,280 feet
1 kilometer (km) = 1,000 meters	
Weight	
1 kilogram (kg) = 1,000 grams (g)	1 pound (lb) = 16 ounces (oz)
Capacity	
1 liter (L) = 1,000 milliliters (mL)	1 pint (pt) = 2 cups (c)
	1 quart (qt) = 2 pints, or 4 cups
	1 gallon (gal) = 4 quarts

TIME	
1 minute (min) = 60 seconds (sec)	1 week (wk) = 7 days
1 hour (hr) = 60 minutes	1 year (yr) = 12 months (mo), or 52 weeks, or 365 days
1 day = 24 hours	

MONEY
1 penny = 1 cent (¢)
1 nickel = 5 cents
1 dime = 10 cents
1 quarter = 25 cents
1 half dollar = 50 cents
1 dollar ($) = 100 cents

SYMBOLS
< is less than
> is greater than
= is equal to
°F is degrees Fahrenheit

TEKS Grade 3

Texas Essential Knowledge and Skills

TEKS
Number, Operation, and Quantitative Reasoning
3.1 The student uses place value to communicate about increasingly large whole numbers in verbal and written form, including money. The student is expected to:
(A) use place value to read, write (in symbols and words), and describe the value of whole numbers through 999,999;
(B) use place value to compare and order whole numbers through 9,999; and
(C) determine the value of a collection of coins and bills.
3.2 The student uses fraction names and symbols (with denominators of 12 or less) to describe fractional parts of whole objects or sets of objects. The student is expected to:
(A) construct concrete models of fractions;
(B) compare fractional parts of whole objects or sets of objects in a problem situation using concrete models;
(C) use fraction names and symbols to describe fractional parts of whole objects or sets of objects; and
(D) construct concrete models of equivalent fractions for fractional parts of whole objects.
3.3 The student adds and subtracts to solve meaningful problems involving whole numbers. The student is expected to:
(A) model addition and subtraction using pictures, words, and numbers; and
(B) select addition or subtraction and use the operation to solve problems involving whole numbers through 999.
3.4 The student recognizes and solves problems in multiplication and division situations. The student is expected to:
(A) learn and apply multiplication facts through 12 by 12 using concrete models and objects;
(B) solve and record multiplication problems (up to two digits times one digit); and
(C) use models to solve division problems and use number sentences to record the solutions.

TEKS Continued

TEKS
3.5 The student estimates to determine reasonable results. The student is expected to:
(A) round whole numbers to the nearest ten or hundred to approximate reasonable results in problem situations; and
(B) use strategies including rounding and compatible numbers to estimate solutions to addition and subtraction problems.
Patterns, Relationships, and Algebraic Thinking
3.6 The student uses patterns to solve problems. The student is expected to:
(A) identify and extend whole-number and geometric patterns to make predictions and solve problems;
(B) identify patterns in multiplication facts using concrete objects, pictorial models, or technology; and
(C) identify patterns in related multiplication and division sentences (fact families) such as $2 \times 3 = 6$, $3 \times 2 = 6$, $6 \div 2 = 3$, $6 \div 3 = 2$.
3.7 The student uses lists, tables, and charts to express patterns and relationships. The student is expected to:
(A) generate a table of paired numbers based on a real-life situation such as insects and legs; and
(B) identify and describe patterns in a table of related number pairs based on a meaningful problem and extend the table.
Geometry and Spatial Reasoning
3.8 The student uses formal geometric vocabulary.
The student is expected to identify, classify, and describe two- and three-dimensional geometric figures by their attributes. The student compares two-dimensional figures, three-dimensional figures, or both by their attributes using formal geometry vocabulary.
3.9 The student recognizes congruence and symmetry. The student is expected to:
(A) identify congruent two-dimensional figures;
(B) create two-dimensional figures with lines of symmetry using concrete models and technology; and
(C) identify lines of symmetry in two-dimensional geometric figures.

TEKS
3.10 The student recognizes that a line can be used to represent numbers and fractions and their properties and relationships.
The student is expected to locate and name points on a number line using whole numbers and fractions, including halves and fourths.
Measurement
3.11 The student directly compares the attributes of length, area, weight/mass, and capacity, and uses comparative language to solve problems and answer questions. The student selects and uses standard units to describe length, area, capacity/volume, and weight/mass. The student is expected to:
(A) use linear measurement tools to estimate and measure lengths using standard units;
(B) use standard units to find the perimeter of a shape;
(C) use concrete and pictorial models of square units to determine the area of two-dimensional surfaces;
(D) identify concrete models that approximate standard units of weight/mass and use them to measure weight/mass;
(E) identify concrete models that approximate standard units for capacity and use them to measure capacity; and
(F) use concrete models that approximate cubic units to determine the volume of a given container or other three-dimensional geometric figure.
3.12 The student reads and writes time and measures temperature in degrees Fahrenheit to solve problems. The student is expected to:
(A) use a thermometer to measure temperature; and
(B) tell and write time shown on analog and digital clocks.

TEKS Continued

TEKS
Probability and Statistics
3.13 The student solves problems by collecting, organizing, displaying, and interpreting sets of data. The student is expected to:
(A) collect, organize, record, and display data in pictographs and bar graphs where each picture or cell might represent more than one piece of data;
(B) interpret information from pictographs and bar graphs; and
(C) use data to describe events as more likely than, less likely than, or equally likely as.
Underlying Processes and Mathematical Tools
3.14 The student applies Grade 3 mathematics to solve problems connected to everyday experiences and activities in and outside of school. The student is expected to:
(A) identify the mathematics in everyday situations;
(B) solve problems that incorporate understanding the problem, making a plan, carrying out the plan, and evaluating the solution for reasonableness;
(C) select or develop an appropriate problem-solving plan or strategy, including drawing a picture, looking for a pattern, systematic guessing and checking, acting it out, making a table, working a simpler problem, or working backwards to solve a problem; and
(D) use tools such as real objects, manipulatives, and technology to solve problems.
3.15 The student communicates about Grade 3 mathematics using informal language. The student is expected to:
(A) explain and record observations using objects, words, pictures, numbers, and technology; and
(B) relate informal language to mathematical language and symbols.
3.16 The student uses logical reasoning. The student is expected to:
(A) make generalizations from patterns or sets of examples and nonexamples; and
(B) justify why an answer is reasonable and explain the solution process.

Glossary

Pronunciation Key

a	add, map	f	fit, half	n	nice, tin	p	pit, stop	yo͞o	fuse, few
ā	ace, rate	g	go, log	ng	ring, song	r	run, poor	v	vain, eve
â(r)	care, air	h	hope, hate	o	odd, hot	s	see, pass	w	win, away
ä	palm, father	i	it, give	ō	open, so	sh	sure, rush	y	yet, yearn
b	bat, rub	ī	ice, write	ô	order, jaw	t	talk, sit	z	zest, muse
ch	check, catch	j	joy, ledge	oi	oil, boy	th	thin, both	zh	vision, pleasure
d	dog, rod	k	cool, take	ou	pout, now	t͟h	this, bathe		
e	end, pet	l	look, rule	o͝o	took, full	u	up, done		
ē	equal, tree	m	move, seem	o͞o	pool, food	û(r)	burn, term		

ə the schwa, an unstressed vowel representing the sound spelled *a* in above, *e* in sicken, *i* in possible, *o* in melon, *u* in circus

Other symbols:
- • separates words into syllables
- ′ indicates stress on a syllable

acute angle [ə•kyo͞ot′ ang′gəl] **ángulo agudo** An angle that has a measure less than a right angle (p. 368)
Example:

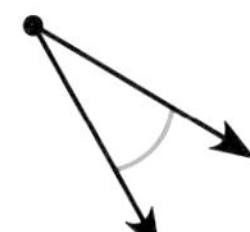

acute triangle [ə•kyo͞ot′ trī′ang•gəl] **triángulo acutángulo** A triangle that has three acute angles (p. 376)

addend [a′dend] **sumando** Any of the numbers that are added (p. 56)
Example: 2 + 3 = 5
↑ addend ↑ addend

addition [ə•dish′ən] **suma** The process of finding the total number of items when two or more groups of items are joined; the opposite operation of subtraction (p. 56)

A.M. [ā em] **a.m.** The hours between midnight and noon (p. 140)

analog clock [a′nəl•og kläk] **reloj analógico** A device for measuring time by moving hands around a circle for showing hours, minutes, and sometimes seconds (p. 134)
Example:

angle [ang′gəl] **ángulo** A figure formed by two rays that share an endpoint (p. 368)
Example:

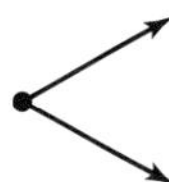

Word History

When the letter "g" is replaced with the letter "k" in the word *angle*, the word becomes *ankle*. Both words come from the same Latin root, *angulus*, which means "a sharp bend."

area [âr′ē•ə] **área** The number of square units needed to cover a flat surface (p. 492)
Example:

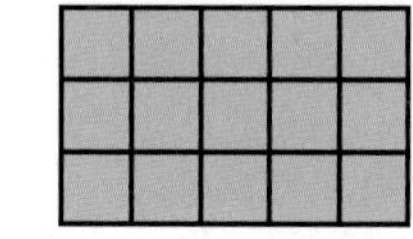

area = 15 square units

array [ə•rā′] **matriz** An arrangement of objects in rows and columns (p. 204)
Example:

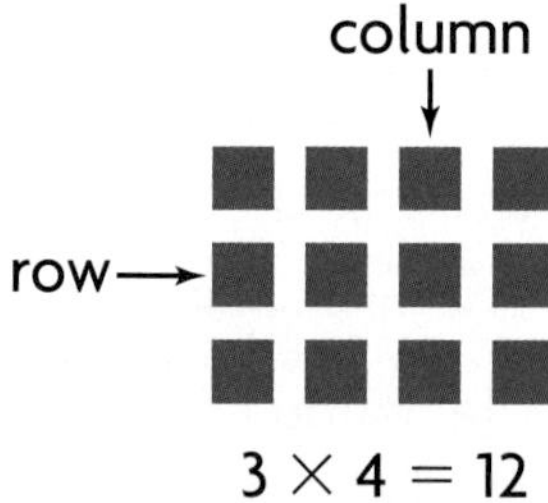

3 × 4 = 12

Associative Property of Addition [ə•sō′shē•ə•tiv prä′pər•tē əv ə•di′shən] **propiedad asociativa de la suma** The property that states that you can group addends in different ways and still get the same sum (p. 56)
Example:
4 + (2 + 5) = 11 and
(4 + 2) + 5 = 11

Associative Property of Multiplication [a•sō′shē•ā•tiv prä′pər•tē əv mul•tə•plə•kā′shən] **propiedad asociativa de la multiplicación** The property that states that when the grouping of factors is changed, the product remains the same (p. 276)
Example:
(3 × 2) × 4 = 24
3 × (2 × 4) = 24

bar graph [bär graf] **gráfica de barras** A graph that uses bars to show data (p. 160)
Example:

capacity [kə•pa′sə•tē] **capacidad** The amount a container can hold (p. 448)
Example:
1 half gallon = 2 quarts

center [sen′tər] **centro** The point in the middle of a circle that is the same distance from anywhere on the circle (p. 382)
Example:

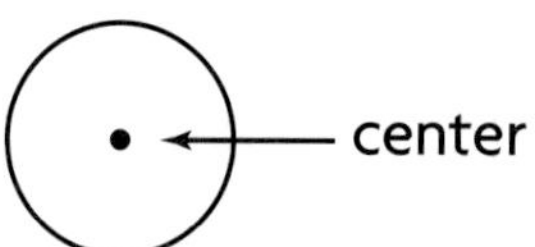

centimeter (cm) [sen′tə•mē•tər] **centímetro** A metric unit that is used to measure length or distance (p. 466)
Example:

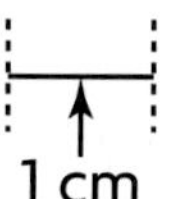

certain [sûr′tən] **seguro** An event is certain if it will always happen. (p. 566)

change [chānj] **cambio** The money you get back if you have paid for an item with coins or bills that have a greater value than the cost of the item (p. 120)

circle [sər′kəl] **círculo** A closed plane figure made up of points that are the same distance from the center (p. 382)

classify [kla′sə•fī] **clasificar** To group pieces of data according to how they are the same; for example, you can classify data by size, color, or shape. (p. 168)

closed figure [klōzd fi′•gyər] **figura cerrada** A shape that begins and ends at the same point
Examples:

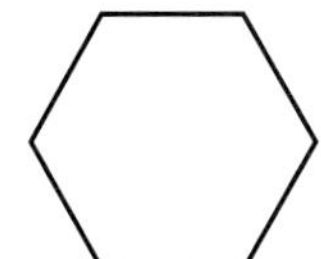

Commutative Property of Addition [kə•myōō′•tə•tiv prä′pər•tē əv ə•di′shən] **propiedad conmutativa de la suma** The property that states that you can add two or more numbers in any order and get the same sum (p. 56)
Example: $6 + 7 = 13$
$7 + 6 = 13$

Commutative Property of Multiplication [kə•myōō•tə•tiv prä′pər•tē əv mul•tə•plə•kā′shən] **propiedad conmutativa de la multiplicación** The property that states that you can multiply two factors in any order and get the same product (p. 205)
Examples: $2 \times 4 = 8$
$4 \times 2 = 8$

compare [kəm•pâr′] **comparar** To describe whether numbers are equal to, less than, or greater than each other (p. 30)

compatible numbers [kəm•păt′ə•bəl num′bərs] **números compatibles** Numbers that are easy to compute mentally (p. 60)

cone [kōn] **cono** A solid, pointed figure that has a flat, round base (p. 416)
Example:

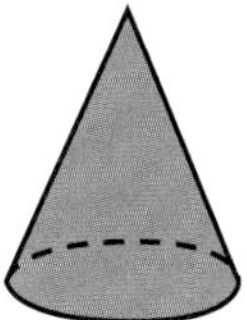

congruent [kən•grōō′ənt] **congruente** Figures that have the same size and shape (p. 396)
Example:

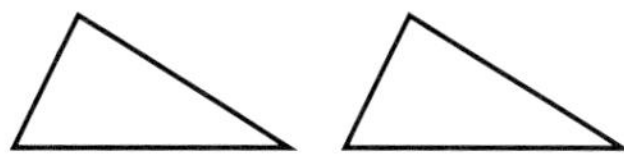

cube [kyōōb] **cubo** A solid figure with six congruent square faces (p. 416)
Example:

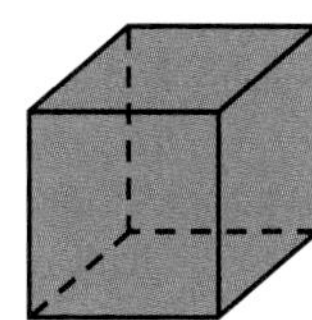

cubic unit [kyōō′bik yōō′nət] **unidad cúbica** A cube with a side length of one unit; used to measure volume (p. 498)

cup (c) [kup] **taza** A customary unit used to measure capacity (p. 448)

cylinder [sil′in•dər] **cilindro** A solid or hollow object that is shaped like a can (p. 416)
Example:

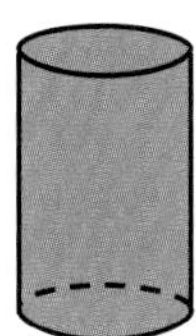

D

data [dā′tə] **datos** Information collected about people or things (p. 152)

decimal point [de′sə•məl point] **punto decimal** A symbol used to separate dollars from cents in money (p. 111)
Example: $4.52
↑ decimal point

decimeter (dm) [de′sə•mē•tər] **decímetro** A metric unit that is used to measure length or distance;
1 decimeter = 10 centimeters (p. 466)

degree Fahrenheit (°F) [di•grē′ far′ən•hīt] **grado Fahrenheit** A customary unit for measuring temperature (p. 454)

denominator [di•nä′mə•nā•tər] **denominador** The part of a fraction below the line, which tells how many equal parts there are in the whole or in the group (p. 514)
Example: $\frac{3}{4}$ ← denominator

difference [dif′rən(t)s] **diferencia** The answer in a subtraction problem (p. 86)
Example: 6 − 4 = 2 ← difference

digital clock [di′jə•təl kläk] **reloj digital** A clock that shows time to the minute using digits (p. 134)
Example:

digits [di′jəts] **dígitos** The symbols 0, 1, 2, 3, 4, 5, 6, 7, 8, and 9 (p. 10)

dime [dīm] **moneda de 10¢** A coin worth 10 cents and equal to 10 pennies; 10¢ (p. 110)

divide [di•vīd′] **dividir** To separate into equal groups; the opposite operation of multiplication (p. 296)

dividend [di′və•dend] **dividendo** The number that is to be divided in a division problem (p. 302)
Example: 35 ÷ 5 = 7 (35 ← dividend)

division [di•vi′•zhən] **división** The process of sharing a number of items to find how many groups can be made or how many items will be in a group; the opposite operation of multiplication (p. 296)

divisor [di•vī′zər] **divisor** The number that divides the dividend (p. 302)
Example: 35 ÷ 5 = 7 (5 ← divisor)

dollar [dol′ər] **dólar** Paper money worth 100 cents and equal to 100 pennies; $1.00 (p. 111)

edge [ej] **arista** A line segment formed where two faces meet (p. 420)
Example:

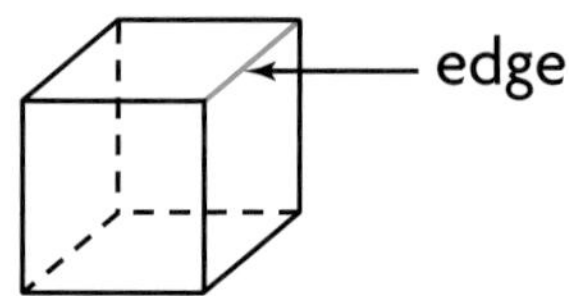

equal sign (=) [ē′kwəl sīn] **signo de igualdad** A symbol used to show that two numbers have the same value (p. 30)
Example: 384 = 384

equal to (=) [ē′kwəl to͞o] **igual a** Having the same value (p. 30)
Example: 4 + 4 is equal to 3 + 5

equally likely [ē′kwəl•lē lī′klē] **igualmente probable** Having the same chance of happening (p. 568)

equilateral triangle [ē•kwə•lat′ər•əl trī′ang•gəl] **triángulo equilátero** A triangle that has three equal sides and three equal angles (p. 376)
Examples:

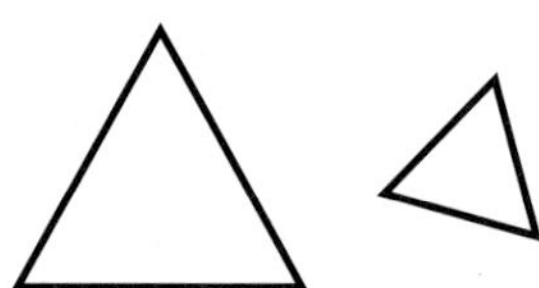

equivalent [ē•kwiv′ə•lənt] **equivalente** Two or more sets that name the same amount (p. 111)

equivalent fractions [ē•kwiv′ə•lənt frak′shənz] **fracciones equivalentes** Two or more fractions that name the same amount (p. 522)
Example:

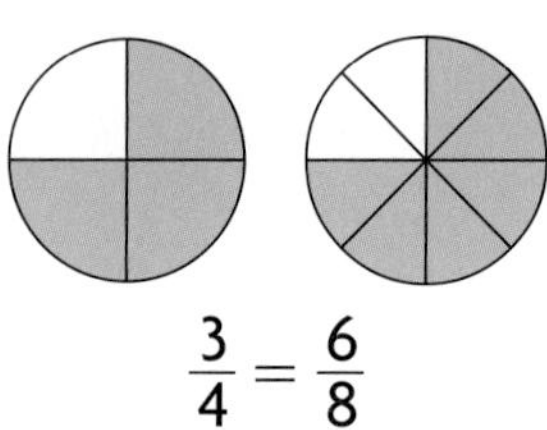

estimate [es′tə•māt] *verb* **estimar (v)**: To find about how many or how much (p. 60)

estimate [es′tə•mit] *noun* **estimación (s)**: A number close to an exact amount (p. 60)

even number [ē′vən num′bər] **número par** A whole number that has a 0, 2, 4, 6, or 8 in the ones place (p. 7)

event [i•vent′] **suceso** Something that might happen (p. 566)

expanded form [ik•spand′id fôrm] **forma desarrollada** A way to write numbers by showing the value of each digit (p. 10)
Example: 7,201 = 7,000 + 200 + 1

experiment [ik•sper′ə•mənt] **experimento** A test that is done in order to find out something (p. 570)

face [fās] **cara** A flat surface of a solid figure (p. 420)
Example:

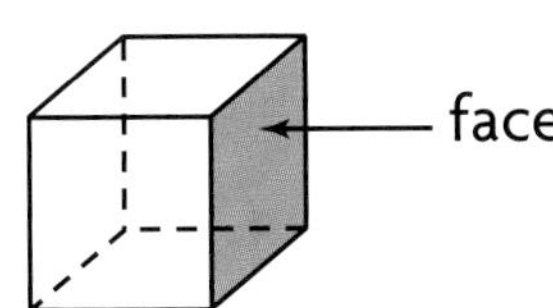

fact family [fakt fam′ə•lē] **familia de operaciones** A set of related addition and subtraction, or multiplication and division, number sentences (pp. 84, 304)
Example:

$4 \times 7 = 28$ $28 \div 7 = 4$
$7 \times 4 = 28$ $28 \div 4 = 7$

factor [fak′tər] **factor** A number that is multiplied by another number to find a product (p. 205)
Example: 3 × 8 = 24
↑ ↑
factor factor

foot (ft) [fo͝ot] **pie** A customary unit used to measure length or distance;
1 foot = 12 inches (p. 440)

fraction [frak′shən] **fracción** A number that names part of a whole or part of a group (p. 514)
Examples:

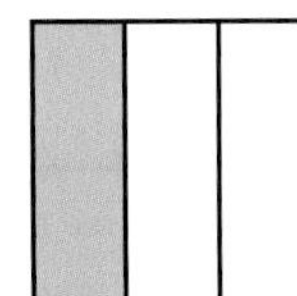

$\frac{1}{3}$

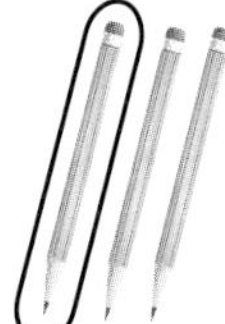

Word History

A *fraction* is part of a whole, or a whole that is broken into pieces. *Fraction* comes from the Latin word *frangere*, which means "to break."

frequency table [frē′kwen•sē tā′bəl] **tabla de frecuencia** A table that uses numbers to record data (p. 152)
Example:

Favorite Color	
Color	**Number**
blue	10
red	7
green	8
yellow	4

gallon (gal) [ga′lən] **galón** A customary unit for measuring capacity;
1 gallon = 4 quarts (p. 448)

gram (g) [gram] **gramo** A metric unit that is used to measure mass (p. 474)

greater than (>) [grā′tər t͟han] **mayor que** A symbol used to compare two numbers, with the greater number given first (p. 30)
Example: 6 > 4

groups [gro͞ops] **grupo** A number of things that have one or more things in common (p. 202)

Grouping Property of Addition [grōō′ping prä′pər•tē əv ə•dish′ən] **propiedad de agrupación de la suma** See Associative Property of Addition.

Grouping Property of Multiplication [grōō′ping prä′pər•tē əv mul•tə•plə•kā′shən] **propiedad de agrupación de la multiplicación** See Associative Property of Multiplication.

growing pattern [groh•ing pat•ern] **patrón acumu lativo** A pattern in which the number of figures increases by the same amount from one figure to the next. (p. 180)

half dollar [haf dol′ər] **moneda de 50¢** A coin worth 50 cents and equal to 50 pennies; 50¢ (p. 110)

half hour [haf our] **media hora** 30 minutes (p. 134)
Example: Between 4:00 and 4:30 is one half hour.

hexagon [hek′sə•gän] **hexágono** A plane figure with six sides and six angles (p. 374)
Examples:

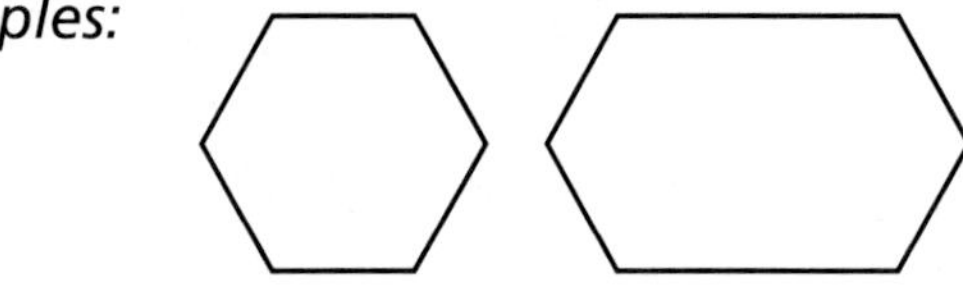

horizontal bar graph [hôr•ə•zän′təl bär graf] **gráfica de barras horizontales** A bar graph in which the bars go from left to right (p. 160)

hour (hr) [our] **hora** A unit used to measure time; in one hour, the hour hand on a clock moves from one number to the next;
1 hour = 60 minutes (p. 134)

hour hand [our hand] **horario** The short hand on an analog clock (p. 134)

Identity Property of Addition [ī•den′tə•tē prä′pər•tē əv ə•dish′ən] **propiedad de identidad de la suma** The property that states that when you add zero to a number, the result is that number (p. 56)
Example: $24 + 0 = 24$

Identity Property of Multiplication [ī•den′tə•tē prä′pər•tē əv mul•tə•plə•kā′shən] **propiedad de identidad de la multiplicación** The property that states that the product of any number and 1 is that number (p. 212)
Examples: $5 \times 1 = 5$
$1 \times 8 = 8$

impossible [im•pä′sə•bəl] **imposible** An event that will never happen (p. 566)

inch (in.) [inch] **pulgada** A customary unit used for measuring length or distance (p. 440)
Example:

intersecting lines [in•tər•sek′ting līnz] **rectas secantes** Lines that cross (p. 372)
Example:

inverse operations [in′vərs ä•pə•rā′shənz] **operaciones inversas** Opposite operations, or operations that undo each other, such as addition and subtraction or multiplication and division (p. 84)

isosceles triangle [ī•sos′ə•lēz trī′ang•gəl] **triángulo isósceles** A triangle that has two equal sides (p. 376)
Example:

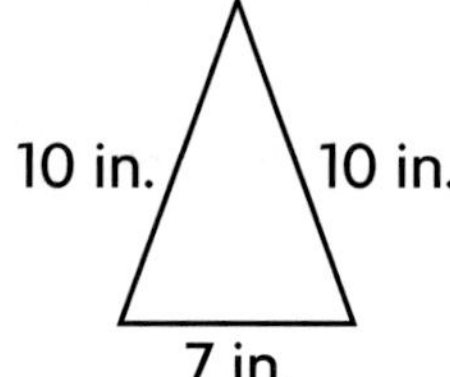

key [kē] **clave** The part of a map or graph that explains the symbols (p. 154)

kilogram (kg) [kil′ə•gram] **kilogramo** A metric unit for measuring mass; 1 kilogram = 1,000 grams (p. 474)

kilometer (km) [kə•lä′mə•tər] **kilómetro** A metric unit for measuring length or distance; 1 kilometer = 1,000 meters (p. 466)

length [leng(k)th] **longitud** The measure of something from end to end (p. 440)

less likely [ən•līk′lē] **poco probable** An event is less likely if it does not have a good chance of happening. (p. 566)

less than (<) [les than] **menor que** A symbol used to compare two numbers, with the lesser number given first (p. 30)
Example: $3 < 7$

like fraction [līk frak′shənz] **fracciones semejantes** Fractions that have the same denominator (p. 539)
Example: $\frac{3}{8}$ and $\frac{7}{8}$

line [līn] **recta** A straight path extending in both directions with no endpoints (p. 368)
Example:

The word *line* comes from *linen*, a thread spun from the fibers of the flax plant. In early times, thread was held tight to mark a straight line between two points.

line of symmetry [līn əv sim′ə•trē] **eje de simetría** An imaginary line on a figure that when the figure is folded on this line, the two parts match exactly (p. 402)
Example:

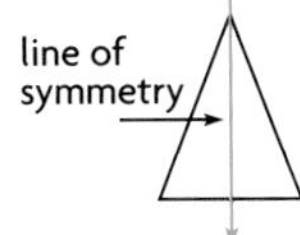

line segment [līn seg′mənt] **segmento** A part of a line that includes two points, called endpoints, and all of the points between them (p. 368)
Example:

liter (L) [lē′tər] **litro** A metric unit for measuring capacity; 1 liter = 1,000 milliliters (p. 472)

mass [mas] **masa** The amount of matter in an object (p. 474)

meter (m) [mē′tər] **metro** A metric unit for measuring length or distance; 1 meter = 100 centimeters (p. 466)

midnight [mid′nīt] **medianoche** 12:00 at night (p. 140)

mile (mi) [mīl] **milla** A customary unit for measuring length or distance; 1 mile = 5,280 feet (p. 440)

milliliter (mL) [mi′lə•mē•tər] **mililitro** A metric unit for measuring capacity (p. 472)

minute (min) [min′it] **minuto** A unit used to measure short amounts of time; in one minute, the minute hand moves from one mark to the next (p. 134)

minute hand [mi′nət hand] **minutero** The long hand on an analog clock (p. 134)

more likely [līk′lē] **probable** An event is more likely if it has a good chance of happening (p. 566)

multiple [mul′tə•pəl] **múltiplo** A number that is the product of a given number and a counting number (pp. 232, 282)
Example:

10	10	10	10	
× 1	× 2	× 3	× 4	← counting numbers
10	20	30	40	← multiples of 10

multiplication [mul•tə•plə•kā′shən] **multiplicatión** A process to find the total number of items made up of equal-sized groups, or to find the total number of items in a given number of groups. It is the opposite operation of division. (p. 202)

multiply [mul′tə•plī] **multiplicar** When you combine equal groups, you can multiply to find how many in all; the opposite operation of division (p. 202)

multistep problem [mul′tē•step prä′bləm] **problema de varios pasos** A problem with more than one step (p. 280)

nickel [nik′əl] **moneda de 5¢** A coin worth 5 cents and equal to 5 pennies; 5¢ (p. 110)
Example:

noon [nōōn] **mediodía** 12:00 in the day (p. 140)

number line [num′bər līn] **recta numérica** A line on which numbers can be located (p. 8)
Example:

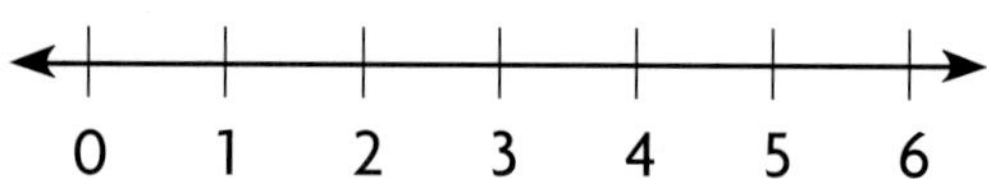

number sentence [num′bər sen′təns] **enunciado numérico** A sentence that includes numbers, operation symbols, and a greater than or less than symbol or an equal sign (p. 308)
Example:
$5 + 3 = 8$ is a number sentence.

numerator [nōō′mə•rā•tər] **numerador** The part of a fraction above the line, which tells how many parts are being counted (p. 514)

Example: $\frac{3}{4}$ ← numerator

obtuse angle [əb•t(y)ōōs′ ang′gəl] **ángulo obtuso** An angle that has a measure greater than a right angle (p. 368)
Example:

obtuse triangle [əb•t(y)ōōs′ trī′ang•gəl] **triángulo obtusángulo** A triangle that has 1 obtuse angle (p. 376)

octagon [äk′tə•gän] **octágono** A plane figure with eight sides and eight angles (p. 374)
Example:

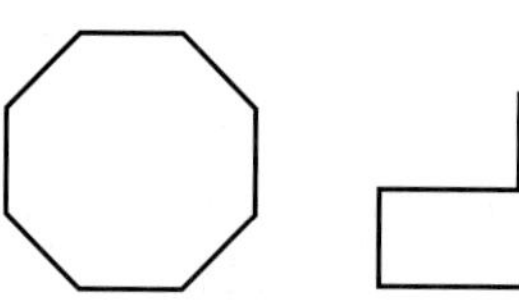

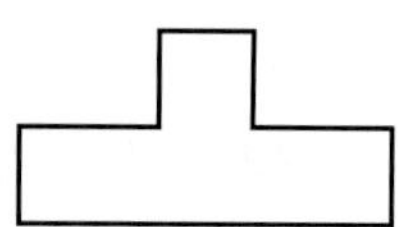

odd number [od num′bər] **número impar** A whole number that has a 1, 3, 5, 7, or 9 in the ones place (p. 7)

open figure [ō•pən fi′•gyər] **figura abierta** A figure that does not begin and end at the same point
Examples:

order [ôr′dər] **orden** A particular arrangement or placement of things, one after another (p. 34)

Order Property of Addition [ôr′dər prä′pər•tē əv ə•dish′ən] **propiedad de orden de la suma** See Commutative Property of Addition.

Order Property of Multiplication [ôr′dər prä′pər•tē əv mul•tə•plə•kā′shən] **propiedad de orden de la multiplicación** See Commutative Property of Multiplication.

ounce (oz) [ouns] **onza** A customary unit for measuring weight (p. 450)

outcome [out′kem] **resultado** A possible result of an experiment (p. 568)

parallel lines [par′ə•lel līnz] **rectas paralelas** Lines that never cross; lines that are always the same distance apart (p. 372)
Example:

Word History

Euclid, an early Greek mathematician, was one of the first to explore the idea for parallel lines. The prefix *para-* means "beside or alongside." This prefix helps you understand the meaning of the word *parallel*.

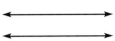

parallelogram [par′ə•lel′ə•gram] **paralelogramo** A quadrilateral whose opposite sides are parallel and have the same length (p. 379)
Example:

pattern [pat′ərn] **patrón** An ordered set of numbers or objects; the order helps you predict what will come next. (pp. 6, 198)
Examples:
2, 4, 6, 8, 10

pattern unit [pat′ərn yo͞o′nət] **unidad de patrón** The part of a pattern that repeats (p. 178)
Example:

penny [pen′ē] **moneda de 1¢** A coin worth 1/100 dollar or one cent; 1¢ (p. 110)

pentagon [pen′tə•gän] **pentágono** A plane figure with five sides and five angles (p. 374)
Example:

perimeter [pə•ri′mə•tər] **perímetro** The distance around a figure (p. 486)
Example:

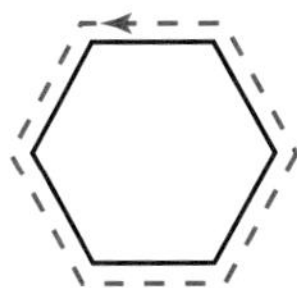

perpendicular lines [pûr′pən•dik′yə•lər līnz] **rectas perpendiculares** Lines that intersect to form right angles (p. 372)
Example:

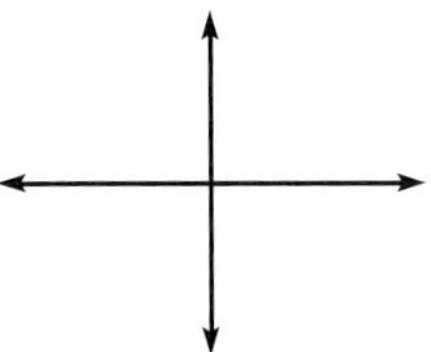

pictograph [pik′tə•graf] **pictograma** A graph that uses pictures to show and compare information (p. 154)
Example:

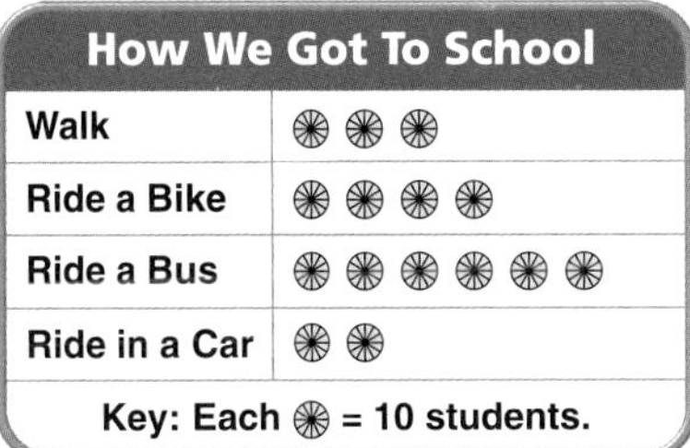

pint (pt) [pīnt] **pinta** A customary unit for measuring capacity;
1 pint = 2 cups (p. 448)

place value [plās val′yo͞o] **valor posicional** The value of each digit in a number, based on the location of the digit (p. 10)

plane figure [plāne fi′•gyər] **figura plana** A closed figure in a plane that is formed by lines that are curved, straight, or both (p. 374)
Example:

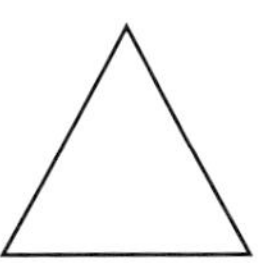

P.M. [pē em] **p.m.** The hours between noon and midnight (p. 140)

point [point] **punto** An exact position or location

polygon [pol′ē•gän] **polígono** A closed plane figure with straight sides that are line segments
Examples:

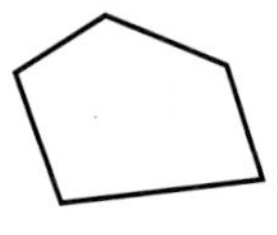 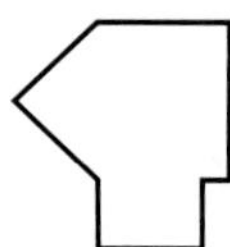 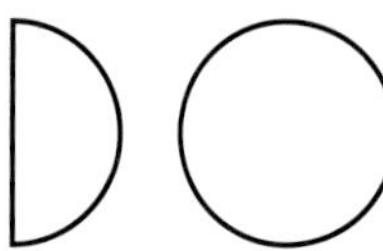

polygons   not polygons

possible [pos′ə•bəl] **po sible** Having a chance of happening (p. 568)

possible outcome [pos′ə•bəl out′kəm] **resultado posible** Something that has a chance of happening (p. 568)

pound (lb) [pound] **libra** A customary unit for measuring weight;
1 pound = 16 ounces (p. 450)

predict [pri•dikt′] **predecir** To make a reasonable guess about what will happen (p. 568)

probability [prä•bə•bi′lə•tē] **probabilidad** The chance that a given event will occur (p. 566)
Example:

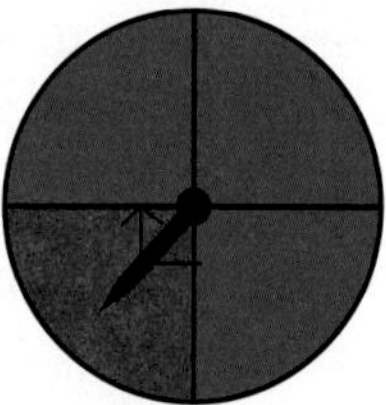

probability of red = 1 out of 4

product [prä′dəkt] **producto** The answer in a multiplication problem (p. 205)
Example: 3 × 8 = 24
↑ product

quadrilateral [kwa•drə•lat′ər•əl] **cuadrilátero** A plane figure with four sides and four angles (p. 374)
Example:

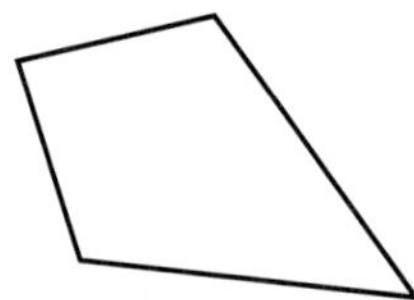

quart (qt) [kwôrt] **cuarto** A customary unit for measuring capacity;
1 quart = 2 pints (p. 448)

quarter [kwôr′•tər] **moneda de 25¢** A coin worth 25 cents and equal to 25 pennies; 25¢ (p. 110)

quarter hour [kwôr•tər our] **cuarto de hora** 15 minutes (p. 134)
Example: Between 4:00 and 4:15 is one quarter hour.

quotient [kwō′shənt] **cociente** The number, not including the remainder, that results from division (p. 302)
Example: 8 ÷ 4 = 2
↑ quotient

radius [rā′dē•əs] **radio** A line segment with one endpoint at the center of a circle and the other endpoint on the circle (p. 383)
Example:

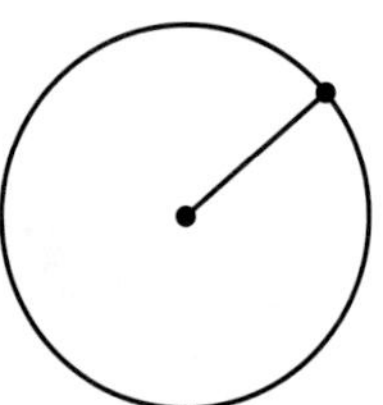

ray [rā] **rayo** A part of a line, with one endpoint, that is straight and continues in one direction (p. 368)
Example: •⟶

rectangle [rek′tang•gəl] **rectángulo** A quadrilateral with 2 pairs of parallel sides, 2 pairs of equal sides, and 4 right angles (p. 378)
Example:

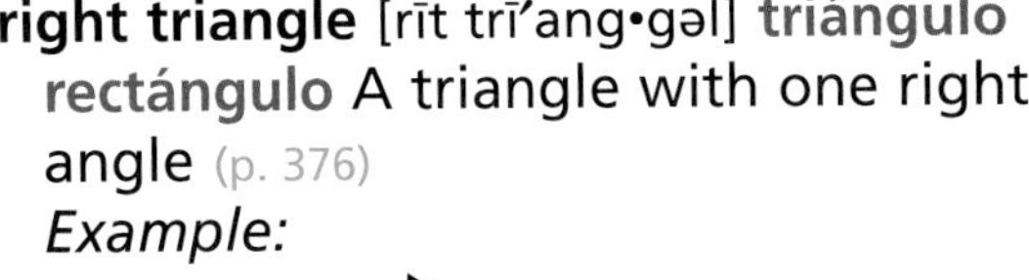

rectangular prism [rek•tan′gyə•lər pri′zəm] **prisma rectangular** A solid figure with six faces that are all rectangles (p. 416)
Example:

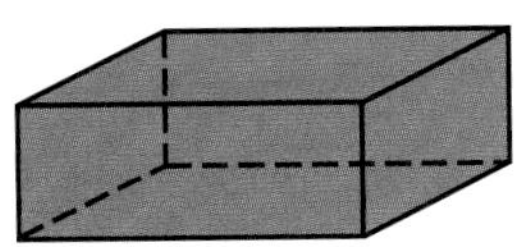

regroup [rē•gro͞op′] **reagrupar** To exchange amounts of equal value to rename a number (p. 62)
Example: 5 + 8 = 13 ones or 1 ten 3 ones

repeating pattern [rē•pēt•ing pat•ern] **patrón que se repite** A pattern which uses the same pattern unit over and over again (p. 180)
Example:

results [ri•zults′] **resultados** The answers from a survey (p. 166)

rhombus [räm′bəs] **rombo** A quadrilateral with 2 pairs of parallel sides and 4 equal sides and four angles (p. 378)
Example:

right angle [rīt ang′gəl] **ángulo recto** A special angle that forms a square corner (p. 368)
Example:

right triangle [rīt trī′ang•gəl] **triángulo rectángulo** A triangle with one right angle (p. 376)
Example:

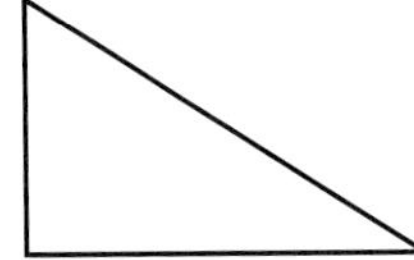

round [round] **redondear** Replace a number with another number that tells about how many or how much (p. 38)

rule [ro͞ol] **regla** An instruction that tells you the correct way to do something (p. 180)

S

scale [skāl] **escala** The numbers on a bar graph that help you read the number each bar represents (p. 160)

scalene triangle [skā′lēn trī′ang•gəl] **triángulo escaleno** A triangle in which no sides are equal (p. 376)
Example:

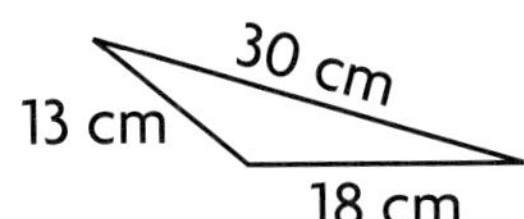

second [sek′ənd] **segundo** A small unit of time 60 seconds = 1 minute (p. 138)

simplest form [sim′pləst fôrm] **mínima expresión** When a fraction is modeled with the largest fraction bar or bars possible (p. 526)

solid figure [sol′id fĭg′yər] **cuerpo geométrico** A figure having length, width, and height (p. 416)
Example:

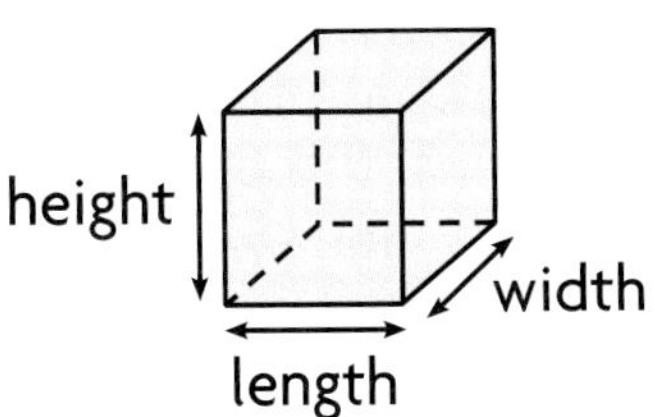

sphere [sfir] **esfera** A round object whose curved surface is the same distance from the center to all its points (p. 416)
Example:

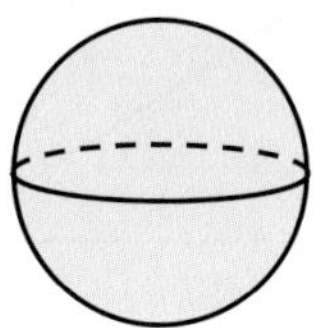

square [skwâr] **cuadrado** A quadrilateral with 2 pairs of parallel sides, 4 equal sides, and 4 right angles (p. 379)
Example:

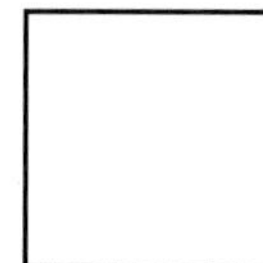

square number [skwâr num′bər] **número cuadrado** The product of two factors that are the same (pp. 204, 269)
Example: $2 \times 2 = 4$, so 4 is a square number

square pyramid [skwâr pir′ə•mid] **pirámide cuadrada** A solid, pointed figure with a flat base that is a square (p. 416)
Example:

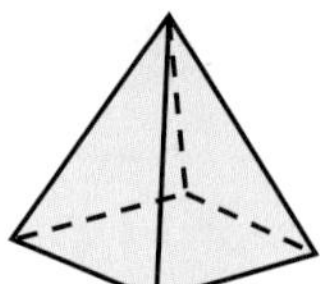

square unit [skwâr yo͞o′nət] **unidad cuadrada** A square with a side length of one unit; used to measure area (p. 492)

standard form [stan′dərd fôrm] **forma normal** A way to write numbers by using the digits 0–9, with each digit having a place value (p. 10)
Example: 345 ← standard form

subtraction [səb•trak′shən] **resta** The process of finding how many are left when a number of items are taken away from a group of items; the process of finding the difference when two groups are compared; the opposite operation of addition (p. 84)

sum [sum] **suma o total** The answer to an addition problem (p. 56)

survey [sər′vā] **encuesta** A method of gathering information (p. 166)

symmetry [sim′ə•trē] **simetría** A figure has symmetry if it can be folded along a line so that the two parts match exactly; one half of the figure looks like the mirror image of the other half (p. 402)

tally table [ta′lē tā′bəl] **tabla de conteo** A table that uses tally marks to record data (p. 152)
Example:

Favorite Sport	
Sport	Tally
Soccer	卌 |||
Baseball	|||
Football	卌
Basketball	卌 |

tessellation [te•sə•lā′shən] **teselación** A repeating pattern made of a closed plane figure that covers a surface with no overlapping or empty space (p. 391)
Example:

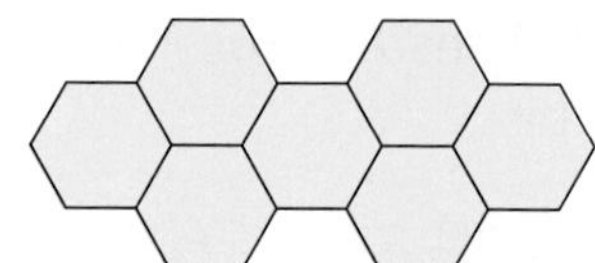

thermometer [thər•mom′ə•tər] **termómetro** An instrument for measuring temperature (p. 454)

three-dimensional figure [thrē′di•men′shən•əl fig′yər] **figura tridimensional** A figure having length, width, and height (p. 416)
Example:

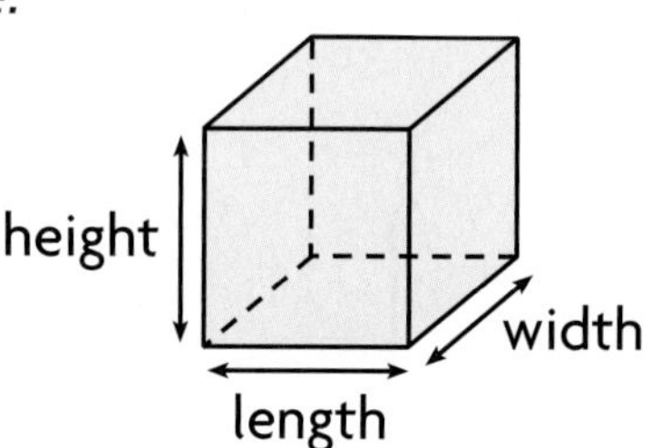

trapezoid [trap′ə•zoid] **trapecio** A quadrilateral with one pair of parallel sides and four angles (p. 378)
Example:

triangle [trī′ang′gəl] **triángulo** A plane figure with three sides and three angles (p. 374)
Examples:

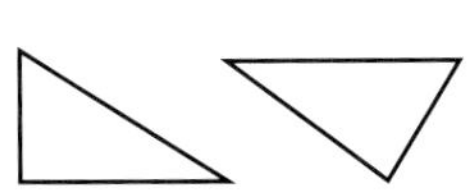

triangular prism [trī•an′gyə•lər pri′zəm] **prisma triangular** A solid figure that has two triangular faces and three rectangular faces (p. 416)
Example:

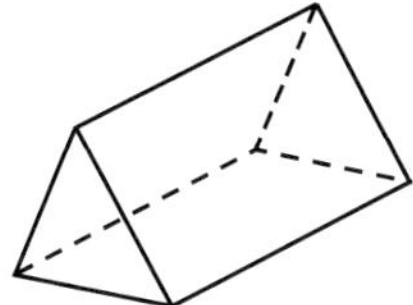

two-dimensional figure [to͞o•di•men′shən•əl fig′yər] **figura bidimensional** A figure having length and width (p. 374)
Example:

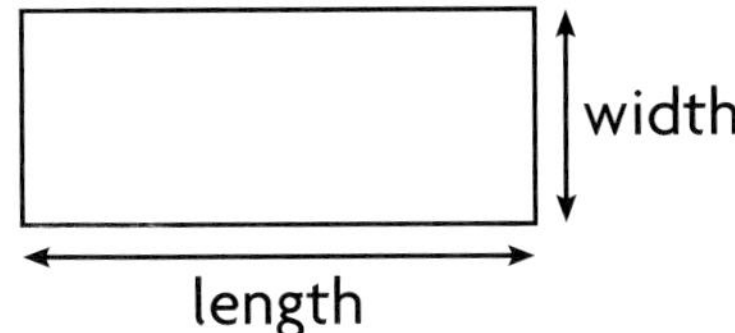

variable [vâr′ē•ə•bəl] **variable** A symbol or a letter that stands for an unknown number (p. 274)

Venn diagram [ven dī′ə•gram] **diagrama de Venn** A diagram that shows relationships among sets of things (p. 381)
Example:

2-Digit Numbers | Even Numbers

35, 17, 29 | 12, 10 | 8, 6, 4

vertex [vûr′teks] **vértice** The point at which two (or more) line segments meet in a plane figure or where three or more edges meet in a solid figure (pp. 368, 420)
Examples:

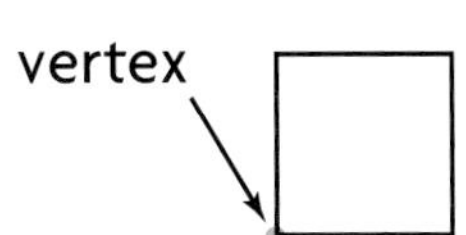

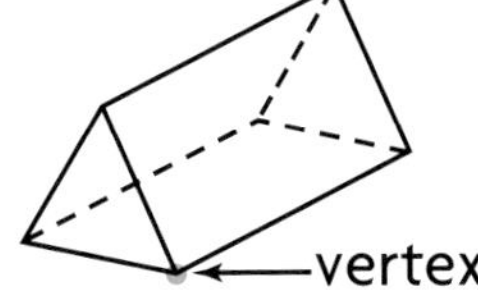

vertical bar graph [vûr′ti•kəl bär graf] **gráfica de barras verticales** A bar graph in which the bars go up from bottom to top (p. 160)

volume [väl′yəm] **volumen** The amount of space a solid figure takes up (p. 498)

weight [wāt] **peso** How heavy an object is (p. 450)

whole number [hōl num′bər] **número entero** One of the numbers 0, 1, 2, 3, 4, ... The set of whole numbers goes on without end.

word form [wûrd form] **en palabras** A way to write numbers by using words (p. 10)
Example: The word form of 212 is two hundred twelve.

yard (yd) [yärd] **yarda** A customary unit for measuring length or distance; 1 yard = 3 feet (p. 440)

Zero Property of Multiplication [zir′ō prä′pər•tē əv mul•tə•plə•kā′shən] **propiedad del cero de la multiplicación** The property that states that the product of zero and any number is zero (p. 213)
Example: $0 \times 6 = 0$

Index

D

E

M

Q

R

S

T

U

V

W

The basket is 18 inches in diameter, and 120 inches off the ground.
The basketball used in high school weighs between 20 and 22 ounces.
It will last approximately 10,000 bounces during its life.

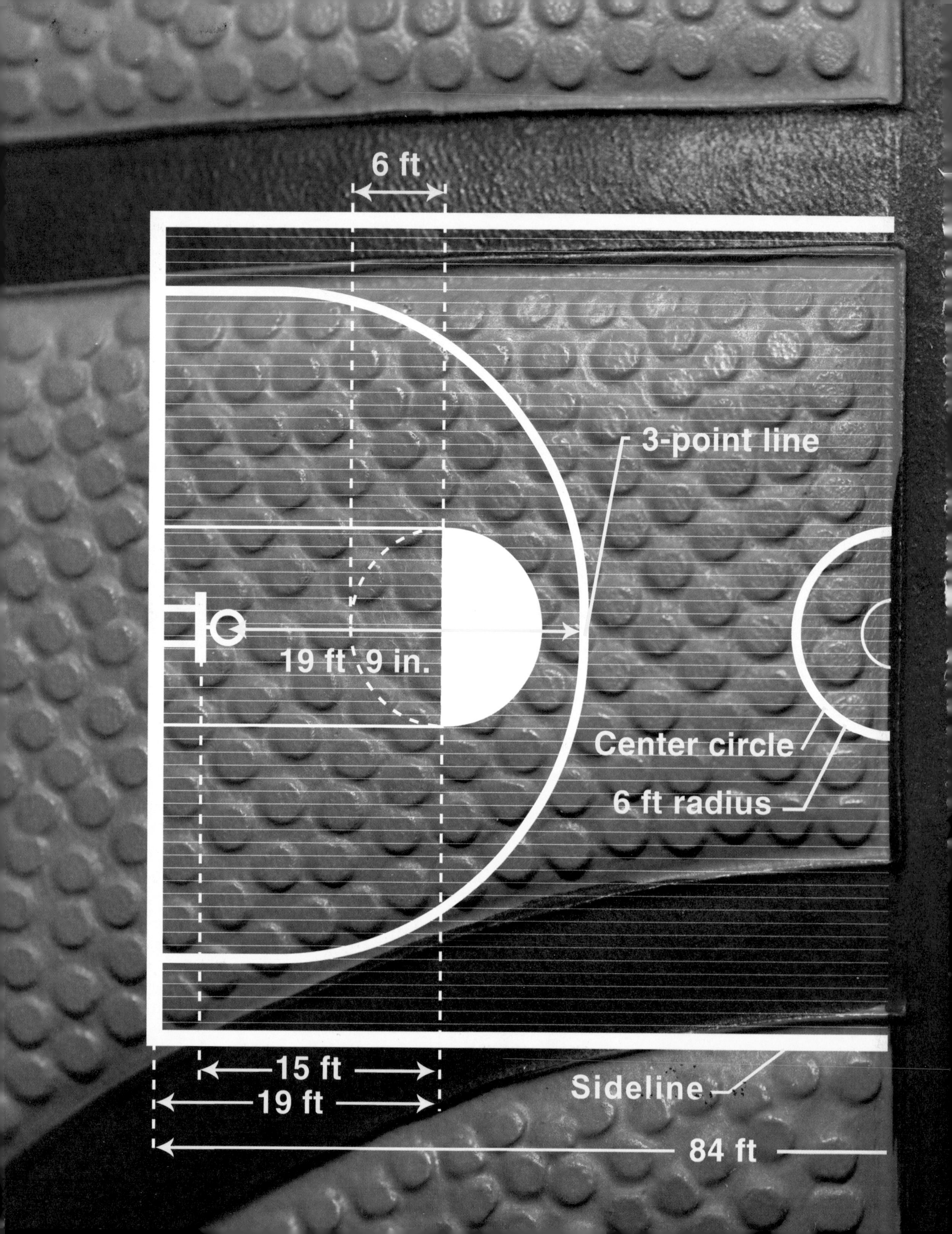

6 ft

3-point line

19 ft 9 in.

Center circle

6 ft radius

15 ft

19 ft

Sideline

84 ft